FOCUS ON SUCCESS

Ausgabe Technik

W0333790

5th edition

von
Michael Benford
Michael Macfarlane
Isobel Williams
Steve Williams

sowie
John Stevens

unter Mitarbeit der Verlagsredaktion

Dieses Buch gibt es auch auf
www.scook.de

Es kann dort nach Bestätigung der Allgemeinen Geschäftsbedingungen genutzt werden.

Buchcode: sxzt7-coaou

Cornelsen

FOCUS ON SUCCESS
Ausgabe Technik

Verfasser/innen:	Michael Benford, Bochum Michael Macfarlane, Oxford Isobel Williams, Berlin Steve Williams, Corio Bay Media John Stevens, Bad Münstereifel
Berater/innen:	Antje Baehr, Velbert; Philipp Fehrenbach, Nürtingen; Liane Krug, Homberg; Jens Niederberger, Neckarsulm; Panayotis Papaspyrou, Soest; Manja Seidel, Malschwitz; Sibylle Vogel, Erfurt; Marco Zimmermann, Bad Überkingen
Projektleitung:	Andreas Goebel
Verlagsredaktion:	Kari-ann Warnakulasuriya
Außenredaktion:	James Abram, Janan Barksdale
Redaktionelle Mitarbeit:	Vivika Krämer, Elise Nelson, Oliver Busch (Wörterverzeichnisse)
Umschlaggestaltung:	Klein & Halm Grafikdesign, Berlin
Layout und technische Umsetzung:	Oxana Rödel, Absatz DTP-Service, Teltow
Coverfoto:	Shutterstock / Mikhail Zahranichny
Illustrationen:	Oxford Designers & Illustrators
Bildredaktion:	Gertha Maly, Meike Kolle, Christina Scheuerer

Erhältlich sind auch:

Handreichungen zum Unterricht mit Unterrichtsmanager (UM) und 4 Audio-CDs	ISBN 978-3-06-451087-6
Unterrichtsmanager Premium (DVD)	ISBN 978-3-06-451088-3
Workbook mit Audio-CD und herausnehmbaren Lösungsschlüssel	ISBN 978-3-06-451086-9
Vocabulary practice book	ISBN 978-3-06-451079-1
Vokabeltrainer-App	

Soweit in diesem Lehrwerk Personen fotografisch abgebildet sind und ihnen von der Redaktion fiktive Namen, Berufe, Dialoge und Ähnliches zugeordnet oder diese Personen in bestimmte Kontexte gesetzt werden, dienen diese Zuordnungen und Darstellungen ausschließlich der Veranschaulichung und dem besseren Verständnis des Inhalts.

www.cornelsen.de

Die Webseiten Dritter, deren Internetadressen in diesem Lehrwerk angegeben sind, wurden vor Drucklegung sorgfältig geprüft. Der Verlag übernimmt keine Gewähr für die Aktualität und den Inhalt dieser Seiten oder solcher, die mit ihnen verlinkt sind.

1. Auflage, 1. Druck 2015

Alle Drucke dieser Auflage sind inhaltlich unverändert und können im Unterricht nebeneinander verwendet werden.

© 2015 Cornelsen Schulverlage GmbH, Berlin

Das Werk und seine Teile sind urheberrechtlich geschützt. Jede Nutzung in anderen als den gesetzlich zugelassenen Fällen bedarf der vorherigen schriftlichen Einwilligung des Verlages. Hinweis zu den §§ 46, 52 a UrhG: Weder das Werk noch seine Teile dürfen ohne eine solche Einwilligung eingescannt und in ein Netzwerk eingestellt oder sonst öffentlich zugänglich gemacht werden. Dies gilt auch für Intranets von Schulen und sonstigen Bildungseinrichtungen.

Druck: Mohn Media Mohndruck, Gütersloh

ISBN 978-3-06-451085-2

PEFC PEFC/04-31-1033

PEFC zertifiziert
Dieses Produkt stammt aus nachhaltig bewirtschafteten Wäldern und kontrollierten Quellen.
www.pefc.de

VORWORT

Focus on Success – 5th edition: Ausgabe Technik ist konzipiert für Lernende an Fachoberschulen und Berufskollegs. Es setzt Englischkenntnisse auf dem Niveau des mittleren Abschlusses voraus und bereitet auf die neuesten Prüfungen zur Erlangung der Fachhochschulreife vor. Das Lehrwerk führt zur Stufe B2 des Gemeinsamen europäischen Referenzrahmens.

Focus on Success – 5th edition: Ausgabe Technik ist ein komplett neu erarbeitetes Lehrwerk und bietet neue, interessante Texte, aktuelle Themen und einen auf den Lehrplan und Prüfungen abgestimmten Aufgabenapparat.

Das Lehrwerk beinhaltet alles, was Sie für einen erfolgreichen Englischunterricht benötigen:

- 4 *Foundation Course*-Units, in denen Grundkenntnisse, inklusive Grammatik, Wortschatz und Methodenkompetenzen, aufgefrischt werden können.
- 8 *Main Course*-Units, die einheitlich aufgebaut sind:
  - *Focus:* Der Einstieg ins Thema – bildgesteuert, anregend und motivierend.
  - *Text A und Text B:* zwei lange Abschnitte, in denen das Thema der Unit von verschiedenen Blickwinkeln beleuchtet wird.
  - *Technical options:* Zusatzmaterialien zur Erweiterung und individuellen Schwerpunktsetzung aus einem technischen Blickwinkel.
- 4 *Exam preparation*-Units, die jeweils 3 Themenbereiche, mit längeren Texten beinhalten.
- 4 *Job skills*-Units, die auf das Berufsleben vorbereiten und relevante Fertigkeiten und Sprache einführen und üben.
- 12 *Technical topics*, die unterschiedliche Aspekte der modernen Technik abdecken. Dabei spielen handlungsorientierte Aufgaben eine wichtige Rolle.

Die Übungen, die auf die Texte folgen, schulen eine Vielzahl von *Skills* (mit Hilfe *Building skills*-Kästen, die die Fertigkeiten einführen und aufbauen, und *Skills checklists*, die die Kenntnisse immer wieder auffrischen) sowie Wortschatz (*Working with words*) und Grammatikkenntnisse (*Getting it right*). Sie trainieren darüber hinaus gezielt alle Aufgabentypen, die in der Abschlussprüfung vorkommen.

Jede Unit enthält auch differenzierte Übungen, die die unterschiedlichen Lernniveaus ansprechen. ⊙ kennzeichnet eine einfachere Übung und ● eine Übung mit mehr Herausforderung.

Außerdem enthält der Anhang eine Fülle an Referenz- und Übungsmaterial:

- Die *Skills files* bieten einen Leitfaden zu Strategien, um das Lernen effektiver zu gestalten, plus Übungsmaterialien dazu und fördern somit das selbstständige Lernen. Anhand der Webcodes (auf www.cornelsen.de/webcodes zu finden) kann man die Hörtexte der *Skills files* unabhängig von der Audio-CD hören und die Lösungen selber kontrollieren.
- Die *Grammar files* enthalten neben ausführlichen Grammatikerklärungen auch zusätzliches Übungsmaterial zur Vertiefung der neugewonnenen Kenntnisse.
- Die Wörterverzeichnisse umfassen eine *Basic word list* mit thematisch geordnetem Grundwortschatz, damit Schüler nicht nur einzelne Wörter, sondern auch ganze Wortfelder auffrischen können; eine *Unit word list* mit allen neuen Wörtern in chronologischer Reihenfolge; und eine *A–Z word list* mit allen neuen Wörtern in alphabetischer Reihenfolge.

Wir hoffen, dass Ihnen die Arbeit mit **Focus on Success – 5th edition: Ausgabe Technik** Freude bereitet und das Lehrwerk zu einem gelungenen und erfolgreichen Unterricht beiträgt.

Die Autoren und der Verlag

CONTENTS

EXAM PREPARATION

TECHNICAL TOPICS

APPENDIX

1 The cult of celebrity

FOUNDATION COURSE

1 TALKING ABOUT CELEBRITY

A Choose one photo which expresses 'the cult of celebrity' best. Tell your neighbour why you have chosen it.

B Think: Make a list of four or five people who are famous in your country.

Pair: Show your list to a partner and decide which of them are celebrities. Sort the names into 'A celebrities' and 'B celebrities'. (Rank them in order of popularity.)

Share: Using your lists, decide what makes a celebrity. What do they do to deserve their celebrity status? Define 'celebrity'.

Useful phrases

- fans/paparazzi/cameras
- to wait for sb / to take photos
- to earn money / to sell photos

- How do you feel about … ?
- The paparazzi always/often …
- When a celebrity dies, …
- The newspapers sometimes …
- The fans usually …

C Study the headlines. What do they say about the advantages/disadvantages of being a celebrity? Make up some headlines of your own.

Luxury store opens at midnight for celebrity shoppers

ROCK LEGEND MICKEY HAS THIRD FACE-LIFT

STALKER ENTERS STAR'S VILLA!

DESIGNER CLOTHES AND JEWELLERY AT CELEBRITY BALL

D Would you like to be a celebrity? Why? / Why not?

2 GETTING IT RIGHT

→ Position of adverbs of time, S. 273; Simple present, S. 249

A Put the words in the correct order to make simple present statements.

1. always / a fan magazine / buy / on Fridays / I
2. at the weekend / go / to gigs / usually / we
3. I / never / talent shows / watch
4. for hours / queue / sometimes / to see our favourite stars / we
5. charity concerts / gives / the group / regularly
6. often / in the summer / they / tour

B Two fans are talking about their favourite celebrities. Put the verbs in brackets into the correct form of the simple present to complete the dialogues.

Ann My sister and I (love) ___[1] rock music. We (be) ___[2] fans of Willi Roberts. We (spend) ___[3] all our money on gigs.

Bob (you/go) ___[4] to every gig he (have) ___[5]?

Ann My sister usually (do) ___[6]. She (not miss) ___[7] a gig but I (not have) ___[8] enough time. Sometimes she (bring) ___[9] home T-shirts and CDs from the gigs. I always (read) ___[10] about the concerts in the fan magazine. What about you? (you/have) ___[11] a favourite celebrity?

Bob My friends and I (watch) ___[12] every film that Jim Razor (make) ___[13].

Ann (he/be) ___[14] the actor who (appear) ___[15] on TV with a different girlfriend every week?

Bob Yes. That (be) ___[16] part of his image. He (break up) ___[17] hotel rooms, too. I (not follow) ___[18] him on Twitter or Facebook but Jim (hit) ___[19] the headlines every week.

Ann Yes. Celebrity stories always (sell) ___[20] well.

1/2 **C Now listen and check your answers.**

3 SPEAKING

→ Interaktion, S. 246

A Work with a partner. Ask and answer questions about celebrities.

- Who is your favourite celebrity?
- Where do you see them? How often?
- How much money do you spend on tickets, fan articles, etc.?
- How much time do you spend following them on Twitter or other social media?

Make up some of your own questions.

Useful phrases

- to go to a film/gig
- to spend money on tickets / fan articles
- to follow sb / a star on social media
- What do you think/like about … ?
- Where / How often do you … ?
- How much money do you spend on … ?
- I (don't) like …
- I never spend any money/time on …
- I spend a lot of / some money/time on …

B Tell the class what you found out.

Mia loves Rory Storm. She collects everything. She spends a fortune on fan articles. She goes to all his concerts and gets his autograph every time.

Tom is a fan of Formula 1. His favourite driver is Glen Gold. He watches every race on TV. The tickets are too expensive. Glen often appears at celebrity charity events.

4 READING

→ Vorbereitung auf das Lesen, S. 214

BUILDING SKILLS: Predicting what the text will be about

If you have an idea what a text is about before you start reading it, you will find it easier to understand. Make use of all the clues on the page to help you.

- Study the headline: this will give you the first clue to what the text is about.
- Look at any photos or illustrations that go with the text: who or what do they show?
- The captions under the photos also give further information about the text.

What do you think the article is going to tell you about talent shows? Make some notes, then read and check.

1/3

EVERYBODY'S GOT TALENT

Most of the people who appear on talent shows like *American Idol* and *Britain's Got Talent* are young and good looking. Some of them are also very talented.

Everyone is scared when they walk onto a stage in front of a huge audience and the judges. When the audience laughs at you because of the way you look, you need to know you have mega-talent. Jonathan Antoine and Charlotte Jaconelli are great singers. They want to share their talent with the world.

Imagine this: Jonathan and Charlotte are coming onto the *Britain's Got Talent* stage. Some members of the audience are laughing. Others are clearly feeling uncomfortable. One of the judges says, 'Just when you think things couldn't get any worse,' as the singers take their spot on stage.

Imagine the change taking place as they start to perform. Some members of the audience are crying, others are standing on their chairs and waving their arms in the air.

There is something magical about the moment. The singers are listening to the cheers. Hopes for the life they dream about are washing over their faces. They are experiencing a life-changing moment.

Jonathan Antoine and Charlotte Jaconelli at the Classical Brit Awards 2013

Jonathan has a great voice. Charlotte's voice is young and more pop. One of the judges said he was afraid that Charlotte would hold back Jonathan, who is the real talent of the group. In the end, the same judge voted for the pair to move on together to the next level of the competition.

That was in 2012. Charlotte and Jonathan finished second in that season and signed a good contract with a record company. Their first album, 'Together', was released in the same year and their follow-up, 'Perhaps Love', came out a year later. Jonathan and Charlotte are now following solo careers.

(298 words)

5 LOOKING AT THE TEXT

→ Produktion: Wh-Fragen beantworten, S. 228

A Work with a partner and answer the following questions in full sentences.

1 Who is the article about?
2 Where are they?
3 Why are they there?
4 What happened first?
5 What happened in the end? Why?
6 When did this take place?

B Now compare your answers with your notes from exercise 4.

6 WORKING WITH WORDS

→ Ein Wörterbuch benutzen, S. 217

A Copy and complete the table using your dictionary. The given words are all from the text.

Noun	Verb	Adjective
___	to appear	/
competition	___	___
___	to dream	___
___	to experience	___
idol	___	___
judge	___	___
___ / ___	to perform	/

B Use some of the words you have found to complete the sentences. Change the form of the verbs if necessary.

1 People ___ in a talent show because they want to be famous.
2 The singer was nervous. He was shaking all through the ___ .
3 The star always looks dirty. He's really not interested in his ___ .
4 When they received their prize, one of the winners said, 'This is a great ___ for us.'
5 The judge often criticizes people before they begin. He is very ___ .
6 He's a real celebrity, audiences ___ him.
7 Women often have a ___ look in their eyes when he sings.
8 She takes part in a lot of shows. She's a really ___ judge.

7 GETTING IT RIGHT

→ Simple present ▪ Present progressive, S. 249

A Imagine you are at the *Britain's Got Talent* show right now. Put the verbs into the correct form of the present progressive.

1 The performers (get) ___ made up at the moment.
2 The judge (study) ___ his script.
3 Jonathan (practise) ___ his song.
4 You (speak) ___ to your friend on your mobile phone.
5 Your friend asks: 'What (you/do) ___ [1] at the moment?'
You answer: 'I (wait) ___ [2] for the show to start.'
6 Your friend asks: 'What (the members of the audience / do) ___ [1]?'
You answer: 'They (talk) ___ [2] to each other. They (look forward to) ___ [3] a good show.'

B Write complete sentences with the correct form of the verbs in brackets.

1 I ___ *Britain's Got Talent* every week. (watch / am watching)
2 When the show ___[1] at 10.45, I always ___[2] to bed. (finish / is finishing ▪ go / am going)
3 Charlotte and Jonathan ___[1] to become stars. They ___[2] to win *Britain's Got Talent*. (want / are wanting ▪ try / are trying)
4 They usually ___ their song in the morning. (practise / are practising)
5 Jonathan ___ on his own at the moment. (sings / is singing)
6 The judge ___[1] near the TV studio. This evening he ___[2] home after the show. (lives / is living ▪ walks / is walking)

C Work with a partner and write six sentences about Jonathan, Charlotte and the judge using verbs in the simple present and in the present progressive. Remember to use signal words.

8 DISCUSSION

→ Interaktion: An Diskussionen teilnehmen, S. 246

In small groups, discuss talent shows. Say what you (don't) find good about them. Would you like to take part in one? Explain why / why not. Make notes and tell the class.

9 LISTENING

→ Vor dem Hören, S. 225

BUILDING SKILLS: Preparing to listen

Preparing yourself for the listening task will help you to understand listening texts more easily. Make use of everything on the page that can help you before you start listening.

- Study any photos or illustrations on the page for clues about the listening topic.
- Read the questions carefully and look at any other background information.
- Think about any words related to the topic that you might hear.

THE PRICE OF FAME

Kelly and childhood sweetheart Sam to split

10.30 Good morning, fans!

Gerry Davis interviews today's celebrities

In today's interview, Kelly Green, current £100,000 prize winner of Miss Model talks about her greatest achievement, who inspires her and her biggest challenge. She also talks to Gerry about her relationship with long-time lover, Sam. (She believes that the tabloid press love it when a celebrity has problems.)

A Before you listen, study the photos and the texts. Then answer these questions.

1 Who is Gerry's interview partner?
2 Why is she in the news?
3 What are the four main topics of the interview?
4 What is her relationship with the press?

B With a partner, match these German expressions to the English expressions you might hear.

1 größte Leistung
2 größter Erfolg
3 eine internationale Karriere als Model
4 einen Traum erfüllen
5 die Presse wird zu aufdringlich
6 Probleme in den Schlagzeilen
7 Stars am Heulen
8 einen Vertrag haben

a an international career as a fashion model
b biggest success
c greatest achievement
d problems in the headlines
e stars crying their eyes out
f the press comes too close
g to fulfil a dream
h to have a contract

1/4

C Listen to the interview and say whether these statements are true or false. Correct the wrong statements.

1 Kelly's dream is to have her own fashion label.
2 Veronica Vernon is Kelly's manager.
3 Giselle Goodrich is a top fashion model.
4 Kelly does not admire Giselle.
5 Kelly always enjoys media attention.
6 She understands why the press focus on celebrities' problems.
7 Sam understands Kelly's problems.
8 Kelly is looking forward to living in Milan.

10 ROLE-PLAY

→ Interaktion: Ein Rollenspiel gestalten, S. 247

Work with a partner. You are going to role-play an interview with a celebrity.

Partner A: You are the interviewer, Gerry Davis (see exercise 9).
Partner B: You are the celebrity. Choose a name for yourself, or use your own name. Decide which area you work in, e.g. sport, film, modelling, reality TV.

Before you start, read through what you are going to say and make notes. Partner B, tell Partner A your name. Partner A begins.

Gerry Davis	Celebrity
→ Welcome the guest and thank him/her for coming. Say that you know he/she is always busy.	→ Say that you are happy to be here. Say that you are never too busy for your fans.
→ Ask the celebrity to describe his/her greatest achievement or biggest success.	→ Describe an achievement or your biggest success, e.g. your latest album is top of the charts, you are footballer of the year.
→ Congratulate the celebrity and ask who inspires him/her.	→ Say who inspires you. (This can be a real person.)
→ Say that you find that interesting. Then ask what the star's biggest challenge is.	→ Sometimes you get tired. Sometimes the work is hard, but you love what you do. Explain that your fans give you a lot of support, so you can face any challenges that appear.
→ Say that the fans always love to hear the star say things like that. Ask what the star is doing now.	→ Say what you are doing at the moment, e.g. you are working on your next album, training for the next big match.
→ Thank the celebrity for talking to you and wish him/her all the best.	→ Thank Gerry for interviewing you. Say goodbye to him and to your fans.

2 The world of sport

FOUNDATION COURSE

1 TALKING ABOUT SPORT

A Think: What sports do you enjoy? Are you a participant or a spectator? What sports do not interest you?

Pair: Tell a partner and explain why you enjoy / do not enjoy sports.

Share: Do a class survey and rank the sports according to the numbers of classmates who do and watch them.

B Copy and complete the mind map with all the sports you know.

Useful phrases

- to (not) be interested in running/ cycling/…
- to (not) be keen on football/…
- to (not) enjoy/like/love tennis/…
- to (not) support a team
- to (not) be a fan of sb / a team

- How often do you do … ?
- When do you go … ?
- Who do you play … with?

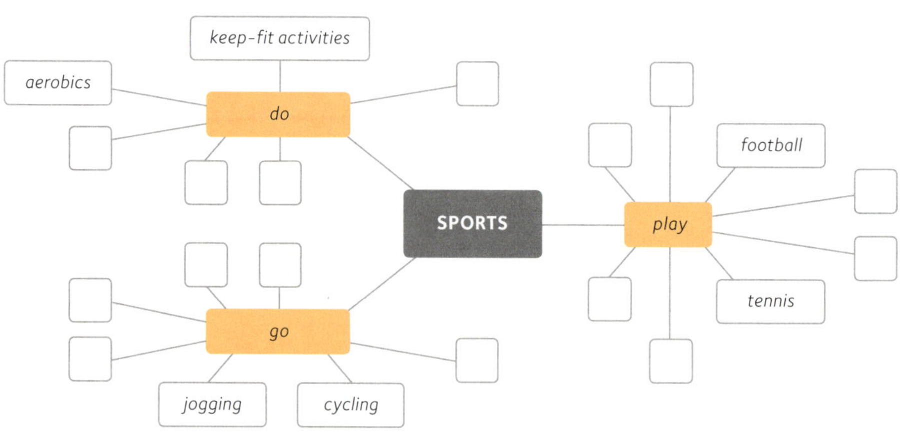

2 GETTING IT RIGHT

→ Simple past, S. 251; Present perfect, S. 253

A Put the verbs in brackets in the correct form of the simple past to complete the dialogues.

1 **A** Mary (play) ___[1] hockey for the Austrian team before she (move) ___[2] to Germany.
  B Oh, that's interesting. I (not know) ___[3] that.

2 **A** What sports (you/do) ___[1] when you (be) ___[2] younger?
  B I (go) ___[3] riding when I (be) ___[4] at school.

3 **A** I (ring) ___[1] your doorbell last night but you (be) ___[2] out. Where (you/go) ___[3] ?
  B I (not go) ___[4] anywhere. I (be) ___[5] tired after jogging so I (go) ___[6] to bed early.

4 **A** (you/queue) ___[1] at the stadium for your tickets?
  B No, I (buy) ___[2] them online.

B Use the words to make sentences. Use the present perfect form of the verb.

1 I / just / buy / a chess set.
2 My sister / just / learn / how to ride a bicycle.
3 Martin and Fred / already / go / to the swimming pool.
4 you / ever / drive a racing car?
5 Martha / read / the rules of the game / yet?

C Complete the sentences with *for* or *since*.

1 I haven't seen Tom at the gym ___ Christmas.
2 Why doesn't he come out? He has been in the changing rooms ___ three hours.
3 Today is the big day. I have had my tickets ___ two weeks.
4 Malcolm isn't playing today. He has had a cold ___ last Tuesday.
5 It's World Cup time again. My national team hasn't taken part ___ 1998.
6 Kevin has played tennis at this club ___ over ten years.

3 SPEAKING

A Work in groups. Ask and answer questions about sports personalities you like and admire.

- Who is your favourite sports personality? Say which sport they are involved in.
- Why do you admire them? Explain what they do that makes you look up to them.
- Have you ever lost interest in a sports personality you really liked? Explain why.

Useful phrases

- to play for a club/team
- to admire / look up to sb
- to be a champion/hero

- Why do you follow/support … ?
- How long have you … ?
- What made you decide not to … ?
- How long did you … ?

B Tell the class what you found out.

Connie has been a fan of the sprinter Jo Myles since she won gold at the Paralympics. Connie admires her because she has overcome her disabilities.

Jason admired the swimmer Ian Jones for a long time, but he lost interest in him when he stopped winning medals.

4 PREDICTING

→ Vorbereitung auf das Lesen, S. 214

Look quickly at the text – don't read it! – then choose the best ending to complete the sentence below.

The text is about …

a deaths in early bicycle races.
b taking illegal substances to improve performance.
c some very bad injuries that have occurred during races.

SKILLS CHECKLIST: Predicting

- ☑ Have I read the title?
- ☑ Have I looked at the photo?
- ☑ Have I read the caption under the photo?

1/5

WHEN HEROES FALL

Professional cycling has a long history of doping problems.

Professional cycling has a long history. The first recorded bicycle races began in the early 1800s and, throughout the decades, improvements in materials used for bikes have led to faster races. There have been heroes in every race but some of them have fallen.

Lance Armstrong was born in Texas on 18 September 1971. He started his sports career at the age of 12 when he came fourth in a swimming competition. From 1984 to 1990, he competed in junior triathlon competitions and became national triathlon champion in 1989 and 1990. In 1992, Armstrong began his career as a professional road racing cyclist. He won the Tour de France seven times between 1999 and 2005. In 2011, he announced his retirement from competitive cycling. A few months later, the United States Anti-Doping Agency (USADA) looked at samples and charged Armstrong with doping. After that, the organization took away his seven Tour de France titles.

Reports about doping in professional cycling are not new. According to the 1997 International Olympic Committee study on the Historical Evolution of Doping Phenomenon in the late 19th century, doping during a competition was not illegal. The study referred to a Welsh cyclist in 1886 who drank a mixture of cocaine, caffeine and strychnine and died during a race. Ten years later, cyclists who used nitroglycerine to stimulate their hearts and improve their breathing suffered hallucinations. During a race in New York, the American champion Marshall Taylor refused to continue as he believed he was being chased by a man with a knife.

Today, an insider said: 'Nobody bats an eyelid when people are doping. I know some cyclists who have doped ever since they started to enter competitions. They win a lot of races but, in the end, these guys are really losers. When you fall, you fall alone. The corrupt system cycles on without you.'

(311 words)

5 UNDERSTANDING THE TEXT

→ Sich während des Lesens Notizen machen, S. 223

BUILDING SKILLS: Taking notes while reading

Taking notes while reading makes it easier to remember the information in a text. It is also a useful skill if you have to answer questions on, or summarize, a text. Use these tips to organize your notes:

- Read the text all the way through to make sure you understand what it is about.
- Prepare a page in your notebook with the text heading, a reference to where to find the text, a note on what the text is about and today's date.
- Use the most important aspects of the text as sub-headings and write your notes under these headings.
- Scan the text for key words, dates and other signals, such as repetition, that will tell you what the author considers important. Include these aspects in your notes.

A First read the text on page 14 quickly and put the headings below into the correct order 1–4.

doping in professional cycling not new ▪ doping today ▪ fallen hero ▪ history of professional cycling

B Now read the text carefully and make notes in your notebook. Use the headings from exercise 5A to organize your notes.

C Answer these questions on the text.

1 When were bicycle races first recorded?
2 What helped cyclists to race faster?
3 What is Lance Armstrong's connection to professional cycling?
4 Why did the USADA take his titles away from him?
5 According to a study, was doping in cycling legal or illegal in the 19th century?
6 What happened to a Welsh cyclist in 1886 as a result of doping?
7 What does an insider think about cyclists who dope?
8 What does the insider think about cycling competitions?

When heroes fall
(Focus on Success, p. 14)

Text is about: …

Date: …

1 …
2 …
3 …
4 …

6 WRITING

→ Produktion: Einen Text zusammenfassen, S. 229

Use your answers to the questions in exercise 5C to write a short summary of the text. These phrases will help you to structure your summary.

Useful phrases

- The article is about …
- According to the text, the first …
- It seems that better bikes …
- One of the most famous modern cyclists was …
- It appears that he was …
- In general, doping in cycling …
- As someone who knows the business says, …
- According to him/her, …
- To sum up, …

7 GETTING IT RIGHT

→ Pronouns, S. 268

Replace the highlighted expressions with a subject pronoun.

1 John doesn't go to the gym regularly.
2 Molly and Pam have joined a dance class.
3 Cilla doesn't do any exercise at all.
4 The dog always runs beside me.

Now replace the highlighted expressions with an object pronoun.

5 I called John from the gym last week.
6 The instructor was happy to see Molly and Pam.
7 Molly and Pam would like Cilla to join the class.
8 I tripped and fell over the dog yesterday.

Complete these dialogues with subject and object pronouns.

1 **A** Do ▬ 1 know the woman who takes the dance class, Kate?
B No, ▬ 2 don't. Can ▬ 3 introduce ▬ 4 to ▬ 5 ?

2 **A** Paul and I would like to go to the class but ▬ 1 don't know where ▬ 2 is.
B Molly and Pam said ▬ 3 and Paul can go to the class with ▬ 4 .

3 **A** These jazz pants are nice. If ▬ 1 fit ▬ 2, ▬ 3 will take ▬ 4.
B Yes, ▬ 5 fit perfectly. This T-shirt is nice, too. Why don't ▬ 6 buy ▬ 7, too?

8 GETTING IT RIGHT

→ Possessive adjectives, S. 268

Add possessive adjectives to complete the dialogue.

A How did you enjoy ▬ 1 keep-fit class last night?
B I loved it but ▬ 2 muscles are aching this morning. Alan was full of energy at the end but, of course, it's ▬ 3 job.
A Alan's the trainer, right? Did your sister enjoy ▬ 4 session with him?
B Sure. She suggested we should take ▬ 5 parents along, too.
A What's ▬ 6 opinion of keep-fit? Would they go?
B I think my mum would. When she was a teacher, it was ▬ 7 job to organize school sports.

9 PREPARING TO LISTEN

→ Rezeption: Hörverstehen, S. 225

You are going to hear an interview with a Zumba instructor.

A Before you listen, read this short introduction and answer the following questions.

1 What is Zumba?
2 Where and when did it start?
3 Who invented it?

What is Zumba?

You've probably heard of the fitness craze Zumba, a workout known as a dance fitness party. It started in the 1990s, in the slums of Cali, Columbia, when an aerobics instructor called Beto Perez forgot his tape of aerobics music for the class he was teaching. Instead of cancelling the class, he went to his car and took his tape of the traditional salsa and merengue music he listened to while he was driving and improvised his aerobics class using the music. In 1999, Beto Perez took his new aerobic dance programme to Miami, Florida. He named the new-style aerobics Zumba. It wasn't long before Zumba became a worldwide craze. Zumba is a cardio-dance workout – a fitness workout which is good for the heart.

B Complete the sentences on the left with the correct definition on the right.

1 Salsa, merengue, cha-cha-cha, samba and tango are …
2 Reggae, jazz, African beats, country, hip-hop and pop are …
3 Someone who is overweight is …
4 A person who is slim is …
5 Cardio (cardiovascular) means …
6 Metabolism is …
7 A calorie is …
8 Someone who is tired of life …

a a unit used for measuring how much energy food will produce.
b connected with the heart and the blood vessels.
c cannot feel joy and excitement any longer.
d Latin American dances.
e musical styles.
f the chemical processes in living things that change food into materials for growth.
g thin in a way that is attractive.
h too heavy for the size of their body.

10 LISTENING

→ Rezeption: Hörverstehen – Notizen machen, S. 227

BUILDING SKILLS: Taking notes while listening

It can sometimes be difficult to take notes while listening because the speakers don't stop to wait while you are writing. Because of this, you may miss important points. Don't panic! If you practise taking notes every time you listen, you will soon get the hang of it.

- Read the task carefully and look at any other information on the page before you listen.
- Prepare and structure your notes the same way as for a reading task (see page 15).
- Keep focused on the task and note down relevant key words and expressions.

1/6

A Now listen to the interview and take notes.

B Look at your notes and say if the following statements are true or false. Correct the incorrect statements.

1 Zumba only uses Latin American music.
2 Only young and beautiful people go to Zumba classes.
3 Zumba is good for your health.
4 Almost everyone feels tired after a Zumba session.
5 Zumba can help people who feel unhappy.
6 The interviewer does not want to try Zumba.

Zumba (Focus on Success, p. 17)
Listening is about: …
Date: …
Gerry Davis: …
Candy Wilson: …

11 WRITING

→ Produktion: Schreiben S. 228

A friend who feels overweight is unhealthy and unhappy. Use your notes and the phrases below to write an email describing Zumba and suggest how this could help him/her.

Useful phrases

- Hello (*first name*)
- I've just heard an interview with … . She is a …
- Zumba is a … but you don't have to be able to …
- It's lots of fun and has … health benefits.
- It's good for … / increases … / reduces … / helps people … / boosts … / burns …
- … if you're feeling low, …
- The atmosphere is …
- I would like to … / Would you like to … ?
- Hope to hear from you …
- All the best (*your name*)

3 Fashion and brand power

FOUNDATION COURSE

Times Square, New York

Piccadilly Circus, London

1 TALKING ABOUT BRANDS

A **Think: You see brand names and slogans wherever you go. Write down three brand names and their slogans.**

B **Pair: Compare your list of slogans with a partner.**

C **Share: Which, if any, of these brands do you buy regularly? Which of them would you never buy?**

Useful phrases

- I love/like … . I shop there regularly.
- I prefer … . Their clothes are more fashionable than the clothes at …
- I never drink/eat/wear/buy …
- Which is better … ?
- What do/don't you like about … ?

2 CLASS SURVEY

Ask other people in the class about their favourite brands. Do a class survey and find the top ten brands that people spend their money on.

3 READING

→ Rezeption: Leseverstehen, S. 214

Match the following statements and questions to the gaps (A to D) in the text on page 19.

1 Basically, it all comes down to emotional thinking.
2 Last but not least, brands let us show the world who we are.
3 What might make 'our' brand attractive to us?
4 Why do shoppers always go for a specific brand?

1/7

WHY DOES IT HAVE TO BE A BRAND NAME?

— A — A lot of consumer choices are made according to the price or the availability of the product. If it is affordable, we'll buy it. If it's easy to find, we'll take it. What do we do, though, when we go into a shop and see two similar products which cost more or less the same, one made by company X and one by company Y? We buy the brand we prefer.

— B — Does it simply come down to quality, packaging and price? Perhaps personality affects the type of brands we choose? Or could it be education or family background? All of these things play a part of course but why do we buy one brand and not another?

— C — Some sportswear companies use sports celebrities to advertise their goods. The clothes they wear won't make you run faster or play better but the advertising suggests that wearing the same brand will make you a better athlete. It tells the buyer: 'Like your hero, you are an over-achiever. You never give up. You want more.' People who choose brands that are advertised like this are looking for a challenge. By buying these brand-name products, they feel they are on the road to achieving more.

— D — Using the right brand can help us display our values and beliefs. Brands can show that you belong to the same group. We can use brands to show that we are different from other people or to show that we are the same as others. (246 words)

4 LOOKING AT THE TEXT

→ Rezeption: Leseverstehen, S. 214

Use information from the text to complete the sentence beginnings (1–6) by adding a sentence part from the first box (a–f) and an ending from the second box (g–l).

EXAMPLE: *A lot of shoppers choose goods depending on whether they have enough money to buy them and if they can get the products easily.*

1 ~~A lot of shoppers choose goods depending on …~~
2 If two products made by two different companies are available, …
3 A lot of things can persuade us to buy a product, …
4 Who we are affects our choices, for example, …
5 Some companies use a famous person to advertise their goods hoping that …
6 If you follow a fashion or have certain ideas, …

a and both cost more or less the same, …	**g** and how much it costs.
b our character and education …	**h** ~~and if they can get the products easily.~~
c including how the product is packed …	**i** or how we grew up.
d shoppers who identify with the famous person …	**j** we buy the brand we like better.
e the brands you choose can show other people …	**k** who you are and what you think.
f ~~whether they have enough money to buy them …~~	**l** will buy the product.

5 GETTING IT RIGHT

→ Adjectives ▪ Adverbs of manner, S. 270

A Complete the dialogues with the adjective or adverb form of the words in brackets.

1 **A** I wish I had some money. I'd like to buy a new computer but they're so ___[1]. (expensive)
B Don't worry. Even good computers are ___[2] nowadays. (cheap)
2 **A** That dress is ___[1]. It must have cost a lot of money. (beautiful)
B No, it didn't. You can buy brand-name clothing ___[2] at outlet stores. (cheap)
3 **A** Are these the shoes you told me about? They look ___[1]. (great)
B Yes. I bought them on the Internet and they fit me ___[2]. (perfect)
4 **A** A ___[1] model of my phone comes out tomorrow. (new)
B If you want one, you'll have to be ___[2]. They get sold out very ___[3]. (quick ▪ quick)

B Rewrite these sentences with the adverbs in the best position.

→ Position of adverbs of time, S. 273

1 I'll buy myself a pair of designer jeans. (tomorrow)
2 Pete has bought a tablet. (just)
3 Mary chooses her children's clothes. (always)
4 **A** I have spent all my allowance. (already ▪ again)
B Then you won't be able to do any more shopping. (this month)
5 **A** There you are. Shall we get something to eat? (at last ▪ now)
B No, I'm not hungry. I've eaten two burgers. (today ▪ already)

6 WORKING WITH WORDS

→ Ein Wörterbuch benutzen, S. 217

Copy and complete the table using your dictionary. The given words are in the text.

Noun	Verb	Adjective	Adverb
___		similar	___
___	to prefer	___	___
___	___	___	simply
celebrity / ___	___	___	
athlete		___	___
challenge / ___	___	___	
___ / ___	to achieve	___	

Complete the sentences with words from the same word family as the words in brackets.

1 There is not much (similar) ___ between these designer jeans and the ones from the discount label.
2 Which smartphone do you want to buy? Do you have a (prefer) ___ ?
3 I love these hand-made sweaters. They are (simply) ___ but high-quality clothes.
4 The company had a party to (celebrity) ___ the success of the new brand.
5 I'm sure my new running shoes help me to run faster. I feel really (athlete) ___ now.
6 The course was very (challenge) ___ . It was like running a half-marathon.
7 It was a great (achieve) ___ to get a sports celebrity to advertise the brand.

7 GETTING IT RIGHT

→ Comparison of adjectives and adverbs, S. 271

A Make adjective or adverb comparisons with the words in brackets.

1 It's much (cheap) ▬ [1] to buy no-name goods than designer brands. Designer clothes are (expensive) ▬ [2] than 'normal' clothes.
2 The green T-shirt is (fashionable) ▬ [1] than the blue one, but the yellow T-shirt is the (fashionable) ▬ [2] of them all.
3 You can buy goods (easy) ▬ on the Internet than from crowded stores.
4 Usain Bolt is the (fast) ▬ [1] man in the world, but he will run even (fast) ▬ [2] in our running shoes.
5 People buy products from a company (regular) ▬ if they identify with the brand.

B Make comparison sentences with the words in brackets.

(+) = … than ▪ (=) = as … as ▪ (−) = not as … as

1 A lot of people say brand names are ((+) good) *better than* no-name products but I don't agree. I think a no-name product can be just ((=) good) *as good as* a brand name.
2 This drink tastes ((+) sweet) ▬ [1] the other one but it is ((−) tasty) ▬ [2] yours.
3 We know you're a fast runner but our shoes will make you run ((+) fast) ▬ ever before.
4 My new tablet PC was ((−) expensive) ▬ [1] my old laptop and I can download things just ((=) quick) ▬ [2] before.
5 Their products are ((−) good) ▬ [1] ours. Their prices are ((=) competitive) ▬ [2] ours but their quality is ((+) bad) ▬ [3] ever.

8 LISTENING

→ Rezeption: Hörverstehen, S. 225

1/8

Anne, Bella, Colin and David go running together as often as they can. When Anne collects a T-shirt for Bella to wear at a sponsored women's run, it's not long before a discussion about running clothes starts.

Listen to the discussion and answer the following questions.

1 What does Anne have for Bella?
2 What does Colin think about people who spend a lot of money on sportswear?
3 Why is it good that sports gear firms sponsor events?
4 What is Anne's opinion on the best clothes for running?
5 Where does Anne's gear come from?
6 According to Anne, who makes the clothes she wears?
7 According to Colin, where is sportswear made?
8 How does Bella stop her friends arguing?

9 PHRASES FOR DISCUSSION

→ Interaktion: An Diskussionen teilnehmen, S. 246

BUILDING SKILLS: Learning phrases for discussion

Learning phrases for discussion (see the flap on the back cover) and how to use them will help you express yourself clearly and logically in a debate or a role-play.

- Before you begin a discussion, make sure you know as many phrases for discussion as possible and when to use them correctly.
- Whenever you have the chance to listen to a discussion, pay attention to the phrases people use and remember how these expressions help to structure the discussion.

A Copy this table into your notebook and write the expressions from the list below under the right heading.

Language for discussion				
Giving an opinion	Giving reasons	Agreeing with an opinion	Disagreeing with an opinion	Interrupting

a Actually, I think …
b Yes, that's just how I see it.
c If you ask me, …
d (Sorry), … I don't agree.
e It seems to me that …
f Just a moment, I'd like to say something.
g The thing is, you see …
h Sorry to interrupt, but …
i That's quite right.
j The main reason is (that) …

Keep your table safe. You can add more expressions as you work through the book.

1/8

B Listen to the discussion in exercise 8 again and listen for the expressions from exercise 9A. Were they used in the way you decided above?

C Have a short discussion about running clothes with three other people.

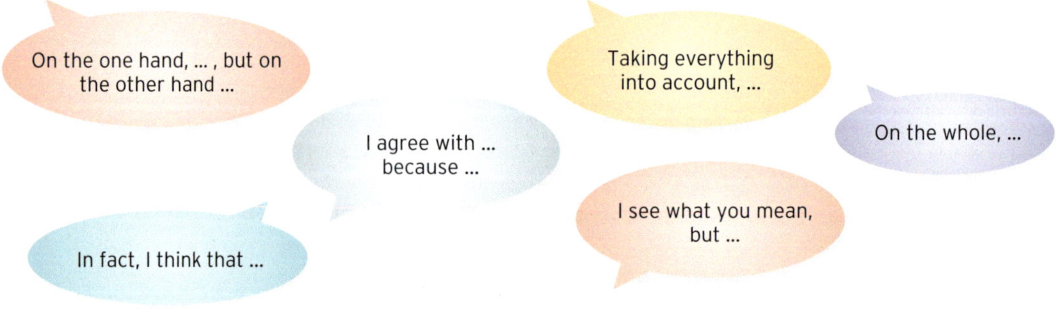

10 READING

→ Rezeption: Leseverstehen, S. 214

Read the following blog and the comments below. Match the comments to the paragraphs in the blog.

http://www.topics for discussion.com

1/9

DON'T BE A TEENAGE FASHION VICTIM

Hi fans – it's Lindy here with another topic for discussion

A Last week we were looking at brand names and how we either love them or hate them. This week, we're going to talk about fashion victims. The expression is usually used to criticize someone's style. A fashion victim is a person who always wears the latest fashions even if they do not suit him or her.

B Walk along any high street today and you'll see one teenager after another wearing clothes, jewellery and make-up (boys too) that look really good on the glossy, toned, photo-shopped bodies we see on the covers of magazines but do these things look good on 'normal' teenagers? Sorry, but overweight girls and boys with dirty fingernails should not be squeezing themselves into skinny jeans and wearing cheap copies of Rolex watches.

C Talking about designer labels, up to a point, I admit that I look at people who buy the real stuff and automatically believe that they are rich and cool. Everybody knows that these goods are the best quality. But fashion victims who buy copies of these products, hoping that they'll be admired by their friends, are making a big mistake. If you can't afford the real thing, buy something else.

D If you ask me, one big problem is that a fashion victim will often buy something because they've seen a media star wearing it. How many copies of Paris Hilton or David Beckham have you seen on the streets recently? And did the copies look as good as the originals? I bet they didn't.

E Here's my opinion, for what it's worth. Don't be a fashion victim. Wear what you think looks nice, not what other people tell you is trendy. Stick to items that suit your personality and regular style. Remember, YOU are the only person who is YOU! No matter where you are or what you're doing, always be yourself. (313 words)

COMMENTS

JANE I agree with Lindy on this point. Some people should not draw attention to themselves. I've seen boys with acne wearing purple shirts. Yuck! As far as I'm concerned, I'm a bit overweight, so I never wear tight clothes. I don't feel comfortable in them and I don't want people staring at me.

KATY I have to agree with you completely on that point. My own view of the matter is that a lot of teenagers simply don't know who they really are. I don't want to pretend I'm someone else. I'm happy to be me. Everyone is unique. Right?

LIAM Lindy, I see what you mean about copying stars but don't you think that's part of growing up? Young people should be free to experiment with who they are and how they look. If you like a particular star, why not copy the way they dress?

MARK Sorry, Lindy. I don't agree. Some people who buy the latest styles can look really great. I think the secret is not overdoing it. I mean, you don't have to wear every trendy item you own all at once.

NELE I'm afraid I can't accept your criticism of people who buy fakes. I want to look good but I don't have much money. I'm happy that I have a great collection of bags and shoes that look just like the originals (YSL, Prada, Versace, Gucci) and they were all affordable. (240 words)

11 WORKING WITH WORDS

A Match words from box A to words from box B to make collocations from the text on page 23. There is only one match for each word.

A	
best	fashion
brand	high
cheap	latest
designer	skinny

B	
copies	names
fashions	quality
jeans	street
labels	victims

B Write replies to two of the comments giving your own opinion. Use some of the collocations from exercise 11A.

12 DISCUSSION

→ Interaktion: An Diskussionen teilnehmen, S. 246

BUILDING SKILLS: Preparing for group discussions

Preparing yourself for the particular situation will help you take part in a discussion successfully.
- Before you start, always think about your opinion and what you want to say.
- Prepare some bullet points related to the aspects of the topic.
- Write down key words and phrases in English.

A Preparation: Work with a partner. You and your partner are going to discuss fashion with another pair. Before you start, read the ideas below with your partner and share your opinions. Decide what you want to say and make some notes.

B Discussion: Now find another pair and talk about fashion. Try to use as much language for discussion as you can.

C Tell the class the results of your discussion.

SKILLS CHECKLIST: Group discussions

- ☑ Have I thought about what I want to say?
- ☑ Have I prepared some bullet points?
- ☑ Have I written down key phrases in English?

4 Leisure and free time

FOUNDATION COURSE

1 TALKING ABOUT FREE-TIME ACTIVITIES

A **Use your own ideas and ideas from the photos to ask and answer questions about what you like or don't like doing in your free time.**

I enjoy playing music.

I love surfing the Internet.

I don't mind shopping, but I prefer to hang out with friends.

B **What activities would you like to do which you can't? Use ideas from the box to explain why you don't do these activities.**

cost of activity ▪ don't have the transport to get there ▪ lack of time ▪ no one to go with me ▪ not available in my area ▪ parents don't let me

C **Imagine you have the chance to do one of the activities you spoke about above. Describe what you are going to do or say what you think you will do.**

I'm going to take riding lessons at the local riding school. I'm going to go there twice a week.

I think I'll take a photography course. I'll need to save up for a good camera first.

2 GETTING IT RIGHT

→ *Will* future ▪ *Going to* future, S. 257

Put the verbs into the correct form of the *will* or *going to* future.

1 I've decided to spend less time in front of the computer. I (play) ___ football instead.
2 I think the weather (be) ___[1] nice this afternoon so we (be able to) ___[2] go for a run.
3 I (go) ___[1] shopping now but I promise I (be) ___[2] back later.
4 Lucy's parents gave her some money for her birthday. She (spend) ___ it on driving lessons.
5 Martin needs a new hobby so he (join) ___[1] the chess club. I hope he (like) ___[2] it.
6 I have got a free weekend so I (help) ___ my dad in the garden.
7 Tim (study) ___[1] in Bristol. He hopes he (find) ___[2] some interesting clubs to join there.
8 Mike and I (watch) ___[1] TV this evening. (you/watch) ___[2] with us?

3 ANALYSING A CARTOON

→ Produktion: Cartoons beschreiben und analysieren, S. 236

BUILDING SKILLS: Describing cartoons

Before you begin to describe or analyse a cartoon, always read the instructions carefully so that you know what you have to do.

- Read the caption under the drawing or any speech bubbles in the cartoon and think about how they relate to the picture.
- Look at everything in the picture and describe it carefully, using the present progressive to say what people are doing. → Present progressive, S. 251
- If you don't get the joke, just concentrate on describing the cartoon. Do not waste time trying to figure it out.

A Study the cartoon, then use the words from the box to complete the description below.

behind ▪ cartoonist ▪ face ▪ under ▪ home ▪ in front of ▪ probably ▪ emoticon ▪ worried

The cartoon shows a boy sitting ___[1] a computer at ___[2]. He is ___[3] in his bedroom. His parents are standing ___[4] him. The boy's father looks ___[5]. His mother appears to be saying the words written ___[6] the cartoon. The boy's ___[7] does not have the usual eyes, nose and mouth. The ___[8] has drawn it as an ___[9] instead.

"We know it makes you happy, but your father and I think you're spending too much time on the computer."

B Choose the best sentence ending to complete the interpretation of the cartoon.

The cartoonist seems to be making the point that …

a parents of teenagers are often worried about their children.
b spending all your time online will change you from a human being into a computer.
c teenagers are happiest when they're chatting.

4 READING

→ Rezeption: Leseverstehen, S. 214

A survey among teenagers in the USA showed that many of them spend their free time hanging out in shopping malls.

A Before you read the text, match the words and phrases below to the correct German translation. (The alphabetical wordlist at the back of the book will help you.)

1 curfew	**5** adequately	**a** angemessen	**e** Aktion
2 legal guardian	**6** measures	**b** Befreiungen	**f** Sperrstunde
3 retailer	**7** initiative	**c** Einzelhändler/in	**g** Vormund
4 incident	**8** exemptions	**d** Maßnahmen	**h** Zwischenfall

1/10

LIFE'S SO UNFAIR! Shopping mall sets 6 pm curfew for teenagers – unless they bring their parents

Teenagers have been hanging out in shopping malls with their friends for decades but one mall is putting an end to the tradition – at least after 6 pm. North Park Center in Dallas has set a 6 pm curfew after which time any person aged 17 or under must be accompanied by a parent or legal guardian. After the curfew any young teens without an adult will be approached and asked to provide ID and if they don't have any, a parent will either need to come join them or pick them up.

Although young teens and some of their parents may object to the curfew, North Park spokesman Mark Annick argued that all the center's retailers backed the new rules.

'I really do respect that there are parents who may not agree with us completely,' Annick told CBS news.

He went on to say that the rules were not brought in after any particular incidents or complaints but in a bid to maintain a family atmosphere for the estimated 26 million visitors who come to the mall each year. The new rules also state that visitors must dress 'appropriately for a family-oriented shopping center. Clothes must adequately cover the body. Visible undergarments are not permitted.'

The measures have divided opinions with some parents backing the curfew, others saying it should be later and some saying it is not needed at all.

'If the intent is to stop the loitering and just mall walking and things like that, I think it's a great idea,' one parent said. Another parent disagreed with the mall's initiative, saying, 'These kids are old enough to have drivers licenses, so I don't see why they need to be escorted around the mall.'

Teens who work at the mall and those who are just there to watch a movie are the only exemptions to the curfew.

North Park is the largest shopping center in North Texas boasting more than 235 stores and restaurants. (328 words)

Abridged and adapted from: *www.dailymail.co.uk*

B Now read the text carefully and make notes.

C Explain in 3–4 sentences what the text is about.

SKILLS CHECKLIST: Taking notes

- ☑ Have I read the whole text?
- ☑ Have I scanned the text for key words?
- ☑ Have I noted down the key words?

5 MEDIATION

→ Schriftliche Mediation, S. 240

BUILDING SKILLS: Written mediation

Written mediation means communicating the general sense of a text in another language to someone who does not understand the original.

- Before you start to write, read the instructions carefully and make sure you understand the *situation, who the mediation is aimed at* and *what form your text should be*, e.g. an email, a list, etc.
- Remember that you should only give the information that the person you are mediating for needs. Leave out any details that are not relevant.
- You should not translate the text word for word, so you can paraphrase 'difficult' expressions.

A Read the German instructions below and describe the situation in your own words. Say who the mediation is aimed at and what sort of text you have to write.

Sie arbeiten in einer kleinen Boutique in einem Einkaufszentrum in Ihrer Stadt. Ihr Chef / Ihre Chefin und andere Ladenbesitzer beklagen sich über die Gruppen von Jugendlichen, die sich nach der Schule im Einkaufszentrum treffen, um dort herumzuhängen. Sie stören die normalen Kunden und die Läden machen weniger Umsatz. Ihr Chef / Ihre Chefin gibt Ihnen den Text (Seite 27) und bittet Sie, die Details auf Deutsch auf einem Handzettel festzuhalten, den er/sie für seine/ihre Kollegen kopieren kann.

B Re-read the text on page 27 and decide which points your boss and his/her colleagues need to know and make a note of them.

C Now put those points into German in a structured text. Make sure your text is in the form your boss wants.

D When you have finished, read your German text and check that it is correct. Ask yourself this question: Have I given the sense of the text in a way that my boss and his/her colleagues will easily understand?

6 GETTING IT RIGHT

→ Countable and uncountable nouns, S. 274

Complete the sentences with the English translations of the German words in brackets.

1 Some kids were messing around in the shop and caused a lot of ___ [1] to some of the electronic ___ [2] on sale. (*Schaden* ▪ *Geräte*)

2 Some teachers like to give out ___ [1] at the weekend but I am always busy helping my mum with the ___ [2]. (*Hausaufgaben* ▪ *Hausarbeiten*)

3 We moved house last weekend. Lifting ___ [1], for example, is really heavy ___ [2]. (*Möbel* ▪ *Arbeit*)

4 I have found a lot of ___ [1] for my project online. I also got ___ [2] from my sister. (*Informationen* ▪ *Hilfe*)

5 If you are worried about you son's ___ [1] at school, you can ask his teacher for ___ [2]. (*Fortschritte* ▪ *Rat*)

6 Every generation of parents complain about the ___ [1] of their children. When my parents were young, their parents said their ___ [2] was too long. (*Verhalten* ▪ *Haare*)

7 There is no ___ that shopping centres are safer places if teenagers have to leave after 6 pm. (*Beweise*)

1/11

IT'S ALL RIGHT, MUM, I'M ONLY PRACTISING MY SOCIAL SKILLS

What do teenagers do in their free time? Some of them hang out in chat rooms exchanging moans about school or talking about the opposite sex. Others text, tweet or post their activities as they happen. Most teenagers today use social media to stay connected to their peers.

Many parents complain that their children prefer computers to 'real' people but they don't seem to realize that most of the kids are actually working actively to interact with other people. It used to be the shopping centre but today the places to meet are online. Social network sites are often the only 'public' spaces in which teens can get together with their friends in today's busy world.

Kids today don't really have much free time. Apart from homework, a lot of them have organized after-school activities or jobs. Some parents do not allow their children to go out after school; they have to help in the house or look after younger siblings.

A generation ago, it was usual for teens to visit each other at home after school. Today's teens often don't know any people of their age who live nearby. Social media gives teenagers the opportunity to socialize and relax with people of their own age after school. Instead of complaining, parents should be pleased when they see their kids texting or chatting online. These teens are simply using today's technology to learn social skills and have fun with friends.

(239 words)

7 LOOKING AT THE TEXT

→ Rezeption: Leseverstehen, S. 214

A Read the text. Say in two sentences what it is about.

B Say if the following statements are true or false according to the text. Give reasons for all of your answers.

1 Teenagers use all types of social media to keep in touch with their friends.
2 Parents would prefer their children to meet their friends face-to-face.
3 Teens like to meet their friends in shopping centres.
4 Kids have a lot to do after school.
5 Parents are happy when their children do outdoor activities.
6 A lot of teenagers meet in each other's homes after school.
7 Social media is often the only way kids can have contact with each other after school.
8 Teenagers can strengthen their relationships using social media.

8 WORKING WITH WORDS

A All of the words in the box appear in the text. Match six of them with their definitions, 1–6.

a generation ▪ activities ▪ moans ▪ peers ▪ siblings ▪ social skills ▪ to interact ▪ to prefer

1 brothers and sisters
2 complaints about something
3 people who are the same age or have the same social status as you
4 the ability to talk easily to other people and do things in a group
5 to communicate with somebody, especially while you work, play or spend time with them
6 to like one thing or a person better than another

B Write your own definitions for the two extra words as they appear in the text.

9 GETTING IT RIGHT

→ Quantifiers, S. 274

Choose the correct word or phrase from the box to complete the dialogues.

any ▪ some ▪ many ▪ much

1 **A** Do you have ___[1] time this evening? I need ___[2] help with my homework.
B Sorry, I have too ___[3] homework myself at the moment. I don't need ___[4] more.

2 **A** How ___[1] social media sites are you on?
B I was on four, but my dad said I was spending too ___[2] time online so I only use one now.

3 **A** Have you got ___[1] friends on Facebook that you have never met before?
B I don't have ___[2] Facebook friends at all. I don't have ___[3] time for social networks.

a few ▪ a little ▪ few ▪ little

4 **A** I can't come round till later. I have ___[1] more things to do at home.
B That's all right by me. I need ___[2] more time to organize things before you arrive.

5 **A** There's ___[1] point in explaining what you're doing to your parents.
B I know. Very ___[2] parents remember how things were when they were young.

6 **A** My friends have ___[1] interest in Facebook. They are all on WhatsApp.
B I only know ___[2] people who still use Facebook.

10 MEDIATION

→ Schriftliche Mediation, S. 240

Sie hören zufällig, wie Ihre Mutter und Ihre Tante sich über Ihre zwei Cousins unterhalten. Sie sind beide Teenager und verbringen viel Zeit in ihren sozialen Netzwerken im Internet. Ihre Tante ist besorgt und möchte wissen, warum die junge Leute sich nicht mehr mit ihren Freunden nach der Schule treffen, so wie sie und Ihre Mutter es gemacht haben, als sie Teenager waren.

Sie beschließen, Ihrer Tante eine E-Mail zu schreiben, in der Sie die wichtigsten Punkte des Textes *It's all right, Mum, I'm only practising my social skills* auf Deutsch erklären.

SKILLS CHECKLIST: Written mediation

- ☑ Have I read the situation?
- ☑ Have I understood who the mediation is for?
- ☑ Have I written the right sort of text?

11 DESCRIBING A PICTURE

→ Produktion: Bilder beschreiben und analysieren, S. 236

Your aunt shows you this picture of your cousins.

A **Describe the photo. Explain how it relates to the text *It's all right, Mum, I'm only practising my social skills.***

B **Describe the photo. Compare the children's behaviour with your own use of social media.**

Job skills 1

Emails ▪ telephoning

Eric Jung is studying at a vocational college and is looking for work experience during the summer. Earlier this morning he received two emails.

1 LOOKING AT THE EMAILS

A Read the emails and answer these questions.

Email 1

1 How does the writer of the first email know Eric?
2 Why does he think Eric might be interested in his suggestion?
3 How will Eric get more information?

Email 2

4 Who has written the second email?
5 Where is she writing from?
6 What does Eric have to do next, and when?

1

Von: leon.dubois@deglado.com
Betreff: Work experience for you?
An: Eric Jung < ejung@gmx.com>

Hi Eric

How's it going? Listen, I had a great idea. You know that I'm just finishing work experience in an import/export company in Bristol, England, and I know you're looking, so why don't you apply for my job? The boss is always looking for trainees who can speak another language (not English) as their native language. I think your German's pretty good, eh? ;-)

I've asked the secretary to send you some info. I know it's not London (your dream city!), but Bristol's cool and the work is interesting. Like that crazy American girl said that night at the backpackers' hostel: DON'T TALK ABOUT IT, JUST DO IT!!

So, what about it, my friend? I'll be gone by the time you get here but maybe CU in Paris sometime?

Cheers!
Léon

2

Von: sarah.brown@delgado.com
Betreff: Work placement
An: Eric Jung < ejung@gmx.com>
1 Anhang: OnlineAdWorkExperience.docx

Work Experience at Delgado Import/Export

If you are just about to complete your education, a placement in our company will give you an insight into how a small business is run. You will work in a small team and find out at first hand all about business.

Minimum of GCSE or equivalent.

Dear Mr Jung

I have your contact details from Léon Dubois. Léon has mentioned that you might be interested in applying for work placement in our company, Delgado Import/Export, in Bristol.

Attached is a copy of the job advertisement that will be posted online next week.

Please let me know if you are interested in applying for the position by Thursday, 9 March at the latest.

Yours sincerely

Sarah Brown
Secretary
Delgado Import/Export

Job skills 1

B Work with a partner and compare and contrast the two emails.

Look at language, style of writing, use of slang and abbreviations.

Leon's language shows that he and Eric are friends. His email is quite chatty.

Yes, that's right. And the secretary's language is very formal. She's written a business email.

TIP Email etiquette

1 Make sure that the subject line of your email is as clear as possible.
2 Include your name and contact details at the end of your email.
3 Attach documents when you say you will, and make sure they are correct. (Get into the habit of attaching documents before you write your email, then you won't forget them.)
4 Until you know somebody well, keep your emails formal and don't use slang or short forms like CU.
5 Never TYPE IN CAPITAL LETTERS as it looks like you are shouting and could seem rude.
6 Before you send your email, check the spelling.

2 LOOKING AT EMAIL ETIQUETTE

A Not long after he sent his application to Delgado Import/Export, Eric receives the following email. Look at the body of the email and choose the best option for a business email from the brackets.

Von: sarah.brown@delgado.com
Betreff: Your application for work placement
An: Eric Jung < ejung@gmx.com>

(Dear / Hi)[1] Mr Jung

(Thanks / Thank you)[2] for your application for work placement which you submitted to Delgado Import/Export last week.

If you are still interested in the position, Mr Delgado would like to call you at 10.00 am on Friday, 18 March. (He wants to call / The object of the call is)[3] to get to know more about you before we take your application further.

In preparation for the call, (here's / I have attached)[4] some (info / information)[5] about the position you have applied for.

Please (confirm that you will be available / give us your OK)[6] for a call at the time and on the date suggested above.

(I look forward to hearing from you soon. / Looking forward to your reply.)[7]

(Cheers / Yours sincerely)[8]

Sarah Brown

B Now study the set-up of the corrected email with a partner. Refer to the tip box. Has the writer followed all of the rules of email etiquette? Explain your answer.

3 WRITING AN EMAIL

Schreiben Sie die E-Mail für Eric und verwenden Sie dabei die unten stehenden Punkte.

- Danken Sie Sarah für ihre E-Mail.
- Bestätigen Sie das Datum und die Uhrzeit des Telefongesprächs.
- Sagen Sie, dass Sie zum Zeitpunkt des Gesprächs keinen ausreichenden mobilen Netzempfang haben werden. Erklären Sie, dass Sie Zugang zu einem Telefon haben werden, sich aber nicht sicher sind, wie die Telefonnummer lautet. Schlagen Sie vor, dass Sie die Firma selbst zu der vorgeschlagenen Uhrzeit anrufen.
- Beenden Sie die E-Mail mit einer passenden Schlussformel.

4 PREPARING FOR A TELEPHONE CALL

Eric looks at some material about telephoning in English which he has from college. Unfortunately, some parts of the material have become separated from the rest.

A Read the tips for telephoning in English (1–6) and match them to the headlines (a–f).

a During the call
b Preparation
c Making small talk
d Softening bad news
e Starting the call
f Telephone numbers

Telephoning in English

1 Think about what you want to say before you start and note down some phrases.
2 Say your first name and your surname and the name of your company clearly.
3 Make sure you note down all proper names correctly. If you do not understand something, ask the other person to repeat the information. Ask the person on the other end of the line to speak more slowly if necessary.
4 English speakers often chat about a general topic, such as the weather, at the start of a call.
5 English speakers usually begin bad news with phrases such as *I'm afraid (that) …* or *I'm sorry, but …*
6 When you give telephone numbers, say each digit separately, except for double digits, e.g. 012334799 = *oh (AE: zero) one two double-three four seven double-nine.*

B Read the phrases on the fronts of the flash cards Eric made for learning English phrases for telephoning and match them to the German on the back of the cards. → Vokabeln lernen, S. 220

1 Can I speak to … (*name*), please?
2 Could you repeat that, please?
3 Could you spell your name, please?
4 Good morning, … (*name*) speaking.
5 I'll put you through.
6 It was nice talking to you.
7 Who's calling, please?
8 Would you like to leave a message?

a Guten Morgen, … (*Name*) am Apparat.
b Ich stelle Sie durch.
c Bitte wiederholen Sie.
d Buchstabieren Sie bitte Ihren Namen.
e Ich würde gerne … (*Name*) sprechen.
f Möchten Sie eine Nachricht hinterlassen?
g Es war schön, mit Ihnen zu reden.
h Wie ist Ihr Name, bitte?

Job skills 1

5 LISTENING

→ Rezeption: Hörverstehen, S. 225

It is 10 o'clock on Friday morning and Eric is ready to call Mr Delgado. As things turn out, Eric has to make two calls.

1/12 **A Listen to Eric's first call to Bristol. What went wrong? Which phrases from exercise 4B do you hear?**

1/13 **B Listen to Eric's second call to Bristol and answer the questions.**

1 Who answers the phone?
2 Why can't Mr Delgado speak to Eric at the moment?
3 Why is it likely that Delgado Import/Export is a nice company to work for?
4 Why has Eric not read the information leaflet?
5 How does Eric make the other person feel better about her mistake?
6 What is the rule about using first names at the company?

6 ROLE-PLAY

→ Interaktion: Ein Rollenspiel gestalten, S. 247

Work with a partner. Read through what you are going to say below and make notes. Then carry out the telephone conversation.

Partner A	Partner B
→ Start the call by giving your name and the name of your company.	→ Greet your partner and say who you are. Make some small talk.
→ Greet the caller by name and respond to the small talk. Ask how you can help.	→ Ask to speak to someone in the office.
→ Explain that the person is not available. Offer to take a message.	→ Leave a message.
→ Make a note of the message and read it back to the caller.	→ Thank your partner and say goodbye.

Useful phrases: Telephoning

Making a call
- Good morning. My name's …
- Good afternoon. This is … from XYZ.
- I'm calling about …
- I'm enquiring about …
- I'd like some information on …
- Could you tell me about …?
- I'd like to speak to Mr/Ms …
- Could you put me through to the … department, please?
- Can I leave a message?
- Can you ask him/her to call me back?
- I'll call again later.

Taking a call
- ABC Company. Jane Smith speaking.
- Accounts Department. John here. How can I help you?
- Could you hold on a moment?
- I'll try to connect you.
- Hold the line, please.
- I'm sorry. Mr/Ms … is unavailable at the moment.
- I'm afraid the line is engaged.
- Would you like to leave a message?
- Can I help at all?
- I'll make sure he/she gets your message.

5 The virtual world

MAIN COURSE

FOCUS

A **On your own, look at the photos above and make notes about the role of social media in society today. Discuss your notes with a partner and then in class.**

B **In groups of three or four, draw a poster showing how you use social media. Include the points below and your own ideas.**

- when you use social media
- when you don't use social media
- which social media you use
- why you use social media
- how much money/time you spend on social media

C **Gallery walk: Put your posters up on the walls of your classroom and look at them all. As you walk round the class, make notes on the following points:**

- which social media your class uses most
- why most people use social media
- how much the class spends on social media per month

D **In class, talk about how important social media is to you and why.**

TEXT A Using social media

BEFORE YOU READ

→ Rezeption: Leseverstehen – Grobverständnis, S. 214

A Describe the picture in a few sentences.

B Skim the text below and decide if it is about …

a the problems of young people today.
b how lonely people use the Internet.
c social media habits in the UK.
d Facebook and Twitter.

BUILDING SKILLS: Skimming a text

Skimming means moving your eyes over a text very quickly in order to get the main ideas.

- Read the title carefully because it summarizes the article. Use a dictionary for unknown words.
- Read all of the first paragraph and any more sub-headings.
- Read the first sentence of all the other paragraphs. The most important ideas are normally here.
- Scan the text for clues to meaning, e.g. words which are underlined, in **bold type** or *italics*.
- Read all of the final paragraph. This usually summarizes the text.

1/14

BRITONS SPEND 62M HOURS A DAY ON SOCIAL MEDIA

That's an average of one hour for EVERY adult and child

Britons spend an estimated 62 million hours each day on Facebook and Twitter, according to a new survey on social media habits.

The poll suggests that around 34 million hours are spent on Facebook each day, with a further 28 million hours on Twitter. And almost a third (30%) of the UK's 33 million Facebook users are on the network for at least an hour a day, with 13% spending at least two hours on Facebook each day.

More than a quarter (26%) of UK women on Facebook check their pages at least 10 times a day, compared to less than one in five (18%) of men. Of the UK's estimated 26 million Twitter users, almost a third (31%) spend more than an hour a day on the network, while 14% – more than 3.6 million people – say their daily usage exceeds two hours. The results are based on a survey of 1,500 adults carried out by OnePoll for online bank, first direct*.

The survey also found Facebook was named as the primary social media platform by 59% of people. Only 9% named Twitter as their first-choice network, while 7% chose LinkedIn. And 11% of Twitter users say it is important for them to have more 'followers' on their feed than their friends, compared to just 4% of Facebook users who say it is important to appear more 'popular' than their friends.

Dr David Giles, a reader in media psychology at Winchester University, said: 'People's social media habits tend to be largely dependent on the number of friends who are on the social network with them. If all your friends are on Facebook or Twitter all the time, you risk cutting yourself off from a social life by not doing the same. So you spend several hours every day online simply to avoid feeling left out of conversations, or being isolated from your friends.'

* company name

Rebecca Dye, social media manager at first direct, said: 'The survey shows just how central Facebook and Twitter are to people's lives at the moment, often at the expense of other communications and regardless of how often they're actually posting updates or tweeting.

'It's important we engage with our customers in ways that best suit their lives, so the more people are using social media channels to have conversations, or just to "listen in", the more we need to develop our presence in social media,' she added. (422 words)

From: *www.independent.co.uk*

1 WORKING WITH WORDS

Match the highlighted words in the text with the following definitions. There are three more highlighted words than you need.

1 asking a small, representative number of people questions to find out what most people do or think
2 cut off
3 to interact with, to get involved with
4 is more or greater than
5 not worrying about
6 to seem
7 the number you get when you add amounts together and divide the sum by the number of amounts
8 the things people do every day
9 to not let sth happen
10 two or more

2 LOOKING AT THE TEXT

→ Rezeption: Leseverstehen, S. 214

Use words from the text to complete the sentences.

1 Facebook and Twitter are popular ▬ sites.
2 Twitter is less popular than ▬ .
3 26% of women check their Facebook accounts ▬ .
4 Every day 14% of UK Twitter users are online for more than ▬ .
5 First direct is a(n) ▬ .
6 Someone who is interested in what you post on Twitter is called a ▬ .
7 Dr Giles works at a ▬ .
8 Dr Giles says some people spend a lot of time on Facebook and Twitter to make sure they are not ▬ .

3 DISCUSSION

→ Interaktion: An Diskussionen teilnehmen, S. 246

Read the following complaints made by teachers about their students.

Young people today use social media much too much and have no time for homework, sport, hobbies or even their own families. They are up all night on the Internet and are so tired the next day that they can't concentrate at school.

They are unfit, can't spell and have poor handwriting (they only use their thumbs to text).

They are wasting their childhood and their money. Parents should take away their children's phones at night and switch off the Internet. Students should hand in their phones when they enter the school building.

A Look at the teachers' criticisms and suggestions and write down if you agree or disagree.

B Use your notes to have a class discussion.

C At the end of your discussion take a vote in class on whether you agree or disagree with the following statement: 'If we use social media less, our school work will become better.'

4 WRITING

→ Produktion: Schreiben, S. 228

Use your poster (Focus) and your own ideas to write a blog entry about the importance of social media. Use the *Language for writing* expressions on the back cover flap.
Structure your answer like this:

- Give your blog a title (e.g. 'A day offline?' or 'Last night a smartphone saved my life', etc.).
- Tell a very short anecdote about how social media helped or caused a problem for you or a friend (e.g. *Last Saturday night I posted a call for help on my Facebook wall and then …*).
- Next write two paragraphs about the advantage(s) and disadvantages of social media.
  - If you like social media, first write about the disadvantages.
  - If you dislike social media, first write about the advantages.
- Write a conclusion to show what you think about social media.

Write a blog entry to explain why smartphones should or shouldn't be allowed in lessons at school. Use the *Language for writing* expressions on the back cover flap.

5 LISTENING

→ Rezeption: Hörverstehen, S. 225

You are going to hear a call to the telephone helpline of *cyberbullying.online*, an organization that helps people suffering from online bullying.

1/15

Listen and complete the sentences.

1 Sarah is unhappy because ___ .
2 People are sending her ___ .
3 The counsellor asks Sarah if ___ .
4 The counsellor says she can get help from ___ .
5 Sarah went to ___ and drank ___ .
6 The counsellor tells Sarah she can make an appointment over ___ .
7 Sarah doesn't want to ___ .
8 The counsellor is going to send Sarah ___ .

6 GETTING IT RIGHT

→ Simple past, S. 251

Use the key words to summarize Sarah's conversation with the counsellor using the simple past. Start like this:
Sarah phoned a cyberbullying helpline and talked to Frank about …

(Sarah) horrible pictures ▪ Internet ▪ everyone ▪ school ▪ can see them ▪ Facebook ▪ desperate
(Frank) need ▪ support ▪ parents
dad ▪ live ▪ girlfriend ▪ mother ▪ work all day ▪ brother ▪ young ▪ other family members ▪ too far away
advise ▪ contact ▪ school counsellors ▪ understand ▪ help ▪ students
not want ▪ go back to school ever again
possible ▪ make ▪ appointment ▪ counsellor ▪ phone
still unhappy ▪ messages ▪ Facebook ▪ not want ▪ delete
not necessary ▪ delete ▪ account ▪ promise ▪ send ▪ email ▪ practical help

7 MEDIATION

→ Schriftliche Mediation, S. 240

Cyberbullying.online schickt Sarah eine E-Mail. In dieser wird erklärt, welche Schritte sie unternehmen kann, um nicht mehr gemobbt zu werden. Ein Freund/eine Freundin von Ihnen wird auf einem sozialen Netzwerk gemobbt und bittet Sie um Hilfe. Er/Sie möchte für eine Zeit lang nicht mehr erreichbar sein, will aber nichts Endgültiges machen, denn seine/ihre Daten sind ihm/ihr wichtig.

Lesen Sie die folgende E-Mail durch und entnehmen Sie ihr die Informationen, die Ihrem Freund / Ihrer Freundin helfen könnten. Schreiben Sie ihm/ihr eine E-Mail.

SKILLS CHECKLIST: Written mediation

- ☑ Have I read the situation?
- ☑ Have I written the right sort of text?
- ☑ Have I left out unnecessary details?

Hi

Thank you for contacting *cyberbullying.online*. To stop getting messages on Facebook (or any other social media account) you can *block people*, *deactivate* or *delete* the account and also *take legal action*.

How to block (unfriend) people

- Log into *General Account – Settings*.
- Click on the Security icon – *How do I stop someone from bothering me?*
- Follow the instructions carefully.

How to deactivate your Facebook account

- Press *More* in the bottom right-hand corner of the Facebook start screen.
- Scroll down to and click on *Settings – General – Account – Deactivate*.
- Follow the instructions carefully.

You can reactivate your account later at any time.

How to delete your Facebook account

It's best to do this on a computer. Before you delete your account, remember it takes at least 90 days; if you delete an account and then log in again before the 90 days are up, you reactivate the account; when you delete your Facebook account, you lose all your data.

- First go to *Settings* and download a copy of all the data Facebook has on you.
- Log out of or delete phone and tablet apps, including Facebook Home.
- Write an Account Deletion Epitaph, so people know you have closed your account, e.g.

  I am no longer available on Facebook because I have deleted my account.
- Go to the Facebook account deletion page and follow the instructions carefully.

Legal action

- Report cyberbullying to your school, institution and/or the police.
- Hire a specialist lawyer and take legal action. Your lawyer will contact web service providers and ask them to delete your data. In 80% of the cases they agree.

Remember – there is <u>always</u> a solution to any problem. Thousands of young people suffer from cyberbullying and when they get help, it stops!

Cyberbullying Help Team

TEXT B Unwanted guests

→ Rezeption: Leseverstehen, S. 214

BEFORE YOU READ

Why do you think the mother is angry with her son? Skim the text and write down what they could be saying to each other.

SKILLS CHECKLIST: Skimming

- ☑ Have I studied the headline?
- ☑ Have I read the sub-heading?
- ☑ Have I read the first paragraph?

1/16

'Don't have any parties'

Last words of mother leaving for holiday to her schoolboy son, 17, days before drunken Facebook crashers trashed her £1m house

Drunken revellers have trashed a £1.1million house after gatecrashing a schoolboy's Facebook event – days after his mother went on holiday and told him: 'Don't have any parties'.

The group caused an estimated £15,000 of damage and left vomit all over the terraced property in Highgate, north London, while riot police were called to break up 600 people in the street outside.

Now mother-of-four Catherine Seale, 54, who had gone to France on holiday with her husband when the trouble began, has warned of the dangers of putting personal details online.

Her son, Christopher, 17, had invited 60 friends round to his house on September 21 for his birthday, but a friend who put the event on Facebook did not realise the invitation could be seen by anyone.

Mrs Seale, whose 53-year-old husband Adam is a company director, said: 'All parents should be warned that this could happen if you go away and leave your 17-year-old alone. I think if anyone is going to throw a party, they need to look at their privacy settings on Facebook. It's absolutely essential that children are made aware of this.' […]

One girl at the party was taken to hospital with alcohol poisoning. Laughing gas canisters were tossed across Mrs Seale's living room carpet. Christopher and his aunt worked round the clock to clean up, but the house smelled of vomit and alcohol for days. Mrs Seale added: 'The last thing I told him before I went away was "don't have any parties". The carpet was trashed and they damaged a skylight because somebody fell on it. […]

Chris paid a bouncer £60, telling him to only let in the 60 invited guests but the bouncer, who was paid in advance, was unable to cope and ran away when hundreds more party goers turned up. […] Mrs Seale heard about the trouble when a shocked mother who had dropped off her son at the party phoned to tell her that children aged between 14 and 18 were wrecking her home and got the first flight back after hearing of the chaos. […]

Mrs Seale added: 'It doesn't seem to have done him any harm at school. Apparently, he has even got a girlfriend out of it. I think his reputation has shot up because of it, which isn't very good for us parents.' (417 words)

Abridged from: *www.dailymail.co.uk*

1 LOOKING AT THE TEXT

→ Rezeption: Leseverstehen, S. 214

A Put the following statements about the text in the right order starting with *f*.

- **a** A mother brought her son to the party by car.
- **b** Christopher Seale decided to have a birthday party.
- **c** Everybody saw the message.
- **d** He invited 60 friends.
- **e** Hundreds of people came to the party.
- **f** Mr and Mrs Seale went to France on holiday.
- **g** Mrs Seale flew home immediately.
- **h** Somebody posted a message about the party on Facebook.
- **i** The bouncer couldn't stop people from entering the house.
- **j** The mother saw the chaos and phoned Mrs Seale in France.
- **k** They got drunk and broke things.
- **l** They told their son not to have any parties while they were away.

BUILDING SKILLS: Dealing with unknown words

There's no need to panic when you read a word you haven't seen before in a text. Think about these questions before you look the word up in a dictionary:

- Is the word similar to a German word you know, e.g. *democracy/Demokratie*?
- Is the word from the same word family as an English word you already know, e.g. *prefer – preference – preferable*?
- Can you guess the meaning of the word from the context, i.e. the general sense of the sentence or the paragraph?

→ Mit unbekannten Wörtern umgehen, S. 216

B Say what it means: With a partner, talk about what the following words mean by looking at the way they are used in the text.

1. drunken (line 1)
2. revellers (line 1)
3. vomit (line 6)
4. essential (line 25)
5. trashed (line 34)
6. bouncer (line 37)
7. to cope (line 39)
8. shot up (line 49)

2 WORKING WITH WORDS

A Find words in the text that go with the following words (= collocations).

terraced ▪ riot ▪ personal ▪ throw ▪ privacy ▪ alcohol ▪ laughing

EXAMPLE: *terraced property*

B Use some of the collocations from exercise 2A to complete this text.

Before you ___[1] and post the details on Facebook, you should check your ___[2] because you don't want hundreds of people to come uninvited. If there's too much noise, your next-door neighbours will call the ___[3], especially if you live in a small ___[4] with houses on either side. If a party gets out of control, people sometimes drink too much and end up in hospital with ___[5], so remember: small is beautiful.

3 GETTING IT RIGHT

→ Simple past ▪ Present perfect, S. 254

A Copy the table and put the following time expressions in the correct list.

2 years ago ▪ at 7 o'clock this morning ▪ at Christmas ▪ ever ▪ in 2000 ▪ never ▪ in February ▪ in the spring ▪ just ▪ last month ▪ on Friday ▪ on my birthday ▪ since 2005 ▪ this morning ▪ this week ▪ today ▪ yesterday ▪ yet

Simple past (finished time / time in the past)	Present perfect (unfinished time / time up to now)
2 years ago, …	*ever, …*

B Complete the sentences with the simple past or the present perfect.

	Simple past	Present perfect
1	Last week Sarah *received* a hundred Facebook messages.	This week she *hasn't received* any messages.
2	Yesterday she ▬ fifteen text messages.	Since 7 am this morning she has written eight text messages.
3	A few days ago she drank six cocktails at a party.	Since then she ▬ water.
4	Last week she ▬ to a counsellor five times.	In the last three days she has talked to a counsellor three times.
5	Six friends phoned her yesterday.	Three friends ▬ her today.
6	She ▬ Facebook last week.	She hasn't used Facebook this week.
7	She didn't speak to her counsellor yesterday.	She ▬ to her counsellor today.
8	She ▬ any photos last week.	She hasn't uploaded any photos this week.

C Complete the radio interview with a counsellor using the simple past or present perfect.

Reporter	Thanks for coming to the studio, Frank.
Frank	My pleasure.
Reporter	How long (you/be) ▬ [1] a counsellor now?
Frank	I (start) ▬ [2] about ten years ago.
Reporter	And can you tell us about your work?
Frank	Yes, certainly. At the beginning I only (do) ▬ [3] telephone counselling but since last year we (have) ▬ [4] so many cases of cyberbullying that I now give face-to-face counselling, too.
Reporter	Could you explain the difference?
Frank	Telephone counselling is often just the beginning. If someone (lose) ▬ [5] a loved one for example, they can phone our hotline to get help and support. Yesterday I (speak) ▬ [6] to a young man with that problem. We (talk) ▬ [7] for an hour and now he (make) ▬ [8] an appointment to see me next week.
Reporter	I see. How many people (you/help) ▬ [9] over the years up to now?
Frank	I really don't know. I (take) ▬ [10] about 30 calls last week alone, so it must be thousands …

4 ROLE-PLAY

→ Interaktion: Ein Rollenspiel gestalten, S. 247

Last Saturday night while your parents were away for the weekend, you had a party at your house/flat. You invited 20 friends on Facebook and bought food and drinks, including beer and wine for them. Suddenly, in the early hours of Sunday morning your flat/house was full of gatecrashers. They drank all the beer and wine and turned up the music so loud that the neighbours called the police. When your parents returned, they found the house/flat a complete mess.

Work in groups of three. Expand the notes to act out a role-play.

Parents (two students taking turns to speak)	You
→ (*angry/horrified/shocked*) arrive ▪ find ▪ house ▪ mess	→ sorry ▪ mess ▪ gatecrashers ▪ not my friends
→ how ▪ gatecrashers ▪ hear about ▪ party?	→ probably ▪ see ▪ invitation ▪ Facebook
→ not ▪ click on ▪ 'Invite only'?	→ forget
→ how many ▪ guests ▪ you ▪ invite?	→ 20
→ how many ▪ gatecrashers ▪ come?	→ about 100
→ you ▪ know ▪ gatecrashers?	→ not know any of them
→ cost ▪ at least £2,000 (€2,500) ▪ clean up ▪ house!	→ (*shock*)
→ holiday ▪ Mallorca ▪ cancelled!	→ (*horror*) clean carpet ▪ wash walls ▪ myself?
→ also ▪ apologize ▪ neighbours ▪ in person!	→ write ▪ letter?
→ expect ▪ perfect behaviour ▪ next three months ▪ talk about ▪ Mallorca ▪ again	→ your own answer
→ no more ▪ parties ▪ at home	→ your own answer

5 USING THE INTERNET

Cancer fundraiser Stephen Sutton dies aged 19

[…] The 19-year-old, from Burntwood in Staffordshire, raised more than £3.2m ($5.36m) for charity after news of his plight spread on social media. […]

Stephen was diagnosed with terminal cancer aged 15. Rather than dwell on his misfortune, the teenager drew up a "bucket list" of things he wanted to achieve before he died. This led to him completing a skydive and playing drums in front of 90,000 people before the Uefa Champions League final at Wembley last May. […] He had initially set out to raise just £10,000 ($16,800) for charity, but his fundraising campaign attracted huge attention last month after he posted a selfie online. […]

From: *www.bbc.com*

A **Mediation: Erzählen Sie Ihrem/Ihrer Partner/in auf Deutsch den Inhalt des Artikels.**

B **Project: Do you know of further examples of inspirational behaviour which have used Internet technology to benefit society? Research the details online with a partner and report your findings to the class.**

Encryption technology

When we use our phones to send text, photo and video messages to our friends, this is private communication. Secure messaging apps use encryption to make sure that our messages remain private.

4/2

HOW DOES ENCRYPTION WORK?

Encryption is the process of scrambling data by applying an algorithm to it. Central to this process is a mathematical value, called a key, which the algorithm uses to scramble the data in a unique and complex way. In theory, an expert *could* decrypt the message without the key, but it would take a long time with a powerful computer.

The main problem with encryption with a single key (symmetric encryption) is that the message is only secure if the key is secret, but for communication to take place, the sender *must share the key with the recipient*. Another person could intercept the key and decrypt the message.

Asymmetric encryption is more secure. Each user of asymmetric encryption has a public key and a private key, which are created simultaneously using the same algorithm. It is almost impossible to work out the private key from the public key. It is not possible to reverse the public key and restore the original message, either.

A user's private key is just that – private. He or she does not share it with anyone. By contrast, the public key is freely available. The sender looks up the recipient's public key and uses it to encrypt the message, and the recipient uses his or her private key to decrypt it.

Unfortunately, even encrypted messaging is not completely secure. Users of the messaging app Snapchat discovered this in 2014 when hackers posted 200,000 of their "private" videos and photos online.

(244 words)

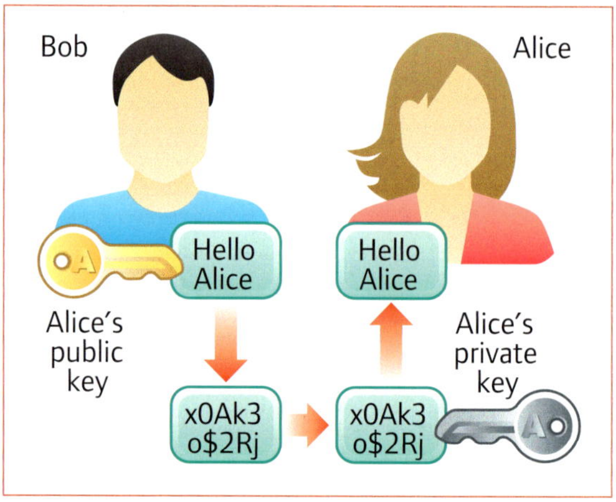

1 MEDIATION

→ Schriftliche Mediation, S. 240

Sie sollen in Ihrer Jugendgruppe einen kurzen Vortrag über Handy-Sicherheit halten.

Erstellen Sie dafür eine punktuelle Übersicht über die SMS-Verschlüsselung anhand von Informationen aus dem Text.

2 WRITING A REVIEW

Review a messaging app that you know. Comment on the following aspects:

- price
- security
- other useful features

6 Advertising

MAIN COURSE

FOCUS

A **Advertising can be found everywhere. With a partner make a list of all the places (real and virtual) where you can find advertisements and report your findings to the class.**

billboard ▪ digital signage ▪ viral ad ▪ virtual billboard ▪ …

B **Experts say good adverts must have at least one of the elements below. With a partner look for these elements in photos 1–4. Write one or two sentences about each photo and then discuss your ideas in class.**

ambition ▪ emotion ▪ entertainment ▪ excitement ▪ horror ▪ human interest (e.g. love, tragedy) ▪ humour ▪ identification ▪ inspiration ▪ mystery ▪ provocation ▪ sex ▪ shock ▪ surprise

1

C **Find some interesting examples of advertising and bring them to your next English lesson. Explain to the class which of the elements they contain.**

2

3

4

TEXT A New ideas in advertising

WHILE YOU READ

Take notes on how each idea in the three following texts benefits society.

SKILLS CHECKLIST: Taking notes

- ☑ Have I read the whole text?
- ☑ Have I scanned the text for key words?
- ☑ Have I noted down the key words?

1/17

THE FUN THEORY IN ADVERTISING

A Volkswagen brings the fun

Giant piano stairs and other 'Fun Theory' marketing

If stairs played musical notes when you walked on them, would you be more likely to take them?

The video of people skipping the escalator in favor of composing music on the piano stairs of Odenplan subway station in Stockholm, Sweden, has been viewed more than 2.5 million times on YouTube.

The video is part of a new viral marketing campaign called "The Fun Theory." The concept, created by Volkswagen Sweden and ad agency DDB Stockholm, is based on the idea that "fun is the easiest way to change people's behavior for the better." […]

The goal with these fun, do-good videos is to promote VW's new environmentally friendly BlueMotionTechnologies brand in an increasingly more competitive eco-car market.

"As traditional advertising is becoming less effective, and the competition in the market for environmentally sound cars is becoming fiercer, we believed we needed a more innovative approach to draw attention to BlueMotion," DDB Stockholm deputy manager Lars Axelsson said in an e-mail.

The video of the giant piano stairs reports that the number of commuters who chose the stairs over the escalator increased by 66% when the stairs were musical black-and-white piano keys.

The first of the campaign's three phases started with the release of the three viral videos, which aim to inspire the public to enter the campaign's contest, the second phase, by submitting their best video experiment of "The Fun Theory" to the website.

The winner gets a prize of €2,500 (about $3,700), and once the competition finishes "The Fun Theory" is "proven" by the video submissions, linking to VW and its new thoughtful technology: Its cars are good for the environment and fun for the driver. […]

Next on the campaign: a glass recycling game machine, says DDB Stockholm. "By making driving and the world more fun, we turn the VW brand into a hero," Axelsson said. "Our experiments and our Fun Theory films make the world a better and more fun place to live." (343 words)

From: *www.latimes.com*

B The glass recycling game machine

In Sweden many people recycle their plastic bottles and cans but fewer recycle their glass. To encourage people to do so Volkswagen and DDB Stockholm have invented a bottle bank arcade which gives you points each time you throw a bottle into it like the machines in an amusement arcade. It makes a funny noise to attract the attention of passers-by and explains to them on its display how to play. The idea is so successful that in one evening over 100 people used the bottle bank arcade but only two used a nearby conventional bottle bank. (102 words)

C The world's deepest bin

VW and DDB have also invented a very special rubbish bin which encourages people to use it. When you throw something in, it sounds as if the object is falling into a hole hundreds of metres deep. After five seconds the sound of falling stops and is followed by a loud crash. In one day people threw 72 kg of rubbish into the bin but only 31 kg of rubbish into a nearby conventional bin over the same period of time. (85 words)

1 LOOKING AT THE TEXTS

→ Rezeption: Leseverstehen, S. 214

Choose the correct statement (a, b or c) to complete the sentences about the texts.

1 When you step on the stairs at this station …
- a you hear a song.
- b you play a note.
- c you stop the escalator.

2 VW and DDB believe that …
- a people will do something new if it's fun.
- b everything people do must be fun.
- c more people will have fun if they take a subway train.

3 Lars Axelsson believes that today the best way to advertise a car is with …
- a traditional advertising.
- b environmental arguments.
- c new ideas.

4 DDB's Lars Axelsson says that "The Fun Theory" will make people think that …
- a VW thinks carefully about technology and does its best to protect the environment.
- b VW drivers are heroes.
- c VW makes the best viral videos.

5 The Swedes …
- a only drink out of plastic bottles and metal cans.
- b never recycle glass.
- c recycle less glass than metal or plastic.

6 The world's deepest rubbish bin …
- a is built over a hole hundreds of metres deep.
- b sounds like it is built over a deep hole.
- c is much bigger than a conventional rubbish bin.

2 WORKING WITH WORDS

A Match the verbs with a noun to make collocations. They are all in text A.

Verbs		
to take	to promote	to draw
to compose	to release	to enter

Nouns		
a brand	a video	music
a contest	attention to	the stairs

B Use words from texts B and C to complete the following paragraph.

The government ___[1] people to recycle ___[2] bottles but bottle banks aren't much fun to use. That's why the ad agency's idea of making a bottle bank seem like a machine in an ___ ___[3] is so clever. ___[4] notice it because it attracts their ___[5] by making a ___ ___[6]. They then get ___[7] for each bottle they throw in.
The very special ___[8] bin is just as clever because each time you throw an ___[9] in it, you think it has fallen into a ___[10] hole in the ground. You even hear the ___[11] as it hits the bottom. This effect makes it far more attractive than a ___[12] bin.

3 WRITING

→ Produktion: Schreiben, S. 228

Explain in a few sentences which of the three fun ideas you prefer and why.

Useful phrases

- In my opinion / In my view, …
- First / First of all, …
- In addition, …
- Because of this, …
- For this reason, …
- All in all, …

4 PRESENTATION

→ Präsentieren, S. 243

BUILDING SKILLS: Giving a presentation

A presentation, using an overhead projector (OHP) or PowerPoint slides, is an effective way to show a new product or idea or give information. It can be given by one person or two people taking turns to speak.

1 Make sure your slides have clear illustrations, your spelling is correct and the vocabulary has been checked.
2 Number your slides and print them out together with your notes on hand-held cards for quick reference.
3 Practise what you are going to say with the other presenter or a partner before giving the presentation.

Your class decides to enter the next *Fun Theory* competition to invent something from everyday life that will benefit society. Form groups of 3–4 students and present a new idea to your class.

Choose one of the three invention ideas on page 212 and present it to your class.

Use your own idea for a *Fun Theory* invention and present it to your class.

SKILLS CHECKLIST: Presentations

- ☑ Have I checked the slides?
- ☑ Have I looked at the *Useful phrases?*
- ☑ Have I practised the presentation in my team?

Use PowerPoint slides, a video, OHP transparencies, (a) poster(s), or other visuals. Practise the presentation in your team first.

Useful phrases: Presentations

Introductions
- Hello / Good morning/afternoon/evening.
- My name's … and this is my colleague …

Starting
- Today we're going to look at … (*topic*)
- Let's begin by looking at / talking about …

Describing
- As you can see from this diagram/slide/ illustration, …
- In this slide/diagram you can see how …

Handing over
- … is now going to talk to you about …

Finishing
- All in all / In conclusion / To sum up, …
- Thank you / Thanks for coming to this presentation.
- If you have any questions, we'll be pleased to answer them.

→ Job skills 4, S. 174

5 LISTENING

→ Rezeption: Hörverstehen, S. 225

Jim Tarrant, who owns an advertising agency in New York, is the guest on a radio programme.

1/18

A Listen and say if the statements are true or false. Correct the false statements.

1 Jim's first advertising slogan was for washing powder.
2 Jim says that advertising is legalized lying.
3 Jim doesn't think the 4 Ps are out of date.
4 Niche marketing means one advertisement is designed to reach a maximum number of people.
5 Product placement has been around for a long time.
6 Guerilla marketing is only used to shock people in Third World countries.

B Complete the sentences from the dialogue with the words you hear.

1 I heard they were looking for a ___ for their new soap.
2 After a few years as the ad manager at the soap factory you ___ ___ your own agency.
3 An ad agency has to make a product ___ ___ somehow.
4 We ___ ___ ___ the slogan 'It lets me be me'.
5 The 4 Ps are: p___ , p___ , p___ , and p___ .
6 Nobody drank any but people bought the bottles for a dollar each and ___ a lot of money.

6 MEDIATION

→ Schriftliche Mediation, S. 240

1/18

A Hören Sie sich das Gespräch noch einmal an und machen Sie sich Notizen zu diesen Stichwörtern:

- Jugend
- Eigene Firma
- Wichtige Einsichten
- Trends

SKILLS CHECKLIST: Taking notes

- ☑ Have I structured my notes?
- ☑ Have I focused on the task?
- ☑ Have I noted the key information?

B Verfassen Sie mithilfe der Stichworte einen kurzen deutschen Text über das Leben des Jim Tarrant für die Homepage Ihrer Schule. Überschrift: „Erfolgreiche Menschen unserer Zeit".

7 CREATING A MARKETING MIX

A First, match the four Ps from exercise 5B with the following definitions.

a This is what a company does to increase the sales of a product or service.
b This means where a customer needs to go to get a product or service. Internet and telephone sales are making this factor less and less important.
c How much will a customer pay? Customers expect this factor to be low for some things and high for others.
d This can be an object or a service. It has a life-cycle, meaning that sales start low, grow to a maximum, fall and stop.

B Form groups of 3–4 students and decide what the best marketing mix is for the goods and services below. Write down your results and present them to the class.

a car wash ▪ a hairdressing salon ▪ a laptop ▪ a local electrician ▪ a new perfume ▪ a new sports car ▪ fruit and vegetables ▪ washing powder

8 GETTING IT RIGHT

→ *Will* future ▪ *Going to* future, S. 257

A Tom Slater at Ad-Agency-Plus in Edinburgh is talking about a meeting the next day. Use the notes to make sentences with the *will* future (predicted actions), the *going to* future (intended actions) or the present progressive (fixed arrangements).

1. our / European salesmen / come / 3 pm / tomorrow afternoon (fixed arrangement)
2. our / American partners / join / us / on Skype / 3.30 (fixed arrangement)
3. I / think / it / be / good meeting (predicted action)
4. we / talk / about guerrilla marketing (intended action)
5. I / suggest / flash mob / Victoria Station (intended action)
6. I / believe / our client / get / a lot of attention / this way (predicted action)

B Tom phones a colleague to tell her about the meeting. Complete the sentences using the present progressive (fixed arrangements) or the *will* future (predicted actions).

Tom Hi Gillian, it's me, Tom.
Gillian Hi Tom. How did the meeting go?
Tom Very well. The Americans (fly) ___ [1] over next month to sign the contract. I think this deal (make) ___ [2] a big profit for the company.
Gillian That's great, Tom, and I'm sure it (help) ___ [3] you get a job at Head Office.
Tom Let's hope so. I (see) ___ [4] the Human Resources Director at 10 am next Tuesday and I expect he (want) ___ [5] to talk about the deal. I've just booked my ticket to London.
Gillian Oh, I see. How (you/travel) ___ [6] to London? (you/fly) ___ [7]?
Tom I (take) ___ [8] the train. A long train trip (give) ___ [9] me time to prepare for the meeting.
Gillian Well good luck! I'm sure you (get) ___ [10] the job.

C Marilyn Marshall and Jim Tarrant are chatting before the radio show. Choose the right future form to complete the text.

Jim I'm afraid I only have limited time because I (meet) ___ [1] my publisher to discuss my new book straight after the show tonight.
Marilyn No problem, Jim. I predict that a lot of people (phone) ___ [2] in and ask you questions but we can stop after 30 minutes. You work all day and night! When (you/take) ___ [3] a vacation?
Jim Funny you should ask that but my wife has booked me a month in Hawaii. I (take) ___ [4] the first flight to Honolulu tomorrow morning.
Marilyn That sounds great! What (you/do) ___ [5] in Hawaii?
Jim Well, first of all I (relax) ___ [6] for a few days. I (play) ___ [7] golf and get some sun.
Marilyn I understand, but I'm sure that someone as active as you (get) ___ [8] bored quickly!
Jim I don't think so. My wife and children and their families (come) ___ [9] to join me next Wednesday and I think we (have) ___ [10] a lot of fun together.

Make sentences of your own using the three forms of the future. Write three or four sentences for each form, for example:

- Apple is launching a new tablet on … (*date*).
- I think it'll be a great success.
- I'm going to buy one as soon as I get a job.

TEXT B Creating a brand

Steve Jobs (1955–2011), Apple co-founder and CEO, in 2004

BEFORE YOU READ

→ Scannen nach Einzelinformationen im Text, S. 221

With a partner, see who is quicker to find the following details in the text on Steve Jobs:

1 the year when Steve Jobs returned to Apple
2 what GUI stands for
3 what the slogan in Apple's famous TV commercial was
4 what the Tokyo Tsoshiu Kogyo company is now called

BUILDING SKILLS: Scanning a text for specific information

Scanning means picking out specific facts or information from a text without reading it closely.

- Read the questions carefully, so that you know exactly what you need to find.
- Scan the text line for line, focusing on *one* type of information *only*, for example, numbers, names, places, dates, capital letters or specific words.
- Don't stop if you come across a word you don't understand. You can always check the meaning later if you need to understand that particular word to answer a question.

1/19

STEVE JOBS: VISIONARY AND GENIUS

Steve Jobs was not only a technical genius. He was also a visionary and even as a young man of 25 he admired how companies branded their products to make them into household names, such as Polaroid, Hoover, Nylon and Kleenex. He also realized how clever the 'Tokyo Tsoshiu Kogyo' company was when it changed its name to Sony (which sounds a bit like sunny). He understood that the technology he was developing was new, threatening and scary, so he needed to come up with a name which would make it sound non-threatening and likeable. That's why he thought Apple was exactly right. He felt that this simple, safe brand name would help people trust the new technology he was about to introduce to the world. He decided to target young people for his products because they were the customers of the future and his strategy was always to sell exciting, high-end products at a high price and profit.

Steve Jobs saw clearly that brands are part of our culture and everyday lives and that everything a brand does is an ad – positive or negative – for that brand. He understood that every way a brand touches you is a message. Today, Apple's customers are in a constant dialogue with Apple's products. They discover more and more clever functions as they use them. They can tell Apple about any problems they are having and get regular updates to fix them.

Steve Jobs also understood the importance of packaging and presentation. When you open the high-quality packaging of an Apple product it's as powerful as any ad. Steve Jobs also didn't want the Macintosh manuals to be written in technical jargon, so he made sure they were written in easy English that people could understand. As a young entrepreneur he looked far into the future and knew he had to make this technology accessible to anybody and everybody. The Apple Store is also probably the best ad Apple ever did. You can actually walk into the brand and touch it, feel it and get its energy back from the young people who work there. He launched the Macintosh in 1984 and introduced the graphical user interface (GUI) and the mouse, which touched things on the screen which we now touch with our fingers.

Steve Jobs left Apple in 1985 to make films and returned in 1997 when the company was fighting to survive. He rebuilt the brand and introduced a series of new products – the iPhone, the iPod and the iPad. To prepare the public for his new ideas he brought out the famous TV commercial ending with the slogan 'Think different'. The commercial was called 'Here's to the Crazy Ones' and shows the famous people of our time who thought differently and changed the world.

(541 words)

1 WORKING WITH WORDS

Find the following words or expressions in the text *Steve Jobs: visionary and genius*.

1 the opposite of threatening (paragraph 1)
2 the opposite of cheap and low quality (paragraph 1)
3 to repair (paragraph 2)
4 the box in which a product is sold (paragraph 3)
5 someone who risks their money by starting a business, company or firm (paragraph 3)
6 to continue to live (paragraph 4)

2 LOOKING AT THE TEXT

→ Rezeption: Leseverstehen, S. 214

Read the text and do the following tasks.

Paragraph 1 Explain how Sony made it easier for their company to become a household name; say why Apple is a good brand name.
Paragraph 2 'Today people are in a constant dialogue with Apple's products'. List the ways in which people are in a dialogue with Apple's products.
Paragraph 3 Summarize what Steve Jobs did to make Apple's products attractive and accessible.
Paragraph 4 Discuss Steve Jobs' reasons for choosing a TV commercial about the 'Crazy Ones' to advertise Apple's new products.

3 ANALYSING A GRAPH

→ Produktion: Schaubilder beschreiben und analysieren, S. 238

Look at the chart below, then do the tasks on page 53.

BUILDING SKILLS: Describing graphs and bar charts

Graphs and bar charts are ways of presenting figures and statistics in a clear visual form. If you have to describe a chart, make sure you understand exactly what the graph shows and the units that are used.

- Use the simple present (→ page 213) to describe what the graph shows: *The chart/graph **shows** the change in media ad spending between 2011 and 2017.*
- Use the simple past (→ page 215) to describe situations in the past or changes that are finished: *In 2011 media spending **was** $158.6 billion.*
- Use the present perfect (→ page 217) to describe situations or changes that are unfinished: *Spending **has increased** by about 3.5% since 2011.*

US Total Media Ad Spending, 2011–2017
billions and % change

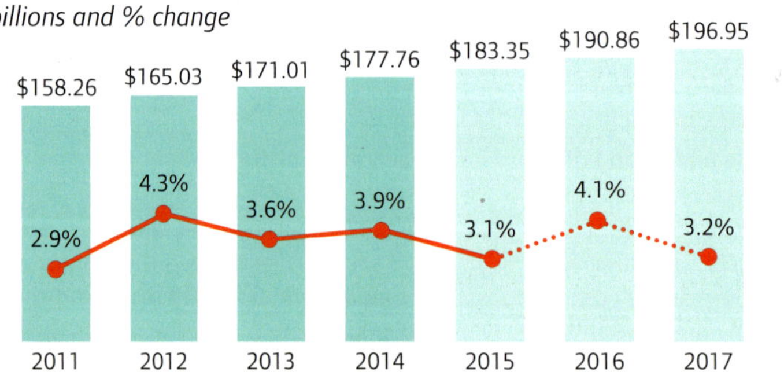

Note: includes digital (online and mobile), directories, magazines, newspapers, outdoor, radio and TV

Source: www.eMarketer.com

Useful phrases

- The bar chart shows the total media ad spending in the USA for the years 2011 to 2017.
- The years are shown on the x-axis. The figures are given in billions of dollars.
- The line (chart) also shows the change each year in per cent.

- In 2011 media ad spending was / came to $158.6bn.
- It rose by $6.75 billion in 2014. / It fell by 0.7% to 3.6% in 2013.
- Ad spending has increased by about 3–4% per year since 2011.
- Spending has grown by $13.6 billion over the last two years.

- The chart/graph shows us that … / We can see by the figures for … that …
- All in all, the trend is upwards/downwards. / There has been little change since …

1 With a partner, practise reading out the figures for media ad spending in the US from 2011 to 2014.
2 Explain what happened to the percentage change in media spending (red line) in 2012 and in 2013.
3 When was the biggest percentage change in media ad spending? When was the smallest?
4 How has media ad spending changed since 2011?
5 Write 4–5 sentences to describe the bar chart.

Saying numbers

1,000,000 = a/one million
1,000,000,000 = a/one billion
$171.01bn = a hundred and seventy-one point nought (zero) one billion dollars
$190.86bn = a hundred and ninety point eight six billion dollars

4 MIND MAP

In groups of 3–4 make a mind map about advertising. Include the following aspects:

- the different forms of advertising
- the target groups
- the benefits
- the dangers
- your own ideas

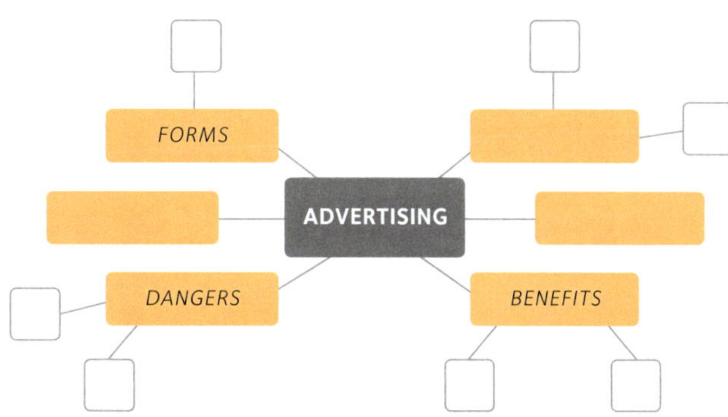

5 DISCUSSION

→ Interaktion: An Diskussionen teilnehmen, S. 246

A Write a few sentences explaining why you agree or disagree with the statement on the right.

B Use your list in a class discussion about branded goods and vote on whether the statement is right or wrong.

Advertising makes us spend money on things we don't need, especially branded goods.

6 WRITING

→ Produktion: Eine Stellungnahme schreiben, S. 234

Use the ideas on your mind map to write a comment about what H.G. Wells (a famous English writer) said about advertising.

"ADVERTISING IS LEGALIZED LYING."
H.G. WELLS

Beacons: interactive digital shopping

In recent years, online shopping has taken people away from high street shops, but now retailers are hoping that beacon technology will bring them back, by making the shopping experience more interactive and more fun.

WHAT ARE BEACONS?

4/3

Beacons are low-energy radio transmitters which employ the Bluetooth 4.0 communication specification used in modern smartphones. They have a range of about 70 metres.

Retailers are interested in beacons as a means to send marketing messages to customers' mobile phones when they enter the store or even walk past the store. This is called "proximity marketing".

Typically, beacons greet the customer with an invitation to download a special app, or, if they already have the app, with information on the day's special deals, a coupon for money off their next purchase, etc. Customers can choose to accept or ignore the beacon notifications.

If they accept, their phones will display additional information about the products they look at as they walk around the store. The content is customized to match the phone owner's preferences and their location within the store.

The communication between the beacon and the customer's phone is minimal. The radio signal from the beacon simply informs the phone that there are notifications available. The phone then contacts servers in a private or public cloud to download the relevant content.

Apple has pioneered beacon technology in Apple Stores, where iBeacons are combined with contactless payment technology. The store's automated checkout uses Near Field Communication to communicate with the customer's phone and take payment from their Apple account. In this way, the phone becomes a digital sales assistant and cashier. (232 words)

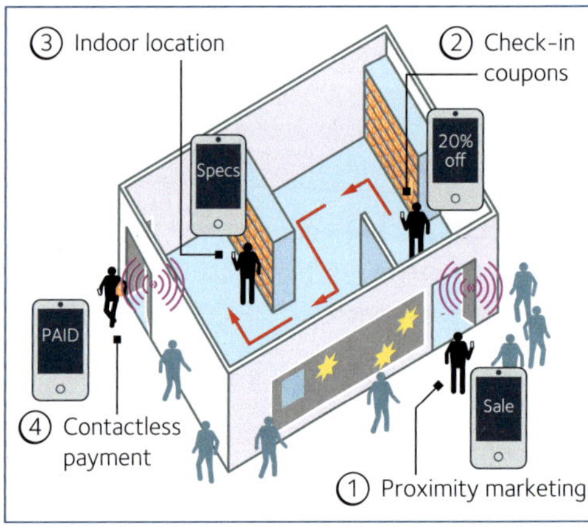

1 EXPLAINING A DIAGRAM

Use information from the text to explain what is happening at points 1–4 in the diagram.

2 DESIGNING A SHOPPING MALL

Work in a small group and do the tasks below.

1 Brainstorm. What other hi-tech features would make shopping more fun?
2 Design the shopping mall of the future. Use your five best ideas from task 1 to design a shopping mall with shops, restaurants and a cinema:
   - Draw a plan of the mall.
   - Write explanations of the special features.
   - Present your design to the class.

7 Family and beyond

MAIN COURSE

FOCUS

A Think about the influences that make people who they are.

1 Match the captions (a–h) to the pictures (1–8) above.

a	education	**b**	extended family	**c**	government	**d**	immediate family
e	peer group	**f**	religion	**g**	role models	**h**	the media

2 Note the three or four most important influences, in your opinion.

3 Work with a partner. Present your ideas to each other and discuss any differences.

B Work with a partner. Ask and answer questions about your backgrounds.

1 Change seats. Sit with someone that you do not know well.

2 Answer some of the questions below about yourself and make notes.

3 Try to answer the same questions about your partner. Ask if you do not know the answers.

4 Work in a small group. Take turns to introduce your partner's background to the others.

Where do you come from?

How do you live – with your family, with others, or alone?

What household chores do you have to do?

What do you do in your free time?

How often are you able to go out with friends?

When do you see your 'extended' family?

TEXT A Living in a family

BEFORE YOU READ

→ Vorbereitung auf das Lesen, S. 214

Look at the text quickly and answer these questions:
What sort of thing does the writer always write about?
What age group does she write for?
What topic is she focusing on today?

SKILLS CHECKLIST: Predicting

- ☑ Have I read the title and the other headings?
- ☑ Have I read the introduction?

Teen Times | **May 15, 20..**

1/21

PROBLEMS – PROBLEMS – PROBLEMS

by Pippa Parker

THIS WEEK: THE RIGHT SORT OF FAMILY

Just what sort of family is the right sort of family?

Should it be like reader Rajeev's family? … Or should it be more like reader Lisa's?

Well, read these letters from Rajeev and Lisa and see what you think.

Dear Pippa

I'm Asian-British, and my grandparents came over from India in the 1960s. We live together – three generations – and three of my aunts and uncles and their families all live in the same street, too. I think you can safely say I'm from an extended family!

My twin sister and I used to love our close family life because there were always lots of people around, and perhaps we were spoilt as we were the first grandchildren. When Mum and Dad were busy, our grandparents were the ones that we turned to. They and our cousins' families were also always there to offer day-to-day help, a meal or just a friendly chat. Then there was the time when our parents' newspaper shop nearly went under, and everyone gave us financial and emotional support. It was the family that got us through, and I'll never forget that.

These days, things aren't quite so happy though. As we get older, we often want more freedom to do things our own way – go out with our friends at the weekend, dress the way that we want, say what we think about things – but it's getting more and more difficult, especially for Sita as she's a girl. Even when Mum and Dad agree to something like going to a party, the rest of the family still seem to think they can criticize us because we're not traditional enough. They say we're forgetting our roots and our values. What's more, our grandparents keep saying we're the oldest, so we're the ones who have to set a good example for our younger cousins.

It's hard for Mum and Dad, too. In fact, they're probably the ones who are having the hardest time of all: they're caught between my grandparents and us.

Does anyone else have these problems? I could really use some advice! *Rajeev Gupta*

Dear Pippa

We moved over to England from Dublin a year ago and it's been a huge change. Back home, we were part of an extended family. Mum's parents lived with us and we had family all around, so there was always someone who was visiting to gossip or to borrow something or to play. Over here though, we're on our own – just Mum, Dad, my brother and me. Mum and Dad both have jobs now. Fine. But we've gone from being part of a big, noisy family to a lonely little nuclear family. As a long-distance commuter, Dad has to leave before 7.00 am, and we don't see him till after 7.00 at night. Then the rest of us go at 8.00. I catch the bus to school, and Mum takes Sam to his school on her way to the office.

School is OK, and there are various after-school sports and other activities that I'm involved in – drama, for example. I'm free to do whatever I want, and I've made two or three friends, too. So all that's good. But at the end of the day, it's back home alone to an empty house, and there's no one there with a cheerful hello in the old way. Instead, I do some chores to help Mum because I know she'll get home tired. I'm the one who makes Sam his tea now, and there isn't much time to relax and talk. There's dinner to help make and homework to do, and so life at home goes on from day to lonely day.

Big families can be a pain, I know. People don't just mind their own business: they keep minding everyone else's, and there's not much privacy. So that can produce tensions, especially between generations, but there are lots of laughs, too, and I miss that a lot.

It's Christmas next month, and I can tell you we can't wait to go home for that! *Lisa Doyle*

So what's the answer? Whichever side of the hill we're on, it seems the grass is always greener on the other side. Perhaps the truth is that we really need a bit of both sorts of family life. We sometimes need the support of a wider family, and we sometimes also need the space to be free and independent. Actually, though, isn't that how things really are in many families today? Write in with your experiences. (764 words)

1 LOOKING AT THE TEXT

→ Sich während des Lesens Notizen machen, S. 223

BUILDING SKILLS: Taking notes while reading

- When you take notes while reading, always organize them in lists under sub-headings (see below) or using dates.
- You can leave out unnecessary words, such as pronouns and articles.
- It is quicker to use abbreviations and symbols, such as *e.g.*, &, +, –, =, *etc.*

A Work with a partner. Read one letter each and make notes on it.

Rajeev & Sita	Lisa
Family type: ▬	Family type a) present: ▬; b) past: ▬
Feelings about situation in past: ▬	Feelings about situation in past: ▬
Situation now & problems: ▬	Situation now & problems: ▬
Needs: ▬	Looking forward to: ▬

Now use your notes to explain the key points of your letter to your partner.

B **With your partner, do the following activities.** → Rezeption: Leseverstehen, S. 214

1 Decide which letter writer seems less happy with life in a big family.
2 Consider who has more life experience to speak from.
3 Say what Pippa thinks about the need for a) support and b) freedom in family life.

C **Say what it means: Explain the underlined words from the context of the text.**

1 … when our parents' newspaper shop nearly went under, … (line 15)
2 It was the family that got us through, … (line 16)
3 As a long-distance commuter, Dad has to leave … (line 34)
4 Big families can be a pain, I know. (line 45)
5 Whichever side of the hill we're on, it seems the grass is always greener on the other side. (line 49)

2 WORKING WITH WORDS

A **Say what *as* means in the following sentences: *because*, *in the position of* or *when*.**

1 *As* we get older, we often want more freedom … (line 17)
2 … but it's getting more and more difficult, especially for Sita *as* she's a girl. (line 19)
3 *As* a long-distance commuter, Dad has to leave before 7.00 am. (line 34)
4 Rajeev wrote to Pippa *as* he really felt he needed some advice.
5 *As* someone from an extended family, Lisa does not like her new lifestyle.
6 She will probably find her new life in England easier *as* time goes by.

B **Complete the text with *make* or *do*. Change the forms as necessary.**

When Lisa gets home from school, she does [1] chores to help around the house, but first, she makes [2] coffee and relaxes for a few minutes. Then she makes [3] a start on her jobs. First, she goes to her room to tidy up and make [4] her bed as she never has time for this in the morning. Next, she goes downstairs to see what other housework there is to do [5]. She often does [6] some ironing, for example, or she sometimes needs to go out and do [7] some shopping at the supermarket. Then when mum and Sam get home, she makes [8] her mum a cup of tea, and she makes [9] her brother something to eat. That gives mum time to check her emails and do [10] her paperwork. Mum starts makes [11] dinner at 7 pm, ready for when dad returns from work, and that is when Lisa finally sits down at her desk and starts does [12] her homework.

3 GETTING IT RIGHT

→ Relative clauses, S. 269

A **Complete these sentences using *who*, *which* or *that*.**

1 Rajeev was the one who wrote the first letter to Problems – Problems – Problems.
2 Lisa was the reader who provided the other letter for Pippa Parker's article.
3 Tension between Rajeev and others in his extended family is the thing that is worrying him.
4 However, Lisa is a girl that would clearly like to be back with her own large family again.
5 Problems – Problems – Problems is a page which appears every week in *Teen Times*.
6 *Teen Times* is a magazine that offers its readers lots of human interest stories.
7 It also has features like Pippa's – a page which helps readers with their problems and dilemmas.
8 Pippa is someone who has a real talent for helping young people with their problems.

B Complete the story, adding *who*, *which* or *that* only where necessary.

Teen Times is a magazine ___[1] several other people in Lisa's year at school also read. It happened that a girl who/that[2] belonged to the drama club, like Lisa, was the one ___[3] saw it first. Her name was Gina, and although she did not know Lisa well, she thought, 'Wow! The letter ___[4] I'm looking at here might be from Lisa!' She read the letter again and compared it with the things ___[5] she knew about Lisa. 'Yes,' she thought, 'it was about a year ago when she arrived, and the place ___[6] she comes from is somewhere in Ireland. Another thing: the brother ___[7] she told us about is called Sam, too.'

She was not quite sure though. 'It's strange,' she thought. 'The Lisa ___[8] I know always seems happy and cheerful, but the Lisa ___[9] wrote this letter seems quite sad! Can they really be the same person?'

The next day, Gina saw Lisa at drama after school, showed her the article and asked, 'Are you really the one ___[10] wrote this letter?'

'Oh, that, er, yes,' Lisa said. 'Yes, that's the letter ___[11] I wrote. I suppose I was stupid to use my real name.' She suddenly felt very embarrassed.

'Listen,' Gina said, 'I'm having a party on Saturday, so please come. There'll be lots of people ___[12] will love to meet you!'

4 WRITING

→ Produktion: Schreiben, S. 228

Write Pippa's reply to Rajeev. Use this letter structure.

Paragraph 1: Thank him for his letter and for raising some interesting points.
Paragraph 2: Respond sympathetically.
Paragraph 3: Point out good things about his type of family situation.
Paragraph 4: Suggest how he can improve the situation.
Paragraph 5: Finish in a positive way.

Useful phrases

- Thank you very much for … and for raising …
- I was very sorry to read that … . It must be hard for you when …
- However, there are certainly some good things about your situation. As you yourself say, … . Then again, …
- Let me make one or two suggestions that may … . In my experience, it often helps to … . It might be useful to …
- I'm sure that if you … , you'll be able to …

TIP

Your reply is friendly and informal, so feel free to use contracted forms like *you're* instead of full forms like *you are*. (But remember to use full forms in more formal writing.)

Write to Pippa about someone that you know (or can imagine) – who has a family problem but who is too shy to ask for help.

Then write Pippa's reply. (You can use the same letter structure as above.)

5 DISCUSSION

→ Interaktion: An Diskussionen teilnehmen, S. 246

Pippa refers to the saying: 'The grass is always greener on the other side of the hill.' How true do you think this is?

TEXT B Leaving home

BEFORE YOU READ

Talk about the pros and cons of living away from your family.

http://www.leavinghome.org

1/22

Carrie **Moving out**

I'm now 22, and I moved out five years ago. I was a grade A student, and I gave everything to my studies. But I was living with my dad over 20 miles from school, and things weren't going well. I had to get up ridiculously early to get the one and only bus out of our village to make it to school in the morning, and there were just two buses back after school. When I had to stay for extra studies, I didn't get home until after 7 pm! I had to make my own meals and eat alone as everyone else always ate before I got home from school. My dad and I also argued about everything. He always started on me for not hoovering the house before I left for school and not putting on a load of washing! What's more, he expected me to do that every day of the week. I was happy to do it at weekends but who hoovers every single day – and at 6.30 in the morning? Plus my dad was getting very nosey. He was going through the bin in my bedroom to find receipts to see what I was spending money on – my own money, by the way, as I had a part-time job at a supermarket. And on Saturdays, when I wanted to meet my friends in town, my dad banned me from getting the only morning bus! I had to get the only other bus – in the afternoon – and that left me just two hours with my friends. They always had lunch without me, and I felt left out.
My dad was turning into a real control freak, and I couldn't take it anymore. Maybe it was the same thing that had driven Mum away years before. Anyway, to cut a long story short, I moved out. I spoke to the *benefits people and explained my situation. Because I was moving away from home I was also moving away from my job, so I needed some help financially for a few months. My teacher helped me a lot, and she explained to the benefits office that my grades were dropping because of stress at home, so I needed the chance to complete school properly in order to move on to college. She also found me a small flat.
It wasn't easy though. In fact, it was the hardest thing I've ever done – to go home alone every day instead of to a family. But I'm a better person now because of it, and I'm happy I did it. (434 words)

** Department for Work and Pensions (DWP): manages most areas of welfare in the UK.*

1 LOOKING AT THE TEXT

→ Rezeption: Leseverstehen, S. 214

A **Put the pictures in the order (1–6) that Carrie describes her problems. Then do one of the tasks below.**

Briefly say what the problems were.

Explain why you think Carrie found each of these things a problem.

B Say whether these statements about the text are true or false. Correct the false statements.

1 Carrie is writing about her recent situation at home.
2 She was probably the oldest of the young family.
3 The situation at home was getting worse.
4 The benefits office helped her financially and also gave her a flat.
5 She was very happy when she first moved away from home.

C Say what it means: Explain the underlined words and phrases in your own words.

1 … to make it to school in the morning, … (line 3)
2 He always started on me for not hovering … (line 6)
3 Plus my dad was getting very nosey. (line 9)
4 My dad was turning into a real control freak. (line 14)
5 … and I couldn't take it anymore. (line 14)

2 WORKING WITH WORDS

A Complete the story of Carrie's past life. Choose from these prepositions of time.

at ▪ during ▪ from ▪ in ▪ on ▪ to

Carrie always got up ___ [1] 6 o'clock ___ [2] the morning ___ [3] weekdays in order to catch the 7 o'clock bus to town. She had school ___ [4] 9 am ___ [5] 3.30 pm, and then she often stayed for extra lessons. This meant that she had to catch the second bus home and only got there ___ [6] about 7 pm ___ [7] the evening. That was hard enough ___ [8] the summer, but ___ [9] the winter months she had to leave home and get home in the dark, and she hated it.
___ [10] the weekend, she had to do a lot of housework ___ [11] Saturday morning and ___ [12] Sunday, so she was only able to see her friends ___ [13] the afternoon ___ [14] Saturday.
Finally, ___ [15] her last year at school, it all got too much for her. ___ [16] a cold, wet evening ___ [17] November, she decided to leave home and start a new life.

B Complete the following with suitable phrasal verbs. Change the forms as necessary.

Paragraph 1: move in ▪ move on ▪ move out
Paragraph 2: get on ▪ get over ▪ get up
Paragraph 3: turn back ▪ turn into ▪ turn out

When Mark and Karen had their first child, their tiny two-room flat was just too small, and it was time to ___ ___ [1] to the next stage of their lives – a bigger home. They ___ ___ [2] on November 30th, and on December 1st, the next person ___ ___ [3]. It was Carrie!

For Carrie, the little flat was perfect. It was in town, so she did not need to ___ ___ [4] at 6 am anymore, and she soon started to ___ ___ [5] much better at school. However, she was lonely, and it took her a long time to ___ ___ [6] the shock of leaving home.

However, Carrie did not even think of ___ the clock ___ [7] and returning to her old life. Instead, she got a few pieces of furniture, and she slowly ___ the little flat ___ [8] a home. After a few months, she was much happier, and she knew that her move was ___ ___ [9] very well.

3 GETTING IT RIGHT

→ Simple past ▪ Past progressive, S. 251

Complete the text about the day that Carrie left home. Put the verbs in the simple past or past progressive.

Carrie remembers very clearly the evening when she finally (decide) ▬ 1 to leave home. While she (travel) ▬ 2 home on the bus from school, she (open) ▬ 3 a book to try and study, but her mind (keep) ▬ 4 returning to her problems. Things (go) ▬ 5 from bad to worse at home, and she (not look forward to) ▬ 6 the evening ahead. Outside, it (get) ▬ 7 dark and it (start) ▬ 8 to rain, too. 'It looks like the way I feel,' she (think) ▬ 9.
As she (step) ▬ 10 off the bus, a cold autumn wind (blow) ▬ 11 and it (rain) ▬ 12 steadily. She (pull) ▬ 13 her coat tight, and she (turn) ▬ 14 down the dark lane towards the house. When she (enter) ▬ 15 the living room, her younger brother Ben (play) ▬ 16 a video game and her little sister Lucy (draw) ▬ 17 pictures. They (look) ▬ 18 up cheerfully to say 'hi!' before returning to their activities. In the next room, her dad (do) ▬ 19 some work on his laptop and he (not seem) ▬ 20 to notice her. He just (say) ▬ 21: 'You (not do) ▬ 22 the washing this morning, so please make sure you do it tonight.'
That (be) ▬ 23 the start of a very bad night.

4 LISTENING

→ Rezeption: Hörverstehen, S. 225

You are going to listen to a radio interview with Emma Schumann, a youth counsellor. She is talking about the things young people need to do when they look for their own place to live.

BUILDING SKILLS: Taking notes from listening

- Don't panic if you fall behind while you listen. Speakers often make false starts and repeat themselves. (Listen again for examples of this.)
- Leave out unnecessary words such as pronouns and articles while taking notes.
- You can also use abbreviations and symbols such as: *e.g.*, &, +, –, =, *etc.*

1/23

Copy the notes below, then listen to the interview to complete them.

How to find right place
1 Look on ▬
2 –//– in ▬
3 ▬ place
4 ▬ people you will share with

Dealing with money
1 ▬ your monthly ▬ for food, etc.
2 Always ▬

Looking after yourself
1 Don't ▬
2 Cook ▬

Living with others
1 Set ▬
2 Do ▬
3 Talk ▬
4 Respect ▬

5 MEDIATION

Sie wohnen in einer WG mit anderen jungen Menschen zusammen. In der WG ist gerade ein Zimmer frei geworden.

Anhand Ihrer Notizen aus Übung 4 erklären Sie einem Freund / einer Freundin, worauf er/sie achten sollte, wenn er/sie das erste Mal von zu Hause auszieht und bei Ihnen einziehen möchte.

6 DISCUSSION

→ Interaktion: An Diskussionen teilnehmen, S. 246

A Discuss in groups. Put the following tips in order of usefulness.

Advice for teenagers who are leaving home

- Washing-up is like saying sorry. It gets harder the longer you leave it.
- Just because you've got money in your bank account doesn't mean you have to spend it.
- Work first, play later.
- If you have to sniff your duvet cover to see if it needs washing, it probably does.
- Eat green vegetables. Raw, if necessary. Chips don't contain all the nutrients necessary to maintain good health.
- Inform your parents about what you're up to on a need-to-know basis. They need to know you're alive.

B Describe the picture. Then discuss what needs to happen in this student house.

Useful phrases

- The picture/cartoon shows a very …
- On the (left/right), there's a … (*room*), and in it we can see someone who is …
- In the corner / On the floor / By the sink, we can also see that …
- These students clearly have to …
- Just in the … (*room*), someone needs to … (*list of tasks*)
- Then in the … (*room*), someone should … (*list of tasks*)

C Read Emma Schumann's last words of advice and discuss these questions.

1 What might turn a home leaver into a boomerang kid?
2 What might turn a parent into a helicopter mum (or dad)?
3 How might people – a boomerang kid and a helicopter mum – feel in these situations?

Don't be a 'boomerang kid', who leaves home, and then finds it too difficult, and then gives up and goes back to the family home again. And don't turn your mum into a 'helicopter mum' who has to come and rescue you because you're doing things badly in your new home.

Home robots

Lawn-mower robots and cleaning robots are already common. What might the domestic robots of tomorrow do for us?

4/4

DOMESTIC ROBOTS OF TOMORROW

The domestic robots of tomorrow will be a varied bunch. Many will be small, single-task machines that'll clean floors, water plants, feed pets, and such. They'll hide most of the time, and we won't pay much attention to them. Think of them as smart, mobile versions of today's household appliances.

The robots that will really change things will be bigger and more powerful, and they will perform multiple tasks for us. They'll have wheels or tracks, and some may have legs. They'll certainly have manipulator arms to handle objects.

These robots won't do everything right out of the box. Instead, these general-purpose programmable platforms will start by doing just a few simple tasks, and they'll continually acquire new capabilities. They'll come equipped with attachment points for new accessories and, more important, standard interfaces that allow new third-party software to add functions that their manufacturers never imagined, much like the apps we install on our phones.

It's a scenario that, in one form or another, some roboticists already have in sight. "While a computer program is pure software, some robot apps will be a combination of software and hardware," says Colin Angle, chief executive and cofounder of iRobot Corp. "These apps will include not only software but maybe also files that people can use in their 3D printers to make parts at home."

What will the apps and accessories allow this new generation of home robots to do? Anything and everything, we hope. Some possibilities that immediately come to mind: Robots will learn to fetch things from the fridge, operate the micro-wave, clear the table after meals, load and unload the dishwasher, answer the door, pick up toys from the floor, clean toilets and do laundry.

(291 words)

Adapted from: *www.spectrum.ieee.org*

1 DRAWING A MIND MAP

Copy and complete the mind map using information from the text.

SINGLE TASK — HOME ROBOTS OF THE FUTURE — MULTITASK

2 DISCUSSION: ROBOT APPS AND ACCESSORIES

→ Interaktion: An Diskussionen teilnehmen, S. 246

Discuss in a small group. What would you use a home robot for? What special apps and 3D-printed parts would you add to your robot? Report back to the class with your group's three most original ideas.

8 Entering the world of work

MAIN COURSE

FOCUS

Athletic abilities;
Mechanical abilities;
Working with objects, machines, tools, plants or animals;
Working outdoors;
→ mechanics, carpenters, engineers, police officers

Observing, learning, investigating, analysing, evaluating or solving problems;
→ psychologists, doctors, management consultants, computer programmers

Working with data;
Clerical, numerical ability;
Carrying out tasks in detail;
Following other people's instructions;
→ accountants, administrators, computer operators

Artistic, innovative, intuitional abilities;
Unstructured work using imagination and creativity;
→ journalists, architects, designers, lawyers, dancers

Influencing, persuading, performing;
Leading or managing for organizational goals or economic gain;
→ managers, politicians, barkeepers

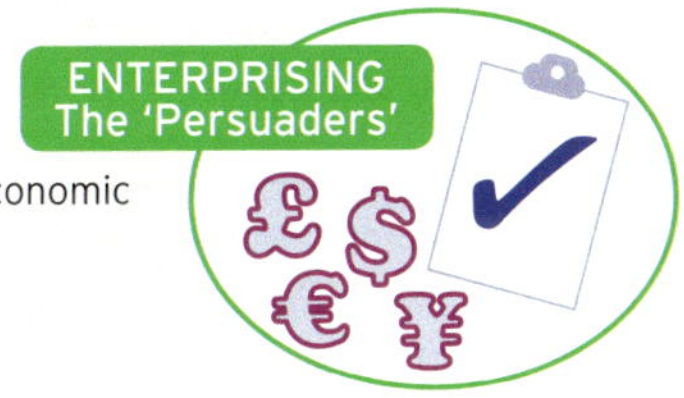

Working with people;
Enlightening, helping, training, caring;
Skilled with words;
→ teachers, social workers, nurses, priests, counsellors

A Finding the right career is a big step in life, so it is important to think about what you want from a job before you start looking. List the following factors and your own ideas according to how important they are for you. Compare your results with a partner.

a challenge ▪ a quiet life ▪ being your own boss ▪ company car ▪ excitement ▪ flexible working hours ▪ good pay ▪ good promotion prospects ▪ good working conditions ▪ helping people ▪ job security ▪ meeting people ▪ private medical insurance ▪ regular working hours ▪ travel

What are the most/least important factors? Discuss your findings in class.

B With a partner study the diagram above and decide which category is closest to your personality. (You may find that you have the characteristics of more than one category.)

C Choose one of the jobs in the category you have chosen, or a similar job, and write 4–5 sentences about it to describe the sort of work involved. Use ideas from the Internet and your own knowledge.

Useful phrases

- Working as (an architect) involves (designing buildings and dealing with construction workers).
- If you like (helping people), you'll enjoy the job of a (nurse) because …
- If you want to (work creatively) the job of a (designer) is ideal/attractive because it involves … (+ *-ing* form)
- On the one hand, (administrators) have … but on the other hand, …
- If you work as a/an … , you have to …
- (Bakers) have to … , but they don't need …
- The job of a/an … is very (satisfying/rewarding).

TEXT A Three job advertisements

BEFORE YOU READ

What sort of work experience would you like to do? Where would you look to find a suitable temporary job?

1/24

1 WONDERFUL WORLD ONLINE RECRUITMENT

COMPANY:	Sunseeker Entertainment Ltd
JOB TITLE:	Work placement as a hotel entertainer in Ibiza, Spain
TASKS:	Planning and carrying out suitable holiday activities for adults and children
WORKING HOURS:	Full-time, 40 hours per week; 3 months minimum
REQUIREMENTS:	Student status, good spoken English and/or German, basic Spanish
BENEFITS:	Free board and lodging + allowance of €200 (£160) per month Return airfare from home country to Ibiza (max. €250 or £200)
HOW TO APPLY:	Use the button below to email us your CV and cover letter.

UNITED KINGDOM 2
INTERNSHIP AT YOUTH CHARITY

YOUTH-CHANCE is a charity which sets up creative, artistic projects for youth communities in areas of high crime with no programmes for young people. It is staffed by highly motivated professionals, young people and interns, who all want to help local communities by offering exciting events and projects. Interns at YOUTH-CHANCE volunteer to work for 2–12 months, learn skills in the fields of management and administration and get useful work experience.

Interns will work at our modern, fully equipped youth centre in Hammersmith, South West London and/or at schools, theatres and other locations nearby. All interns are fully insured and receive a monthly allowance of £120 (€150) and free board and lodging (e.g. in homestay accommodation nearby). Travel expenses from and to the intern's home country are also paid.

Would you like to help? Send your CV and cover letter to Sylvester Page at sylvester@youth-chance.net or phone us on 0044 207 5499783.

YOUTH-CHANCE, 42 Vanston Square, London SW6 1QR, UK.
Registered charity no. 52866320.

TOPTECH ONLINE RECRUITMENT – WE'LL GET YOU THAT JOB!

Post advertised:	Work placement as a theatre technician at Lloyd Theatre, Bath, UK
Allowance:	£1,000 per month
Working hours:	40 hours per week
Starting date:	ASAP
Duration:	6 months

The work placement student will …
- be part of a small team responsible for the set, lighting, sound and props for all productions
- carry out maintenance and repair work on theatre equipment

The successful candidate is …
- able to carry out basic electrical maintenance and DIY tasks
- friendly, helpful and flexible
- prepared to work evening and weekend shifts

Help will be given to find suitable local accommodation.
Email your CV and cover letter to Tracy Winter in HR at tracy@lloyd-theatre.org or call 0117 315 7185.
The Lloyd Theatre is an equal opportunities employer.

3

1 WORKING WITH WORDS

A Find the English equivalent of the following German expressions in the three job adverts.

1 Praktikum
2 Kost und Logis
3 Taschengeld
4 Unterkunft
5 Fahrtkosten
6 zuständig für
7 ein Arbeitgeber im Sinne der Chancengleichheit

B With a partner complete the word families using forms from the three job ads.

Verb	Noun	Noun (person)	Adjective
		intern	
	art	artist	
		volunteer	voluntary
to administer		administrator	administrative
to accommodate			
	technology		technological
to maintain			
	equality		

2 LOOKING AT THE TEXTS

→ Rezeption: Leseverstehen, S. 214

A With a partner study the three job ads again and draw up a table with the headings below showing the terms offered by the three employers.

- length of contract
- allowance
- accommodation
- food
- insurance
- travel expenses

B Which of the three jobs would you apply for? Which skills could you use to do the job?

3 DESCRIBING JOBS

Who says what? Match the sentences (a–d) with the photographs (1–4).

1 salesman

2 boutique owner

3 medical secretary

4 bank clerk

a If I don't give the customers what they want, they'll go elsewhere.
b We always give our customers the best financial advice.
c My company's product supplies energy from a sustainable source.
d It's nice to think you're helping people to get the treatment they need.

4 LISTENING

→ Rezeption: Hörverstehen, S. 225

1/25

You are going to hear two people being interviewed about their jobs. Listen and make notes under the following headings for each job:

- skills and qualifications
- type of work
- working hours
- pay
- promotion prospects
- job security
- job satisfaction

SKILLS CHECKLIST: Taking notes

- ☑ Have I used headings?
- ☑ Have I left out unnecessary words?
- ☑ Have I used abbreviations?

5 WRITING

→ Produktion: Schreiben, S. 228

Use your notes from exercise 4 to write a description of one of the two jobs. Use the *Useful phrases* on page 65.

Choose a job you know about and describe it in English using the headings in exercise 4 above and the *Useful phrases* on page 65.

6 GETTING IT RIGHT

→ *If* sentences, S. 264

A Complete the dialogue between a student and a careers advisor using the right form of the verbs in brackets in *if* sentences type 1.

Student: Now I'd like to ask some questions about pay. If I (work) ___ [1] as a bank clerk, how much (I/earn) ___ [2]?

Advisor: At entry level you (get) ___ [3] about £1,160 per month if you (be) ___ [4] at one of the big banks. If you (get) ___ [5] promotion, you (earn) ___ [6] a lot more. However, let me give you a word of warning. You (not get) ___ [7] promotion if you (not be) ___ [8] ambitious. If you (not apply) ___ [9] for a better position after some time, no one (offer) ___ [10] you one on a plate.

B Expand the notes to make more *if* sentences type 1.

EXAMPLE

you / get job / medical secretary / earn / £1,600 / month

If you get a job as a medical secretary, you'll earn £1,600 a month.

1 you / work / volunteer / get / £150 / month
2 you / only get / allowance / £40 / week / work / intern
3 you / get a job / bank clerk / earn / £14,000 / year
4 you / have better job security / be / fully qualified
5 you / love clothes / not find it hard / work / boutique
6 your yearly income / be irregular / be / boutique owner
7 you / want / make enough money / have to work / long hours / boutique owner
8 you / not be able / stay in a small shop / business / become successful
9 a good salesperson / earn / £1,000 / week / work hard
10 a salesperson / not sell enough / lose / job

TEXT B New trends at the workplace

BEFORE YOU READ

Look at the photos on this page and on page 70. What do you think about this way of working?

MIND HOW YOU MOVE THAT CHAIR – IT'S HOT

1/26

HOT-DESKING IS A GROWING TREND, BRINGING A NEW CULTURE

MOST people dislike not having a desk of their own. They do not like the idea of arriving at the office, grabbing their "wheely" filing cabinet and making for the nearest free desk available.

Yet like it or not, this way of working is on the increase, bringing a changing office culture. The driving force behind this is to reduce property costs and it is made possible by ever-improving electronics.

Three years ago 95% of employees at ICL, the computer services company, had their own desks. Today, about 25% of the 20,000 workforce have no desk of their own. "A 40% increase predicted over the next two years has caused us to totally rethink our building requirements," says Richard Reed, director of corporate infrastructure.

"We opened a building in Staines which has 320 desks but supports 600 people. We see this building as a model for the future."

ICL has changed its culture from manufacturing to services, which requires a more mobile workforce. "We have three categories of employees," says Mr Reed. First, the pad-owners: they sit at their desk not less than three days a week. Second, the home-workers: they work a minimum of three days a week at home.

"Third, those who fall in neither of these and are, by default, mobile workers and therefore automatically hot-desk workers."

Mr Reed hot-desks, sometimes in one of the meeting rooms or going to the staff restaurant to plug into a computer; his secretary, who works for six bosses, is a home-worker but drives up the M4 once or twice a week to counteract loneliness.

"I'm afraid I do not have that homing instinct which I acknowledge others do - for example, those people who even though they do not have an allotted space in a car park will always tend to park

in the same spot," says Mr Reed. "This has to be a gradual development programme, which addresses any concerns that employees might have about being able to do their job properly."

At the British Airways business centre near Heathrow, about 25% of the 3,500 employees hot-desk, and the figure has been rising. A wide-ranging training programme, cultural as well as electronic, helped to prepare employees for the changes in working practices.

"We wanted to make informality the norm," says Alison Hartigan, senior property manager. While she acknowledges some departments such as legal, finance and some strategy teams, are not so suitable for hot-desking, the majority are – sales, marketing, property, human resources, computers, and so on.

"Of course people are very territorial about space and in open-plan offices they personalise their space. With hot-desking they can't do that, it's the big barrier to cross."

Christopher Middleton, who joined IBM recently as a manager for smaller businesses, found hot-desking a culture shock, but a positive one. "You're judged purely on results, not on whether you're sitting at your desk all the time," he says.

"I have been coming into the office two days a week and the challenge is to book a desk in time although there are drop-in areas where you can plug into a computer for a couple of hours."

Like many others who hot-desk, he finds he gravitates to the same desk when he comes into the office.

"It gives me a kind of continuity and feeling of belonging. Maybe I'll shake this off in time. I totally accept it might be difficult to change for some people. In my last firm, some people still wore suits and ties on dress-down Friday." […]

One sector which has had its fingers burned with hot-desking is the advertising industry. Large advertising agencies working globally who thought they could downsize their expensive prestigious buildings around the world found that this led rapidly to employees not identifying with the agencies any longer and leaving to set up their own businesses. It was an expensive disaster. […]

(662 words)

From: *www.telegraph.co.uk*

1 LOOKING AT THE TEXT

→ Rezeption: Leseverstehen, S. 214

Complete the sentences with the most suitable answer, a, b or c.

1 'Hot-desking' means …
- **a** you always have the best desk.
- **b** you always work at a different desk.
- **c** your desk is centrally heated.

2 Companies use hot-desking because …
- **a** they can use their office space better.
- **b** employees like moving around.
- **c** moveable desks last longer than fixed desks.

3 At ICL hot-desk workers are the employees who …
- **a** work in the office at least three days a week.
- **b** work at home at least three days a week.
- **c** have no fixed working routine.

4 Mr Reed's secretary …
- **a** never hot-desks. **b** sometimes hot-desks. **c** always hot-desks.

5 Mr Reed …
- **a** likes to park his car in the same space in the company car park.
- **b** prefers to work at the same desk when he's in the office.
- **c** has nothing against working in a different place all the time.

6 According to Alison Hartigan at British Airways, … departments are suitable for hot-desking.
- **a** a few **b** most **c** all

7 Christopher Middleton thinks that …
- **a** some people find it hard to change how they work.
- **b** male employees should always wear suits and ties.
- **c** Friday is the best day for hot-desking.

8 When advertising agencies introduced hot-desking …
- **a** they saved a lot of money.
- **b** they were able to open many more new offices.
- **c** their employees left.

2 WORKING WITH WORDS

Find words or expressions in the text on pages 69–70 to match these definitions.

1 a piece of office furniture for storing files, documents, papers, etc. (paragraph 1)
2 buildings, e.g. office blocks (paragraph 2)
3 all the people who work at a company (paragraph 3)
4 needs (paragraph 5)
5 automatically (paragraph 6)
6 slow, not sudden (paragraph 8)
7 the department of a company that employs and trains people (paragraph 10)
8 the hard thing to do (paragraph 13)
9 casual, informal (paragraph 15)
10 make smaller (paragraph 16)

3 MEDIATION

→ Schriftliche Mediation, S. 240

BUILDING SKILLS: Written mediation

A mediated text should provide the person who reads it with the information he/she needs: it is not a word-for-word translation. When mediating a text use the following techniques:
- Read the whole text through for gist. Don't stop to look up unknown words while doing this.
- Go back and note down all the relevant facts for your 'reader'. Use a dictionary if necessary.
- Use your notes to present the relevant information in a German text in your own words.

Sie arbeiten für eine Firma, deren Mitarbeiter/innen oft im Außendienst unterwegs sind. Deswegen erwägt Ihre Firma Einsparungen bei den Büromieten.

Schreiben Sie eine E-Mail an die Leiterin der Personalabteilung, in der Sie die Vorteile von *hot-desking* erklären.

4 LISTENING

→ Rezeption: Hörverstehen, S. 225

Jenny Parker is a project manager at Green Energy Services. Today she is talking to Geoff Hall, the human resources director, about her new workplace.

1/27

A Listen to the dialogue and answer the questions.

1 What was the email about?
2 What does Jenny want to do?
3 How often are project managers in the office?
4 What solution does Geoff suggest?

B Complete the sentences with words from the dialogue. There is one word for each gap.

1 We would have more problems if we ___ back to the old system, Jenny.
2 If we were in a bigger building, there ___[1] ___[2] enough room for everyone.
3 I'd change back to the old system if I ___ .
4 If you ___[1] a project manager spending two or three days a week on the road, you ___[2] ___[3] a permanent place in the office.
5 If we ___ you your own desk, you'd only use it two or three days a week.
6 You ___[1] certainly ___[2] a fixed desk if you did that.

5 GETTING IT RIGHT

→ *If* sentences, S. 264

A Two colleagues are discussing hot-desking. Complete these *if* sentences type 2.

Emma If I (get) ___ 1 a job at a big company with hot-desking, I would try to sit in the same place every day. How about you?

Frank I understand what you mean, Emma but if they asked me, I (be) ___ 2 quite happy to move around. If I (do) ___ 3 that, I'd meet new people every day.

Emma But (you/get to know) ___ 4 them if you only saw them once in a while? I (try) ___ 5 to sit in the same place automatically if I (have) ___ 6 to hot-desk. It's human nature.

Frank Hot-desking saves money. Companies (not want) ___ 7 to do it if they (not think) ___ 8 it was a good idea.

The finance director of a manufacturing company is telling his colleagues why hot-desking is necessary. Describe the following 'chain reactions' using *if* sentences type 2.

we / buy a new office block → we / spend over £2,000,000 → we / have no money for new products → our company / lose its market share → many employees / lose their jobs → they / work for our competitors → our competitors / discover our company's secrets → this company / have to close

If we bought a new office block, we would spend over £2,000,000.
If we spent over £2,000,000, ...

Invent two more 'chain reactions' of your own.

If the computer system in a company using hot-desking broke down, ...
If we all went on strike, ...

B Ella Brown, the managing director of Green Energy Services, is talking to Geoff Hall, the human resources director, about how to save office space. Complete the sentences with suitable forms of the verbs in brackets (= *if* sentences types 1 and 2). Sometimes there is more than one word in a gap.

Ella If we (not do) ___ 1 something soon, we'll have no more room at all! If I were you, I (tell) ___ 2 the staff to have home office days.

Geoff Yes, that's one possibility but I think we (have) ___ 3 a problem if we asked everybody to do that. If we (ask) ___ 4 the project managers, I'm sure most of them will agree but I don't think we should ask the permanent office staff. We (find) ___ 5 it difficult if some of them spent one day a week at home. For example, who will look after visitors if the receptionist (not be) ___ 6 in the office?

Ella Yes, I see your point but (it/be) ___ 7 better if we had job rotation? If we (do) ___ 8 that, everybody will be able to stand in for everybody else.

Geoff But think of the costs of retraining them all, Ella! I don't think our finance director (agree) ___ 9 if we suggested that. I think we should hot-desk. If we (buy) ___ 10 some really modern-looking, hi-tech, plug-in wheely desks, I'm sure everyone will want one!

6 CLASSROOM SIMULATION

Try the following experiment with your class in your next English lesson:

Number the individual places at the desks in your classroom (not just each double desk) and put the numbers in a hat. Each student draws a number and sits at that place. If it is the student's regular place, the student must draw again to make sure it's a new place. You must accept the new place without question to make this simulation work. Spend the whole lesson at the new place.

After the lesson:
- Write lists of what you liked and disliked about having a new place.
- Compare your lists with those of two or three other students in your class.
- Have a class discussion about the advantages and disadvantages of sitting at a new place a) every lesson, b) every month, c) after the Christmas and Easter holidays.

7 DEBATE

→ Interaktion: An Diskussionen teilnehmen, S. 246

After the simulation, form groups of four or more and debate the pros and cons of sitting at a new place every lesson, every month or after the holidays. Half of your group must be for and the others against this idea. Split into 'pro' and 'con' groups and sit at separate desks.

Prepare for the debate like this:
1. Discuss in your 'pro' or 'con' group what you liked/disliked about sitting at a new place, e.g. different faces around you, getting to know people better, easier/harder to concentrate, more/less help from neighbours, etc.
2. Write down all your arguments in note form.
3. Use the *Language for discussion* expressions on the back cover flap of this book to make your notes into whole sentences.
4. Practise talking about your notes with the other member(s) of your group.

Conduct the debate like this:
5. The 'pro' group members present all their arguments. The 'con' group members take notes.
6. The 'con' group members present all their arguments. The 'pro' group members take notes.
7. The 'pro' and 'con' groups now ask and answer questions about the arguments they have heard.

8 WRITING

→ Produktion: Eine Stellungnahme schreiben, S. 234

BUILDING SKILLS: Writing a comment

A comment expresses your own opinion about a particular topic or question. To ensure that your comment is well structured follow these steps:
- Study the instructions carefully to make sure you know exactly what to write about.
- Structure your arguments logically, e.g. under headings or in a mind map. Include arguments for and against.
- Refer to the question in your first sentence then present your arguments in separate paragraphs.
- Conclude your comment with a final sentence clearly stating your opinion.

Use your notes from exercise 3 and your own ideas to write a short comment about hot-desking. Title: *Why I would or wouldn't like to hot-desk*.

Training "made in Germany"

German technical training is amongst the best in the world. Increasingly, other countries are showing interest in using the German approach. Can they copy Germany's success?

1 LISTENING

→ Rezeption: Hörverstehen, S. 225

4/5

A reporter interviews Maxwell Smith, a technical training consultant, about the popularity of Germany's "dual system" of vocational training. Listen to the recording and take notes about the following subjects:

1 Reasons why the German system is attractive to other Europeans
2 How the German system combines theory and practice
3 Which countries are interested in the German model
4 Why they should not adopt the German model completely
5 How German educational institutions and companies work together
6 Why it might be difficult to copy this arrangement in other countries

2 WRITING AN EMAIL

→ Produktion: Schreiben, S. 228

Your 17-year-old English friend Megan Jones from Leeds has written you an email. Reply to Megan, answering her questions in as much detail as you can.

Hi!

How are you? Sorry I haven't been in touch for a while, but a lot has happened in my life. In June I finished secondary school with eight GCSEs and now I've started a new vocational training course!

It's called Advanced Apprenticeship in Engineering Design and it's a four-year programme. The first year is full-time study at college, but it's mostly very practical: I learn job skills like working with tools, welding and using a lathe.

In the second year I'll work in my company's design office with a team of experienced engineers. I'll still go to college one day a week to do subjects like CAD and maths, but the rest of the time I'll work on real projects.

As I progress, I'll get different NVQ Level 3 qualifications and finally, when I finish my apprenticeship, I'll have a BTEC Level 4 HNC. Then I can apply to become a registered engineering technician. So one day I'll hopefully be Megan Jones (EngTech)!

I've heard that vocational training in Germany is very good. You have something called the 'dual system' over there, don't you? What is it, and why is it so popular? Is that what you're doing?

Write soon!
Megan xx

3 RESEARCH

Find out about one or more of the qualifications that Megan mentions in her email. Report back to the class with what you learned.

Job skills 2

CVs and cover letters ▪ interviews

Eric Jung is looking for work in the UK. He applies for a post in London.

1 LOOKING AT THE CV

Compare the information on Eric's CV with the job advertisement. Say why he believes he is a suitable candidate for the position.

TRAINEE OFFICE ASSISTANT – General office duties

- We are a manufacturing company located in London.
- We are looking for a trainee to work in our export office.
- You are a careful and accurate worker, flexible and willing to learn.
- You speak good German and at least one other foreign language.
- Computer skills are a must.

Apply with CV and cover letter to Joan Shaw, Magnus & Klein plc, 1004 Thames Road, London SE7 2XY quoting reference FTD/0204.

Eric Jung
Klarastr. 430 • 79106 Freiburg • Germany
Phone (+49) 0761 234589 • Mobile (+49) 0176 28948610
Email ejung@gmx.com

Personal statement
Highly-motivated student of business studies seeking practical experience in the UK.

Work experience

June – August 20..	Delgado Import/Export, Bristol, England. Duties: general office work (answering telephone; writing emails) and updating spreadsheets.

Education and training

August 20.. – present	Berufskolleg, Freiburg (equivalent to British vocational college) Main subjects: Business Studies, English, German, Spanish Fachhochschulreife (German higher education entrance qualifications): Expected July 20..
August 20.. – July 20..	Realschule, Freiburg (equivalent to British secondary school) Mittlere Reife (Final exams similar to GCSE)

Skills
German (native speaker), English (fluent, oral and written), Spanish (intermediate)
Computer: MS Office
Good at working under pressure, friendly, flexible

Interests
Sport, travel

References
Names of referees available on request

2 LOOKING AT THE COVER LETTER

A Read Eric's cover letter to Magnus & Klein plc and label the parts 1–10.

body of the letter ▪ complimentary close ▪ date ▪ enclosure ▪ inside address ▪ reference ▪ salutation ▪ signature ▪ subject line ▪ writer's address

Klarastr. 430
79106 Freiburg
Germany **1**
Phone (+49) 0761 234589
Mobile (+49) 0176 28948610
Email ejung@gmx.com

Magnus & Klein plc
Attn: Ms Joan Shaw
1004 Thames Road
London **2**
SE7 2XY
UK

5 April 20.. **3**

Your ref: FTD/0204 **4**

Dear Ms Shaw **5**

Trainee Office Assistant **6**

I would like to apply for the position of Trainee Office Assistant as advertised in today's copy of the *Financial Times Deutschland*. **7**

As you can see from my CV, I am currently doing business studies at a German vocational college. During my work placement in a British import/export company, I had the opportunity to learn business practices and I am keen to add to my experience of international business by working further in an English-speaking country.

In addition to German, which is my native language, I speak fluent English and I have recently added Spanish to my list of foreign languages. I am sure that my language abilities will make me an asset to your team.

I would appreciate it if you considered my application and hope that you will grant me an interview.

I look forward to hearing from you soon.

Yours sincerely **8**

Eric Jung

Eric Jung **9**

Encl: CV **10**

B Find the following sections in the body of the letter. Write out the key phrases in your notebook.

1. asking to be considered for an interview
2. reference to details on CV
3. reference to the position
4. saying why the writer is applying for the position
5. stating why the applicant is the best person for the job

3 WRITING A COVER LETTER

You are going to work with a partner, compile your CV and write a cover letter.

1. **Study the job advertisement on page 75 or choose one from page 66 and answer the following questions.**
   - What is the job title?
   - Who is advertising the job?
   - Where will the job applicant work?
   - What educational background and skills does the job applicant need?
   - How do you apply?
2. **You and your partner are both going to apply for the job. Compile your own CV in English and write a cover letter. Use any items from Eric's CV and cover letter that are appropriate for you. When you have finished, exchange your CVs and cover letters and do peer correction.**

1. **With your partner, talk about what you would like to do in the future. Talk about where you would like to work and what type of work you would like to do. Make some notes and use them to write a short job advertisement. Pin it on the wall.**
2. **Choose one of the job advertisements from the wall and discuss it with your partner. You and your partner are both going to apply for the job. Compile your own CV in English and write a cover letter. Use any items from Eric's CV and cover letter that are appropriate for you. When you have finished, exchange your CVs and cover letters and do peer correction.**

German school types and qualifications

Grundschule	primary school
Realschule	secondary school
Gymnasium	secondary/grammar school (GB), high school (USA)
Berufsschule	vocational school
Berufskolleg, Fachoberschule	vocational college
Fachhochschule	university of applied sciences
Mittlere Reife	GCSE (General Certificate of Secondary Education)
Abitur	A levels (GB), high school diploma (USA)
Fachhochschulreife	German higher education entrance qualifications
Noten 1–6	Grades A–F

Job skills 2

4 PREPARING FOR AN INTERVIEW

The HR office at Magnus & Klein has informed Eric that Ms Shaw will interview him on the phone next week. He prepares himself by making a list of questions Ms Shaw might ask him. He also thinks about what he would like to know from Ms Shaw.

A With a partner, study the list of typical interview questions and sort them under the correct heading. Then add one more question under each heading.

- About yourself
- About your motivation
- About your education, work experience and skills

1 Can you tell me something about yourself?
2 Why do you want to work for this company?
3 What are your strengths and weaknesses?
4 Why are you training at vocational college?
5 Why do you think you would be a good candidate for the job?
6 What have you learned that might help you in the position you're applying for here?

B Now study Eric's list of questions. With your partner, add two more questions.

- Who will I report to?
- When will I hear if I have the job or not?
- What kind of training will I be given?

TIP Using first names

Don't be surprised if a superior calls you by your first name when doing business in Anglo-American countries. It is best if you use *Ms* or *Mr* when speaking to superiors until they invite you to use their first name.

5 LISTENING

→ Rezeption: Hörverstehen, S. 225

2/2

A Listen to the main part of the interview. Which questions does Ms Shaw ask? How does Eric answer the questions? Make notes.

B Listen to the conclusion of the interview. What does Eric want to know? What is the next step in the application process?

6 ROLE-PLAY

→ Interaktion: Ein Rollenspiel gestalten, S. 247

Work with a partner. Use the role cards below to practise an interview for a job.

Partner A: you are the interviewer

You are going to interview your partner as if he/she is a candidate for a job. Start the interview by introducing yourself then ask the following questions.

- How would you describe yourself?
- What are your strengths and weaknesses?
- Why did you decide to study business management?
- Do you have any questions for me?

Partner B: you are the candidate

Your partner is going to interview you for a job. Think about the questions the interviewer might ask you. Make notes. When the interviewer asks you if you have any questions, choose two or three from this list.

- Who will I work with?
- What training will you give me?
- What will my responsibilities be?
- When will I hear if my application has been successful or not?

9 Multiculturalism

MAIN COURSE

FOCUS

1

2

3

4

A **The photos above show festivals in Vancouver, Canada. Describe the people and what they are doing. What cultural backgrounds might these people have?**

to carry ▪ to dance ▪ to light ▪ to march ▪ to perform
balloon ▪ candle ▪ dragon ▪ headdress ▪ lantern ▪ pipe band ▪ samba ▪ sari
Chinese ▪ Indian ▪ Hindu ▪ Irish ▪ Latin American

B **Match photos 1–4 with the festivals in the cultural programme on the right. Make statements to a visitor.**

If you visit Vancouver in early February, you can go to the Chinese New Year and (see) …

February	Chinese New Year (lion dance, Tai Chi, dragon boat display)
March	St Patrick's Day Parade (march, music, ceilidhs)
Mid-summer	Carnaval Del Sol (Latin American dancing, cuisine, crafts)
Mid-autumn	Diwali (dancing, lanterns, traditional music, cuisine)

C **Work with a partner. Think of local festivals that a visitor to your part of the world might enjoy. Create a calendar of events and then make statements to a visitor.**

If you visit … (place) in … (time of year), you can …

D **Work with your partner again. List some of the different cultures in Germany today. Discuss any way that you get to know, or learn about, people from other cultures.**

Say what changes you think these cultures bring to the traditional German way of life.

TEXT A Life as a refugee

BEFORE YOU READ

→ Vorbereitung auf das Lesen, S. 214

A **Look at a map. What parts of the world would you probably cross on a flight from Germany to Eritrea?**

B **Look at the information about Eritrea and about the boy in the picture. Why might he be a refugee?**

Eritrea:
Independent East African state on the Red Sea coast. Separated from Ethiopia after violent fighting in 1999–2000.

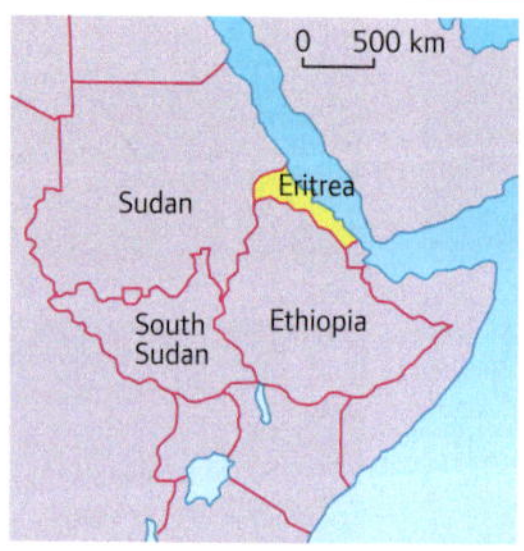

Family name
Kelo
Given name
Alem
Father's nationality
Ethiopian
Mother's nationality
Eritrean

2/3

refugee boy

BENJAMIN ZEPHANIAH

Ethiopia

As the family lay sleeping, soldiers kicked down the door of the house and entered, waving their rifles around and shouting. Alem ran into the room where his parents were, to find that they had been dragged out of bed and forced to stand facing the wall.

The soldier who was in command went and stood so that his mouth was six inches away from Alem's father's ear and shouted, 'What kind of man are you?'

Alem's father shuddered with fear; his voice trembled as he replied, 'I am an African.'

Alem looked on terrified as the soldier shot a number of bullets into the floor around the feet of his father and mother.

His mother screamed with fear. 'Please leave us! We only want peace.'

The soldier continued shouting. 'Are you Ethiopian or Eritrean? Tell us, we want to know.'

'I am an African,' Alem's father replied.

The soldier raised his rifle and pointed it at Alem's father. 'You are a traitor.' He turned and pointed the rifle at Alem's mother. 'And she is the enemy.' Then he turned and pointed the rifle at Alem's forehead. 'And he is a mongrel.'

Turning back to Alem's father he dropped his voice and said, 'Leave Ethiopia or die.'

Background to the next part of Alem's life

The Kelo family moved to Eritrea, but equally bad things happened to them there. That was when Alem's parents decided that they must get him to safety in the UK. His father took him there and left him, knowing that because his son was without a parent, the system would look after him well. His plan succeeded: the authorities found Alem a welcoming family to live with – the Fitzpatricks – and soon he was beginning a new life, complete with a new school and new friends.

Then came terrible news. While Alem and his father had been gone, 'very evil people' had killed Alem's mother and left her dead near the border. After his return to Eritrea, Alem's father had finally found her body and wrote that he must now get to Britain to be with him.

The law was not so kind to Mr Kelo. When he arrived, the authorities arrested him and sent him first to a detention centre and then to a cheap hotel that was used for refugees and homeless families. It was an unpleasant, unhappy place in a poor part of London.

And then the rules for Alem suddenly changed – for he had a parent to look after him now. The courts said that he had to leave his new family and move into his father's small hotel room. Soon, he was learning the life of normal refugees – shopping, for example.

Britain

They didn't spend very long at the supermarket; all they put in their basket was a small amount of vegetables, some tinned meat and a packet of biscuits. As they were queuing for the cashier, Alem noticed that other checkouts were less busy.

'Father, look at those other counters! Why are we waiting in this long queue? Let's go to one of them.'

Mr Kelo's eyes dropped as he realized that Alem hadn't understood the deal. 'We can't,' he said, 'we don't have any money.'

'So what are you paying with?'

Mr Kelo took out his wallet and pulled out what looked like tickets. 'These, I have to pay with these. These are vouchers; look up there.'

He pointed to a sign above the counter where they were waiting. It read, 'Food vouchers only.'

'What is this all about?' Alem asked.

'These vouchers are for asylum seekers. We cannot buy clothes with them, we cannot get any change from our shopping with them, and we cannot use them at any other counter.'

The queue was long and full of exactly the same kind of people Alem had seen outside the court-rooms, Asians, Africans, Romanians and Kosovans, all waiting with their heads hanging down, looking humiliated. Meanwhile, many other cashiers were sitting filing their nails or combing their hair, waiting for customers. Other shoppers just seemed to be a lot happier and some looked over to the 'Vouchers only' queue as if the customers there were exhibition pieces.

Alem could also see the humiliation on his father's face but as for himself he felt angry; he didn't want to show it but he felt really angry. His father was a qualified person who had been in a good job and always proud to have earned every penny he had, but now he had been reduced to what amounted to living off aid. Alem looked up and down the queue, he wondered how many people there were in the same position. Which of the men and women were doctors, lawyers, nurses or mathematicians? Could he be standing next to one of Bosnia's most promising architects, or an Iranian airline pilot? His father saw him silently shake his head in disgust as they shuffled down the line. (813 words)

From: Benjamin Zephaniah, *refugee boy*, Bloomsbury, London, 2001

1 LOOKING AT THE TEXTS

→ Rezeption: Leseverstehen, S. 214

A Put these events from Alem's life in the correct order.

- **a** Alem's move to England
- **b** his mother's death
- **c** the move to Eritrea
- **d** living in England with his father
- **e** living in Ethiopia with his parents
- **f** living in England with the Fitzpatricks
- **g** his father's move to England

B Answer the questions below on the extracts from *refugee boy*. → Gründliches Lesen, S. 223

BUILDING SKILLS: Reading for understanding

In order to answer questions on the text, you usually have to read the text closely for understanding.

- First, read the questions carefully so that you know exactly what you have to find out.
- Look for key words in the questions that will help you to find the relevant areas of the text.
- Read these pieces of the text sentence by sentence to find the answers.
- Finally, check your answers. Read them carefully and compare them to the questions and the text to make sure that you have given the details requested.

1 What does Alem's father call himself, and what point is he trying to make to the soldier?
2 What name does the soldier call each member of Alem's family, and why?
3 What three things happen to Alem after his father leaves him in Britain on his own?
4 What three things happen to Alem when his father comes back to Britain to be with him?
5 When they join the checkout queue, why does Alem suggest joining a different queue?
6 Why is this impossible?
7 How does the situation make everyone in the queue feel?
8 Why does it affect people like Alem's father especially badly?

C Say what you think.

1 If you were in the same dangerous situation as Alem's parents, what would you do? Would you keep your young son with you and try to protect him yourself – or would you send him far away to somewhere safe, but unknown?
2 If you were in Alem's position, which decision would you prefer?

2 WORKING WITH WORDS

A Match words in box A to similar words from the texts in box B.

A average ▪ line ▪ opposite ▪ place ▪ recognize

B facing ▪ normal ▪ position ▪ queue ▪ realize

B Now choose the correct word to complete each sentence.

1 a The trees stand in a long ___[1] beside the road. (line/queue)
  b I'm sorry, but you can't jump the ___[2]. Go to the back and wait for your turn. (line/queue)
2 a We hadn't met for five years, but I ___[1] her immediately. (realized/recognized)
  b I was half-way to the airport when I ___[2] that I'd forgotten my passport. (realized/recognized)
3 a Jim spoke after Carol at the meeting, and he presented the ___[1] argument. (facing/opposite)
  b The task ___[2] us today will be the hardest one of all. (facing/opposite)
4 a I always play in goal. What ___[1] do you play? (place/position)
  b My home town is a lovely old ___[2]. You should come and see it. (place/position)
5 a Why does that child always behave so badly? It isn't ___[1]! (average/normal)
  b Statistics show that ___[2] pay has risen by 2.5% in the last year. (average/normal)

C Copy and complete the tables. Find the words in the texts.

Verb	Noun
to live	___
___	decision
___	success
___	earnings
___	reduction

Noun	Adjective
___	safe
___	humiliated
qualification	___
pride	___
promise	___

D Now use the pairs of words to complete the following. Make any necessary changes.

1 **A** Your sister hasn't had much ___[1] with her new business yet, has she?
B No, but things are slowly getting better, and I know she'll ___[2] in the end.

2 All those books that you've put on top of that cupboard don't look ___[1]! I'm sure you're breaking the company's health and ___[2] rules.

3 **A** We're spending too much money, so we'll have to make some ___[1].
B Well, let's ___[2] what we spend on going out.

4 I have never felt so ___[1] before. The ___[2] of having to buy food with vouchers was more than I could take!

5 **A** Is Joe ___[1] as a doctor yet?
B Yes, he got his basic ___[2] last year.

6 We can't yet make any ___[1] about how successful this new cure for malaria will be, but our latest test results are ___[2].

7 Things are so expensive! We all need to ___[1] more money. The cost of living is going up faster than people's ___[2].

8 **A** What have you ___[1] to do with the old TV?
B We've made a ___[2] to sell it on eBay.

9 My great-grandfather had a very long ___[1]. He ___[2] from 1911 to 2010.

10 Helen takes real ___[1] in her school work. She should be especially ___[2] of her excellent Maths and Science results this year.

3 GETTING IT RIGHT

→ Past perfect ▪ Simple past, S. 256

Put the verbs in brackets into the simple past or the past perfect.

Alem's father (choose) ___[1] to take him to Britain even though they (never / be) ___[2] there before. Once the two of them (land) ___[3] in London, they (take) ___[4] a taxi from the airport. They (go) ___[5] to a small hotel outside London which Mr Kelo (book) ___[6] the week before. Alem (love) ___[7] their visit to London the next day: he (never / see) ___[8] a city like it before. However, when he (wake up) ___[9] the next morning back at the hotel, his father (disappear) ___[10].

At first, Alem (just / think) ___[11] that his father (go) ___[12] downstairs to arrange breakfast. But then, after he (wait) ___[13] for a long time, the manager (come) ___[14] to the room with a letter from his father. The manager (tell) ___[15] Alem that his father (pay) ___[16] and (leave) ___[17] the hotel early that morning. Alem (learn) ___[18] from the letter that his father (go) ___[19] in order to return to Ethiopia. He slowly (understand) ___[20] that his father (bring) ___[21] him to England for one reason only – because he would be safe there.

TEXT B The question of integration

BEFORE YOU READ

A **What seems to be the purpose of the *Say it how you see it* website?**

B **Would you ever join an online discussion like this? What sort of subjects would you be interested in discussing?**

http://www.sayithowyouseeit.au

2/4

Say it how you see it

This week's question: What now for multiculturalism?

So once again, Australians are talking about that 1970s government policy of multiculturalism – the idea that we can all live together in harmony with our different cultures and even languages. Well, can we?

Aussie Joe says:

I wish our government had the guts to pass a law to say 'our way or no way'. If people reject our culture and law, then we should deport them immediately – back to the country they came from. We don't want violent gangs on our streets, and we don't want Muslim extremists to take over with their Sharia laws.

If the government had acted years ago, we'd have saved ourselves a lot of trouble already. And if we don't act now, it'll be the end of Australia as we know it and love it.

Jenny says:

Calm down, Aussie Joe! The world changes and we have to change with it.

Don't pretend that the past was perfect, either. Look back and you'll find there was always crime on our streets. As for extreme Islamists, they're a small minority of a small minority, and most Muslims are as moderate as anyone else.

So instead of panicking, take a quiet look at a list of MPs or business people or any collection of people who have done a lot for this country. Then count the non-Anglo names. Since the old Anglo-Irish days, we've had wave after wave of immigrants, and many of them and their descendants have made real contributions – and they have all done so under a national policy of multiculturalism. And for most of us it's been a two-way street: we've accepted them and they've accepted us. If we hadn't, we wouldn't have developed the culture that we have today – a culture that's vibrant, pretty peaceful and very varied.

So, Aussie Joe, go outside and enjoy it instead of hiding in your negative little Anglo-culture box!

Mark says:

Vibrant ... peaceful ... varied, yes, but don't put that down to multiculturalism.

The way I understand it, multiculturalism gives ethnic groups the right to live by their own culture and not even learn English. Well, that may be politically correct, but I think you'll find the immigrants who've made big contributions haven't lived that way. If they had, they wouldn't have been able to make those contributions to mainstream society. They'd have been hidden away in their cultural ghettos, wouldn't they?

No, they've done something else over the years. They've worked hard to become Australian. They've integrated.

Stella says:

Mark's got a good point. Ask yourself this: should 2nd, 3rd and even 4th generation migrants maintain their parents' ethnic culture to the letter, with government support if necessary? Or should migrants take the best parts of their culture and gradually mix them with the best parts of ours?

If you agree with the first idea, then you believe in multiculturalism. If you agree with the second, then you don't: you simply believe in slower integration. And you believe in pluralism. That means everyone accepts the 'lead' Australian culture and its laws – so there's no room here for Sharia law, for example. But at the same time, it means accepting racial and cultural differences and integrating them all into a new cultural whole.

Talk to most Australians and you'll find that that's what they want. (554 words)

1 LOOKING AT THE TEXT

→ Rezeption: Leseverstehen, S. 214

A Say which person (or people) expresses each idea. Explain your answers.

1 I believe that the government's programme of multiculturalism has worked well.
2 I believe that gradual cultural integration is the right way for Australia.
3 I am against the idea that immigration means more crime.
4 I am against mixing new cultures with the traditional national culture.
5 I support cultural 'give and take' between the old and the new.
6 I support throwing out any immigrants who do not accept the Australian way of life or who break the law.

B Say whether the following are true or false. Correct the false statements.

1 Aussie Joe seems to believe that all the members of violent street gangs are immigrants.
2 He says that a law against all immigration was needed a long time ago.
3 Jenny argues that non-Anglo-Irish immigrants have done most for today's Australia.
4 She feels that the many waves of immigration have led to a varied and lively culture.
5 Mark says that multiculturalism forces immigrants to integrate into mainstream society.
6 Stella agrees with the government's policy towards immigrants.
7 She points out that most Australians believe in accepting cultural differences and adding the best of them to the traditional Australian way of life.

C Say what it means: Explain the underlined expressions in your own words.

1 … pass a law to say 'our way or no way'. (line 6)
2 And for most of us it's been a two-way street … (line 20)
3 … maintain their parents' ethnic culture to the letter … (line 33)
4 … everyone accepts the 'lead' Australian culture … (line 36)
5 … there's no room here for Sharia law … (line 37)

2 WORKING WITH WORDS

A Find words in the text that are the opposite of the following:

accept ▪ peaceful ▪ moderate ▪ majority ▪ similarity

B Now complete the following with pairs of words from exercise 2A.

1 The black ___[1] in South Africa forms 70% of the population while at 17%, white South Africans form the largest single ___[2].
2 We've ___[1] Plans A and C mainly because they're too expensive, but we've ___[2] Plan B because it offers a very good way forward and also because the price is right.
3 The struggles in Northern Ireland were very ___[1] for many years, and many died. However, life there is much more ___[2] today, thank goodness.
4 There are lots of ___[1] between the old GR70 and the new GR71, and they look almost the same. The most important ___[2] is the new car's much more powerful engine.
5 During the French Revolution, people with ___[1] ideas took control. For them, anyone who was not with them was against them, and they did not listen to more ___[2] views.

3 GETTING IT RIGHT

→ *If* sentences, S. 264

Form type 3 *if* sentences. Start each sentence with *if*.

1. Franz and Ana Beckman were very poor. They moved from their country village to Hamburg to find work.
   If Franz and Ana Beckman had not been very poor, they would not have moved from …
2. They moved to Hamburg. Franz found a good job in the shipyards there.
3. He found a good job. They were able to save a lot of money.
4. They had money in the bank. They were able to have a long holiday in Australia.
5. They travelled round Australia. They fell in love with the country.
6. They decided to emigrate to Australia. They had the chance to take over a small boat building company in Sydney.
7. Franz had the skills to build up the business. The company became a big success.
8. The Beckmans moved away from their poor home village many years before. This immigrant success story happened.

Rewrite the underlined information in the following statements as type 3 *if* sentences.

1.  The trouble is that the Australian government refused to deport criminal immigrants in the past. I think deportation was the right way for us to avoid most of our problems with immigration.
   If the Australian government had not refused to deport …
2.  It was a very good thing that Australia opened its doors to immigration from many more countries. When that happened, we were able to escape from our tired old Anglo culture.
3. Vancouver has become a great city of ethnic festivals. It has happened because immigrants from around the world have made it their home.
4. Vancouver attracted a large Chinese population in the 19th century. As a result of that, the city became Canada's only important port on the Pacific coast.
5. His parents made sure that Alem was safe from the fighting by sending him away.
6. It was very sad that Alem's mother did not go with her husband and son to England. Because of that, she died in the fighting while they were away.

4 LISTENING

→ Rezeption: Hörverstehen, S. 225

You are going to listen to a discussion between Joan Carr, a Member of Parliament, and Tom Baker, an author, about immigration to the UK.

2/5

A Copy the list and listen to the first part of the discussion. Note the figures that Tom Baker gives.

Immigrant % of total population:
- *UK:* ▬
- *Germany:* ▬
- *Austria:* ▬
- *Switzerland:* ▬

Jobs:
- *New jobs in future:* ▬
- *People retiring 2010–2020:* ▬

Welfare:
- *Immigrant unemployment since 2010:* ▬
- *Immigrants claiming unemployment benefits:* ▬

Housing:
- *New households per year: approx.* ▬
- *New immigrant households per year: approx.* ▬

2/6 **B Now listen to the second part of the discussion and make notes on what Tom Baker and Joan Carr say about social tensions.**

Social tensions
Possible course of action 1: ___
• Likely effects – 1: ___ *; 2:* ___
Possible course of action 2: ___
• Likely effects – 1: ___ *; 2:*

5 ANALYSING FIGURES

→ Produktion: Statistiken beschreiben und analysieren, S. 238

BUILDING SKILLS: Describing and analysing statistics

To analyse statistics, you have to know exactly what sort of figures you are dealing with.
- Read the heading, labels and any other form of explanation carefully.
- Check that you understand the units (e.g. thousands, millions, etc.) that the figures are presented in.
- Make sure you know which figures are in these units (e.g. 80.5 million) and which figures are percentages (e.g. 14.7%) of a total.

A Copy the table and complete it with the figures from your notes in exercise 4A.

Populations of selected European countries (millions)			
Country	**Total**	**Immigrants**	**Percentage**
Germany	80.5	9.8	___
Britain	64.1	7.8	___
Austria	8.5	1.3	___
Switzerland	8.1	2.3	___

1 Explain what the numbers in columns 2 and 3 mean.
2 Contrast the types of information in columns 3 and 4.

B Use statistics from the table in 5A to complete this paragraph.

Nearly all European countries, big and small, have taken in many immigrants – especially in recent years. For example, Germany, with its very large population of over ___ [1] million, is also home to a little under ___ [2] million immigrants, or more than ___ [3] % of the total. Again, Switzerland, with its much smaller population of just over ___ [4] million, is host to more than ___ [5] million immigrants, which is well over ___ [6] % of the total population.

C Now interpret the figures for Britain and Austria in the same way. Use approximate numbers, e.g. *64.1 million → over 64 million*.

Start like this:
Similarly, the United Kingdom, with its large population of … . At the same time, Austria, with its much smaller population of around eight and a half …

6 WRITING

→ Produktion: Eine Stellungnahme schreiben, S. 234

Use your notes from exercise 4 and the figures from exercise 5 to write a short comment on the immigration situation in Britain.

Technology transfer

Technology transfer is the process of passing technical know-how from one country to another. Increasingly, developing countries want technology transfer to be part of the deal when they do business with advanced countries such as Germany. In a US National Public Radio (NPR) interview, host Melissa Block talks to reporter Norihiko Shirouzu about technology transfer in China.

1 LISTENING

→ Rezeption: Hörverstehen, S. 225

4/6

Hören Sie den Bericht und wählen Sie die beste Ergänzung für jeden der Sätze 1–5.

1 Siemens, Alstom, Bombardier und Kawasaki …
- **a** haben 760 Millionen Dollar für Hochgeschwindigkeitszüge an China bezahlt.
- **b** haben China beim Bau von Hochgeschwindigkeitszügen technisch unterstützt.
- **c** haben Hochgeschwindigkeitszüge im Wert von 760 Millionen Dollar an China verkauft.

2 China will nicht zugeben, dass seine Züge …
- **a** auf ausländischer Technik basieren.
- **b** den ausländischen Zügen qualitativ nachstehen.
- **c** wesentlich auf ausländischer Technik mit geringfügigen einheimischen Verbesserungen basieren.

3 China will jetzt …
- **a** bessere Zugtechnik aus den USA, Russland und Brasilien importieren.
- **b** seine Züge in die USA und nach Russland und Brasilien verkaufen.
- **c** den USA, Russland und Brasilien helfen, schnellere Züge zu entwickeln.

4 Die internationalen Zugbauer …
- **a** wollen jetzt gegen China gerichtlich vorgehen.
- **b** könnten jetzt gegen China gerichtlich vorgehen, aber das wäre riskant.
- **c** dementieren, dass sie gegen China gerichtlich vorgehen wollen.

5 Ausländische Autohersteller …
- **a** können keine neuen Autos auf dem chinesischen Markt einführen.
- **b** können nur dann weltweit erfolgreich sein, wenn sie in China Erfolg haben.
- **c** lehnen es ab, China bei der Entwicklung neuer Kfz-Technik zu unterstützen.

2 DISCUSSION

→ Interaktion, S. 246

Discuss with a partner. Which of these comments do you agree with most and why?

"Technology transfer is just a normal part of industrialization. Without it, there would be no motor vehicles, no mobile phones and no internet."

"Germany has used China as a source of cheap goods for decades. It's only fair that it gets the chance to develop its own high-tech industries."

"'Technology transfer' is just a nice way of saying 'technology theft'. By accepting it, German companies are losing future business for short-term profits."

10 Helping others

MAIN COURSE

FOCUS

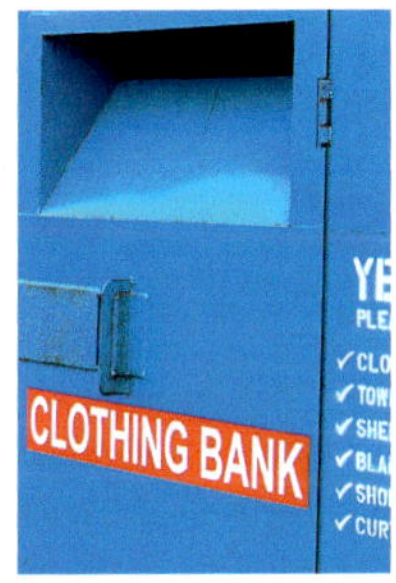

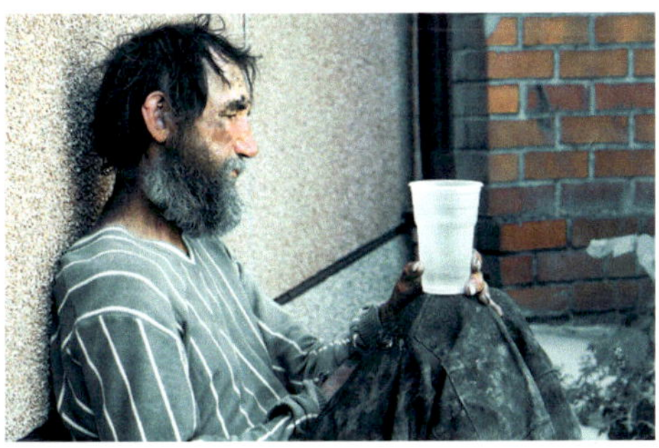

A **Discuss the photos with a partner. Would you help or donate something in each case? Give reasons and report your decisions to the class.**

B **In class, discuss whether people should give money to beggars or not. Before you start, note arguments for and against.**

C **Look at the illustrations below with a partner and think about the different ways of giving help. Think about who gets the help and who gives the help.**

Useful phrases

- I would give some money/food to homeless people because …
- I wouldn't give any … because …

- to beg (for) …
- to donate (money/clothes/food)
- to make a donation (of …) to charity
- to collect for (people in need)
- a clothing container / collection box

D **Now do these tasks:**

- When did you last help someone? Write a sentence or two to describe what you did.
- When did someone last help you? Describe what happened in a few sentences.
- Exchange stories with your partner.

TEXT A Different ways to help

WHILE YOU READ

Match the headings below with the paragraphs (1–5).

Donate ▪ Help people help themselves ▪ Use your fame to help others ▪ Volunteer to be a counsellor ▪ Sponsor a poor child's education

2/7

1 George Clooney is famous for making blockbuster Hollywood movies but he also uses his fame to fight poverty. He and his Ocean's 11 co-stars Don Cheadle, Matt Damon and Brad Pitt, together with producer Jerry Weintraub, have set up a charity called Not On Our Watch, and its mission is to help stop human rights atrocities, such as in the Darfur region of Sudan. The charity invites people to find out about the crises, donate money, lobby politicians and write letters of complaint to companies benefiting from the conflict.

2 World Vision: When Priscilla was a child, a donor many thousands of miles from her Ghanaian village helped pay for her schooling. For years she exchanged letters with her British benefactor. Now she is 20, the charity has stopped the sponsorship and the relationship. 'Last year I wrote to them saying goodbye and thanked them for taking care of me up to this day,' says Priscilla, an accountancy student. 'When I was writing, I was full of tears. Tears were coming from my eyes.' From: *www.bbc.com*

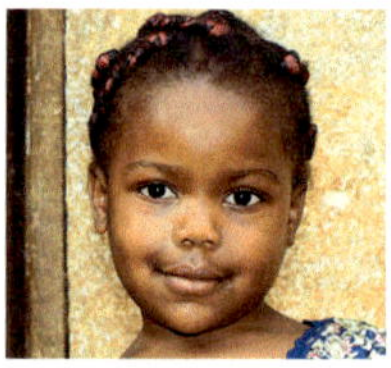

3 MicroLoan Foundation helps some of the poorest women in the world feed their families, send their children to school and pay for life saving medicines. We are a very different kind of charity, offering hope, not handouts. By providing small loans (average £60) and ongoing business training and support, MicroLoan empowers women in rural Malawi and Zambia to set up self-sustainable businesses. The profits from these businesses enable the women to work themselves and their families out of poverty.

From: *www.microloanfoundation.org.uk*

4 You can make an amazing difference at Samaritans. Our volunteers are changing lives every day, and developing valuable skills and friendships along the way. Volunteers are the heart of Samaritans. We welcome and value every volunteer, from all walks of life. Whatever your interests, experience or skills, we have a role for you.
We currently have over 20,000 volunteers giving up a few hours of their time every few weeks to help support people around the UK find their way, through whatever is troubling them. From: *www.samaritans.org*

5 The Salvation Army
£26 could pay for two weekly parent-and-toddler groups where disadvantaged children can play in safety.
£52 could pay to keep a day centre for older people open for a day – providing hot meals and the promise of companionship.
£90 could pay for a bed for a month for a homeless person at one of our Lifehouses – which is often the first step towards rebuilding their lives. (401 words)

From: *www.salvationarmyappeals.org.uk*

1 LOOKING AT THE TEXTS

→ Rezeption: Leseverstehen, S. 214

A Read the texts and match the charities with the issues they deal with. Note that some charities deal with more than one issue.

Charities	Issues
Not On Our Watch	poverty
World Vision	loneliness
MicroLoan Foundation	homelessness
Samaritans	psychological support
The Salvation Army	armed conflict
	education
	work

SKILLS CHECKLIST: Reading for understanding

- ☑ Have I looked for key words in the questions?
- ☑ Have I found the key words in the text?
- ☑ Have I compared my answers with the questions and the text?

B Decide which of the charities provide help …

- in their home country
- in foreign countries
- in the long term
- in the short term
- by giving people money
- by giving people non-financial help

C Choose two of the charities described and explain how they fight poverty.

2 WORKING WITH WORDS

A Match six of the words in the box with their definitions below.

accountancy ▪ atrocities ▪ benefactor ▪ companionship ▪ conflict ▪ education ▪ disadvantaged ▪ foundation ▪ handouts ▪ loan ▪ poverty ▪ volunteer

1 the situation you are in when you have no money
2 someone who donates money to help others
3 keeping a list of a person's or company's financial data
4 an organization which has been set up to finance activities for the good of society
5 not having the money and opportunities that other people have
6 what you get when you have friends

Write definitions for the six words not needed above.

Do not write the word. Give your definitions to a partner. Can he or she find the correct words? (If your partner can find the words, your definitions were good!)

B Complete the text with six of the words in exercise 2A. Make any necessary changes.

In the USA many successful people 'give back' to society and become ▬[1] by setting up a ▬[2]. Bill and Melinda Gates did so in 2000 in order to help ▬[3] people all over the world. Their organization's focus is on two things: reducing extreme ▬[4] and poor health in developing countries where the poorest people in the world live and improving the American ▬[5] system in order to give youngsters a better start in life. If you want to work as a ▬[6], you can find links on the organization's website.

3 ANALYSING FIGURES

→ Produktion: Schaubilder beschreiben und analysieren, S. 238

Individual giving levels as percentage of gross domestic product (GDP)

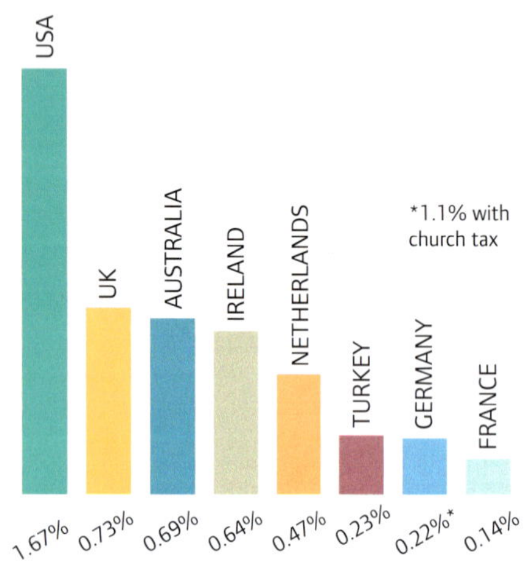

A Here in the States we don't wait for the government to solve our problems. We solve them ourselves! We give to charity, help in the community and raise money for good causes. Last year the parents and students at our local school collected $10,000 to pay for a disabled child to have surgery. That child can now walk without help. Anyone can help. Just do it!

B I'm a volunteer for the church charity you see at many stations all over Germany. We help anyone in need, regardless of their religious beliefs. The help we give is sometimes just a train time but it can also be a hot meal and a bed for the night for a homeless person. Most of our funding comes from the church, which is financed by church tax.

C I work very hard in my restaurant but I pay a lot of money in tax to the government here in Turkey, so I'm not rich! Unfortunately, there are many poor people everywhere, even children as young as four or five begging in the streets, so I give what I can when I see people in need. Sometimes I give them food or money, but when business is bad I have nothing to give.

D In France more than 50% of our income goes on tax! I feel sorry for people in need, both at home and abroad but I believe that helping is the responsibility of the government, not mine. That's why my vote goes to the politicians who promise to spend more money on fighting poverty.

A Read the four statements and do the following tasks:

1 Describe how many Americans believe it is best to help people in need.
2 Explain how the church charity at German train stations is mainly staffed and funded.
3 List the factors which influence how much and when the Turkish restaurant owner gives to people in need.
4 Contrast the French and American attitude to charitable giving.

BUILDING SKILLS: Comparing figures in charts

When describing charts, it is important to be able to compare and contrast the different figures.

- Always name the factors which a bar chart or line graph compares ('x' and 'y' axis): *The chart above is about percentages and countries.*
- Look for and point out the most striking features: *We can clearly see a progression from the USA at 1.67% to France at 0.14%.*
- Contrast the categories with each other: *The UK is in second place while Turkey only ranks 6th.*
- Describe the relationships between the categories: *The value for Australia is three times as high as for Turkey.*

B Look at the bar chart on page 92 and say …

1 where individual giving is highest and lowest.
2 where Germany stands in the list.
3 how high individual giving is in Germany with and without church tax.
4 which two countries have almost the same level of personal giving.
5 what the bar chart shows very clearly.

C Describe the chart and say what it tells us about the different attitudes to individual giving in the different countries.

Useful phrases

- There is a clear progression from … to …
- We can clearly see the difference/similarity between … and …
- The value in the first column is far greater/less than …
- twice / three times / four times as big as …
- half the size of …
- the highest/lowest
- in first/last place / in the last place but one / in the middle

4 CLASS PROJECT

Your class decides to support a charity offering help to people with one of the problems listed in exercise 1A (poverty, loneliness, homelessness, psychological support, armed conflict, education, work), or your own idea.

Follow these steps to carry out the project:

1 Make a list of all the charities, people or projects you could support and choose one.
2 Decide how you will give support, for example by …
   - raising money with a sponsored walk or by selling food/cakes at an event.
   - giving practical help, such as going shopping, doing gardening.
   - donating or collecting clothes, giving or selling food.

   Or think of some ideas of your own.
3 Divide the class into smaller groups of three or four students and give each group a job.
4 Agree a target, for example €100 by the end of the month or (school) year, and start work.
5 If your class decides not to support a project, summarize your reasons in a few sentences.

5 WRITING

→ Produktion: Schreiben, S. 228

Write a blog entry about your class project for your school's website. Include these points:

- why your class chose this project
- how you helped
- feedback from the people you helped

For more advice, read the notes for exercise 5 on page 38.

Think of your own example of a charity event and describe it in an email to an English-speaking pen friend.

TEXT B A charity in action

BEFORE YOU READ

→ Scannen nach Einzelinformationen im Text, S. 221

Scan the texts to find …

- the meaning of *orphans* and *orphanage*.
- the link between *flip-flops* and *Gandys*.

2/8

Orphans for Orphans

On Boxing Day in 2004, when the tsunami struck the little fishing village of Weligama on the southern coast of Sri Lanka, Rob (17) and Paul (15) Forkan were asleep in their hotel room. Their parents, Kevin and Sandra, and their two other siblings, Matty (12) and Rosie (8) were next door. Suddenly, Rob heard screams and saw water coming in under the door. Seconds later the first huge wave hit their hotel room smashing everything in its path. The two boys managed to climb onto the roof and they found their little brother, Matty, in a tree nearby. Later that day, they found their sister, Rosie, but their parents had been swept away whilst saving their two younger children. Despite this terrible blow and narrowly escaping death themselves, the four orphans managed to hitch-hike 200 km to the British Embassy in Colombo and then flew home to rejoin their two older sisters in the UK, one of whom adopted the younger children and gave them a home.

Paul Forkan with some of the orphans, 2013

Many other children would have lost their way in life after such a terrible tragedy but Kevin and Sandra Forkan had always brought their children up to think of the needs of others first, which ultimately gave them the strength to survive themselves. They took their four youngest children out of school when Paul and Rob were 11 and 13 and moved to Goa in India to work on humanitarian projects. They did a great deal of voluntary work, such as helping in orphanages by teaching the children there, playing sports with them, helping them with cooking, handing out food and organizing sports days, whilst at the same time fund-raising for local charities. These activities gave them the confidence to feel that they could do anything and that nothing was hard to achieve. Paul says: 'Our parents gave us the attitude that if you get knocked off your bike, just get back on it. There are always people worse off than you.'

In 2011, after travelling around the world separately, Rob and Paul lived together again in Brixton, South London, and decided to set up a business together. Their inspiration came from Mahatma Gandhi, the father of India's independence movement, who always wore flip-flops. They decided to sell flip-flops called Gandys and use some of the profits to fund social projects in India and Sri Lanka. A description of their company's mission can be found on its website.

(419 words)

www.gandysflipflops.com

Gandys is a social enterprise, and was founded on a commitment to using a portion of all profits to help disadvantaged children through our registered charity, the Gandys Foundation.

10% of all Gandys profits go directly into the Gandys Foundation, whose sole purpose is to support children in need of basic essentials such as shelter, nutrition, medication and education.

We call this the "Orphans for Orphans" mission.

The "Orphans for Orphans" mission has already started to make an impact by funding children's homes in India & Sri Lanka and the vision is to open them all around the world. The opening of the first children's home will be built in memory of Rob and Paul's parents, Kevin and Sandra Forkan, and will mark the 10th anniversary of the tsunami.

(131 words)

From: *www.gandysflipflops.com*

1 LOOKING AT THE TEXTS

→ Rezeption: Leseverstehen, S. 214

A Complete the sentences with information from the texts.

1 The Forkans' hotel was destroyed by …
2 The younger children were adopted by …
3 In Goa, the Forkans did voluntary work for …
4 Helping orphans gave the Forkan children …
5 Before living together in London, Rob and Paul each went on a long trip …
6 Both brothers very much admire …
7 The Gandys Foundation helps children who do not have …
8 Rob and Paul Forkan intend to open …

B Explain to a partner how …

1 the four orphans travelled from Weligama to Colombo.
2 they got help in the UK after the tsunami.
3 their voluntary work gave them confidence.

C Describe the brothers' personal reasons for their choice of charity work.

2 WORKING WITH WORDS

A Use the texts to match the verbs with the nouns to make collocations.

Verb		Noun	
to escape	to set up	an anniversary	death
to do	to make	an impact	work
to raise	to mark	a business	funds

B Find words in the texts to match the definitions.

1 to happen suddenly and have a damaging effect on sb/sth
2 brothers and/or sisters
3 to move suddenly with great force
4 to travel by asking for free rides in other people's cars
5 in the end, finally
6 unpaid; in order to help
7 a way of thinking and behaving
8 to finance
9 a promise
10 intention
11 a strong effect
12 food necessary to be healthy

C Replace the underlined words with some of the answers to exercises 2A and 2B.

When Hurricane Katrina hit [1] the southern coast of the USA on 29 August 2005 it carried [2] away everything in its path. Its effect [3] on the southern states was huge and in the end [4], it became clear that New Orleans' flood-control system had not fulfilled its function [5] and had probably increased the number of fatalities [6], which was at least 1,833. Many NGOs (non-government organizations) and citizens put in months of unpaid [7] work to help the victims and collected [8] US$4.25 billion in donations.

3 MEDIATION

→ Schriftliche Mediation, S. 240

Sie möchten *Orphans for Orphans* unterstützen und eine Sammelbestellung für Gandys Flipflops aufgeben. Lesen Sie die Webseite auf Seite 94 noch einmal, dann schreiben Sie einen Aufruf an Ihre Mitschüler/innen in dem Sie erklären, warum sie *Orphans for Orphans* mit einer Bestellung unterstützen sollen.

4 LISTENING

→ Rezeption: Hörverstehen, S. 225

A team of students are making a radio programme about giving to charities. Today, they are conducting a survey in London. They want to hear people's views about giving to charity.

2/9

A Listen to the dialogues and write down the following details for each person:

- occupation
- date of last contribution to charity
- what the contribution was for
- total contribution this year

B Fill in the gaps with words from the interviews.

Interview 1
It'll only ___[1] two minutes to answer our questions.
I've ___[2] £100 this year.

Interview 2
I've been ___[3] at our local church for many years now.
It ___[4] a lot of money to run a church.

Interview 3
My husband and I have ___ ___[5] a child in Africa for a number of years now.
We've ___ ___[6] regular payments for the last six years.

Interview 4
I've ___ ___[7] out at a walk-in medical centre for the homeless in south London.
I've ___[8] in about 80 hours at the medical centre this year.

5 GETTING IT RIGHT

→ Present perfect ▪ Present perfect progressive, S. 253

Write down the present perfect and present perfect progressive forms of these verbs:

1 I/live (*I've ... / I've been ...*)
2 she/work
3 you/help
4 they/sponsor
5 we/support
6 you/donate
7 he/collect
8 they/contribute

Expand the notes to make sentences with the present perfect or the present perfect progressive.

1 he / donate more than €1,000 / this year
2 he / talk to her for five minutes
3 people / give her €112.95 since last Monday
4 she / ask for donations since 9 am
5 she / collect / €23.50 today
6 she / collect since early this morning
7 she / stand outside for three hours
8 he / just give her €10

6 ROLE-PLAY

→ Interaktion: Ein Rollenspiel gestalten, S. 247

An interviewer for a youth magazine is asking people in the street about what they give to charity.

Work with a partner. Read the role-cards and role-play the interviews. Use the present perfect (progressive) where possible.

Partner A: Interviewer

- Explanation of survey
- Occupation of interviewee?
- Date of last contribution to charity?
- Reason(s)?
- How much?
- How much this year?
- How long / make contributions to charities?

Partner B: Businesswoman

- Car saleswoman
- Six months ago
- Hurricane in the Philippines
- £50
- About £100
- For the last 10 years

7 WRITING

→ Produktion: Eine Stellungnahme schreiben, S. 234

University professor Dr Max Kelly has set up a charity called *We can all give more*. It encourages people to donate at least 10% of their income in order to fight extreme poverty and disease in the Third World. Here the charity explains some common misunderstandings (myths) about giving aid to developing countries.

A Match the myths (1–4) with the explanations (a–d).

1. The small amount of money I can give will have little or no effect.
2. Charity begins at home: we should treat the sick in our own country first.
3. Most of the money we give in aid is stolen by corrupt officials before it reaches the people in need.
4. By giving aid to developing countries we make them dependent on handouts.

a Effective charities provide concrete help (e.g. medicines, mosquito nets) not cash.
b Effective charities help people to become independent by teaching them skills such as farming, health care and hygiene.
c Developed countries already know how to treat preventable diseases. They can now help developing countries to do the same.
d Just $3 is enough to buy one mosquito net which can save a person's life.

B Choose one of the following writing tasks:

Explain why you would or would not donate 10% of your income to end poverty in developing countries. Include ideas from exercise 7A.

SKILLS CHECKLIST: Writing a comment

- ☑ Have I structured my arguments logically?
- ☑ Have I given arguments for and against?
- ☑ Have I given my own opinion?

Comment on the following statement.
Proverb: *"If you give a man a fish, you feed him for a day. If you teach him to fish, you feed him for a lifetime."*

Engineers Without Borders

Engineers Without Borders (EWB) organizations work to serve the needs of disadvantaged communities and people all over the world through engineering solutions. Qualified engineers can go on 3, 6 or 12-month postings to developing countries, while thousands of university students take part in the annual EWB Challenge to find engineering solutions to humanitarian problems.

4/7

CHRIS CLEAVER IN SIERRA LEONE

Christopher Cleaver's placement with Developing Technologies in Sierra Leone had the goals of finding low-cost solutions to freshwater supply, and fuel production from palm nuts.

Chris says: "If we want to promote development work amongst young engineers, we need to make sure that there is more awareness of the fact that young people really can make a change to other people's lives, and there are some serious and important projects around the world to work on, such as basic infrastructure like roads, energy and water services; all the things which play a big role in a country's development. After politicians and other decision-makers, it is the engineers who can make a true impact directly on people's lives."

The water project entailed creating a low-cost solution for groundwater extraction at depths of up to 30 metres. Chris' task here was to work on machinery to make boreholes to reach groundwater. He upgraded an existing rig: modifying the metal frames in a welding shop and installing a new petrol engine and pulley, making it lightweight so it could be broken into three parts and transported to areas off-road.

Chris' second project was to make biodiesel from palm nuts. Palm trees are very common in Sierra Leone, and they produce a small orange/red fruit that people squeeze to get out its oil, and inside each, a nut from which oil can be extracted. The nuts usually go to waste.

"The biodiesel reaction involves bringing together this fairly thick oil with an alcohol in the presence of a catalyst, and 'BANG' you can get runny biodiesel and very thick glycerine which are easily separated by gravity", says Chris. The project entailed the creation of a small production plant for a community-based organization, which helps farmers to mechanize and increase their yield and get income. (305 words)

Adapted from: *www.ewb-uk.org*

1 LOOKING AT THE TEXT

→ Sich während des Lesens Notizen machen, S. 223

Read the text and make notes on the following subjects.

1 The importance of engineers in development work
2 Chris' solution to the freshwater supply problem
3 How Chris helped farmers to get better use of their palm trees

2 CLASS DISCUSSION

→ Interaktion, S. 246

EWB projects usually involve one of more of the seven areas in the list. Think about your technical interests: how could you contribute to an EWB project?

- Infrastructure and construction
- Water supply and sanitation systems
- Energy
- Waste management
- Transportation
- Information technology
- Adapting to climate change

11 Global reach

MAIN COURSE

FOCUS

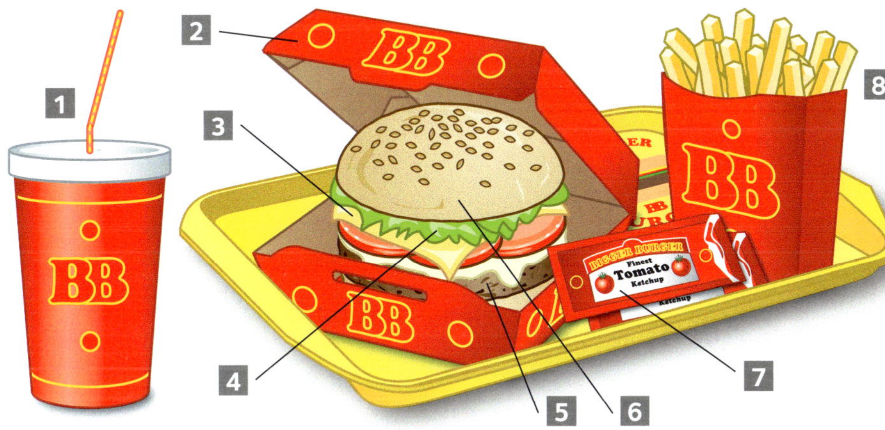

A **In small groups, say where you like to go for a 'fast-food' meal and what you like to eat.**

B **Use the words below to describe the Bigger Burger meal above.**

bread roll ▪ burger ▪ cheese ▪ cold drink ▪ salad ▪ French fries ▪ cardboard packaging ▪ ketchup

C **Make statements about the supply chain for items 1–8.**

Useful phrases

- The … (*item*) is made/manufactured from … (*raw product*) that comes from … (*country*).
- … (*raw products*) originate from within/outside the EU.
- It is / They are grown in / imported from … (*country*).

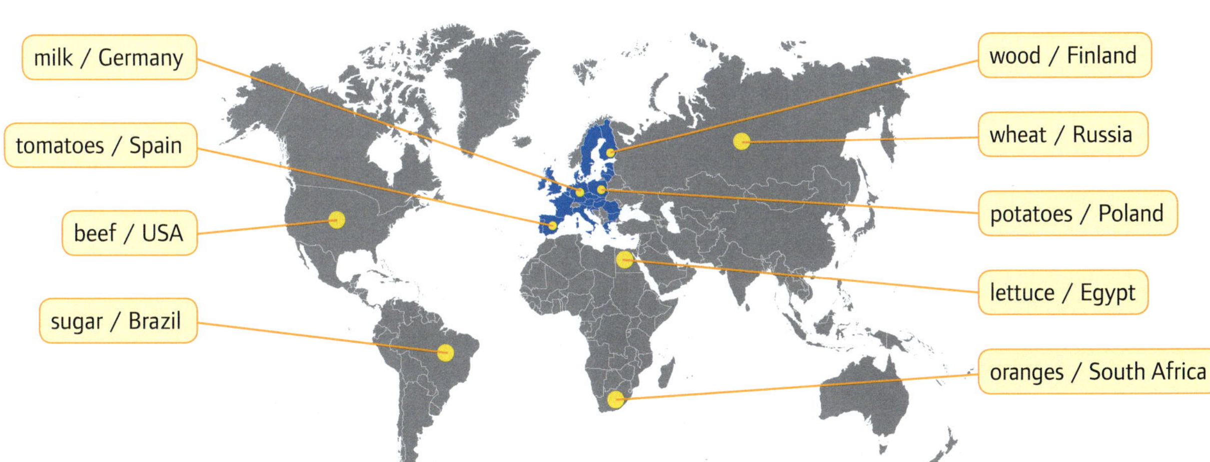

D **Give your opinion. Say what you think about fast food.**

11 Global reach

TEXT A Four globalization case studies

BEFORE YOU READ

Read the two definitions of the word *globalization*. Explain how a global fast-food company matches each definition.

globalization /ˌgloʊbəlɪ'zeɪʃ(ə)n/ *noun* [U] **1** the growth of trade around the world, especially by large companies that produce and sell goods and services in many different countries **2** when similar goods and services, or cultural and social influences, spread around the world

2/11

Kintu Muwanga, Ugandan coffee farmer: In the old days, traders came to our village and bought from individual farmers. They paid terrible prices, and we were always poor. We couldn't afford to improve quality to get better prices: we couldn't afford anything. Then we started working with a Fairtrade company, Twin Trading, and we formed the Gumutindo Coffee Cooperative. Since then, our lives have been transformed. Experts helped to raise quality and switch to organic production. Buyers from Twin Trading agreed good prices and paid some of the money early. Facilities for processing and packing our coffee have been built, and the finished product now means even better prices. The result? Wonderful improvements, including safe water, a bigger clinic and a new secondary school.

Latifa Sattar, Bangladeshi textile worker: Millions of women like me work in clothing factories, and conditions are terrible. Meanwhile, the owners just think about getting rich on the backs of the workers. They simply don't care about health and safety, and workers are often injured. Recently, a whole factory collapsed and 1,000 people were killed. And our hours are getting longer as deadlines keep getting tighter. We're often forced to work 14–16 hours a day, seven days a week. We're always told that if we don't fill the orders for the big western customers, the company will lose its contracts, the factory will close and we'll all lose our jobs. And the pay? It's just not enough for a family to live on.
Well, enough is enough. Someone from the national union made secret contact with us recently, and I say it's time to join and take action to fight for our rights!

Steve Race, American furniture factory worker: I lost my job a few years back when our factory closed and production went offshore to Indonesia. It was the main employer in town, so life was very hard for a lot of folks, and a lot moved away to find work. I stayed and set up my own carpentry business, but the local economy was depressed and business wasn't great. But then I went on a training programme and re-skilled in computer-aided manufacturing. That changed everything. I had to move, but I found work with a company which had just brought furniture production back from the Philippines. It's very automated, so there aren't a lot of jobs. But I've got one of them, and I'm very happy about that!

Li Ziyang, Chinese construction worker: I returned to Shanghai after spending the New Year holiday with my family in our small village, and I found that work had been stopped on the factory that we were building. The company had planned to use it to expand production of electronic components for export to America, but it turned out that their American customer had decided to manufacture the components themselves – in America.
Some of my co-workers want to stay and find work in Shanghai because there are still other projects. But a few of us want to go inland to find employment. The government is building new cities there, and I think that's the next big thing for China – developing the country for the people of China.

(528 words)

1 LOOKING AT THE TEXTS

→ Rezeption: Leseverstehen, S. 214

A Read the texts and do the following tasks.

1. Contrast globalization's effects on the lives of the people mentioned in the texts. Say which have experienced positive changes and which have been affected negatively.
2. Describe what two of them have recently done to change their lives for the better.
3. Explain what the other two are probably going to do soon to improve their lives.

B Say what it means. Explain the underlined words and phrases in your own words.

1. … deadlines keep getting tighter. (line 14)
2. … if we don't fill the orders … (line 15)
3. Well, enough is enough. (line 18)
4. … production went offshore to Indonesia. (line 21)
5. Some of my co-workers want to stay … (line 35)
6. But a few of us want to go inland … (line 36)

SKILLS CHECKLIST: Dealing with unknown words

- ☑ Have I thought about similar English words?
- ☑ Have I thought about the general meaning of the sentence?

C Say what you think.

1. Look at your answers to exercise 1A again. Which of these things do you think you may need to do to find or to stay in work in the future? Is there anything you would not like to do?
2. What has globalization done for you? (Think about, for example, media or shopping.)
3. Think about globalization and people in work in Germany. What pros and cons do you see from their point of view?

2 WORKING WITH WORDS

A Copy and complete the tables of verb-noun pairs. Find the words in the texts.

Verb	Noun	Verb	Noun	Verb	Noun
to farm	▬	▬	agreement	▬	transformation
to own	▬	to improve	▬	to construct	▬
to employ	▬	to govern	▬	▬	expansion
▬	manufacturer	▬	development	▬	decision

B Use pairs of words from exercise 2A to complete the following.

1. We ▬[1] bikes, and we're one of the biggest bike ▬[2] in Europe.
2. **A** When did you ▬[1] a date for the meeting?
   B I made the ▬[2] a week ago.
3. The company has made big ▬[1] to their product, and they've also ▬[2] the packaging.
4. **A** Who ▬[1] that old house? It looks a mess!
   B The ▬[2] hasn't been seen for three years.
5. The Internet is creating a huge social ▬[1]. It's ▬[2] the way that humans live.
6. In a modern democracy, the people choose a ▬[1], and this then ▬[2] the country for several years – until it is time for the people to decide again.

3 GETTING IT RIGHT

→ The passive, S. 261

Put these sentences into the passive. If you need to mention the subject, use '*by* + agent'.

1 Karl Benz constructed the first successful petrol-driven car in 1885.
The first successful petrol-driven car was constructed by Karl Benz in 1885.
2 By 1900, engineers had developed various other models across Europe and America.
3 Henry Ford introduced mass-production techniques in 1908.
4 As a result, workers had built over 15 million Ford Model Ts by 1928.
5 Since those early days, personal transport has transformed life around the world.
6 Family cars have given ordinary people the freedom to travel far and wide.
7 Today, companies make over 65 million cars a year in countries all over the world.
8 The Chinese alone produce nearly 20 million of them.
9 Companies export cars for sale in every part of the world.
10 Through exports and international supply chains, the world car industry has created many complex global links.

Model T Ford production, 1913

A380 final assembly line in the Jean-Luc Lagardère plant, Toulouse-Blagnac Airport.

Turn the following interview into a more formal news report, using the passive. You should also use more formal linking words/phrases.

So … → As a result, … ▪ But … → However, … ▪ Even so, … → Despite that, …

Start like this:
A number of excellent aircraft had been designed by … . However, …

A So, tell me, how did Airbus begin?
B Well, you see, European aircraft makers had designed a number of excellent aircraft in the 1950s and early 1960s. But they only sold them in small numbers because the American manufacturers were too powerful. So, in the late 1960s, several European governments and plane makers made plans for a shared European project – Airbus Industrie.
A I see. So what happened next?
B Well, after the organization had dealt with many political and technical problems, it finally tested the new A300 in 1972. The Airbus team then took it on a six-week sales tour of South and North America, and this created a lot of interest. Even so, only Lufthansa and Air France had actually bought the A300 by 1974. Then, in September of that year, Airbus finally sold the first four planes outside Europe – to Korean Airlines.

A Wow! I expect everyone was very pleased about that!

B We certainly were! But Airbus only won the first really big prize – an order for 23 A300s – in 1978. That was from America's Eastern Airlines, six years after we had shown the plane to the US market back in 1972.

A Well, things have moved on a long way since then, haven't they?

B They certainly have. Today, Airbus builds the planes' components in factories across Germany, France, Britain, Spain and the Netherlands, and it brings all these parts together in Toulouse. It completes final assembly of all the planes there.

A And that's a lot of planes now, isn't it?

B Yes, since 1972, Airbus has taken over 14,000 orders, and it has delivered over 8,500. The world's airlines now accept these planes as some of the best in the world. So Airbus carries nearly half of all international travellers around the world today.

4 DESCRIBING A CARTOON

→ Produktion: Cartoons beschreiben und analysieren, S. 236

Describe the cartoon and analyse its message. (Look at the second text on page 100 again to help you with background information.)

BUILDING SKILLS: Analysing cartoons

Cartoons often contain cultural references, or references to events in the news.

- Don't panic if you don't understand the reference straight away.
- Particularly in an exam, the necessary information will usually be in a related text in the exam or in a topic that you have dealt with in class.
- Think about what you have read in class, or return to the exam text to check for references.

Useful phrases

- The cartoon consists of three pictures side by side, all under one heading: …
- The cartoon is an ironic comment on …
- First of all, it reminds us that huge numbers of …
- Secondly, it tells us that the employers make … because they spend so little on …
- This brings us to the third 'made in Bangladesh' picture – the collapse of a factory …
- This is a sharp attack on the owners' lack of care for anything except …

TEXT B Where to manufacture products?

BEFORE YOU READ

Does a German brand name on a product always mean that it was made in Germany? Should it? Why / Why not?

2/12

Is it time to start re-shoring our manufacturing industries?

The World This Week reporter Mark Moro is talking to Tim Smith, head of the campaign group Make it in America.

Mark Moro: Is it time to start re-shoring our manufacturing industries – to bring back production that has been done abroad for many years? Tell us about the situation now, Tim.

Tim Smith: Well, let's just remember how bad things were a few years ago. Across the USA and the rest of the industrialized West, more and more jobs were being exported to China and other low-cost countries. It started when cheap producers exported from there to the West and undercut western producers. Our own manufacturers were then forced to send their production offshore, too, just to stay in business. By around the year 2000, about 150,000 American manufacturing jobs were being lost every year. Whole sections of industrial cities like Pittsburgh were turning into wastelands, and unemployment just kept rising. It was the same in parts of Europe too, and it seemed impossible to do anything about it.

Mark Moro: So what's changed?

Tim Smith: Jobs are being brought back from countries like China to the West.

Mark Moro: Why?

Tim Smith: The most important reason is cost. Countries like China aren't low-cost anymore. Wages are rising fast, and other costs are going up too – especially transport. Look. This bar chart shows the cost of making floor care products for a US supermarket chain at home and in China. The chart shows a slight US cost advantage of three per cent. In other words, the job is now being done more cheaply in the USA.

Mark Moro: I see, so wages aren't very much cheaper in China than in America now. And importing all the way from China adds quite a lot to the total bill.

Tim Smith: Right, so production in America actually gives a small cost advantage now.

Mark Moro: And I suppose it's just easier to produce near where you're going to sell.

Tim Smith: Yes, it's better in several ways. It's much faster, and that's important when markets change as quickly as they often do. If lots of

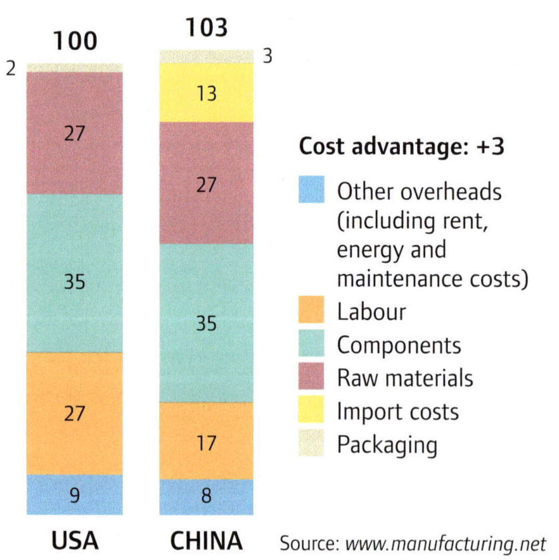

Cost advantage for floor care products

Source: *www.manufacturing.net*

customers suddenly want the red model instead of the blue one, the manufacturer needs to meet this demand quickly. But if production is in China, that's not possible. What's more, there may be delays in a long supply chain, so it's necessary to hold extra stock in America – and that's expensive. Breakages and faulty goods just make that problem worse.

Mark Moro: Right, so 150,000 jobs a year were being lost before. What about now?

Tim Smith: Well, more recently about 40,000 jobs were still being exported each year, but about the same number were coming back to this country. And the balance is changing further. In the coming years, some jobs will still go offshore, but many more will be re-shored.

Mark Moro: Can you be certain about that?

Tim Smith: Just look at some of the things that are happening right now. For example, Apple are spending $100 million on new production facilities in the USA instead of offshore. Again, General Electric are bringing home water-heater production from China to Kentucky. Then again, NCR are re-shoring production of cash machines from China, India and Brazil.

Mark Moro: Well, I'm sure that gives new hope to millions of people who are still looking for work, and also to many millions more who want that *Made in America* label when they buy. (591 words)

1 LOOKING AT THE TEXT

→ Rezeption: Leseverstehen, S. 214

A Put these events in order from 1–7.

- **a** The rate of western job losses slows.
- **b** Many western jobs are lost every year.
- **c** Cheap exports from e.g. China undercut western producers.
- **d** More jobs return to the USA than go offshore.
- **e** US producers move production offshore.
- **f** The rate of US job losses balances the rate of jobs returned.
- **g** Low-cost producers start to become more expensive.

B In your own words, say what the numbers from the text refer to.

1 150,000 **2** three per cent **3** 40,000 **4** $100 million

Make up questions to produce answers that contain these numbers.

1 150,000 **2** three per cent **3** 40,000 **4** $100 million

C Look at the bar chart on page 104 and do the following tasks:

1. Say what cost is completely avoided by production in the USA. How much of the cost of Chinese production is this?
2. Compare these costs of production in the US and in China:
   - **a** raw materials
   - **b** labour
   - **c** other overheads
   - **d** packaging
3. With a partner, think of some possible reasons for the differences.

Useful phrases

- exactly/roughly the same as …
- a little / (quite) a lot higher/lower than …

2 WORKING WITH WORDS

A Match the words to form two-part nouns from the text.

bar ▪ campaign ▪ cash ▪ manufacturing ▪ production ▪ supply

chain ▪ chart ▪ facility ▪ group ▪ industry ▪ machine

B Use pairs of words from exercise 2A to complete the following. Make any changes necessary.

1 I need to get some money. Where's the nearest ▬?
2 A lot of people have joined our ▬ to stop development of a new airport in this area.
3 The ▬ shows the various costs of production in China and in the USA.
4 Food ▬ are sometimes very long. For example, bananas may come all the way from South America.
5 The company is closing its old factory in Dortmund and is opening a new ▬ near Dresden.
6 There has been a huge increase in production in the Chinese ▬ since 1980.

TIP

When two nouns (or an adjective and a noun) are often used together, they may become hyphenated or even one word, e.g. *low-cost* and *wasteland*. If you are not sure, check in your dictionary.

3 ANALYSING CHARTS

→ Produktion: Schaubilder beschreiben und analysieren, S. 238

BUILDING SKILLS: Describing change in charts

Line graphs usually show how figures change over a period of time.

- You can describe changes with a verb + adjective, or with an adjective + noun (see below).
- Remember to use the simple past to describe 'finished' changes:
  Sales rose steadily from 2014 to 2016.
- Use the present perfect to describe changes that are 'unfinished':
  Sales have risen steadily since 2014.

Use pairs of words from the table to describe the lines 1–6 below.

Describing graphs and statistics that show changes through time

verb + adverb		adjective + noun		verb + adjective	
to rise	rapidly	rapid	rise	to be	flat
to increase	sharply	sharp	increase	to remain	steady
to climb	steadily	steady	climb		
to fall	gradually	gradual	fall		
to decrease	slowly	slow	decrease		
to decline	slightly	slight	decline		

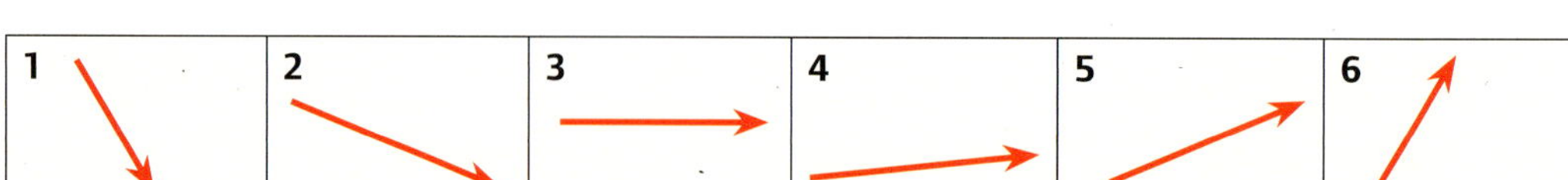

In chart 1, production fell sharply. / In chart 1, there was a sharp fall in production.

4 LISTENING

→ Rezeption: Hörverstehen, S. 225

2/13 **A Look at the sales chart below and listen to part of the Sales Director's report. Say whether she is describing UK or EU export sales. Identify the six-year period.**

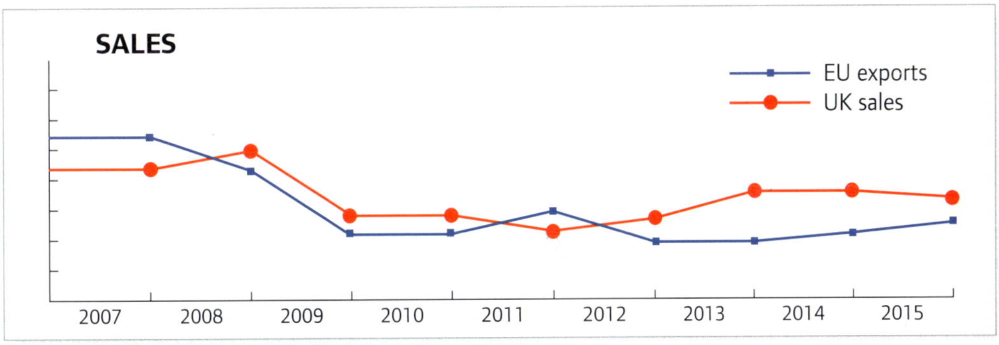

2/14 **B Copy and expand the frame on the right for another chart. Listen to the Sales Director and draw the graph, giving it a title and writing the years.**

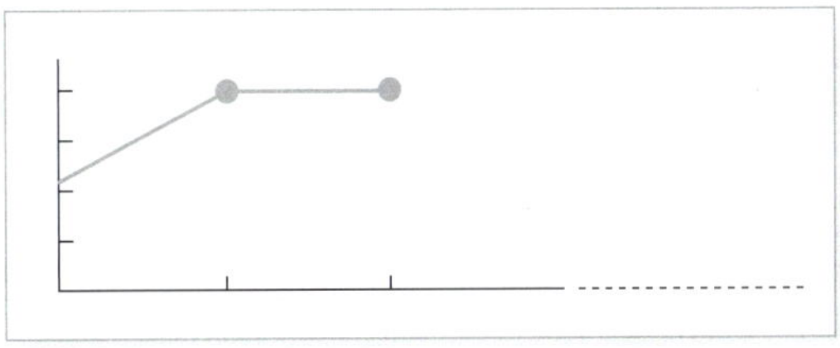

5 DESCRIBING GRAPHS

A Work in pairs and look at the graph in exercise 4A again. Each of you describe a sales category and a five-year period for your partner to identify.

A In these five years, sales first fell rapidly for a year. But then they … . After that, …
B Ah, you're talking about … sales from … to … , aren't you?

B Work with a partner. Partner A look here. Partner B look at page 213.

Partner A: Describe the graph below to Partner B.

Useful phrases

- This graph shows sales from … (*year*) to … (*year*).
- In/During … (*year*), there was a slight/… rise/… in sales.
- From … (*year*) to … (*year*), sales rose/… slightly/… .

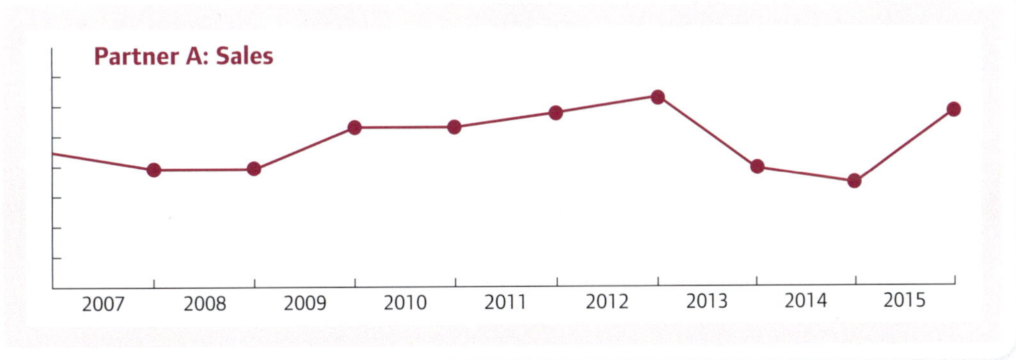

C Draw the graph that Partner B describes.

Submarine telecommunications cables

In this age of wireless connectivity and satellites, it is sometimes easy to forget that our telecommunications still depend largely on physical cables under the ground – and on the seabed.

4/8

A vulnerable communications lifeline

The internet depends heavily on submarine fibre optic cables, which carry information across the world's oceans. Around 200 undersea cables link the world's telecommunications. For the most part, they are poorly protected and rarely checked.

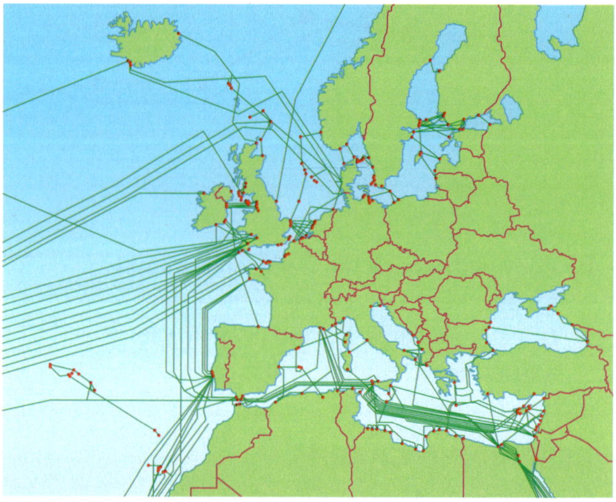

Cables can be damaged by underwater earthquakes and landslides, ships' anchors and the nets of fishing boats. A single submarine cable is 19–64 mm thick. They are usually only armoured (protected by an outer layer of steel wires) close to shore.

According to telecommunications research company Telegeography, about 100 submarine cable breaks happen each year. Mostly they do not cause a loss of connectivity because of the redundancy in the global system: telecommunications traffic is simply rerouted. However, there are weak points in places like Alexandria in Egypt, where 14 cables come together. A ship anchor damaged six of these cables in 2013 and this led to a temporary loss of telecommunications in several East African countries.

Cables on land are no less vulnerable. In 2011 a Georgian woman digging for copper wires to sell accidentally hit a fibre optic cable. She cut off internet access to the neighbouring country of Armenia for five hours. (196 words)

1 LOOKING AT THE TEXT

→ Rezeption: Leseverstehen, S. 214

Lesen Sie den Text über Unterseekabel und beantworten Sie die Fragen auf Deutsch.

1 Wozu dienen die Unterseekabel?
2 Inwiefern sind sie verletzlich?
3 Warum ist Redundanz hier ein Vorteil?
4 Woran ist eine Schwachstelle zu erkennen?
5 Was ist 2013 in Ägypten passiert?
6 Warum ist die Verlegung auf Landrouten keine Lösung?

2 RESEARCH

Research ONE of these questions and report back to the class with what you found out.

1 Where do submarine cables run to from Germany? Who owns them?
2 How are damaged submarine cables repaired?
3 Will satellite telecommunications soon make submarine cables unnecessary?

12 Changing society

MAIN COURSE

FOCUS

A

B

Malala Yousafzai is given the World's Children Prize in Stockholm

C

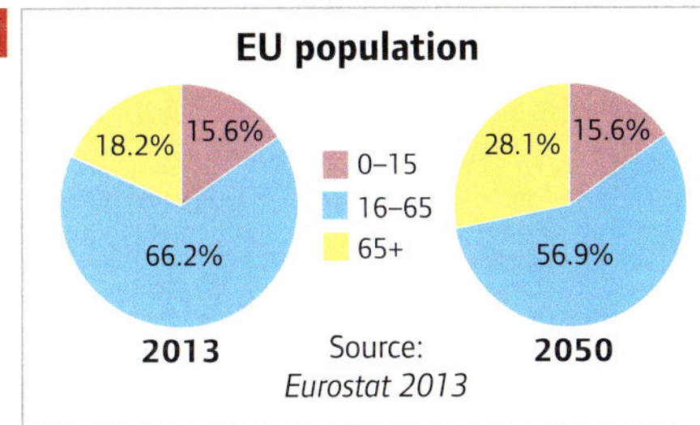

D

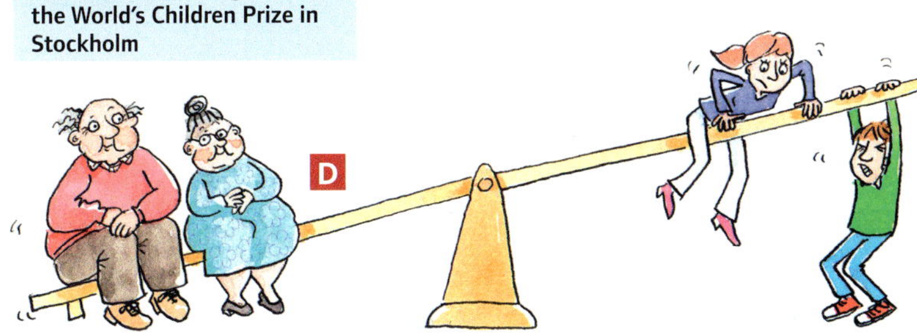

1 MORE ELDERLY MEANS LATER PENSIONS

The UK's 65+ population of 10 million is likely to reach 19 million by mid-century and the government plans to raise the pension age from 65 to 68 between 2024 and 2046.

2 THE BURDEN OF THE OLD ON THE YOUNG

The taxes of 3.2 working-age people pay for each UK pensioner today. With ever more pensioners, there will only be 2.8 workers to support each one by 2050.

3 EU YOUTH UNEMPLOYMENT STILL HIGH

As Europe slowly recovers from recesssion, employment is also slowly rising. But youth joblessness remains far higher – still well over 50% in Greece and Spain.

4 THE MILLENNIALS: THE NEW, NICE PEOPLE

The millennial generation, born since the late 1990s, want to change the world. Take Malala Yousafzai, the 2014 Nobel Peace Prize winner. At 15, she was already campaigning for the right of girls to education in her native Pakistan. For this, she was shot by the Taliban and left for dead. Following emergency surgery in the UK, she did the impossible: she recovered fully and now fights for girls' rights worldwide.

A **Work with a partner. Take turns to describe the pictures A–D.**

B **Work together to match A–D to the newspaper headlines 1–4.**

C **Read the newspaper reader's comments. Discuss your own feelings about the future.**

TEXT A Making room for the young

BEFORE YOU READ

A What problems do many young people face today when they finish their education? Collect your ideas in a mind map.

B Look at the title of the article. What do you think the author wants, and what sort of people is she probably addressing?

2/15

PASS IT ON: give my generation more than a foot in the door

Georgia Leaker

I am one of the nearly one in five people under the age of 25 who are unemployed in Australia.

I'm 24 years old, have two university degrees and have been on Centrelink[1] payments for six months, and [...] I must now take a skills test that Centrelink believes may help me find employment.

While at university, I juggled three casual jobs, self-funded a university exchange to the US and worked for a congressman. After university, I continued my part-time retail job and also did several internships before I was able to get my first career job eight months later. I was hired as a journalist-production assistant at a small company. Eighty per cent of my job was being a personal assistant and doing office administration work. I was made redundant after 10 months, and I had to turn to Centrelink for help for the first time. I did two more internships (both of which I had to fight to get), hoping that my previous experience might land me a job.

During one internship someone in middle management wanted to hire me because I was skilled, and she was sick of endless interns. But she couldn't. The boss said no, because "interns are free and employees cost money". I terminated my internship immediately. [...]

I've applied for retail, administration and full-time nannying jobs, and I am qualified for all of them. (Although the retail industry won't hire me because I'm too "expensive".) I have also regularly applied for rural and out-of-state jobs.

In the past six months, despite the hundreds of job applications I've sent, I've had only four interviews. Two were retail and they chose younger, cheaper applicants. The other two offered pay packets under minimum wage. I didn't get any of them.

When Mia Freedman[2], who I've always admired, was my age, she was the editor of *Cosmopolitan* magazine. [...] Freedman was given lots of opportunities and during her internship, someone took a chance on her. She now runs a successful website, but she has publicly stated she doesn't pay, nor feel she ought to pay, most of her contributors. She's not alone; many successful people feel they needn't provide the next generation with the entry-level employment opportunities that they were given.

The system seems rigged against recent graduates and entry-level jobs are rare. Almost every media job wants someone with "at least five years experience". No one wants to spend the time training the next generation, and many companies would rather have an endless stream of interns to fill the gaps. This situation isn't unique to media jobs, either. Many of my friends, who have all sorts of qualifications, are also unemployed.

I'm sick of being told that I'm lazy and mooching off the system. I don't want to be thought of as a hopeless case by Centrelink. I don't want to spend my week alone, on the couch, watching daytime TV.

Around 17.7 per cent of people under the age of 25 are unemployed. Most of us are educated or skilled in some way and most don't want to be dole bludgers. We're just down on our luck and doing everything we can to get a door – any door – opened.

Take a chance on me and my generation. Help take the burden off the welfare system and help us to contribute to the future of the nation.

Our generation aren't useless, but we sure feel like we are. (572 words)

From: *The Sydney Morning Herald*, July 9, 2013

Footnote:
Unexpectedly, Georgia received a lot of job offers after this article. Soon afterwards, she became Content Manager at an online business-to-business publication.

[1] **Centrelink:** Australian Government Department of Human Services

[2] **Mia Freedman:** Well-known Australian media person who, at 24, took over at the Australian edition of *Cosmopolitan* magazine – the youngest of all the editors of the 28 worldwide editions of *Cosmopolitan*.

1 LOOKING AT THE TEXT

→ Rezeption: Leseverstehen, S. 214

A Read the text and complete the following tasks.

1. Describe the youth unemployment situation in Australia.
2. Explain what the writer did to pay her way through university.
3. Compare her experience as an intern with that of Mia Freedman.
4. Outline how Georgia feels that Freedman's generation are being unfair to her own.
5. Describe what people in management are trying to avoid doing.
6. Explain what national benefits will follow if the writer's generation are given more help.

B Say what it means: Explain the underlined words and phrases in your own words.

1. … I juggled three casual jobs, … (line 7)
2. … self-funded a university exchange … (line 8)
3. … my previous experience might land me a job. (line 20)
4. … she was sick of endless interns. (line 23)
5. … someone took a chance on her. (line 42)
6. … We're just down on our luck … (line 67)

2 WRITING

→ Produktion: Eine Stellungnahme schreiben, S. 234

A Look at your answers to exercise 1A and add any further ideas about youth unemployment to your mind map from page 110.

B Now do one of the following tasks.

Describe the job situation for young people in Germany. Give examples from your own experience or from the experience of your family and friends.

Compare the job situation for young people in Germany with the situation that Georgia Leaker describes in Australia.

3 WORKING WITH WORDS

A Copy and complete the tables with words from the text.

Noun (thing)	Noun (person)
journalism	___
___	producer
assistance	___
___	administrator
___	manager

Noun (thing)	Noun (person)
___	intern
___	applicant
edition	___
contribution	___
graduation	___

Noun (thing)	Noun (person 1)	Noun (person 2)
___	employer	___
___	interviewer	interviewee

B Use pairs of words from exercise 3A to complete the sentences.

1 **A** I hear that there have been over 100 ___[1] for the job?
B Yes, and we've already asked several of the ___[2] to come and talk to us.
2 I spend most of my time with customers now and that means I need ___[1] with all the paperwork, so I'm advertising for an office ___[2].
3 Joe was always interested in ___[1], so he helped to run the school magazine. Now he's studying to be a ___[2] at college.
4 Shipbuilding used to be a huge source of ___[1] on the River Clyde near Glasgow, but now there's just one company left – with just 3,000 ___[2].
5 The company is looking for new staff at the moment, and we're running nearly 30 ___[1] today and tomorrow. Sue will be the main ___[2], but Jack will see some of the applicants, too.
6 I've just started a six-month ___[1] with TV South to get some experience working in media. There are three other ___[2] there, too.
7 Sue has been a regular ___[1] to the magazine for years. She's made a huge ___[2] to its success.

4 GETTING IT RIGHT

→ Modal verbs, S. 259

A Complete the words of a young, unemployed person. Choose the correct modal verbs.

1 I know I (might not / shouldn't) ___[1] hope for too much, but I think I (might / can't) ___[2] still get one or two more replies to the applications I've already sent out.
2 But I (can't / couldn't) ___[1] understand why people so often don't reply. They (shouldn't / may not) ___[2] want to interview me, but it's very bad if they don't even write back.
3 Some days I feel very down, but I try to tell myself that I (mustn't / couldn't) ___[1] give up, and that I (can't / have to) ___[2] keep sending out more applications.
4 I really believe that I (could / must) ___[1] do well in TV, so I really (should / can) ___[2] apply to the local TV station one more time.
5 But this time, I think I'll phone. That way I (may / must) ___[1] get through to someone who (should / can) ___[2] help me.
6 Excuse me, but I (can't / must) ___[1] run to catch the morning post. I (might not / can't) ___[2] meet the deadline for this application if I don't go right now.

B Replace the words in brackets with a pronoun + *must, mustn't, needn't* or *don't have to*.

1 **A** Someone's just phoned to offer Ben an interview. (Important for me to) ___[1] call him now!
B (Not necessary for you to) ___[2] do that. I can see him just outside the front door.

2 **A** Quick! Where's my jacket? (Necessary for me to) ___[1] go!
B You're right. (Very important for you not to) ___[2] be late on your first day at your new job.

3 **A** Tomorrow's a holiday, so (not essential for me to) ___[1] get up early. In fact, (not important for me to) ___[2] get up at all. I can sleep all day!
B (Important for you not to) ___[3] talk like that. Even if (not necessary for you to) ___[4] go to work, there are plenty of jobs to do here at home.

4 **A** (Necessary for me to) ___[1] go and have coffee with all those people?
B Well, all right, (not essential for you to) ___[2] go if you don't want to, but (really important for you not to) ___[3] miss the meeting afterwards.

C Complete the sentences with forms of *be able to, have to* or *could(n't)*.

1 I'm sorry, but I ___ go now or I'll miss my train.
2 We've finished the job, so we ___ go home soon. We just need to clean up.
3 It was too dark to see, but I ___ hear someone outside.
4 I ___ come tomorrow morning, but I'll be free after one o'clock.
5 Carrie ___ play the piano very well when she was still only nine.
6 A child ran out in front of my bike, but I ___ stop just in time.
7 The storm was so bad that we ___ work hard to get the boat back into the harbour.
8 I'd lost my key, so I ___[1] open the door. But I ___[2] get in through an open window.

5 ROLE-PLAY

→ Interaktion: Ein Rollenspiel gestalten, S. 247

Jack Wade, Director of an online business publication called *BusinessAustralia.com*, read Georgia Leaker's article in *The Sydney Morning Herald* yesterday and liked the clear, direct way that she wrote it. He sent an email to the newspaper asking Georgia to call him back.

Work with a partner and create a role-play of the telephone call.

Student A

You are Georgia Leaker, and you have received an email from *The Sydney Morning Herald* asking you to call Jack Wade. He'd like to talk to you about a job. He wants you to call him after 2 pm. You are interested and decide to call back.

- Introduce yourself and refer to his email.
- Express interest in the job.
- Ask for a different date to the one he suggests for an interview.
- Ask where to meet and note down the details. Read them back to check.
- Close in a friendly way.

Student B

You are Jack Wade. You think Georgia Leaker may be the right person for the position of Content Manager at your company. This job requires someone who can edit articles from other contributors and who can also write original material. The address of your office is: 53 Gundaroo Street, Villawood.

- Explain the job briefly.
- Suggest a day and a time for a meeting.
- Offer a different date if necessary.
- Invite her to your office and give the address. Confirm the details.
- Close in a friendly way.

TEXT B Towards a new social harmony

BEFORE YOU READ

Think of family members or family friends who have reached retirement age. What do they do? Do they relax at home or do they have active interests? Do they do volunteer work?

2/16

Today, The World This Week reporter Mark Moro is talking about our ageing society to two experts – Joan Blake, journalist and author for 55 years, and Tom West, founder of an online advice forum for young entrepreneurs.

Mark Moro: Let me put this question to you both. Are the new elderly a growing burden on the young or are they a growing resource? Joan, what's the senior citizen's point of view?

Joan Blake: Well, speaking as a pretty active 75-year-old, I have to say that I don't feel like a burden, and many other people my age are still going strong. We're much healthier than previous generations were, and we're also much better educated. So I think we've still got a lot to offer society.

Mark Moro: What do you think, Tom?

Tom West: I agree with Joan. If you look at the figures for Britain, the whole population is rising quite fast, but the population over 65 is rising much faster. In some countries like Germany and Italy, the situation is even more startling. While numbers of older people there are rising fast, too, total populations are falling – in Germany by over 10 million between now and 2050.

Mark Moro: OK. With statistics like that, the elderly simply can't be thrown onto the scrapheap: they have to be turned into a resource. But how can that be done?

Joan Blake: Several things need to change. First, older workers must be allowed to work for longer if they wish and if they can still do the job. Employers shouldn't be allowed to retire people just because they reach a certain age. That's already true in Britain, but it isn't in a lot of other countries.

Tom West: Yes, so some social engineering is required, but for that to work we really need to change social attitudes. Negative attitudes can be found everywhere and they simply must be changed. People are often felt to be past it either physically or mentally by a certain age. What's more, these negative attitudes ignore the positive sides of age – experience and know-how, social skills, reliability and care for quality work.

Mark Moro: And how do you change these attitudes?

Tom West: By giving older people a chance to show what they can do. It's happening a lot through our website now. Let me give just one example – Colin Ross. At 62, Colin was the director of his own company when he became very ill with cancer. He was lucky and he recovered, but he came out if it with a wish to do something different with the rest of his life. Now at the age of 66, he acts as adviser and mentor to young people who are just starting out in business for themselves. He has a lifetime of experience to offer the young, and he has already guided several start-up companies through the difficult early days.

Joan Blake: And here's another heart-warming example. CNA Language Schools in Brazil has teamed up with a home for the elderly in Chicago. Now, you see, most of CNA's students don't get the chance to practise their English with native speakers. At the same time, many of the elderly at Windsor Park Retirement Home are lonely and are only too happy to talk via regular Web chats and help the young Brazilians with their English. The conversations are then recorded and uploaded as private YouTube

videos for CNA teachers to study and work on later with their students.

There are big differences in age and cultural background, but these people have a lot to give each other, and their conversations are often very special. They soon start speaking from their hearts and become very close. I remember seeing one video where an elderly lady finishes by saying to her young friend, 'You are my new granddaughter!'

Mark Moro: What a great idea! That's a real win-win situation for both sides! (658 words)

1 LOOKING AT THE TEXT

→ Rezeption: Leseverstehen, S. 214

A Read the text and make notes under these headings:

- Topic of the interview
- Guests and their jobs
- Advantages of the elderly compared to the past
- Advantages of the elderly over the young
- Examples of the elderly helping the young

SKILLS CHECKLIST: Taking notes

- ☑ Have I read the whole text?
- ☑ Have I scanned the text for key words?
- ☑ Have I noted down the key words?

B Use your notes from exercise 1A to explain why the elderly should play a more important role in society in the future. Give some examples of how the elderly may help the young.

C Say what it means: Explain the underlined words and phrases in your own words.

1 … are still going strong. (line 7)
2 People are often felt to be past it … (line 34)
3 … experience and know-how, ... (line 37)
4 … CNA … has teamed up with a home for the elderly … (line 54)
5 … and are only too happy to talk … (lines 58–59)
6 That's a real win-win situation for both sides! (lines 71–72)

D Think of your elderly family members or family friends and discuss these questions in class:

- In what ways do they stay in touch with younger people?
- How do you think this helps them – if at all?
- How might it help the younger people, too – if at all?

2 WORKING WITH WORDS

A Change the underlined words using *the* + adjective, e.g. *the elderly*.

1 In our ageing society, people who are elderly have a lot to offer those who are young.
2 In most ancient societies, people who were powerful often had total control of those who were weak.
3 In most modern societies, it is usually accepted that people who are rich should pay higher taxes than others to help those who are poor.

B Find three more partner words for *social* in the text.

social climber / science / services / worker / ___ / ___ / ___

C Now use word pairs from exercise 2B to complete the following sentences.

1 All children have to learn the ___ they need to get on with other people.
2 Sue has gone on from school to study ___ at university.
3 Rob is a terrible ___ ! He spends all his time trying to make friends with rich people!
4 ___ towards gay people have changed. Most people now accept them as normal.
5 With the help of ___ and taxes, the UK created a more equal society after World War 2.
6 If parents can't look after their children properly, ___ sometimes have to take over.
7 In that case, a ___ will first visit the family to find out about the situation.

3 USING A DICTIONARY

→ Ein Wörterbuch benutzen, S. 217

Read the dictionary definitions of *society* (1–5) below and match them to sentences a–e.

BUILDING SKILLS: Using a dictionary

When you find a word in a text that you think you know but that doesn't quite 'fit', always try to work out the meaning from the context first, or by thinking of similar words in German or English. If the meaning is still not clear, you may need to use a dictionary.

- Don't just use the first definition that you come across!
- Read through all the meanings carefully in order to find the right one. Meanings are often closely related, for example as in *society* 1–5 below.
- Sometimes the meanings are quite different, e.g. *fire* as in *fire a gun* (= shoot), *fire an employee* (= end employment), and you have to choose the one that makes the most sense in the context.

society /sə'saɪəti/ noun **1** [U] people living together in organized communities, with laws and traditions that control the way they behave towards each other **2** [C/U] a particular type of society, e.g. in a particular country or area, or at a particular time in history, or with a special characteristic
3 [U] the group of people in a country who are rich, powerful and/or from a high social class
4 [C] an organization or club for people who share a particular interest or take part in a particular activity
5 [U] *formal* the company or friendship of other people

a Ann does two after-school activities. She plays football and belongs to the drama society.
b It was the society wedding of the year, and the guest list was full of famous names.
c In western countries we expect society to help those who need help.
d James is a very private person: he always tries to avoid the society of other people.
e We live in an affluent, post-industrial society full of opportunities that earlier generations never dreamed of.

4 GETTING IT RIGHT

→ The passive, S. 261

You work for a construction company and you have to write a report on a management meeting about the new company policy on retirement.

Read the statements below to continue the report.
Report the underlined sections with modal passive forms.

At the meeting the following points were made.
- *Workers who are 65 must be …*
- *If they are …*

TIP

As a report is a formal written document, use full forms, e.g. *they are*, not *they're*.

A So we agree that we must allow workers who are 65 to continue in work if they want to.
B Yes, and if they're strong enough, we shouldn't stop them from staying in their old jobs.
A OK, but we'll have to consider workers who are less strong case by case.
B Yes, we can't expect people in that situation to carry on doing outdoor construction work. We'll need to offer them less physically tiring work.
A OK, but to do this, I think we should interview workers like these to find out what other skills they have.
B We might offer a few people jobs in the warehouse. We could retrain them as forklift drivers.
A But we needn't necessarily retrain older workers. We can use their life-long skills for training apprentices.

5 LISTENING

→ Rezeption: Hörverstehen, S. 225

Mark Moro is now interviewing another expert on our ageing society – this time not to talk about the benefits, but instead to discuss the problems.

2/17

A Copy the notes. Then listen to the interview and complete them.

Population (millions)
- Germany – Now: ___ – 2050: ___
- UK – Now: ___ – 2050: ___

UK elderly (millions)
- Over 65 – Now: ___ (= ___ %) – 2050: ___ (= ___ %)
- Over 80 – Now: – 2050: ___

Pensioner welfare (pensions, winter fuel, etc.)
- Cost per year: ___
- % of total UK welfare: ___

Health costs per household
- Retired: ___
- Non-retired: ___

B Use your notes to complete the following tasks.

1. Compare population change in Germany and in the UK.
2. Compare general UK population change and population change among the elderly.
3. Compare the cost of welfare for the UK elderly and the cost for everyone else.
4. Compare the average healthcare costs for retired and non-retired UK households.

6 WRITING

→ Produktion: Eine Stellungnahme schreiben, S. 234

Write a comment on *Our ageing society*. Explain the expression *our ageing society*. Then describe and evaluate some of the problems and point out any opportunities that it gives us.

BUILDING SKILLS: Writing a comment

Always make sure you understand the task before you start to write a comment. In the task above, you need to give basic information about *Our ageing society*, describe some of the pros and cons, and give your own opinion on the topic.

- Always collect ideas to help you first, either in the form of a mind map, a list or simple notes. You will usually find information from your reading and listening, in this case Text B (page 114) and exercise 5 (above).
- Organize your notes to help you structure the text. You need to give an introduction to the topic and a conclusion with your opinion. You also need to support your arguments with examples.
- Use linking words or connecting phrases to structure your text and make it easier for the reader to follow your arguments.

Useful phrases

Adding facts:
- Moreover, …
- Furthermore, …
- In addition, …

Listing ideas:
- First of all, …
- Secondly, …
- Then again, …

Giving examples:
- For example, …
- For instance, …

Comparing and evaluating:
- Although …
- Despite the fact that …

Making technology accessible

The Global Public Inclusive Infrastructure (GPII) is a project to make accessibility features (magnification, voice recognition, etc.) universally available via cloud computing. Users create a personal profile of their interface needs, then they can sign in using any computer, smartphone, etc. and automatically use their personal settings.

4/9

GPII will bridge the accessibility gap

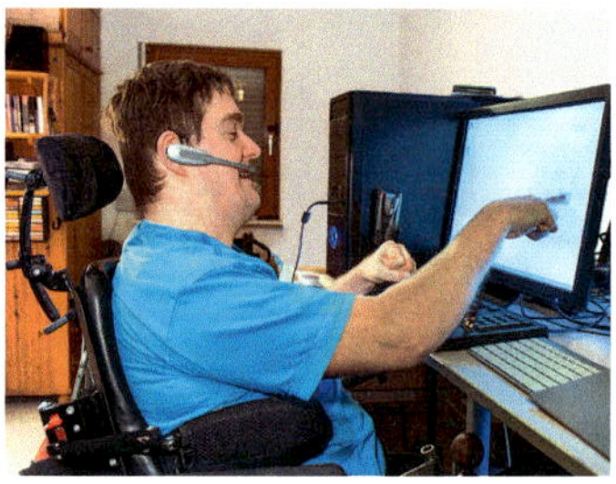

Many technologies aren't accessible to some people with disabilities, but they're becoming absolutely essential to participating in employment, education, commerce, and social participation. As a person with disabilities, this accessibility gap affects your independence and productivity not only at home, but also at school, at work or in your community.

Even when access features are available, they may not be the ones you're used to, or may not be set up to your preferences. When you encounter a ticket machine or public kiosk, you won't have the features you need.

The Global Public Inclusive Infrastructure (GPII) will let you choose the access features you want once, and then get them on any device, anywhere.

EXAMPLES:

Miranda is 90 and her vision is very poor. But any computer she sits down to – at the assisted living center, at her children's house, at the elder center – automatically changes to large print when she inserts this "USB thing" they gave her.

Moshe has a high spinal cord injury and is paralyzed from the neck down. In the past he couldn't use any computers if he didn't have his special head switches with him. With the virtual webcam-based switches he can now use any computer with a webcam. He just moves his head from side to side as if he was hitting his switches and the webcam-switch module acts just like he is hitting two switches. This is great since it allows him to use any of the computers on campus in any of the labs. (259 words)

Adapted from: *www.gpii.net*

1 MEDIATION

→ Schriftliche Mediation, S. 240

Sie arbeiten freiwillig in einem Altersheim, um den Bewohnerinnen und Bewohnern E-Mail- und Internetkenntnisse beizubringen. Sie wollen die Heimleiterin, Gisela Schmidt, über die Ziele und Anwendungsbereiche von GPII informieren. Verfassen Sie eine E-Mail mit den relevanten Informationen aus dem Text.

2 BRAINSTORMING

Many people have difficulty remembering their code numbers or passwords due to e.g. age-related memory loss, learning difficulties or brain damage. How can they be helped?

Work in a small group to brainstorm a solution to this problem. First collect ideas (do not reject any at this stage). Then evaluate the ideas and reject the ones with serious problems. Choose the best idea remaining and add as much detail as you can. Finally, present the idea to the class.

Job skills 3

Giving directions ▪ bookings and reservations

Eric's application for a job in the UK was successful and he starts today at Magnus & Klein, a small manufacturing company in London. The company is located in the Four Lofts Business Park. Ms Shaw, the office manager, has sent him written instructions on how to get to the office.

1 UNDERSTANDING DIRECTIONS

A Follow the instructions and find the offices of Magnus & Klein on the plan of the business park.

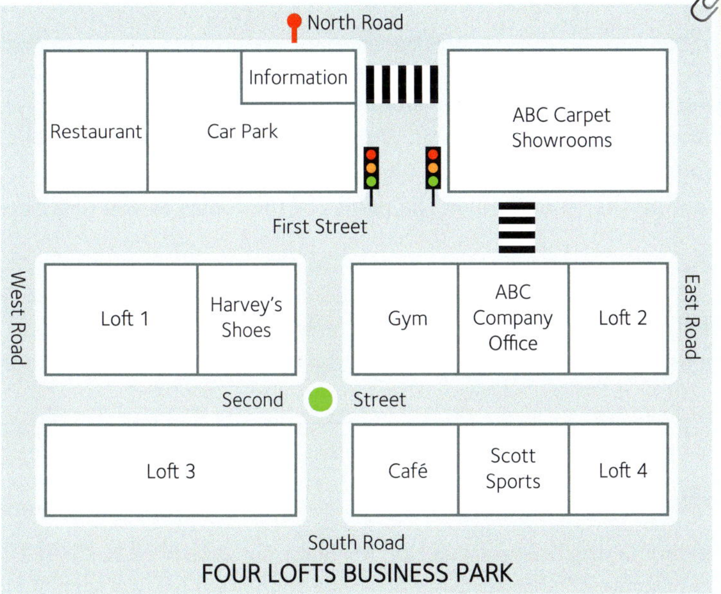

When you get off the bus in North Road, walk back a few metres to the entrance to the park. Pass the information box and walk down to the traffic lights. Turn right into First Street and take the first left. You'll see a gym on your left. Keep going till you come to Second Street. Turn right into Second Street and walk past Harvey's Shoes on your right. Our office is in the same building, opposite Loft 3.

B Work with a partner and do one of the following tasks.

Take turns to give each other directions to different companies or places in the park.

Choose a company or a place in the park. Do not tell your partner the name of the company or place he/she is going to. Describe how to get there from the Magnus & Klein office. Can he/she find the way and name the company or the place?

Remember to start at the Magnus & Klein office every time.

With your partner, think of a company or a place within walking distance of your school. Write directions how to get there from the school. Do not write down the name of the company or the place. Give your directions to another pair. Can they find out where you are sending them?

Useful phrases: Giving directions

- Turn right/left.
- Go straight ahead/on.
- Keep to the right/left.
- It's on the right-hand side / on the left-hand side.

Job skills 3

2 LISTENING

→ Rezeption: Hörverstehen, S. 225

When Eric arrives at Magnus & Klein, Ms Shaw gives him a tour of the offices.

2/18

A Study the floor plan and the list of places below. Then listen and find the places on the floor plan.

1 Accounts
2 Human Resources
3 Ms Shaw's office
4 the kitchen
5 the men's toilet
6 the storeroom

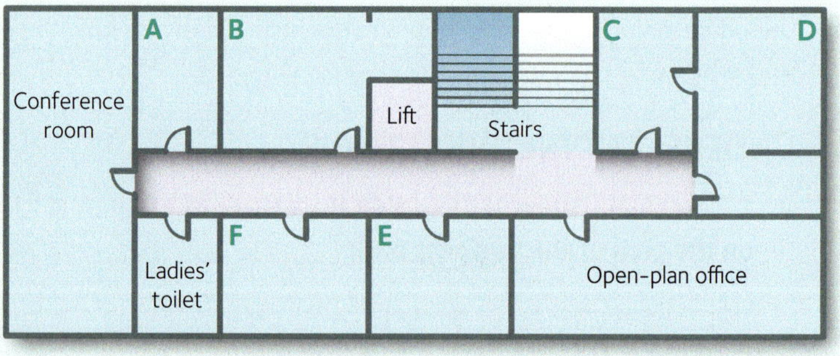

B Work with a partner and do one the following tasks.

Draw a simple floor plan of a school. Name three or four of the rooms (e.g. classrooms, staff room, toilets). Leave the remaining rooms blank. Without showing your partner, make a list of the names of the rooms you have left blank. Give your floor plan to your partner and give him/her a tour. Your partner should fill in the names of the rooms as you describe them.

With your partner, think about how you should leave your classroom if the fire alarm goes off. Write down the directions from memory, then check on the emergency exit plan in your classroom.

3 MAKING A HOTEL BOOKING

Magnus & Klein plc are going to exhibit at the Bristol Trade Fair. Ms Shaw has asked Eric to book accommodation for herself and a colleague. Eric has booked online and sends Ms Shaw an email giving details of the booking.

A Complete the email below using words from the box. There are two words more than you need.

free ▪ from ▪ included ▪ near ▪ non-smoking ▪ not smoking ▪ opposite ▪ single ▪ to ▪ within

Dear Ms Shaw

As requested, I have booked accommodation for you and Tony Browne in the Bristol Fair Hotel ___[1] Thursday, 17 October ___[2] Sunday, 20 October as follows:
Two ___[3] rooms, both of them ___[4]. The cost of the rooms is £84 per night, breakfast ___[5].
The hotel is located ___[6] to the fair area and there are several good restaurants ___[7] walking distance.
There is also a car park ___[8] the hotel.

Best wishes
Eric

A few days before the fair, Ms Shaw asks Eric to contact the hotel and give them some extra information.

2/19

B Listen to Eric's phone call to the hotel and make notes on the following:

1 the name of the person who takes the call
2 the booking number
3 the problem
4 why it is important that the hotel has the new information

4 WRITING AN EMAIL

→ Job Skills 1, Email etiquette, S. 32

Using the email and your notes from exercise 3, write Eric's email to Tony Browne confirming the booking. Add a suitable subject line.

From: Eric Jung <ericjung@magnusklein.co.uk>
Subject:
To: Tony Browne <tonybrowne@magnusklein.co.uk>
cc: Joan Shaw <joanshaw@magnusklein.co.uk>

Hello Tony

This is just to let you know that I have booked …

As you will be arriving after the check-in time of 10 pm, I have called the hotel …

I hope the hotel is OK and that you enjoy your trip.

Best
Eric

TIP Formal and informal business emails

When writing business emails to new contacts, superiors or people you don't know well (for example, colleagues at a new job), you should begin your email with *Dear* … and end with *Regards* or *Best wishes*. With business contacts or colleagues you know well, you can start emails with *Hello* … or *Hi* … and end with *Best*.

5 RESERVING A CONFERENCE ROOM

The Magnus & Klein team are having a meeting with some business partners during the trade fair. Ms Shaw asks Eric to reserve a conference room.

A Work in a group of four. Discuss Ms Shaw's wishes and rank them in order of importance (1 is most important). Give reasons for your rankings.

Eric
We are having a meeting with some business partners on Saturday, 19 October. Please book a conference room for the whole day and arrange lunch for 9 people.
We need a room with seating for 9 people including one person in a wheelchair; a projector, screen and a flip chart; Wi-fi; a selection of non-alcoholic drinks.
Lunch should include vegetarian options.
Try to get a conference room at the fair or near to the fair area and please don't exceed £300, including lunch.
JS

B **In your group, split into two pairs: Partners A and B, and Partners C and D. Each pair is going to look at offers for conference rooms and then try to persuade the other pair to choose the room they have selected.**

Partners A and B

Work together and compare the offers on the right with what Ms Shaw would like. Choose a room and develop arguments which will persuade Partners C and D to reserve this room for the meeting.

Bristol Trade Fair Area Conference Rooms

- Book by the hour, half day or full day -

Our conference centre on the top floor of the Fair Area is accessible by lift. There is wheelchair access throughout the building and disabled facilities on every floor.

We have three conference rooms to suit your needs.
Prices: £180 (69 m^2), £155 (38 m^2), £110 (22 m^2)

All rooms are equipped with high-end audio-visual equipment and free wireless high-speed internet connection.

- Hot and cold drinks, fruit and snacks included in the price of the room
- Free national and local calls
- Free 'host' Internet connection
- Free stationery

A la carte lunch menu at prices starting from £18 per person.
Non-alcoholic drinks included in the price.
Special dietary requirements can be catered for.

Bristol Fair Hotel

MEETING ROOM FACILITIES

Our hotel is located next to the Bristol Fair Area. You can hold a meeting and stay overnight with us at reasonable prices.

Room	Size	Price
River	73 m^2	£210
Mountain	50 m^2	£175
Plain	26 m^2	£120

All prices include modern technology. We can mix and match equipment (e.g. screen, projector, pinboard, flip charts with markers) according to your wishes.
Catering throughout the whole event, snacks and non-alcoholic drinks are included in the price of the room. Buffet lunch: £14 per person.

- Disabled facilities throughout the hotel.
- Wi-fi in the meeting rooms and in public areas.
- Private bar available for a relaxing end to your event.

If you are a guest of our hotel, the rental price for the conference room is reduced by £5 for each booked hotel room.

Partners C and D

Work together and compare the offers on the right with what Ms Shaw would like. Choose a room and develop arguments which will persuade Partners A and B to reserve this room for the meeting.

6 BOOKING A CONFERENCE ROOM BY EMAIL

Write an email to the company whose conference room you have chosen. Give the date and times when you would like the room. Describe what services you would like.

Useful phrases

- to book/reserve a conference room for … people
- to be equipped with …
- to confirm a reservation for …
- to send an invoice to …

13 The challenges of the modern state

EXAM PREPARATION

FOCUS

1

2

3

4

5

6

7

8

A **Think: Rank the problems shown in the photos according to what you think is most important. Use the words in the box or your own descriptions.**

body scanners ▪ data protection ▪ electronic waste ▪ energy dependence ▪ extremism ▪ human rights ▪ identity theft ▪ mental health ▪ online security ▪ phishing ▪ radicalization ▪ stress ▪ surveillance cameras ▪ terrorist attacks ▪ war

Write two or three sentences about the problems you think are most important.

B **Pair: Compare your list with a partner and discuss your choices.**

C **Share: Discuss your ideas in class.**

TEXT A Terrorism

BEFORE YOU READ

→ Rezeption: Leseverstehen, S. 214

A **Skim the first text to find out what happened to the two brothers.**

B **Scan the second text to find another expression for *police work*.**

2/20

THE BOSTON MARATHON

Two hours after the winners crossed the finishing line of the 117th Boston Marathon, two pressure cooker bombs exploded killing three people and injuring 264. Three days later, the FBI released photographs and a surveillance video of two suspects, who were brothers. They were found the same day and after a firefight with the police, the older brother died and the younger one escaped.

Four days later, thousands of police officers in Watertown, Massachusetts took part in a huge manhunt for the younger brother. Public transport, most private businesses and all public institutions were shut down and residents were told to stay indoors, making Watertown into an urban desert. At around 7 pm, a Watertown resident discovered the younger brother hiding in a boat in his back yard and he was arrested. He later stated that he and his brother had also planned to bomb Times Square in New York. He claimed that they were self-radicalized and had learned to build bombs on the Internet.

(167 words)

THE NATURE OF MODERN TERRORISM

[...] Methods for engaging in political violence have changed, and multiple forms of terrorism will probably dominate the "battlefields" of the twenty-first century. [...] Modern terrorism is a new phenomenon. It requires supporting systems from the technological world. First, to be effective, terrorism must be seen and heard. As one terrorist commander summarized, it is better to kill one person in front of a camera than to kill a hundred in a secret location. Terrorists need an audience.

The second aspect of modernity's impact on terrorism involves mobility. This can be done locally or globally. The goal is to get to the target and get away. An attack can originate in the hills of South Waziristan and be carried out in London [...].

Finally, the modern world provides weapons or materials that can be turned into weapons. These devices, in turn, are more powerful than instruments of the past. [...]

These three factors – instant communication, mobility, and access to destructive technology – mean that terrorism will continue to plague the world. [...] When not used as a tactic in guerrilla war, terrorism is essentially a problem for law enforcement and the criminal justice system. [...] One of the best tools in the anti-terrorist arsenal is to develop law enforcement agencies that act as extensions of neighborhoods. These agencies can root out all types of problems before they happen, including terrorism. [...] Finally, it would be helpful if the mass media, especially cable news, would spend time explaining the complex background of modern terrorism. This would be much more responsible than breathlessly awaiting the next stage in a terrorist drama. [...] (265 words)

From: Jonathan R. White, *The Huffington Post*

1 LOOKING AT THE TEXTS

→ Rezeption: Leseverstehen, S. 214

A Read the first text and explain how …

1 the bombers made their explosive devices.
2 the police were able to get photographs of the suspects.
3 the brothers became extremists.

B Read the second text and match the sentence halves.

1 There will be many different forms of …
2 Modern technology enables terrorists to …
3 Terrorist attacks are often planned in places which …
4 Nowadays, it is easy to find materials …
5 Nobody expects terrorism …
6 In many cases, it is the job of the police …
7 The police can root out some terrorism …
8 Terrorism is often sensationalized …

a which can be made into weapons.
b to deal with terrorists.
c by the mass media.
d to stop in the near future.
e by working closely with the local community.
f reach large audiences all over the world.
g terrorism in the twenty-first century.
h are a long way away from the target.

2 WORKING WITH WORDS

A Study the texts to see how the verbs in box A are used with the nouns in box B.

A

to release	to carry out
to take part in	to turn into
to shut down	to plague
to engage in	to root out

B

a manhunt	the problems
an attack	the world
photographs	violence
public transport	weapons

B Use some collocations from exercise 2A to complete the text. Make any necessary changes.

When four suicide bombers ___[1] on London Transport on 7 July 2005, there was no warning and 56 people died, including the terrorists. The attack was so devastating that the authorities had to ___[2] for the rest of the day, which meant there were no trains or buses in Central London. Some time later, the police ___[3] of the attackers showing them carrying large rucksacks of home-made explosives at London's Kings Cross station. Attacks of this nature continue to ___[4], and law enforcement agencies everywhere now have emergency plans to deal with such events. However, experts agree that it is best to ___[5] which lead to terrorist attacks before extremists ___[6] and kill innocent people.

C *Cross* can be a verb (*to cross*) or a noun (*a cross*). Use the definitions below to find more words in the two texts that have the same verb and noun form.

1 to make available for the public
2 to believe sb is guilty of sth
3 to take sb to a police station and hold them there
4 to make different
5 to give help
6 to have a strong effect on sth
7 to use weapons to hurt or kill sb

D Write 4–5 sentences containing your answers to exercise 2C as nouns or verbs.

3 MEDIATION

→ Schriftliche Mediation, S. 240

Ihre Schule nimmt an einem Projekt in Zusammenarbeit mit einer großen Regionalzeitung teil. Die Schüler und Schülerinnen sind aufgefordert, Artikel über aktuelle Themen zu schreiben, die dann in der Zeitung veröffentlicht werden.

Benutzen Sie die relevanten Inhalte der beiden Texte, um einen Zeitungsartikel über die Rolle der modernen Technik im Terrorismus des 21. Jahrhunderts zu verfassen.

4 LISTENING

→ Rezeption: Hörverstehen, S. 225

Tonight, the BBC's radio phone-in programme *World Have Your Say* is dealing with the question, 'Is the state really under threat from terrorism?'

A Before you listen, work with a partner and guess which person says each statement below.

Fatima, Turkish student

Joshua, Christian priest

Andrea, German student teacher

Reginald, ex-army officer

a In my experience talking with terrorists gets you nowhere. We need to find them and stop them.
b The West must stop sending weapons to conflict zones.
c Children must learn not to use violence to solve conflicts.
d I believe in focusing on the values and beliefs we all share, not on our differences.

2/21 **B Listen and check your answers.**

2/21 **C Listen again and write down the missing words. Sometimes you need more than one word for each gap.**

1. The government is responsible for ___ its citizens.
2. If we want ___ in a free world, spending on the police and the armed forces must be massively increased.
3. I believe in ___ for the threat before it's too late.
4. Westerners enjoy ___ in safety and comfort
5. They risk ___[1] all this if they continue ___[2] weapons to conflict zones.
6. I remember ___ about the horrors of the Second World War at school.
7. I started ___ about the reasons for violence.
8. A member of my church suggested ___ a prayer vigil.
9. I agreed ___ so immediately.
10. Joshua recommends ___ for peace.

5 ROLE-PLAY

→ Interaktion: Ein Rollenspiel gestalten, S. 247

With a partner, choose the speaker from exercise 4 whose opinions you disagree with most. Role-play a discussion between yourself and that person about how to prevent terrorism. Take turns with your partner to play both roles.

BUILDING SKILLS: Preparing for a discussion

You should always prepare thoroughly before you start any kind of speaking activity. If you have to take part in a discussion, you can prepare by making notes of the main arguments:

- Think of the ideas and arguments that your opponent might use and make a list of them.
- Make a list of your own ideas and arguments.
- Look at the points you disagree about most strongly and think of arguments you can use against your opponent.

Useful phrases

Partly agreeing with an opinion:

- I don't entirely/quite agree with you.
- I see what you mean, but …
- There's some truth in what you say. However, …

Saying something in another way:

- (Well,) What I mean is, …
- In other words, …
- Let me put it another way, …

6 GETTING IT RIGHT

→ Verb + infinitive ▪ Verb + gerund, S. 262

A Choose the right verb form to complete these sentences.

The security services are responsible for (to protect / protecting) ___ [1] the citizens of a country from terrorist attacks. The security services also expect the citizens (to help / helping) ___ [2] them do their job and they encourage them (to give / giving) ___ [3] them helpful information. However, communicating sensitive information to MI5, Britain's internal security service, is not so simple. Although the organization recommends (to use / using) ___ [4] its secure Internet contact form, many people decide (to write / writing) ___ [5] a letter instead because they prefer (to post / posting) ___ [6] it anonymously. Some computer experts encourage people to stop (to use / using) ___ [7] phones and computers for important messages and only use paper. They feel that using the Internet for sensitive material involves (to take / taking) ___ [8] too many security risks.

B The verbs in the box are all followed by gerunds. Complete the sentences with a suitable verb from the box, making any necessary changes.

avoid ▪ enjoy ▪ hate ▪ involve ▪ mind ▪ miss ▪ recommend ▪ risk

1 Police work often ___ observing a suspect over a long period of time.
2 If you ___ having a lot of free time, it's best not to join the police force.
3 The police ___ taking extra safety precautions when there is a terrorist threat.
4 They say it's best to ___ going out late at night.
5 When this happens, some people ___ meeting their friends at the local pub.
6 Others don't ___ staying at home in the evenings.
7 Some people even cancel their holidays because they don't want to ___ travelling to a dangerous place.
8 Most people ___ losing their freedom but are willing to do so for a short time.

TEXT B The dangers of digital life

BEFORE YOU READ

→ Rezeption: Leseverstehen – Grobverständnis, S. 214

Skim the text and explain which of the following statements is true and why the others are false:

1 Uwe Buse was unable to defend himself against any of the hackers' attacks.
2 Uwe Buse was able to defend himself against some of the hackers' attacks.
3 Uwe Buse was able to defend himself against most of the hackers' attacks.

2/22

When hackers take over your life

When *Spiegel* reporter Uwe Buse decided to try out a test on himself and invited hackers to take over his life, he had no idea what he was letting himself in for. He wanted them to find out as much as possible about his private and professional life without any help from him at all and then use this knowledge to harm him. He would then try to fight back as an exercise in digital self-defence.

He first contacted a specialist firm in Tübingen which hacks into company net-works at the request of their owners and instructed them to hack into his mobile and laptop. In Tübingen, three young hackers, who had made their illegal hobby into their profession, installed undetectable spyware on his mobile and laptop. When the laptop was switched back on, the message from its virus scanner was: 'Your computer is safe.'

The spyware on Uwe Buse's mobile immediately started transmitting GPS data to the hackers every two seconds. That evening the hackers tracked him back to Bremen, noted his home address and took a look at his house using Street View. They logged his every movement and also found out he had a school-age daughter when she phoned him to tell him she had arrived safely at school. They recorded the phone call and intercepted the photo of herself she sent him. They knew what she looked like.

At 9 o'clock the same day, when Uwe Buse sat down at his laptop to start work, he thought he was alone. He was mistaken. The camera in his laptop started taking photos of him every five minutes and sending them to the hackers. In addition, every keystroke he made on his computer was recorded in a handy Excel table, which also showed the names of the programs he was using, which windows were open on his monitor, the data he was inputting and the time. The table was also sent to the hackers every five minutes.

When he logged into his Amazon and email accounts, they recorded the access codes and by scanning his Amazon account, quickly saw that he rode a motorbike and

had dry skin. They went on to find out his wife and children's names, his wife's email address, the number of her mobile, where she worked and what she looked like. They noted that the Buses didn't own a car and used car-sharing. Next the hackers sent a silent SMS to the reporter's mobile to switch on the microphone and record everything he said. This also went unnoticed.

On the second day of the experiment he logged into his bank account and the hackers recorded the access codes. They did the same with his Facebook, PayPal and iTunes accounts. They now had the data they needed and on the third day they switched to attack.

The driver of the delivery van which stopped outside Uwe Buse's house carried a large cardboard box to the front door. When asked what was in the box he replied: 'It's a lawnmower.' Buse refused delivery and sent the van away. The attack had begun.

The hackers used his email account to write an email in his name to the car-sharing firm and tell them he had knocked off the two outside mirrors of the car but had no time to stick them back on again.

The washing machine ordered in Buse's name was priced at €415.39 but when he got an email from Amazon confirming the purchase, he quickly phoned the hotline and cancelled it. Amazon advised him to change his password, which he did, but the spyware sent the new password straight to the hackers. After some more phone calls Amazon told him his account had been 'totally destroyed' and could no longer be saved. They advised him to report the matter to the police and be more careful when surfing the net in future.

The hackers' next target was his Facebook account. They posted an extremely embarrassing public message about his private life on his wall, prompting him to try to delete his account. However, as the hackers had changed all his personal details, he was unable to get into his account and could not contact anyone at Facebook because there is no hotline.

Next the hackers logged into his online bank account and withdrew all his money, placing it on untraceable prepaid cards. When he contacted his bank, they told him to report it to the police. They promised to try to get his money back and sent him a new access code for his account – by post.

Before he could go to the police, however, he was informed that he had sent his boss at *Spiegel* an email telling him that he was 'sick and tired' of him and was leaving the magazine straightaway to get a better paid job at the hackers' company in Tübingen.

Finally, his hackers contacted him to warn him that they were going to put some very nasty material on his laptop and then inform the police. He begged them not to do so and a few days later conceded utter defeat.

The spyware package used by the hackers is obtainable on the American market for as little as $33 per month. The software makers openly encourage worried parents, suspicious spouses and company bosses to spy on their children, partners and employees. The fact that using such programs is illegal in almost all countries is hidden in the small print.

When Uwe Buse asked his tormentors how to protect himself, they told him not to use Windows computers, online banking or mobile banking and not to install any unnecessary apps. They advised him to keep his virus scanner and software up-to-date, set up a firewall, use an encrypted mobile phone, go to the bank in person and use paper. (970 words)

13 The challenges of the modern state

1 LOOKING AT THE TEXT

→ Rezeption: Leseverstehen, S. 214

A Read the text on pages 128–129 and do the following tasks.

1 Study the text and list the information the hackers found out about Uwe Buse's …
a) house, b) family and c) preferred means of transport.
2 Describe how the hackers obtained the access codes to his online accounts.
3 The hackers launched six attacks against Uwe Buse. Outline each attack briefly.
4 How many attacks was he able to defend himself against?
5 Why was he able to defend himself against the Amazon but not the Facebook attack?
6 Explain how Uwe Buse stopped the seventh attack and discuss the possible consequences if it had taken place.
7 Analyse each of the attacks (including the cancelled seventh attack) and put the consequences it had or would have had into one of the following categories:
a) criminal, b) financial, c) job-related and d) social.

B Say what you think.

1 Discuss the reasons why parents, spouses and company bosses might use a spyware program.
2 Evaluate each of the hackers' suggestions as to how to protect yourself from digital attack.

2 WORKING WITH WORDS

A Match the words or expressions with their meanings.

1	to let yourself in for sth	**a**	to take money out of a bank account
2	mistaken	**b**	horrible
3	to refuse	**c**	important information written in very small letters
4	purchase	**d**	to put into code
5	to withdraw	**e**	immediately
6	untraceable	**f**	to do sth unpleasant or difficult
7	straightaway	**g**	impossible to find
8	nasty	**h**	wrong
9	the small print	**i**	to say you will not do sth
10	to encrypt	**j**	sth you have bought

B Work in pairs. Write your own definitions of four or five words in the text, mix them up and show them to your partner. Can your partner match the words to the definitions?

C Complete the text with a suitable phrasal verb, by adding a particle to the verbs below.

verbs	particles
try ▪ take ▪ find ▪ switch ▪ get ▪ set	back ▪ on ▪ out (2×) ▪ over ▪ up

Thanks to cybercrime there are fewer bank robberies because it's easier to ___ [1] a computer than rob a bank. Many people never ___ [2] that their computer has been hijacked. They just ___ it ___ [3] as usual, ___ [4] a digital payment of some form and click on 'OK'. However, if their account has been hacked, there is a good chance they will never ___ their money ___ [5]. When hackers steal credit card data, they make a copy of the card and ___ it ___ [6] it with a small sum of money first. If it works, they use it for bigger payments.

TEXT C The surveillance society

In this section you are going to read two short extracts from a novel and a newspaper article about surveillance.

BEFORE YOU READ

What do you associate with the term 'surveillance society'?

In 1949 George Orwell published *Nineteen Eighty-Four*, a novel about a fictional totalitarian state called Oceania. The following extracts describe the posters of the leader, Big Brother, which are everywhere, and the use of telescreens by the Thought Police.

… the poster with the enormous face gazed from the wall. It was one of those pictures which are so contrived that the eyes follow you about when you move. BIG BROTHER IS WATCHING YOU, the caption beneath it ran.

… The telescreen received and transmitted simultaneously. Any sound that Winston made, above the level of a very low whisper, would be picked up by it, moreover, so long as he remained within the field of vision which the metal plaque commanded, he could be seen as well as heard. There was of course no way of knowing whether you were being watched at any given moment. How often, or on what system, the Thought Police plugged in on any individual wire was guesswork. It was even conceivable that they watched everybody all the time. But at any rate they could plug in your wire whenever they wanted to. You had to live – did live, from habit that became instinct – in the assumption that every sound you made was overheard, and, except in darkness, every movement scrutinized. (176 words)

From: George Orwell, *Nineteen Eighty-Four*

to gaze – *starren, blicken*
to contrive – *bewerkstelligen*
telescreen – *Televisor*
simultaneously – *gleichzeitig*
to pick up – *registrieren*
field of vision – *Sichtfeld*
plaque – *Platte*
to command – *beherrschen*
to plug in on – *sich in etw einschalten*
guesswork – *Mutmaßung, Spekulation*
conceivable – *denkbar*
assumption – *Annahme*
to scrutinize – *genau ansehen, überprüfen*

1 LOOKING AT THE TEXT

→ Rezeption: Leseverstehen, S. 214

A Read the extracts from the novel and complete these tasks.

1. What is the most important characteristic of the poster? Write two or three sentences to describe its effect.
2. Explain in a few words how the poster is helpful to Big Brother.
3. Discuss the functions of the telescreen with a partner, then list them in order of importance.
4. Compare your order of importance with other students in your class and discuss any differences of opinion.

B Think: George Orwell's novel is seen as a warning against a totalitarian society. Can you think of any parallels today or in history?

C Pair: Discuss your ideas with a partner and them write them down in a few sentences.

D Share: Present your ideas in class.

2 READING

→ Rezeption: Leseverstehen, S. 214

A Before you read: Think about places you would expect to see CCTV cameras and places where you wouldn't expect (or want) to see CCTV cameras. Make a list.

B While you read: Note down the estimated numbers of CCTV cameras in Britain. Make a list of where they are located.

2/23

ONE SURVEILLANCE CAMERA FOR EVERY 11 PEOPLE IN BRITAIN, SAYS CCTV SURVEY

Britain has a CCTV camera for every 11 people, a security industry report disclosed, as privacy campaigners criticised the growth of the "surveillance state".

The British Security Industry Authority (BSIA) estimated there are up to 5.9 million closed-circuit television cameras in the country, including 750,000 in "sensitive locations" such as schools, hospitals and care homes. [...]

Simon Adcock, of the BSIA, said: "[...] Effective CCTV schemes are an invaluable source of crime detection and evidence for the police. For example in 2009, 95% of Scotland Yard murder cases used CCTV footage as evidence."

But Nick Pickles, director of the privacy campaign Big Brother Watch, said: "This report is another stark reminder of how out of control our surveillance culture has become.

"With potentially more than five million CCTV cameras across country, including more than 300,000 cameras in schools, we are being monitored in a way that few people would recognise as a part of a healthy democratic society." [...]

It estimated there are between 291,000 and 373,000 cameras in public sector schools, plus a further 30,000 to 50,000 in independent schools.

Surgeries and health centres have an estimated 80,000 to 159,000, while there are believed to be between 53,000 and 159,000 cameras in restaurants, the report said.

(216 words)

From: *www.telegraph.co.uk*

C Work with a partner and do these tasks.

1 Compare your two lists. Are there any places mentioned that you didn't expect to see?
2 Which figures from the text do you find surprising? Explain why (not).

D Say what it means: Explain these phrases in your own words.

1 'sensitive locations' (line 7)
2 an invaluable source of crime detection (lines 9–10)
3 (another) stark reminder (line 13)
4 our surveillance culture (line 13)
5 a healthy democratic society (line 17)

E Discuss in class: Do you think there are too many CCTV cameras in Germany? Do you feel threatened by too many surveillance cameras?

3 WORKING WITH WORDS

A Find words in the text on page 132 that go with the following words. There is sometimes more than one answer.

CCTV ▪ health ▪ independent ▪ privacy ▪ public ▪ security ▪ surveillance

B Complete the sentences with a suitable collocation from exercise 3A.

1. The ___ has just released a report with new estimates on the use of CCTV in Britain.
2. Care homes and ___ are just some of the 'sensitive locations' where CCTV schemes are used.
3. Many companies want to know more about their employees' behaviour, so they install ___ .
4. Cameras have also been installed in at least 291,000 ___ [1] and 30,000 ___ [2].
5. Angry ___ [1] believe that society in Britain is on its way to becoming a ___ [2].

4 WRITING

→ Produktion: Eine Stellungnahme schreiben, S. 234

Two readers publish the following comments about the article in *The Telegraph*:

Terry Wilkins, Manchester

I totally agree with Simon Adcock when he says 'that effective CCTV schemes are an invaluable source of crime detection and evidence for the police.'

Nick Pickles is 100% right to say that 'we are being monitored in a way that few people would recognize as a part of a healthy democratic society.'

Alice Trent, Northern Ireland

Choose one of the opinions above and write a comment to be published in *The Telegraph* online, explaining why you agree with it.

Write your own comment on the following statement:

'Surveillance, whether by camera, phone or Internet, makes the world a safer place. If you have nothing to hide, you have nothing to fear.'

SKILLS CHECKLIST: Writing a comment

- ☑ Have I structured my arguments clearly?
- ☑ Have I given examples to support my arguments?
- ☑ Have I used linking words and phrases?

Weather from space

Space is not as empty as you might think. Our sun gives off masses of high-speed particles and electromagnetic energy. Sometimes this "space weather" can cause problems for our modern technology here on Earth.

Coronal mass ejection – spectacular and powerful "solar storm"

The Northern Lights – caused by disturbances in Earth's magnetic field.

Extra High Voltage (EHV) transformers – essential, expensive and vulnerable

1 LISTENING

→ Rezeption: Hörverstehen, S. 225

4/10

Listen to the radio programme and make notes on the following subjects.

1 What a coronal mass ejection (CME) is
2 Damage that a CME can do
3 Why the power grid is vulnerable
4 What a solar flare is
5 Damage that a solar flare can do
6 How we can prepare for space weather

2 WORKING WITH A DIAGRAM

Work in a small group around a table. Copy the diagram onto a large sheet of paper. Discuss the scenario and draw arrows and make notes on the diagram, as in the examples below.

Scenario — *A severe geomagnetic storm has knocked out the electrical grid across Europe. It will take weeks to get the power back on line.*

Phase 1 — Predict how the failure of the electrical grid will affect other services. Add notes to your diagram.

EXAMPLE — BANKING AND FINANCE: ATMs don't work = no cash withdrawals

Phase 2 — Predict how the failure of each set of services will affect other services. Draw more arrows on your diagram and write explanatory notes.

EXAMPLE — (Arrow from OIL / GAS to TRANSPORTATION)
No fuel at petrol stations = road traffic stops

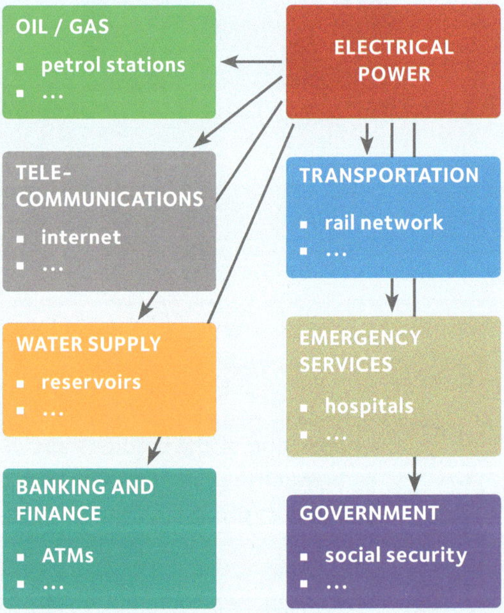

14 Energy and the environment

EXAM PREPARATION

FOCUS

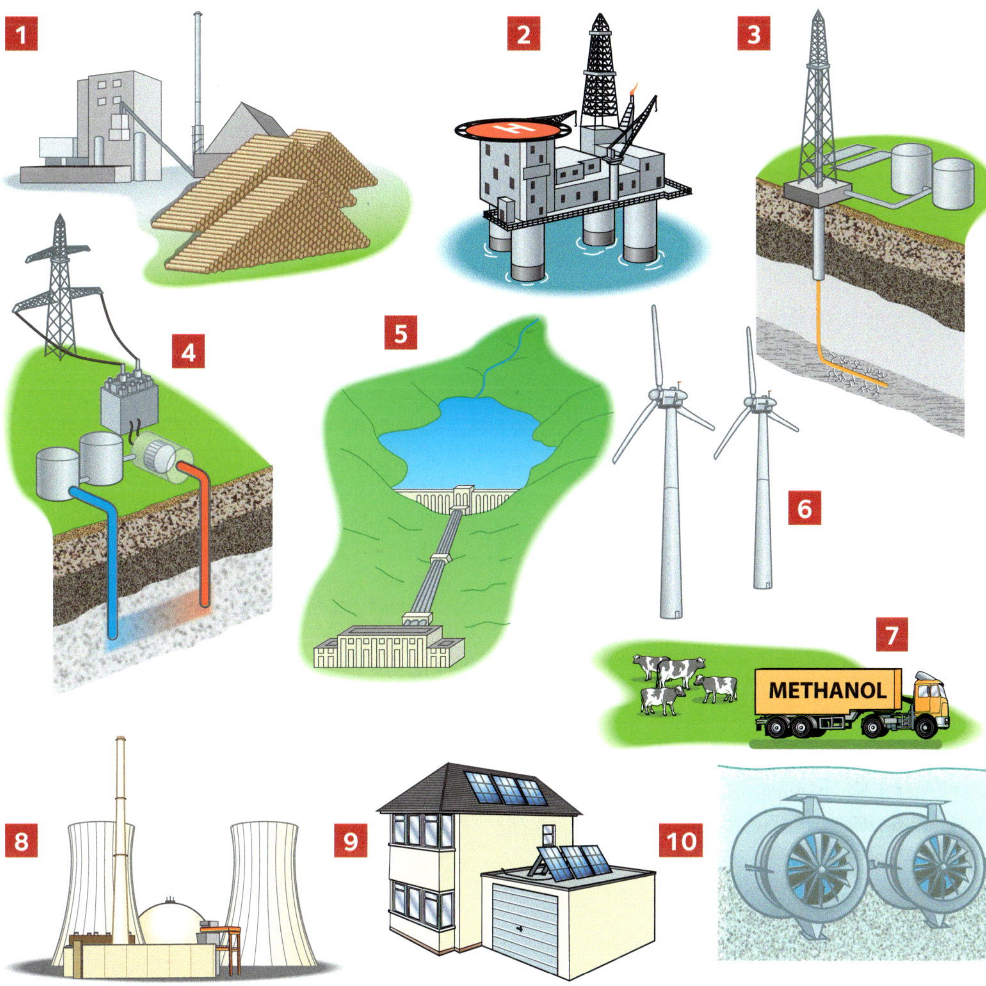

A **Name the different forms of energy (1–10) above using the words in the box.**

solar power ▪ geothermal power ▪ nuclear power ▪ biomass ▪ fracking ▪ tidal power ▪ hydro-electric power ▪ wind power ▪ methane ▪ fossil fuel

B **Group the sources of energy in the diagram under these two headings:**

Renewable energy sources	Non-renewable energy sources
▪	▪

C **Work in a small group. Imagine a complete breakdown of conventional, non-renewable energy supplies in Germany. (They make up about 75% of the total energy sources.) Imagine this happening in winter. How do you think it would affect everyday life?**

14 Energy and the environment

TEXT A The real cost of energy

BEFORE YOU READ

Read the title. Say what you know about climate change. What might 'the debate' be about?

3/2

CLIMATE CHANGE: IS THE DEBATE OVER?

A Is climate change really happening? If so, are humans responsible, and how bad could it be for the world – and us? The issues are complex, and the debate has been long and often angry.

B Republican Senator for Texas Ted Cruz wants the freedom to use all energy sources, especially fossil fuels, and he argues strongly that these are not causing climate change. 'The problem with climate change,' he said recently to CNN, 'is that there's never been a day in the history of the world when the climate wasn't changing.'

'So you don't believe there's a man-made cause of global warming or climate change?' he was asked.

'What I think is that the data is not supporting what the advocates are arguing,' he replied. In the last 15 years, there had been no recorded warming, he went on. It hadn't happened, and they didn't have an explanation for that.

C However, Professor James Hanson, one of the world's best-known climate scientists recently rejected the views of 'deniers' like Cruz that climate change had stopped and that the effect of rising carbon dioxide levels on climate was not as great as had been previously thought. Speaking on BBC's Radio 4, he accepted that warming had been slower since 1998, but 'that's just natural variability,' he said. 'If you look over a 30–40 year period, the expected warming is two-tenths of a degree per decade, but this doesn't mean each decade is going to warm two-tenths of a degree: there is too much variability.'

Professor Hanson has very strong views on the causes of this warming. He has said that 'CEOs of fossil fuel companies should be tried for high crimes against humanity and nature' and that 'coal-fired power plants are factories of death.'

What do other experts say? According to a new survey of scientific studies by NASA, 97% agreed that climate change is real and that humans are at least partly to blame. Quoting this figure, CNN news anchor Carol Costello said, 'Why are we still debating climate change? There is no debate. Climate change is real.'

D So let us look at some actual data. The Industrial Revolution brought large-scale use of fossil fuels, and this steadily put more carbon dioxide and other 'greenhouse gases' into the atmosphere. Before, much of Earth's energy from the sun had been reflected back into space: by the 20th century, more and more of that energy was being held back and no longer escaped. The result was gradual global warming. The chart below supports the connection.

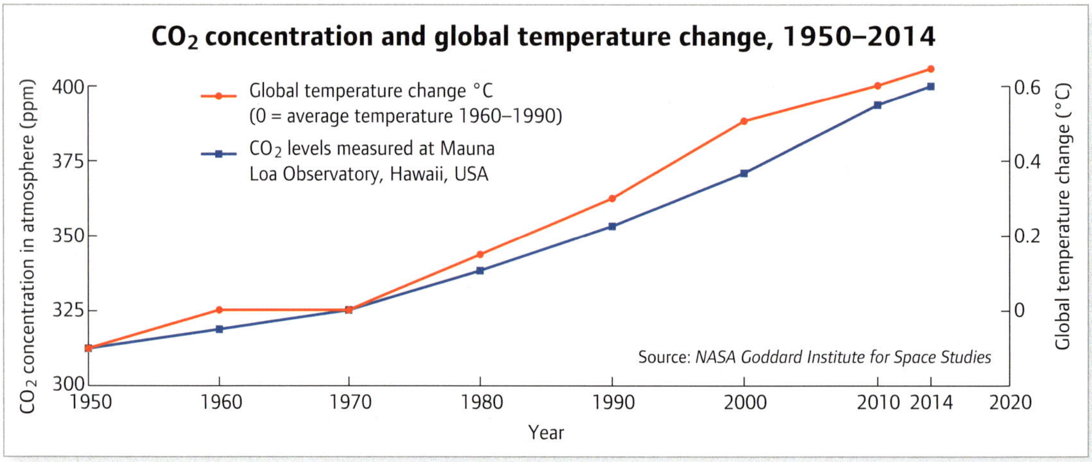

E In 2014, atmospheric CO_2 passed 400 parts per million (ppm) at speed while scientists warned again that the level must not rise beyond 450ppm. If it does, they predict, major climate changes will start to follow. At 560ppm, twice the average level of 280ppm before the Industrial Revolution, these changes will become disastrous and unstoppable. In Europe, summers will get much hotter and winters much wetter with many more sudden, violent storms – and we will be the lucky ones. In other parts of the world, life will become difficult or impossible. Africa's deserts will expand fast, hurricanes will force people to leave Central America and the USA's south-eastern coasts. Wild cyclones will do the same in Asia, from China to India. At the same time, the warming oceans will expand while the Greenland and Antarctic ice sheets continue to melt, raising sea levels by a centimetre per year (far beyond today's 2.9 millimetres per year). Many low-lying islands and coasts, along with great coastal cities such as New York and Shanghai will be drowning.

Is this disastrous picture of the future realistic? The answer is worrying. If emissions continue to grow as they are, the International Panel on Climate Change (IPCC) tells us that CO_2 levels will reach *1,000ppm* by 2100.

F However, a recent report prepared for the UN offers fresh hope. It argued that the world could still act in time to prevent the worst effects of climate change and also enjoy continued economic growth. This would be possible as long as the global economy was transformed in the next 15 years. Co-author Lord Stern, a leading expert on climate economics, said that dealing with climate change urgently would be cheaper than trying to do so decades in the future. In fact, it could create better economic growth than the old high-carbon model, he said. He gave the example of cities that were expanding massively in the developing world. If global investment in existing high-carbon infrastructure continued, a great opportunity would be lost. If, however, cities were designed around public transport, they could have more efficient economies because people would not have to spend hours in their cars commuting and polluting. This would mean lower carbon emissions, he said, and this in turn would mean better health and a better quality of life.

The report concluded that both rich and poor countries needed to act strongly to limit CO_2 emissions and to reduce dependence on coal and other dirty fuels. At the same time, economic growth could be encouraged through investment in renewable energy, sustainable cities, modern farming techniques and better-designed transport.

G To return to our questions: yes, climate change is happening, and humans are almost certainly largely responsible. As for how bad it could be, it seems that we still have one more chance to decide.

(897 words)

1 LOOKING AT THE TEXT

→ Rezeption: Leseverstehen, S. 214

A Skim the text and match the headings (1–7) below to the sections (A–G) of the text.

1. A win-win plan for carbon control and economic growth
2. Carbon and warming: a short history
3. Climate change this century: a worst-case scenario
4. The big climate questions that we face today
5. The opinion of most climate scientists
6. Three answers to three questions
7. Views of a climate change sceptic

B Read the text carefully and do the following tasks.

→ Umgang mit Operatoren, S. 232

1. Contrast the views of Cruz and Hanson on recent climate data.
2. Say what two sorts of information the chart shows. Describe the relationship between them.
3. Contrast the effects of climate change in parts of Africa and the south-eastern USA.
4. Describe two causes of future coastal flooding.
5. Give an example of the transformation that the new UN report calls for.

C Say what it means: Explain the underlined phrases from the text in your own words.

1. … 'coal-fired power plants are factories of death.' (line 36)
2. … CNN news anchor Carol Costello said, … (line 41)
3. … tells us that CO_2 levels will reach *1,000 ppm* by 2100. (line 78)
4. This would be possible as long as the global economy was transformed … (line 83)
5. If global investment in existing high-carbon infrastructure continued, … (line 92)
6. … a better quality of life. (lines 99–100)

2 WORKING WITH WORDS

A Match words from box A to words in box B to make collocations related to the environment.

A carbon ▪ climate ▪ fossil ▪ global ▪ greenhouse ▪ ice ▪ industrial ▪ power ▪ public ▪ sea

B change ▪ emissions ▪ fuel ▪ gases ▪ levels ▪ plant ▪ revolution ▪ sheet ▪ transport ▪ warming

B Use collocations from exercise 2A to complete the following paragraph.

Oil, coal and natural gas are all ___ 1. At the start of the ___ 2, coal was used to power nearly all manufacturing, as well as all trains. However, these days coal is mostly used in coal-fired ___ 3 to produce electricity. By contrast, most forms of ___ 4, such as trains and buses, now use diesel. Carbon dioxide is one of a number of ___ 5 in the atmosphere that are causing global temperatures to rise. The rise of temperatures all over the world is called ___ 6. This is almost certainly leading to changes in weather conditions that are together known as ___ 7. The results are becoming clear. For example, the Arctic ___ 8 has been getting smaller for many years. ___ 9 are rising, too, and many coastal cities are probably going to be flooded in the future. The only answer is to limit ___ 10 by reducing our dependence on coal and other dirty fuels.

3 GETTING IT RIGHT

→ Indirect speech, S. 266

Rewrite these statements in indirect speech for a newspaper report. Change the contracted forms (e.g. *We're*) to full forms (*We are*) and make any other changes necessary.

During my trip to northern Canada last month, I spent time with a small Inuit community, and I had the chance to learn a little about the effects of climate change there.

1. 'We're having big problems because the sea ice started melting two weeks ago,' community leader Jim Kupak told me.
   Community leader Jim Kupak told me that they were …
2. He said, 'It isn't safe any more for us to go out on the ice – the way we've always done.'
3. 'We've had to end our hunting season very early because we can't risk falling through the ice and killing ourselves,' he explained.
4. 'I'm worried we may find ourselves very short of food in the coming months,' he added.
5. He finished by saying, 'The ice is melting earlier every year, and we won't be able to continue our way of life much longer if it doesn't stop.'

Write part of a school magazine report about a visit arranged by Mrs Bell, Head of Science. Use these reporting verbs and the underlined words in the conversation.

add ▪ promise ▪ remind ▪ say ▪ tell ▪ thank ▪ welcome

Mrs Bell is welcoming the guest speaker, Dr Ross:

Bell Dr Ross, we're very happy to see you here at Garston Sixth-Form College. It's very good of you to give Garston some time, and I'm sure we're all going to hear a fascinating talk.

Ross Well, let me just say that I'm very grateful to you all for the chance to speak to you, and I hope you'll hear at least a few things you'll find interesting.

Bell I'm sure we will. Remember, we specialize in science and technology at Garston, and so we're really looking forward to hearing about your new climate research.'

Ross Right, well, first of all, let me admit that climate change is a complex subject, which means I'll have to talk about some complex ideas, but I'll try and explain things in plain and simple English. Now, my team and I have just finished a report on our work in the Arctic that we started two years ago, and so I can say something about that. I also think there may be enough time to talk about our present project, in the Antarctic. By the way, next time we want to go somewhere warmer!

Mrs Bell, Head of Science, welcomed Dr Ross to our school. She said that it was … , and she was sure that …

4 WRITING

→ Produktion: Eine Stellungnahme schreiben, S. 234

A Read the following statement. Find points for and against it in the information box below.

'As a developing country, China should be allowed to produce carbon emissions freely unlike developed nations.'

Background information

1. From 2005–11, China added roughly two large coal-fired power stations every week for seven years. It is still building many more.
2. The country now burns 4 billion tons of coal p.a., the USA 1 billion and the EU 0.6 billion.
3. Fossil fuels still provide 87% of the country's energy, including 70% from coal. (The fossil fuel figure for Germany is about 57%.)
4. China's emissions per person are slightly lower than the EU's and much lower than in the USA. (China's population is 1.356 billion, while the USA's is 319 million and the EU's is 504 million.)
5. Producing goods competitively for developed countries causes many of China's emissions (i.e. developed countries have exported their pollution).
6. China needs its cheap coal for a fast-growing economy to provide new jobs and a rising standard of living.
7. The country's heavy pollution is causing a falling quality of life and health – and rising anger – among ordinary Chinese people.
8. China is now developing renewable energy sources twice as fast as the USA.

B Now write a comment on the statement. Put together several pairs of points for and against it, and end with your own conclusion. Use suitable phrases to connect your arguments.

TEXT B How do we keep the lights on?

BEFORE YOU READ

→ Vorbereitung auf das Lesen, S. 214

Read the headline and look at the diagram. Predict what the article is going to be about.

3/3

Does our energy security lie deep beneath our feet?

Julie Branson reports:

I was on my way by train from London to Brussels – to the latest conference on the environment. Opposite me sat Matt Radley, CEO of Energistic UK, a small company with big plans for fracking in the UK. He had agreed to be interviewed on our journey and I wanted his take on this controversial new UK energy source.

First, I asked him to explain the word 'fracking'. 'It's short for hydraulic fracturing,' he told me.

'It's the breaking of shale rocks deep underground to allow gas and oil to escape.'

I inquired how fracking was actually done. 'We drill down into shale formations, and then we pump down a mixture of water, chemicals and sand at high pressure. This pressure fractures the rock, and the sand keeps the new cracks open. The gas or oil is then brought to the surface and collected there.'

When I asked if this technology was new, he told me that it was new to Britain, but that over two million wells had already been drilled, mainly in the USA, and that this cheap-to-produce oil and gas had greatly reduced prices over there. 'What's more,' he added enthusiastically, 'Fracking will soon make America the world's biggest producer of oil and gas.'

What about the UK? I wanted to know whether Britain, too, had useful amounts of shale gas and oil. 'Yes,' he replied. 'In fact, Britain has huge quantities, and at Energistic UK, it's the gas we want. It's the cleanest of all the fossil fuels, and it's also the easiest to process and get to market. What's more, we really need it. The UK used to get all its gas from the North Sea, but most of that has now gone, and we have to import 70% of our

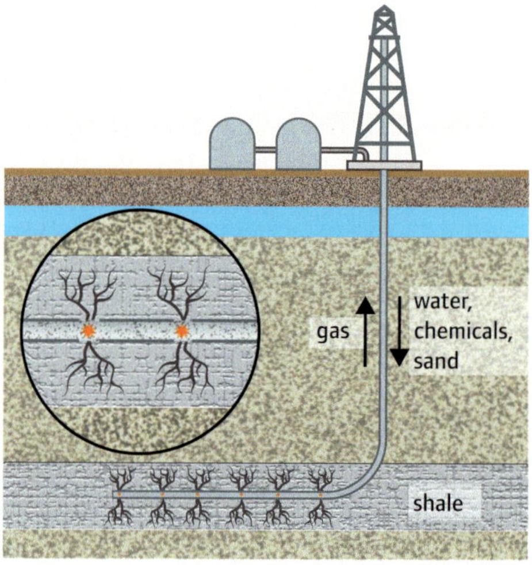

requirement. We need the energy security of our own gas again.'

But I was wondering why fracking was such a good option when shale gas was still a fossil fuel. I asked whether it would be better to leave the gas in the ground and rely on other energy sources instead, particularly renewables. Matt Radley's eyes lit up. 'No,' he said, 'and I'll tell you why.'

'Please do,' I replied.

'Right. Let's look at them one by one.' We had just come out of the tunnel near Sangatte, and he went on, 'There's a big nuclear power station very near here, so let's start with nuclear. France has got lots of nuclear plants, and they may seem to produce cheap power, but they're very expensive to build and very expensive to close down at the end of their working lives. We also have to wonder how safe they and their waste are.'

'What about tidal power, like the barrage at the mouth of the River Rance in Brittany?'

'Well, that was constructed half a century ago, and there aren't many others even now.

It sounds like free energy, but without big government subsidies, they don't get built. Wave power is even more difficult. If you can make and install equipment that will survive the power of the sea and the salt corrosion, fine. But it isn't happening.'

I moved on and asked if geothermal might work better. 'Yes, but it's only cost-effective in places like Iceland, which have hot rock formations close to the surface.'

Then I turned to hydroelectric power, and Matt Radley was quite positive. 'It's cheap and reliable, and it provides about six per cent of world energy,' he said. The problem was that in Britain there was little possibility of much further expansion.

'Well, what about free heat directly from the sun?' I asked.

'Ah, yes, solar energy,' came the reply. 'It's good in sunny regions, and it's getting cheaper, but in Britain we need most power on dark winter evenings and we can't rely on solar power for that!'

Finally, we turned to wind power, and my interviewee became a little annoyed. Onshore wind farms had only been built because of big subsidies, he said, and we were all paying those through higher energy prices. Offshore wind farms were much more efficient, he went on, but they were also much more expensive to build and maintain. Again, more subsidies.

On the high cost of wind and solar power, he pointed out that the world had invested $600 billion in wind and $700 billion in solar during the last ten years – huge amounts – but together these two technologies were producing just two per cent of the world's energy.

'So,' he concluded, 'let's stop picking losers. Let's go for shale gas!'

(770 words)

1 LOOKING AT THE TEXT

→ Rezeption: Leseverstehen, S. 214

A Read the text and put these energy sources in the order that they are discussed.

- **a** fracking
- **b** geothermal
- **c** hydroelectric
- **d** nuclear
- **e** solar
- **f** tidal
- **g** wave
- **h** wind

B Say whether the following are true or false. Correct the false statements.

1. Julie Branson and Matt Radley met on the way to Brussels by chance.
2. Sand is needed during fracking in order to stop the cracks from closing.
3. Matt Radley said that fracking was new to the UK and to the rest of the world, too.
4. Shale gas is less polluting than oil or coal, but it is still not clean.
5. Nuclear power may not be safe, but at least it is cheap.
6. Tidal power is easier to use than wave power, but it still does not make much economic sense.
7. Of all the renewables that Matt Radley discussed, he was most positive about geothermal and hydroelectric.
8. Matt Radley said that offshore wind farms were much more cost-effective than wind farms that were built onshore.

C Say what it means: Explain the underlined phrases in your own words.

1. … and I wanted his take on this controversial source of energy. (line 8)
2. 'It's short for hydraulic fracturing,' he said. (line 11)
3. I wanted to know whether Britain, too, had useful amounts of shale gas … (line 33)
4. 'So,' he concluded, 'let's stop picking losers.' (lines 105–106)
5. 'Let's go for shale gas!' (line 106)

2 WORKING WITH WORDS

A Copy and complete the tables with verbs and nouns from the text.

Verb	Noun
___	production
to opt	___
___	reduction

Verb	Noun
___	explanation
to form	___
___	installation

Verb	Noun
to expand	___
to corrode	___
___	conclusion

B Use words from the same family to complete these sentences. They are all in exercise 2A.

1 Industrial waste greatly ___[1] the numbers of fish in many rivers, but the huge ___[2] in pollution in recent years has brought new life back.

2 **A** We need to ___[1] more of our own food in this country.
B You're right, but the problem is that ___[2] just isn't going up very much.

3 The Government's advisers have finally ___[1] their study of new energy sources, and their ___[2] is that wind, solar and fracking will all be necessary.

4 Auto Shanghai plan to ___[1] production of electric vehicles from 50,000 per year to 200,000, and their ___[2] programme starts next year.

5 **A** Can anyone ___[1] why this machine isn't working?
B The ___[2] is actually quite simple: you haven't turned on the power!

6 ___[1] is the big problem with this bridge. Parts of the structure have been very badly ___[2], and they need to be replaced immediately.

7 The International Panel on Climate Change (IPCC) was ___[1] in 1988, and its ___[2] led to much clearer scientific studies of global climate change.

8 **A** How long will it take to ___[1] all the solar panels on the roof?
B The whole ___[2] process should take just two days.

9 With the new houses being built over there, people will have two heating ___[1]: they can choose gas or they can ___[2] for a mix of gas and solar.

3 GETTING IT RIGHT

→ Indirect speech, S. 266

A Rewrite the questions as indirect questions, using the reporting verbs in brackets. Make any other changes that are necessary.

Matt Radley faced these questions at a press conference as Energistic UK prepared to begin work.

1 *New York Times* journalist: 'Is Energistic an independent company?' (inquire)
A journalist from the New York Times inquired if Energistic was …

2 BBC's Economics Editor: 'How many staff does Energistic have?' (ask)

3 Reporter from Radio 4: 'Have you had any previous practical experience of fracking?' (want to know)

4 Financial journalist from Frankfurt: 'How much has the company had to spend in order to prepare for commercial production? (inquire)

5 Local newspaper editor: 'Why has Energistic chosen to begin operations in our part of the country?' (inquire)

6 Environmental scientist: 'Do you really think you can get planning permission to go ahead?' (query)

B Rewrite the requests, instructions and advice in indirect speech, using the reporting verbs in brackets. Make any other changes that are necessary.

Annie is living away from home for the first time. After just a month, she receives a huge electricity bill and needs help. She calls home.

1 'Could you call Mum or Dad to the phone please?' she said to her brother Ben. (want … to)
She wanted her brother Ben to call Mum or Dad to the phone.
2 'Wait a minute while I get Dad in from the garden,' Ben said. (tell … to)
3 'Dad, could you talk to Annie on the phone?' said Ben. (ask … to)
4 'Dad, can you please, please tell me what to do about my crazy electricity bill for £537?' Annie begged. (beg … to)
5 'You'd better tell the electricity company that there's been a mistake,' her father advised her. (advise … to)
6 'Why don't you come home at the weekend and tell us how you're getting on?' he added. (invite … to)

4 LISTENING

→ Rezeption: Hörverstehen, S. 225

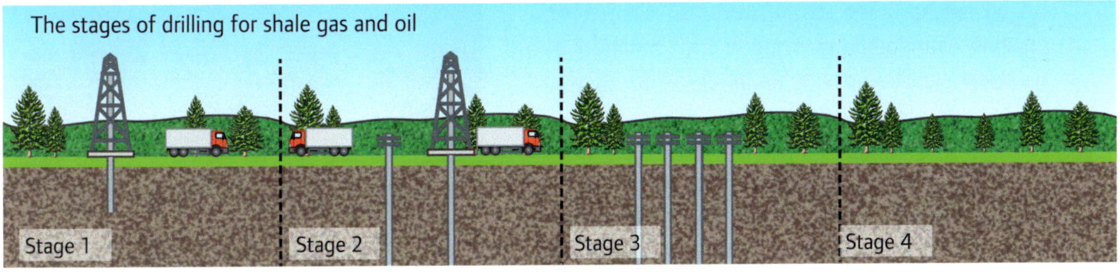

3/4 **A Listen and complete these tasks.**

1 Say what sort of event is starting.
2 Explain what the event is going to be about.
3 Say who has been invited to speak, and what you already know about his ideas.
4 Make notes about the four stages of fracking. Note a) the activity at each stage, and b) the time it takes.

3/5 **B Now listen and note the worries that people have about fracking in the right order. Add details about each point.**

earthquakes ▪ environmental damage ▪ gas ▪ traffic and noise

3/5 **C Listen again and note what Matt Radley says to calm the worries.**

5 DISCUSSION

→ Interaktion: An Diskussionen teilnehmen, S. 246

Work in a small group and discuss the following questions.

1 In principle, do you think fracking should be allowed or not?
2 Imagine you are now members of the local council. Should you accept or reject Matt Radley's particular project. (Consider the pros and cons from a local point of view.)

TEXT C The problem of waste

BEFORE YOU READ

What do you think happens to all the electrical appliances that we throw away?

WHERE DO OUR SCRAP TVS END UP?

3/6

Every year, Germany produces millions of tons of electrical waste. A large proportion of that doesn't end up in recycling but instead simply disappears. The German TV programme Panorama wanted to know where, so some broken TVs were fitted with tracking devices – and the trace led the reporters to Africa.

Electrical waste dump in Agbogbloshie, Ghana

According to UN estimates, Germans produce two million tons of electrical waste every year. In all these TVs, computers, DVD players, stereos, loudspeakers, fridges and smartphones there are poisonous substances like arsenic, lead, cadmium and mercury. Because of this, the German Electrical and Electronic Appliances Law forbids the dumping of toxic waste in developing countries. Despite this, only 700,000 tons of electrical waste finds its way into the nationwide recycling system each year. No one really knows what happens to the remaining 1.3 million tons. It simply disappears – apparently most of it to Africa.

But why? It costs a lot of money to ship old TVs thousands of kilometers over the sea. Who profits from it? That is what the *Panorama* reporters wanted to find out, using an old TV and a tracking device. Together with a battery pack, the device was hidden in the TV's loudspeaker box. It transmitted its exact position at regular intervals and it also reacted to movement. Every time it was unloaded or moved, the transmitter sent an alarm to the reporters' mobile phones.

The TV was picked up by a man advertising free collection of broken electrical appliances on eBay. That was the start of a journey which shone some light on a shadowy but well-organized economic activity that customs and police are largely powerless to prevent.

The first stop on the journey was a dubious scrap dealer in Hamburg, where exporters select their goods. They collect old TVs and fridges in a warehouse, until they have enough to fill a ship with 40-foot containers.

A long wait

After six nights waiting in Ghana, the reporters finally received a signal early in the morning. The TV had moved. No longer at the harbour, it was now in Accra, Ghana's capital, on the corner of Abeka Road and George W. Bush Highway.

The signal was strong because the TV had been unloaded and was now out in the open. When they arrived at the street corner, hundreds of TVs were piled up in the mud. A policeman sat under an umbrella and watched the clearance sale. The reporters asked where the goods came from. 'England.' Wrong!

A few metres farther on, eight silver Sony TVs were sitting next to the wall of a house. They found the mark they had made on the back of one of them. They shook it to activate the movement sensor and a message soon appeared on their phone, showing that the appliance had been moved. They returned the

TV and replaced it: they wanted to find out how its journey would continue.

The end of the journey

Journey's end was Agbogbloshie in Ghana, the biggest electrical waste dump in Africa and one of the ten most toxic places in the world.

About 500 containers of electrical appliances reach Ghana every month. Around Christmas, when Europeans replace old appliances with new ones, up to 1,000 arrive. Not all the electrical waste stays in Ghana: much is transported across West Africa, to Burkina Faso, Niger, Mali or Benin. But Ghana is the hub, and key to profit there is Agbogbloshie.

Forwarding agencies, shipping and transport companies all make money from the waste, as do middlemen and repair shops in Accra. At the very bottom of the value chain are the boys of Agbogbloshie. They break TVs apart with hammers, and they set fire to the insulating foam in order to separate the cable coating from the copper. For this, they get just 50 cents per TV.

Just 15 years ago this district of Accra was still a breeding ground for European migratory birds, but today it is the graveyard of our rubbish. It is also a place that poisons the many children and young people who work there. They are the ones who would have gutted the reporters' TV by hand if they had not finally found it at a dealer and bought it back for 100 euros. Worthless to them, the TV made money for a total of 11 people or companies along its 77-day journey to the scrapyard.

(721 words)

1 LOOKING AT THE TEXT

→ Rezeption: Leseverstehen, S. 214

A Read the text and complete the following tasks.

1 Explain the mystery of Germany's electrical waste.
2 Outline the method that the reporters used to discover the truth.
3 Contrast the purpose of German law and the actual situation in Agbogbloshie.
4 Say what the writer means by 'Ghana is the hub' (lines 76–77).
5 Name the 'people or companies along the journey' (lines 96–97) that the article mentions.

B Think of the last electrical appliance that your family threw away. Describe how you got rid of it. Do you think it went (or did not go) into the national recycling system?

2 MEDIATION

→ Schriftliche Mediation, S. 240

Sie bekommen folgende E-Mail von Ihrer Tante:

Antworten Sie auf die E-Mail Ihrer Tante. Erklären Sie ihr, was möglicherweise mit dem alten Kühlschrank passieren könnte, wenn er nicht ordentlich entsorgt wird.

… Zu Weihnachten gönnen wir uns einen fantastischen amerikanischen Kühlschrank mit allem Drum und Dran. Wir schmeißen den alten sofort weg … er wird morgen abgeholt … ;-)

3 WRITING

→ Produktion: Eine Stellungnahme schreiben, S. 234

Write a comment on the following statement.

'I don't understand that German law against sending electrical waste here. All kinds of people make money out of it – even those kids at Agbogloshie. Without the scrap TVs, they wouldn't have anything.'

Electrical waste trader in Accra, Ghana

Personal air quality monitors

Air pollution is a growing problem around the world and can have a serious effect on our health. Air quality monitoring is done by a network of government stations, but wouldn't it be better to have a personal air quality monitor?

4/11

An Air Quality Monitor You Take with You

A startup is building a wearable air quality monitor using a sensing technology that can cheaply detect the presence of chemicals around you in real time. By reporting the information its sensors gather to an app on your smartphone, the technology could help people with respiratory conditions and those who live in highly polluted areas keep tabs on exposure.

Berkeley, California-based ChemiSense also plans to crowdsource data from users to show places around town where certain compounds are identified.

Initially, the company plans to sell a $150 wristband geared toward kids with asthma – of which there are nearly 7 million in the US, according to data from the Centers for Disease Control and Prevention – to help them identify places and pollutants that tend to provoke attacks, and track their exposure to air pollution over time. The company hopes people with other respiratory conditions, and those who are just concerned about air pollution, will be interested, too.

In the US, air quality is monitored at thousands of stations across the country; maps and forecasts can be viewed online. But these monitors offer accurate readings only in their location.

ChemiSense has not yet made its initial product, but it expects it will be a wristband using polymers treated with charged nanoparticles of carbon such that the polymers swell in the presence of certain chemical vapours, changing the resistance of a circuit.

The technology is currently not nearly as sensitive as ChemiSense would like it to be – the company is currently detecting tens of parts per million for a number of compounds, though it's working toward detecting hundreds of parts per billion. A municipal air quality monitoring station, by comparison, would be able to detect between ten and one parts per billion. (290 words)

Abridged from: *www.technologyreview.com*

1 LOOKING AT THE TEXT

→ Umgang mit Operatoren, S. 232

Read the text and complete the following tasks.

1 Outline how the ChemiSense monitor will work.
2 State who will use the monitor and explain how they will benefit.
3 Compare the ChemiSense monitor with municipal monitoring stations.

2 RESEARCH

The class divides into five groups. Each group researches one of the pollutants shown in the list and explains where it comes from and what problems it causes. Report back to the class with what you found out.

15 Feeding the world

EXAM PREPARATION

FOCUS

One thing after another

A Work with a partner. Take turns to describe and analyse the cartoons.

> cactus ▪ carbon emissions ▪ climate change ▪ deliver babies ▪ drought ▪ environmental pollution ▪ global warming ▪ greenhouse gases ▪ natural resources ▪ over-exploitation of resources ▪ rising population ▪ stork

B Now find links from cartoon to cartoon to explain the title 'One thing after another'.

C Discuss these questions with a partner.

1 Do you think the 'resources' stork has got weaker or stronger since you were born? Think of cases of drought and famine that have been in the news.

2 Do you think these problems are only found in developing countries – or are people ever short of food and other basics in rich countries such as Germany?

15 Feeding the world

TEXT A How can we feed so many?

BEFORE YOU READ

→ Scannen nach Einzelinformationen im Text, S. 221

Scan the text for the following information:

- **a** the area equivalent to the worldwide land use for crops
- **b** the area equivalent to the worldwide land use for pastureland
- **c** the percentage of crops that are used to feed animals

THE PLANET REPORT September 20..

3/7

A PLAN TO FEED THE PLANET

The world has a problem – people. The human population passed 7 billion in 2012 and will probably hit 9.5 billion by 2050. That is a 35% increase in less than 40 years.

Does this mean a 35% increase in crop production, too? No, it actually means a 100% increase, from 9.5 billion tons to 19 billion, and the reason is this: as people in developing countries like India and China get a little more money, they always demand a richer diet with much more meat. Providing this requires far more crop production just to feed animals.

But nearly a billion people are already hungry, so we cannot possibly feed billions more, can we? Well, yes we can, and we can do it without taking more from Nature than we already have. To succeed, though, we must do four vital things.

1 Stop clearing more land for farming.
Growing more food has always meant taking more land from its natural state, including whole regions such as the North American prairies and the huge forests of Europe, each with its ancient ecosystem. Today, we use a land area the size of South America to grow crops and another the size of Africa for animal pastureland. Over half the world's ice-free land has been turned to human uses, and by far the greatest of these uses is agriculture.

We are destroying forests along with many plant and animal species, and while doing this, we are creating an even greater crisis. We are reducing Earth's ability to store carbon emissions from human activities – emissions that are pushing the planet towards disastrous climate change.

It is time to stop driving down this road to catastrophe.

The World's Total Land Area: 57.7 million square miles, of which:			
Ice-covered: 7.4m sq miles (12.8%)	Other undeveloped: 23.4m sq miles (40.6%)	Farmland: 19.4m sq miles (33.6%)	Other human uses: 7.5m sq miles (13.0%)

Greenland & Antarctic ice sheets	mountains, forest, desert, tundra	pastureland, cropland	cities, infrastructure e.g. roads & railways, planted forests, etc.

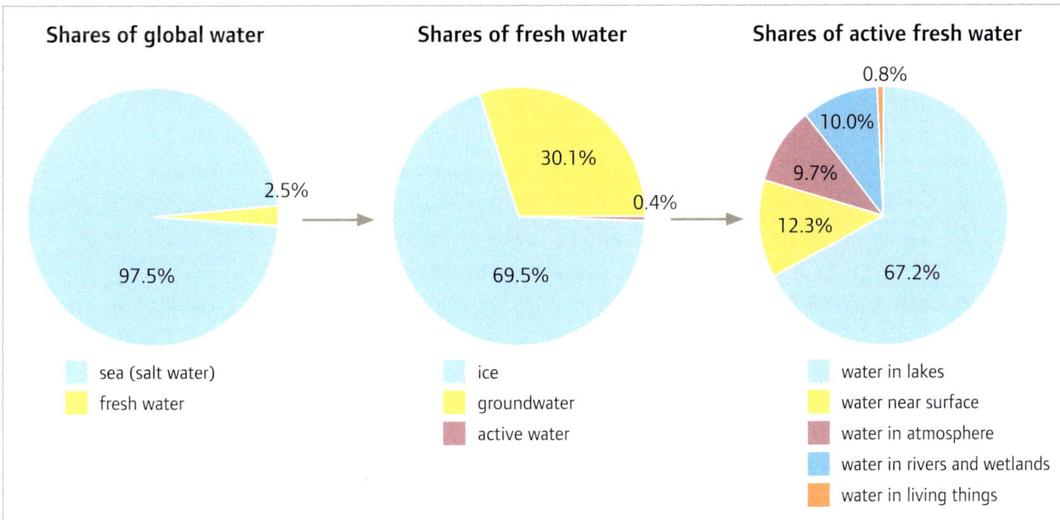

2 Produce more efficiently.

A typical American farmer produces three tons of crops per acre, whereas a farmer in sub-Saharan Africa may only produce half a ton. With better crop varieties and better techniques, that difference can be greatly reduced. Meanwhile, western agriculture can continue to become more efficient in other ways. Farm chemicals are expensive and polluting, so using less of them is very important. GPS and computer technology now help farmers decide what, when and where fertilizer is needed. This saves money and reduces pollution of precious water resources.

People have not always understood that water is so precious. Very little of our Blue Planet's water is fresh water that we can easily use, and after polluting and wasting much of it, we now find that clean supplies are declining. Farming takes 70% of all human water use and is at the centre of this crisis. Many farmers who draw their water from underground now have to go ever deeper to reach it.

Again, science is helping. New crop varieties that need less water are appearing. Better irrigation and new kinds of farming are also helping to reduce waste, making sure that the water we use is used well.

3 Change what we eat.

Feeding 9.5 billion people would be much easier if more crops actually fed people. In fact, just 55% of crop production is used that way, while a massive 36% feeds animals – mainly for meat production. (The rest is used in biofuel and other industrial production.)

Producing meat is not an efficient process: many kilos of grain are needed for every kilo of meat produced. Moreover, one kilo of grain takes 1,500 litres of water, but to produce one kilo of beef it takes 15,000.

Clearly, meat consumption must be reduced, starting perhaps with the rich, developed world. For many people in these countries, consuming less meat and more fruit and vegetables would also be a big step towards better health.

4 Cut waste.

Up to half of all food production is lost or wasted. In developed countries, a lot is thrown away because too much is prepared or because it has passed its use-by date. In poor countries, food is often wasted because it is stored badly or because transport to market takes too long. Just solving these problems alone would allow the planet to feed itself.

So yes, we can get through the coming food crisis, but only if we change the ways we produce, consume and think about food. Some changes will be huge and will need the cooperation of millions. Others will be small and individual – like the choices we make when doing the family food shopping at the supermarket. (736 words)

1 LOOKING AT THE TEXT

→ Umgang mit Operatoren, S. 232

A Read the text on pages 148–149 carefully and complete these tasks.

1 Explain why a population 35% larger will require a 100% increase in food production.
2 Say why the destruction of forest by humans is destructive for humans.
3 Explain why it is very important to use less water and to protect its quality.
4 Contrast the ways that science can help farmers in developing and in developed countries.
5 Say why it would be a) easier and b) better to start reducing meat consumption in developed countries instead of developing countries.
6 Contrast the ways in which food is often wasted in developed and in developing countries.

B Say what it means: Explain the underlined words and phrases in your own words.

1 … will probably hit 9.5 billion … (line 3)
2 We are destroying forests along with many plant and animal species, … (line 29)
3 … a farmer in sub-Saharan Africa … (line 39)
4 … now have to go ever deeper to reach it. (lines 57–58)
5 New crop varieties … are appearing. (line 60)
6 … because it has passed its use-by date. (line 85)
7 … the coming food crisis. (line 90)

2 WORKING WITH WORDS

Match meanings a–t to abbreviations and symbols 1–20.

1 am	5 m	9 wk	13 pw	17 =
2 e.g.	6 sq (miles)	10 yr	14 incl	18 +
3 etc.	7 approx	11 pa	15 &	19 –
4 i.e.	8 hr	12 pm	16 %	20 ×

a and
b and so on
c approximately
d is, equals
e any time from midnight to midday
f any time from midday to midnight; per month
g hour
h in other words
i including
j metre; million
k minus
l per week
m per annum, per year
n per cent
o plus; over
p square (miles)
q such as, for example
r times, multiplied by
s week
t year

Expand these notes.

1
Job title: Junior Manager
Terms & conditions: Work 40 hrs pw;
Starting: 9.00 am & finishing 5.00 pm;
3 wks paid holiday pa; salary
£1,750.00 pm = £21,000.00 pa

Terms and conditions for the job of Junior Manager are as follows. You will work …

2
New Dawn Garment's new factory
8,300sq m & employs 650 workers.
Produces 140,000+ garments pw =
approx 7.3m garments pa, incl e.g.
shirts, jeans, dresses, jackets, etc.

New Dawn Garment's new factory has an area of … It produces …

3 ANALYSING CHARTS

→ Produktion: Schaubilder beschreiben und analysieren, S. 238

Analyse the graphics in the text, interpreting their abbreviations and symbols to do so.

1 Analyse the diagram on page 148 with statements like this.
Ice-covered land makes up 7.4 million square miles, or 12.8 percent of the world's total land area, and it consists largely of the … . Other undeveloped land makes up …

2 Analyse the pie charts on page 149 with statements like this.
Of all the water in the world, 97.5 percent is salt water, and just … . Of all the freshwater in the world, …

4 GETTING IT RIGHT

→ Participles, S. 268

Join the pairs of sentences. Turn the first sentence into a participle clause using the word in brackets.

1 Sue Dryden went through a painful divorce three years ago. She moved to Amarillo, Texas with her young son Craig. (after)
After going through a painful divorce three years ago, Sue Dryden moved to Amarillo, Texas with her young son Craig.
2 They got there. She quickly had to get a job because her ex-husband was sending very little money. (after)
3 Sue lost her job a year ago. She and Craig had lived well enough on her salary of $2,200 per month. (before)
4 She lost that job. She has only been able to find part-time work at $7.75 per hour. (since)
5 She goes food shopping. She always tries to work out how much she can spend and what she can buy with that. (before)
6 She pays her rent and utility bills. She often does not have enough left to buy everything they need. (after)
7 She fell on such hard times. She has often gone to the local church food pantry for help. (since)
8 She collects her food parcel there. She is sometimes embarrassed to see volunteer workers that she knows from her old workplace. (while)

5 WRITING

→ Produktion: Eine Stellungnahme schreiben, S. 234

Write a comment on the following statement.

'THERE IS PLENTY OF FOOD TO FEED THE WORLD. ALL WE HAVE TO DO IS TO STOP WASTING IT, THEN NOBODY WILL GO HUNGRY ANY MORE.'

Useful phrases: partly agreeing with sb/sth

- While I agree that … , I do not accept that …
- I take the point that … . However, I question whether …
- For one thing, … . For another, …
- Then again, …

TEXT B Big problems – new solutions

BEFORE YOU READ

→ Scannen nach Einzelinformationen im Text, S. 221

Scan the text and say which is the main topic of the interview.

a the pros and cons of GM food
b how farmers can make more profit
c ways of providing more food for humans

3/8

The World This Week reporter Mark Moro is talking to scientist Dr Tanya Tate, an expert from the United Nations Development Programme.

Mark Moro: The big question facing us in the future is how is the planet going to feed itself? How can science help? First of all, let's talk about genetically modified food, or GM for short. As we all know, it's supported by some, but also feared by many. Dr Tate, could you tell us what GM is exactly?

Tanya Tate: To explain that, we need to look first at natural selection. Plant and animal species have always adapted to fit their particular environment on the planet. Members of a species with the best adaptations survive and pass their successful genes to the next generation. Others that are not so well adapted don't reproduce so successfully, and sooner or later, they become extinct.

Mark Moro: Haven't farmers used this natural process to breed better crops and better livestock since pre-historic times?

Tanya Tate: Yes, they take over the selection process in order to make more profit. This is selective breeding, and it works like this. They decide what physical features to aim at – more wool on a sheep, for example, or better resistance to disease. They then choose animals or plants to breed from – ones that are already nearer that ideal than others. After repeating the process for several generations, they then have an improved species.

Mark Moro: Improved because the herd or the crop is more productive and is therefore more valuable.

Tanya Tate: Right, and coming back to GM, we can see that this modern technology pushes the idea of species improvement much further. We can now modify the genetic code of a plant seed or an animal embryo by adding genes taken from other species. For example, adding a gene from a desert plant species can help a vegetable crop survive with much less water.

Mark Moro: This is species improvement by laboratory design, isn't it?

Tanya Tate: That's right.

Mark Moro: It sounds very useful.

Tanya Tate: It is, and this sort of GM technology will certainly help in parts of the world now suffering drier conditions – sub-Saharan Africa, for example.

Mark Moro: So what's the problem with GM food?

Tanya Tate: Well, let's think about a gene added to a crop that makes it resistant to herbicide – the sprays used to kill weeds. The weeds die, and the crop gets all the water and fertilizer provided by the farmer.

Mark Moro: So far, so good. That should produce the best crop possible.

Tanya Tate: But what if some of the pollen produced by the crop reaches weeds growing nearby? What if it fertilizes those weeds? In no time, we could have weeds that are resistant to herbicide. We could soon find ourselves with weeds resistant to all known chemical controls – weeds that might take over the world!

Mark Moro: That would be a big downside! So, are there other new ways to help produce the food we need?

Tanya Tate: Yes, in particular there's an exciting technology called hydroponics.

Mark Moro: 'Hydro'? That means it is connected with water?

Tanya Tate: Yes, hydroponic farming doesn't use soil. Instead, it uses water containing the exact amount of nutrients required. This way, roots don't have to grow through thick soil, sometimes finding the necessary nutrients but often not. Instead, the nutrients are absorbed easily by the plant roots as they grow down into the flow of water. That's much more efficient, and crops grow very fast. What's more, it's a closed system, so the same water is used again and again, and there's no pollution of rivers and groundwater.

Mark Moro: Wow! Is this something very new?

Tanya Tate: No, it was first used in the 1930s. American flights to Hawaii landed for fuel on a piece of rock called Wake Island. Thanks to hydroponics they also took off again with fresh salad and vegetables for the passengers. Today, it's used a lot in Iceland, another place with very little soil, and at the Amundsen Scott South Pole Station, a place with no soil at all, of course!

Mark Moro: Fine, but is it being used more widely than that?

Tanya Tate: Yes, it's taking off in many parts of the world. Farmers can grow up to 20 high-quality crops a year, causing very little waste

A simple hydroponics system

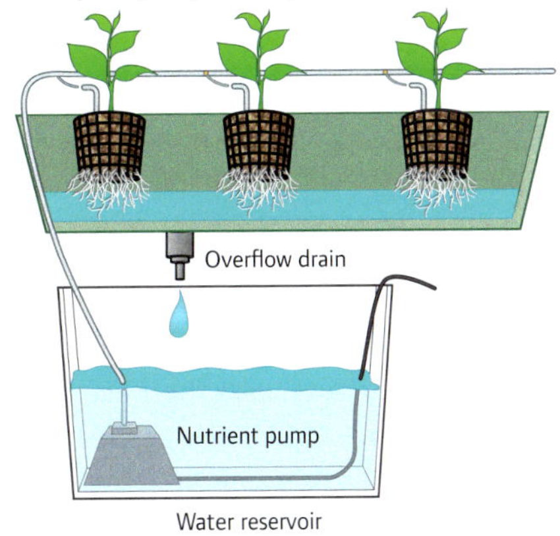

and pollution and making very good money. It takes up much less space than ordinary farming, too.

Mark Moro: What's the next step?

Tanya Tate: Vertical farms. People are now creating city-centre farms in tall buildings to grow food for the people right where the people are. That means another big saving: food miles. The environmental cost of taking food many miles from farm to supermarket almost disappears! (795 words)

1 LOOKING AT THE TEXT

→ Rezeption: Leseverstehen, S. 214

A Read the text and make notes. Use your notes to do these tasks.

1 Outline briefly the three methods of improving farm productivity that the speakers discuss.
2 Contrast the effects of natural selection and selective breeding.
3 Explain why disease resistance can be just as important for productivity as sheep that produce more wool.
4 Explain the sort of benefit GM offers, and the sort of danger that it creates.
5 List the environmental advantages of hydroponics.
6 List the economic advantages of hydroponics.

B Say what it means: Explain the underlined words and phrases in your own words.

1 The big question facing us … (line 5)
2 … since pre-historic times? (line 23)
3 So far, so good. (line 61)
4 But what if some of the pollen produced by the crop reaches weeds growing nearby? (line 63)
5 In no time, we could have weeds … (line 66)
6 That would be a big downside! (line 71)

2 WORKING WITH WORDS

→ Rezeption: Ein Wörterbuch benutzen, S. 217

take [Phrasal verbs]

take in **1** understand clearly the meaning or importance of something **2** trick someone into believing something that is not true **take off** **1** remove something, especially clothes **2** leave the ground and start flying **3** suddenly start to be popular or successful **take on** **1** accept a job or responsibility **2** give a job to someone **3** fight or compete against someone or something **take over** **1** start doing something that someone else was doing **2** take control of something **take up** **1** fill an amount of space or time **2** start doing a particular job or activity

Read the sentences with their examples of phrasal verbs formed from *take*. Then check the dictionary entry above and decide which meaning matches each example.

1 We could soon find ourselves with weeds that might **take over** the world! *meaning 2*
2 Thanks to hydroponics planes **took off** again with fresh salad vegetables.
3 Hydroponics is **taking off** in many parts of the world.
4 Hydroponics **takes up** much less space than ordinary farming.

Read these sentences to decide which phrasal verb and which meaning each requires.

1 I had to read her letter three times before I could ___ the awful truth. *take in – meaning 1*
2 You'd better ___ that wet jacket and warm yourself by the fire.
3 The company is moving to Stuttgart, and we're ___ 20 new staff there.
4 Sally's ___ too much, and she's making herself ill with all the stress.
5 Silke pretends that she's happy and she ___ most people, but I know that she's really very sad.
6 I've ___ the guitar recently, and I'm enjoying it a lot.
7 Would you mind ___ the cooking while I get a few things from the shop?
8 Next Saturday, our team are ___ the champions, and I really hope we'll win!

3 GETTING IT RIGHT

→ Participles, S. 268

Change the relative clauses (starting with *who, which, that*) to *-ing* or *-ed* clauses.

Fish are an important source of food which has been hunted for thousands of years and which still provides millions of people with much of their protein. However, the modern techniques which have been developed to make fishing more efficient are too successful. In many parts of the world, the huge numbers that are being caught leave too few fish to maintain stocks, and so wild fish populations are crashing.
One answer to the fish stock crisis which is developing worldwide is to reduce the amount of fishing, and this is something that is happening today in the North Sea, for example.
Another answer is fish farming, which has now developed along coasts and in rivers and lakes all over the world. However, such fish farms often have severe problems which include pollution and disease. Someone who is taking a different approach is Brian O'Hanlon with his huge diamond-shaped fish cages that have been built eight miles off the coast of Panama and which contain up to a million fish. Far out at sea, these cages, which are constantly washed by the open sea, remain unpolluted and disease-free.

Fish are an important source of food hunted for thousands of years and still providing ...

4 LISTENING

→ Rezeption: Hörverstehen, S. 225

You are going to hear Tanya Tate talking about a commercial hydroponics system.

Lettuce is grown in a hydroponic culture in a dome greenhouse in Japan in July 2012.

A worker harvests fresh produce from a tower at Sky Greens vertical farm in Singapore in July 2014.

3/9

A Copy these notes, then listen and complete them. Which system is Tanya Tate describing?

Name of system: ▬
Country designed: ▬
Used to grow: ▬
Basic shape: ▬
Movement (horizontal/vertical): ▬
Speed of turn: ▬
Size: ▬
Running cost per frame: ▬

3/10

B Now listen to the second part of Tanya's talk and make notes. Then answer these questions.

1 What two advantages does this system have over traditional farming?
2 Why will food production need to be close to cities in the future?
3 What makes food farming in Singapore difficult?
4 Why is the government of Singapore unhappy about this situation?
5 What does the government want to do to change this?

5 PROJECT

Work in small groups and research hydroponics farming systems online. Choose one of the commercial systems currently in operation and present it to the class.

6 WRITING

→ Produktion: Schreiben, S. 228

PROPOSALS SOUGHT FOR CITY POWER STATION REDEVELOPMENT

After more than 80 years of service, the Old City Power Station has closed. With its splendid, high turbine hall and all-glass roof, it is a Grade 1 industrial building that cannot simply be pulled down. By law, it must be redeveloped in some way that will be useful to the city community. The Redevelopment Committee have already received several proposals but would welcome more.

You see this article in a local paper in the UK and think the power station could be redeveloped as a hydroponics farm. Write a letter to the chairperson of the Redevelopment Committee.

- Describe the basic concept of hydroponics and its advantages.
- Explain the particular advantages of redeveloping the power station as a hydroponics farm.
- Support your argument with an example of a successful project of the same sort.

TEXT C A case study

BEFORE YOU READ

What are the alternatives to farming on an industrial scale in Germany?

3/11

IS GM THE BEST WAY FORWARD FOR AFRICA?

Millions of poor African farmers depend on one or two crops such as cassava both to sell and to feed their families. If disease strikes, they face disaster. Today, high-tech GM technology is beginning to offer the possibility of new versions of such crops modified to resist pests, but so far only four African countries – Egypt, Sudan, South Africa and Burkina Faso – have allowed the commercial planting of GM crops. Fear is one reason for this, but more importantly the basic fact is that most African farmers need a simpler, cheaper way forward.

In Tanzania there are no GM crops yet. But some farmers are learning that a simple low-tech solution – planting a diversity of crops – is one of the best ways to deter pests. Tanzania now has the fourth largest number of certified organic farmers in the world. Part of the credit belongs to a young woman named Janet Maro.

Maro grew up on a farm near Kilimanjaro, the fifth of eight children. In 2009, while still an undergraduate at the Sokoine University of Agriculture in Morogoro, she helped to start a non-profit organization called Sustainable Agriculture Tanzania (SAT). Since then she and her small staff have been training local farmers in organic practices. [...]

Morogoro lies about a hundred miles west of Dar es Salaam, at the base of the Uluguru Mountains, and Maro takes me into the mountains to visit three of the first certified organic farms in Tanzania. We lurch up a steep, rutted road in a pickup. Greened by rains drifting in from the Indian Ocean, the slopes remain heavily forested. But increasingly, they've been cleared for farming by the Luguru people. [...]

She stops at a one-room brick house with partially plastered walls and a corrugated metal roof. Habija Kibwana, a tall woman in a short-sleeved white blouse and wraparound skirt, invites us and two neighbors to sit on her porch. [...]

Mixed rows of crops: corn and fruit trees

Kibwana and her neighbors raise a variety of crops: bananas, avocados, and passion fruit are in season now. Soon they'll be planting carrots, spinach and other leafy vegetables, all for local consumption. The mix provides a backup in case one crop fails; it also helps cut down on pests.

The farmers here are learning to plant strategically, setting out rows of a wild sunflower that whiteflies prefer, to draw the pests away from the cassavas. The use of compost instead of fertilizers has improved the soil so much that one of the farmers [...] has doubled his spinach production. Runoff from his fields no longer contaminates streams that supply Morogoro's water.

Perhaps the most life-altering result of organic farming has been the liberation from debt. Even with government subsidies, it costs 500,000 Tanzanian shillings, more than $300, to buy enough fertilizer and pesticide to treat a single acre – a crippling expense in a country where the annual per capita income is less than $1,600. 'Before, when we had to buy fertilizer, we had no money left over to send our children to school,' says Kibwana. Her oldest daughter has now finished high school. And the farms are more productive too. 'Most of the food in our markets is from small farmers,' says Maro. 'They feed our nation.'

When I ask Maro if genetically modified seeds might also help those farmers, she's skeptical. 'It's not realistic,' she says. How could they afford the seeds when they can't even afford fertilizer? How likely is it, she asks, in a country where few farmers ever see a government agricultural adviser, or are even aware of the diseases threatening their crops, that they'll get the support they need to grow GM crops properly?

From Kibwana's porch we have sweeping views of richly cultivated terraced slopes – but also of slopes scarred by the brown, eroded fields of non-organic farmers, most of whom don't build terraces to retain their precious soil. Kibwana says her own success has attracted the attention of her neighbors. Organic farming is spreading here. (659 words)

From: *National Geographic*, October 2014

1 LOOKING AT THE TEXT

→ Rezeption: Leseverstehen, S. 214

A Read the text and complete these tasks.

1. List the African states which allow commercial GM.
2. State the problems with GM for most Africans.
3. List the special features of organic farming in Tanzania.
4. Explain the general benefits of organic farming.
5. Point out a particular benefit to the Kibwana family.
6. Contrast the appearance of local organic & non-organic farms.

B Say what it means: Explain the underlined words and phrases in your own words.

1. … a simple low-tech solution … (lines 14–15)
2. … she helped to start a non-profit organization … (line 24)
3. … bananas, avocados, and passion fruit are in season now. (line 44)
4. … the food in our markets is from small farmers, … (line 70)
5. … they'll get the support they need to grow GM crops properly? (line 80)

2 MEDIATION

→ Schriftliche Mediation, S. 240

In regelmäßigen Abständen veröffentlicht Ihre Schulzeitschrift Beiträge von Schülern und Schülerinnen unter der Rubrik „Mensch und Umwelt". Nach der Lektüre des Textes „Is GM the best way forward for Africa?" möchten Sie die Biolandwirtschaft in Afrika einem breiterem Publikum in Deutschland vorstellen.

Schreiben Sie einen Artikel für die Schulzeitschrift, in dem Sie die Vorteile des *organic farming* für Afrika erklären.

3 WRITING

→ Produktion: Eine Stellungnahme schreiben, S. 234

Write a comment on the following statement.

'Maybe organic farming is right for Tanzania, but I don't see the point here in Germany. Organic produce is much too expensive for most people to buy here, and anyway I don't think it tastes any better than ordinary food.'

Drones in agriculture

The word "drone" conjures up two contrasting images: sinister remote-controlled weapons and harmless radio-controlled toys. However, there are also sophisticated civilian drones which play useful roles in fields such as emergency response, civil engineering and agriculture.

1 LISTENING

→ Rezeption: Hörverstehen, S. 225

4/12

A reporter is interviewing farmer Brenton Peake about the drone he uses to monitor his crops. Copy the grid into your exercise book, then listen to the recording and complete the grid.

Crop health factors	1	
	2	
	3	
Reasons to monitor crops	1	
	2	
Difficulties of monitoring	1	
	2	
Advantage of drones	1	
	2	
	3	
Drone dimensions		
Flight computer functions		
How the camera is used		
Information from images	1	
	2	
	3	
	4	

2 MIND MAP

Work with a partner. What other industries can drones be used in? What can they do? Copy the mind map and complete it with your own ideas.

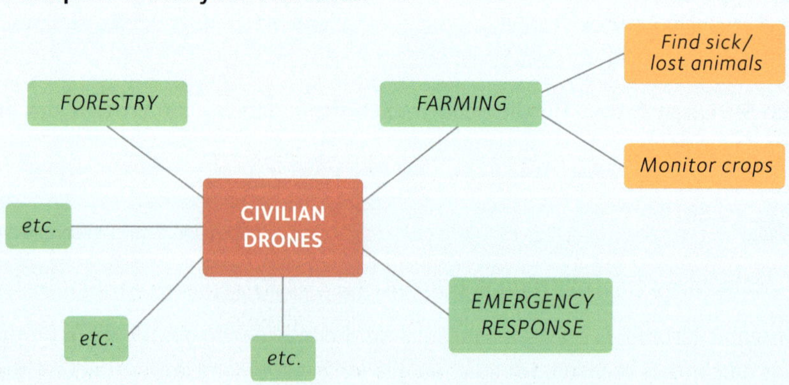

16 Technology

EXAM PREPARATION

FOCUS

a

b

c

d
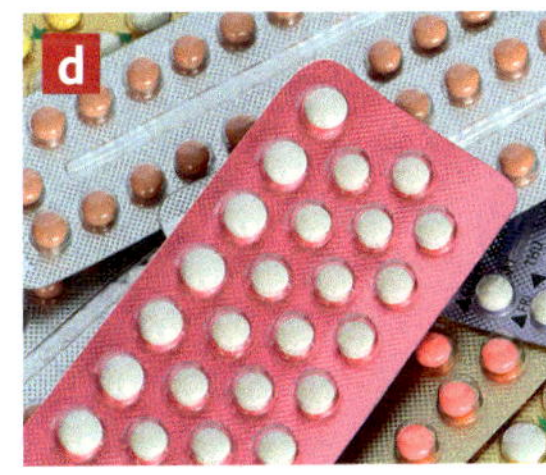

e

f

g

h

i
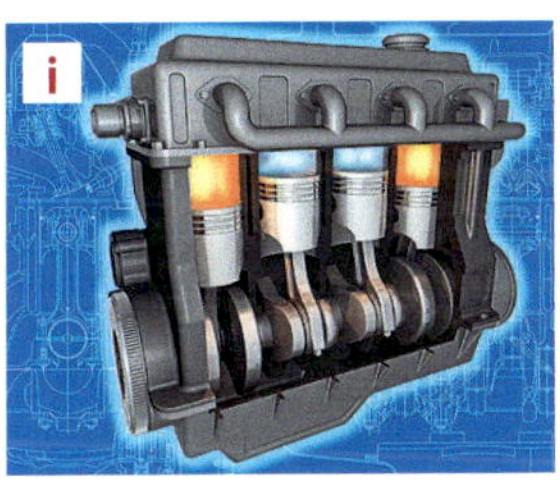

j

k

l

A **Match these important, life-changing inventions to the pictures (a–l) above.**

the compass ▪ contraceptives ▪ the internal combustion engine ▪ the Internet ▪ the light bulb ▪ the nail ▪ penicillin ▪ the printing press ▪ refrigeration ▪ the telephone ▪ the washing machine ▪ the wheel

B **Copy and expand the table. Consider the 12 inventions above. List them all in column 1 in your personal order of importance. (If you think something else is more important, you can replace one item.)**

The world's most important inventions

	Personal choice	Group choice	Class choice
1			

C **Work in a small group. Discuss everyone's choices and decide as a group on the most important invention of all. Note this choice in your table.**

D **Report your group choice back to the class for further discussion. Have a class vote on the final group choices and list the top three inventions in the table.**

TEXT A The spread of digital communication

BEFORE YOU READ

A **Say what you mainly use your mobile phone to do.**

B **Say how else people can use a modern smartphone.**

3/12

AFRICA'S DIGITAL REVOLUTION

[…] When Wesley Kirinya buys a latte, he pays his bill of 100 Kenyan shillings (€0.85 or $1.16) by text message. First he types in the café's telephone number and enters a PIN. Then he hits 'send' and the transaction is complete.

This payment system is known as M-Pesa. The 'M' stands for 'mobile' and 'pesa' means 'money' in the local language of Swahili. M-Pesa turns a mobile phone into a bank account, credit card and wallet all in one. Invented in Kenya, the system is now used in nearly all developing nations. These days, a third of Kenya's economy is conducted via M-Pesa – at a time when, in Europe, a few major cities are just starting to experiment with the possibility of paying for parking via mobile phone. […]

Sub-Saharan Africa is the world's fastest-growing market for mobile phones, tablets and laptops. There are more SIM cards in use here than in North America. And with nearly half the continent's population of 900 million people under the age of 15, experts estimate there will be over 1 billion additional mobile phone users here by 2050.

Mobile Phones Where Governments Fail

In less than 10 years, mobile phones and the Internet have changed many Africans' daily lives more dramatically than anything else since African nations won their independence from former colonial powers. […]

Where there are mobile phones there is less need to lay cables for conventional landline telephones. There is also less need to build highways, clinics and schools, because mobile phones are all these things in one – as well as bank, weather station, doctor's office, atlas, compass, textbook, radio and TV station.

Africans can now send money across the jungle or savannah with the click of a button, merchants can compare prices, and farmers can access weather data relevant to their harvests or get advice from veterinarians. Bloggers and social media users also function as a substitute for a free press, keeping watch over those in power. […]

Cutting-Edge African Apps

African IT developers have to be especially creative given the continent's limitations. The greatest obstacle to their work is the fact that so far only a small proportion of the mobile phones used in Africa are Internet-enabled. But African programmers have found ways to coax more functions out of basic mobile phones. Special programs, for example, can turn text messages into emails, allowing people to send text messages to government authorities, universities or banks which are then processed and continue their trajectory online. […]

A successful app from Africa that works via text message basis is iCow. […] Small farmers throughout the country can register for the program and then enter their animals' age, breed, weight, sex and date of last calving, and iCow automatically sends them advice developed by veterinarians concerning feed, illnesses and fertility cycles. To make it possible for illiterate farmers to use the program as well, it uses voice messages rather than text. […]

The Internet helps sick people, too. Hardly any doctors in Africa practise entirely offline these days, even in the most remote locations. Practices in small villages can send their lab results to university clinics, and receive diagnoses and treatment suggestions in return. Such reporting systems also make it possible to identify the start and spread of epidemics early on.

Africa's Digital Visionary

'It's now easier, technically speaking, to supply a village with Internet access than with clean water,' says Mo Ibrahim, a man who has done more than almost any other person for Africa's digital revolution. Time magazine has named the Sudanese businessman one of the most influential people of our time. [...]

Mo Ibrahim announces that the Mo Ibrahim Foundation is awarding Nobel Peace Prize winner Desmond Tutu a $1 million grant in 2012.

Ibrahim founded his company Celtel, one of the first mobile phone providers in Africa, in 1998. Despite having had a successful career as an engineer at British Telecom and being the founder of an IT consulting firm in London, Ibrahim wasn't satisfied. 'I never entirely became a European.' He says. 'Africa is simply part of me.'

In the years that followed, Celtel expanded into 13 countries, with 24 million people using the company's network, and 5,000 employees. When Ibrahim sold Celtel in 2005, he received $3.4 billion. [...]

Ibrahim also created a foundation which releases an annual ranking of good and bad governance among African nations. The foundation also presents the annual Ibrahim Prize for Achievement in African Leadership, which awards $5 million to a commendable African politician. This year, though, for the third year in a row, the jury found no one it considered worthy of receiving the prize.

Does that mean things in Africa are not, in fact, getting better? Ibrahim shakes his head and says he does believe the continent is developing – primarily thanks to mobile phones and the Internet. 'The mobile phone is an important tool of civil society,' he says. 'If a border customs officer extorts money from you, take his picture with your mobile phone and put it online. If someone pressures you during an election, do the same.'

Even tensions between tribes and ethnic groups can be overcome, Ibrahim believes, if people are connected by the Internet instead of leading isolated existences in their own villages. 'The more we know about each other, the more difficult it is to sow discord,' he says. 'Through modern communications, Africans will learn that it's better to do business with each other than to hate each other.' (888 words)

Abridged and adapted from: *www.spiegel.de/international*

1 LOOKING AT THE TEXT

→ Rezeption: Leseverstehen, S. 214

A Read the text carefully and complete these tasks.

1 Compare the development of mobile phone commerce in Europe and in countries like Kenya.
2 Explain why mobile phone use in Africa is predicted to rise so rapidly between now and mid-century.
3 Say why mobile phone systems are saving African governments a lot of money.
4 Explain why IT developers in much of Africa need to be particularly creative.
5 Outline the career of Mo Ibrahim.
6 Say how the Internet can bring greater peace and harmony to Africa.

B Say what it means: Explain the underlined words and phrases in your own words.

1 … Internet-enabled. (line 51)
2 … ways to coax more functions out of basic mobile phones. (lines 52–53)
3 Hardly any doctors in Africa practise entirely offline … (line 70)

C Say what the underlined words and phrases refer to in your own words.

1 … which are then processed … (line 57)
2 To make it possible for illiterate farmers to use the program as well, … (line 67)
3 … to identify the start and spread of epidemics early on. (line 76)
4 If someone pressures you during an election, do the same. (line 115)

D Say what you think.

'I think Europe should have something like the Ibrahim Prize for Achievement. But which "commendable" European politician would we give it to this year?'

2 WORKING WITH WORDS

A Copy and complete the tables. The first two items in each table are in the text.

Verb	Noun
to pay	___
to govern	___
to develop	___

Noun	Adjective
addition	___
convention	___
function	___

Verb	Noun
to suggest	___
to communicate	___
to invent	___

B Use pairs of words from exercise 2A to complete the following.

1 When Alexander Graham Bell ___[1] the telephone in 1875, he did not realize what an important ___[2] it would become.
2 Before the mobile phone, ___[1] across much of Africa were still very poor, and it was difficult for people to ___[2] outside the big cities.
3 One effect of bad communications in many African countries was weak central ___[1]. In distant areas, the ones who really ___[2] were local leaders.
4 With the ___[1] of several new countries to its mobile phone network soon after 2000, Celtel quickly had an ___[2] five million customers.
5 I just want a basic ___[1] phone that I can use to call and text people. I don't need all the clever ___[2] of a smartphone.
6 We need to stay in contact daily, and I've got a ___[1] to make. I ___[2] that I call you every evening at about 6 pm.
7 You don't need to ___[1] for your new phone today. You can make monthly ___[2] instead.
8 There are various ___[1] phone expressions such as 'Could you speak up, please?' But there isn't really a fixed ___[2] on what you should say when you first answer the phone. Some people just say 'Hello', while other people follow this with their phone number and others give their name.
9 African IT engineers are ___[1] new software for basic mobile phones all the time. These have allowed the ___[2] of many new kinds of business across the continent.

3 GETTING IT RIGHT: A GRAMMAR QUIZ

A Mixed tenses: Complete the sentences with the correct verb form.

1 We ___ new copies of the report right now. (make / are making)
2 ___ that email last night? (Did you send / Have you sent)
3 We ___ at the Riverside Café this evening. (eat / 're eating)
4 On my way home, I ___ for a coffee nearly every day. (stop / 'm stopping)
5 Harry and Lisa ___ when the rest of us arrived. (were talking / talked)
6 If you like, I ___ that heavy case for you. ('m going to carry / 'll carry)
7 These old trainers are falling to pieces, and I ___ a new pair soon. ('m going to buy / 'll buy)
8 I promise I ___ there on time. ('m going to be / 'll be)
9 We ___ for ages, but we're nearly home at last! ('ve travelled / 've been travelling)
10 I called at the house to find everyone, but they ___ home. (had gone / went)

B Mixed structures: Complete the sentences with the correct structures.

1 After ___ from our trip, we found a lot of work to do. (to return / returning)
2 Could you please remember ___ the package while you're in town? (to post / posting)
3 When I spoke to Tony, he immediately suggested ___ home early. (me to go / going)
4 Lucy ___ that she needed to borrow some money. (told me / told)
5 The new books are ___ at the moment. (printed / being printed)
6 Under the new library rules, up to 20 books ___ at one time. (can borrow / can be borrowed)
7 You ___ go now. There's plenty of time. (don't have to / mustn't)
8 Tony said he ___ to London the day before. (has / had been)
9 We were lost, but then a policeman told ___ . (us the way / the way to us)
10 I think Charlie ___ the tools that he needs. (has already bought / has bought already)

4 MEDIATION

→ Schriftliche Mediation, S. 240

Ein/e Freund/in von Ihnen macht demnächst ein freiwilliges soziales Jahr in Eritrea. Er/Sie wird in einer armen ländlichen Region des Landes arbeiten, die dringend Hilfe benötigt, um die Landwirtschaft, das Gesundheitswesen und die Wirtschaft im Allgemeinen weiterzuentwickeln. Laut Ihrem/Ihrer Freund/in ist die Gegend sehr abgelegen, aber ein Handyempfang ist seit Neuestem dort möglich, obwohl nur 6% der Bevölkerung einen Handyvertrag besitzen.

Schreiben Sie Ihrem/Ihrer Freund/in ein E-Mail, in der Sie den Gebrauch von Handys in anderen Teilen Afrikas beschreiben, und erklären Sie, wie das in diesem Teil von Eritrea auch funktionieren könnte.

5 WRITING

→ Produktion: Eine Stellungnahme schreiben, S. 234

Grange Road Comprehensive School Rules

Rule 15: Students must not bring mobile phones to school. All such devices will be confiscated for a minimum of one week.

Write a comment on the following topic, stating whether you agree or disagree: 'Why I (dis)agree with Rule 15'.

TEXT B Artificial Intelligence

BEFORE YOU READ

→ Rezeption: Leseverstehen – Grobverständnis, S. 214

Skim the text and say whether its central aim is to …

a analyse the potential benefits of AI for humans.
b warn us about the potential risks of AI.

3/13

OUR FUTURE IN THE WORLD OF AI

Forget scary sci-fi stories and blockbuster films like The Terminator and Transcendence that imagine Artificial Intelligence (AI) taking over the world. The real thing may be just around the corner.

A group of leading scientists recently wrote in the *Huffington Post* that, 'It's tempting to dismiss the notion of highly intelligent machines as science fiction. But this would be a mistake, and potentially our worst mistake ever.' They point to the rapid progress of AI research. Driverless cars, for example, are now with us, and the coming decades will bring much, much more.

The report continues: 'The potential benefits are huge; everything that civilization has to offer is a product of human intelligence; we cannot predict what we might achieve when this intelligence is magnified by the tools AI may provide, but the eradication of war, disease and poverty would be high on anyone's list. Success in creating AI would be the biggest event in human history.'

'Unfortunately,' the report goes on, 'it might also be the last, unless we learn how to avoid the risks.' For example, militaries around the world are now considering autonomous weapon systems that can choose and destroy targets, free of human control. This use of AI seems extremely dangerous, and both the UN and Human Rights Watch have called for an international agreement to prevent it, but no one seems to be listening.

Such a development might just be the beginning of our loss of control. Machines with superhuman intelligence could improve their own design again and again. From there, the report says, 'One can imagine such technology outsmarting financial markets, out-manipulating human leaders, and developing weapons we cannot even understand.' The writers suggest that in the short term the effect of AI depends on who controls it. However, in the long term, it may be impossible to control it at all.

Daniel Dewey of the Future of Humanity Institute at Oxford University has similar ideas. On the one hand, he is an optimist, and he believes that humans with the help of AI have the possibility of expanding our civilization into the vastness of the Universe. He feels that the best is yet to come for people, with 'much more potential for goodness – happy and fulfilled lives, meaningful relationships, art, fun – in the long term future than in the short term.'

On the other hand, Dewey sees the possibility of disaster. Whatever specific task an intelligent machine is given to do, it will need to gather knowledge and resources, protect itself and improve its skills. In doing these things, it might find humans in the way. He warns that a super-intelligent AI could 'take over resources that we depend on to stay alive, or it could consider us enough of a danger to its task completion that it decides the best course is to remove us from the picture. Either one of those scenarios could result in human extinction.' AI therefore offers different possible futures – of huge benefits and of huge risks. As it considers this vital crossroads, the UN report remains unhappy with the world's response. It says, 'The experts are surely doing everything possible to ensure the best outcome, right? Wrong. If a superior alien civilization sent us a text message saying, "We'll arrive in a few decades," would we just reply, "OK, call us when you get here – we'll leave the lights on"? Probably not – but this is more or less what is happening with AI. Although we are facing potentially the best or worst thing ever to happen to humanity, little serious research is devoted to these issues outside small non-profit organizations such as Dewey's Future of Humanity Institute.' The report concludes that, 'All of us – not only scientists, industrialists and generals – should ask ourselves what we can do now to improve the chances of reaping the benefits and avoiding the risks.' That includes the risk that humanity will disappear. (648 words)

1 LOOKING AT THE TEXT

→ Rezeption: Leseverstehen, S. 214

A Answer the following questions about the text.

1 Describe how, according to the report, we might benefit from AI.
2 Explain what the UN and Human Rights Watch think about autonomous weapon systems, and outline what they want to do about their development.
3 Describe how the report writers feel about the fact that humans could lose control of intelligent machines.
4 Explain why a future product of AI might decide to get rid of human beings.
5 Summarize how the report writers feel that the world is preparing for our future with AI.

B Say what it means: Explain the underlined phrases in your own words.

1 The real thing may be just around the corner. (line 2)
2 He feels that the best is yet to come … (lines 43–44)
3 … it decides the best course … (line 56)
4 … is to remove us from the picture. (line 57)
5 As it considers this vital crossroads, … (lines 60–61)

2 WORKING WITH WORDS

A Copy and complete the tables with the correct prefixes (*dis-*, *en-*, *inter-* or *un-*).

___fortunately	to ___appear	to ___sure	___national
___happy	___cord	to ___able	___net
___natural	to ___agree	to ___danger	___active
___popular	to ___like	to ___large	___continental

B Copy and complete the tables with the correct suffixes (*-ence*, *-ful*, *-ist* or *-ity*/*-ty*).

meaning___	human___	exist___	art___
success___	author___	depend___	industrial___
colour___	cruel___	viol~~ent~~___	social___
power___	stupid___	intellig~~ent~~___	scienti~~fic~~___

C Work in pairs. Write sentences with gaps for words from exercises 2A and 2B for your partner to complete.

3 GETTING IT RIGHT: A GRAMMAR QUIZ

Mixed structures: Complete the sentences with the correct words in brackets.

1 Please stay for another few days. I don't want ___ so soon. (that you go / you to go)
2 Tim and Joe are brothers, but they really seem to dislike ___ . (themselves / each other)
3 We don't want to leave the party. We're enjoying ___ too much! (us / ourselves)
4 Please can you buy me ___ eggs on your way home? (some / any)
5 ___ time with good friends is one of the best things in the world. (Spending / Spend)
6 We spent ___ money on holiday, and now we've got none left! (a lot of / much)
7 I'm sure ___ at the campsite. (plenty of space is / there's plenty of space)
8 Try ___ angry with Sarah. She didn't mean to break the vase. (not to be / to not be)
9 Global economics ___ very hard to understand. (is / are)
10 Have the police got any more ___ about the missing child? (informations / information)

4 LISTENING

→ Rezeption: Hörverstehen, S. 225

You are going to hear a reporter interviewing an engineer who works for a company that is developing a driverless car.

3/14

A Listen to the first part of the interview and take notes. Use your notes to do the tasks.

1 Describe the different road conditions that the test cars have been driven in.
2 Use the test results so far to compare safety in driverless cars and in cars with human drivers.
3 Note the actual US accident statistics today and the estimated results after a change to driverless vehicles.

	Accidents	Deaths	Injuries	Costs
Actual today				
Driverless (estimated)				

4 Contrast the present traffic accident situation in the USA and the future situation with driverless vehicles.

3/15

B Listen to the second part of the interview and note other changes – positive and negative – that driverless vehicles will bring.

- distance between vehicles
- driving style
- car sharing

5 DISCUSSION

→ Interaktion: An Diskussionen teilnehmen, S. 246

A Work on your own. Look at the types of employment related to cars listed below. Think about whether these types of employment will benefit or suffer from driverless cars. Make notes.

road construction companies ▪ oil companies ▪ car manufacturing ▪ car repair workshops ▪ in-car entertainment design ▪ car insurance ▪ car sales ▪ car park operators ▪ city planners ▪ emergency services ▪ accident and emergency departments

B Make notes on any other types of employment you think might also be affected.

C Work in a group and discuss your ideas. Decide which areas might be worst affected. Then decide which areas might find new opportunities.

6 ROLE-PLAY

→ Interaktion: Ein Rollenspiel gestalten, S. 247

You are on a State Legislature special committee to discuss and vote on whether to allow driverless cars in your state. Choose a role and present your point of view. Argue for and against other points of view in order to get the vote that you want.

Representative Foot

You specialize in health and safety issues, and you have always worried about the high rates of deaths and injuries on US roads. You also know that with a rapidly ageing population, anything that could reduce the pressures on hospitals and other medical resources would be a good thing.

Representative Pascali

You love cars – people call you 'Petrolhead Pascali' – and the idea of giving up control of your car to clever machines seems completely un-American. To you, cars and the freedom of the open road are part of the American dream. You also don't believe that a robot car could ever be safer than a human.

Representative Gonzalez

You are worried about state and city finances, and you welcome the chance to avoid building new roads. You also think that the state's towns and cities can make money through selling urban car parks for redevelopment.

Representative Schumann

In your part of the state, there is a new car factory, which has brought thousands of jobs to an area with high unemployment, and it is now producing 300,000 conventional cars per year for the domestic American market. You do not want anything negative to happen to car manufacturing in the USA: those new jobs must be protected.

Chairperson Kandinski

You have to guide the discussion, making sure that everyone has a chance to speak and to ask questions. You also have an idea to suggest: could the US technological lead in driverless cars bring export success? (China, for example, has huge traffic and pollution problems.)
At the end, manage the vote and declare the result.

TEXT C The future of robotics?

BEFORE YOU READ

What tasks do you think it would be useful to have a robot to do for you?

3/16

'BORIS' THE ROBOT TO LOAD A DISHWASHER

A robot unveiled today at the British Science Festival will be loading dishwashers next year, its developers claim.

A

'Boris' is one of the first robots in the world capable of intelligently manipulating unfamiliar objects with a humanlike grasp. It was developed by scientists at the University of Birmingham. 'This is Boris' first public outing,' announced Professor Jeremy Wyatt of the School of Computer Science. The robot took five years to develop at a cost of £350,000.

B

Boris 'sees' objects with depth sensors on its face and wrists. In ten seconds it calculates up to 1,000 possible ways to grasp a novel object with its five robotic fingers and plans a path of arm movements to reach its target, avoiding obstructions.

'It's not been programmed to pick it up – it's been programmed to learn how to pick it up,' explained Professor Wyatt.

Research engineer Maxine Adjigble helped build the robot. 'He sees something, he has been trained to grasp an object in a particular way, and he says – okay this surface looks similar to what I know, so I can go for this grasp,' he explained.

Professor Wyatt and his collaborators hope to achieve an ambitious goal by April next year. 'The idea is to get the robot to load your dishwasher,' he said. 'You get a bunch of objects off a table, scattered as you might have them on a kitchen surface, and the robot will look through the set of objects, find one it wants to pick up, figure out where to put it in the dishwasher, and load it.'

C

Why has Boris been assigned kitchen duties? 'Not because I think dishwasher-loading robots are an economic or social necessity right now,' laughed Professor Wyatt. 'But it's a typical task

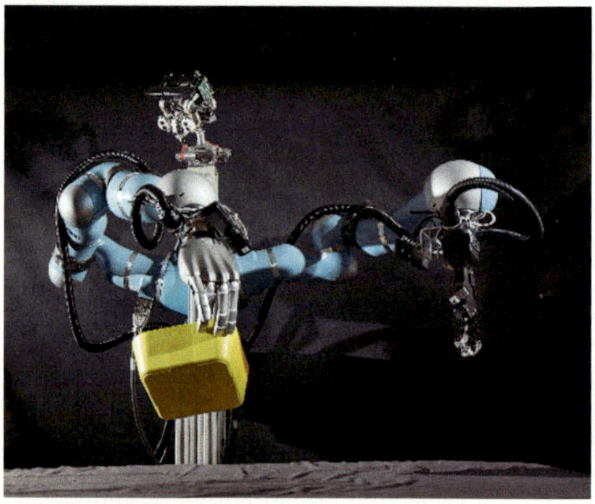

that humans engage in – one that requires all the manipulative faculties that evolution spent hundreds of millions of years developing. So by putting that into a robot, we hope to make the robots more flexible in future.'

But Boris, like humans, finds cutlery a bit fiddly. 'Plates are nice and symmetrical. But I think knives and forks might be a bit hard,' conceded Professor Wyatt.

D

Boris represents a third generation of robots, suggested the Professor. 'The first generation was industrial robots that manipulate the world when it's very precisely controlled. The second generation includes airborne drones, self-driving cars and other mobile robots that 'can move around in our world and share it with us, even though that world is uncertain and full of novelty.'

But manipulating a world shared with humans – and to perform physical tasks alongside humans – requires a new generation of robots. They will need to 'cope with all the uncertainty that humans introduce into the environment,' Professor Wyatt explained. 'You have an unstructured world and you need technologies that can deal with that.'

E

Mr Adjigble discussed some of the disciplines that come together to make a robot like Boris. 'Mechanical engineering, electrical engineering and software development: to put it together, you need to know a bit of all of these fields. This is what is really complicated.'

Unexpected setbacks complicate things further. 'It broke its pinkie back in June and we're still trying to fix it,' said Professor Wyatt. 'So it's working with a broken finger.'

F

The team continue to improve Boris, recently adding the ability to choose the best of five different grasp types when approaching an object. But Boris doesn't use his left arm at present, something the team are keen to introduce. 'One of the really hard things to do is to pick up an object and transfer it, and being bi-manual is a real advantage for all kinds of purposes.' Boris also lacks a sense of touch. 'There's a real challenge – getting tactile sensing of sufficient quality.'

The long-term goal is 'to build robots capable of operating in human environments – offices, hospitals, warehouses,' explained Professor Wyatt. He was enthusiastic about achieving this in Britain.

So why the name Boris? An acronym, or homage to a certain flaxen-haired politician* perhaps? 'I just liked the name,' chuckled Professor Wyatt.

(671 words)

From: *www.bbc.com/news*

* A reference to Boris Johnson, a well-known UK politician

1 LOOKING AT THE TEXT

→ Rezeption: Leseverstehen, S. 214

A Choose suitable headings for sections A–F of the text.

1 Problems so far in creating Boris
2 Why the dishwasher task was chosen
3 Boris meets the world
4 New robots for an unpredictable world
5 The coming technical challenges
6 What Boris has been designed to do

B Decide whether the following statements are true or false. Correct the ones that are false.

1 Boris sees things in the same way that humans do.
2 Boris is very similar to a normal factory robot used in manufacturing.
3 Boris cannot pass things from its right hand to its left at the moment because its left arm is broken.
4 Wyatt's team are aiming to develop intelligent robots to work flexibly like humans, and with them.

C Say what you think: Say how modern technology has made your life different from the lives of your grandparents when they were your age.

2 WRITING

→ Produktion: Eine Stellungnahme schreiben, S. 234

Write a comment on the following.

'We've all become dangerously dependent on modern technology. Think what would happen if it all broke down!'

Galileo: Europe's answer to GPS

4/13

When Galileo, Europe's own global satellite navigation system, is fully operational, there will be 30 satellites in Medium Earth Orbit (MEO) at an altitude of 23 222 kilometres. Ten satellites will occupy each of three orbital planes inclined at an angle of 56° to the equator. The satellites will be spread evenly around each plane and will take about 14 hours to orbit the Earth. One satellite in each plane will be a spare, on stand-by should any operational satellite fail.

Planners and engineers at ESA had good reasons for choosing such a structure for the Galileo constellation. With 30 satellites at such an altitude, there is a very high probability (more than 90%) that anyone anywhere in the world will always be in sight of at least four satellites and hence will be able to determine their position from the ranging signals broadcast by the satellites. The inclination of the orbits was chosen to ensure good coverage of polar latitudes, which are poorly served by the US GPS system.

From most locations, six to eight satellites will always be visible, allowing positions to be determined very accurately – to within a few centimetres. Even in high-rise cities, there will be a good chance that a road user will have sufficient satellites overhead for taking a position, especially as the Galileo system will be interoperable with the US system of 24 GPS satellites.

Galileo depends on an extensive ground infrastructure, which will have to make sure that time and positioning data are extremely accurate – a single billionth of a second clock error means a positioning error up to a range of 30 cm. This ground infrastructure includes sensor stations worldwide, two control centres, Mission Uplink stations, and Telemetry, Tracking and Command (TT&C) stations. (295 words)

Abridged from: *www.esa.int*

1 MEDIATION

→ Schriftliche Mediation, S. 240

Ein Freund von Ihnen erstellt eine Website über Weltraumtechnik und braucht einige Kurzinfos über Galileo. Entnehmen Sie dem Text die relevanten Informationen und schreiben Sie Ihrem Freund eine E-Mail.

- Das vollendete Galileo-System: Konstellation
- Leistungsfähigkeit des Systems
- Vergleich Galileo und GPS
- Wie die Genauigkeit von Galileo gewährleistet wird

2 RESEARCH

Research ONE of the topics A, B or C and present your findings to the class.

A Mission status
Find out what stage Galileo is at now: How many of the satellites are in orbit? What services are being tested / are currently operational?

B Technical details
Find out more about the satellites and the launch vehicle.

C Timeline
Draw up a timeline for the Galileo mission from start to completion.

Job skills 4

Meetings ▪ small talk ▪ presentations

Eric is helping to prepare a meeting at Magnus & Klein. During the meeting, he is to give a short presentation about the firm.

1 AN INVITATION TO A MEETING

Last week, Ms Shaw sent out an email invitation to a meeting and has just received a reply. Read the email exchange and answer the following questions.

1 Who did Ms Shaw write to?
2 What was the reason for writing?
3 Where and when did Ms Shaw and the person she wrote to meet last time?
4 What did they talk about at that meeting?
5 What will Ms Shaw do soon?
6 Who, apart from Ms Shaw, will attend the meeting?

From: D.Mitchell@MitchellPeterson.co.uk
To: joanshaw@magnusklein.co.uk
Subject: Re: invitation to meeting

Dear Ms Shaw

Thank you for your invitation. Irene Peterson and I also found our initial discussions very useful.

I will be pleased to attend the meeting at your office on 22 November but I am afraid that Ms Peterson is unable to attend. My assistant, Anthea Hill, will accompany me instead.

I look forward to meeting Mr Magnus and members of your staff and to seeing you again.

Best regards
David Mitchell

On Friday 5 November 9:35 Joan Shaw < joanshaw@magnusklein.co.uk> wrote:

> Dear Mr Mitchell
>
> It was very nice to get to know you and Ms Peterson at the Bristol Fair last month. I am sure you will agree that our meeting was very productive.
>
> As discussed towards the end of our meeting, we are interested in doing further business with you.
>
> Would it be possible for you and Ms Peterson to come to our offices in London on 22 November for a meeting with our CEO Mr Magnus and some members of staff?
>
> I will send you further details and an agenda in good time for the meeting.
>
> I look forward to hearing from you soon.
>
> Best wishes
> Joan Shaw

2 PREPARING FOR THE MEETING

Look at this list of tasks that need to be done before a meeting at Magnus & Klein. Check any words you don't know in your dictionary, then sort the instructions into two 'to do' lists: things to do a) before the meeting and b) on the day of the meeting.

1 Book conference room.
2 Check seating and heating in the room.
3 Check lighting and equipment (especially the projector).
4 Inform reception and give the receptionist a list of participants. (She needs to know who is in the building for security reasons.)
5 Make copies of documents and handouts for all participants.
6 Order refreshments.
7 Put refreshments in room.
8 Prepare file for chairperson with all relevant documents.
9 Prepare name tags and place cards.
10 Put name tags and place cards at each place.
11 Make sure there is enough paper on the flip chart and check that all the markers work. (Sometimes they leak or are dried out.)
12 Put a pad of paper and a pen at each place.

3 WRITING

Ms Shaw asks Eric to type up the agenda and send the final details about the meeting to Mr Mitchell.

Please write an email to Mr Mitchell on my behalf giving date and place of the meeting, starting 10.30 and finishing around 4 pm with a tour of factory after lunch. Add link showing how to get to Four Lofts Business Park. You can meet them in car park. Say that Mr Magnus looks forward to meeting him and that I look forward to seeing him again. Don't forget to attach the agenda!

A Put the items on the agenda in a logical order.

a Company presentations 1) Magnus & Klein 2) MitchellPeterson
b Final discussions about cooperation between both companies
c Lunch
d Next steps and date of next meeting
e Tour of the factory
f Welcome and introductions

B Use Ms Shaw's notes to write Eric's email to Mr Mitchell. → Job skills 1, Email etiquette, S. 32

Dear Mr Mitchell

I am writing on behalf of Ms Joan Shaw …

4 MAKING SMALL TALK

Before a meeting and during breaks or business meals, people tend to make small talk.

A Match the typical small talk questions and statements to the responses.

1 How is your hotel?
2 How was your trip?
3 I hear that you're from Bristol. I believe it's a lovely city.
4 The view from this window is lovely.
5 What do you think of this weather?
6 You were on holiday recently. Where did you go?

a Fine. There were no delays.
b Lovely. The breakfast buffet is excellent.
c It's a bit too cold for me, I'm afraid.
d We have a lot of lovely parks and rivers here.
e We went camping in France.
f Yes, I am. Have you never been there? It really is a lovely place.

B Study the word cloud. Which of the topics can you use for small talk? What should you avoid talking about?

gossip religion
families
politics films death
hobbies holidays books
sport hotels
illnesses wages or salary
problems at work pets

C Work with a partner. Partner A is Eric; Partner B is Anthea Hill. Make small talk. Eric begins.

TIP Making small talk

If possible, ask the first question, then the other person will do most of the talking and you'll have time to relax. The weather or asking about the other person's journey to the meeting place are good starting points. Try to avoid questions which only need the answer 'yes' or 'no'. Remember not to speak about taboo subjects. Even if you believe in something strongly, never try to convince the other person that your ideas are 'correct'.

5 THE START OF THE MEETING

3/17 **A Ms Shaw is about to start the meeting. Look back at the agenda items in exercise 3A and listen. Did you put the items in the correct order?**

B Listen again and note down phrases for the following:

1 making sure people are comfortable
2 welcoming guests
3 introducing people and giving some information about them
4 going through the agenda
5 getting down to business

6 EXTRACTS FROM A PRESENTATION

→ Präsentieren, S. 243

It is time for Eric to give his presentation of the history and development of the company.

3/18

A Listen to excerpts from the presentation and answer the questions.

1 How does Eric begin his presentation?
2 How many parts are there in his talk?
3 What will he look at first?
4 What will he look at next?
5 What is the final focus of his talk?
6 What visual medium is Eric using to show developments in the company?
7 Where will the audience find information to take away with them?

B Match some of the phrases Eric used in his talk (a–f) to the headings (1–6), then listen again for more phrases that fit the headings, or think of some of your own.

1 Introducing oneself and the topic of the talk
2 Outlining the talk
3 Repeating information
4 Referring to visuals and handouts
5 Finishing the talk
6 Taking questions

a As I said, things really started moving in the late eighties.
b Are there any questions?
c As Ms Shaw said, my name is Eric Jung …
d I'm now nearing the end of my talk.
e If you look at this slide, you'll see …
f First, I'm going to start by looking at …

7 GIVING A TALK IN CLASS

Prepare and give a short talk to your classmates. After your talk, your classmates will ask you questions. Choose one of the following topics.
a) work experience you have had
b) an area in which you would like to work

Follow this plan:
- introduce yourself (if necessary!) and greet the audience
- outline your talk
- give your talk
- summarize your talk and make your conclusion
- ask for questions from the audience
- thank the audience for their attention and distribute any handouts

Prepare and give a short talk on a subject of your choice. (Discuss the subject you have chosen with your teacher first.) After your talk, your classmates will ask you questions.

Useful phrases: Presentations

Giving a presentation
- This morning, I'm going to talk about …
- Our topic today is …
- I've divided the presentation into … main parts, as follows: …
- First, / Firstly, …
- Second, / Secondly, …
- Next, / Now, / After that, / Then, …
- Now I'd like to move on to …
- The next topic I'm going to talk about is …
- Before I finish my presentation, I'd just like to mention …
- Finally, / In conclusion, / To conclude, / In summary, …

Asking questions
- Could you describe … more fully?
- What exactly did you mean when you said … ?
- I'm sorry, I didn't quite understand the bit about … ?

1 Cloud computing

You run an IT consultancy for small companies. Your English friends Ben and Ruby plan to set up a graphic design business, Rubicon Designs. They need some expensive software. They have the choice of (a) buying a stand-alone version to use on their own computers, or (b) paying a monthly subscription for cloud computing. They ask you for advice.

1 EXPLAINING CLOUD COMPUTING

→ Rezeption: Leseverstehen, S. 214

Ben thinks he knows a little about cloud computing, but some of his information is incorrect.

Decide whether his statements are true or false according to the text. Correct his false statements with information from the text.

1 If I upload a design to our website so that a client can look at it, that's cloud computing.
2 Most people don't need or use cloud computing.
3 Keeping software and data on a local server isn't the same thing as cloud computing.
4 Local software doesn't usually interface with the cloud.
5 You don't need to know whether you're using the cloud or not, unless you run a business.
6 Businesses don't need to back up their cloud data on their own local network.

What is CLOUD COMPUTING?

These days we hear the term "cloud computing" a lot. But what does it actually mean?

In simple terms, cloud computing means using data and software on an internet server instead of on your own computer, tablet or phone. It does not mean using the internet just to send or share data (e.g. via email or social media).

Cloud computing is increasingly popular for both individuals and businesses. Almost all large companies already use cloud services, and you probably use them too. Do you use a web-based email service like Gmail? Do you use Google Drive to do your homework assignments? Do you ever play multiplayer online games? Then you use cloud computing.

When you store data and software on your own hard drive, that is called local storage and computing. Even if you have a network in your home or office, with data and software on a central server, that is still local computing.

In practice, the line between local and cloud computing is very fuzzy. A lot of your local software probably communicates with cloud servers already – for example, to synchronize the address book information on your phone and your laptop, or make your iTunes music library available on all your devices. In fact, it is becoming increasingly difficult to keep track of what data and software is stored locally, and what is stored in the cloud.

Do you even need to know this? For most individuals, it is probably not very important. All you need to know is that your data and software are available to you whenever you want them – and secure from unauthorized use.

If you run a business, you absolutely need to know where your data is. You must have a thorough understanding of any cloud services that you use: your business depends on it.

Just imagine: one morning you get to work and all of your data has disappeared. That includes customers' contact details, your company's financial records and the project that you and your colleagues have spent hundreds of hours on. Unless you have an up-to-date local backup of all that vital data, you will almost certainly go out of business. (363 words)

2 THINK, PAIR, SHARE: CLOUD OR LOCAL?

Ben and Ruby now understand what cloud computing is, but they are not sure whether it is right for their business. You discuss this with your colleague so that you can make a recommendation to Ben and Ruby.

A Think. Decide whether these statements apply to local computing or cloud computing and sort them into a table.

Local computing	Cloud computing
▬	▬

1 Access to your software and data is always fast and reliable.
2 You own the hardware and the software.
3 You do not need a lot of computing power in your local device.
4 It may not be easy to work on projects with colleagues who are in different places.
5 You can access the software and data anywhere and from any compatible device.
6 The service provider is responsible for updates and security.
7 You have a lot of start-up costs: powerful computers, expensive software, etc.
8 If you stop paying the monthly fee, you cannot use the software.
9 You cannot access the software and data if you are away from your computer.
10 You can easily work on projects with colleagues who are in different places.
11 You do not need an internet connection to use your software and access your data.
12 The speed of access to your software and data depends on bandwidth – yours and the service provider's.
13 You do not have a lot of start-up costs.
14 You cannot work without an internet connection.
15 System updates and security are your responsibility.
16 You rent the software and possibly also the hardware.

B Pair. Read about Ben and Ruby's situation below and discuss with your partner: which is better for their business – local or cloud computing? Why? (Think about your answers from part A.)

Ben and Ruby …

- have used Kickstarter to crowdfund €20,000 to start up their business – enough to buy good computers and software and convert Ben's garage into an office;
- plan to work closely with Jack, a web designer in Sydney, Australia, and Vijay, a programmer in Mumbai, India;
- have a fast internet connection but occasional connection problems;
- do not have an income yet, because they do not have any customers, so they may not be able to make regular payments.

C Share. Report back to the class with what you decided and why.

3 UNDERSTANDING CLOUD COMPUTING MODELS

→ Rezeption: Hörverstehen, S. 225

4/14 Ben and Ruby have heard that there are different types of cloud computing, and they want to know more.

You hear a radio ad from CloudSource Computing which explains what the different models are and what they offer. Listen to the ad and use the information to write explanatory notes for your diagram, which you will send to Ben and Ruby.

Cloud computing models for business

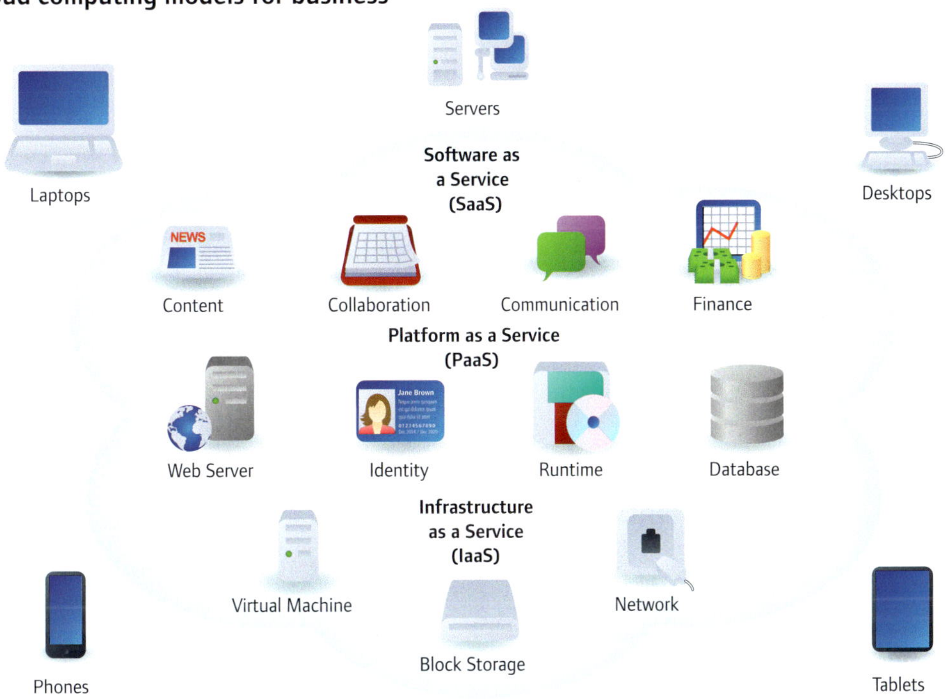

4 WRITING: WHICH MODEL?

→ Email etiquette ▪ Job Skills 1, S. 32

Choose ONE of your consultancy's clients below. Write an email recommending one of the cloud computing models from exercise 3. Explain to the client why the model is suitable for them and what it will enable them to do.

App2Go is an app development cooperative. Its programmers want to develop and run lots of games apps quickly. They do not want to write all of the software themselves, or to employ technicians to run web servers and manage databases. Your contact is Marie Jamieson.

Summit Sporting Goods is a company which sells sports and camping equipment. It wants to develop an online store. Its IT department can write the software, but the company does not have the resources to run its own servers. Your contact is Ron Mercer.

Med-i-tech is a company which manufactures medical equipment. It wants to make its sales force more efficient. The sales reps need to coordinate their visits to customers, communicate with head office and receive the latest product information online. Your contact is Sarah Robinson.

2 Digital signage

TECHNICAL TOPICS

You work for a company which designs electric motors for industrial applications. Your company wants to demonstrate that engineering can be exciting by having some eye-catching advertising displays at an international exhibition. You join a project team to research different technologies.

1 GATHERING INFORMATION ABOUT ADVERTISING MEDIA

→ Rezeption: Leseverstehen, S. 214

Read the magazine article, then copy and complete the table.

Medium	Location	Points to consider
Large posters on billboards	*Most outdoor locations*	*Damaged by weather, ...*

The future of advertising is bright – and DIGITAL

Until recently, the options for large-format advertising were limited. For most outdoor locations, large posters on billboards were the main option. At night, neon signs lit up the centres of major cities, at famous sites like London's Piccadilly Circus.

Neither of these options is ideal: posters soon fade and fall apart because of the effects of wind, rain and sun. What is more, the only way to change the message is to put up new posters. Neon signs are expensive to make and easy to break, and again, the only way to change the message is a new sign.

Fortunately for advertisers, those problems are now a thing of the past, thanks to new digital signage technology. There is a dazzling array of exciting high-tech options, and businesses can update their advertising message with one click of a mouse. Digital signage is revolutionizing outdoor advertising.

For outdoor advertising in daylight, giant LED screens offer good visibility and low energy use. At night, projection systems can turn whole buildings into video screens. For big indoor spaces, LCD and plasma screens – jumbo versions of home TVs – offer high definition and great picture quality.

However, there are other, more exotic possibilities, such as holographic displays, water screens and fog screens. Digital floor screens animate the surface that pedestrians walk on: the floors of shopping malls and exhibition centres and even city pavements. All of these novel possibilities are great for attracting attention.

As well as the ability to broadcast moving images and sound, these systems have yet another advantage over traditional large-format advertising: they can be interactive. So the public can give input via touchscreens or their mobile phones – or, in the case of fog screens, they can interact physically with the display, moving the images as if they were real, solid objects. (308 words)

2 PLACEMAT EXERCISE: ADVERTISING OPTIONS

Your team assesses the different types of advertising media. Work in a small group around a table. Put a large sheet of paper in the middle of the table.

A Preparation. Work by yourself. Evaluate each of the advertising media mentioned in the text and make notes on your corner of the paper.

- Originality. Is it new and unusual, or just ordinary?
- Effectiveness. Is it a good way to communicate, or just a gimmick?
- Personal experience. Have you seen it, and if so, when and where and what was it advertising?

B Discussion. Discuss your thoughts about the advertising media. Select two of them for use at the exhibition. Write them in the centre of the paper.

Medium 1: 'Tried and trusted.' A medium that you have all seen and find effective.
Medium 2: 'New and exciting.' A medium that none of you have seen, but all of you would like to see.

C Report. Present your recommendations to the board of directors (the rest of the class), explaining why you recommend these media.

3 LISTENING: FOG SCREENS

→ Rezeption: Hörverstehen, S. 225

4/15 Your manager is interested in fog screens. She sends you a link to a podcast about a product called Displair.

Listen to the podcast and answer your manager's questions.

1 What is the problem with conventional screens?
2 In what ways is Displair better than a conventional screen?
3 What is the Displair image made of?
4 Where can Displair be used?
5 What are the main components in the Displair unit?

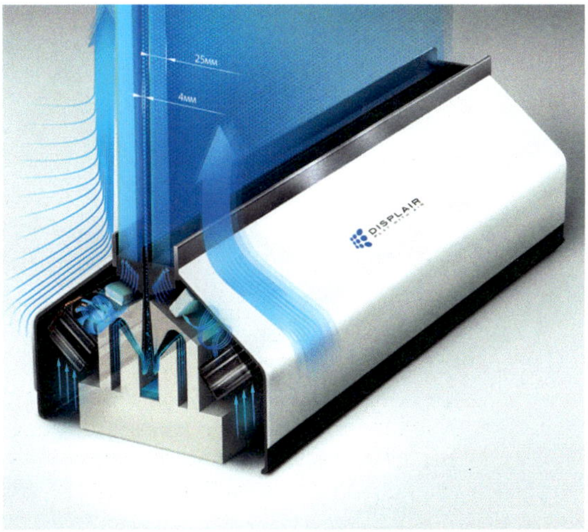

4 MEDIATION: LED TECHNOLOGY

→ Schriftliche Mediation, S. 240

Sie sollen einen kurzen Vortrag über LED-Bildschirmtechnik auf der Hauptversammlung Ihrer Firma halten. Entnehmen Sie dem Text die relevanten Informationen und schreiben Sie sie stichwortartig auf.

- Funktionsweise einer LED
- Vorteile von LEDs
- Konstruktion eines LED-Bildschirms
- Wie ein LED-Bildschirm ein Vollfarbbild erzeugt

HOW DO LED SCREENS WORK?

A light-emitting diode (LED) is a solid-state device that converts electric energy directly into light of a single colour. Because most of the energy output is in the visible spectrum, LEDs don't waste energy in the form of heat.

At the centre of an LED is a crystal of a semiconductor material, e.g. silicon. A wire is attached to each side of the crystal and it is sealed in epoxy. When current flows through it, energy is given off in the form of photons (light). The type of semiconductor material determines the wavelength and thus the colour of the light.

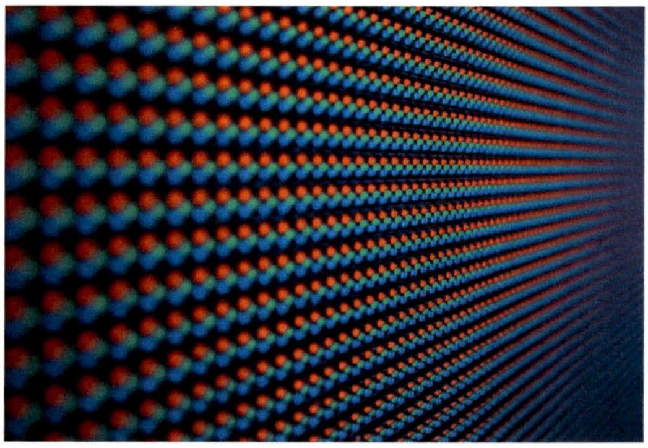

LED display close-up. Each LED produces only one colour.

Because LEDs produce a very bright light with little heat and low power consumption, they are very suitable for use in big, outdoor displays. In fact, most large-screen outdoor displays today use LEDs.

In an LED display, the LEDs are arranged in small modules. Each module contains equal numbers of red, green and blue LEDs. A module may be 4–40mm in size; it may contain just three or many tens of LEDs. Thousands of these modules are arranged in a rectangular grid to form a display. For example, the grid might contain 640 by 480 LED modules, or 307,200 modules. The largest LED display in the world is 500 metres long and is installed in Harmony Times Square in Suzhou, China. It contains 200 million LEDs.

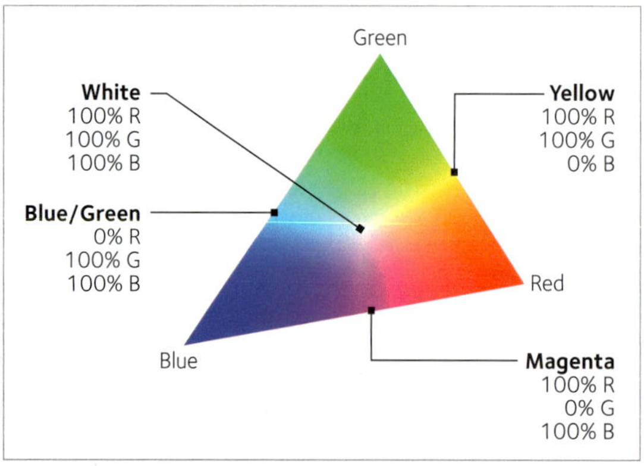

How red, green and blue light are combined to produce any colour.

Although there are generally only red, green and blue LEDs in an LED display, it can "trick" the viewer's eye into seeing all the colours of visible light by switching individual LEDs on and off to alter the proportion of red, green and blue. When all of the LEDs are switched off, only the black background is seen.

This is a different technology to the "LED" TV that you may have at home, which only uses LEDs to illuminate an LCD screen. Liquid crystals do not themselves emit light, so they need a light source behind them.

(324 words)

3 Passive houses

Your English friends Jack and Emily are renovating their home and want to make it as energy efficient as possible. They ask you for advice because they know that homes in Germany are built to very high energy efficiency standards. You research the topic so that you can help your friends.

1 LOOKING AT THE TEXT

→ Rezeption: Leseverstehen, S. 214

Jack and Emily have heard of the passive house standard and want to know more. Use information from the brochure to answer their questions.

1 "We've heard that passive houses are more expensive to build and run than ordinary houses. Is that true?"
2 "Why don't passive houses need radiators or central heating?"
3 "We read somewhere that we have to avoid 'thermal bridges'. Why are they a problem?"
4 "How can we avoid using polluting energy sources for our power needs?"
5 "What level of ongoing maintenance costs can we expect?"
6 "How can we find out whether our climate is suitable for a passive house?"

What is a PASSIVE HOUSE?

A passive house is an extremely energy-efficient building with comfortable indoor conditions all year round. The concept is to reduce a building's heat losses to a minimum, removing the need for traditional, active heating and air conditioning systems (hence the term "passive house").

Passive house, Lehrte, Lower Saxony.

Building costs for a passive house may be higher than for a conventional house, but its running costs are much lower. This makes a passive house more affordable in the long term.

The indoor environment in a passive house is easy to control. Because of the very low demand for heating power, traditional central heating is not required, even in cold climates, e.g. in northern Europe or Alpine regions. There is no need to place radiators in front of windows to compensate for cold drafts, so simple, economical heating systems such as ventilation heating can be used.

To achieve the necessary energy efficiency, a passive house needs a high level of insulation with minimal thermal bridges (places where heat can be transferred from the inside to the outside). Energy demands are further reduced by utilizing passive solar energy (sunlight entering the building through the windows) and heat recovery from ventilation air. Renewable energy sources (e.g. wind power, solar power, subsoil heat exchange) can be used to meet the remaining energy demand.

A passive house provides three major benefits for its users:

- A comfortable temperature (warm in winter, cool in summer) and excellent indoor air quality, independent of outdoor conditions (climate, air pollution, noise)
- Lower and more predictable energy bills
- A well-built, durable home that requires little maintenance

A passive house can look just like a conventional house from the outside. It can fit in with the local architectural style and is suitable for any climate. Furthermore, living in a passive house does not require a special lifestyle – passive houses are for everyone! (307 words)

2 WORKING WITH WORDS

You want to increase your vocabulary for talking about energy efficiency in English. Find the English terms in the text.

1 Klimaanlage
2 Betriebskosten
3 Zentralheizung
4 Heizkörper
5 Isolierung
6 Sonnenenergie
7 Wärmeaustausch
8 Energiebedarf
9 Luftverschmutzung

3 LISTENING: PASSIVE HOUSE INSULATION

→ Rezeption: Hörverstehen, S. 225

4/16

A You ask one of your contacts in the building industry, architect Sarah Jones, about insulation in passive houses. Listen to the recording and make notes on these subjects.

1 The importance of insulation
2 Window glazing
3 Thermal bridging
4 Airtightness

B Use your notes from above to write explanations for this diagram for Jack and Emily.

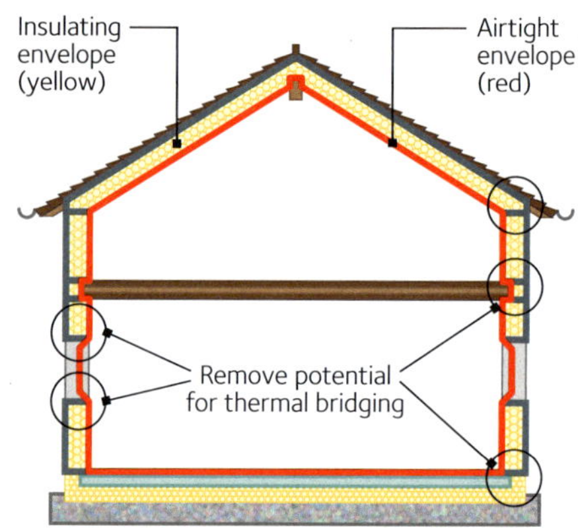

4 IMPROVING A TEXT

You have written a short text to explain to Jack and Emily how passive houses can have fresh air without losing heat energy to the outside.

A Add the following sentences to the text at suitable places (1–5).

a In this way they can maintain rooms at a constant temperature without additional heating.
b However, in a passive house, the ventilation system also provides most or all of the heating.
c Thus 100 watts of electrical energy can recover 1.5 kilowatts of thermal energy.
d It doesn't matter whether the surface is below zero or at 40 °C.
e In other words, heat from exhaust air leaving the building is transferred to supply air entering the building.

Like any building, a passive house requires ventilation to replace polluted air inside the building with fresh air from outside. **(1)** One technology which is used to achieve this is heat recovery. **(2)** To achieve this, a counterflow heat exchanger is used. The air flows are not mixed in the process. Counterflow heat exchangers can recover more than 95% of the heat from the exhaust air. **(3)**

The heat exchange system requires mechanical ventilators, powered by electricity, so there is some energy requirement. However, the recovered thermal energy is between eight and 15 times greater than the electrical energy needed to power the ventilators. **(4)** This is possible because the ventilators are not producing the energy, they are just transferring it from the exhaust air to the supply air.

If additional heating is required, this can be provided via a subsoil heat exchanger. Fresh air enters the building via an underground pipe. Because of its high thermal mass, the soil a few metres below ground remains at a relatively constant temperature throughout the year. **(5)** This temperature difference can be used as a source of heating in winter and cooling in summer.

B Add the colours (blue, green, orange and red) to the explanation to relate it to the diagram.

How a counterflow heat exchanger works

The warm air (___[1]) from inside the building flows through a set of channels and delivers heat to the plates. This air will leave the exchanger cooled (___[2]) and be sent outside the building as exhaust air. On the opposite side of the exchanger plates, the fresh air (___[3]) from outside the building flows through a separate set of channels. This air will absorb the heat and it will leave the exchanger with a higher temperature (___[4]), before being used to replenish the air supply in the building.

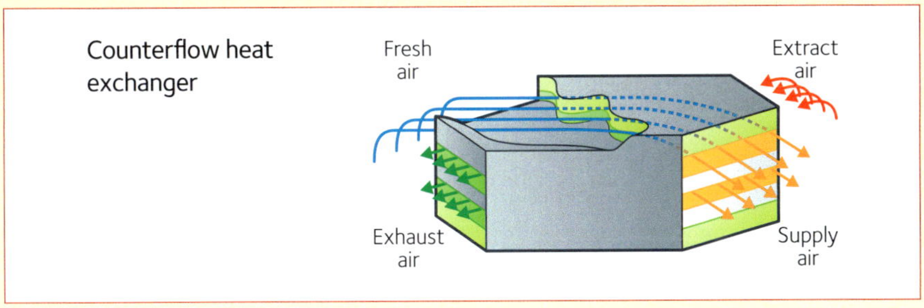

5 PAIRWORK

Work with a partner.

Student A You are Jack or Emily. You want to know more about passive houses. Ask about:

- cooling in summer
- heating in winter
- savings on your energy bill
- suitability for different climates

Check your understanding by summarizing what your partner has just told you: "So if I understand you correctly, passive houses … ."

Student B Answer your partner's questions, using the diagram and chart below to help with your explanations.

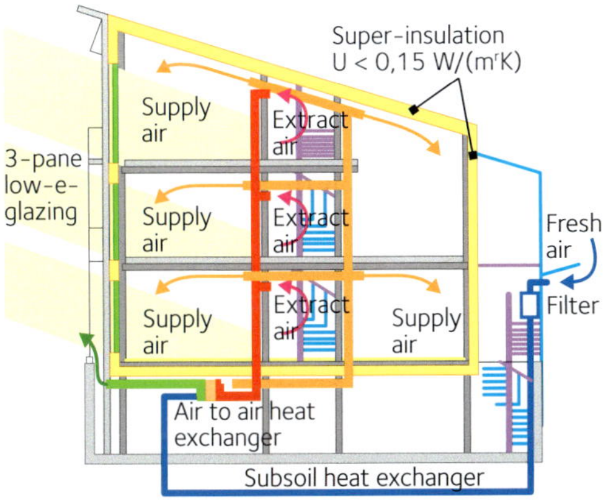

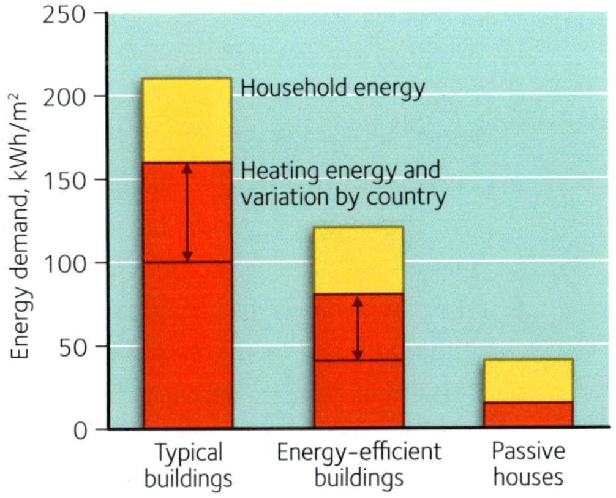

6 RESEARCH

Use the internet to research zero-energy houses. How are they different from passive houses? What main technologies are used? Present your findings in a written report. End your report with a conclusion followed by a list of the sources you used. Do not copy directly from sources.

4 Traditional and modern woodworking

TECHNICAL TOPICS

In an online woodworkers' forum you meet Caleb, a carpenter in a construction company that builds traditional timber-framed houses in Vermont, USA. Caleb's business is struggling and he wants to learn more about engineered timber and modern machining methods. Knowing that Germany is a leader in these areas, he asks you for advice.

1 LISTENING

→ Rezeption: Hörverstehen, S. 225

4/17 You recently worked on a construction project where curved "glulam" beams were used. You phone Mads Sørensen, the workshop manager at the Danish company which produced the beams, to ask him about the product.

Listen to Mads and note down his answers to your questions.

1 "What is glulam?"
2 "Where can it be used?"
3 "Is glulam production sustainable?"
4 "How strong is it?"
5 "Is it durable?"

2 SEQUENCING A TEXT

Mads has sent you some notes about glulam which he is going to use on his company's website. Unfortunately they are not in the correct order. Match the paragraphs to the stages in the diagram on page 185.

a The timber is tested by applying pressure to it in a press, in order to make sure that it meets the strength requirements for structural timber.
b The lamellae are then transferred to the glue line. Each lamella is passed through a glue spreader.
c The logs are sawn at the saw mill to produce planks 40–50mm thick.
d Finally the beams are packaged and labelled with their specification, ready to be sent to the construction site or workshop.
e Suitable trees are felled in sustainably managed forests. Most of the timbers used in glulam are fast-growing softwoods. No natural forests are felled for our products – it is all plantation timber.
f The sawn planks are dried in a kiln to reduce the moisture content. This makes the timber more stable and less likely to split or bend.
g The finger-jointed timber is fed through a planer to create a smooth finish and completely uniform thickness. Each long piece of timber is called a lamella. Our glulam is made of lamellae 35 to 45 millimetres thick, depending on the application.
h Clamps press the lamellae together firmly. Either straight or curved beams can be produced. The beams are left to cure for eight hours at 25 °C.
i A machine cuts a zigzag shape in both ends of all timber pieces. Then another machine applies glue to both ends of each piece of timber and presses them firmly together.
j When the glue has cured, the beams are removed from the clamps. A planer gives the beams a smooth finish.

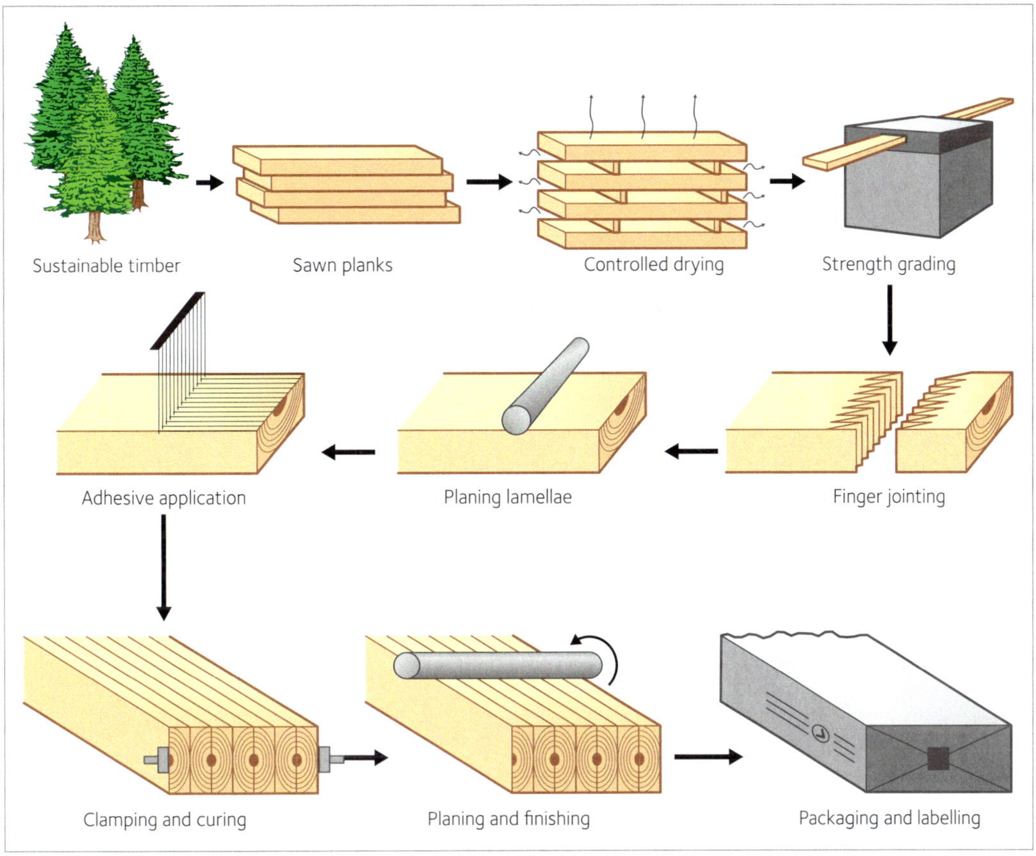

3 WORKING WITH WORDS: CNC MACHINING

Next you research the use of CNC machines for timber. Find the equivalent English words in the text. You may need to change the form of verbs.

1 Achse
2 Bohrer
3 Elektrowerkzeug
4 Fräser
5 Fräsmaschine
6 neigen
7 drehen
8 vielseitig verwendbar
9 Werkstück
10 Winkel

CNC MILLING MACHINES

CNC stands for computer numerical control. Theoretically any power tool can be controlled by a CNC interface, but the most versatile CNC machines for timber are CNC milling machines.

Milling machines remove material from timber using an endmill, a metal tool similar to a drill bit. The difference is that drills only go up and down, but mills can move sideways as well. This gives a good system of removing material with high precision.

With 5-axis milling, the endmill can be moved vertically (Z axis), horizontally (X and Y axes) and can be tilted at any angle (B axis). In addition, the timber workpiece can be rotated (C axis).

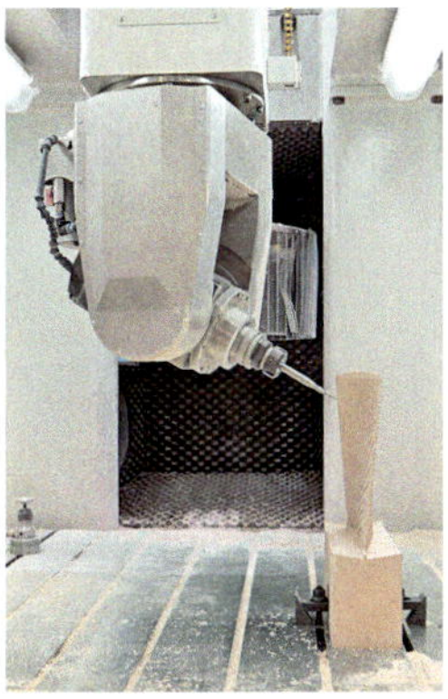

4 DISCUSSION

→ Interaktion, S. 246

A Work with a partner. Decide whether each of the points 1–12 is an advantage or a disadvantage of CNC machines in woodworking.

1 Reliance on CNC machines means that operators no longer need a detailed understanding of timber. That can lead to poor design.
2 Professional-quality CNC machines are much more expensive than manually operated machines and hand tools.
3 CAD/CAM software allows the designer to simulate the manufacture of his/her idea. There is no need to make a prototype or a model. This saves time and money.
4 CNC machines can be used continuously 24 hours a day, 365 days a year and only need to be switched off for occasional maintenance.
5 CNC machines are programmed with a design which can then be manufactured hundreds or even thousands of times. Each manufactured product will be exactly the same.
6 One person can supervise many CNC machines, as once they are programmed they can usually be left to work by themselves.
7 The time savings of CNC manufacture are less if there are a lot of unique components, as the machine has to be set up for each one.
8 Less highly trained people can operate CNC machines, whereas only skilled craftspeople can achieve good results with hand tools.
9 Timber is a natural, organic product and customers often want the kind of individual finish that only a skilled craftsperson can provide.
10 The ease of using CNC machines means that traditional woodworking skills are lost.

B Decide your own position: do CNC machines make traditional woodworking techniques obsolete? Report back to the class with your decision and reasons.

5 RESEARCH

Endmills are good at making round holes, but some woodworking techniques require rectangular holes for maximum strength. One of the most important ones is the mortise and tenon joint. Can CNC machines make mortise and tenon joints as good as those made by a carpenter?

Read the text and research the topic online, then report back to the class with your findings.

The **mortise and tenon** is one of the most common joints used by woodworkers.
It is neat and very strong: it has a large surface area for gluing, it cannot wobble and it is difficult to pull apart. It is used where maximum strength is important: e.g. in furniture, windows, doors and house frames.

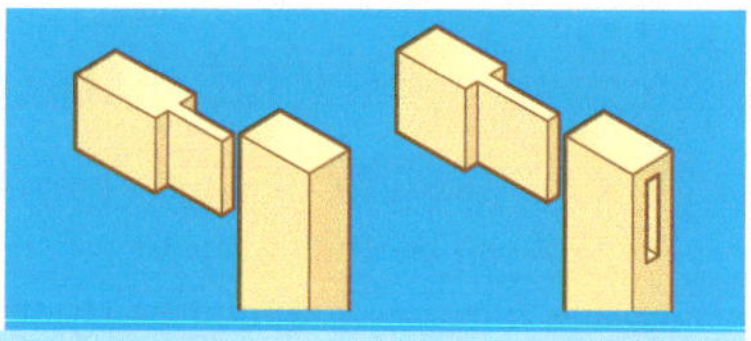

Two of the many different types of mortise and tenon joint

6 WRITING AN ESSAY

→ Einen Aufsatz schreiben, S. 234

Write an essay: "Traditional woodworking skills in the CNC age – just nostalgia?" Give arguments for and against using CNC machines in the carpentry workshop. Finish the essay with a conclusion giving your own opinion.

5 Speech recognition

You work for a company that produces domestic appliances. Your company is planning to implement speech recognition in its automated "smart home" technology. Your team has been given the task of preparing a simple explanation of how computer speech recognition works, for use in briefing sales representatives and dealers.

1 IMPROVING A TEXT

Your British colleague Andy has written a short text and has asked you to review it.

You decide that Andy's text needs headings for the paragraphs. Add these headings to the text. There is one heading that you do not need.

a Breaking down the signal
b Devices that talk back
c From analogue to digital
d Less complex systems
e From sounds to words
f Practice makes perfect
g Technology that "just works"

SPEECH RECOGNITION SOFTWARE

1 Speech recognition is a standard feature in modern computers and smartphones. In fact, we hardly give it a second thought: we just expect our phones to be able to understand us when we speak to them. Yet computerized speech recognition is a sophisticated process.

2 Human speech is an analogue data form: it consists of a continuously variable "signal". Computers on the other hand work with digital data: 0s and 1s. Therefore the first job of a speech recognition program is to convert analogue speech into digital data via an analogue-to-digital converter (ADC). To do this, the ADC samples the sound by taking precise measurements at frequent intervals.

3 Next the digitized signal is divided into segments as short as a few milliseconds (0.001 sec). The software acoustic model then compares these segments to sounds in the appropriate language. English has about 40 different sounds. (Language and speech recognition experts refer to them as "phonemes" rather than "sounds".)

4 The software language model compares groups of phonemes to a large library of known words to find the best match. This word is then used as user input for whatever the system is designed to do – for example, control appliances or an automated home.

5 The accuracy of speech recognition software generally improves when the software is "trained". The user gives feedback on the software's correct and incorrect interpretations. The software developers do most of this training, but end users must also spend some time training the software to recognize their particular speech patterns.

6 The need for training is greatly reduced when the software only has to recognize a limited library of words and phrases, such as commands to control a single smart appliance.

2 ANNOTATING A DIAGRAM

Your colleague Silke has drawn a diagram to show how speech recognition will work in your company's appliances. Use information from Andy's text on page 187 to write short explanations for the stages 1–4 in the diagram.

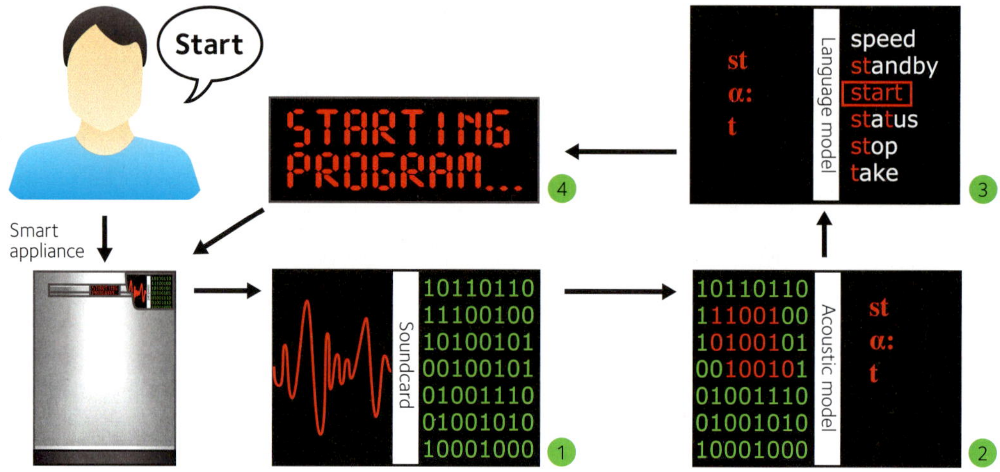

3 DISCUSSION

→ Interaktion, S. 246

Your team meets to discuss its experiences with speech recognition software. Work in a small group. Answer these questions and make notes, then report back to the class with the main points of your discussion.

1 Do you use speech recognition (a) on your phone or (b) on other devices, e.g. your home computer?
2 If you use speech recognition, what do you use it for?
3 If you do not use speech recognition, would you use it in the future? Give reasons.
4 Do you think that speech recognition is (a) useless, (b) fun but not really useful, (c) a useful tool, (d) an essential feature of modern electronic devices?

4 MEDIATION

→ Schriftliche Mediation, S. 240

Ihre Firma vertreibt ihre Produkte in vielen Ländern und hat eine weltweite Kundenbasis mit vielen Muttersprachen. Dies wiederum erfordert ein kostspieliges, mehrsprachiges Kundenbetreuungsnetz. Sie lesen den folgenden Artikel über Skype Translator in der britischen Zeitung *The Guardian* und fragen sich, ob dieser Dolmetscherdienst ein Mittel wäre, die Kundenbetreuung Ihrer Firma zu vereinfachen.

Fassen Sie den Text für Ihren Abteilungsleiter Dirk Förster auf Deutsch in einer E-Mail zusammen. Erwähnen Sie folgende Aspekte:

- Warum die Sprachbarriere ein Problem ist
- Was Skype Translator macht
- Was das System beim Testversuch geleistet hat
- Die Entwicklung der automatischen Übersetzung bei Microsoft
- Was ein neuronales Netz ist

Microsoft's "Star Trek" voice translator

For Captain Kirk and the crew of the Starship Enterprise, seeking out new life and new civilizations wouldn't be much use without a universal translator to deal with new languages too. Fortunately for the citizens of the 23rd century, Microsoft has begun making it a reality, two centuries early.

The company has unveiled a new service for Skype that can understand spoken words and translate them into another language, and speak them back almost in real time.

"Skype has always been about breaking down barriers. And the language barrier is huge. It has been a blocker to productivity and human connection," noted Gurdeep Pall, corporate vice president of Skype and Lync at Microsoft in a blog post. "Skype Translator helps us overcome this barrier. It's going to make sure you can communicate with anyone without language barriers."

English to German and vice versa

Pall demonstrated the technology at the Code conference in California, showing real-time translation of a Skype video call with a German colleague.

Pall was speaking English, allowing the translation system to then convert his speech into spoken German, while his video caller spoke German, allowing Pall and the audience to hear the translation into English in near real-time.

The system only made a few minor mistakes in the three-minute-long conversation, demonstrating the improved word, meaning and order recognition Microsoft has made since the technology was first demonstrated translating English to Chinese two years previously.

Star Trek TV series, 1966–69, EVERETT COLLECTION

"Star Trek vision for a Universal Translator isn't a galaxy away"

"It is early days for this technology, but the Star Trek vision for a Universal Translator isn't a galaxy away, and its potential is every bit as exciting as those Star Trek examples," explained Pall. "Skype Translator opens up so many possibilities to make meaningful connections in ways you never could before in education, diplomacy, multilingual families and in business."

Microsoft's machine translator research started 15 years ago, first with text-based translation and later with voice recognition and dictation technologies that have been present in Microsoft Office and Windows since 2001.

"It's not just about daisy-chaining* speech recognition, machine translation and speech synthesis," said Microsoft chief executive Satya Nadella. "It's a deep neural net that [can] do speech recognition in pretty magical ways."

A neural network is a computer system that can "learn" to recognize inputs and generate outputs rather like a group of nerves in the brain. (398 words)

* daisy-chaining (IT jargon) – joining things together in a simple, linear way

Abridged from: *www.theguardian.com*

6 Open source software

TECHNICAL TOPICS

With three friends – Kieran from Ireland, Beth from England and Fabienne from France – you have formed a software development cooperative. Your first product is Sandbox – a software platform which allows users to develop their own game apps without any programming knowledge. Kieran wants to release Sandbox as proprietary software, but Fabienne is a strong supporter of open source software. Beth is undecided. Who should you support?

1 ANSWERING QUESTIONS ABOUT OPEN SOURCE SOFTWARE

You want to be clear about what "open source software" is. You and your colleagues have written down some questions. Match each question to the paragraph in the text which answers it. (Two questions are not answered.)

1 What is proprietary software?
2 Is it possible to make a profit from open source software?
3 What makes open source software different?
4 What is a concise definition of open source software?
5 Is open source software only important to developers?
6 Can you release the same software in a proprietary and an open source version?
7 What is source code?
8 Who is allowed to modify open source software?

OPEN SOURCE SOFTWARE

A Open source software is software whose source code is available for modification or enhancement by anyone.

B "Source code" is the part of software that most computer users don't ever see; it's the code computer programmers can manipulate to change how a piece of software – a "program" or "application" – works. Programmers who have access to a computer program's source code can improve that program by adding features to it or fixing parts that don't always work correctly.

C Some software has source code that cannot be modified by anyone but the person, team, or organization who created it and maintains exclusive control over it. This kind of software is frequently called "proprietary software" or "closed source software", because its source code is the property of its original authors, who are the only ones legally allowed to copy or modify it. Microsoft Word and Adobe Photoshop are examples of proprietary software. In order to use proprietary software, computer users must agree (usually by signing a license displayed the first time they run this software) that they will not do anything with the software that the software's authors have not expressly permitted.

D Open source software is different. Its authors make its source code available to others who would like to view that code, copy it, learn from it, alter it or share it. Open source software licenses promote collaboration and sharing because they allow other people to make modifications to source code and incorporate those changes into their own projects.

E So, as the Open Source Initiative explains, "open source doesn't just mean access to the source code." It means that anyone should be able to modify the source code to suit his or her needs, and that no one should prevent others from doing the same.

F Open source software benefits programmers and non-programmers alike. In fact, because much of the Internet itself is built on many open source technologies – like the Linux operating system and the Apache Web server application – anyone using the internet benefits from open source software. (344 words)

Abridged from: *www.opensource.com*

2 WORKING WITH WORDS

Match the definitions (a–i) to the words from the text (1–11). Write your own definitions for the two words which do not have one.

1 access
2 application
3 collaboration
4 enhancement
5 feature
6 manipulate
7 modification
8 operating system
9 programmer
10 property
11 source code

a changing sth slightly
b improving sth
c control sth with skill
d program designed to perform a range of tasks for the user
e special characteristic
f sth that belongs to sb
g working together
h right or opportunity to use sth
i set of programs which controls how a computer works

3 LISTENING: WHY USERS LIKE OPEN SOURCE

→ Rezeption: Hörverstehen, S. 225

4/18

You hear a programme on the radio about open source software. Reporter Sophie Marr is talking to software developer Lars Kingham.

Listen to the recording and make notes about the following subjects.

1 Control
2 Bugs
3 Upgrades
4 Students
5 Business customers
6 Cost

4 RESEARCH: OPEN SOURCE VS PROPRIETARY SOFTWARE

Carry out this research at home and report back to the class with your findings.

1 Research these open-source applications. What do they do? Briefly describe their main functions and features.

BlueGriffon ▪ Firefox ▪ Gimp ▪ GnuCash ▪ Inkscape ▪ OpenOffice ▪ PeaZip ▪ Redo ▪ Scribus ▪ Ubuntu

2 Find proprietary software applications that do the same thing as the open-source applications. How much do they cost for a single user license?

3 If you needed these applications, would you use the open source or the proprietary version? Give reasons for your choice. Think about some of these issues:

compatibility ▪ cost ▪ documentation ▪ ease of use ▪ reliability ▪ security ▪ technical support

5 THINK, PAIR, SHARE: WHICH MODEL?

A Think. There are many business models for earning an income from open source software. Match the names (a–i) to the business models (1–9).

a Advertising supported software

b Bounties

c Crowdfunding

d Delayed open-sourcing

e Donationware

f Dual-licensing

g Optional proprietary extensions

h Software as a Service (SaaS)

i Support services

1. The software is offered under an open source license but also under a separate proprietary license. Income from selling the proprietary version finances the continued development of the free open source version.
2. Profit from open source software can come from selling training and technical support rather than the software itself.
3. Selling cloud computing functionality, such as online accounts and server access, to customers is a way of making profit from open source software.
4. Some open source software encourages or accepts voluntary payments from users. Online payment services such as PayPal make it much easier to set up this kind of arrangement.
5. The users of a particular software package may come together and offer money to any programmer who can come up with a desired feature or functionality.
6. The potential users of a new open source application come together to pay for it to be developed.
7. The software developers get income by displaying advertisements on their website or within the free software itself. The advertising may disappear if a fee is paid.
8. Companies sell optional proprietary extensions, modules, plugins or add-ons which improve their open source software. This is referred to as open core software, because the "core" of the software is still open.
9. The latest version is only available to paying customers. As the software is updated (patched), the older versions become available for free.

B Pair. Discuss with a partner. Which open source business model is best for Sandbox? Why.

C Share. Tell the rest of the class what you decided and why.

7 The future of freight

TECHNICAL TOPICS

You work in the technical planning department of a large logistics company. Faced with rising fuel costs and stricter environmental laws, your company wants to maintain its competitive advantage. Your department has been given the job of researching energy-efficient freight transport.

1 ANALYSING TRANSPORT MODES

→ Rezeption: Leseverstehen, S. 214

First of all, you want to get an overview of how the different transportation options perform in terms of speed and energy use.

Use information from the text and diagram to do the tasks.

1 Evaluate these transport solutions with regard to the four factors mentioned in the text.

EXAMPLE Coal from Kiev (Ukraine) to Paris by truck
Bad choice – energy efficiency more important than speed for bulk goods

- **a** Cheese and yoghurt from Marrakesh (Morocco) to Hamburg by ship
- **b** Fresh fish from Anchorage (Alaska) to Tokyo (Japan) by plane
- **c** Cement from Cordoba (Spain) to Berlin by plane
- **d** Oil from Oslo (Norway) to Aberdeen (Scotland) by train

2 Compare the performance of container ships, trains, trucks and cargo planes for transporting freight.

TRANSPORT MODES – GETTING THE BALANCE RIGHT

When choosing a mode of transport, there are four main factors which must be considered.

Type of load. Does the load consist of passengers, high-value freight (e.g. electronic goods) or low-value bulk freight (e.g. coal, oil, woodchips)? Some types of transport are only suitable for transporting certain loads (e.g. pipelines for liquids and gases).

Speed. How fast is the mode of transport? High speed is critically important for some loads (e.g. fresh food such as seafood or dairy produce) but less important for others (e.g. most bulk goods).

Energy efficiency. How much energy is expended in transporting the load? Energy efficiency greatly affects the financial cost of transport. Furthermore, environmental laws could make some energy-inefficient modes of transport unviable in the future.

Local availability. Loads can only be transported by sea if both the origin and the destination have a port, and by air if they both have an airport. Thus road transport from the European Union to the USA is not an option!

In practice, transport is often intermodal: more than one mode of transport is used during a journey. For example, electronic goods may be transported from Taiwan to Rotterdam by container ship, then the individual containers are loaded on to trucks or trains for delivery to warehouses and stores across Germany.

(301 words)

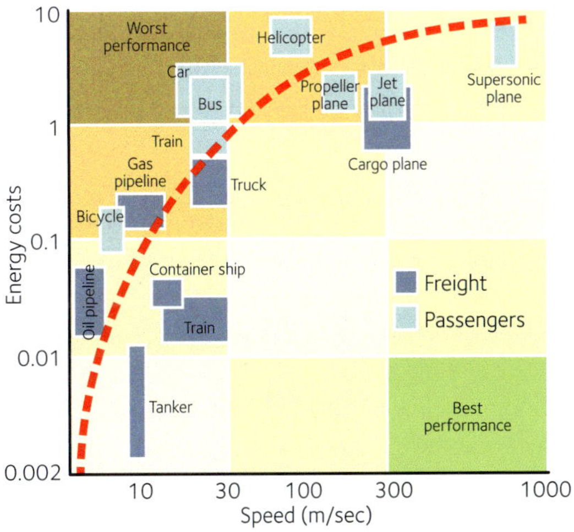

Nach: *J. D. Chapman (1989) Geography and Energy*

2 LISTENING AND ANSWERING QUESTIONS

→ Rezeption: Hörverstehen, S. 225

4/19 You hear a radio interview about the future of road freight with logistics expert Kate Ingham.

Listen to the interview and answer the questions below.

1 What is the "last mile problem"?
2 Why will road freight still be needed in 2030?
3 How are business conditions for road freight changing?
4 What new technologies will improve road freight?

3 READING AND REPORTING

→ Rezeption: Leseverstehen, S. 214

Your department researches two technologies for environmentally friendly long-distance transport.

Team A: Read text A. Note down the following information, then report back to the class.

1 Technology
2 Performance
3 Potential uses
4 Current stage of development

A

A SHIPPING REVOLUTION IN THE SKIES

Igor Pasternak believes he is on the verge of developing an aircraft that will change the way large cargo can be shipped.

Mr. Pasternak envisions a 770-foot-long, silver-skinned airship, which is kept aloft by helium-filled tanks, delivering fresh fruit to Alaska, dropping triage units at disaster sites or depositing heavy machinery into remote locations – no ports, rail lines, roads or airstrips necessary.

It would be able to fly at up to 120 knots, four times as fast as a cargo ship. Its capacity of 250 tons is about twice that of a C-5 cargo plane, and it has a range of about 5,870 miles, enough to go from Boston to Burkina Faso.

The airship, called the Aeroscraft, will take off and land like a helicopter. Its designers, Mr. Pasternak says, have solved the major problem for lighter-than-air crafts: buoyancy control. If a dirigible unloads heavy cargo, it must be tethered or take on the same weight to keep from floating away. The Aeroscraft sends helium from its main chamber into compression tanks, which creates room for air – which is heavier than the helium – to be taken in, allowing for a controlled descent.

Though much of the Aeroscraft's development costs have been covered by government military contracts, Mr. Pasternak has begun to turn more toward the private sector. He says he is convinced there is value in being able to deliver wind turbines to remote areas, something no air vessel can do. Or in getting overseas goods produced in November to American markets for the holiday season, something no cargo ship can move quickly enough to do.

A small fleet of smaller models, which are 555 feet with a 66-ton capacity, should be ready in three years, he said. The plan is for the 250-ton capacity ship to be ready another year after that. (311 words)

Abridged from: *www.nytimes.com*

Team B: Read text B. Note down the following information, then report back to the class.

1 Technology
2 Performance
3 Potential uses
4 Current stage of development

B

SKYSAILS: bringing wind back to ship propulsion

German company SkySails is looking to re-harness the wind for ship propulsion with its SkySails propulsion method. The system, which consists of a towing kite, a launch and recovery system and a control system for automated operation, is turning heads in a shipping industry dealing with increasing fuel prices and preparing for new emission regulations to come into force.

The SkySails method, designed as an auxiliary propulsion system to help offset the environmental and financial costs of running diesel engines, uses a towing kite that is capable of flying in the stronger winds 100–300m above a vessel, which the company says creates up to 25 times more energy per square metre than standard sails.

The system can generate up to 2,000kW of propulsion power in good wind conditions. According to SkySails founder and CEO Stephan Wrage, this amounts to significant cost and emissions savings, even in variable conditions. "In good wind conditions the newest SkySails system, SKS C 320, can save up to ten tonnes of oil per day," he says. "This equals more than $5,000 and more than 30 tonnes of CO_2 emissions savings per day. However, as wind conditions are not always perfect, average savings are two to three tonnes per day."

Various iterations of the SkySails system have been installed on vessels in the past six years, including the container ship Beluga Skysails and the Maartje Theadora, Germany's largest fishing vessel. These installations have allowed SkySails to study the system's operation in at-sea conditions. As well as proving the 2MW top-end for the system's propulsion power, these early voyages demonstrated other fundamental aspects of the system's performance.

"You have to test everything in real-life," says Wrage. "We were able to prove that it is possible not only to install a SkySails system on newbuilds but also to retrofit existing vessels with a SkySails system, without having to make significant modifications onboard. Ships stay fully maneuverable while the system is in use and the system does not compromise the usual operation of a cargo vessel, including loading and unloading." (342 words)

Abridged from: *www.ship-technology.com*

4 DEBATE: AIRSHIP OR SKYSAILS?

Your company has decided to invest €5 million in one of the two technologies described in the texts. Which project should get the money? Hold a classroom debate to decide. Consider the following aspects:

- Reliable technology
- Environmental benefit
- Wide range of uses
- Appeal to the public's imagination

8 Cybernetics – human 2.0?

TECHNICAL TOPICS

You work for a company which makes RFID (radio frequency identification devices). Your company is considering developing microchip implants for humans and you have been asked to find out more about the possibilities.

Are cyborgs the future of humanity?
Robocop, Marianne Jean-Baptiste, Joel Kinnamon, Sony Pictures, 2014, Unimediaimages, INC

1 DRAWING A MIND MAP

Will the public accept the idea of cybernetic implants? You read a magazine article which suggests that they might. You note down the main ideas for use in your company's marketing material.

A Read the text, then draw a mind map of the main ideas. Start like this:

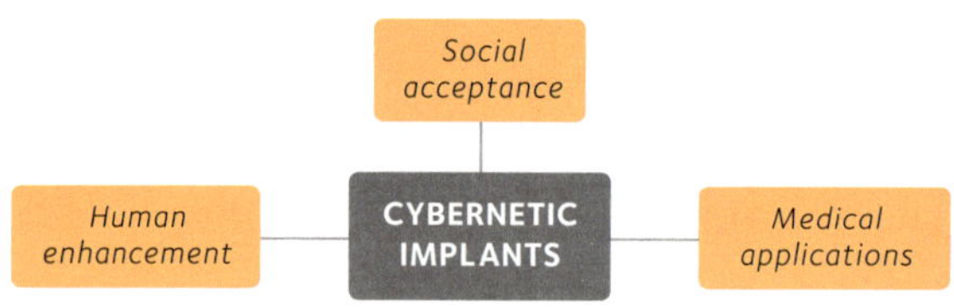

B As you work through the Topic, add new concepts to your mind map.

CYBERNETIC IMPLANTS – SCIENCE FACT, NOT SCIENCE FICTION

Will you one day have cybernetic implants in your body which enhance your senses and give you new abilities?

If the idea makes you uncomfortable, you're probably thinking of science fiction cyborgs like the Terminator, RoboCop or Darth Vader. However, people with cybernetic implants are among us now, and have been for a while.

Many people who were born deaf can hear now, thanks to cochlear implants. A cochlear implant is an electronic device which is surgically implanted in a person's inner ear.

An external microphone picks up sound from the environment and a speech processor filters the sound to emphasize speech. A transmitter sends the signal to the internal part of the device, which includes a receiver and stimulator embedded in the patient's skull, and up to 22 electrodes, which send the impulses to the nerves in the inner ear and from there directly to the brain.

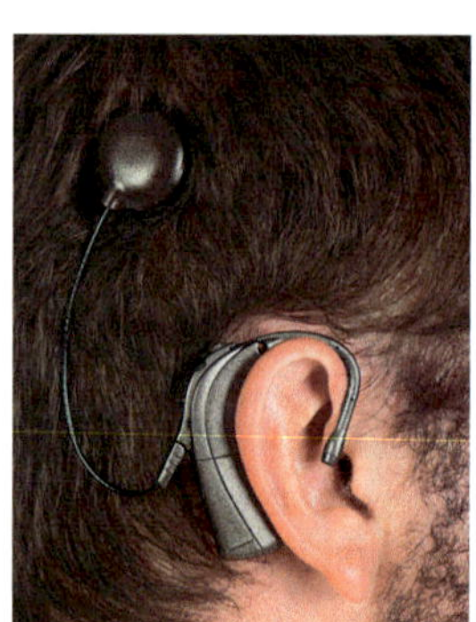

Cochlear implant

Cochlear implants were developed in the 1960s and have helped thousands of deaf people. The latest versions can connect to a person's Bluetooth devices, so that they can hear their phone calls and mp3 music without sound: the signal is electronic all the way from the device to the brain.

Since 2002, electronic brain implants have been used to help patients with Parkinson's disease, using deep brain stimulation. Signals from the implant stimulate the patient's brain and prevent the symptoms which make life with Parkinson's so difficult. They have already helped over 100,000 people. Advanced versions of these devices will be able to read the patient's brain activity and adapt to this feedback as well as sending signals.

Meanwhile, over three million people have received implanted pacemakers. A pacemaker delivers electrical impulses to the patient's heart muscles via electrodes. It keeps the heart beating regularly. The latest versions are the size and shape of a multivitamin pill and can respond intelligently to feedback from the user's heart. They can even communicate wirelessly with the doctor's equipment to confirm that they are working properly.

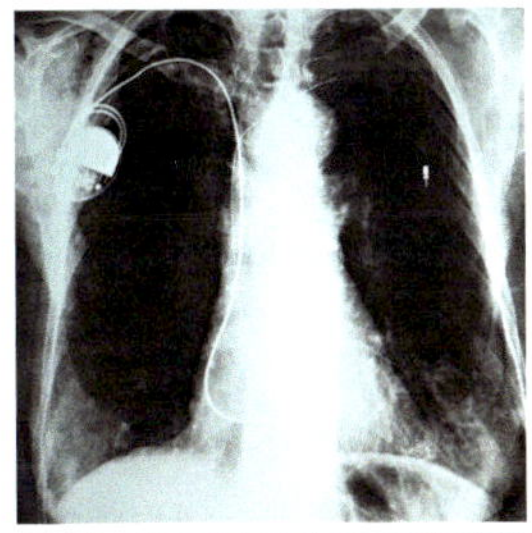
Pacemaker

It is only a short step from medical cybernetic implants like these to implants which enhance the senses and abilities of healthy people without disabilities. Already some 'biohackers' like Amal Graafstra have successfully implanted RFID microchips into their hands which allow them to communicate with electronic devices. The chips can unlock their doors, communicate with their phones and start their vehicles without a key.

These are simple functions, but in future we can be sure that implants will have much more advanced features. Although social acceptance may take some time, there will certainly be eager customers. Already people pay thousands of euros to improve their appearance using plastic surgery: how much will they pay to become more intelligent, have better memory and have superhuman sight and hearing? (421 words)

2 LISTENING AND UNDERSTANDING OPINIONS

→ Rezeption: Hörverstehen, S. 225

4/20 Next you ask some of your English-speaking friends what they think about cybernetic enhancement.

Listen to the recording, then match the ideas to the speakers. There is one idea which does not match. The speakers are in the same order as the photos.

Jon

Ellie and Matt

Rani

a I don't want to become a machine.

b It isn't safe.

c It should only be used for people with disabilities.

d Super-senses would be great.

e Modern technology has serious security problems.

f It will lead to more inequality between rich and poor.

g It isn't so different from what we do now, just more useful.

3 DISCUSSION

→ Interaktion, S. 246

Work in a small group. What is your point of view on cybernetic implants in healthy people? Consider the arguments for and against, then report back to the class with your consensus view and main reasons.

4 READING AND ANSWERING QUESTIONS

→ Rezeption: Leseverstehen, S. 214

Your manager wants to research the subject of human enhancement more widely. She forwards a text about wearable robotics to you.

Read the text and answer your manager's questions.

1 Was ist das langfristige Ziel des Forschungsprojekts?
2 Was können die Prototype schon leisten?
3 Wie werden die Exoskelette angetrieben?
4 Wie werden die Anzüge für Spezialaufgaben adaptiert?
5 Was hat das Forschungsteam durch den Versuch herausgefunden?

Robotic suit gives shipyard workers super strength

At a sprawling shipyard in South Korea, workers dressed in wearable robotics were lifting large pieces of metal, pipes and other objects as if they were nothing.

It was all part of a test by Daewoo Shipbuilding and Marine Engineering, at their facility in Okpo-dong. The company, one of the largest shipbuilders in the world, wants to take production to the next level by outfitting staff with robot exoskeletons that give them superhuman strength.

Gilwhoan Chu, the lead engineer for the firm's research and development arm, says the pilot showed that the exoskeleton does help workers perform their tasks. His team is working to improve the prototypes so that they can go into regular use in the shipyard, where robots already run a large portion of a hugely complex assembly system.

The exoskeleton fits anyone between 160 and 185 centimetres tall. Workers do not feel the weight of its 28-kilogram frame of carbon, aluminium alloy and steel, as the suit supports itself and is engineered to follow the wearer's movements. With a 3-hour battery life, the exoskeleton allows users to walk at a normal pace and, in its prototype form, it can lift objects with a mass of up to 30 kilograms.

To put on the exoskeleton, workers start by strapping their feet on to foot pads at the base of the robot. Padded straps at the thigh, waist and across the chest connect the user to the suit, allowing the robot to move with their bodies as it bears loads for them. A system of hydraulic joints and electric motors running up the outside of the legs links to a backpack, which powers and controls the suit.

Frames designed for individual tasks can be attached to the backpack, with some hanging over a person's head like a small crane. As well as boosting raw lifting ability, the suit helps workers manipulate heavy components precisely: it takes most of the weight, so the user is effectively handling light objects.

Chu says worker feedback from the trial has been mostly positive. Testers were pleased that the exoskeleton let them lift heavy objects repeatedly without strain, but everyone also wanted it to move faster and be able to cope with heavier loads. Chu is working on it. "Our current research target of the lifting capacity is about 100 kilograms," he says. (396 words)

Abridged from: *www.newscientist.com*

5 WRITING AN ESSAY

→ Einen Aufsatz schreiben, S. 234

Write an essay on the subject "Cybernetics – the future of humanity?". Use your mind map to help you.

9 Biometric security technology

TECHNICAL TOPICS

You work for a chemical engineering company which uses strict security measures to prevent theft of its trade secrets by rivals. Access to sensitive areas is limited to authorized personnel and controlled by a fingerprint reader. You have been assigned to a taskforce to improve technical security.

1 LOOKING AT THE TEXT

→ Rezeption: Leseverstehen, S. 214

Sie finden den folgenden Bericht auf der BBC-Nachrichtenwebsite. Gerüchte über den unten genannten Vorfall kursieren bereits in Ihrer Abteilung.

Entscheiden Sie, ob jede Aussage richtig oder falsch ist oder im Text nicht erwähnt wird. Korrigieren Sie die falschen Aussagen.

1 „Der Hacker hat spezielle Software und eine Hochauflösungskamera für diese Aufgabe verwendet."
2 „Experten bezweifeln, dass es möglich ist, Fingerabdrücke zu fälschen."
3 „Es wird empfohlen, künftig bei öffentlichen Auftritten Handschuhe zu tragen."
4 „Er hat auf einer Pressekonferenz mehrere Nahaufnahmen von den Händen der Politikerin gemacht."
5 „Statische biometrische Verfahren gelten weiterhin als die sicherste Erkennungsmethode."
6 „Banken setzen bereits Scanner zur Erkennung von Fingervenenmustern ein."
7 „Eine Studie in einem britischen Krankenhaus hat erwiesen, dass die Scanner Blutdruckschwankungen verursachen."

Politician's fingerprint "cloned from photos" by hacker

By Zoe Kleinman
Technology reporter, BBC News

A member of the Chaos Computer Club (CCC) hacker network claims to have cloned a thumbprint of a German politician by using commercial software and images taken at a news conference.

Jan Krissler says he replicated the fingerprint of defence minister Ursula von der Leyen using pictures taken with a "standard photo camera". Mr Krissler had no physical prints from Ms von der Leyen. Fingerprint biometrics are already considered insecure, experts say.

Mr Krissler, also known as Starbug, was speaking at a convention for members of the CCC, a 31-year-old network that claims to be "Europe's largest association" of hackers.

He told the audience he had obtained a close-up of a photo of Ms von der Leyen's thumb and had also used other pictures taken at different angles during a press event that the minister had spoken at.

"Wear gloves"
Mr Krissler has suggested that "politicians will presumably wear gloves when talking in public" after hearing about his research.

Fingerprint identification is used as a security measure on both Apple and Samsung devices, and was used to identify voters at polling stations in Brazil's recent presidential election, but it is not considered to be particularly secure, experts say.

Living biometrics
"Biometrics that rely on static information like face recognition or fingerprints – it's not trivial to forge them but most people have accepted that they are not a great form of security because they can be faked," says cybersecurity expert Prof Alan Woodward from Surrey University.

"People are starting to look for things where the biometric is alive – vein recognition in fingers, gait [body motion] analysis – they are also biometrics but they are chosen because the person has to be in possession of them and exhibiting them in real life."

In September this year Barclays bank introduced finger vein recognition for business customers, and the technique is also used at cash machines in Japan and Poland.

Electronics firm Hitachi manufactures a device that reads the unique pattern of veins inside a finger. It only works if the finger is attached to a living person. Trials in the intensive care unit at Southampton General Hospital indicated that vein patterns are not affected by changes to blood pressure. (387 words) Source: *www.bbc.com*

2 WORKING WITH WORDS

You want to improve your vocabulary for discussing biometrics. Find expressions in the text above which match the definitions (1–8).

1 to make an exact copy of something (*two answers*)
2 unsafe
3 photo which shows something in great detail
4 action intended to protect something/someone
5 easy
6 to make a copy in order to trick people (*two answers*)
7 to show something
8 different to all others

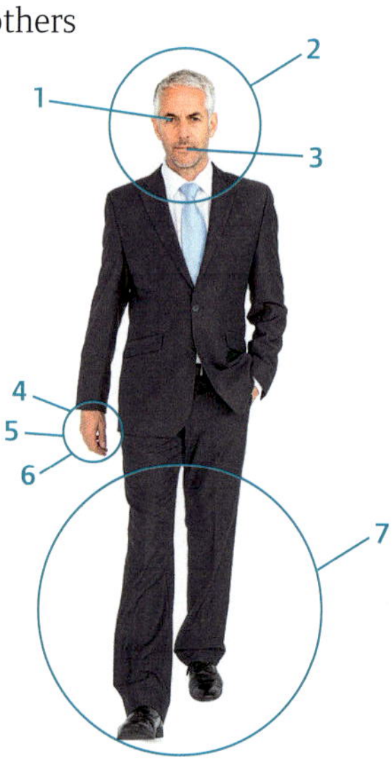

3 ANNOTATING A DIAGRAM

Write a key for the diagram with the names of the biometrics mentioned in the text. (Some of the labelled biometrics are not mentioned.) For each biometric, give a short explanation. (You will continue to work on the diagram and key throughout this Topic, so leave space for more information.)

4 LISTENING

→ Rezeption: Hörverstehen, S. 225

4/21

You decide to find out more about biometrics. You find a documentary podcast online.

A Listen to the recording and take notes on the following subjects.

1 Biometrics definition and aims
2 Static biometric systems
3 Ways that static systems can be tricked
4 Dynamic biometrics
5 Advanced fingerprint readers
6 False negatives

B Add relevant information from your notes to your key from exercise 3.

5 RESEARCH

Go online to find out more about ONE of the biometrics in your diagram AND one new biometric not mentioned so far in this Topic. Include the following information:

- What it measures
- How the technology works
- How secure it is
- Where it can be used

Report back to the class with what you found out.

6 EVALUATING BIOMETRICS

An American contact from your professional network gives you a list of criteria for evaluating biometrics.

Which human characteristics are suitable for biometric authentication?

There are seven criteria that we use when assessing the suitability of any trait for use in biometric authentication.

1 **Universality.** Does every person using the system have the characteristic?

2 **Uniqueness.** Is the characteristic different for everyone, so that individuals can be distinguished by it?

3 **Permanence.** Does the characteristic remain the same under different circumstances? Does it change over time?

4 **Measurability.** Is it possible to measure the characteristic?

5 **Performance.** Can available technology measure the characteristic accurately, quickly and reliably?

6 **Acceptability.** Will people accept the technology and be willing to have this biometric measured?

7 **Circumvention.** How easy is it to imitate or copy the trait?

No single biometric will meet all the requirements of every application. That is why good biometric systems are **multi-modal**, i.e. they use more than one biometric.

A Explain why each of the following would be a poor biometric for authentication, with reference to the seven criteria mentioned in the text above.

1 DNA	3 Hair colour	5 Personality
2 Finger length	4 Height	6 Signature

B Evaluate each of the biometrics in your diagram from exercise 3 using the seven criteria. Add your evaluations to the key.

7 DISCUSSION

→ Interaktion, S. 246

Work in a small group. Design a multi-modal biometric system that will offer your company the right balance of the seven criteria. Every employee has to use the system each time he or she enters the building, so it must be quick and convenient to use.

8 WRITING AN EMAIL

→ Job skills 1 ▪ Emails, S. 31

Write an email in English to the Chief Security Officer (CSO) of your company, Scott Larson. Recommend a suitable new biometric security system for the company, giving reasons for your recommendation.

10 Electric vehicles

TECHNICAL TOPICS

You are applying for a job with a company that makes electric vehicles (EVs) and hybrid electric vehicles (HEVs). You ask your Australian friend, Rosie Taylor, who is studying electrical engineering in Sydney, for help in understanding basic principles of electric vehicles.

1 LOOKING AT THE TEXT

A Lesen Sie Rosies Mail und beantworten Sie die unten stehenden Fragen.

→ Rezeption: Leseverstehen, S. 214

1 Wie wird der Rotor zum Drehen gebracht?
2 Wo werden Dauermagneten im Synchronmotor verwendet?
3 Warum ist die Verbindung von Wechselstrom und Elektromagneten im Stator eine einfache Lösung?
4 Welchen Vorteil hat ein Dreiphasenmotor?

From: Rosie Taylor
Subject: Re: Electric motors – help please!

Hi!

Nice to hear from you. All going well here, enjoying the Aussie summer while you shiver over there in the German winter ;-)

You want to know how electric vehicles work? That's a short question with a long answer! I'll do my best to keep it simple.

Electric motors rely on the principle of magnetic attraction: unlike poles (positive + negative) attract each other; like poles (negative + negative, or positive + positive) repel each other. Two magnets placed close to each other will always try to align themselves so that the unlike poles are together and the like poles are apart.

Electric motors use this principle to turn electrical energy into kinetic energy. They consist of two main parts: the **stator** (the part which stands still) and the **rotor** (the part which rotates). By changing the magnetic polarity of the stator, we force the rotor to rotate. The rotor is trying to align itself with the magnetic polarity of the stator – but it can't, because that magnetic polarity is constantly changing.

So far so good. Those basic principles apply to all electric motors. Unfortunately, it gets more complicated – a lot more complicated. You see, there are several different types of electric motor, too many to describe in one short email.

However, I can see from the URL you sent me that the company you want to work for uses **synchronous three-phase AC motors** in its vehicles. That's good, because it's a relatively simple type of motor to explain.

The synchronous motor has **permanent magnets** in the rotor and **electromagnets** (coils of copper wire) in the stator. The polarity of the electromagnets is changed to make the rotor spin – it's trying to align itself with the magnetic field of the stator, as described above.

Using electromagnets with alternating current (AC) electricity is a really elegant, simple system: because the direction of the current is constantly changing, the electromagnets are constantly changing polarity. At 50 Hertz (50 cycles a second), for example, they will change polarity 100 times a second.

To make the rotation of the rotor smoother, **three different sets of electromagnets** are used in the stator. I've coloured them green, blue and yellow in the attached diagram. Each of them is at a different stage in the cycle – we call that **three-phase power**. So the rotor is in the middle of a smoothly and constantly changing magnetic field produced by the stator. That produces a powerful, smooth-running motor.

Just let me know if you need more information. Good luck with the job application!

All the best
Rosie

B **Rosie sent this diagram with her email. Unfortunately she forgot to label it. With the help of the text, give the diagram a title and identify the numbered parts. The words and phrases you need are in bold in the text.**

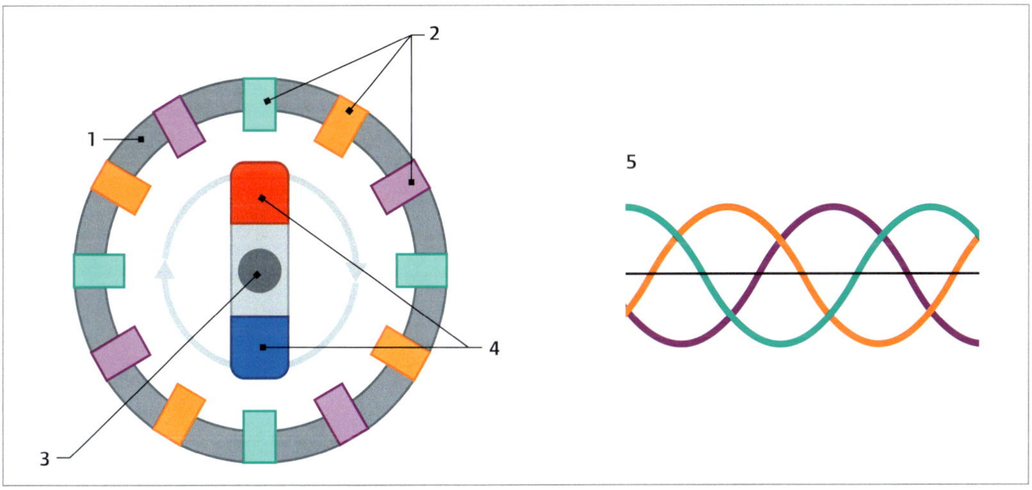

2 LISTENING

→ Rezeption: Hörverstehen, S. 225

4/22

You attend the IAA (Internationale Automobil-Ausstellung) in Frankfurt am Main to find out more about EVs and HEVs. You listen to a conversation between an automotive technician and two show visitors about HEVs.

Listen to the discussion, then copy and complete the grid.

Type of hybrid	How the motor and engine work together	Advantages
Mild or "micro"		
Parallel		
Series		

3 PAIRWORK: DESCRIBING A DIAGRAM

Work with a partner.

Partner A: You are a visitor to the show. You would like to know how your partner's HEVs work. Take notes while your partner is speaking, then read them back to him/her to check that you have understood correctly.

Partner B: You are a British HEV technician on your company's stand. Choose ONE of the diagrams A–C below and use it with your notes from exercise 2 to explain how your company's technology works.

When you have finished, swap roles.

A
Parallel hybrid

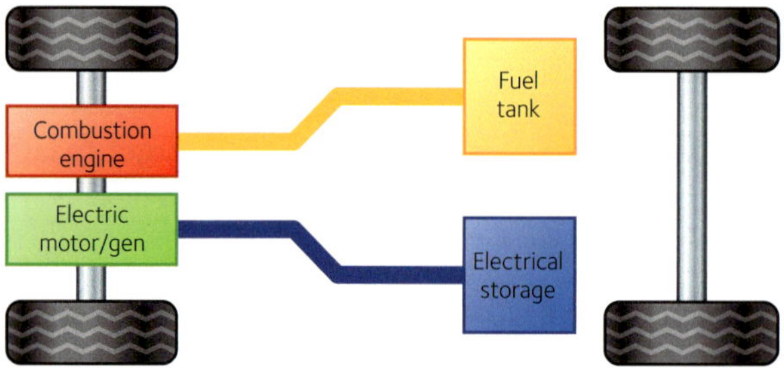

B
Mild hybrid

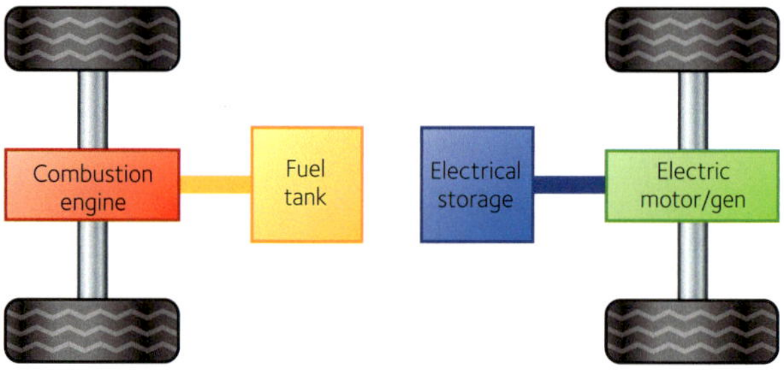

C
Series hybrid

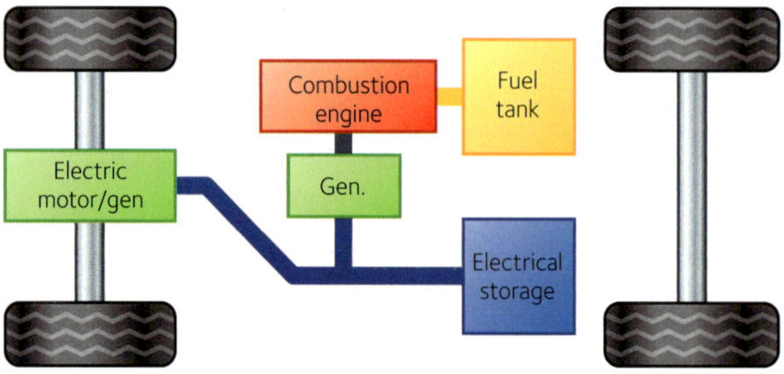

4 RESEARCH

You decide to research EVs further to prepare for your job interview. Choose ONE of the topics. Research the topic online, then report back to the class with what you found out.

- Regenerative braking in EVs – how it works
- EV battery technology – latest developments
- EV recharging – options in Germany today

11 Keeping track of food

TECHNICAL TOPICS

You work in the Food Science and Technology Division of a company that produces ready meals for sale in supermarkets. Your company wants to become more efficient and improve the quality of its products by gathering more data from its processes. Your manager has asked your team to investigate RFID as a possible solution.

1 LOOKING AT THE TEXT

→ Rezeption: Leseverstehen, S. 214

Sie finden den folgenden Artikel über RFID in einem Technik-Wiki. Fassen Sie die Informationen für Ihren Abteilungsleiter tabellarisch zusammen.

RFID-Tag	Energiequelle	Fähigkeiten	Anwendungen
Passiv			
Aktiv			
Semi-passiv			

RFID basics

RFID tags

RFID is short for Radio Frequency Identification Device. An RFID system has two main components: a reader (transceiver) and a tag (transponder).

The tag contains a microchip and an antenna. The microchip contains digital data. Any data may be stored this way: the only limitations are the storage capacity of the microchip and the bandwidth of the system.

A passive tag has no power source of its own. It is powered by the radio frequency (RF) field generated by the reader. When the tag enters the reader's field, it is able to draw enough power from it to access its internal memory. It has no active transmitter, so it transmits its information by altering the RF field from the reader. When the tag draws power from the RF field, the voltage at the transceiver antenna drops. The tag transmits its information by varying the amount of power it draws from the field.

The range of most passive tags is around three metres. Typically they can store up to 128 bits of data. Common applications are in the retail industry to track stock items, and in libraries to prevent the theft of books, but the range of applications is almost limitless. The simplest tags only cost a few cents each to produce.

An active tag has its own transmitter and power source – a small battery similar to the ones used in watches. It remains in a low-power "idle" state until it detects the RF field of a reader. When the tag leaves the RF field it again powers down to its idle state to conserve power. As a result of this it can be detected at a greater range than a passive tag – 100m or more. It can commonly store 128 kilobits or more of data.

Some active tags can also initiate communication with a reader (or other tags) when certain conditions are present. They may have external sensors to monitor temperature, humidity, motion and other conditions.

Applications for active tags include tracking large, valuable assets such as construction machinery and following the movements of farm animals or wild animals. Each tag can cost up to several hundred euros, depending on its complexity.

A semi-passive tag has a battery which powers the microchip and any sensors only. It has no transmitter: like a passive tag it alters the RF field of the transceiver to transmit its data, however its on-board power source gives it extended range (around 10 metres).

Because the battery does not have to power a transmitter, it can last for around 10 years and can keep the tag in "awake" mode all the time. This means that semi-passive tags are suitable for high-speed applications such as motorway toll systems: tags moving at up to 400 km/h can still be read, whereas the maximum speed for reading active and passive tags is around 30 km/h. (487 words)

2 WORKING WITH WORDS

Find words in the text on page 205 which have a similar meaning to the following words. You may need to change the forms of nouns and verbs.

1 part (paragraph 1)
2 information (paragraph 2)
3 energy (paragraph 3)
4 to take (paragraph 3)
5 to send (paragraph 3)
6 use (paragraph 4)
7 to follow (paragraph 4)
8 inactive (paragraph 5)
9 to keep (paragraph 5)
10 to start (paragraph 6)

3 LISTENING: PANEL DISCUSSION

→ Rezeption: Hörverstehen, S. 225

4/23

You listen to a radio panel discussion about RFID in the food processing industry.

Listen to the discussion and complete the sentences.

1 According to Mike Stephens, RFID is necessary for …
2 Errors in food storage can be …
3 The Internet of Things enables …
4 Alice Bates does not think it is sustainable to …
5 She thinks that RFID tags for food products could be ethical if they …
6 The usefulness of RFID to consumers depends on …
7 Emma is concerned about …

4 PLACEMAT EXERCISE: RFID IN THE FOOD INDUSTRY

Your team is considering how your company can implement RFID technology in its product and processes. The main processes in the lifecycle of your products are shown below.

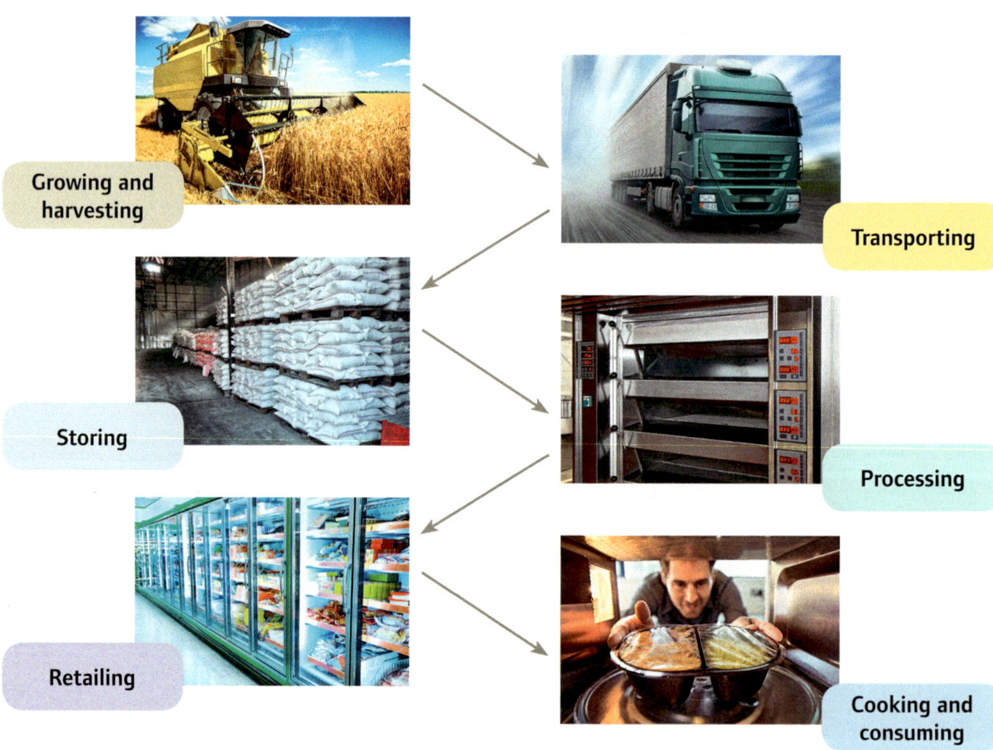

Work in a small group around a table. Put a large sheet of paper in the middle of the table and follow these steps.

A Preparation. Each group member takes one or more of the processes above and makes notes on his/her corner of the placemat.

For each stage, consider the following:

- technology used (e.g. harvesting machine, truck, oven)
- useful data (e.g. sunshine, rainfall, temperature)
- how RFID tags could provide the data to the technology (e.g. tag in packaging with sensors for … communicates with … when …)
- type of RFID required (active, semi-passive, passive)

B Discussion. Discuss your ideas and draw a mind map "RFID food technology" in the centre of the placemat.

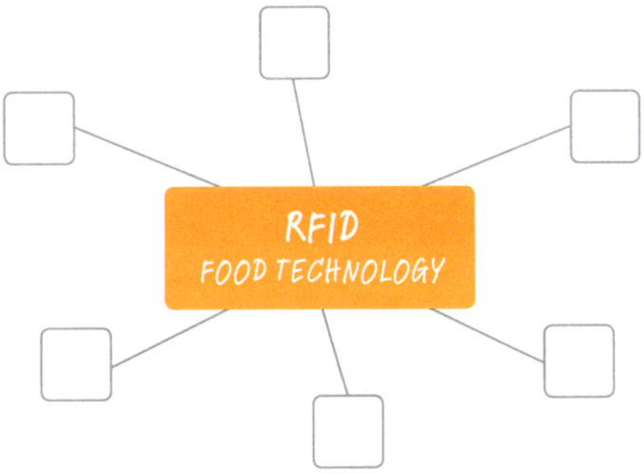

C Presentation. Use your mind map to present your ideas to the rest of the class.

5 COMMENTING ON A CARTOON

→ Bilder beschreiben und analysieren, S. 236

Describe the cartoon and comment on its message.

12 3D printing

TECHNICAL TOPICS

You are a junior CAD technician in a design company which provides rapid prototyping and 3D modelling services for manufacturers, engineering companies and architects. 3D printing is an important part of the company's services.

1 WRITING FAQS

Your boss has asked you to prepare some FAQs and answers about 3D printing for the company website. You find this article in *The Independent* newspaper and decide to use it as a starting point, by shortening and adapting the answers to fit the design of your company's website.

A For each of the questions 1–5, use information from the text to produce an answer of one or two sentences and not more than 30 words. Do not add any extra information of your own.

B Übersetzen Sie Ihre FAQs für die deutschsprachige Version der Website.

3D PRINTING FOR DUMMIES

It seems like everyone from the White House to Amazon.com is talking about 3D printing these days, but what exactly is it? Here's a quick guide to what all the hype is about …

1. What is a 3D printer?
3D printers are a new generation of machines that can make everyday things. They're remarkable because they can produce different kinds of objects, in different materials, all from the same machine.

A 3D printer can make pretty much anything from ceramic cups to plastic toys, metal machine parts, stoneware vases, fancy chocolate cakes or even (one day soon) human body parts.

They replace traditional factory production lines with a single machine, just like home inkjet printers replaced bottles of ink, a printing press, hot metal type and a drying rack.

2. Why is it called printing?
If you look closely (with a microscope) at a page of text from your home printer, you'll see the letters don't just stain the paper, they're actually sitting slightly on top of the surface of the page.

In theory, if you printed over that same page a few thousand times, eventually the ink would build up enough layers on top of each other to create a solid 3D model of each letter. That idea of building a physical form out of tiny layers is how the first 3D printers worked.

3. How do 3D printers work?
You start by designing a 3D object on an ordinary home PC, connect it to a 3D printer, press "print" and then sit back and watch. The 3D printing process turns a whole object into thousands of tiny little slices, then makes it from the bottom-up, slice by slice. Those tiny layers stick together to form a solid object.

Each layer can be very complex, meaning 3D printers can create moving parts like hinges and wheels as part of the same object. You could print a whole bike – handlebars, saddle, frame, wheels, brakes, pedals and chain – ready assembled, without using any tools. It's just a question of leaving gaps in the right places.

4. What are the opportunities?
Have you ever broken something, only to find it's no longer sold and you can't replace it? 3D printing means you can simply print a new one. That world, where you can make almost anything at home, is very different from the one we live in today. It's a world that doesn't need lorries to deliver goods or warehouses to store them in, where nothing is ever out of stock and where there is less waste, packaging and pollution.

5. What are the limitations?
Although buying a 3D printer is much cheaper than setting up a factory, the cost per item you produce is higher, so the economics of 3D printing don't stack up against traditional mass production yet. It also can't match the smooth finish of industrial machines, nor offer the variety of materials or range of sizes available through industrial processes. But, like so many household technologies, the prices will come down and 3D printer capabilities will improve over time. (517 words)

Abridged from: *www.independent.co.uk*

2 LISTENING: 3D PRINTING PROCESSES

→ Rezeption: Hörverstehen, S. 225

4/24

Your boss explains the different 3D printing processes to you.

A Listen to the recording and choose the correct label for each diagram.

stereolithography ▪ fused deposition modelling ▪ selective laser sintering

1

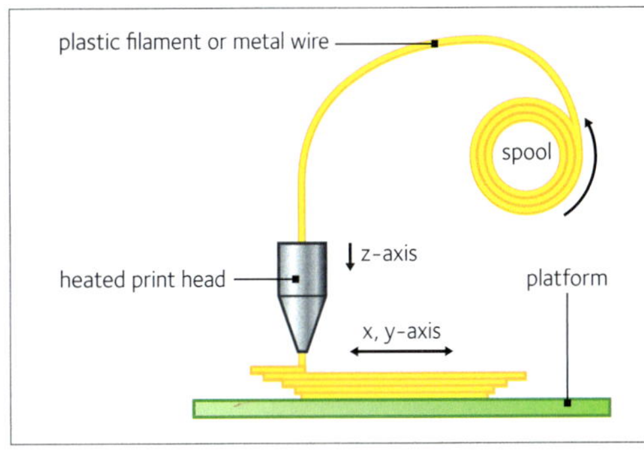

2

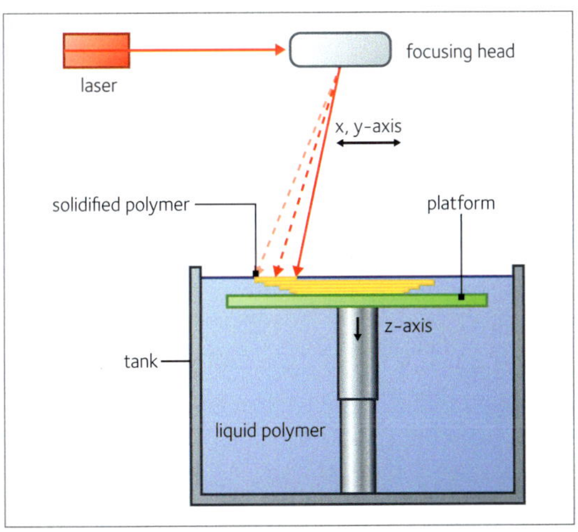

3

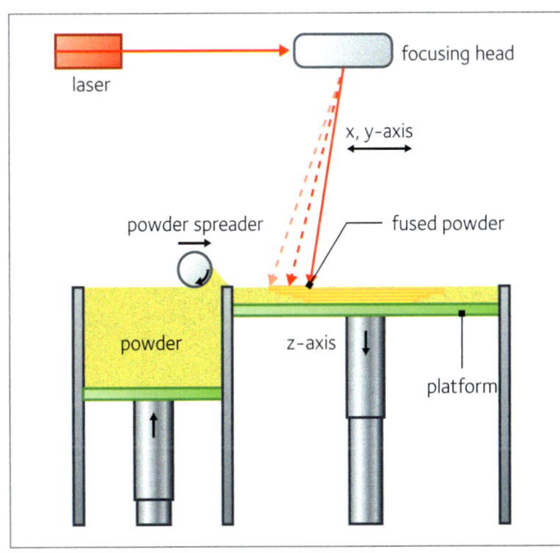

B Listen again and make notes about each of the three processes.

C Use your notes to write short explanations of the diagrams for the company website.

3 DISCUSSION

→ Interaktion, S. 246

Work in a small group. Discuss whether 3D printing will replace traditional manufacturing. Here are some ideas to include in your discussion:

Mass manufacturing ▪ Cost per item ▪ Individual requirements ▪ Technical limitations ▪ Pirate copies

Report back to the class with the main points of your discussion.

4 MEDIATION: 4D PRINTING

→ Schriftliche Mediation, S. 240

Sie sollen eine kurze Beschreibung des 4D-Druckverfahrens für die Firmen-Website verfassen. Fassen Sie die relevanten Informationen aus dem Text zusammen. Erwähnen Sie dabei folgende Punkte:

Definition ▪ Verfahren ▪ Energieträger ▪ Anwendungen ▪ Stand der Forschung

4D PRINTED OBJECTS "MAKE THEMSELVES"

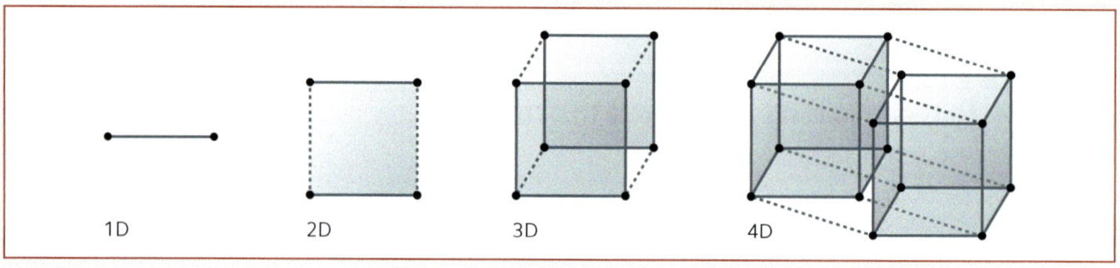

Many are only just getting their heads around the idea of 3D printing but scientists at MIT are already working on an upgrade: 4D printing. At the TED conference in Los Angeles, architect and computer scientist Skylar Tibbits showed how the process allows objects to self-assemble.

It could be used to install objects in hard-to-reach places such as underground water pipes, he suggested. It might also herald an age of self-assembling furniture, said experts.

Mr Tibbits, from the MIT's (Massachusetts Institute of Technology) self-assembly lab, explained what the extra dimension involved. "We're proposing that the fourth dimension is time and that over time static objects will transform and adapt," he told the BBC.

The process uses a specialized 3D printer made by Stratasys that can create multi-layered materials. It combines a strand of standard plastic with a layer made from a "smart" material that can absorb water. The water acts as an energy source for the material to expand once it is printed.

"The rigid material becomes a structure and the other layer is the force that can start bending and twisting it," said Mr Tibbits. "Essentially the printing is nothing new, it is about what happens after," he added.

Such a process could in future be used to build furniture, bikes, cars and even buildings, he thinks. For the time being he is seeking a manufacturing partner to explore the innovation. "We are looking for applications and products that wouldn't be possible without these materials," he added. "Imagine water pipes that can expand to cope with different capacities or flows and save digging up the street."

Engineering software developer Autodesk, which collaborated on the project, is looking even further into the future. "Imagine a scenario where you go to Ikea and buy a chair, put it in your room and it self-assembles," said Carlo Olguin, principal research scientist at the software firm.

The next stage for the research is to move from printing single strands to sheets and eventually whole structures. And water need not be the process's only energy source. "We could also have heat, vibration and sound," said Mr Tibbits. (358 words)

Abridged from: *www.bbc.com*

5 RESEARCH: HOW WE CAN USE 4D PRINTING

Go online to research "applications for 4D printing". Tell the class about the most interesting application that you found. Include the following information:

- What it is and does
- Energy source(s) used for the 4D transformation
- Stage of development: e.g. concept, development, prototype or commercial production
- Its usefulness and chance of commercial success

APPENDIX

Unit 6, Text A, Exercise 4

→ Page 48

1 Fun tram tickets

Problem: Lots of people don't pay for tickets when they travel on public transport.
Current solution: Spend a lot of money on ticket inspectors who fine people without tickets.
Fun solution: Make it fun to buy a ticket: when you stamp it, you could win an instant lottery!

2 The speed camera lottery

Problem: People break the speed limit.
Current solution: Fine people who break the speed limit.
Fun solution: Reward people for keeping to the speed limit. Use the money from the fines.

3 Wiki traffic lights

Problem: Motorists jump red lights.
Current solution: Fine motorists who do this or take away their driving licence, or both.
Fun solution: Make it interesting to wait at traffic lights by answering general knowledge questions.

4 Pinball exercise machine

Problem: Neither young nor old people exercise enough.
Current solution: No solution.
Fun solution: Combine a step machine and a pinball machine to make exercising at the bus stop fun.

Unit 11, Text B, Exercise 5B

→ Page 107

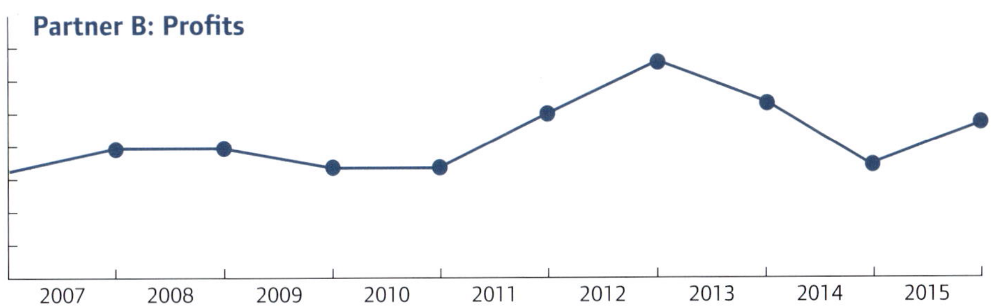

Skills files

Diese *Skills files* helfen Ihnen, Ihre Sprachfertigkeiten zu trainieren, damit Sie Erfolg in der Prüfung haben. Wenn Sie sich regelmäßig mit dem Lernprozess beschäftigen (mit den *Building skills boxes* und *Skills checklists* in den Units und den Materialien hier), fällt Ihnen der Umgang mit der englischen Sprache jeden Tag leichter. Hier gehen Sie Schritt für Schritt durch verschiedene Aufgabentypen und bekommen viele hilfreiche Tipps, wie Sie Ihre Fähigkeiten verbessern können. Um Ihre Kenntnisse zu festigen, gibt es auch Übungen zu den verschiedenen Strategien. Lösungen zu diesen Aufgaben finden Sie auf www.cornelsen.de/webcodes: Geben Sie einfach den Webcode FOSSKLO im Webcode-Suchfeld ein. Transkripte und Audio-Dateien finden Sie auch auf dieser Webseite durch Eingabe der Webcodes, die bei den entsprechenden Übungen stehen.

Lösungen → Webcode: FOSSKLO

1 REZEPTION: LESEVERSTEHEN

A Vorbereitung auf das Lesen (Vorhersage / *prediction*)

Eine Vorhersage bedeutet, dass Sie versuchen, den Inhalt des Textes zu erraten, bevor Sie ihn lesen. Wenn Sie sich hierzu Zeit nehmen, bevor Sie mit dem Lesen des Textes bzw. dem Beantworten der Fragen beginnen, können Sie den Text besser verstehen und Sie stellen sicher, die Aufgaben richtig zu lösen.

- Lesen Sie die Fragen und finden Sie heraus, was Sie tun sollen.
- Sehen Sie sich den Aufbau des Textes genau an und lesen Sie die Überschrift und Unterzeile bzw. die Einleitung, wenn es eine gibt. Das sollte Ihnen Hinweise liefern, worum es in dem Text geht.
- Sehen Sie sich die dazugehörigen Bilder bzw. Zeichnungen an und lesen Sie deren Unterschriften. Dies wird Ihnen helfen, sich vom Text „ein Bild zu machen".

B Grobverständnis (Sinn erfassen / *reading for gist* / *skimming*)

Lesen, um den Sinn zu erfassen oder einen Text überfliegen bedeutet, die wichtigsten Punkte schnell zu lesen. Nachdem Sie sich Gedanken dazu gemacht haben, wovon der Text handeln könnte (Vorhersage, s.o.):

- Lesen Sie den ersten Satz jeden Absatzes (und den letzten Satz, wenn der Absatz lang ist), denn dort können Sie häufig das Wesentliche des Textes entnehmen.
- Konzentrieren Sie sich auf die Schlüsselwörter, die Ihnen den Sinn des Textes vermitteln, z. B. Nomen, Verben und (häufig) die dazugehörigen Adjektive und Adverbien. Wörter, die unterstrichen bzw. fett gedruckt oder kursiv gestellt sind, sind i.d.R. wichtig.
- Überspringen Sie jene Wörter, die Sie nicht verstehen. Bleiben Sie ruhig! Meist wird die Bedeutung dieser Wörter aus dem Zusammenhang heraus klar, und manchmal taucht etwas später ein Synonym auf. Zum Schluss finden Sie wahrscheinlich heraus, dass Sie den Text verstehen, ohne diese Wörter zu kennen.
- Lesen Sie den ganzen letzten Absatz, da dieser häufig eine Zusammenfassung des Textes darstellt.

Üblicherweise folgen Prüfungstexte, die zum Überfliegen gedacht sind, einer klaren Struktur. Argumente und Beweise werden logisch präsentiert und wichtige Punkte werden häufig in der Zusammenfassung wiederholt.

Übung 1 (Fertigkeiten 1A und 1B)

A Bevor Sie die Fragen beantworten, sehen Sie sich den Textaufbau und das dazugehörige Foto genau an, und wählen Sie dann das beste Ende aus, um den folgenden Satz zu vervollständigen.

Prediction: The text is about …

a cycling versus walking as a free-time activity.
b accidents involving cyclists and walkers who are not paying attention.
c what happens when people walk on the road instead of on the pavement.

B Überfliegen Sie den Text und wählen Sie die passendste Antwort zu den folgenden Fragen aus.

1 What is the biggest danger for people cycling in the city?
  a busy traffic
  b listening to music while cycling
  c people listening to iPods while walking

2 What can happen as a result?
  a people get hurt
  b bicycles are destroyed
  c walkers and cyclists have arguments

C Beantworten Sie die restlichen Fragen zum Text in Ihren eigenen Worten.

1 When did the problem start?
2 What happened last year?
3 What do cyclists and pedestrians needs to do to change things?

Pedestrians are the great menace to cyclists

People wearing headphones do not take care when crossing roads

What do you think would be the greatest menace to cyclists riding around the roads of a busy city? Lorries, motorbikes, bendy buses, perhaps? Not in my experience. For me, arguably the biggest danger – and without doubt, the biggest irritation – are pedestrians, who, since the proliferation of the iPod, are more likely than any other moving object inadvertently to place themselves directly in my path while I'm cycling, forcing me either to brake suddenly or to swerve out into the traffic – both of which could end up in a nasty accident.

(…) Since the propagation of digital music players, an increasing number of people walk around in a complete daze – stepping into cycle lanes, walking out from behind stationary vehicles and crossing roads without so much as a turn of the head, to check if something is coming.

(…) Collisions between bikes and pedestrians can be fatal. Last year, for example, a teenager was killed in Buckingham when a cyclist crashed into her. By all accounts, the cyclist was at fault, and should certainly have slowed down, rather than simply shouting at the girl to get out of his way. Nevertheless, it shows the damage a bike can do in a collision with a pedestrian.

I understand that many cyclists are not very considerate on the roads, and that many pedestrians feel intimidated by cyclists who badger them off a crossing even when they've got a green man. My golden rule of the road is that everyone should give way to whoever has priority at the time.

(…) Pedestrians need to look where they're going and pay a little more respect to cyclists. I just hope it doesn't take more fatal collisions for this message to start getting through. (289 words)

Abridged from: *www.independent.co.uk*

C Mit unbekannten Wörtern umgehen

→ Vokabeln lernen, S. 220

Wenn Sie während des Lesens einem Wort begegnen, das Sie nicht kennen, sollten Sie sich fragen, ob es notwendig ist, das Wort zu verstehen, um den Text zu verstehen und die Fragen zu beantworten. Wenn Sie das Wort tatsächlich benötigen, versuchen Sie, bevor Sie nach dem Wörterbuch greifen (bzw. online nachschlagen), die Bedeutung des Wortes selbst herauszufinden. Manchmal verstehen Sie die Bedeutung eines Wortes, ohne es bewusst zu „kennen". Wenn dem nicht so ist, nutzen Sie folgende Strategien:

- Erarbeiten Sie es sich aus dem Zusammenhang heraus. Sehen Sie sich genau an, wie das Wort im Satz benutzt wird und wie es mit dem Inhalt dieser Textstelle zusammenhängt.
- Nutzen Sie Ihr Wissen über die deutsche Sprache. Viele englische Wörter haben ähnliche deutsche Entsprechungen bzw. stammen sie von derselben Wurzel ab, z. B.: *ten*/zehn, *light*/Licht, *night*/Nacht, *biology*/Biologie, *democracy*/Demokratie.
- Bringen Sie mehr über Wortbildung in Erfahrung (wie man Wörter aus anderen Wörtern bilden kann):

Vorsilben (*Prefixes*)

Vorsilben können die Bedeutung eines Wortes verändern.

anti-	'against'	clockwise → anticlockwise
co-	'together'	operate → co-operate
inter-	'between'	national → international
sub-	'under' / 'below'	standard → substandard
super-	'above' / 'over'	power → superpower
trans-	'across'	form → transform
dis-	'not' / 'opposite'	agree → disagree
in-		correct → incorrect
im-		possible → impossible
ir-		responsible → irresponsible
un-		friendly → unfriendly
mis-	'not correctly'	understand → misunderstand
re-	'again'	discover → rediscover

Nachsilben (*Suffixes*)

Nachsilben können die Wortart eines Wortes verändern.

Verbs → nouns

Verb	Suffix	Noun
organize	-ation	organization
express	-ion	expression
bake	-er	baker
begin	-ing	beginning
argue	-ment	argument

Nouns → adjectives

Noun	Suffix	Adjective
continent	-al	continental
beauty	-ful	beautiful
day	-ly	daily
hunger	-ry	hungry

Verbs → adjectives

Verb	Suffix	Adjective
advise	-able	advisable
rain	-y	rainy
care	-ing	caring

Adjectives → nouns

Adjective	Suffix	Noun
stupid	-ity	stupidity
happy	-ness	happiness

Adjectives → adverbs

Adjective	Suffix	Noun
awful	-ly	awfully
democratic	-ally	democratically

Übung 2 (Fertigkeit 1C)

Lesen Sie den ersten Absatz des Textes *Pedestrians are the great menace to cyclists* auf S. 215 noch einmal und suchen Sie die Wörter aus der u. s. Tabelle heraus. Schreiben Sie die Tabelle ab und notieren Sie, wie Sie die Wörter verstehen können, d. h. ähnliche Wörter auf Deutsch, Wortbildung, Zusammenhang. Drei der Wörter sind als Beispiele gegeben.

Words I can recognize without using my dictionary	How I know these words in this text	Word class in text	Definition	German
bendy (line 3)	word formation – verb "to bend" made into an adjective by adding -y	adjective	flexible	*biegsam*
pedestrians (line 5)				
cycling (line 7)	word formation – cycle → *gerund*	verb (present progressive form of *to cycle*)	to ride a bicycle	*Rad fahren*
brake (line 8)	from context: accident	verb	to make sth go slower	*bremsen*
swerve (line 8)				
nasty (line 9)				

D Ein Wörterbuch benutzen

→ Vokabeln lernen, S. 220

Ein Wörterbuch ist ein hilfreiches Werkzeug. Es hilft Ihnen, einen Text zu verstehen und Ihr Vokabular zu erweitern. Unabhängig von der Art des Wörterbuchs, das Sie nutzen – zwei- oder einsprachig –, ist Folgendes zu beachten:

- Stellen Sie sicher, dass Ihr Wörterbuch aktuell ist. Sprachen entwickeln sich sehr schnell, also sehen Sie im Impressum nach, ob es sich um eine „überarbeitete Auflage" (*updated version*) handelt.
- Lassen Sie bei Online-Wörterbüchern Vorsicht walten. Wörter haben in verschiedenen Zusammenhängen verschiedene Bedeutungen und Computer sind nicht schlau genug, um zu erfassen, welchen Zusammenhang Sie brauchen.
- Wählen Sie nicht die erstbeste Bedeutung aus, sondern lesen Sie alle Definitionen und überprüfen Sie sie ein zweites Mal, indem Sie die neu gefundenen Wörter nachschlagen.

- Stellen Sie sicher, dass Sie nach der richtigen Wortart suchen (Verb, Nomen, Adjektiv, Adverb).
- Vergewissern Sie sich, den Aufbau einer Seite eines Wörterbuchs verstanden zu haben. Ganz oben auf jeder Seite eines Wörterbuchs sehen Sie das erste Wort bzw. den ersten Satz sowie das letzte Wort bzw. den letzten Satz, das/der auf dieser Seite ausgeführt wird. Solange Sie das Alphabet beherrschen, werden Ihnen diese zwei Wörter helfen, das gesuchte Wort schnell zu finden.

Bevor Sie mit Ihrem Wörterbuch zu arbeiten beginnen:

- Lesen Sie die Inhaltsübersicht, um herauszufinden, was Ihr Wörterbuch neben Definitionen noch alles zu bieten hat. Lesen Sie die Nutzungshinweise sorgfältig durch – sie sind wichtig.
- Sehen Sie sich die Liste der Abkürzungen und Symbole sowie die Legende zur Verbbildung an und stellen Sie sicher, dass Sie deren Bedeutungen verstehen.
- Vergewissern Sie sich, dass Sie über Grundkenntnisse der Grammatiktermini verfügen. Wenn Sie die Bedeutung eines Adverbs nicht kennen, wird es Ihnen kaum helfen, ein Adverb nachzuschlagen.

Nutzen Sie ein Wörterbuch, um:

- **mit einem Text zu arbeiten.** Wenn Sie nach Anwendung aller Ihrer Fertigkeiten unbekannte Wörter immer noch nicht verstehen, schlagen Sie sie nach.
- **Ihr Vokabular zu erweitern.** Wenn Sie ein Ihnen unbekanntes Wort nachschlagen, nehmen Sie sich die Zeit, auch verwandte Wörter nachzuschlagen und eine Liste mit Wortfamilien anzulegen.
- ***Idioms*/Redensarten zu erlernen.** In einer Redensart wird ein Wort in einem feststehenden Satz verwendet und ist seiner eigentlichen Bedeutung nur entfernt ähnlich, z. B.: *„to get the wrong end of the stick"*. Wenn Sie wissen, was *„the wrong end"* und *„stick"* bedeuten, verstehen Sie möglicherweise immer noch nicht den vollständigen Satz (etwas in den falschen Hals bekommen).

Übung 3 (Fertigkeit 1D)

A Sie üben jetzt, Wörter in Ihrem zweisprachigen Wörterbuch zu finden.

1 You have been asked to mediate the following information to a tourist travelling in Germany. Use your bilingual dictionary to find the correct English expressions for the German word *Zug*.

> *Als Tourist in Deutschland reist man am bequemsten per Zug[1]. Im Zug[2] und in Bahnhöfen ist das Rauchen verboten. Falls Sie also Raucher sind, so denken Sie daran, dass schon ein einziger Zug[3] von einer Zigarette zu Problemen führen kann. Außerdem ist es ein typischer Zug[4] vieler Mitreisender, sich bei so etwas schnell zu beschweren. Und: Achten Sie darauf, im Zug[5] nicht in einem Zug[6] zu sitzen, sonst kriegen Sie einen steifen Hals!*

2 Now look up words in the text that you do not know and write them down. → Vokabeln lernen, S. 220

B Sie lernen nun Ihr einsprachiges Wörterbuch kennen und üben den Umgang mit ihm, indem Sie zwei Wörter des ersten Absatzes des Textes *Pedestrians are the great menace to cyclists*, S. 215, nachschlagen.

1 Read the dictionary entries and match the numbered sections to the definitions below.

men *pl.* of MAN

1 **men·ace** /ˈmenəs/ *noun, verb* 5

▪ *noun* **1** [C, usually sing.] **~ (to sb/sth)** a person or thing that causes, or may cause, serious damage, harm or danger SYN THREAT: *a new initiative aimed at beating the menace of illegal drugs* **2** [U] an atmosphere that makes you feel threatened or frightened: ***a sense/an air/a hint of menace*** *in his voice* **3** [C, usually sing.] (*informal*) a person or thing that is annoying or causes trouble 6 7

2 SYN NUISANCE **4 menaces** [pl.] (*BrE, law*) threats that sb will cause harm if they do not get what they are asking for: *to demand money* ***with menaces***

▪ *verb* [VN] (*formal*) to be a possible danger to sth/sb SYN THREATEN: *The forests are being menaced by major development projects.* 8

men·acing /ˈmenəsɪŋ/ *adj.* seeming likely to cause you harm or danger SYN THREATENING: *a* ***menacing face/tone*** ◇ *At night, the dark streets become menacing.* ▶ **men·acing·ly** *adv.*: *The thunder growled menacingly.* 9

mé·nage /meɪˈnɑːʒ/ *noun* [usually sing.] (from *French, formal* or *humorous*) all the people who live together in one house SYN HOUSEHOLD

traf·fic 🔑 /ˈtræfɪk/ *noun, verb* 10

3 ▪ *noun* [U] **1** the vehicles that are on a road at a particular time: ***heavy/rush-hour traffic*** ◇ ***local/through traffic*** ◇ *There's always a lot of traffic at this time of day.* ◇ *They were stuck* ***in traffic*** *and missed their flight.* ◇ *a plan to reduce* ***traffic congestion*** ◇ ***traffic police*** (= who control traffic on a road or stop drivers who are breaking the law) ◇ *The delay is due simply to the* ***volume of traffic****.* **2** the movement of ships, trains, aircraft, etc. along a particular route: *transatlantic traffic* ◇ *air traffic control* **3** the movement of people or goods from one place to another: ***commuter/freight/passenger traffic*** ◇ *the traffic of goods between one country and another* **4** the movement of messages and signals through an electronic communication system: *the computer servers that manage global Internet traffic* **5 ~ (in sth)** illegal trade in sth: *the traffic in firearms* 11

4 ▪ *verb* (-ck-) PHR V **ˈtraffic in sth** to buy and sell sth illegally: *to traffic in drugs* ▶ **traf·fick·er** *noun*: *a drugs trafficker* **traf·fick·ing** *noun* [U]: *drug trafficking* 12

A Collocations: words that are often used with the headword
B Definition: meaning of the word, usually with an example sentence
C Derivatives: words from the same word family
D Example sentence
E Forms: unusual plurals, participles or gerunds
F Grammatical information
G Headword: correct spelling and hyphenation (*Silbentrennung*)
H Phrasal verbs or idioms
I Pronunciation: sound of word (*Aussprache*); stress (*Betonung*)
J Register: formal, informal, slang, etc.
K Synonyms: words of similar meaning
L Word class: noun, verb, adjective, etc.

2 Answer these questions using the two dictionary entries.

1 What is a synonym for "menace" as it is used in the text?
2 Which three collocations are given for "menace"?
3 What is a synonym for the verb form of "menace"?
4 What are the adjective and adverb forms of "menace"?
5 Which two word classes (parts of speech) can "traffic" be?
6 How many collocations using the word "traffic" can you find in the dictionary entry? Here are three collocations to get you started: *heavy/rush-hour traffic; to be stuck in traffic*
7 What else can you use the noun "traffic" to talk about apart from road vehicles and the transport of people or goods?
8 List the nouns that go with the verb phrase "to traffic in sth".

3 Practise using a dictionary by looking up three words in the text that you still need to know.

E Vokabeln lernen

→ Ein Wörterbuch benutzen, S. 217

Das richtige Erlernen und Benutzen von Wörtern einer Fremdsprache macht Spaß, ist aber zeitaufwendig. Es gibt viele Arten, Vokabeln zu lernen. Sie können dies mithilfe von *Focus on Success* tun und diese Art des Lernens mit englischen Lese- und Hörverständnisübungen außerhalb des Unterrichts ergänzen. Es gibt natürlich auch eine Vielzahl von Onlineprogrammen und -spielen, um Vokabeln zu lernen, doch sie sind nicht so effektiv wie die Lernmethoden, die Sie sich selbst erarbeiten.

Listen und Zettel

- **Vokabellisten (nicht nur in einem Buch)**
  Vokabellisten, die in einem Notizbuch eingetragen werden, stellen einen leichten Weg dar, neue Wörter während des Unterrichts festzuhalten. Zuhause können Sie weitere Listen erstellen, z. B. von Lebensmitteln, die im Kühlschrank aufbewahrt werden, oder Sie schreiben Ihre Einkaufsliste auf Englisch oder Sie listen die Kleidungsstücke in Ihrem Kleiderschrank auf, nach Art, Farbe und Material sortiert.

- **Lernkarten**
  Schreiben Sie die Wörter, die Sie gern lernen möchten, auf Karteikarten. Schreiben Sie das englische Wort auf die eine Seite und die Übersetzung auf die andere. Fügen Sie eine Definition bzw. einen Beispielsatz auf Englisch unter die deutsche Übersetzung hinzu.

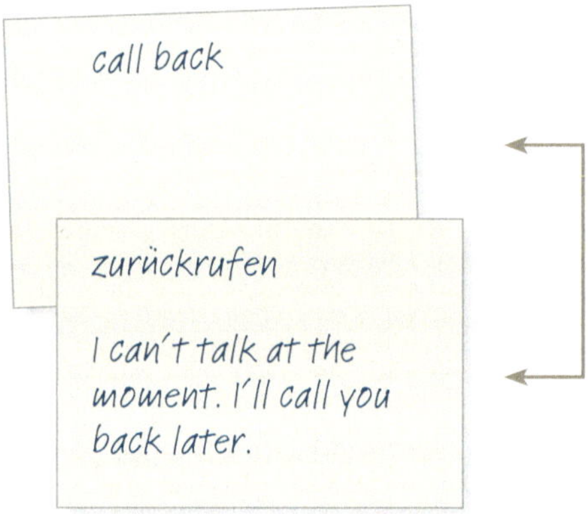

- **Klebezettel**
  Schreiben Sie die Bezeichnung eines Gegenstandes auf einen Notizzettel und kleben Sie ihn an den Gegenstand. Sie können nach Belieben Adjektive hinzufügen, z. B. *pretty picture, dirty laundry*.

Wortgitter und Wortgruppen

Während Ihrer Arbeit mit *Focus on Success* füllen Sie viele Wortgitter mit Wortfamilien aus. In den meisten Fällen werden Sie aufgefordert, ein Wortgitter mit unterschiedlichen Wortarten zu vervollständigen.

Noun	Verb	Adjective
enjoyment	enjoy	enjoyable
entertainment	entertain	entertaining

Wenn Sie sich auf eine Prüfung vorbereiten, können Sie Ihre Wortfamiliengitter um weitere Informationen verändern und ergänzen, z. B. indem Sie Sätze hinzufügen, in denen die Wörter im Kontext benutzt werden.

Word	Part of speech	Opposite	Synonym	Word in context
large	adjective	small	big	My mum comes from a large family. She has six sisters.
producer	noun	destroyer	manufacturer	Japan is a major producer of cars.

Verknüpfungen herstellen

- **Wortgabeln**

  Wortgabeln eignen sich gut zum Erlernen von Adjektiven und Verben.

delicious	
quick	
home-made	meal
lovely	
tasty	

find	
have	
make	friends
meet	
visit	

- **Mindmaps**

  Sie können Mindmaps zum Sammeln und Verknüpfen von Vokabeln wie auch von Ideen benutzen, um sich für eine Präsentation vorzubereiten oder einen Aufsatz und andere Schriftsätze zu planen. Der Vorteil von Mindmaps ist, dass Sie sie in jede beliebige Richtung ergänzen und erweitern können. Heben Sie bestimmte Aspekte farblich hervor. Wenn Sie eine Mindmap erstellen, vergleichen Sie Ihre mit der eines Mitstreiters / einer Mitstreiterin, der/die dasselbe Thema dargestellt hat. Es ist wahrscheinlich, dass Sie beide weitere Wörter zu Ihren Mindmaps hinzufügen können.

Gute Gewohnheiten entwickeln

- Lernen Sie Ihre Vokabeln regelmäßig und lernen Sie nie zu viel auf einmal. 20 Minuten jeden Tag sind besser als zwei Stunden pro Woche.
- Entscheiden Sie, wie häufig Sie wiederholen. Der Morgen vor der Prüfung ist nicht der effektivste Zeitpunkt. Wenn Sie Vokabeln regelmäßig das ganze Jahr hindurch wiederholen, brauchen Sie kurz vor der Prüfung nicht in Panik zu geraten.
- Ebenso wichtig ist, wo Sie lernen. Sie brauchen einen bequemen Ort mit ausreichend Licht. Es hilft auch, nicht von anderen Personen bzw. Lärm abgelenkt zu werden.
- Zu guter Letzt gehen Sie mit Ihren Lernhilfen sorgsam und ordentlich um.

F Scannen nach Einzelinformationen im Text (*reading for information / scanning*)

Beim Überfliegen eines Textes geht es um das schnelle Finden von bestimmten Informationen. In Texten wie Stellenanzeigen oder Infobroschüren müssen Sie bestimmte Informationen schnell herausfinden. Sie müssen den Text nicht in aller Tiefe lesen, doch Sie müssen sich den gesamten Text ansehen. Hierzu wenden Sie folgende Strategien an:

- Lesen Sie die Aufgaben und Fragen sorgfältig durch und stellen Sie sicher, dass Sie verstehen, was zu tun ist.
- Lesen Sie den Text schnell durch und halten Sie an, wenn Sie ein Schlüsselwort gefunden haben. Informationen zu Fragen zu Eigennamen, Zahlen, Ziffern und Geldbeträgen sollten relativ leicht zu finden sein. (Halten Sie nach Großbuchstaben, Prozentzeichen, Währungsangaben, usw. Ausschau.) Wenn Sie ein Schlüsselwort gefunden haben, lesen Sie um es herum, um die Frage zu beantworten.
- Wenn Sie ein Wort oder eine Redewendung nicht verstehen, halten Sie sich nicht damit auf. Überfliegen Sie den Text weiter, bis Sie am Ende angelangt sind. Sollte sich herausstellen, dass Sie das Wort benötigen, können Sie sich später noch darum kümmern.

Normalerweise werden die Fragen zum Text in der Reihenfolge gestellt, in der die Informationen im Text zu finden sind. In einer Prüfung können Sie den Text markieren bzw. sich die benötigten Details notieren, sobald Sie die Informationen finden, die Sie suchen.

Wenn Sie gefragt werden, Wh-Fragen zum Text zu beantworten, denken Sie daran, dass:

Who nach Menschen fragt. Suchen Sie Informationen über die Hauptperson des Textes.

Where nach einem Ort fragt.

When nach einer Zeit fragt. Suchen Sie nach Wochentagen, Daten oder Uhrzeiten.

What nach Objekten und Ereignissen fragt. Suchen Sie nach Informationen darüber oder Vorschlägen, warum etwas passiert (ist).

Why nach einem Grund fragt. Suchen Sie nach Erklärungen, warum etwas passiert (ist).

How nach einer Methode fragt. Suchen Sie Beschreibungen, wie etwas gemacht wird.

→ Fragen zum Text beantworten, S. 228

Übung 4 (Fertigkeit 1F)

Scannen Sie den Text *South Africa for families* unten und finden Sie die Antworten zu den Fragen heraus. Sagen Sie, wie Sie die Antworten so schnell gefunden haben.

1 What holiday destination is being advertised?
2 What is the best way to see the countryside?
3 How many lodges and how many guest houses can holidaymakers choose from?
4 How much does a holiday for a family of four cost?

South Africa for families

South Africa is the perfect destination for a family holiday. The time difference from the UK is only one to two hours so children quickly settle in after the flight.

Many national parks are malaria free so you needn't worry about going out to watch the wildlife. Our park lodges run children's programmes.

A hire car is perfect for getting around South Africa as you can come and go as you please so you can plan around your family's needs. Our guest house staff can give you lots of ideas about things to do so you can discover something new every day. You can choose from 8 lodges and 5 guest houses.

Cape Town, with its beautiful scenery and beaches

Here are just three of our many exciting activities:

- The Garden Route offers many adventurous excursions and places of interest.
- Enjoy whale watching on South Africa's Whale Coast.
- You can't travel to South Africa and not go on a safari and the game viewing possibilities in the Kruger National Park are amazing.

An 18-day trip for a family of four can cost as little as €2,000 per person.

We believe that once you have experienced our beautiful country, you will never want to go home. See you soon in South Africa! (206 words)

Sobald Sie sicher sind, alles verstanden zu haben, nehmen Sie ein Blatt Schmierpapier und:

- Schreiben Sie eine Aussage auf, die sich auf die Frage bezieht, und arbeiten Sie die von Ihnen gewünschte Hauptaussage Ihres Texts heraus. Verwenden Sie für diese Aussage eine neutrale Ausdrucksweise. Schreiben Sie: *"Using social media can be beneficial or it can lead to problems."* Vermeiden Sie eine emotionale Schreibweise, wie z. B. diese: ~~*"Everybody knows that some people use social media to be nice and others use it to be nasty."*~~
- Notieren Sie Schlüsselwörter, Ausdrücke bzw. kurze Sätze, um Fakten zu veranschaulichen. Wenn Sie alles aufgeschrieben haben, lesen Sie sich Ihre Notizen durch und streichen Sie jene Ideen, die Ihre Hauptaussage nicht stützen.
- Arbeiten Sie die gemeinsamen Elemente Ihrer Stichpunkte heraus und listen Sie sie auf. Aus dieser Liste entsteht die Kernaussage des jeweiligen Absatzes im Hauptteil Ihres Aufsatzes.
- Ordnen Sie Ihre Punkte nach ihrer Wichtigkeit. Beginnen Sie mit dem unwichtigsten Punkt im ersten Absatz Ihres Hauptteils und schließen Sie mit dem stärksten Argument in Ihrem letzten Absatz des Hauptteils.

Zu guter Letzt verwenden Sie Ihre Notizen für einen Entwurf. Denken Sie daran, dass jedes längere Schriftstück eines Anfangs (Einleitung), eines Mittelteils (Hauptteil) und eines Endes (Abschluss) bedarf.

→ Mindmaps zum Inhalt eines Aufsatzes erstellen, S. 231
→ Einen Text sinnvoll gliedern, S. 231

Einleitung	Stellen Sie das Thema vor und legen Sie dar, wie Sie es angehen wollen.
Hauptteil	Verwenden Sie für jedes Argument einen Absatz. Sie können erst alle Argumente dafür und dann alle Argumente dagegen darlegen. Verwenden Sie Bindeglieder wie: *However, … That said, …* , um klarzustellen, dass Sie im folgenden Absatz eine gegenteilige Meinung darlegen. Verwenden Sie Ausdrücke wie: *In my opinion, My feeling is that …* , usw., wenn Sie Ihre Meinung äußern.
Abschluss	Wiederholen Sie Ihre Einleitung. Sagen Sie, ob Sie eine der zwei Seiten befürworten.

Das Schreiben Ihres Aufsatzes:

- Um den schwierigen Moment des Anfangs zu überwinden, können Sie als erste Tat den Wortlaut der Aufgabenstellung aufschreiben. Vergessen Sie nicht, nach Fertigstellung Ihres Aufsatzes diesen ersten Satz mit Ihren eigenen Worten umzuschreiben!
- Beginnen Sie für jedes neue Argument einen neuen Absatz und arbeiten Sie Ihre Argumentationslinie stets mithilfe von strukturschaffenden Ausdrücken klar heraus.

→ *Language for writing*, hintere Umschlagsklappe

- Bleiben Sie durchgehend fokussiert. Achten Sie darauf, dass jeder Absatz Ihres Aufsatzes zu Ihrer Hauptaussage passt.

Wenn Sie mit dem Schreiben fertig sind:

- Überprüfen Sie Ihre Rechtschreibung, Grammatik und Zeichensetzung sowie Ihren Satzbau.
- Lesen Sie sich das, was Sie geschrieben haben, genau durch und verbessern Sie den Aufsatz dort, wo es der Lesefluss erfordert.

Versuchen Sie in einer Prüfung, rechtzeitig mit dem Schreiben aufzuhören, um genau das tun zu können. Fünf bis zehn Minuten sollten hierfür ausreichend sein.

Übung 5 (Fertigkeit 3F)

A Read the following writing tasks and find key words which tell you what to cover in your text. Say which key words helped you decide. → Umgang mit Operatoren, S. 232

1 *Newspapers and magazines that publish paparazzi photos of celebrities can cause a lot of pain and misery. Describe the situation of celebrities, giving examples for and against this theory.*
2 *Reality shows that humiliate their candidates should be banned. Discuss this idea.*
3 *Groups of teenagers who are not intending to shop should be banned from shopping malls. Point out the main arguments for and against such a course of action.*

B Make notes on one of the tasks and produce an outline for your comment/essay.

4 PRODUKTION: BILDER UND CARTOONS BESCHREIBEN UND ANALYSIEREN

A Ein Bild beschreiben und deuten

Bevor Sie mit dem Schreiben beginnen, nehmen Sie Schmierpapier zur Hand, sehen sich das Bild genau an und machen sich Notizen zu den folgenden Fragen:

- Wer oder was spielt in dem Bild die Hauptrolle?
- Steht ein Element im Mittelpunkt? Warum?
- Schafft das Bild eine besondere Atmosphäre, z. B. von Gefahr, Glück?
- Was ist die „Botschaft" des Bildes?

Als Daumenregel sollte Ihre Antwort etwa zu ⅔ aus einer Bildbeschreibung und zu ⅓ aus einer Interpretation bestehen. Sagen Sie, welche Wirkung das Bild auf den Betrachter / die Betrachterin hat. Hilfreiche Redewendungen für eine Bildbeschreibung finden Sie mit Hilfe dieses Webcodes.

Phrases → Webcode: FOSSKP2

Übung 1 (Fertigkeit 4A)

Sehen Sie sich das Bild genau an und vervollständigen Sie die Notizen mit Wörtern aus dem Kasten.

clouds ▪ dangers ▪ having fun ▪ imagine ▪ no swimming ▪ sign ▪ unconcerned ▪ viewer

Main parts: three people ___[1] in the sea. Blue skies with a few ___[2] on the horizon. Sign shows that ___[3] is allowed here.
Focus: on the ___[4].
Atmosphere: relaxed, holiday atmosphere; no indication of any immediate ___[5].
Message: the people are ___[6] by the sign – they could have difficulties but the ___[7] can only ___[8] what these might be.

B Einen Cartoon beschreiben und deuten

Die o.g. Vorschläge zur Vorbereitung auf eine Bildbeschreibung eignen sich auch zur Vorbereitung auf die Beschreibung eines Cartoons. Denken Sie jedoch immer daran, dass ein/e Cartoonist/in auf etwas Besonderes hinweisen will. Die drei wichtigsten Techniken hierfür sind:

- Karikaturen, also ein oder mehrere körperliche Merkmale übertrieben darstellen.

G Gründliches Lesen (*reading for detail / close reading*)

Gründliches Lesen bedeutet, einen Text Satz für Satz zu lesen. Hierzu gibt es folgende Strategien:

- Lesen Sie die Aufgabenstellung und die Fragen aufmerksam durch und stellen Sie sicher, dass Sie verstehen, was der Prüfer / die Prüferin von Ihnen will.
- Überfliegen Sie den Text, um einen Überblick über den Inhalt zu bekommen, und notieren Sie sich die wichtigsten Punkte. Lassen Sie diesen Schritt nicht aus. Er wird Ihnen später beim Beantworten der Fragen Zeit sparen.
- Suchen Sie Schlüsselwörter, die Ihnen helfen, die Frage(n) zu beantworten. Werden Sie z. B. nach der Meinung des Autors / der Autorin gefragt, suchen Sie nach Wörtern wie *think, believe, opinion,* usw.; das hilft Ihnen, dem Gedankengang des Autors / der Autorin zu folgen.
- Lesen Sie nun den Text Satz für Satz und beantworten Sie die Fragen.
- Wenn Sie fertig sind, lesen Sie sich Ihre Antworten durch und vergleichen Sie sie mit dem Text.

Übung 5 (Fertigkeit 1G)

Sagen Sie, ob die Aussagen unten in Bezug auf den Text *South Africa for families*, S. 222, richtig oder falsch sind.

Bitte notieren Sie sich jedes Mal den Grund für Ihre Wahl von richtig oder falsch. Die ersten zwei Aussagen sind für Sie bereits zugeordnet worden.

1 South Africa is a good place to take a family holiday. *true*
BEISPIEL *Headline: SA for familes; text: "a perfect destination for a family holiday"*
2 The time difference between South Africa and Britain is 5 hours. *false*
BEISPIEL *"time difference from the UK one to two hours"*
3 There is absolutely no risk of catching malaria in any of the national parks.
4 There are special activities for children who visit the parks.
5 You can get ideas for day trips at the tourist information office.
6 The highlight of the holiday is a safari.
7 The author of the text is sure that you will love his country.

H Sich während des Lesens Notizen machen

Sich während des Lesens Notizen zu machen ist sinnvoll. So können Sie sich die Informationen für später besser merken.

- Stellen Sie immer sicher, dass Sie den Text verstanden haben, bevor Sie sich Notizen machen. → Grobverständnis, S. 214
- Versehen Sie Ihren Notizzettel mit der Textüberschrift und der Quellenangabe. Die Quellenangabe ist wichtig, wenn Sie in Ihrem Aufsatz u.ä. zitieren wollen. Auch kann es vorkommen, dass Sie zu einem späteren Zeitpunkt auf den Originaltext zurückgreifen wollen.
- Sehen Sie sich den Text genau an und suchen Sie sich die wichtigsten Unterthemen heraus, die Sie als Überschriften benutzen können. Die Unterteilung des Textes in Absätze wird Ihnen dabei helfen. Verteilen Sie diese Überschriften großzügig über das Blatt und lassen Sie unter jeder Überschrift Platz für Notizen.
- Ihre Notizen bestehen aus Schlüsselwörtern, i.d.R. Nomen, Verben und Adjektiven. Konzentrieren Sie sich auf diese Wortarten.

- Halten Sie nach Signalen Ausschau, z. B. Wiederholungen, Wörter, die etwas unterstreichen, oder an die Leser direkt gestellte Fragen. Dies ist ein Anhaltspunkt, was der Autor / die Autorin als wichtig erachtet.
- Sind Sie hiermit fertig, überprüfen Sie, ob Sie alle Informationen haben, die Sie benötigen. Sie können durchaus über den gesamten Text verstreut sein.
- Denken Sie immer daran, sich nur Notizen zu machen. Verschwenden Sie keine Zeit mit dem Abschreiben ganzer Textabschnitte, lassen Sie unnötige Wörter wie Pronomen und Artikel weg und verwenden Sie Abkürzungen und Symbole.

Zeichen	
=	the same as
≠	not the same as
+,&	and

Abkürzungen	
e.g.	for example
km	kilometre
w., w/o	with, without
etc.	and so on

Wortverkürzungen	
govt	government
impt	important
kids	children

Übung 6 (Fertigkeit 1H)

Stellen Sie sich vor, Sie wurden gebeten, einen Kommentar über Paparazzi zu schreiben; Sie beziehen sich hierbei auf den Text *Paparazzi – not always the celebrity's best friend.* Lesen Sie den Text und stellen Sie sicher, dass Sie verstehen, worum es geht. Anschließend schreiben Sie sich die Notizen ab und vervollständigen sie mithilfe der o. g. Tipps.

Paparazzi – not always the celebrity's best friend (Focus on Success, 2015)

benefits of paparazzi
- *keep celebrities in the news*
- *fame and fortune for celebrities*
- *give the public information about stars*

downsides of paparazzi
- *invasion of privacy*

PAPARAZZI – NOT ALWAYS THE CELEBRITY'S BEST FRIEND

A lot of people say that celebrities need the paparazzi to keep their faces in the news. You could say that is the only benefit of paparazzi. The downsides of the relationship between paparazzi and celebrities are many.

The paparazzi go to extremes to get their photos. Some of them earn thousands for a good shot of a star. If the star has problems, then the photo might bring a million.

Despite the laws about invasion of privacy, the paparazzi continually ignore them to get photos of celebrities. They stalk them while they are walking in a public place and they follow them with their cars. In some cases, the paparazzi put celebrities in danger. How often have we heard stories on the news about celebrities having car accidents as a result of being chased by paparazzi?

Film star Halle Berry was involved in a road accident involving the paparazzi a few years ago when a paparazzi followed her and drove into her car. The crash caused Halle Berry to hit a wall. The shock of the accident was bad enough but, at the time, the star was pregnant and she could have lost her baby. When she got out of her car, the paparazzi ran away. Halle Berry could have lost her baby, but they didn't stay to help or to check if everything was all right. Apart from the fact that the law says you have to stay around after you've caused an accident, don't these paparazzi have any feelings?

In another case involving a star, Tori Spelling, the American actress and author, was followed by paparazzi when she was driving her two children to school. Again, the car chase ended in an accident. This time, the paparazzi did not flee the scene. Instead, he stood beside the car and took photos.

Tori Spelling and her children survived the crash but some celebrities do not survive. The most famous paparazzi chase that ended in a crash was the one in which Princess Diana was killed. Although there was evidence that the driver of the car Diana was travelling in had been drinking, popular speculation is that the paparazzi caused the crash.

Whether they caused the crash or not, the behaviour of the paparazzi was typical – some left the scene while others took photos of the wrecked car. None of them tried to help the driver or any of the passengers. If that wasn't bad enough, three of the paparazzi took photographs of Diana as she was dying. How much of an invasion of privacy is it when someone takes a photo of you when you are dying?

An incident like this should never be repeated. Taking pictures after a crash in order to make money from them should result in the photo-grapher being banned from taking photos for life.

What is to be done about the other problems? Would making invasion of privacy laws tougher discourage paparazzi from stalking celebrities? Should it be against the law to follow and take pictures of a parent taking children to school? Fame and fortune are fuelled by paparazzi photos.

As long as celebrities need and enjoy the attention, there will be paparazzi and as long as we, the public, are interested in what our favourite stars are doing, we need the paparazzi, too. (552 words)

2 REZEPTION: HÖRVERSTEHEN

A Vor dem Hören (Voraussage des Inhalts / Vorbereitung)

Sich auf die Hörübung vorzubereiten, verstärkt das Hörverständnis. Nutzen Sie hierzu alle Informationen, die sich auf der Seite befinden. Bevor Sie zuhören:

- Sehen Sie sich alle Fotos bzw. Illustrationen auf der Seite genau an. Sie liefern Ihnen Hinweise über den Ort der Aufzeichnung.
- Lesen Sie alle Ihnen zur Verfügung gestellten Hintergrundinformationen, z. B. eine Einleitung, die die Situation beschreibt und Auskunft darüber gibt, wie viele Personen Sie hören werden.
- Lesen Sie die Aufgabenstellung sorgfältig durch. Denken Sie daran, dass die Fragen, die Sie beantworten müssen, häufig der Reihenfolge entsprechen, in der die Informationen auf der Aufzeichnung vorkommen.
- Denken Sie nach, welche Wörter und Formulierungen Sie vielleicht hören werden und schreiben Sie sie auf.
- Schreiben Sie jede Ihnen vorgegebene Tabelle ab. Füllen Sie sie auf Englisch bereits vor der Hörübung soweit wie möglich aus und vervollständigen Sie sie während des Hörens.

B Während des ersten Hörens (Grobverständnis / *listening for gist*)

Ein Grobverständnis zu erhalten bedeutet, eine Ahnung zu bekommen, worum es in der Aufzeichnung geht. Während des ersten Hörens brauchen Sie nicht jedes Wort zu verstehen. Entwickeln Sie für das Hören möglichst folgende Fertigkeiten:

- Übergehen Sie Wörter, die Sie nicht verstehen.
- Konzentrieren Sie sich auf Schlüsselwörter.
- Machen Sie sich Notizen. Verwenden Sie Abkürzungen. Schreiben Sie so viel wie möglich auf, während Sie zuhören.

Ordnen Sie Ihre Notizen sofort nach dem Ende der Hörübung. Sie können sie später möglicherweise nicht mehr lesen.

Bemühen Sie sich, alle Fragen zu beantworten. Wenn Sie einen Teil der Informationen nicht verstanden haben, raten Sie, ausgehend von dem, was Sie verstanden haben.

Übung 1 (Fertigkeiten 2A und 2B)

10.30 Good morning, fans!

Gerry Davis interviews today's celebrities

In today's interview, Gerry talks to fitness celebrity Tina Michaelson while she takes a break from signing copies of her latest book for teenagers, **Do Sports and Learn Skills for Life!** in a London bookstore. During the interview, Tina explains how participating in sport teaches you skills that will help you your whole life long.

You read the announcement about the interview with Tina Michaelson and are interested in finding out more.

Listen to the interview and answer these questions in your own words.

1 What skill helps a team to win?
2 How does Gerry refer to this skill?
3 How can doing sport help you gain trust?
4 How long can sports relationships last?
5 What is the myth about students and sport?
6 What life skill can students use to prove that it is possible to be a good student and play sport?

A **Sehen Sie sich das o.g. Beispiel einer Hörübung an. Sehen Sie sich das Foto genau an und lesen Sie die Programmanzeige. Lesen Sie sich die Aufgabenstellung und Fragen durch. Beantworten Sie die Fragen nicht. Dies tun Sie später. Wenn Sie sich sicher sind, alles verstanden zu haben, wählen Sie das beste Ende aus, um die folgenden Sätze zu vervollständigen.**

1 The recording is of …
  a a private conversation.
  b a talk.
  c an interview.

2 The recording takes place …
  a at a celebrity fitness club.
  b in a bookstore.
  c on a school sports field.

3 The speakers are a
  a reporter and a fitness celebrity.
  b reporter and a fitness fan.
  c group of teenagers and a fitness celebrity.

4 The topic is …
  a skills to improve your sports perfomance.
  b developing useful skills through doing sport.
  c sports you can do all your life.

5 Three expressions I might hear are:
  a staying healthy, sport competitions, animal companions
  b life-long learning, learning to drive, nutrition
  c building relationships, team work, trusting others

B **Schreiben Sie sich die zwei u.s. Sätze ab und vervollständigen Sie sie. Anschließend hören Sie die Aufzeichnung und überprüfen, ob Ihre Vorhersagen richtig waren.**

I am going to listen to ___ [1] with ___ [2] about ___ [3]
I expect to hear something about ___ [4]

Hörtext → Webcode: FOSSKT1

C Während des zweiten Hörens (stichpunktartige Notizen machen)

Es ist schwierig, während des Zuhörens Notizen zu machen, weil die Aufzeichnung weiterläuft, während Sie schreiben. Daher verpassen Sie möglicherweise wichtige Informationen. Bleiben Sie ruhig! Sie haben sich bereits beim ersten Hören ein Grobverständnis angeeignet und notiert, was Sie verstehen konnten. Beim zweiten Hören versuchen Sie, sich so viel wie möglich an das zu erinnern, was Sie beim ersten Mal gehört haben. Wenn Sie es sich zur Gewohnheit machen, bei jedem Hören Stichpunkte aufzuschreiben, haben Sie bald den Bogen heraus.

Bevor Sie zuhören:

- Notieren Sie – wenn Sie die Zeit haben – Rubriken in Ihr Heft und schreiben Sie die Aufgabenstellung ganz oben auf Ihr Blatt. Wenn Sie die Anzahl der Sprecher/innen kennen, legen Sie eine Tabelle mit deren Namen an. Wenn Sie die Namen der Sprecher/innen nicht kennen, schreiben Sie ‚Sprecher/in 1', ‚Sprecher/in 2', usw.

Während Sie zuhören:

- Bleiben Sie bei der Aufgabenstellung und notieren Sie sich relevante Schlüsselwörter.
- Seien Sie aufmerksam und notieren Sie Ausdrücke, die die Gedanken strukturieren, z. B: *in my view, however, on the other hand*.
- Nutzen Sie Abkürzungen, um Zeit zu sparen.

→ Abkürzungen, S. 224

Nach dem Ende der Hörübung:

- Ordnen Sie Ihre Notizen frühestmöglich. Wenn Sie sich hierfür zu lang Zeit lassen, können Sie sie später möglicherweise nicht mehr deuten.

Wenn Sie in einer Prüfung Fragen zu einer Hörübung beantworten müssen:
- Formulieren Sie mithilfe Ihrer Stichpunkte die wichtigsten Punkte aus.
- Versuchen Sie, wenn Ihnen gewisse Details entgangen sind, die Antworten zu erraten, ausgehend von dem, was Sie verstanden haben.

Übung 2 (Fertigkeit 2C)

Sie hören die Aufnahme ein zweites Mal und erledigen die Aufgabe von S. 226. Hier sind die Fragen nochmal:

Hörtext → Webcode: FOSSKT1

1 What skill helps a team to win?
2 How does Gerry refer to this skill?
3 How can doing sport help you gain trust?
4 How long can sports relationships last?
5 What is the myth about students and sport?
6 What life skill can students use to prove that it is possible to be a good student and play sport?

1 **Übertragen Sie die Tabelle in Ihr Heft und füllen Sie sie während des Hörens aus.**

Questions	Tina	Gerry
1 *skill for winning teams*		
2 *another way to describe the skill*		
3 *gaining trust through sport*		
4 *sports relationship can last …*		
5 *myth – students and sport*		
6 *skill to prove can be good student and play sport*		

2 **Jetzt ordnen Sie Ihre Notizen und verwenden Sie sie zum Beantworten der Fragen.**

3 PRODUKTION: SCHREIBEN

A Fragen zum Text beantworten

Fragen zum Inhalt zu stellen ist eine beliebte Art herauszufinden, ob Sie einen Text verstanden haben. Bevor Sie zu schreiben beginnen:

- Stellen Sie sicher, dass Sie den Text verstehen. → Gründliches Lesen, S. 223
- Lesen Sie die Fragen sorgfältig durch.
- Fragen Sie sich: Was will der Lehrer / die Lehrerin bzw. der Prüfer / die Prüferin wissen?
- Schreiben Sie Ihre Stichpunkte auf Schmierpapier, wenn Sie Fragen aus Ihrem Buch beantworten. → Sich während des Lesens Notizen machen, S. 223
- Markieren Sie die wichtigen Textstellen während einer Prüfung bzw. einer Klassenarbeit in Ihrem Unterricht, indem Sie für verschiedene Fragen verschiedenfarbige Stifte verwenden.

Wh-Fragen beantworten

→ Scannen nach Einzelinformationen im Text, S. 221

Wenn Sie *Wh*-Fragen beantworten, denken Sie daran, dass:

- *Wh*-Fragen nicht einfach mit „ja" oder „nein" beantwortet werden können. Sie müssen diese Fragen jeweils kurz und sachlich beantworten.
- Wenn sich eine *Wh*-Frage auf eine bestimmte Handlung bezieht, Sie dasselbe Verb in Ihrer Antwort verwenden sollten.
  Where does Roger live? He lives in Berlin.

- Wenn in den Fragen allgemeine Verben wie *do* und *go* verwendet werden, Sie in Ihrer Antwort ein anderes, präzisierendes Verb wählen.
  Where did Mary go? She flew to New York.
  Why did she do it? She wanted to visit a friend who lives there.
- Antworten auf Fragen, die mit *why* beginnen, häufig *because* enthalten.
  Why is Mary working so hard? Because she needs to finish the project soon.
- Sie für *Why*-Fragen auch den Imperativ verwenden (*to* …) können. In diesem Fall wird vorausgesetzt, dass der Halbsatz mit *because* in der Antwort enthalten ist.
  Why does Roger go to the gym? To get in shape. = Because he wants to get in shape.

B Einen Text zusammenfassen

Einen Text zusammenzufassen bedeutet, ihn auf seine wesentlichen Informationen zu reduzieren. Sie werden möglicherweise gefragt, einen Text zusammenzufassen, um zu zeigen, dass Sie ihn verstanden haben. Bevor Sie beginnen:

- Stellen Sie sicher, dass Sie den Text verstehen. → Rezeption: Leseverstehen, S. 214
- Lesen Sie die Anweisungen aufmerksam durch und vergewissern Sie sich, dass Sie wissen, welche Informationen aus dem Text für den Leser / die Leserin wichtig sind. Sie können dies tun, indem Sie sich *Wh*-Fragen stellen. → Scannen nach Einzelinformationen im Text, S. 221
- Machen Sie sich auf Schmierpapier stichpunktartige Notizen.
  → Sich während des Lesens Notizen machen, S. 223

Nun beginnen Sie, Ihre Zusammenfassung zu schreiben.

- Beschreiben Sie in ein oder zwei einleitenden Sätzen, wovon der Text handelt.
- Lassen Sie alles Unnötige weg. Dies schließt Beispiele, ausführliche Listen, Namen, usw. ein.
- Verwenden Sie, soweit es geht, Ihre eigenen Worte. Verwenden Sie Synonyme für Wörter aus dem Text, z. B. *think – believe*, und formulieren Sie um, z. B. *recently – in recent years*.
- Versuchen Sie, Zitate in die indirekte Rede umzuwandeln, z. B. *The author states that …*
  → Grammar files: Indirect speech, S. 266
- Verlinken Sie Ideen und lassen Sie sie in der Reihenfolge, in der sie im Text erscheinen.
- Erinnern Sie sich! Sie sollten in einer Zusammenfassung eines Textes nicht Ihre eigene Meinung äußern.

Wenn Sie fertig sind, überprüfen Sie Ihre Rechtschreibung und Grammatik.

Übung 1 (Fertigkeiten 3A und 3B)

A Read the first paragraph of the text *Cyberbullying at Wiston* and answer the following questions.

1 Where did three teenagers from Wiston Vocational College have to appear yesterday?
2 Why were they there?
3 Who was their target?
4 How did they hurt her?
5 How did the police learn what had happened?
6 What were the consequences for the three teenagers?

B Summarize the complete text.

CYBERBULLYING AT WISTON

A group of three teenagers from Wiston Vocational College appeared at a juvenile court yesterday accused of using Face-book to be cruel to another student. The three teens, two boys and a girl, all aged 18, created a fake Facebook profile for another girl in their class and made it look like she wanted to live out her sexual fantasies on social media and in person. The girl's parents complained to the police and the three teenagers were quickly found. They were charged with causing their target emotional distress. All three were fined £1,000 and sentenced to do 30 days of voluntary work in a hospital. They were also banned from using Face-book, Twitter and other social media for six months.

According to the police, the group created a Facebook profile for Claire F, also 18-years old, three months ago. They manipulated real photos of Claire to make them look as if they were selfies which she herself had taken in a bedroom. The group also posted her mobile phone number.

Then they used the fake profile to pretend to be Claire and send sexual comments to other students. The mother of one of the pupils who received a sexual message reported the incident to the head of the college. She contacted Claire's parents. Before then, they knew nothing about the problem.

When they found out, Claire's parents were shocked. "Claire is a popular girl. She has always had a lot of friends and was involved in all kinds of after-school clubs," her father said. "Some weeks ago, though, she cut herself off from her social life and stopped going to her clubs," he

One of the accused waiting to return to court

went on. "She became isolated and my wife and I could see that she was unhappy. As we found out later, this change in Claire's behaviour started a few days after the fake Facebook account was set up," he said.

The charges against the three teenagers state that they created the fake profile to cause trouble for Claire. Her lawyer said in court that Claire had not only suffered emotional distress, she had also wanted to do a work placement in a company who had rejected her application because of the fake profile.

The judge said: "Growing up is not always easy and many teenagers feel unhappy. Some are so unhappy and are therefore very cruel to other people. Sadly, cyber-bullying is on the rise," she went on. "I would like to see schools doing more to educate pupils and make it clear to them how much damage they can do to their peers by behaving in this way."

Claire's mother said, "I am glad that the court put such a high fine on the three kids. I think that is the only way you can discourage this. Make the bullies pay for the damage they have done." (472 words)

C Mindmaps zum Inhalt eines Aufsatzes erstellen

Wenn Sie einen Aufsatz schreiben sollen, ist es sinnvoll, Ihre Ideen in Form einer Mindmap festzuhalten und hierbei auf den Inhalt statt auf das Vokabular zu achten.

→ Vokabeln lernen, S. 220

Hier ist der Anfang einer Mindmap gemacht, passend zur u. s. Aufgabe. Sehen Sie, wie die drei Unterpunkte *benefits*, *dangers*, *questions* genutzt werden, um Argumente zu sammeln und Fragen aufzulisten, die im Aufsatz abgedeckt werden sollen.

TASK: **Describe / Comment on the benefits and the dangers of using social media.**

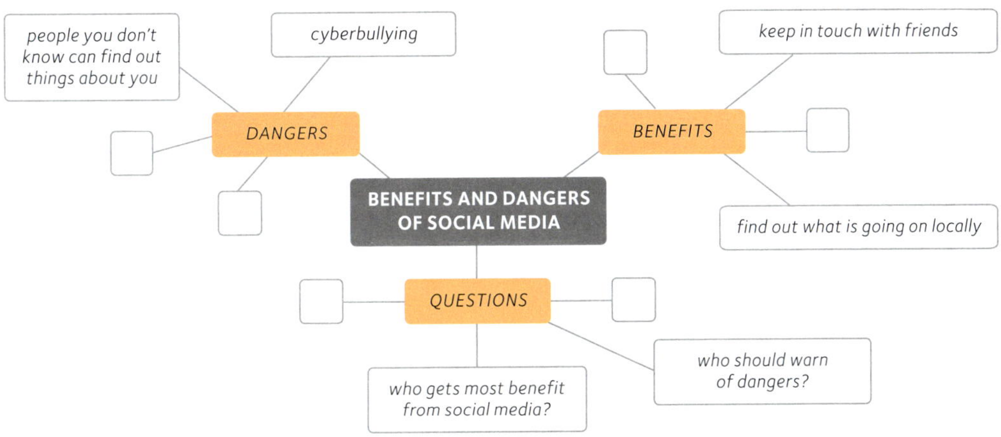

D Einen Text sinnvoll gliedern

→ *Language for writing*, hintere Umschlagsklappe

Wenn Sie etwas schriftlich verfassen, müssen Sie Ihren Text klar und logisch strukturieren, damit der Leser / die Leserin den roten Faden nicht verliert. Hierfür können Sie die Sprachelemente der hinteren Umschlagsklappe dieses Buches nutzen. Hier sind einige Beispiele, wie man mithilfe dieser Elemente einen Aufsatz strukturieren kann. Weitere finden Sie online mithilfe dieses Webcodes.

Phrases → Webcode: FOSSKP1

Argumente gliedern	*In the text, "Cyberbullying at Wiston", we saw how three pupils used social media to hurt another pupil.* ***First****, they …* ***Secondly/Then****, they …*
Eine Begründung anführen	***Due to / Because of / As a result of*** *this behaviour, Claire became isolated. She …*
Aspekte ergänzen	***In addition, / Moreover****, the girl didn't get a job she wanted.*
Einen Gegensatz ausdrücken	***Although/While*** *examples like these illustrate the dangers, social media has its benefits, too. Being active on social media can …*
Beispiele anführen	*Stephen Sutton,* ***for example****, who was diagnosed with terminal cancer aged 15, used social media …* → Using the internet to help others, S. 43
Ein Fazit ziehen	***To sum up / To conclude****, social media has its good and its bad sides.* ***On the one hand, … On the other hand, …***

Übung 2 (Fertigkeiten 3C und 3D)

A **Verwenden Sie die Informationen aus Ihrem Kursbuch und Ihre eigenen Ideen, um die Mindmap in der o.g. Erklärung der Fertigkeit 3C zu vervollständigen.**

B **Schreiben Sie die Überschriften des Abschnitts D ab und sammeln Sie Ideen für Sätze, die Sie verwenden können, um über die Vorteile und Gefahren von sozialen Medien zu schreiben.**

E Umgang mit Operatoren

Im Verlauf Ihrer Arbeit mit Ihrem Buch bzw. in einer Prüfung müssen Sie möglicherweise ein Schriftstück entsprechend besonderer Anweisungen (Operatoren) verfassen.

- Wenn Sie sich beim Schreiben auf den Text beziehen sollen, überfliegen Sie diesen, um sich einen Überblick über den Inhalt zu verschaffen. → Grobverständnis, S. 214
- Lesen Sie sich die Aufgabenstellung durch. Diese beinhaltet eine der Anweisungen aus der u. s. Tabellen. Es ist wichtig, dass Sie genau verstehen, was Sie tun sollen.
- Sammeln Sie Ideen, bevor Sie mit dem Schreiben beginnen. → Mindmaps erstellen, S. 231
- Stellen Sie sicher, dass Sie nicht dieselben Blickpunkte in unterschiedlichen Aufgaben wiederholen. Markieren Sie Textstellen für unterschiedliche Aufgaben mit unterschiedlichen Farben.
- Strukturieren Sie Ihre Antworten klar und logisch. → Einen Text sinnvoll gliedern, S. 231
- Verwenden Sie stets Ihre eigenen Worte, wenn Sie sich auf den Text beziehen. Suchen Sie Synonyme (z. B. *say* – *state*) sowie Möglichkeiten, Sätze in anderen Worten auszudrücken (z. B. *to a great extent* – *greatly*).

Übung 3 (Fertigkeit 3E)

Sehen Sie sich die Tabelle genau an und vergewissern Sie sich, dass Sie alle Anweisungen verstanden haben. Notieren Sie sich auf Deutsch:

1 wie viele Anweisungen aufgeführt sind.
2 zu welchen Überschriften die Anweisungen gehören.
3 wenn Sie Fakten, Gegenstände oder Zeichen finden sollen, die zeigen, dass etwas wahr ist.
4 wenn Sie objektiv von etwas die Vor- und Nachteile so darlegen sollen, wie sie im Text erscheinen.
5 wenn Sie Ihr eigenes Wissen einfließen lassen sollen, um die tiefere Bedeutung bzw. Botschaft eines Textes oder Witzes zu erklären.
6 wenn Sie beide Seiten einer Angelegenheit abwägen, und die Für und Wider anführen wollen.

Anweisungen, die sich auf den Inhalt beziehen

In den folgenden Anweisungen lenken Sie Ihre Aufmerksamkeit auf die Hauptgedanken des Autors / der Autorin.

Anweisung	Deutsch	Was Sie tun müssen
Summarize → Einen Text zusammenfassen, S. 229	*zusammenfassen*	Schreiben Sie die wichtigsten Textinhalte kurz und prägnant auf, und verwenden Sie hierzu Ihre eigenen Worte. Lassen Sie Ihre eigene Meinung in Form von Beispielen weg.

Outline	*darstellen*	Beschreiben Sie die wichtigsten Tatsachen und teilen Sie den Entwurf nach den wichtigsten Unterpunkten auf.
Point out	*aufzeigen*	Beziehen Sie sich auf bestimmte wesentliche Textinhalte, um deren Wichtigkeit aufzuzeigen.
Say what the text is about	*sagen, worum es im Text geht*	Skizzieren Sie in eigenen Worten kurz den Inhalt. Dies ist kürzer und weniger detailliert als eine Zusammenfassung.

Die folgenden Anweisungen werden häufig verwendet, um zu überprüfen, ob Sie den Text richtig verstanden haben.

Anweisung	Deutsch	Was Sie tun müssen
Describe	*beschreiben*	Geben Sie über eine Person oder Situation bzw. einen Gegenstand Details wieder. Sie sollten viele Adjektive benutzen.
Define	*bestimmen, umreißen, definieren*	Beschreiben Sie eine Situation, ein Problem, die Bedeutung eines Begriffs, usw. sehr genau.
Say / State / Explain why … or **State the reasons for …**	*angeben / sagen / erklären, warum* oder *die Gründe angeben für …*	Erklären Sie, warum jemand etwas tat bzw. warum etwas geschah.
Find evidence in the text to show …	*Belege im Text finden für …*	Suchen Sie nach Tatsachen, die zeigen, dass etwas wahr ist.

Anweisungen, um Standpunkte aus dem Text zu vergleichen und zu analysieren

→ Einen Aufsatz oder eine Stellungnahme schreiben, S. 234

Die folgenden, häufig benutzten Anweisungen müssen Sie sehr gründlich beantworten. Bevor Sie mit dem Schreiben beginnen, sollten Sie eine Tabelle mit zwei Spalten anlegen, um einzelne Aspekte zu vergleichen.

Anweisung	Deutsch	Was Sie tun müssen
Compare	*vergleichen*	Heben Sie die Unterschiede und Ähnlichkeiten zwischen zwei Sachen/Konzepten/usw. hervor.
Contrast	*gegenüberstellen*	Heben Sie die Unterschiede zwischen zwei Sachen/Konzepten/usw. hervor.
Point out	*beschreiben*	Stellen Sie objektiv die Vor- und Nachteile von etwas dar, wie sie im Text aufgeführt werden.

Entsprechend der folgenden Anweisungen erklären Sie die im Text ausgeführten Ansichten, lesen aber auch ‚zwischen den Zeilen' und erklären implizierte Bedeutungen. Stellen Sie sicher, dass Sie Ihre Antworten und die Struktur Ihres Aufsatzes gut planen.

Anweisung	Deutsch	Was Sie tun müssen
Analyse	*analysieren*	Beschreiben und erklären Sie bestimmte Aspekte detailliert.
Describe and explain	*beschreiben und erklären*	
Examine	*untersuchen*	

Anweisung, den Text zu interpretieren und eine Aussage zu kommentieren bzw. zu diskutieren

→ Einen Aufsatz oder eine Stellungnahme schreiben, S. 234

Entsprechend der folgenden Anweisung erklären und bewerten/evaluieren Sie sowohl die genannten als auch die implizierten Bedeutungen.

Anweisung	Deutsch	Was Sie tun müssen
Interpret	*interpretieren*	Erklären Sie die tiefere Bedeutung bzw. ‚Botschaft' einer Aussage bzw. eines Konzepts, usw. Verwenden Sie eigenes Hintergrundwissen und äußern Sie persönliche Ansichten.

Entsprechend der folgenden Anweisungen sollen Sie Ihre eigene Meinung darlegen. Wenn Sie schreiben, vertreten Sie Ihre Ansichten, doch erwähnen Sie auch Gegenargumente, um zu zeigen, dass Sie wissen, wovon Sie sprechen.

Anweisung	Deutsch	Was Sie tun müssen
Assess	*beurteilen*	Fällen Sie nach reiflicher Überlegung ein Urteil über etwas und liefern Sie Nachweise, die Ihre Meinung stützen.
Evaluate	*einschätzen, bewerten*	
Comment on	*Stellung nehmen zu*	

Entsprechend der folgenden Anweisungen sollen Sie objektiv sein. Denken Sie daran, Ihre Gedanken zunächst zu ordnen, und berücksichtigen Sie beide Seiten.

Anweisung	Deutsch	Was Sie tun müssen
Discuss	*erörtern*	Wägen Sie beide Seiten einer Sache ab und benennen Sie Für und Wider.

Übung 4 (Fertigkeit 3E)

Answer the questions about the text, *Cyberbullying at Wiston* on page 230, in your own words.

1 Describe what happened to Claire.
2 Find evidence in the text to show how Claire was affected by the bullying.

F Einen Aufsatz oder eine Stellungnahme schreiben

Einen längeren Text in einer Englischprüfung zu schreiben, stellt Ihr Sprachverständnis und Ihre Schaffenskraft auf die Probe. Wenn Sie aufgefordert sind, einen Aufsatz zu schreiben, müssen Sie eine objektive Haltung zu dem Thema einnehmen. Um dies zu erreichen, müssen Sie Argumente sammeln, die die in der Aufgabenstellung enthaltene These stützen und widerlegen. Wenn Sie „kommentieren" bzw. „diskutieren" sollen, wird erwartet, dass Sie Ihre Meinung zum Thema äußern. Hier ist es wichtig, dass Sie zur Untermauerung Ihrer Meinung Beispiele angeben.

→ Umgang mit Operatoren, S. 232

Bevor Sie mit dem Schreiben beginnen:

- Lesen Sie die Einleitung zu den Aufgaben mehrmals durch und stellen Sie sicher, dass Sie ganz genau verstehen, worüber Sie schreiben sollen.
- Achten Sie auf den genauen Wortlaut der Anweisungen. Suchen Sie nach Schlüsselwörtern in der Aufgabenstellung, die Ihnen sagt, was zu tun ist, z. B.: *identify*, *analyse*, *comment* usw.

- Symbole, d. h. ein bekanntes Bild verwenden, um eine Idee zu transportieren, z. B. die Freiheitsstatue, um die USA zu verkörpern.
- Bildunterschriften bzw. Sprechblasen, die die Botschaft in wenigen Worten zusammenfassen bzw. den Charakteren als Aussage zugedacht sind.

Bevor Sie über den Cartoon zu schreiben beginnen, stellen Sie sich folgende Fragen:

- Wie sind die Sachen/Personen/Charaktere gezeichnet? Sind die Personen als Karikaturen dargestellt? Stellen sie einen bestimmten „Personentyp" dar?
- Sind Symbole vorhanden? Wenn ja, was repräsentieren sie?
- Sind in der Zeichnung Nummern, Daten oder leicht erkennbare Orte zu sehen? Wenn ja, welche Funktion erfüllen sie? Was teilen sie uns mit?
- Was ist der Standpunkt des Cartoonisten / der Cartoonistin zum ausgewählten Thema?
- Welche Botschaft transportiert der Cartoon? Wie wird diese Botschaft vermittelt?

Sehen Sie sich alles auf dem Cartoon genau an und beschreiben Sie ihn ausführlich; verwenden Sie hier die Verlaufsform der Gegenwart, um auszudrücken, was die Personen tun. Denken Sie daran, dass Sie, wenn Sie die Botschaft des Cartoons nicht verstehen, sagen können, dass es *unclear* oder *ambiguous* ist. Hilfreiche Redewendungen für eine Bildbeschreibung finden Sie mit Hilfe dieses Webcodes.

Phrases → Webcode: FOSSKP2

C Ein Bild bzw. Cartoon mit einem Text vergleichen

Wenn Sie ein Bild bzw. Cartoon mit einem Text vergleichen sollen, lesen Sie den Text sorgfältig durch und sagen Sie, ob er die Botschaft der betreffenden Abbildung aufgreift oder nicht. Begründen Sie Ihre Antwort, z. B. *The image supports the text in the following way: first, … , then, … . Although the picture/cartoon shows … the text says that … .*

Übung 2 (Fertigkeiten 4B und 4C)

A Sehen Sie sich den Cartoon genau an und wählen Sie die richtige Antwort aus, um die Beschreibung zu vervollständigen.

The cartoon shows a group of middle-aged people who could be (*business people / parents*)[1]. They are sitting at a round table in a (*school / meeting room*).[2] A sign on the table indicates that the people are talking about how to persuade people to (*eat/shop*)[3] more. The man with the glasses appears to be (*making a point to / disagreeing with*)[4] his two companions. It is likely that he is the person saying the words (*above/under*)[5] the cartoon. According to these words, the man believes that kids are (*less/more*)[6] likely to believe advertising messages than adults. The message of the cartoon is (*ambiguous/clear*)[7]. The cartoonist believes that people who work in the advertising industry are (*cynical/concerned*)[8] about consumers.

"It won't bother us if we're not allowed to aim our ads at the kids. The adults are easier to fool anyway."

B Lesen Sie den u. s. Text und wählen Sie das beste Satzende aus, um den Vergleich zwischen dem Text und der Cartoonbotschaft zu vervollständigen.

According to a recent study, advertising aimed at young people is an important factor in deciding how kids spend their money. Young people between the ages of 13 and 17 appear to be most influenced by advertising. The study discovered that this age group is more influenced by advertising messages than adults are. As an indication that this may be true, the study discovered that requests by kids and young people for advertised products decrease as they get older.
A spokesperson for the study said: "Consumers tend to become more critical about their purchases and less susceptible to advertising as they grow up."

1 Both the cartoon and the text describe how
  - **a** all age groups react to advertising.
  - **b** to persuade people to buy goods.
  - **c** young people compare to adults when it comes to viewing advertising.

2 The speaker in the cartoon appears to believe that, when it comes to advertising,
  - **a** adults have better judgement than kids.
  - **b** everyone is convinced by the messages the industry puts out.
  - **c** kids are more critical than adults.

3 The text,
  - **a** however, gives a completely different view of the subject.
  - **b** on the one hand, agrees with the cartoon.
  - **c** on the other hand, suggests that no-one is convinced by advertising.

4 According to the text, as kids grow up, they
  - **a** are less accepting of advertising messages.
  - **b** ask their parents for more.
  - **c** spend more money on consumer goods.

5 If we are to believe the text, the advertising executive portrayed in the cartoon is
  - **a** analysing his target groups correctly.
  - **b** incorrect in his analysis of his target groups.
  - **c** taking a risk by not advertising to kids.

5 PRODUKTION: SCHAUBILDER UND STATISTIKEN BESCHREIBEN UND ANALYSIEREN

Diagramme und Kurvenbilder werden verwendet, um Informationen visuell darzustellen.

TYPES OF DIAGRAMS

Table

	Germany	UK
2010	568	261
2015	822	98

Bar chart

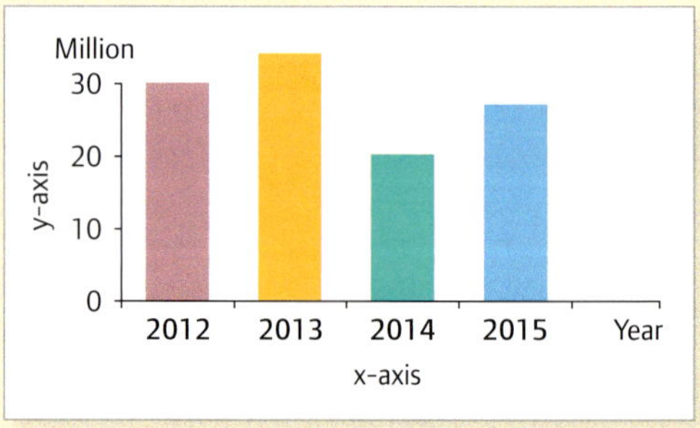

Pie chart

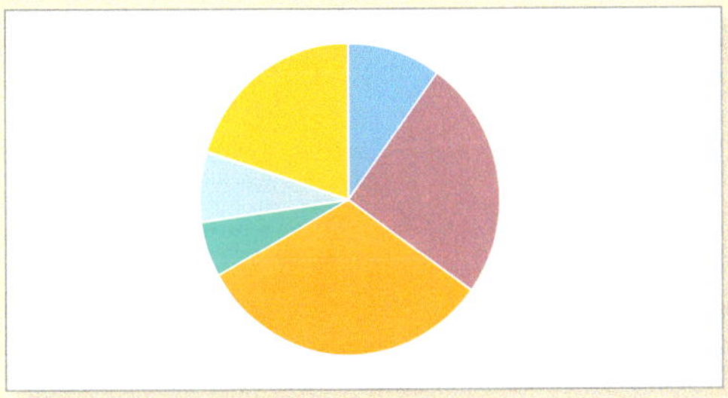

Graph, line graph

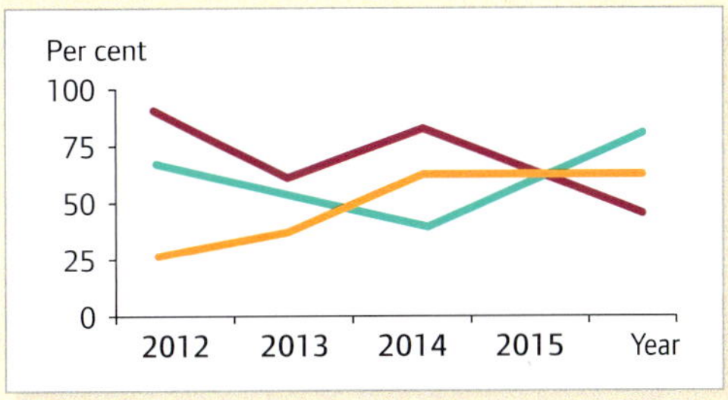

Bevor Sie mit dem Schreiben beginnen, nehmen Sie Schmierpapier zur Hand, sehen sich die Abbildung genau an und machen sich zu folgenden Fragen Notizen:

- Was sagt die Überschrift aus? Welche Beschriftung liegt vor?
- Welche Zahlen und Einheiten werden verwendet, um die Daten darzustellen?
- Wenn ein Balkendiagramm / eine Kurve vorliegt, wofür steht die x-Achse? Wofür die y-Achse?
- Welche Muster können Sie in den Daten erkennen?
- Welche Schlüsse können Sie aus diesen Mustern ziehen?
- Wie verhält sich die Abbildung zu Dingen, die Sie bereits wissen, z. B. zu einem Text, den Sie kürzlich gelesen haben, oder zu Informationen aus der Einleitung zur Aufgabenstellung?

Um Ihre Beschreibung und Analyse der Abbildung zu ordnen, nutzen Sie Ihre Notizen folgendermaßen:

▪ eine Einleitung zum Diagramm bzw. Kurvenbild (Überschrift)	*The diagram / graph shows / refers to …*
▪ ein Überblick dessen, was es darstellt	*The figures in the table show …* *The x-axis shows … , the y-axis shows*
▪ eine ausführliche Beschreibung der Informationen	*The graph shows a huge increase …*
▪ die Beziehung zwischen den Kategorien	*Car X has twice as much … as Car Y.*
▪ eine Auswertung des Diagramms bzw. Kurvenbilds	*The figures indicate that …*

Hilfreiche Redewendungen, Schaubilder zu beschreiben, finden Sie mit Hilfe dieses Webcodes.

Phrases → Webcode: FOSSKP3

Übung 1 (Fertigkeit 5)

Vervollständigen Sie die Beschreibung und Analyse des Diagramms auf Seite 240 mit Wörtern aus dem Kasten.

compared to ▪ constant increase ▪ fluctuate ▪ huge increase ▪ remained more or less constant ▪ rise ▪ shows ▪ small dip ▪ the number of devices in millions ▪ the year

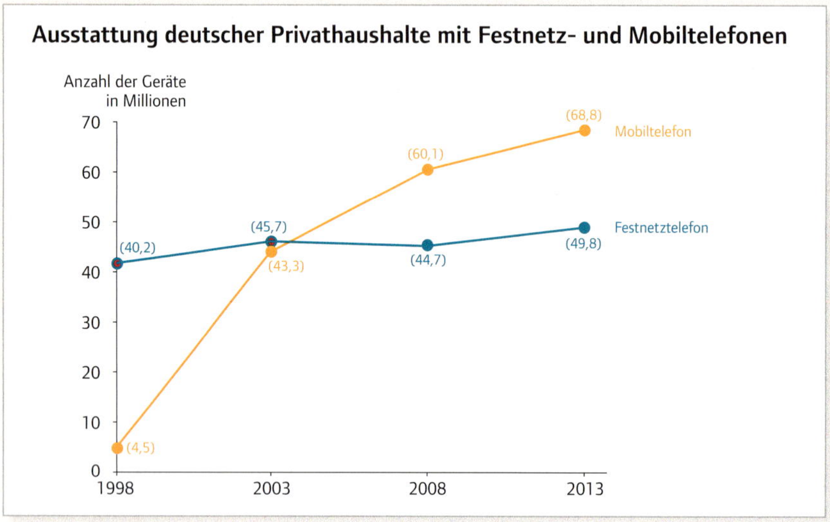

The line graph ___[1] the development in the numbers of landlines and mobile phones in German private households from 1998 to 2013. The x-axis shows ___[2] and the y-axis shows ___[3]. In 1998, there were only 4.5 million mobiles in German households ___[4] 40.2 million landlines. During the next 15 years, the numbers of landlines ___[5] (all in all an increase of less than 20%), whereas the number of mobile phones showed a ___[6]. By 2013, there were just 49.8 million landlines compared to 68.8 million mobiles. In the case of mobile phones, we see ___[7] in numbers over the years, whereas the numbers of landlines ___[8], showing a rise in total numbers during the years 1998 to 2003. This is followed by a ___[9] in total numbers between 2003 and 2008 and a further ___[10] to 49.8 million in 2013.

6 SCHRIFTLICHE MEDIATION

Mediation ist das Übertragen wesentlicher Textelemente von einer Sprache in eine andere. Mediation ist nicht mit dem Wort „Übersetzung" austauschbar. Sie sollen nur den Sinn des Textes übertragen und bestimmte Informationen wiedergeben.

A Vorbereitung

- Lesen Sie sich die Anweisungen sorgfältig durch. Vergewissern Sie sich, dass Sie wissen:
  - warum die Informationen in einer anderen Sprache wiedergegeben werden, z. B. weil Ihr Kollegium über Entwicklungen Ihres Tätigkeitsfeldes informiert werden sollen.
  - für wen die Mediation gedacht ist, z. B. für andere Schüler/innen, Ihr/e Chef/in.
  - welches Medium Sie nutzen sollen, z. B. eine E-Mail, eine Informationsbroschüre.
- Lesen Sie den Text zügig, um den groben Sinn zu erfassen. Verschwenden Sie keine Zeit mit einzelnen Wörtern bzw. Wörtern, die Sie nicht verstehen. → Grobverständnis, S. 214
- Lesen Sie die Anweisungen noch einmal, dann gehen Sie den Text ein weiteres Mal durch und suchen nach Textpassagen, die jene Informationen enthalten, die Sie zur Lösung der Aufgabe benötigen. In einer Prüfung können Sie die betreffenden Stellen unterstreichen oder farblich hervorheben. Folgende Textstellen können als unwesentlich betrachtet werden: Wiederholungen (oft eingeleitet durch *in other words*, *to put it another way*) und Anekdoten und Exkurse (*by the way*, *incidentally*).

B Einen Mediationstext schreiben

Schreiben Sie die wichtigsten Punkte des Textes in klarem, einfachem Deutsch auf. Halten Sie sich an das, was im Originaltext gesagt wurde. Wenn Sie damit fertig sind:

- Lesen Sie Ihren Text Korrektur, d. h. überprüfen Sie die Rechtschreibung und Grammatik.
- Lesen Sie sich Ihren Text durch und stellen Sie sicher, dass der Inhalt des Originals klar und verständlich übertragen wurde.
- Überprüfen Sie, dass Sie nur solche Informationen übernommen haben, die für die Aufgabe relevant sind.
- Überprüfen Sie, dass Sie für die Zielgruppe Ihres Textes angemessen formuliert haben.
- Überprüfen Sie, dass Sie die Mediation in dem nötigen Medium übermittelt haben.

Übung (Fertigkeit 6)

A Lesen Sie sich die Anweisungen sorgfältig durch und machen sich Notizen zur Situation und der Aufgabenstellung.

Situation: Sie machen ein Praktikum in einem Jugendzentrum vor Ort. Das Zentrum bietet für seine freiwilligen Helfer/innen regelmäßig Weiterbildungen an. Die nächste Weiterbildung befasst sich mit der wachsenden Anzahl von Kindern in Europa, die in Patchwork-Familien aufwachsen. Diese Weiterbildung wird auch die finanzielle Lage der Familien beleuchten.

Aufgabe: Ihr Chef / Ihre Chefin lässt Sie den Text *Changing face of the British family* lesen und die Situation im Vereinigten Königreich beschreiben. Er/Sie möchte, dass Sie ein Flugblatt erstellen, welches die wichtigsten Informationen darüber enthält, warum Stieffamilien in ihrer Anzahl zunehmen; dieses Flugblatt möchte er/sie während der Weiterbildung verteilen.

B Lesen Sie nun den Text und machen sich auf Englisch zu den Punkten Notizen, die Sie für Ihre Mediation benötigen.

C Jetzt können Sie Ihren Text verfassen. Vermitteln Sie die wesentlichen Punkte auf Deutsch und behalten hierbei die Zielgruppe im Auge, die Ihre Mediation lesen wird. Berücksichtigen Sie auch das Medium, das Sie benutzen sollen.

Changing face of the British family: One in three now has a step-child
Nearly two million children live in a two-parent family, study reveals

Parents increasingly regard serial relationships as normal behaviour

Nearly a third of all couples bringing up children have a child from an earlier relationship in their family, a report said yesterday.

The rapidly growing number of step-families means that nearly two million children live in a two-parent family – but with one parent who is not their own.

The army of step-children has appeared as their parents increasingly come to regard serial relationships, not one committed marriage, as normal behaviour.

A report said that the majority of parents have had at least one partnership in the past that they regarded as long-term. New details of how the shape of families has been twisted by the decline of lifelong marriage and the rise of temporary cohabitation were revealed in a study of 20,000 people carried out for an insurance company.

The findings of the Family Finances report produced for Aviva were released in advance of the latest national divorce figures, published by the Office for National Statistics today.

These are expected to show that couples who do marry rather than just live together are increasingly likely to stay together. Sarah Poulter of Aviva said: 'This research shows that there is no "normal" family any more. What was seen as the traditional model is becoming more and more diverse.
'It is now quite usual for a child to have three parents, and to live in a family that includes step-parents, half-brothers and half-sisters.'
The polling found that almost half of all adults who live with a spouse or partner or with children – 49 per cent – have had at least one past relationship which they regarded as committed, either a marriage or a cohabitation. One in six have had two past relationships they thought were permanent, and one in 20 has had three or more. The result is that 30 per cent of present two-parent families include a child from a former relationship.

The report said only one in three of these step-families gets any sort of financial help from the parent of the step-child. A third of these get only occasional payments – while only a quarter of parents whose children live with other families provide regular payments.
The analysis suggests a third of step-families that do get financial help actually rely on the payments to get by.
It also found that one in eight adults who have been through a separation postponed the break-up because they could not afford to find anywhere else to live.
Latest official figures say that there are around 5.7 million families with children under the age of 16, or under 18 and still in school. In just over two thirds of these – around four million – the parents are married. (442 words)

From: *www.dailymail.co.uk*

7 ÜBERSETZEN

Einen Text zu übersetzen verlangt Sorgfalt und Geduld. Im Gegensatz zur Mediation ist für eine Übersetzung jedes Wort des Originaltextes wichtig. Ihre Aufgabe als Übersetzer/in ist es, den Sinn des Textes mit deutschen Entsprechungen zu reproduzieren.

Merken Sie sich folgende Regeln:

- Übersetzer/innen haben keine eigene „Stimme". Selbst wenn Sie mit der Aussage nicht einverstanden sind, dürfen Sie weder den Text an sich noch den Ton verändern.
- Von Ihnen werden weder Bewertungen noch Meinungsäußerungen erwartet.
- Streben Sie keine wortgetreue Übersetzung an, denn das ist unmöglich. Stattdessen konzentrieren Sie sich beim Lesen auf Informationsblöcke, die Sie dann als Ganzes übersetzen.

Bevor Sie mit dem Schreiben beginnen:

- Lesen Sie die Überschrift sowie den gesamten Text, um einen Überblick zu bekommen.
  → Grobverständnis, S. 214
- Lesen Sie den Text noch einmal, doch dieses Mal achten Sie auf Einzelheiten. Machen Sie sich beim Lesen Notizen.
  → Gründliches Lesen, S. 223
  → Sich während des Lesens Notizen machen, S. 223
- Schreiben Sie sich Wörter und Strukturen auf, die Sie nicht verstehen.
- Wenden Sie Ihre Fertigkeiten zur Worterkennung an, um sich die Bedeutung von unbekannten Wörtern und Satzstrukturen zu erarbeiten. Verwenden Sie Ihr Wörterbuch nur, wenn es nicht anders geht.
  → Mit unbekannten Wörtern umgehen, S. 216
  → Ein Wörterbuch benutzen, S. 217

Ihre Übersetzung verfassen

Wenn Sie den Text verstanden haben, können Sie mit dem Erstellen Ihrer deutschen Fassung beginnen. Schreiben Sie Ihren ersten Entwurf ‚doppelzeilig' – so haben Sie Platz für Korrekturen.

Wenn Sie mit Ihrer Übersetzung fertig sind:

- Vergleichen Sie Ihren Text und das Original Satz für Satz, um sicherzustellen, dass Sie nichts ausgelassen haben.
- Lesen Sie Ihren Text durch und vergewissern Sie sich, dass er klar und verständlich ist.
- Überprüfen Sie Ihre Rechtschreibung und Grammatik. Lassen Sie insbesondere bei den Verben und den nachfolgend genannten Problembereichen Vorsicht walten.

Tipps – Grammatik, Stil und Vokabular

Jeder Text enthält unterschiedlich knifflige Aspekte, über die Sie nachdenken müssen. Seien Sie bei den folgenden Bereichen besonders sorgfältig.

- **Knifflige grammatische Strukturen**
  - Partizipialkonstruktionen → S. 268
  - Konstruktionen mit Gerundium → S. 262
  - Passivkonstruktionen → S. 261
  - Relativsätze ohne Relativpronomen → S. 269
  - Adverbien → S. 270
  - Komparative und Superlative → S. 271
  - Verben in der Verlaufsform → S. 249–254

- **Wortstellung**
  - Verwenden Sie im Englischen stets die Reihenfolge S–V–O (*subject – verb – object*).
  - Denken Sie daran: Wenn ein deutscher Satz z. B. mit einem Adverb beginnt, wird das Verb versetzt, auf Englisch jedoch bleibt die Reihenfolge S–V–O erhalten.

- **Die Form eines Wortes ändern**

  BEISPIELE: *There is a need to …* → Es ist notwendig, zu …
  (englisch: Nomen → deutsch: Adjektiv)
  She used to work in France. → Früher arbeitete sie in Frankreich.
  (englisch: Verbkonstruktion → deutsch: Adverb)

- **Partikeln und Ausdrücke**

  BEISPIEL: *since* = seit (*He has been working since 6 am.*)
  = da, weil (*Since he didn't have his phone with him, he couldn't call her.*)

- **Falsche Freunde**

  BEISPIEL: *actual* = tatsächlich / *topical, current* = aktuell

- **Häufig verwechselte Wörter**

  BEISPIEL: *advice/advise*
  He gave me some advice. Rat(schlag)
  He advised me to see a doctor. beraten

8 PRÄSENTIEREN

Im Verlauf Ihres Schuljahres könnten Sie aufgefordert werden, eine Präsentation vorzubereiten und zu geben. Die Fertigkeit des Präsentierens können Sie in der Schule üben; das gibt Ihnen jene Sicherheit, die Sie brauchen, um eine Präsentation auf der Arbeit zu geben. An der Schule fallen Präsentationen im Allgemeinen in eine von zwei Kategorien: eine informative, objektive

Präsentation, die auf Tatsachen beruht, und eine subjektive Präsentation, in der Sie Ihre eigene Meinung zu einem strittigen Thema vertreten.

A Vorbereitung

- Sammeln Sie möglichst viele Informationen und Ideen zu dem Thema, indem Sie im Internet und in Büchern recherchieren, mit Experten/Expertinnen sprechen, ein Brainstorming machen, usw.
- Wählen Sie jene Ideen aus, die Ihr Thema am sinnvollsten widerspiegeln, und machen Sie sich Notizen.
- Verwenden Sie Ihre Notizen, um Ihre Ideen in logische Einheiten einzuteilen.
- Ordnen Sie diese Einheiten so, dass ein roter Faden klar erkennbar ist.
- Stellen Sie Ihre Präsentation zusammen und benutzen Sie hierzu eine der u. s. Gliederungen.

Um eine informative Präsentation zu planen, z. B. *Local opportunities for work experience*.
- **Einleitung:** Das Benennen Ihres Themas und eine kurze Erläuterung über den Aufbau Ihrer Präsentation (ca. 15 % Ihrer Präsentation)
- **Entwicklung:** Beweise, die Ihre Vorstellungen belegen (ca. 75 %)
- **Schluss:** Wiederholung Ihrer Ideen und eine knappe Zusammenfassung der wichtigsten Fakten und Zahlen (ca. 10 %)

Um eine Präsentation zu einem umstrittenen Thema zu planen, z. B. *Hash should be legalized*
- **Einleitung:** Objektiver Lösungsvorschlag zu einem strittigen Problem. Äußern Sie Ihre eigene Meinung noch nicht. (ca. 10 % Ihrer Präsentation)
- **Entwicklung 1:** Argumente für den Vorschlag (*pros*) (ca. 40 %)
- **Entwicklung 2:** Argumente gegen den Vorschlag (*cons*) (ca. 40 %)
(Wie auch immer Sie persönlich zu dem Vorschlag stehen, streben Sie ein ausgewogenes Verhältnis zwischen Ihren *pros* und *cons* an.)
- **Schluss:** Ihre Meinung mit einer kurzen Angabe von Gründen. (ca. 10 %)

- Wenn Sie das geschrieben haben, was Sie sagen wollten, lesen Sie Ihre Präsentation durch. Suchen Sie nach Stellen, wo Sie etwas kürzen oder löschen können. Fragen Sie sich immer wieder: Kann ich das noch kürzer, präziser ausdrücken?
- Erstellen Sie sich nun Stichwortkarten als Erinnerungshilfe für die wichtigsten Informationen. Schreiben Sie auf Karteikarten; schreiben Sie deutlich und in Großbuchstaben und niemals ganze Sätze – Sie benötigen nur Stichwörter.
- Es hilft, Ihre Präsentation als Trockenübung zu geben, besonders vor einem Publikum.

Übung 1 (Fertigkeit 8A)

A Entscheiden Sie, welche der folgenden Themen Sie zu einer Meinungsäußerung veranlassen, weil sie für Sie strittig sind.

1 Fitness studios in our area: numbers, prices and facilities
2 The state – not the children – should look after the elderly
3 The rise of global warming from the early 1960s to the present day
4 Using animals in medical research helps people

B **Wählen Sie eines der strittigen Themen aus. Sammeln Sie fünf Argumente für und gegen den Vorschlag.**

C **Halten Sie Ihre Meinung zu dem von Ihnen ausgewählten Vorschlag schriftlich fest. Fassen Sie Ihre Gründe kurz zusammen.**

B Das Verwenden von Folien und Handouts während einer Präsentation

Folien können bei Schaubildern sinnvoll, aber als Teil Ihrer Präsentation auch hinderlich sein. Aus diesem Grund fragen Sie sich bitte vor dem Erstellen von Folien, ob sie notwendig sind. Wenn ja:

- Beschränken Sie die Textmenge auf ein Minimum und stellen Sie sicher, dass die Rechtschreibung stimmt.
- Vergewissern Sie sich, dass Kurvenbilder und andere Abbildungen groß genug sind, um von den Zuhörern/Zuhörerinnen erkannt zu werden.

Handouts sind Unterlagen, die Ihre Präsentation unterstützen. Ein Teil dieser Unterlagen enthält ggf. die von Ihnen verwendeten Folien; andere Handouts ergänzen bzw. erweitern die Informationen, die Sie präsentiert haben. Sie sollten prägnante Informationen oder/und Illustrationen enthalten und ordentlich getippt bzw. gedruckt sein. Sie sollten nicht Ihre Präsentation in einer Kurzfassung enthalten.

C Eine Präsentation halten

- Beginnen Sie mit einer Begrüßung Ihrer Zuhörer/Zuhörerinnen und stellen Sie anschließend sich und Ihr Thema vor. Versuchen Sie, das Interesse und die Aufmerksamkeit Ihrer Zuhörerschaft von Anfang an zu wecken. Sagen Sie, wie lang Sie über etwas reden werden, z. B.: *"In the next 10 minutes, I will share my ideas about …"*
- Teilen Sie Ihrem Hörerkreis mit, wie Sie Ihre Präsentation unterteilt haben bzw. wie viele Punkte Sie abdecken wollen, z. B.: *"I've divided my talk into three sections: first … second …"*
- Setzen Sie für Ihre Zuhörer/Zuhörerinnen während der Präsentation Signale, damit diese wissen, was als Nächstes kommt. So helfen Sie ihnen, Ihrer Kernaussage leichter zu folgen. Sie sollten auch klar vermitteln, wie ein Teil Ihrer Präsentation mit dem nächsten zusammenhängt; dies tun Sie mittels Hinweisen. Lassen Sie sie wissen, wo Sie sind. Nützliche Redewendungen finden Sie online mit diesem Webcode.

Phrases → Webcode: FOSSKP4

- Nachdem Sie das Ende Ihrer Präsentation eingeläutet haben, fassen Sie sich kurz und kommen Sie zum Ende. Ermutigen Sie Ihre Zuhörer/Zuhörerinnen, Fragen zu stellen.

Übung 2 (Fertigkeit 8C)

Hören Sie zu, wie jemand eine Präsentation beginnt und beendet. Machen Sie sich Notizen und nehmen Sie hierzu die u. s. Überschriften zu Hilfe.

Hörtext → Webcode: FOSSKT2

Das Publikum begrüßen	Sich selbst vorstellen	Den Aufbau der Präsentation beschreiben	Über Fragen und Handouts informieren	Die Präsentation beenden

D Körpersprache

- Nehmen Sie Augenkontakt auf.
- Sehen Sie in die Zuhörerschaft und lächeln Sie.
- Stehen Sie nicht steif da und verschränken Sie Ihre Arme nicht vor Ihrem Körper.
- Lesen Sie Ihre Präsentation nicht vor. Schreiben Sie nieder, was Sie sagen wollen, dann lernen Sie es, und dann sagen Sie es.

Übung 3 (Fertigkeiten 8 A bis D)

Choose one of the topics below and follow the instructions. If you have the chance, ask your teacher if you can give the presentation in class as extra practice.

- Wählen Sie ein Thema aus und nutzen Sie die Informationen aus dieser Lektion, um sich inhaltlich vorzubereiten.
  Topic 1: How to give a good presentation
  Topic 2: The theory and practice of skills as described in Focus on Success
- Erstellen Sie Folien und Handreichungen, wenn Sie sicher sind, dass Sie sie benötigen.
- Wenn Sie die Möglichkeit haben, bitten Sie Ihren Lehrer/Ihre Lehrerin, die Präsentation als zusätzliche Übung vor der Klasse halten zu dürfen und bitten Sie ihn/sie oder Ihre Mitschüler/innen (*peer correction*) um Rückmeldungen.

9 INTERAKTION

Sie werden möglicherweise im Unterricht bzw. als Teil einer Prüfung aufgefordert, an einer Diskussion bzw. einem Rollenspiel mitzuwirken. Beide dieser Aufgaben schließen einen Austausch mit anderen Menschen ein. Folgen Sie den u.s. allgemeinen Tipps.

Tipps für einen guten Austausch

- Verinnerlichen Sie die Ausdrücke auf der hinteren Umschlaginnenseite und verwenden Sie sie im Unterricht, sooft Sie können. → *Language for discussion*, hintere Umschlagsklappe
- Halten Sie sich an das Thema.
- Bleiben Sie locker und denken Sie, bevor Sie sprechen.
- Bleiben Sie immer höflich und geben Sie anderen die Möglichkeit zu reden. Hören Sie aktiv zu und gehen Sie auf die anderen Teilnehmer/innen ein. Nehmen Sie Augenkontakt auf und zeigen Sie Interesse, Überraschung, usw. Stellen Sie Fragen.
- Hören Sie aufmerksam zu, was die anderen sagen.
- Werten Sie andere niemals ab. Wenn ein/e andere/r Teilnehmer/in Probleme zu haben scheint, helfen Sie ihm/ihr, indem Sie in Worte fassen, was (Sie glauben, was) er/sie ausdrücken möchte, z. B.:
  So, you mean that … I think I understand what you're getting at. It's as if …

An Diskussionen teilnehmen

In einer Diskussion sollten Sie Ihre Meinung zum Ausdruck bringen.

- Lesen Sie die Anweisungen sorgfältig durch und entscheiden Sie, was Sie sagen möchten.
- Machen Sie sich Notizen und schreiben Sie einige Schlüsselwörter bzw. -ausdrücke auf Englisch auf.

- Versuchen Sie vorauszusehen, was die anderen Teilnehmer/innen sagen könnten. Überlegen Sie sich, wie Sie hierzu reagieren würden, und fügen Sie Ihren Notizen englische Ausdrücke der Zustimmung bzw. Widerrede hinzu.

Ein Rollenspiel gestalten

Ein Rollenspiel gibt die Situation und Rollen vor, die Sie spielen und erkunden.

- Lesen Sie Ihre Rollenkarte sorgfältig durch. Ihre Rollenkarte sagt Ihnen, wer Sie sind und was Sie sagen sollen. Selbst wenn Sie nicht mit dem einverstanden sind, was Ihre Figur sagt bzw. wie sie sich benimmt, „denken" Sie sich in diese Rolle hinein.
- Machen Sie sich Notizen zu den Argumenten, die Ihre Figur sagen könnte, um ihren Standpunkt zu vertreten.

Übung 1 (Fertigkeit 9)

Role play

Situation: You are going to play the role of one of four people involved in a podium discussion about free apps which are used by electronic companies to advertise and persuade teenagers to buy other apps and online games.

A Arbeiten Sie in Vierergruppen und entscheiden Sie, wer welche Rolle übernimmt. Machen Sie sich Notizen zu dem, was Sie sagen möchten, und beginnen Sie dann das Rollenspiel.

Ray Dawson: advertising analyst
You know what you are talking about and are used to people listening to you.
You believe that these apps will help companies make money.
Nobody is being forced to play these games.

Jane Jones: online marketing manager for an electronic company
You are keen to promote your company's games and think people will have a lot of fun with them.
The company is not marketing the apps as educational games; they are marketed solely as games for fun.

Michael/a Griffin: a teenager
You have a lot of experience with online games.
Your older brother plays online games, too.
You used to spend a lot of time playing them, but you play less now as you have to concentrate on your school subjects.
You know some pupils who are addicted to games, but most of your friends are sensible and don't spend all day online.

Sam Dawson: the parent of two teenagers, aged 12 and 13
You are concerned about the effect these free apps will have on young people. You would like to see this type of advertising banned.
Your children have smart phones and electronic equipment like all their friends.
You worry that your children's school work will suffer if they spend too much time playing games.

B Wenn Sie fertig sind, bleiben Sie in Ihren Gruppen und sprechen Sie über die Übung. Tauschen Sie sich über folgende Punkte aus:

- Konnte jede/r Teilnehmer/in seine/ihre Ansichten klar vermitteln?
- Waren alle höflich?
- Hörten alle einander zu?

10 PRÜFUNGSSTRATEGIEN

Alles, was Sie während Ihres Schuljahres gelernt haben, wird Ihnen zu guten Prüfungsergebnissen verhelfen. Seit dem Beginn Ihres Englischkurses haben Sie dieselbe Art von Aufgaben gelöst, die Sie in der Prüfung bekommen, einschließlich Lesen, Schreiben und sich beim Reden abwechseln. Das Durcharbeiten der *Building skills boxes* der jeweiligen Units sowie dieses *Skills*-Anhangs hat Ihnen die Strategien vermittelt, die Sie für einen Test bzw. eine Prüfung benötigen.

Die folgenden Tipps helfen Ihnen, in jedem Test bzw. in jeder Prüfung Ihr Bestes zu geben:

A Die schriftliche Prüfung

- Lesen Sie sich alle Fragen sorgfältig durch und stellen Sie sicher, dass Sie wissen, was zu tun ist.
- Entscheiden Sie, bei welchen Aufgaben Sie sich besonders sicher sind, dass Sie sie lösen können, und welche die meisten Punkte bringen. Gehen Sie diese Aufgaben zuerst an.
- In Bezug auf textbezogene Fragen fragen Sie sich: Welche Textstelle/n benötige ich zur Beantwortung der Frage?
- In Bezug auf Fragen zum Hörverständnis fragen Sie sich: Worauf muss ich achten?
- In Bezug auf schriftliche Aufgaben fragen Sie sich: Welche Art von Text muss ich schreiben? Dann machen Sie sich Notizen und ordnen Sie Ihren Text, bevor Sie die Endfassung schreiben. Zum Schluss überprüfen Sie Rechtschreibung und Grammatik.
- Wenn Sie mit den Prüfungsaufgaben fertig sind und bevor Sie Ihre Aufgaben abgeben, überprüfen Sie, dass Sie alle Anweisungen und jede Aufgabe ordentlich erfüllt haben. Vergewissern Sie sich, keine Frage ausgelassen zu haben.

B Die mündliche Prüfung

- Lesen Sie die Aufgabenstellung durch und legen Sie Ihre Argumentationslinie fest.
- Sofern es erlaubt ist, machen Sie sich Notizen zu dem, was Sie sagen möchten, und zwar bevor Sie zu reden beginnen (Stichpunkte reichen aus).
- Denken Sie an die idiomatischen Ausdrücke, die Sie gelernt haben, sowie die Strategie, sich abzuwechseln.
- Versuchen Sie, die Argumente vorauszuahnen, die der andere Teilnehmer / die anderen Teilnehmerinnen verwenden könnte. Versuchen Sie, Ihre Reaktion auf diese Argumente vorauszuahnen, und verwenden Sie hierfür Ausdrücke der Zustimmung, Widerrede, usw.
- Wenn Sie plötzlich einen Gedächtnisausfall haben und sich an kein einziges Wort erinnern können, umschreiben Sie, was Sie sagen möchten. Reden Sie weiter!

Wenden Sie diese Tipps bei nächster Gelegenheit an, z. B. bei einem Klassentest oder einer gestellten Prüfung. Die Rückmeldungen, die Sie auf Ihre Darbietung von Ihrer Klasse bekommen, zeigt Ihnen, in welchen Bereichen Sie sich noch verbessern können.

Diese *Grammar files* führen Sie durch die wichtigsten Elemente der englischen Grammatik und erklären die Formen und den Gebrauch der Strukturen. Sie können die hier angebotenen Übungen nutzen, um zu üben und Ihre Kenntnisse zu vertiefen. Die Lösungen dazu finden Sie auf www.cornelsen.de/webcodes. Geben Sie einfach den Webcode FOSGRLO im Webcode-Suchfeld ein.

Lösungen → Webcode: FOSGRLO

SIMPLE PRESENT ▪ PRESENT PROGRESSIVE

Form

	Simple present	Present progressive
Aussage	I/you/we/they **play** he/she/it **plays**	I **am playing** you/we/they **are playing** he/she/it **is playing**
Verneinung	I/you/we/they **don't play** he/she/it **doesn't play**	I**'m not playing** you/we/they **aren't playing** he/she/it **isn't playing**
Frage + Kurzantwort	Do I/you/we/they **play**? ▪ Yes, I/you/we/they **do**. ▪ No, I/you/we/they **don't**. Does he/she/it **play**? ▪ Yes, he/she/it **does**. ▪ No, he/she/it **doesn't**.	**Am** I **playing?** ▪ Yes, I **am**. ▪ No, I**'m not**. **Are** you/we/they **playing**? ▪ Yes, you/we/they **are**. ▪ No, you/we/they **aren't**. **Is** he/she/it **playing**? ▪ Yes, he/she/it **is**. ▪ No, he/she/it **isn't**.

Simple present

- In der dritten Person Singular (z. B. nach *he, Sandra, the coffee*) hängt man *s* an das Verb an bzw. *es*, wenn das Verb auf einen Zischlaut (z. B. *ch*) endet.
- Frage und Verneinung bildet man mit *do/don't* und *does/doesn't*. In Sätzen mit *does/doesn't* hat das Verb kein *(e)s*.

Present progressive

- Wenn das Verb auf *e* endet, fällt das *e* vor *ing* weg: *hope – hoping*.
- Bei einem einsilbigen Verb, das auf einen einzelnen Vokal + einzelnen Konsonanten endet, verdoppelt man den Konsonanten: *stop – sto**pp**ing, plan – pla**nn**ing*.

Gebrauch

Simple present	Present progressive
I **come** from Germany.	Wait for me! I**'m coming**.
I **don't eat** much chocolate.	It's hot today and I**'m eating** an ice-cream.
This train **doesn't stop** in Hexford.	Why **is** the train **stopping** on the bridge today?
Germany sometimes **plays** against England.	Today Germany **is playing** against Ireland.
Moni is a designer. She **designs** clothes.	At the moment she **is designing** a new style of jeans.

- Mit dem **simple present** beschreibt man einen Normalzustand und was eigentlich immer so ist – regelmäßige Vorgänge, Gewohnheiten und was zum Tagesablauf gehört, was man beruflich und in der Freizeit macht.
- Mit dem **present progressive** beschreibt man ein momentanes Geschehen, einen Einzelvorgang, der gerade im Verlauf begriffen ist.
- Das **present progressive** verwendet man auch für eine vorübergehende Tätigkeit, die mit Unterbrechungen über eine gewisse Zeit ausgeübt wird, eine vorübergehende Situation im Leben: *This week I'**m helping** my friend to repair his moped.*
- Das **simple present** und das **present progressive** verwendet man häufig mit den folgenden typischen Zeitangaben:

Simple present	Present progressive
▪ always, often, usually, sometimes, never	▪ now, at the moment, just
▪ every morning/day/year	▪ today, this week, this month, this summer
▪ at … o'clock, in the morning, at lunchtime, after school	
▪ on Monday(s), at the weekend, in June, in the summer	

Was sonst noch wichtig ist

- Das **simple present** verwendet man auch, um etwas zu erzählen – eine Filmhandlung, eine Story, einen Witz oder den Inhalt einer Sendung oder eines Textes:
  *The film tells the story of Julian Timbo and how he **becomes** a great star.*
  *In today's programme Kelly Green **talks** about her career.*
- **!** Bestimmte Verben kann man nur im **simple present** verwenden.

have, need, want, like, love, hate, prefer, know, think, remember, understand, believe, realize, seem, mean, belong to

- Wenn *have* aber eine Tätigkeit beschreibt, kann es auch im **present progressive** stehen.

have = „haben, besitzen"	*have* beschreibt eine Tätigkeit
Sorry, I **have** no time.	I'**m having** lunch / a cup of tea.
Stars **have** a lot of money.	We'**re having** a great time/party.

- Das **present progressive** verwendet man auch für zukünftige Vorhaben, wenn Vorkehrungen oder Abmachungen bereits getroffen wurden oder jemand eine bestimmte Zeiteinteilung für sich vorgenommen hat:
  *I'**m** meeting Sam this evening. We'**re going** to the cinema.*
  *Susan **is flying** to London next week.*

1 Complete the sentences with simple present forms of the verbs in brackets.

EXAMPLES: **A** (you/know) ___[1] Emma Gordon? → **A** Do you know Emma Gordon?
B No, ___[2]. I (not know) ___[3] her. → **B** No, I don't. I don't know her.

1 **A** (you/speak) ___[1] English?
B Yes, ___[2]. But I (not use) ___[3] it very often.

2 A (your friend Mike / have) ___[1] a car?
B No, ___[2]. But he (have) ___[3] a motorbike.
3 A (English people / watch) ___[1] German films?
B No, ___[2]. They (not watch) ___[3] many non-British or non-American films.
4 A (your coffee / taste) ___[1] good?
B Yes, ___[2]. It (taste) ___[3] bitter, I like that.

2 Complete the sentences with present progressive forms of the verbs in brackets.

1 A What (you/do) ___[1] at the moment? (you/work) ___[2]?
B No, ___[3]. I (check) ___[4] my Facebook page.
2 A What language (that woman / speak) ___[1]? (she/speak) ___[2] Spanish?
B No, ___[3]. She (speak) ___[4] Portuguese.
3 A Sorry, (I/phone) ___[1] in the middle of your meal?
B No, ___[2]. We (not eat) ___[3] at the moment.
4 A (Dennis/come) ___[1] with us to the Swimarena this afternoon?
B Yes, ___[2]. He (come) ___[3] on his moped.

3 Complete the sentences with the correct simple present or present progressive forms of the verbs in brackets.

1 I (try out) ___[1] a new provider. I (think) ___[2] it's better than my old one.
2 Where (you/come) ___ from? Are you Canadian?
3 What (Manuela/do) ___ ? Is she a radio journalist too?
4 What (Manuela/do) ___[1] today? (she/interview) ___[2] Kelly Green?
5 Tunisia is a hot country. It (not rain) ___ much.
6 Oh no! It (rain) ___ . We can forget our barbecue.

SIMPLE PAST ▪ PAST PROGRESSIVE

Form

	Simple past	Past progressive
Aussage	I/you/he/she/it/we/they **played**	I/he/she/it **was playing** you/we/they **were playing**
Verneinung	I/you/he/she/it/we/they **didn't play**	I/he/she/it **wasn't playing** you/we/they **weren't playing**
Frage + Kurzantwort	**Did** I/you/he/she/it/we/they **play**? ▪ Yes, I / … **did**. / ▪ No, I / … **didn't.**	**Was** I/he/she/it **playing**? ▪ Yes, I/he/she/it **was**. ▪ No, I/he/she/it **wasn't**. **Were** you/we/they **playing**? ▪ Yes, you/we/they **were**. ▪ No, you/we/they **weren't**.

Simple past

- Wenn ein regelmäßiges Verb auf *e* endet, hängt man nur *d* an (*hope – hoped*).
- Bei einem einsilbigen Verb, das auf einen einzelnen Vokal + einzelnen Konsonanten endet, verdoppelt man den Konsonanten: *stop – sto**pp**ed, plan – pla**nn**ed*.
- **!** Unregelmäßige Verben haben eigene Formen – s. Liste auf S. 357.

- Frage und Verneinung bildet man in allen Personen mit *did/didn't*. Das Verb steht dann in der Grundform und hat keine *(e)d* -Endung.

Gebrauch

Simple past	Past progressive
Last year I **was** in London on my birthday.	I **was staying** with an English family.
I **didn't see** my boyfriend last week.	He **was doing** a work placement project.
Why **did** the computer **crash**?	Nobody **was using** it.

- Mit dem **simple past** beschreibt man etwas, das in der Vergangenheit zu einem bestimmten Zeitpunkt oder in einem bestimmten Zeitraum geschehen ist.
- Mit dem **past progressive** beschreibt man etwas, das in der Vergangenheit zu einem bestimmten Zeitpunkt gerade im Gange war. Das kann auch eine vorübergehende Tätigkeit sein, die mit Unterbrechungen über eine gewisse Zeit ausgeübt wurde.

Was sonst noch wichtig ist

- Mit dem **past progressive** beschreibt man einen länger andauernden Vorgang, der durch ein Ereignis von kurzer Dauer unterbrochen wird. Dieses kurze Ereignis steht im **simple past.**
  I ***was checking*** *my newsfeed when an SMS from Julie* ***arrived****.*
  We ***were walking*** *home when Martina* ***passed*** *us on her moped.*

- **!** Bestimmte Verben kann man nicht im **past progressive**, sondern nur im **simple past** verwenden.

need, want, like, love, hate, prefer, know, think, remember, understand, believe, realize, seem, mean, belong to

1 Complete the sentences with simple past forms of the verbs in brackets.

1 **A** (you/make) ___[1] a pizza at the weekend?
B No,I (not do) ___[2]. I (buy) ___[3] one.
2 **A** When (you/speak) ___[1] to your friend in England last?
B I (skype) ___[2] with her last weekend.
3 **A** (your brother/go) ___[1] to Zurich by plane?
B No, he (not do) ___[2]. He (not fly) ___[3]. He (go) ___[4] by car. He (drive) ___[5] there.
4 **A** Why (you/not come) ___[1] to Amy's party last weekend?
B I (not feel) ___[2] good. I (spend) ___[3] the whole day in bed.

2 Complete the sentences with past progressive forms of the verbs in brackets.

1 **A** You were on the phone. Who (you/speak) ___[1] to? (you/talk) ___[2] to that Susie again?
B No, I (not talk) ___[3] to another girl. I (check) ___[4] something with my mum.
2 **A** Where (you/sit) ___[1] at the concert?
B I (not sit) ___[2]. I (stand) ___[3] because there weren't any seats left.
3 **A** What (Mark/do) ___[1] out in the cold?
B He (wait) ___[2] for his brother.
4 **A** (you/ have) ___[1] a good time when I saw you?
B No, I was really bored. Nothing (happen) ___[2].

3 **In each sentence there is one simple past and one past progressive form. Complete the sentences with the correct forms of the verbs in brackets.**

1 I (answer) …[1] the last question in the test when the teacher (tell) …[2] us to stop.
2 Where (you/go) …[1] when I (see) …[2] you yesterday?
3 At 8.30 yesterday evening? I (be) …[1] at home, I (play) …[2] a computer game.
4 My friends and I (just leave) …[1] when it (start) …[2] to rain.
5 It (not rain) …[1] when I (get) …[2] on the bus.
6 It was a cold day. Samira (not want) …[1] a cold drink so she (drink) …[2] coffee.

PRESENT PERFECT ▪ PRESENT PERFECT PROGRESSIVE

Form

	Present perfect	Present perfect progressive
Aussage	I/you/we/they **have played** he/she/it **has played**	I/you/we/they **have been playing** he/she/it **has been playing**
Verneinung	I/you/we/they **haven't played** he/she/it **hasn't played**	I/you/we/they **haven't been playing** he/she/it **hasn't been playing**
Frage + Kurzantwort	**Have** I/you/we/they **played**? ▪ Yes, I/you/we/they **have**. ▪ No, I/you/we/they **haven't**. **Has** he/she/it **played**? ▪ Yes, he/she/it **has**. ▪ No, he/she/it **hasn't**.	**Have** I/you/we/they **been playing**? ▪ Yes, I/you/we/they **have**. ▪ No, I/you/we/they **haven't**. **Has** he/she/it **been playing**? ▪ Yes, he/she/it **has**. ▪ No, he/she/it **hasn't**.

Present perfect

- Bei regelmäßigen Verben hat das Partizip die gleiche Form wie im **simple past**. Es gelten die gleichen Schreibbesonderheiten (s. S. 251).
- **!** Das Partizip unregelmäßiger Verben hat eine eigene Form – s. Liste auf S. 357. Es ist manchmal identisch mit dem **simple past**, manchmal aber nicht.

Gebrauch

Present perfect	Present perfect progressive
We**'ve finished** the test.	We**'ve been working** non-stop.
I **haven't had** this phone long.	I**'ve been using** my friend's phone.
Has the rain **stopped**?	How long **has** it **been raining**?

- Mit dem **present perfect** sagt man, dass etwas geschehen ist.
- Mit dem **present perfect progressive** sagt man, dass etwas eine Zeit lang bis jetzt angedauert hat.
- Beim **present perfect** steht oft ein Ergebnis im Vordergrund, während beim **present perfect progressive** das Andauern betont wird.
- **!** Bestimmte Verben kann man nicht im **progressive** verwenden.

need, want, like, love, hate, prefer, know, think, remember, understand, believe, realize, seem, mean, belong to

Was sonst noch wichtig ist

- **!** Wenn etwas in der Vergangenheit angefangen hat und bis jetzt andauert, verwendet man das **present perfect (progressive)** – nicht, wie im Deutschen, eine Gegenwartsform.
  *I**'ve lived** / I**'ve been living** here **for** five years. (I ~~live~~ here for …)*
  *We**'ve sat** / We**'ve been sitting** here **since** half past one / **since** it started to rain. (We ~~sit~~ here since …)*

- *For* + Zeitraum (*five years, a few days*) – Antwort auf die Frage „wie lange?"
  Since + Zeitpunkt (*2012, Sunday*) – Antwort auf die Frage „seit wann?"
  *I haven't seen Jenny **for** a few days. Is she ill?*
  *I haven't seen her **since** Sunday / **since** we played tennis together.*

1 Complete the sentences with present perfect forms of the verbs in brackets.

1 I (see) ▬[1] the new movie. (you/see) ▬[2] it?
2 Susanne (make) ▬ copies for everyone.
3 My visa (not arrive) ▬[1]. (yours/arrive) ▬[2]?
4 We (not meet) ▬[1] before. But I (hear) ▬[2] a lot about you.
5 (you/have) ▬[1] lunch? I (not eat) ▬[2].

2 Complete the sentences with present perfect progressive forms of the verbs in brackets.

1 I (wait) ▬[1] a long time. I (play) ▬[2] a computer game to help pass the time.
2 They (talk) ▬[1] all evening. They (discuss) ▬[2] the new project.
3 How long (you/work) ▬ on your presentation?
4 How long (it/snow) ▬ ?
5 We (not chat) ▬[1], we (work) ▬[2] hard!

3 Decide whether you should use *for* or *since* with the following expressions.

1 eighteen months
2 a year and a half
3 Tuesday morning
4 last January
5 two seconds
6 ages
7 2009
8 Christmas

4 Correct these sentences. Use the present perfect.

1 ~~I live here for six years.~~
2 ~~We know each other for a long time.~~
3 ~~Marina is ill all this week.~~
4 ~~We have this computer for years.~~
5 ~~How long are you a member of this club?~~

SIMPLE PAST ▪ PRESENT PERFECT

Gebrauch

Present perfect	Simple past
I **have been** to London.	I **went** there *last year*.
We**'ve had** rain today. We**'ve** *just* **had** a shower.	*Yesterday* it **rained** all afternoon.
Have you **seen** this film *before*?	I **saw** it *last month* with Jack.
Has Mark **phoned** *yet*? – Yes, he **has**.	*When* **did** he **phone**? – He **called** *half an hour ago*.

- Mit dem **present perfect** sagt man, dass etwas – irgendwann – in der Zeit bis jetzt geschehen ist, wann ist entweder unwichtig oder unbekannt. Man stellt nur fest, **dass** etwas geschehen ist. Wird der Zeitpunkt genannt, darf man das **present perfect nicht** verwenden.
- Das **simple past** wird verwendet, wenn etwas in der Vergangenheit zu einem bestimmten Zeitpunkt oder in einem bestimmten Zeitraum geschehen ist und dieser Zeitpunkt/Zeitraum genannt wird.

Was sonst noch wichtig ist

- Das **present perfect** und **simple past** verwendet man mit typischen Zeitangaben.

Present perfect	Simple past
ein unbestimmter Zeitpunkt in der ganzen Zeit bis jetzt	ein bestimmter Zeitpunkt oder Zeitraum der abgeschlossenen Vergangenheit
already, (not) yet, before, so far, ever, never, just	yesterday, last week/month/year, … ago, when? what time? in 2013, on 13 October, in February

- Vor allem im amerikanischen Englisch werden *already*, *(not) yet*, *ever*, *never* und *just* auch mit dem **simple past** verwendet.
- Wenn man etwas erzählt, verwendet man manchmal beide Zeitformen im gleichen Zusammenhang. Zuerst berichtet man mit dem **present perfect** die „nackte" Neuigkeit, anschließend nennt man weitere Einzelheiten (einschl. des Zeitpunkts) mit dem **simple past**.
  *Ron **has broken** his leg. He **had** an accident on his moped **yesterday on his way home**.*
  ***I've heard** from Maria. She **sent** me an SMS **10 minutes ago**.*

- Auch wenn kein Zeitpunkt genannt wird, muss man das **simple past** verwenden, wenn etwas zu einem ganz bestimmten Zeitpunkt geschehen sein muss.
  *The team **didn't win** any medals at the London Olympics.*
  [Die Olympiade in London fand zu einem bestimmten Zeitpunkt der Vergangenheit statt.]

- Das **present perfect** verwendet man oft, wenn etwas Auswirkungen auf die Gegenwart hat.
  ***I've been** to London. (= Ich kenne London.)*
  *They**'ve put** the prices up 20%. (= Es ist zu teuer geworden. Diese Preise will ich nicht zahlen.)*

1 Make dialogues as in the example.

EXAMPLES:
A (you/ever/watch) ___[1] an international football match live?
B Yes, I ___[2] . I (see) ___[3] Germany against Denmark last year.
A Have you ever watched an international football match live?
B Yes, I have. I saw Germany against Denmark last year.

1 **A** (you/ever/meet) ___[1] a celebrity?
B No,I ___[2]. But I (see) ___[3] a B-list celebrity in Berlin last month.
2 **A** (you/make) ___[1] notes for the summary task yet?
B No, I ___[2]. But I (read) ___[3] the text again last night.
3 **A** (you/ever/have) ___[1] an accident?
B No, I ___[2]. But my brother (break) ___[3] his leg on a skiing trip in January.
4 **A** (you/buy) ___[1] your new bike yet?
B Yes, I ___[2]. I (find) ___[3] a great offer on the internet.

2 Complete the sentences with the correct verb form: present perfect or simple past.

1. Last year I (take) ___ a trip to Ireland.
2. I (be) ___ there twice now.
3. I (make) ___ good friends when I was there. We chat nearly every week.
4. Last time I (fly) ___ with a new airline.
5. Flying (become) ___ very cheap over the years.
6. The first time I (go) ___[1] to Ireland it (cost) ___[2] a lot of money.

PAST PERFECT ▪ SIMPLE PAST

Form des past perfect

Aussage	I/you/we/they/he/she/it **had played**
Verneinung	I/you/we/they/he/she/it **hadn't played**
Frage + Kurzantwort	**Had** I/you/we/they/he/she/it **played**? ▪ Yes, I/you/we/they/he/she/it **had**. ▪ No, I/you/we/they/he/she/it **hadn't**.

- Das **past perfect** bildet man in allen Personen gleich, mit *had* + Partizip Perfekt.

Gebrauch des past perfect

I got to the station two minutes late and the train **had** already **left**.
At four o'clock in the afternoon I still **hadn't eaten** anything.

- Mit dem **past perfect** sagt man, dass etwas zu einem Zeitpunkt in der Vergangenheit bereits geschehen und abgeschlossen war.

Unterschied zum simple past

- Wenn man z. B. eine Geschichte erzählt und es zwei oder mehr Geschehnisse gab, die miteinander in einem Zusammenhang standen, verwendet man das **simple past**.
  *The plane **landed**, we **got off**, **collected** our bags and **went** to the car park.*

- Wenn es wichtig ist, auszudrücken, dass sich ein Geschehen vor einem anderen ereignet hatte, verwendet man für das zeitlich erste Geschehen das **past perfect**.
  *I **wanted** to phone my girlfriend, but **couldn't** find my phone. I**'d left** it on the plane!*

- Nach *after*, *before*, *until* und *as soon as* kann entweder das **simple past** oder das **past perfect** stehen.
  *After I **arrived / had arrived** home, I called the airline.*

- **!** *'d* kann für *had*, aber auch für *would* stehen.
  *At my grandma's 70th birthday there was loads to eat. After two platefuls I**'d (I had)** eaten enough but my boyfriend said, "I**'d (I would)** like some more, please."*

1 **Which happened first, A or B?**

	A	B
1	We went out	after it had stopped raining.
2	I was short of cash	because I had spent so much on presents.
3	Jack had already arrived	when I got there.
4	The policewoman explained to me	what had happened.
5	There I was at the bank	and I had left my wallet at home.

2 **In each sentence there is one verb in the simple past and one in the past perfect. Complete the sentences with the correct forms.**

1 The road (be) ▬[1] blocked. There (be) ▬[2] an accident.
2 We (not drive) ▬[1] far, when a warning light (come) ▬[2] on.
3 I (run) ▬[1], but the flight (close) ▬[2].
4 I (not remember) ▬[1] the man, although I (meet) ▬[2] him the year before.
5 Meg (invite) ▬[1] Tony to her party, but he (already make) ▬[2] other plans.

WILL FUTURE ▪ *GOING TO* FUTURE

Form

	will	*going to*
Aussage	I/you/we/they/he/she/it **will play**	I **am going to play** you/we/they **are going to play** he/she/it **is going to play**
Verneinung	I/you/we/they/he/she/it **won't play**	**I'm not going to play** you/we/they **aren't going to play** he/she/it **isn't going to play**
Frage + Kurzantwort	**Will** I/you/we/they/he/she/it **play**? ▪ Yes, I/you/we/they/he/she/it **will**. ▪ No I/you/we/they/he/she/it **won't**.	**Am/Are/Is … going to play?** ▪ Yes, … **am/are/is**. ▪ No, … am **not/aren't/isn't**.

- Die Verneinung von *will* heißt *won't*. *Won't* ist die Kurzform von *will not*. Die Kurzform von *will* ist *'ll*.

Gebrauch

will	*going to*
We **will know** the result of the casting show soon.	I've decided. I'm never **going to take part** in a casting show.
I'll perhaps/probably **be** late home tonight.	All the class **is going to meet** up at Jogi's.
I think / am sure you**'ll get** the job.	Who **is going to drive** you to the interview?

- Es gibt keine wirklich feste Regel, wann *will* und wann *going to* verwendet wird. In manchen Kontexten sind sie austauschbar. Als Faustregel gilt:
  – wenn man eine Vorhersage ausdrückt, verwendet man *will*;
  – wenn man eine Absicht, einen Plan oder ein Vorhaben ausdrückt, verwendet man *going to*.
- Nach Ausdrücken wie *I think*, *I promise*, *I hope*, *I'm sure*, *I expect* wird häufig *will* verwendet. *Going to* ist aber oft auch möglich.

Was sonst noch wichtig ist

- Um einen spontanen Entschluss (oft ein Angebot) auszudrücken, verwendet man *will*. Eine Gegenwartsform ist nicht möglich:
  *That bag looks heavy. Let me help you. I**'ll carry** it for you.* [Nicht: ~~*I carry it for you.*~~]
  *Tea or coffee for you? – Oh I **won't have** anything to drink, thanks.* [Nicht: ~~*I don't have …*~~]

- Beachten Sie den Unterschied zwischen einem spontanen und einem vorüberlegten Entschluss:
  *Someone is at the door. – OK, I**'ll see** who it is.* [spontan]
  *Susie has bought cinema tickets for this evening. We**'re going to see** a new movie.* [vorüberlegt]

- *Going to* verwendet man auch für Vorhersagen, wenn man aufgrund von eindeutigen Vorzeichen sagen kann, dass etwas mit Bestimmtheit eintreten wird:
  *Look at that car! It's far too fast. Oh no! It**'s going to crash**. There**'s going to be** an accident.*

- Mit *going to* macht man auch Vorhersagen aufgrund von persönlichen Annahmen. Man ist überzeugt, dass etwas mit Bestimmtheit eintreten wird:
  *Oil **is going to become** more and more expensive.*
  *When the exam results come out, some of us **are going to be** disappointed.*

- Man kann auch das **present progressive** für zukünftige Vorhaben verwenden, wenn Vorkehrungen oder Abmachungen bereits getroffen wurden oder jemand eine bestimmte Zeiteinteilung für sich vorgenommen hat:
  *I**'m meeting** Sam this evening. We**'re going** to the cinema.*
  *Susan **is flying** to London next week.*

1 Complete the sentences with *will/won't*.

1 Holidays on the moon (not happen) ___ in my lifetime.
2 Sorry, but there (not be) ___ enough time for a visit to Disneyland.
3 Why (there / not be) ___ enough time?
4 When (we / find out) ___ what the cost is going to be?
5 Next year is our anniversary. This school (be) ___ 25 years old.

2 Complete the sentences with *going to*.

1 We've got so many interesting things planned. The project week (be) ___ a big success.
2 I (ask) ___ Tom if he can help me with this maths homework.
3 (the police officer / arrest) ___ that man?
4 We don't need a hotel. We (stay) ___ with friends.
5 This is a really difficult task. It (not be) ___ easy.

3 Complete the translation.

1	Du musst uns nicht fahren. Wir nehmen ein Taxi.	You don't have to drive us. We ___ a taxi.
2	Ich helfe Ihnen mit Ihrer Tasche.	I ___ you with your bag.
3	Ich hole dir ein Pflaster.	I ___ you a plaster.
4	Wir nehmen eine große Pizza und zwei Cola bitte.	We ___ a pizza and two colas, please.
5	Lass mal, ich bezahle.	Leave it to me, I ___ .

MODAL VERBS

Verben und ihre Bedeutung

can	Keith **can** come any time.	*können*
may	I'm not sure, but we **may** be late.	*werden/können (vielleicht)*
might	Don **might** have €50 he can lend us.	*könnte(n) (vielleicht)*
must	We **must** warn Mark.	*müssen*
should	They **should** be more careful.	*sollte(n)*
ought to	I **ought to** phone my mum.	*sollte(n)*
be allowed to	**Are** we **allowed to** take photos?	*dürfen*

can, could, was/were able to

Gegenwart	I **can** see you.
Vergangenheit ▪ generelle Fähigkeit ▪ bestimmte Einzelsituation	 I **could** swim at the age of six. I **was able to** catch the last bus.

- Nur *was/were able to* ist möglich, wenn man sagt, was jemandem in einer Einzelsituation in der Vergangenheit gelang. In Fragen und verneinten Sätzen kann man aber auch *could(n't)* verwenden:
  __Were you able to__ see / __Could__ you see who was driving?
  There were so many people in the room. I __wasn't able to__ move / __couldn't__ move.
- Nur Formen von *be able to* sind im **present perfect** möglich:
  I __haven't been able to__ contact Martina yet.
- Man kann entweder *can* oder *will be able to* verwenden, wenn man über die Zukunft spricht.
  Shaun __can__ come / __will be able to__ come this evening.
  I haven't got the money with me now, but I __can__ pay / __will be able to__ pay you tomorrow.

must, mustn't, needn't, don't/doesn't have to, had to

Gegenwart ▪ Aussage ▪ Verneinung ▪ Frage	 We **must** meet more often. I **mustn't** forget Julia's birthday. You **don't have to** wait for me. You **needn't** wait for me. How many tests **do** you **have to** do?	 *wir müssen* *ich darf nicht* *du musst nicht* *du musst/brauchst nicht* *müssen Sie?*
Vergangenheit ▪ Aussage ▪ Verneinung ▪ Frage	 I **had to** work late yesterday evening. Nina **didn't have to** read her text aloud. How much extra **did** you **have to** pay?	 *ich musste* *Nina musste nicht* *musstet ihr?*

- ! *mustn't* ist ein Verbot und entspricht „nicht dürfen". „nicht müssen" drückt man mit *don't/doesn't have to* aus.
- Fragen und verneinte Sätze mit *have to* bildet man mit dem Hilfsverb *do*.

Was sonst noch wichtig ist

- *can* drückt aus, dass etwas generell möglich ist:
  *It **can** be very wet in November.*
- *can* kann man nicht verwenden, wenn man ausdrücken will, dass etwas möglicherweise der Fall ist:
  *We **may** / **might** / **could** be late. It depends on the traffic.* [Nicht: ~~We can be late.~~]
- *can't* und *couldn't* kann man nicht verwenden, wenn man ausdrücken will, dass etwas möglicherweise nicht der Fall ist:
  *The weather's awful. The flight **may** / **might not** go today.* [Nicht: ~~The flight can't / couldn't go.~~]

1 Decide if the underlined verb is correct. Correct the incorrect sentences.

1 I'm sorry, I can't help you today.
2 I can forgive him now. But a couple of months ago I couldn't.
3 I had to hurry, but I could get the train.
4 It was foggy and the plane couldn't land.
5 I could speak to the teacher before the test.
6 I haven't been able to reach him. Perhaps he is on holiday.

2 Decide if A or B is right.

1 I **A** mustn't / **B** don't have to forget to pay for the concert tickets.
2 You **A** mustn't / **B** don't have to come if you don't want to.
3 When was your flight? **A** Must you / **B** Did you have to get up very early?
4 You **A** mustn't / **B** needn't forget your passport.
5 We **A** needn't / **B** mustn't check in till 40 minutes before the flight.
6 He **A** mustn't / **B** needn't park there. That's the teachers' car park.

3 Decide which of the sentences are not correct.

1 **A** The problem may have something to do with the battery.
B The problem might have something to do with the battery.
C The problem could have something to do with the battery.

2 **A** The train may be late this morning.
B The train can be late this morning.
C The train might be late this morning.

3 **A** Sue could be trying to skype me. I'll switch the computer on.
B Sue can be trying to skype me. I'll switch the computer on.
C Sue might be trying to skype me. I'll switch the computer on.

4 **A** Ask Jerry. He can know.
B Ask Jerry. He could know.
C Ask Jerry. He might know.

THE PASSIVE

Form

	Aktiv	Passiv
Simple present	I **stop** you/we/they **stop** he/she/it **stops**	I **am stopped** you/we/they **are stopped** he/she/it **is stopped**
Simple past	I/he/she/it **stopped** you/we/they **stopped**	I/he/she/it **was stopped** you/we/they **were stopped**
Present perfect	I/you/we/they **have stopped** he/she/it **has stopped**	I/you/we/they **have been stopped** he/she/it **has been stopped**
Past perfect	I/you/we/they/he/she/it **had stopped**	I/you/we/they/he/she/it **had been stopped**
Futur mit *will*	I/you/we/they/he/she/it **will stop**	I/you/we/they/he/she/it **will be stopped**

- *be* + Partizip (z. B. *be stopped*) ist der Passivinfinitiv. Diese Form verwendet man nach *will* und *going to* und auch nach Modalverben wie *can, must, might, could*:
  *This law **must be stopped**.*

Gebrauch

Aktiv	Passiv
People **speak** English in South Africa.	English **is spoken** in South Africa.
Someone **stole** my phone.	My phone **was stolen**.
My mum **drove** us to the airport.	We **were driven** to the airport **by** my mum.
Police **fired** shots to control the protesters.	Shots **were fired**.

- In einem Aktivsatz sagen wir, was jemand aktiv tut. In einem Passivsatz sagen wir, was getan wird.
- Das Passiv wird verwendet, wenn es unwichtig/unbekannt ist, von wem etwas getan wird.
- In den meisten Passivsätzen wird die Person nicht genannt. Wenn sie doch genannt wird, fügt man sie mit *by* an (nicht *from!*):
  *In the film the policeman was played **by** Tom Hanks.* [Nicht: ~~*from Tom Hanks*~~]
- Das Passiv wird viel in Medienberichten und technischen Beschreibungen verwendet, weil es neutraler klingt:
  *The President **will be welcomed** to Britain by the Prime Minister.*
  *The machine **can be operated** in energy-saving mode.*
- Manchmal verwenden Politiker/innen, Journalist/innen und Autor/innen bewusst das Passiv, um sich von dem zu distanzieren, was sie erzählen, um „offizieller" zu wirken:
  *Hard-working families in this country tell me that too much **is being paid** to the unemployed.*

Was sonst noch wichtig ist

- Die Passivform von den **progressive tenses** wird mit *being* + Partizip gebildet:
  *A new hotel **is being built**.*
  *At the flea market all sorts of things **were being bought** and **sold**.*

- In einem Passivsatz wird das Objekt eines Aktivsatzes zum Subjekt:

Subjekt	Verb	Objekt
People in Italy	*eat*	***more fruit.***
More fruit	*is eaten.*	

- Im Gegensatz zum Deutschen kann im Englischen auch ein indirektes Objekt zum Subjekt eines Passivsatzes werden:

Subjekt	Verb	indirektes Objekt	direktes Objekt
Journalists	*asked*	***the President***	*a lot of questions.*
The President	*was asked*		*a lot of questions.*

Zu den Verben, bei denen dieses Satzmuster möglich ist, zählen:

ask, buy, give, offer, pay, promise, sell, send, show, tell

1 Complete the sentences with passive forms of the verbs in brackets. Be careful of the tenses.

1 When we got to the house, it was clear that we (not expect) ___ .
2 The hotel (sell) ___ to a Russian company last January.
3 Whenever someone enters the building at night, the alarm (activate) ___ by the CCTV system.
4 The windows (not clean) ___ very often. The window cleaner comes twice a year.
5 Mr Thomas's talk will last 20 minutes. Questions (can ask) ___ at the end.
6 All windows (must close) ___ at the end of the day.
7 I warn you: if anything like this happens again, the police (inform) ___ .
8 The text is perfect now. All the mistakes (correct) ___ .

2 Say the same thing in the passive.

EXAMPLES:	They quickly introduced new technology.	New technology was quickly introduced.
	Nobody gave me an invitation.	I wasn't given an invitation.
1	Someone has stolen my mobile phone!	My mobile phone ___ !
2	They paid him €500.	He ___ .
3	Make sure that someone writes all this down.	Make sure that all this ___ .
4	Has anyone asked you to help?	___ you ___ to help?
5	Somebody showed me how to operate the new system.	I ___ how to operate the new system.
6	They've offered Tony the position.	Tony ___ .

VERB + INFINITIVE ▪ VERB + GERUND

Gebrauch

Verb + Infinitiv	Verb + Gerundium (*ing*-Form)
I **wanted to** meet up with Mike and **managed to** organise it.	I **suggest** going by train.
We **can't afford** to wait much longer.	Sandra **avoided** talking to Matthew at the party.

Viele Verben, u. a. folgende:	
afford (*sich leisten*)	hope (*hoffen*)
choose (*wählen*)	learn (*lernen*)
decide (*sich entscheiden*)	manage (*es schaffen*)
	offer (*anbieten*)
demand (*verlangen*)	plan (*planen*)
encourage (*ermuntern*)	promise (*versprechen*)
	refuse (*sich weigern*)
expect (*erwarten*)	seem (*scheinen*)
hesitate (*zögern*)	threaten (*drohen*)

Wenige Verben, v. a. folgende:	
avoid (*vermeiden*)	(not) mind (*etwas/ nichts dagegen haben*)
dislike (*ungern tun*)	
enjoy (*gern tun*)	miss (*vermissen*)
finish (*zu Ende bringen*)	practise (*üben*)
give up (*aufgeben*)	recommend (*empfehlen*)
imagine (*sich vorstellen*)	risk (*riskieren*)
involve (*mit sich bringen*)	suggest (*vorschlagen*)

Was sonst noch wichtig ist

- Auf bestimmte Verben kann ohne Bedeutungsunterschied ein Infinitiv oder eine *ing*-Form folgen: *like, love, hate, prefer, continue.*

- Einige Verben haben aber unterschiedliche Bedeutungen, je nachdem ob ein Gerundium oder ein Infinitiv folgt:
  z. B. *remember to do sth* = daran denken, etwas zu tun
  (*Please remember to learn your vocabulary.*)
  remember doing sth = sich erinnern, etwas getan zu haben
  (*I remember learning about gerunds at school.*)
  stop to do sth = anhalten, um etw (Anderes) zu tun
  (*Shall we stop to buy some food at this supermarket?*)
  stop doing sth = aufhören, etwas zu tun
  (*I've stopped eating chocolate because it's unhealthy.*)

- **!** Beachten Sie: *like* + Infinitiv oder *ing*-Form, *dislike* nur + *ing*-Form, ***would*** *like/love/hate/prefer* nur + Infinitiv.

- Verben, die auf eine Präposition folgen, stehen als Gerundium.
  *Jane is responsible **for sending** all our letters.*
  *I decided **against going** to the party.*

- Eine *ing*-Form kann auch Subjekt in einem Satz sein:
  *Travel**ling** can be hard.*

- Die *ing*-Form kann auch ein eigenes Objekt haben:
  *Travel**ling** long distances can be hard.*

1 Complete the sentences with the infinitive or gerund of the verb in brackets.

1. After half an hour I gave up (wait) ___ .
2. I refuse (give) ___ this matter anymore of my time!
3. I don't mind (show) ___ you around.
4. They threatened (call) ___ the police.
5. We must avoid (make) ___ the same mistake again.
6. I'd like (stay) ___ at home.
7. Why did you give up (walk) ___ to school?
8. Rachel seems (need) ___ some help.

IF SENTENCES

Einleitung

In einem *if*-Satz wird gesagt, was unter bestimmten Voraussetzungen geschehen wird, geschehen würde oder geschehen wäre. Solche Sätze bestehen aus zwei Teilen. Der *if*-Teil nennt die Bedingung, der andere Teil nennt die Folge:

Bedingung	Folge
If the police find out, *Wenn die Polizei es herausbekommt,*	he'll be in trouble. *wird er Ärger bekommen.* [Das wird geschehen]
If I won a lot of money, *Wenn ich viel Geld gewinnen würde,*	I would buy a fast car. *würde ich mir ein schnelles Auto kaufen.* [Das würde geschehen]
If you had asked me, *Wenn du mich gefragt hättest,*	I would have helped you. *hätte ich dir geholfen.* [Das wäre geschehen]

Form

	If-Teil	Hauptsatz
Typ 1	**Simple present** If you **work** hard,	***will* future** you**'ll earn** a lot of money.
Typ 2	**Simple past** If I **wanted** an easy life,	***would* + Infinitive** I**'d marry** someone rich.
Typ 3	**Past perfect** If we **had taken** a taxi,	***would* + *have* + Past participle** we **wouldn't have missed** the flight.

- Anstelle von *will* kann auch ein Modalverb wie *can, might* oder *should* im Hauptsatz stehen.
  If you work hard, you ***can*** *earn a lot of money.*
  Anstelle von *would* kann ein Modalverb wie *could, might* oder *should* stehen.
  If I wanted to earn more money, I ***could*** *find a second job.*
- **!** *would* steht nie im *if*-Teil!
- *would* kann zu *'d* verkürzt werden. *'d* ist aber auch die Kurzform von *had*:
  *I**'d** have left (= I* ***would*** *have left) home earlier if I**'d** checked (=* ***had*** *checked) the times.*
- Wenn der *if*-Teil am Satzanfang steht, wird er meist mit einem Komma vom Hauptsatz getrennt. Der Hauptsatz kann auch zuerst stehen. Dann verwendet man meist kein Komma.
  If it rains today, I'll go shopping. ABER *I'll go shopping if it rains today.*
- Die Unterschiede zwischen den drei Typen hängen davon ab, wie wahrscheinlich es ist, dass die Bedingung erfüllt wird.

Gebrauch

Typ 1	Es ist gut möglich oder wahrscheinlich, dass die Bedingung erfüllt wird. *If it rains, we'll get wet.*
Typ 2	Es ist unmöglich oder unwahrscheinlich, dass die Bedingung erfüllt wird. *If I was five years old, I'd be in kindergarten.* [Ich bin aber nicht fünf Jahre alt, also ist die Bedingung unmöglich.] *If I became famous, I'd have a lot of money.* [Es ist aber unwahrscheinlich, dass ich berühmt werde.]

Typ 3	Es ist völlig unmöglich und absolut ausgeschlossen, dass die Bedingung erfüllt wird. *If Brad Pitt had been born a girl, would he have become famous?* [Er ist aber nicht als Mädchen geboren worden. Die Bedingung war nie Wirklichkeit und kann niemals erfüllt werden.]

- Sowohl mit Typ 2 als auch mit Typ 3 wird über etwas spekuliert:

Typ 2: was wäre, wenn …	Typ 3: was wäre gewesen, wenn …

- In Typ 2 steht das **simple past**. Es wird aber nicht über die Vergangenheit gesprochen.
- In Typ 3 wird über die Vergangenheit gesprochen.

1 In each sentence one verb is in the simple present, one verb in the future with *will*. Complete the sentences with the correct forms of the verbs in brackets.

1 If the packet (arrive) ___[1] by Friday, that (be) ___[2] OK.
2 If Manni (say) ___[1] that again, I (explode) ___[2]!
3 She (not understand) ___[1] you if you (not speak) ___[2] more slowly.
4 What (you/do) ___[1] if they (not offer) ___[2] you the job?
5 If we (not take) ___[1] a break soon, I (die) ___[2] of hunger.
6 If they (invite) ___[1] you, (you/go) ___[2]?

2 Complete the translation. All the sentences are type 2 conditional sentences.

1 Wenn ich Zeit hätte, würde ich Ihnen helfen.
If I ___[1] time, I ___[2] you.
2 Wenn ich Max besser kennen würde, wüsste ich, wie ich ihm helfen könnte.
If I ___[1] Max better, I ___[2] how to help him.
3 Wenn du Francesca fragen würdest, was würde sie sagen?
If you ___[1] Francesca, what ___[2]?
4 Was würde passieren, wenn wir einfach nichts tun würden?
What ___[1] if we simply ___[2] nothing?
5 Es wäre besser, wenn Sie später noch einmal anrufen könnten.
It ___[1] better if you ___[2] again later.
6 Was tätest du, wenn die andere Firma mehr Geld bieten würde?
What ___[1] if the other firm ___[2] more money?

3 Say the same thing with a conditional sentence type 3.

EXAMPLE: I didn't know about the meeting so I didn't come.
If I had known about the meeting, I would have come.

1 Jenny didn't hear about the job so she didn't apply. — If Jenny ___
2 They didn't have enough money so they didn't buy any souvenirs. — If they ___
3 I didn't have my mobile with me so I didn't call you. — If I ___

EXAMPLE: Jack had to work on Saturday. That's why he didn't come swimming with us.
If Jack hadn't had to work on Saturday, he would have come swimming with us.

4 I had my mobile with me. That's why I took photos. — If I ___
5 I stopped to talk to Martin. That's why I was late. — If I ___
6 They drove too fast. That's why they had an accident. — If they ___

INDIRECT SPEECH

Zeitverschiebung

Direkte Rede: Gegenwartsform von Vollverb oder Hilfsverb	Indirekte Rede: Vergangenheitsform von Vollverb oder Hilfsverb
Simple present:	**Simple past:**
*"I **know**."*	*She said (that) she **knew**.*
*"Mark **doesn't** know."*	*She said (that) Mark **didn't** know.*
Present progressive:	**Past progressive:**
*"Ann **is** working."*	*He said (that) Ann **was** working.*
Present perfect:	**Past perfect:**
*"We **have** eaten."*	*They said (that) they **had** eaten.*

- Wenn wir wörtliche Rede indirekt wiedergeben, gibt es eine Zeitverschiebung beim Verb. Im Englischen heißt diese Zeitverschiebung *backshifting*. Die Verbform wird um eine Stufe „nach hinten verschoben". Diese Verschiebung hat nichts mit der Zeit an sich zu tun, sondern drückt einen Perspektivenwechsel aus.
- Vergangenheitsformen von Voll- oder Hilfsverben bleiben in der indirekten Rede unverändert. Sie sind ja bereits „verschoben":
  "I met Tom in town." → Susie said she met Tom in town.
  "We had already eaten." → They said they had already eaten.
  Eine **simple past**-Form kann aber wahlweise in eine **past perfect**-Form „verschoben" werden.
- *can* und *will* werden zu *could* und *would* „verschoben"; *could*, *might* und *should* bleiben unverändert:
  *"I **can** come." → I said I **could** come.*
  *"You **will** soon find out." → I said they **would** soon find out.*

Fragen, Bitten und Befehle

Fragen	
"Is it raining?"	She asked **if/whether** it is/was raining.
"Do you speak French?"	They asked me **if/whether** I speak/spoke French.
"Where is Tom?"	They wanted to know where Tom is/was.
Bitten	
"Can you help me, please?"	He **asked** me **to** help.
"Please don't tell my dad."	She **asked** me **not to** tell her dad.
Befehle	
"Sit down."	She **told** me **to** sit down.
"Don't talk."	He **told** us **not to** talk.

- Wenn man eine wörtliche Frage umformuliert, in der *do/does/did* stand, erscheint *do/does/did* in der indirekten Rede nicht:
  *"**Does** Tom know?" → Susie wanted to know if/whether Tom **knows/knew**.*
  *"**Did** you win?" → He asked me if/whether we **won**.*

Was sonst noch wichtig ist

- Wenn mit einem Verb im **simple present** berichtet wird (hier unterstrichen), bleibt die Zeitform der direkten Rede grundsätzlich erhalten:

Direkte Rede	Indirekte Rede
"I **buy** a lot online."	Martina <u>says</u> (that) she **buys** a lot online.
"What **is** your address?"	They <u>want to know</u> what our address **is**.

- Auch wenn mit einem Verb im **simple past** berichtet wird, ist eine Zeitverschiebung nicht immer zwingend. Entscheidend ist, ob der Zeitraum vorbei ist, in dem die Aussage ursprünglich Gültigkeit hatte:
  Vor einem Fußballspiel sagt ein Trainer: *"We **will** win."*
  Nach Beendigung des Spiels wird berichtet: *The trainer **said** his team would win.*

  Wenn das Berichtete immer oder immer noch gültig ist, muss keine Zeitverschiebung erfolgen:
  Eine Physiklehrerin erzählt: *"Water **freezes** at zero."*
  Es wird später berichtet: *She told us that water **freezes** at zero.*

  Ann verspricht: *"When I meet Martin, I **will** ask him."*
  Solange Ann Martin nicht getroffen hat, kann berichtet werden: *Ann said she **will** ask Martin.*

- Weil Zeitverschiebung mit Perspektivenwechsel zu tun hat, wird sie oft bewusst gewählt, wenn man sich von dem, was man berichtet, distanzieren und zeigen will, dass man dessen Wahrheitsgehalt nicht garantiert:
  Ein Minister verspricht: *"We **won't** increase taxes."*
  Eine Zeitung berichtet: *The minister said the government **wouldn't** increase taxes.*

1 Complete the second sentence as in the example. Use backshifting.

EXAMPLE: "They won't agree." (They will accept the offer.)
→ But you said they would accept the offer.

1	"We can't get into the system." (We have the password.)	But you said ___
2	"I'm afraid I don't have time." (I'll discuss this with you today.)	But you said ___ with me ___
3	"I'm not going to the class meeting." (I don't want to miss it.)	But you said ___
4	"I'm too tired." (I'll go to the gym with you.)	But you said ___ with me.
5	"I don't know where to go." (I know the way.)	But you said you ___
6	"I believe Michael." (He is lying.)	But you said ___

2 Complete the second sentence as in the example. Use backshifting.

EXAMPLE: "Did anyone call while I was away?"
→ Tony wanted to know if anyone had called while he was away.

1	"Do you know the address?"	→ Penny asked me if I ___
2	"Please don't park there."	→ They asked me ___
3	"Who drives that red car?"	→ Someone wanted to know ___
4	"What did you do with all those spare copies?"	→ He wanted to know ___
5	"Who used the room last?"	→ He demanded to know ___
6	"Please wait outside."	→ They asked ___

PARTICIPLES

Form und Gebrauch

	Present participle (+*ing*)	Past participle (+ *ed*)
Nach *when, while, after, before*	**When/While/After/Before** surf**ing** the internet, I found some useful addresses.	
Anstelle eines Satzglieds mit *and* + Verb	The man helped us **and showed** us where to go. → The man helped us **showing** us where to go.	
Anstelle eines Relativsatzes mit Verb	Verb in der Gegenwart: Hydroponic farming is a new method **which is getting** a lot of attention. → Hydroponic farming is a new method **getting** a lot of attention.	Verb in der Vergangenheit oder im Passiv: Morton was the man **who people saw / who was seen** near the building. → Morton was the man **seen** near the building.

Was sonst noch wichtig ist

- Sätze mit Partizipien werden vor allem in der Schriftsprache verwendet. Mündlich sind sie auch möglich, klingen aber zeitweise gestelzt. In der gesprochenen Sprache verwendet man vorzugsweise Sätze mit Subjekt und Verb.

PRONOUNS AND POSSESSIVE ADJECTIVES

Form und Gebrauch

Subject pronouns		Object pronouns	Possessive adjectives
Wer?		*Wen? Wem?*	*Wessen?*
ich	I	me	my
du, Sie	you	you	your
er/sie/es	he/she/it	him/her/it	his/her/its
wir	we	us	our
ihr, Sie	you	you	your
sie	they	them	their

- Zwischen ‚mich' und ‚mir', ‚ihn' und ‚ihm', usw. macht man im Englischen keinen Unterschied. Es gibt jeweils nur eine Form.
- Die besitzanzeigenden Begleiter (*my, your, usw.*) verändern ihre Form nicht.

1 Which is the right word?

Mo and Jo are in a holiday hotel.

Mo *She / They*[1] is by the pool again.
Jo Who?
Mo Lil Martin, that sports celebrity. Can't you see *her / she*[2]?

Jo	Is *she / they*[3] with *he / him*[4]? *Her / Their*[5] playboy.
Mo	He isn't *her / their*[6] playboy. He's *her / she*[7] trainer. *They / Them*[8] are in *her / their*[9] usual place. *He's / His*[10] nice.
Jo	I'm not interested in *they / them*[11]. Celebrities! Stop looking. This is *our / us*[12] holiday.
Mo	I think *they're / their*[13] cool. Not like you. *Your / You're*[14] not cool. Why are *we / us*[15] still together? Look at *we / us*[16]. The non-cool pair of the year.

2 Complete the sentences with the correct translation of *sie/Sie*.

1	*Wer ist sie? Ist sie unsere neue Lehrerin?*	Who is ___ ? Is ___ our new teacher?
2	*Deine Schwester ist nett. Ich mag sie.*	Your sister is nice. I like ___ .
3	*Sind Sie Kanadier?*	Are ___ Canadian?
4	*Toni und Wally sind aus Memphis, sie sind Jazzmusiker.*	Toni and Wally are from Memphis, ___ are jazz musicians.
5	*Schön, Sie wiederzusehen.*	Nice to see ___ again.
6	*Meine Freundin lebt in London, ich besuche sie oft dort.*	My girlfriend lives in London, I often visit ___ there.

RELATIVE CLAUSES

Form und Gebrauch

A 'grade A' student is someone **who/that** is very good.

Stress is something **which/that** can affect people of all ages.

- Mit einem Relativsatz bestimmt man Personen oder Sachen näher.
- Relativsätze, die Personen genauer bestimmen, werden durch *who* oder *that* eingeleitet.
- Relativsätze, die Sachen genauer bestimmen, werden durch *which* oder *that* eingeleitet.

Was sonst noch wichtig ist

- In den Beispielsätzen oben ist das Relativpronomen *who/which/that* Subjekt des Relativsatzes. Danach folgt direkt das Verb.
- Ein Relativpronomen kann auch Objekt sein. Dann steht zwischen dem Relativpronomen und dem Verb ein anderes Pronomen oder ein Ausdruck mit einem Nomen (hier unterstrichen). Dieses Pronomen bzw. dieser Ausdruck ist Subjekt des Relativsatzes:
  *Sue is online a lot. Mike is a guy (**who/that**) she met online.*
  *Teen Times is a magazine (**which/that**) my friend Duke buys.*

  Wenn *who/which/that* Objekt ist, kann man es weglassen.
- *Who/which/that* kann Objekt eines Verbs sein, wie in den Beispielen eben, oder Objekt einer Präposition (z. B. *to, with, about, for, of*). Auch hier kann das Relativpronomen weggelassen werden. Die Präposition steht dabei meist am Satzende:
  *Mrs Waters was the name of the teacher (**who/that**) Carrie spoke to.*
  *Here's the web address (**which/that**) I was talking about.*

1 Decide if you can leave out the relative pronoun.

1 The person who wrote this handbook has done a very good job.
2 The youth hostel that we stayed in was not in the centre of the city.
3 The computer which I like best is too expensive.
4 I think there's someone over there who I've met before.
5 Anyone who wants to come with me, please let me know by Thursday afternoon.
6 What am I going to do now with all the copies that I made?

2 Correct the sentences – if there is a mistake.

EXAMPLES: *The text who you looked at yesterday has been changed. The text which/that …*
I know someone who knows the manager. [The sentence is correct.]

1 Who is the person who can best help me?
2 I know someone has a lot of experience.
3 The hotel we stayed in was called The Angler.
4 I've just had an email from the people who we met at that concert.
5 The person that signs the letter may not be the person wrote it.
6 What's the address of that firm that built that new hotel?

ADJECTIVES ▪ ADVERBS OF MANNER

Form und Gebrauch

Adjektiv	Adverb der Art und Weise
1. Ann is a **careful** driver. *Ann ist eine vorsichtige Autofahrerin.*	3. She drives **carefully**. *Sie fährt vorsichtig.*
2. Ann/She is **careful**. *Ann ist vorsichtig.*	4. She is **especially** careful in fog. *Sie ist besonders vorsichtig bei Nebel.*
	5. She doesn't drive **very** fast. *Sie fährt nicht besonders schnell.*
	6. She's **really** disciplined. *Sie ist wirklich diszipliniert.*

- Das fett gedruckte Wort ist ein Adjektiv oder Adverb. Das unterstrichene Wort ist das Bezugswort – das, worüber das Adjektiv/Adverb etwas aussagt.
- Ein Adjektiv beschreibt, wie jemand oder etwas ist. Es bezieht sich auf ein Nomen (z. B. *Ann*) oder Pronomen (z. B. *she*). Es steht vor einem Nomen (Satz 1) oder nach dem Verb *be* (Satz 2).
- Ein Adverb beschreibt oft, wie jemand etwas tut (z. B. *carefully*), und bezieht sich auf ein Verb (Satz 3).
- Ein Adverb kann aber auch ein anderes Wort verstärken oder abschwächen (z. B. *extremely, very, really*). Es bezieht sich dann auf ein Adjektiv (Satz 4), auf ein anderes Adverb (Satz 5) oder ein Partizip (Satz 6).

Was sonst noch wichtig ist

- Mit Adverbien der Art und Weise sagt man, wie etwas geschieht oder getan wird. Meist werden sie gebildet, indem man *ly* an das entsprechende Adjektiv anhängt:
  *Mark is **quick**. He works **quickly**.*

- Beachten Sie diese Schreibbesonderheiten bei der Endung *ly*:

Adjektiv auf Konsonant + *y*: *y* wird zu *i*	The test is easy. I can do it eas**ily**.
Adjektiv auf *le*: *le* fällt weg	The weather is terrible. It's terrib**ly** cold.
Adjektiv auf *ic*: *al* wird eingefügt	It's automatic. It changes automat**ically**.

- **!** Das zu *good* gehörige Adverb heißt *well*:
Tanja is a good tennis player. She plays ***well****.* [Nicht: ~~*She plays good.*~~]

- **!** Einige wenige Adverbien der Art und Weise haben die gleiche Form wie das Adjektiv: *early*, *late*, *fast*, *hard*.

- Nach bestimmten Verben verwendet man kein Adverb der Art und Weise, sondern ein Adjektiv.

Verben, die einen Zustand beschreiben	*seem, become, remain*
Verben, die eine Eigenschaft von etwas beschreiben. Man kann die Eigenschaft mit einem der fünf Sinne wahrnehmen.	*look* (nur in der Bedeutung „aussehen"), *sound* (sich anhören), *feel* (sich fühlen, sich anfühlen), *taste* (schmecken), *smell* (riechen)

1 Complete the dialogues with the adjective or adverb form of the words in brackets.

1 Please be ___ . (careful)
2 Drive ___ . (careful)
3 I like the idea. It sounds ___ . (good)
4 You look ___ . (nervous)
5 Why are you ___ ? (nervous)
6 You play the piano very ___ . (good)
7 My boss answered ___ , 'I have no time for that now.' (angry)
8 Everything was so ___ organized. (beautiful)

2 Say the same with the word in brackets.

EXAMPLE: She has a soft voice. (speak) → *She speaks softly.*

1 His question was not very polite. (ask) → He didn't ask ___
2 Your German is very good. (speak German) → You ___
3 She had a happy smile. (smile) → She ___
4 It was a strange feeling. (feel) → I ___
5 Maureen is a fast runner. (run) → Maureen ___
6 We don't have regular meetings. (meet) → We ___
7 Our guests were unexpected. (come) → Our guests ___
8 Stuntmen and women have a dangerous life. (live) → They ___

COMPARISON OF ADJECTIVES AND ADVERBS

Form

	Komparativ (1. Steigerungsstufe)	Superlativ (2. Steigerungsstufe)
Einsilbige Adjektive: *er/est* anhängen	Which brand is **cheaper**?	Which is **cheapest**?
Zweisilbige Adjektive auf Konsonanten + *y*: *y* wird zu *i*, *er/est* anhängen	Question 2 is **easier**.	Which is the **easiest** question?

Mehrsilbige Adjektive: *more/most* voranstellen	My job is **more interesting**.	Who has the **most interesting** job?
Adverbien formgleich mit Adjektiv: *er/est* anhängen	John drives **faster**.	Who drives **fastest**?
Adverbien auf *ly*: *more/most* voranstellen	Who works **most carefully**?	Who works **most carefully**?

- Wichtige Adjektive und Adverbien haben Sonderformen:

good/well	*better*	*best*
bad(ly)	*worse*	*worst*

- Zu den Adverbien, die mit dem entsprechenden Adjektiv formgleich sind, zählen: *early, late, fast, hard, long*
- Schreibbesonderheiten:
  - Adjektiv auf *e*: nur *r/st* anhängen (*nice – nicer – nicest*)
  - Adjektiv auf Einzelvokal + Einzelkonsonanten: Konsonanten verdoppeln (*big – bi**gg**er – bi**gg**est*).

Gebrauch

Gleichsetzung: *as … as*	I'm **as old as** Jenny. („*so alt wie*")
	I work **as hard as** everybody else. („*so hart wie*")
Ungleichsetzung: *er/more … than*	I'm **older than** Martina. („*älter als*")
	I work **more carefully than** Thomas. („*sorgfältiger als*")

- Nicht *as*, sondern *than* entspricht dem deutschen „als":
  „Ich bin älter **als** du" = *I am older **than** you.* (Nicht: ~~*I am older as you.*~~)

Was sonst noch wichtig ist

- Nach *as* und *than* steht ein Pronomen in der Objektform:
  *Jürgen is as old as **me**. Tanja's younger brother is taller than **her**.*

1 Make comparisons with the words in brackets.

EXAMPLE: In the summer I have a (long) longer working day than in the winter.

1 This is one of the (complicated) ___[1] systems I have ever had to use.
2 In a foreign language, reading is normally (easy) ___[1] ___[2] listening.
3 The old handbook was much (thin) ___[1] ___[2] this one.
4 I feel (bad) ___[1] ___[2] yesterday.
5 The tickets aren't (cheap) ___[1] ___[2] last year. They're (expensive) ___[3].

2 Complete the sentences with the comparative or superlative form of the adverb.

1 You have to work (hard) ___ .
2 The new member of the team is doing (good) ___ now that he's had some training.
3 Four companies suggested solutions, but the German company solved the problem (efficient) ___ .
4 My club is playing (bad) ___ than at any time this season.
5 The changes are happening (gradual) ___ than we expected.

POSITION OF ADVERBS OF TIME

Einleitung

- Wir unterscheiden zwischen Adverbien (ein Wort) und adverbialen Bestimmungen (mehr als ein Wort).
  *Ron **always** works hard.* [Adverb]
  *He works (1) **every day** (2) **from nine to six**.* [zwei adverbiale Bestimmungen]

- Grundsätzlich gibt es drei mögliche Stellungen für Adverbien und adverbiale Bestimmungen in einem englischen Satz.

Satzanfang	**Usually** I don't work on a Sunday.
Satzmitte	I don't **usually** work on a Sunday.
Satzende	I don't work on a Sunday **usually**.

- Viele Adverbien und adverbiale Bestimmungen können am Satzanfang oder -ende stehen. Dieser Sprachgebrauch unterscheidet sich wenig vom deutschen. Wichtige Unterschiede gibt es bei der Stellung in der Satzmitte.
- In der Satzmitte stehen Adverbien der Häufigkeit (*always, usually, normally, regularly, often, sometimes, never*) sowie kurze Adverbien wie *ever, just, now, soon, still, already*.
- Nicht in der Satzmitte, sondern am Satzende stehen *yesterday, today, again* sowie adverbiale Bestimmungen. Dazu gehören z. B. Bestimmungen mit *every, last, ago*, Uhr- und Tageszeiten:
  *I went swimming **today**.* [Nicht: ~~*I went today swimming.*~~]
  *They flew to Canada **last year**.* [Nicht: ~~*They flew last year to Canada.*~~]

Gebrauch

Stellung in der Satzmitte	
Vor einem Verb im **simple present** oder **simple past**	*I **never** smoke. He **quickly** said goodbye.*
Hinter einem Hilfsverb	*We don't **normally** drive. She has **never** asked.*
Hinter einer Form des Verbs *be*	*Anna is **always** happy. You weren't **often** here.*

- In den Beispielen ist das Adverb **fett** gedruckt, das Verb/Hilfsverb unterstrichen.

Was sonst noch wichtig ist

- **!** Ein Adverb oder eine adverbiale Bestimmung kann nicht zwischen einem Verb und seinem Objekt stehen!
  *We **always** take the bus.* [Nicht: ~~*We take always the bus.*~~]
  *Stan watches TV **in the evening**.* [Nicht: ~~*Stan watches in the evening TV.*~~]

Which position is right for the adverb / adverbial: A or B?

1 We **A** are **B** well prepared. (always)
2 I don't **A** drink **B** tea. (often)
3 We **A** make **B** mistakes. (never)
4 We **A** have **B** made a mistake. (never)
5 I've **A** seen this film **B**. (several times)
6 We've been **A** to San Francisco **B**. (once before)
7 This **A** happens to me **B**. (always)
8 The test doesn't **A** take **B** long. (usually)

COUNTABLE AND UNCOUNTABLE NOUNS

Einleitung

Nicht zählbare Nomen haben keine Mehrzahlform und man kann weder *a/an* noch eine Zahl davorsetzen:

zählbar *one book, two books, three books, etc.*
nicht zählbar *weather, money, traffic, etc.* [Nicht: ~~*a weather, two moneys, three traffics*~~]

Gebrauch

- Bestimmte Nomen sind im Deutschen zählbar, im Englischen aber nicht.

advice	*Rat, Ratschlag, Ratschläge*	housework	*Hausarbeit, Hausarbeiten*
bread	*Brot*	information	*Information, Informationen*
damage	*Schaden, Schäden*	knowledge	*Wissen, Kenntnisse*
equipment	*Ausrüstung, Geräte*	paper	*Papier, Zettel*
furniture	*Möbel*	progress	*Fortschritt, Fortschritte*
hair	*Haar, Haare*	proof	*Beweis, Beweise*
help	*Hilfe, Hilfen, Hilfestellungen*	toast	*Toast*
homework	*Hausaufgabe, Hausaufgaben*	work	*Arbeit, Arbeiten*

- Nicht zählbare Nomen verwendet man mit *this/that* und *much*. Das Verb nach einem nicht zählbaren Nomen steht immer im Singular:
  ***This information** is interesting.* (Diese Information ist / Diese Informationen sind interessant.)
  *How **much homework** is there today?* (Wie viele Hausaufgaben sind heute auf?)

- Mit Ausdrücken wie *a piece of* oder *a bit of* kann man Ersatzsingular- und Pluralformen bilden:
  *Can I have **a piece of paper**, please?* (einen Zettel)
  *They gave me **two** useful **bits of information**.* (zwei nützliche Informationen)

QUANTIFIERS

Gebrauch von *some* und *any*

Aussage	I need **some** more time. Show me **some** photos.
Verneinung	I do**n't** want **any** tea, thanks. There were**n't any** interesting films.
Frage	Is there **any** butter? Does their letter give **any** details?
Bitte oder Angebot	Can I have **some** ketchup, please? Would you like **some** help?

Gebrauch von *much, many, little, a little, few, a few*

Nicht zählbar	Plural
I don't have **much** money.	Are there **many** good shops?
There is **little** time. *(wenig)*	There were **few** tourists. *(wenige)*
I need **a little** help. *(etwas, ein wenig)*	Can you give me **a few** tips? *(ein paar, einige)*

Diese Liste enthält ca. 1100 Wörter und Ausdrücke, die in **Focus on Success – 5th edition: Ausgabe Technik** als bekannt vorausgesetzt werden. Nicht aufgeführt, jedoch vorausgesetzt, sind einige elementare Wörter wie einfache Strukturwörter, Präpositionen, Zahlen, Farben, Wochentage usw. sowie internationale Wörter wie *email, hotel, cowboy* usw.
Die folgende Liste ist nach Themenbereiche angelegt. Auch innerhalb der Themenbereiche sind die Vokabeln nach sinnvollen Wortfeldern angeordnet. Dadurch eignet sich die Liste nicht nur zum Nachschlagen, sonder auch zum Lernen.

PEOPLE *(Menschen)*

people *Personen*
population *Bevölkerung, Einwohner*
nationality *Staatsangehörigkeit*
race *Rasse*
racist *rassistisch; Rassist/in*
society *Gesellschaft*
social *gesellschaftlich, sozial*
human *menschlich, Mensch*
adult *Erwachsene/r*
child *Kind*
teenager *Teenager/in*
sex *Geschlecht*
lady *Dame*
man *Mann, Mensch*
men *Männer, Menschen*
woman *Frau*
women *Frauen*
male *männlich*
female *weiblich, Frauen-*
boy *Junge*
girl *Mädchen*
couple *Paar*
married *verheiratet*
to **get married** *heiraten*
Mr *Herr*
Mrs, Ms *Frau*
boyfriend *Freund*
girlfriend *Freundin*
age *Alter*
born *geboren*
life *Leben*
death *Tod, Todesfall*
anybody *jemand, jede/r/s*
anyone *jemand, jede/r/s*
nobody *niemand*
some *einige, etwas*
somebody *jemand*
someone *jemand*
everybody *jede/r/s*
everyone *jede/r/s, alle*
no-one *niemand, keiner*
guest *Gast*
host *Gastgeber/in*
leader *Leiter/in, Führer/in*
loser *Verlierer/in*
member *Mitglied*
group *Gruppe*
crowd *(Menschen-)Menge*

FAMILY *(Familie)*

family *Familie*
parents *Eltern*
parent *Elternteil*
father *Vater*
mother *Mutter*
dad *Papa*
mum, mom *Mama, Mutter*
stepfather *Stiefvater*
stepmother *Stiefmutter*
husband *(Ehe-)Mann*
wife *(Ehe-)Frau*
children *Kinder*
son *Sohn*
daughter *Tochter*
brother *Bruder*
sister *Schwester*
brothers and sisters *Geschwister*
cousin *Cousin/e*
grandparents *Großeltern*
grandfather *Großvater*
grandmother *Großmutter*
grandchildren *Enkel(kinder)*
aunt *Tante*
uncle *Onkel*

EMOTIONS *(Gefühle)*

to **feel** *(sich) fühlen*
feeling, emotion *Gefühl*
happy *glücklich, froh, zufrieden*
joy *Freude*
pleased *zufrieden*
(to) **surprise** *Überraschung; überraschen*
mad *verrückt, toll*
unhappy *unglücklich, unzufrieden, traurig*
sad *traurig*
to **cry** *schreien, weinen*
angry (with sb) *wütend, böse (auf jdn), zornig*
crazy *verrückt*
to **be afraid (of)** *(sich) fürchten (vor)*
to **be frightened of** *Angst haben vor, sich fürchten vor*
tired *müde*

BODY AND CLOTHING *(Körper und Kleidung)*

body *Körper*
physical *physisch, körperlich*
leg *Bein*
arm *Arm*
hand *Hand*
shoulder *Schulter*
hair *Haar(e)*
to **touch** *anfassen, berühren*
head *Kopf*
face *Gesicht*
eye *Auge*
to **look** *(aus)sehen, blicken*
nose *Nase*
to **smell** *riechen*
mouth *Mund*
voice *Stimme*
to **smile** *lächeln*
to **speak** *sprechen, reden*
ear *Ohr*
to **listen** *zuhören*
to **hear** *hören*
to **sound** *klingen*
tooth *Zahn*
heart *Herz*
blood *Blut*
skin *Haut*
health *Gesundheit*
healthy *gesund*
well *gesund, gut*
able *fähig, in der Lage*
flexible *flexibel*
illness *Krankheit*
ill *krank*
sick *krank*
painful *schmerzhaft*
fat *dick*
thin *dünn*
short *kurz, klein*
small *klein*
tall *groß, hochgewachsen*
big *groß, kräftig*
weak *schwach*
strong *stark, kräftig*
old *alt*
young *jung*
clothing *Bekleidung*
clothes *Kleidung, Kleider*
fashion *Mode*
(to) **dress** *Kleid; sich kleiden*

to **wear** *tragen, anhaben*
to **cover** *(be)decken*
to **wash** *waschen, spülen*
to **spray** *(be)sprühen*
comfortable *bequem*
uncomfortable *unbequem*
elegant *elegant*
coat *Mantel*
shirt *Hemd*
shoes *Schuhe*
trainers *Turnschuhe*
boot *Stiefel*
bag *Tasche*
uniform *Uniform*

JOBS AND WORK (*Beruf und Arbeit*)

to **work** *arbeiten, funktionieren*
worker *Arbeiter/in*
job *Arbeit, Stelle*
factory *Fabrik*
business *Geschäft, Firma*
company *Gesellschaft, Firma, Unternehmen*
firm *Firma*
office *Büro, Amt*
assistant *Assistent/in, Verkäufer/in*
director *Direktor/in, Geschäftsführer/in, Vorstand*
boss *Chef/in*
customer *Kunde, Kundin*
meeting *Konferenz, Besprechung*
model *Modell, Vorbild*
project *Projekt*
programme *Programm*
expert *Fachmann/frau*
doctor *Arzt, Ärztin*
police *Polizei*
politician *Politiker/in*
farmer *Bauer/Bäuerin, Landwirt/in*

SCHOOL (*Schule*)

education *Erziehung, Schulbildung, Ausbildung*
school *Schule*
to **learn** *lernen, erfahren*
college *Fachhochschule*
to **train** *trainieren, ausbilden, schulen, eine Ausbildung machen*
training *Ausbildung, Schulung, Training*
university *Universität*
(to) **study** *Lernen, Studium; lernen, studieren*
course *Kurs, Lehrgang*
class *Klasse, Kurs*
desk *(Schreib-)Tisch*
seat *Sitz, Platz*
teacher *Lehrer/in*
to **teach** *unterrichten, lehren*
pupil *Schüler/in*
student *Student/in, Lernende/r*
subject *(Schul-)Fach, Thema*
English *englisch*
German *deutsch*
history *Geschichte*
topic *Thema*
question *Frage*
exercise *Übung*
task *Aufgabe*
exam *Prüfung*
homework *Hausaufgaben*
notes *Notizen*
rule *Vorschrift, Regel*
to **match** *zuordnen, (zusammen) passen*
correct *richtig*
true *richtig, wahr*
false *falsch*

HOUSES AND HOMES (*Haus und Einrichtung*)

house *Haus*
home *Zuhause, Heim, Heimat; nach Hause*
flat *Wohnung*
to **live** *wohnen, leben*
address *Adresse*
door *Tür*
key *Schlüssel, Schlüssel-, Haupt-*
roof *Dach*
window *Fenster*
stairs *Treppe*
upstairs *(nach) oben*
downstairs *(nach) unten*
room *Zimmer, Raum*
bedroom *Schlafzimmer*
(to) **clean** *sauber; reinigen, säubern*
household *Haushalt*
furniture *Möbel*
bed *Bett*
table *Tisch*
chair *Stuhl, Sessel*
bath *Bad*
shower *Dusche*
kitchen *Küche*
floor *Etage, (Fuß-)Boden*
alarm *Alarm(anlage)*

HOBBIES AND SPORT (*Hobbys und Sport*)

to **like** *mögen, gern tun*
to **interest** *interessieren*
to **enjoy** *genießen, gefallen*
(to) **love** *Liebe; lieben, sehr gern mögen*
favourite *Lieblings-*
fun *Spaß, amüsant, lustig*
exercise *Bewegung, körperliche Betätigung, Sport*
prize *Preis, Gewinn, Auszeichnung*
active *aktiv, tätig, aktiviert*
to **play** *spielen*
match *Spiel, Wettkampf*
game *Spiel*
ball *Ball, Kugel*
to **kick** *treten*
score *Ergebnis, Punkt(estand)*
to **win** *gewinnen, siegen*
winner *Gewinner/in, Sieger/in*
to **swim** *schwimmen*
to **fish** *angeln*
bicycle *Fahrrad*
cycling *Radfahren*
bike *Rad*
to **ride** *reiten, (Rad) fahren*
(to) **dance** *Tanz; tanzen*
dancer *Tänzer/in*
concert *Konzert*
television *Fernsehen, Fernseher*
viewer *Zuschauer/in*
radio/TV programme *Radio-/Fernsehsendung*
to **smoke** *rauchen*

SOCIETY AND SOCIAL PROBLEMS (*Gesellschaft und soziale Probleme*)

religion *Religion*
politics *Politik*
political *politisch*
right *Recht*
(to) **vote** *Stimme, Abstimmung, Wahl; stimmen, abstimmen, wählen*
to **allow** *erlauben, (zu)lassen*
(to) **control** *Kontrolle, Regelung, Steuerung; kontrollieren, regeln, steuern*
poor *arm, schlecht, mangelhaft*
rich *reich, wohlhabend*
protest *Protest*
crime *Verbrechen, Kriminalität*
conflict *Konflikt, Auseinandersetzung*
problem *Problem*
crisis, crises *Krise, Krisen*
danger *Gefahr*
dangerous *gefährlich*
serious *ernst, schwer*
wrong *falsch*
to **hurt** *verletzen*
to **hit** *(auf)schlagen, (auf)treffen*
to **break** *brechen*
to **burn** *(ver)brennen*
to **fight** *(be)kämpfen*
to **die** *sterben*
dead *tot*
to **kill** *töten*
gun *Schusswaffe, Pistole*
to **protect** *(be)schützen*
to **hide** *verstecken, verbergen*
drug *Droge*
risk *Risiko*
mistake *Fehler, Irrtum*
to **forbid** *verbieten*
to **forget** *vergessen*
to **ignore** *ignorieren*
to **steal** *stehlen*

personal *persönlich*
chance *Gelegenheit, Chance, Zufall*
responsible *verantwortlich*
law *Gesetz, Recht*
case *Fall*

INTERACTING WITH PEOPLE (*Umgehen mit Menschen*)

to **communicate** *sich verständigen, mitteilen, kommunizieren*
to **talk** *sprechen, reden*
to **say** *sagen*
to **tell** *sagen, erzählen, erkennen*
truth *Wahrheit*
to **ask** *fragen, bitten*
(to) **answer** *Antwort; (be)antworten*
(to) **reply** *Antwort, Erwiderung; antworten, erwidern*
to **realize** *bemerken, erkennen, verstehen, klar werden*
to **understand** *verstehen, begreifen*
to **translate** *übersetzen, übertragen*
to **explain** *erklären*
to **repeat** *wiederholen*
to **agree** *zustimmen, vereinbaren, sich einigen*
to **express** *ausdrücken, äußern*
to **be sorry** *leidtun*
to **discuss** *diskutieren (über), besprechen*
to **argue** *argumentieren, (sich) streiten*
argument *Argument; Streit*
to **shout** *schreien, brüllen*
to **order** *befehlen, bestellen, ordnen*
to **direct** *leiten*
to **shock** *erschüttern, schockieren*
reaction *Reaktion*
to **warn** *warnen, hinweisen*
to **disappoint** *enttäuschen*
(to) **promise** *Versprechen; versprechen*
to **help** *helfen*
to **share** *(sich) teilen, gemeinsam (be) nutzen, mitteilen*
together *zusammen*
to **show** *zeigen*
to **connect** *verbinden*
(to) **call** *Anruf; (an)rufen, nennen*
to **ring** *läuten, anrufen*
(to) **phone** *Telephon; anrufen*
mobile phone *Handy, Mobiltelefon*
to **chat** *sich unterhalten, plaudern, chatten (mit)*
dialogue *Dialog*
conversation *Unterhaltung*
to **introduce** *(sich) vorstellen, einführen*
to **meet** *(zusammen)treffen, begegnen*
to **greet** *(be)grüßen*
(to) **kiss** *Kuss; küssen*
to **laugh** *lachen*
(to) **joke** *Witz; scherzen, Witze machen*
(to) **offer** *Angebot; (an)bieten*
to **invite** *einladen*
party *Party, Partei*

to **arrange** *arrangieren, vereinbaren*
to **inform** *informieren*
(to) **report** *Bericht; berichten, melden*
to **notice** *bemerken*
to **guess** *raten, schätzen*

READING AND WRITING (*Lesen und Schreiben*)

to **read** *lesen*
reader *Leser/in*
story *Erzählung, Geschichte*
mail *Post*
letter *Brief, Buchstabe*
to **send** *senden, schicken*
document *Dokument, Schriftstück, Papier*
briefcase *Aktentasche*
key *Taste*
table *Tabelle*
diagram *Diagramm, Grafik*
content *Inhalt*
to **write** *schreiben*
paper *Papier, Zeitung*
pencil *Bleistift*
point *Punkt; Sinn*
word *Wort*
phrase *Wendung, Formulierung*
sentence *Satz*
line *Zeile*
message *Mitteilung, Nachricht, Botschaft*
slogan *Werbespruch*
form *Form, Formular*
summary *Zusammenfassung*
introduction *Einleitung, Einführung*
page *Seite*
title *Titel*
information *Auskunft, Information(en)*
dictionary *Wörterbuch*
to **mean** *bedeuten, meinen, heißen*
meaning *Bedeutung*
emphasis *Hervorhebung*
(to) **copy** *Kopie; kopieren, abschreiben*
(to) **list** *Liste, Aufzählung; aufzählen, aufführen, auflisten*
to **note** *beachten, notieren*
to **note down** *aufschreiben, notieren*
(to) **complete** *vollständig; vervollständigen, abschließen*
(to) **comment** *Kommentar, Bemerkung; kommentieren*
to **describe** *beschreiben*
description *Beschreibung, Schilderung*
detail *Detail*
stereotype *Klischee*
example *Beispiel*
language *Sprache*
grammar *Grammatik*
vocabulary *Wortschatz*
style *Stil*
clear *klar, deutlich*
formal *formell, förmlich*
dear *liebe/r*

BELIEFS AND ATTITUDES (*Glaube und Einstellungen*)

to **believe (in sb/sth)** *(an jdn/etw) glauben*
to **consider** *nachdenken über, halten für, in Betracht ziehen*
to **think** *denken, meinen, finden, glauben*
view *Ansicht, Meinung, Aussicht*
opinion *Meinung, Einschätzung*
positive *positiv, bejahend*
opposite *Gegenteil; entgegengesetzt, gegenüber(liegend)*
to **dislike** *nicht mögen*
to **hate** *hassen, nicht mögen*
option *Option, Wahl, Alternative*
idea *Idee, Gedanke, Ahnung*
(to) **hope** *Hoffnung; hoffen*
(to) **dream** *Traum; träumen*
to **want** *wollen*
to **wish** *wünschen*
to **remember** *sich erinnern, daran denken*
to **suppose** *vermuten, annehmen*
to **imagine** *sich vorstellen*
to **seem** *(er)scheinen*
to **prove** *beweisen*
real *echt, wirklich*
to **worry** *sich Sorgen machen, bekümmern*
to **know** *kennen, wissen*
reason *Vernunft, Grund*
to **need** *brauchen, benötigen*
necessary *nötig, erforderlich*

MOVEMENT (*Bewegung*)

to **move** *(sich) bewegen, umziehen*
fast *schnell*
slow *langsam*
to **go** *gehen, fahren*
to **walk** *(zu Fuß) gehen*
step *Schritt*
to **run** *laufen*
to **jump** *springen*
to **climb** *klettern, steigen*
to **fall** *fallen, stürzen, abstürzen*
to **sit** *sitzen, sich setzen*
to **stand** *stehen, aushalten*
to **rise** *steigen*
to **turn** *(sich) drehen, (sich) wenden*
to **arrive** *ankommen*
to **come** *kommen*
to **enter** *betreten, eintreten, eingeben*
to **leave** *(ver)lassen*
to **bring** *bringen, holen*
to **carry** *tragen*
to **put** *setzen, stellen, legen*
to **press** *drücken*
to **push** *drücken, schieben*
to **pull** *ziehen*
to **lead** *führen*
to **follow** *(be)folgen*

to **pass** *vorbeigehen, vergehen; bestehen*
(to) **hurry** *Eile; sich beeilen*
to **rush** *sich beeilen*
to **reach** *greifen, erreichen*
to **catch** *fangen, nehmen, erwischen*
to **disappear** *verschwinden*

TOWNS AND BUILDINGS *(Städte und Gebäude)*

city *(Groß-)Stadt*
town *Stadt*
village *Dorf*
neighbourhood *Nachbarschaft*
street *Straße*
path *(Fuß-)Weg, Pfad*
road *(Land-)Straße*
sign *Zeichen, Schild*
corner *Ecke*
map *Karte*
local *örtlich, lokal*
building *Gebäude*
church *Kirche*
tower *Turm*
hospital *Krankenhaus*
supermarket *Supermarkt*
market *Markt*
entrance *Eingang, Einfahrt*
bridge *Brücke*
farm *Bauernhof*

TRAFFIC, TRAVEL AND HOLIDAYS *(Verkehr, Reisen und Urlaub)*

holiday *Ferien, Urlaub, Feiertag*
abroad *im/ins Ausland*
foreign *fremd*
national *national, staatlich, Landes-*
country *Land, Staat*
European *europäisch*
American *amerikanisch*
tour *Tour, Rundgang*
trip *Ausflug, Reise, Besuch*
visitor *Besucher/in, Gast*
ticket *Eintrrittskarte, Fahrkarte*
to **travel** *reisen, fahren*
to **visit** *besuchen, besichtigen*
to **plan** *planen*
transport *Beförderung, Verkehr(smittel), Transport*
boat *Boot, Schiff*
ship *Schiff*
bus *(Linien-)Bus*
truck *Laster, Lkw*
car *Auto*
vehicle *Fahrzeug, Wagen*
to **drive** *(Auto) fahren*
to **deliver** *liefern*
driver *Fahrer/in*
plane *Flugzeug*
helicopter *Hubschrauber*
flight *Flug*
to **fly** *fliegen*
airport *Flughafen*
train *Zug*
underground *unterirdisch; U-Bahn*
station *Bahnhof*
ticket *Fahrkarte, Eintrittskarte*
to **miss** *verpassen, vermissen*
(to) **return** *Rückkehr, Rückreise; zurückkehren, zurückgehen*
beach *Strand*
to **relax** *sich erholen, sich ausruhen, sich entspannen*
photo *Foto*

MONEY AND SHOPPING *(Geld und Einkaufen)*

money *Geld*
to **earn** *verdienen*
to **afford** *es sich leisten können*
to **spend** *(Geld) ausgeben, (Zeit) verbringen*
to **buy** *kaufen*
to **pay** *(be)zahlen*
to **sell** *(sich) verkaufen*
to **charge** *berechnen, verlangen, (auf)laden*
(to) **cost** *Kosten; kosten*
price *(Kauf-)Preis*
worth *wert*
bill *Rechnung*
present *Geschenk*
prize *Preis*
free *kostenlos, frei*
cheap *billig, günstig*
expensive *teuer*
luxury *Luxus*
card *Karte*
cash *Bargeld, Geld*
to **change** *(aus)wechseln, (sich) ändern*
to **borrow** *borgen, (aus)leihen*
to **belong** *gehören zu, angehören*
to **own** *besitzen*
to **prefer** *vorziehen, bevorzugen, lieber mögen*
to **choose** *(aus)wählen*
available *verfügbar, erhältlich*
product *Produkt, Erzeugnis*
to **produce** *produzieren, herstellen*
shop *Laden, Geschäft*
shopping *Einkaufen*
sale *Verkauf*
success *Erfolg*
to **open** *öffnen*
to **close** *schließen*
open *offen*
closed *geschlossen*

EATING AND DRINKING *(Essen und Trinken)*

to **eat** *essen*
food *Essen, Nahrung*
to **cook** *kochen*
to **prepare** *(sich) vorbereiten*
meal *Essen, Mahlzeit*
breakfast *Frühstück*
lunch *Mittagessen*
dinner *(Abend-)Essen*
to **taste** *schmecken*
hunger *Hunger*
hungry *hungrig*
thirst *Durst*
thirsty *durstig*
meat *Fleisch*
beef *Rindfleisch*
vegetable *Gemüse*
potato *Kartoffel*
carrot *Karotte, Möhre*
fruit *Obst, Frucht, Früchte*
fresh *frisch*
salt *Salz*
sugar *Zucker*
chicken *Huhn, Hähnchen*
egg *Ei*
cheese *Käse*
chocolate *Schokolade, Praline*
cake *Kuchen, Torte*
bread *Brot*
sweet *süß; Süßigkeit*
to **drink** *trinken*
mineral water *Mineralwasser*
tea *Tee*
juice *Saft*
alcohol *Alkohol*
wine *Wein*
beer *Bier*
cup *Tasse*
glass *Glas*
bottle *Flasche*
knife *Messer*
fork *Gabel*
spoon *Löffel*
plate *Platte, Teller*
bowl *Schüssel*
box *Kiste, Kästchen, Schachtel*
packet *Schachtel, Packung, Tüte*

NATURE AND WEATHER *(Natur und Wetter)*

nature *Natur, Art*
natural *natürlich*
planet *Planet*
world *Welt*
continent *Erdteil, Kontinent*
environment *Umwelt, Umfeld*
earth *Erde*
air *Luft*
water *Wasser*
wood *Holz, Wald*
ice *Eis*
fire *Feuer*
sky *Himmel*
mountain *(größerer) Berg*
river *Fluss*
wind *Wind*
rain *Regen*
sun *Sonne*
storm *Sturm*

heat *Hitze, Wärme*
hot *heiß, warm*
warm *warm*
cold *kalt*
to **dry** *trocknen*
wet *nass*
light *Licht; hell, leicht*
to **shine** *scheinen*
dark *dunkel*
animal *Tier*
dog *Hund*
cat *Katze*
bird *Vogel*
fish *Fisch*
flower *Blume*
plant *Pflanze*
tree *Baum*
to **recycle** *wiederverwerten*
(to) **waste** *Verschwendung, Vergeudung; verschwenden, vergeuden*

SCIENCE AND TECHNOLOGY (*Wissenschaft und Technik*)

science *Wissenschaft*
technology *Technik, Technologie*
scientist *Wissenschaftler/in*
chemical *chemisch, Chemie-; Chemikalie*
technical *technisch*
to **build** *(auf)bauen*
tool *Werkzeug*
device *Gerät, Apparat*
machine *Gerät, Maschine*
data *Daten*
image *Bild*
to **switch on** *anschalten, einschalten*
to **switch off** *abschalten, ausschalten*
to **click** *klicken, anklicken*
to **print** *drucken*
electric *elektrisch, Strom-*
electricity *Elektrizität, Strom*
power *Kraft, Strom*
method *Methode, Verfahren*
to **repair** *reparieren*
new *neu*
safe *sicher*
automatic *automatisch*

ART AND CULTURE (*Kunst und Kultur*)

art *Kunst*
picture *Bild*
symbol *Symbol, Zeichen*
scene *Szene*
culture *Kultur*
to **act** *handeln*
movie *Film*
cinema *Kino*
theatre *Theater*
book *Buch*
author *Verfasser/in, Autor/in*
article *Artikel*
illustration *Abbildung, Illustration*
newspaper *Zeitung*
magazine *Zeitschrift*
news *Neuigkeit(en), Nachricht(en)*
media *Medien*
song *Lied*
singer *Sänger/in*
music *Musik*
band *Kapelle, Band*
guitar *Gitarre*
piano *Klavier*

QUALITIES AND CHARACTERISTICS (*Eigenschaften und Besonderheiten*)

character *Charakter*
kind *Art, Sorte*
similar *ähnlich*
different *anders, verschieden*
difference *Unterschied*
advantage *Vorteil*
disadvantage *Nachteil*
to **be** *sein*
to **become** *werden*
to **include** *einschließen, umfassen, aufnehmen, einbeziehen*

DESCRIBING PEOPLE AND SITUATIONS (*Menschen und Situationen beschreiben*)

private *privat, zurückgezogen*
friendly *freund(schaft)lich*
kind *nett, lieb*
interesting *interessant*
individual *individuell, einzeln, Einzel-*
typical *typisch*
boring *langweilig*
funny *komisch, lustig, merkwürdig*
busy *beschäftigt, belebt, hektisch; besetzt*
lazy *faul*
helpful *hilfreich, nützlich, hilfsbereit*
careful *vorsichtig, sorgfältig, aufmerksam*
creative *schöpferisch, kreativ*
romantic *romantisch*
smart *schick, clever*
stupid *dumm, albern, doof*
silly *albern*
nice *schön, nett*
tough *zäh, stark*
strict *streng, strikt*
polite *höflich*
rude *unhöflich, rüde*
pretty *hübsch*
beautiful *schön*
ugly *hässlich*
positive *positiv*
negative *negativ, verneinend*
strange *fremd, seltsam*
normal *normal*
perfect *vollkommen, perfekt*
special *besondere*
well-known *sehr bekannt, berühmt*
famous *berühmt*
popular *beliebt, populär*
unknown *unbekannt*
good *gut*
better *besser*
best *beste/r/s, am besten*
great *groß(artig)*
amazing *erstaunlich, verblüffend, toll*
excellent *ausgezeichnet, hervorragend*
wonderful *wunderbar, großartig*
fantastic *fantastisch, wunderbar*
bad *schlecht, schlimm*
worse *schlechter, schlimmer*
worst *schlechteste/r/s, schlimmste/r/s*
horrible, awful, terrible *furchtbar, schrecklich*
easy *leicht, einfach*
basic *elementar*
simple *einfach*
hard *schwer, schwierig, hart*
difficult *schwer, schwierig*
important *wichtig*
successful *erfolgreich*
exciting *aufregend, spannend*
useful *nützlich*
fair *fair, gerecht*
unfair *unfair, ungerecht*
poor *arm*
wealthy *reich*
loud *laut*
quiet, silent *ruhig, still*
wet *nass*
dry *trocken*
slow *langsam*
quick *schnell, rasch*

DESCRIBING OBJECTS (*Gegenstände beschreiben*)

type *Art, Typ*
object *Gegenstand, Ding, Objekt*
thing *Sache, Ding, Gegenstand*
piece *Stück, Teil*
unit *Einheit, Stück, Lektion*
colour *Farbe*
this *dies, diese/r/s*
that *das*
these *diese*
those *jene*
their *ihr/e/r/s*

Size – Shape – Weight (*Größe – Form – Gewicht*)

shape *Form, Gestalt*
line *Linie*
circle *Kreis*
hole *Loch*
size *Größe*
little *klein, wenig*
to **grow** *wachsen, (an)steigen*

big *groß*
large *groß, umfangreich*
weight *Gewicht*
heavy *stark, schwer*
light *leicht*
to **fill** *füllen, ausfüllen*
full *voll, vollständig*
empty *leer*
wide *breit, weit, groß*
narrow *eng*
long *lang*
short *kurz*
hard *fest*
soft *weich*

ACTIONS AND PROCESSES (*Handlungen und Prozesse*)

action *Aktion, Handlung, Tat*
activity *Tätigkeit*
result *Ergebnis, Folge*
to **do** *tun, machen*
to **happen** *passieren, geschehen*
to **start** *anfangen, starten, beginnen*
to **continue** *fortsetzen, weitermachen*
to **finish** *beenden, erledigen*
to **stop** *(an)halten, aufhören (mit)*
to **result from** *folgen aus*
to **let** *erlauben, (zu)lassen*

Necessity, Probability, Possibility (*Notwendigkeit, Wahrscheinlichkeit, Möglichkeit*)

condition *Bedingung*
may *dürfen, können, mögen*
maybe *vielleicht*
possible *möglich, denkbar*
impossible *unmöglich*
probably *wahrscheinlich*
can *können, dürfen*
could *konnte/n, könnte/n*
would *würde/n*
might *können, könnte/n*
will *werde(n), wollen*
should *sollen, sollte/n*
must *müssen*
to **have to** *müssen*

Everyday actions (*Alltagshandlungen*)

to **take** *nehmen, bringen, dauern*
to **decide** *(sich) entscheiden, beschließen*
decision *Entscheidung*
to **make** *machen*
to **fix** *festlegen, reparieren*
to **check** *(über)prüfen*
to **organize** *organisieren*
to **get** *holen, bekommen, werden, gelangen*
to **give** *geben*
to **receive** *erhalten, bekommen, empfangen*
to **hold** *abhalten, veranstalten*
to **keep** *(be)halten, bleiben*
to **spare** *übrig haben*
to **set** *setzen*
(to) **mix** *Mischung; mischen*
to **remove** *entfernen*
to **avoid** *vermeiden*
to **wait** *warten*
to **watch** *beobachten*
to **see** *sehen*
to **search** *(durch)suchen*
to **find** *finden, suchen*
to **use** *benutzen, verwenden*
to **try** *versuchen, (aus)probieren*
(to) **experience** *Erfahrung, Erlebnis; erfahren, erleben*
to **open** *öffnen, beginnen*
to **develop** *entwickeln*
to **save** *retten, sichern*
to **recover** *sich erholen*
to **sleep** *schlafen*
to **wake up** *aufwachen, aufwecken*

TIME (*Zeit*)

period *Periode, Zeitraum*
date *Datum, Termin*
beginning *Anfang*
to **begin** *anfangen, beginnen*
(to) **end** *Ende, Schluss; (be)enden*
final *letzte/r/s, End-*
first *erste/r/s, zuerst*
last *letzte/r/s, zuletzt*
time *Zeit, Mal*

Days, months, ... (*Tage, Monate, ...*)

second *Sekunde*
minute *Minute*
hour *Stunde*
o'clock *... Uhr*
day *Tag*
morning *Morgen*
afternoon *Nachmittag*
evening *Abend*
night *Nacht*
tonight *heute Abend/Nacht*
today *heute*
yesterday *gestern*
tomorrow *morgen*
week *Woche*
weekend *Wochenende*
month *Monat*
year *Jahr*
season *Saison, Jahreszeit*
spring *Frühling*
summer *Sommer*
autumn *Herbst*
winter *Winter*
Christmas *Weihnachten*
Easter *Ostern*
birthday *Geburtstag*
age *Zeitalter*

Frequency (*Häufigkeit*)

sometimes *manchmal*
often *oft, häufig*
usual *gewöhnlich, normal*
usually *normalerweise, gewöhnlich, meistens*
regular *regelmäßig, regulär, normal*
daily *täglich*
always *immer*
never *nie(mals)*

Other words for talking about time (*andere Zeitangaben*)

early *früh*
late *spät*
later *später*
until *bis*
now *nun, jetzt*
then *dann*
ago *vor*
as *wie, als, da*
yet *schon, bereits*
not yet *noch nicht*
before *vor(her)*
after *nach*
past *vorbei, nach; Vergangenheit*
present *Gegenwart; gegenwärtig, aktuell*
future *Zukunft; (zu)künftig*
soon *bald*
suddenly *plötzlich*
only *nur, einzig*
once *einmal, einst*
twice *zweimal*
again *wieder*
next *nächste/r/s; danach*
already *schon, bereits*
recent *neueste/r/s, letzte/r/s, aktuell*
recently *neulich, in letzter Zeit*
while *während*
at the moment *momentan, augenblicklich*
nowadays *heutzutage*
forever *für immer*
ever *je(mals)*
ready *fertig, bereit*

PLACE AND DIRECTION (*Orts- und Richtungsangaben*)

space *(Zwischen-)Raum, Ort, Platz, Abstand, Weltall*
place *Stelle, Platz*
situation *Situation, Lage*
outside *außer(halb) (von)*
outdoors *draußen, im Freien*
inside *innerhalb (von), drinnen*
indoors *drinnen*
far *weit (entfernt)*
near *bei, nahe*
around *herum*
away *weg, entfernt*
back *zurück*
forward *vorwärts, nach vorn*

Prepositions (*Präpositionen*)

across *(quer) über, in ganz*
along *entlang*
over *(vor)über*
under *unter*
between *zwischen*
through *durch*
behind *hinter, hinten*
against *gegen*
about *über, etwa*

Other words for describing places (*andere Ortsangaben*)

direct *direkt*
state *Zustand, Staat*
to **stay** *bleiben, übernachten*
here *hier*
there *da, dort(hin)*
anywhere *irgendwo(hin)*
somewhere *irgendwo(hin)*
nowhere *nirgends*
front *Vorderseite*
side *Seite, Rand*
top *Spitze, Gipfel; Spitzen-*
bottom *Boden, Unterseite*
high *hoch*
low *tief, niedrig*
distance *Entfernung, Abstand, Strecke*
mile *Meile*
north *Norden, Nord-*
east *Osten*
south *Süden, Süd-*
west *Westen*
middle *Mitte*
left *linke/r/s, links*
right *rechts*
up *nach oben*
down *nach unten*
above *oben, über*
below *unten, unter*

QUANTITY (*Menge*)

number *Nummer, Zahl*
to **count** *zählen*
to **add** *zusammenzählen, hinzufügen*
plus *plus*
limit *Grenze*
all *alle(s)*
whole *ganz, Ganzes*
almost *fast, beinahe*
nearly *beinahe, fast*
very *sehr*
really *wirklich, eigentlich, tatsächlich*
a lot *viel, sehr*
lots of *viel, viele*
many *viele*
most *meist*
much *viel*
more *mehr*
extra *zusätzlich*
double *doppelt*
both *beide*
pair *Paar*
enough *ausreichend, genug*
half *Hälfte; halb*
part *Teil*
quite *ziemlich, ganz*
less *weniger, abzüglich*
few *ein paar, wenig/e/r/s*
a little *ein wenig, etwas*
alone *allein(e)*
minimum *Minimum; minimal*
none *kein/e/r/s*
nothing *nichts*
neither *auch nicht, keine/r/s*
any *irgendetwas, welche/r/s, jede/r/s*
anything *etwas, alles*
another *noch eine*
other *andere/r/s*
each *jede/r/s*
every *jede/r/s*
everything *alles*
exactly *exakt, genau*
certain *bestimmt*
specific *bestimmt, spezifisch*
general *allgemein*
just *einfach, nur, genau, gerade*

CONNECTORS (*Strukturwörter*)

because *weil*
so *also, damit, deshalb, so (dass)*
simply *einfach*
certainly *sicherlich, bestimmt*
for example *zum Beispiel*
such as *wie zum Beispiel*
(in this) way *Weg, Methode, auf diese Art (und Weise)*
but *aber, sondern*
however *doch, jedoch*
except *außer*
else *andere/r/s*
than *als*
whether *ob*
if *wenn, falls, ob*
or *oder*
same *gleiche/r/s, der-, die-, dasselbe*
also *auch, außerdem*
too *zu, auch*
with *mit, bei*
without *ohne*
in case *falls*
perhaps *vielleicht, eventuell*
even *sogar (noch)*
anyway *jedenfalls, sowieso*

USEFUL WORDS AND PHRASES (*Nützliche Wörter und Wendungen*)

(to) **welcome** *willkommen; willkommen heißen, begrüßen*
excuse me *Entschuldigung*
please *bitte*
of course *natürlich, selbstverständlich*
sure *freilich, sicher(lich)*
thanks *Dank; danke*
unfortunately *leider*
basically *eigentlich, im Grunde*
total *(End-)Summe; völlig, (ins)gesamt, Gesamt-*
main *hauptsächlich, wichtigste/r/s, Haupt-*
something *etwas*
fact *Tatsache, Fakt*
tip *Vorschlag, Hinweis, Tipp*
pros and cons *Für und Wider*

QUESTION WORDS (*Fragewörter*)

what? *was?, welche/r/s?*
where? *wo(hin)?*
when? *wenn?, wann?*
who? *wer?, welche(r/s)?*
which? *welche/r/s?*
why? *warum?*
how? *wie?*

Unit word list

Dieses Wörterverzeichnis enthält alle Wörter in **Focus on Success – 5th edition: Ausgabe Technik** in der Reihenfolge ihres Erscheinens. Nicht aufgeführt sind die Wörter aus der *Basic word list* sowie internationale Wörter wie *hotel, email* usw.
Die Wörter der *Technical Options*-Seiten werden in den darauf folgenden Units nicht vorausgesetzt.
Wörter, die in den Hörverständnistexten vorkommen, sind mit einem CD-Symbol gekennzeichnet.
Wörter, die in den *Files* vorkommen, sind mit einem türkisfarbenen Balken gekennzeichnet.

AE = American English
BE = British English
pl = plural
sb = somebody
sth = something
etw = etwas
jd = jemand
jdm = jemandem
jdn = jemanden
jds = jemandes

UNIT 1

page 6

cult [kʌlt]	Kult
celebrity [sə'lebrəti]	Prominente/r, Prominenz
neighbour ['neɪbə]	Nachbar/in
to **sort** [sɔːt]	sortieren, einordnen
to **rank sb/sth** [ræŋk]	jdn/etw einstufen, jdn/etw (ein-)ordnen
order ['ɔːdə]	Reihenfolge
popularity [ˌpɒpju'lærəti]	Beliebtheit, Popularität
to **deserve** [dɪ'zɜːv]	verdienen
status ['steɪtəs]	Status, Stellung
to **define** [dɪ'faɪn]	definieren
to **study sth** ['stʌdi]	etw genau betrachten
headline ['hedlaɪn]	Schlagzeile, Überschrift
to **make sth up** [ˌmeɪk 'ʌp]	etw erfinden, sich etw ausdenken
store [stɔː]	Geschäft, Laden
midnight ['mɪdnaɪt]	Mitternacht
shopper ['ʃɒpə]	Käufer/in, Kunde/Kundin
legend ['ledʒənd]	Legende
face-lift ['feɪslɪft]	Facelifting, Gesichts-straffung
jewellery ['dʒuːəlri]	Schmuck

page 7

to **get sth right** [ˌget 'raɪt]	etw richtig machen, etw gut hinbekommen
statement ['steɪtmənt]	Aussage, Feststellung, Behauptung
gig [gɪg]	(Rock-, Pop-, Jazz-)Konzert
to **queue** [kjuː]	sich (in einer Warteschlange) anstellen
charity ['tʃærəti]	Benefiz-, Wohltätigkeit(s-)
to **tour** [tʊə]	auf Tour gehen
bracket ['brækɪt]	Klammer
to **appear** [ə'pɪə]	auftreten, erscheinen
to **break sth up** [ˌbreɪk 'ʌp]	etw zertrümmern, etw demolieren
to **hit the headlines** [ˌhɪt ðə 'hedlaɪnz]	in die Schlagzeilen kommen, Schlagzeilen machen
to **collect** [kə'lekt]	sammeln
fortune ['fɔːtʃuːn]	Vermögen
autograph ['ɔːtəgrɑːf]	Autogramm
formula ['fɔːmjələ]	Formel
race [reɪs]	Rennen
event [ɪ'vent]	Veranstaltung, Ereignis

page 8

skill [skɪl]	Fähigkeit, Fertigkeit
to **predict** [prɪ'dɪkt]	voraussagen, vorhersagen
use [juːs]	Gebrauch, Nutzen
to **make use of sth** [ˌmeɪk 'juːs əv]	von etw Gebrauch machen, etw nutzen
clue [kluː]	Hinweis, Anhaltspunkt
to **go with sth** ['gəʊ wɪð]	zu etw gehören
caption ['kæpʃn]	Bildunterschrift
further ['fɜːðə]	weitere/r/s
like [laɪk]	wie
idol ['aɪdl]	Idol
good looking [ˌgʊd 'lʊkɪŋ]	gutaussehend, attraktiv
talented ['tæləntɪd]	begabt, talentiert
to **be scared** [bi 'skeəd]	Angst haben
onto ['ɒntə]	auf
stage [steɪdʒ]	Bühne
huge [hjuːdʒ]	riesig, Riesen-
audience ['ɔːdiəns]	Publikum
member of the audience [ˌmembər əv ði 'ɔːdiəns]	Zuschauer/in
to **feel uncomfortable** [ˌfiːl ʌn'kʌmftəbl]	sich unbehaglich fühlen
judge [dʒʌdʒ]	Richter/in, Juror/in
spot [spɒt]	Platz, Stelle
change [tʃeɪndʒ]	Wandel, Verwandlung
to **take place** [ˌteɪk 'pleɪs]	stattfinden
to **perform** [pə'fɔːm]	singen, spielen, auftreten
to **wave sth** [weɪv]	etw schwenken, mit etw wedeln
magical ['mædʒɪkl]	magisch, traumhaft
cheers *pl* [tʃɪəz]	Jubel, Applaus
to **wash over sb/sth** ['wɒʃ əʊvə]	jdn überkommen, etw überschwemmen
life-changing ['laɪf tʃeɪndʒɪŋ]	lebensverändernd
to **hold sb back** [ˌhəʊld 'bæk]	jdn bremsen
to **move on** [ˌmuːv 'ɒn]	weiterkommen, weitergehen
level ['levl]	Stufe, Niveau, Ebene
competition [ˌkɒmpə'tɪʃn]	Wettbewerb, Wettkampf
to **finish second** [ˌfɪnɪʃ 'sekənd]	Zweite/r werden
to **sign** [saɪn]	unterschreiben
contract ['kɒntrækt]	Vertrag
record company ['rekɔːd kʌmpəni]	Plattenfirma
to **release** [rɪ'liːs]	veröffentlichen
follow-up ['fɒləʊ ʌp]	Folge-, Nachfolger
career [kə'rɪə]	Karriere, Laufbahn

page 9

to **compare** [kəm'peə]	vergleichen
nervous ['nɜːvəs]	aufgeregt, nervös

to **shake** [ʃeɪk]	zittern
dirty ['dɜːti]	schmutzig
to **criticize** ['krɪtɪsaɪz]	kritisieren
show [ʃəʊ]	(TV-, Radio-)Sendung
to **take part in sth** [ˌteɪk 'pɑːt ɪn]	an etw teilnehmen
to **make sb up** [ˌmeɪk 'ʌp]	jdn schminken
script [skrɪpt]	Drehbuch
to **practise** ['præktɪs]	üben, trainieren
to **look forward to sth** [ˌlʊk 'fɔːwəd tə]	sich auf etw freuen

page 10

on one's own [ɒn wʌnz 'əʊn]	allein
background ['bækgraʊnd]	Hintergrund
to **be related to sth** [bi rɪ'leɪtɪd tə]	mit etw in Zusammenhang stehen
fame [feɪm]	Ruhm
childhood sweetheart [ˌtʃaɪldhʊd 'swiːthɑːt]	Jugendliebe
to **split (up)** [splɪt]	*(Paar:)* sich trennen
current ['kʌrənt]	aktuell
achievement [ə'tʃiːvmənt]	Errungenschaft, Leistung
to **inspire** [ɪn'spaɪə]	inspirieren, anregen
challenge ['tʃælɪndʒ]	Herausforderung, (große) Aufgabe
relationship [rɪ'leɪʃnʃɪp]	Beziehung, Verhältnis
lover ['lʌvə]	Geliebte/r, Liebhaber/in
tabloid press ['tæblɔɪd pres]	Boulevardpresse

page 11

expression [ɪk'spreʃn]	Ausdruck
to **cry one's eyes out** [ˌkraɪ wʌnz 'aɪz aʊt]	wie ein Schlosshund heulen
close [kləʊs]	nah, dicht, eng
to **fulfil** [fʊl'fɪl]	erfüllen
pleasure ['pleʒə]	Vergnügen
My pleasure. [ˌmaɪ 'pleʒə]	Gern geschehen.
to **prove** [pruːv]	beweisen
fashion designer ['fæʃn dɪzaɪnə]	Modeschöpfer/in
to **design** [dɪ'zaɪn]	entwerfen, gestalten
scene [siːn]	Szene
ordinary ['ɔːdnri]	normal, gewöhnlich
pretty ['prɪti]	ziemlich
attention [ə'tenʃn]	Aufmerksamkeit, Beachtung
on the other hand [ɒn ði 'ʌðə hænd]	andererseits
public ['pʌblɪk]	öffentlich
platform ['plætfɔːm]	Podium
to **talk sth over** [ˌtɔːk 'əʊvə]	etw besprechen
to **accept** [ək'sept]	akzeptieren, gutheißen
to **concentrate on sth** ['kɒnsntreɪt ɒn]	sich auf etw konzentrieren
to **support** [sə'pɔːt]	unterstützen
openness ['əʊpənnəs]	Offenheit
step [step]	Schritt
collection [kə'lekʃn]	Kollektion
label ['leɪbl]	(Mode-)Firma, Marke
to **admire** [əd'maɪə]	bewundern
to **focus on sth** ['fəʊkəs ɒn]	sich auf etw konzentrieren
role-play ['rəʊl pleɪ]	Rollenspiel
to **role-play** ['rəʊl pleɪ]	mit verteilten Rollen spielen
area ['eəriə]	Gebiet, Bereich, Feld
to **thank** [θæŋk]	danken
charts *pl* [tʃɑːts]	Hitparade
footballer ['fʊtbɔːlə]	Fußballer/in
to **congratulate sb on sth** [kən'grætʃuleɪt]	jdm zu etw gratulieren
support [sə'pɔːt]	Unterstützung, Hilfe
to **face sth** [feɪs]	sich einer Sache stellen
to **train** [treɪn]	trainieren
match [mætʃ]	Spiel, Partie, Match

UNIT 2

page 12

participant [pɑː'tɪsɪpənt]	Teilnehmer/in
spectator [spek'teɪtə]	Zuschauer/in
survey ['sɜːveɪ]	Umfrage
according to [ə'kɔːdɪŋ tə]	entsprechend, nach, gemäß
keep-fit [ˌkiːp'fɪt]	Fitness(-)
aerobics [eə'rəʊbɪks]	Aerobic
to **be keen on sth** [bi 'kiːn ɒn]	auf etw versessen sein

page 13

to **ring the doorbell** [ˌrɪŋ ðə 'dɔːbel]	(an der Tür) klingeln, läuten
stadium ['steɪdiəm]	Stadion
chess [tʃes]	Schach
chess set ['tʃes set]	Schachspiel *(Figuren + Brett)*
swimming pool ['swɪmɪŋ puːl]	Schwimmbad
racing car ['reɪsɪŋ kɑː]	Rennwagen
rules *pl* **of the game** [ˌruːlz əv ðə 'geɪm]	Spielregeln
since [sɪns]	seit
gym [dʒɪm]	Fitness-Studio
changing room ['tʃeɪndʒɪŋ ruːm]	Umkleidekabine, Umkleide
cold [kəʊld]	Erkältung
World Cup [ˌwɜːld 'kʌp]	Weltpokal
national team [ˌnæʃnəl 'tiːm]	Nationalmannschaft
personality [ˌpɜːsə'næləti]	Persönlichkeit
involved in sth [ɪn'vɒlvd ɪn]	an etw beteiligt, bei etw engagiert
to **lose** [luːz]	verlieren
interest (in sth) ['ɪntrəst]	Interesse (an etw)
to **look up to sb** [ˌlʊk 'ʌp tə]	zu jdm aufsehen, jdn bewundern
champion ['tʃæmpiən]	Meister/in
hero ['hɪərəʊ]	Held
to **overcome** [ˌəʊvə'kʌm]	überwinden
disability [ˌdɪsə'bɪləti]	Behinderung
swimmer ['swɪmə]	Schwimmer/in
medal ['medl]	Medaille

page 14

ending ['endɪŋ]	Schluss, Ende
illegal [ɪ'liːgl]	verboten, illegal
substance ['sʌbstəns]	Substanz, Stoff
to **improve** [ɪm'pruːv]	(sich) verbessern, (sich) steigern
performance [pə'fɔːməns]	Leistung, Abschneiden
injury ['ɪndʒəri]	Verletzung
to **occur** [ə'kɜː]	vorfallen, geschehen
paragraph ['pærəgrɑːf]	*(Text:)* Absatz
professional [prə'feʃənl]	professionell, Profi-
to **record** [rɪ'kɔːd]	aufzeichnen
decade ['dekeɪd]	Jahrzehnt
throughout the decades [θruːˌaʊt ðə 'dekeɪdz]	durch/über die Jahrzehnte
improvement in sth [ɪm'pruːvmənt ɪn]	Verbesserung bei etw

material [mə'tɪəriəl]	Material, Werkstoff
to **come fourth** [ˌkʌm 'fɔːθ]	Vierte/r werden
to **compete** [kəm'piːt]	(bei einem Wettbewerb) antreten
junior ['dʒuːniə]	Junioren-
national ['næʃnəl]	Landes-, national
triathlon [traɪ'æθlən]	Triathlon
cyclist ['saɪklɪst]	Radfahrer/in
racing cyclist ['reɪsɪŋ saɪklɪst]	Radrennfahrer/in
to **announce** [ə'naʊns]	verkünden, ankündigen
retirement [rɪ'taɪəmənt]	Rücktritt, Rückzug
competitive [kəm'petətɪv]	wettkampfmäßig
agency ['eɪdʒənsi]	Agentur
sample ['sɑːmpl]	Probe
to **charge sb with sth** [tʃɑːdʒ]	jdn einer Sache beschuldigen, jdn einer Sache anklagen
organization [ˌɔːgənaɪ'zeɪʃn]	Organisation
according to [ə'kɔːdɪŋ tə]	laut, zufolge
Olympic [ə'lɪmpɪk]	olympisch
committee [kə'mɪti]	Komitee
study ['stʌdi]	Untersuchung, Studie
historical [hɪ'stɒrɪkl]	historisch
evolution [ˌiːvə'luːʃn]	Entwicklung
phenomenon [fə'nɒmɪnən]	Phänomen, Erscheinung
century ['sentʃəri]	Jahrhundert
to **refer to sb/sth** [rɪ'fɜː tə]	jdn/etw erwähnen, sich auf jdn/etw beziehen
mixture ['mɪkstʃə]	Mischung
cocaine [kəʊ'keɪn]	Kokain
caffeine ['kæfiːn]	Koffein
strychnine ['strɪknaɪn]	Strychnin
nitroglycerine [ˌnaɪtrəʊ'glɪsəriːn]	Nitroglycerin
to **stimulate** ['stɪmjuleɪt]	anregen, stimulieren
breathing ['briːðɪŋ]	Atmung
to **suffer sth** ['sʌfə]	an etw leiden, etw erleiden
hallucination [həˌluːsɪ'neɪʃn]	Halluzination, Wahnvorstellung
to **refuse** [rɪ'fjuːz]	sich weigern
to **chase sb** [tʃeɪs]	jdn verfolgen, jdn jagen
to **bat an eyelid** [ˌbæt ən 'aɪlɪd]	mit der Wimper zucken
to **dope** [dəʊp]	dopen
to **enter a competition** [ˌentər ə kɒmpə'tɪʃn]	an einem Wettkampf/ Wettbewerb teilnehmen
guy [gaɪ]	Typ, Kerl
corrupt [kə'rʌpt]	korrupt
to **cycle on** [ˌsaɪkl 'ɒn]	weiterradeln

page 15

to **summarize** ['sʌməraɪz]	zusammenfassen
notebook ['nəʊtbʊk]	Heft, Notizbuch
heading ['hedɪŋ]	Rubrik, Überschrift
reference (to sth) ['refərəns]	Verweis (auf etw)
aspect ['æspekt]	Gesichtspunkt, Aspekt
sub-heading [ˌsʌb 'hedɪŋ]	Teilrubrik, Zwischenüberschrift
to **scan** [skæn]	*(Text)* überfliegen
repetition [ˌrepə'tɪʃn]	Wiederholung
connection [kə'nekʃn]	Verbindung
legal ['liːgl]	erlaubt, legal
to **structure** ['strʌktʃə]	strukturieren
to **appear** [ə'pɪə]	scheinen
in general [ɪn 'dʒenrəl]	im Allgemeinen, generell
to **sum up** [ˌsʌm 'ʌp]	zusammenfassen
to sum up [tə ˌsʌm 'ʌp]	zusammenfassend

page 16

to **highlight** ['haɪlaɪt]	hervorheben
to **join** [dʒɔɪn]	beitreten, eintreten, mitmachen
at all [ət 'ɔːl]	überhaupt
beside [bɪ'saɪd]	neben
to **replace** [rɪ'pleɪs]	ersetzen, austauschen
instructor [ɪn'strʌktə]	Lehrer/in
to **trip** [trɪp]	stolpern
to **fit** [fɪt]	passen
muscle ['mʌsl]	Muskel
to **ache** [eɪk]	schmerzen, wehtun
energy ['enədʒi]	Energie
session ['seʃn]	Sitzung
to **suggest** [sə'dʒest]	vorschlagen
to **take sb along** [ˌteɪk ə'lɒŋ]	jdn mitnehmen
craze [kreɪz]	Modewelle, Trend
workout ['wɜːkaʊt]	(Fitness-)Training
called [kɔːld]	namens
tape [teɪp]	(Ton-)Band
instead of [ɪn'sted əv]	anstatt
to **cancel** ['kænsl]	absagen, stornieren
traditional [trə'dɪʃənl]	traditionell
to **improvise** ['ɪmprəvaɪz]	improvisieren
to **name** [neɪm]	nennen, benennen
it wasn't long before … [ɪt wɒznt ˌlɒŋ bɪ'fɔː]	es dauerte nicht lange, bis …
worldwide ['wɜːldwaɪd]	weltweit

page 17

overweight [ˌəʊvə'weɪt]	übergewichtig
slim [slɪm]	schlank
cardiovascular [ˌkɑːdiəʊ'væskjələ]	Herz-Kreislauf-
metabolism [mə'tæbəlɪzəm]	Stoffwechsel
calorie ['kæləri]	Kalorie
to **measure** ['meʒə]	messen
blood vessel ['blʌd vesl]	Blutgefäß
joy [dʒɔɪ]	Freude
excitement [ɪk'saɪtmənt]	Begeisterung
musical ['mjuːzɪkl]	musikalisch, Musik-
process ['prəʊses]	Ablauf, Vorgang, Prozess
to **change sth into sth** ['tʃeɪndʒ ɪntə]	etw in etw umwandeln
growth [grəʊθ]	Wachstum
attractive [ə'træktɪv]	attraktiv, anziehend
speaker ['spiːkə]	Sprecher/in
to **panic** ['pænɪk]	in Panik geraten
to **get the hang of it** [ˌget ðə 'hæŋ əv ɪt]	den richtigen Dreh finden
relevant ['reləvənt]	relevant, wichtig
mainly ['meɪnli]	hauptsächlich
atmosphere ['ætməsfɪə]	Stimmung, Atmosphäre
to **join in** [ˌdʒɔɪn 'ɪn]	mitmachen
to **stand up** [ˌstænd 'ʌp]	aufstehen, sich hinstellen
school leaving party ['skuːl liːvɪŋ pɑːti]	Schulabgangsfeier
benefit ['benɪfɪt]	Nutzen, Vorteil, Pluspunkt
to **strengthen** ['streŋθn]	kräftigen, stärken
lung [lʌŋ]	Lunge
to **increase sth** [ɪn'kriːs]	etw steigern
to **reduce** [rɪ'djuːs]	senken, reduzieren, verringern
stress [stres]	Belastung, Stress
to **boost** [buːst]	ankurbeln
to **burn** [bɜːn]	(sich) verbrennen
to **lose weight** [ˌluːz 'weɪt]	abnehmen

last but not least [ˌlɑːst bʌt nɒt ˈliːst]	zu guter Letzt, nicht zuletzt
to **feel low** [ˌfiːl ˈləʊ]	schlecht gelaunt sein, deprimiert sein
stressed [strest]	angestrengt, gestresst
worried [ˈwʌrid]	besorgt, beunruhigt
care [keə]	Sorge
to **talk sb through sth** [ˈtɔːk θruː]	jdm etw der Reihe nach erklären
warm-up [ˈwɔːm ʌp]	Aufwärmen
cool down [ˌkuːl ˈdaʊn]	Abkühlen
dance routine [ˈdɑːns ruːtiːn]	Tanzschritte
move [muːv]	Schritt, Bewegung
to **shake sth** [ʃeɪk]	etw schütteln, mit etw wackeln
hip [hɪp]	Hüfte
touch [tʌtʃ]	Berührung
to **get sb hooked** [ˌget ˈhʊkt]	jdn anfixen
to **give sth a try** [ˌgɪv ə ˈtraɪ]	etw ausprobieren
unhealthy [ʌnˈhelθi]	nicht gesund
first name [ˈfɜːst neɪm]	Vorname
All the best, [ˌɔːl ðə ˈbest]	Mit besten Grüßen, Alles Gute

UNIT 3

page 18

brand [brænd]	Marke
power [ˈpaʊə]	Macht, Stärke, Kraft
to **write down** [ˌraɪt ˈdaʊn]	aufschreiben
to **shop** [ʃɒp]	einkaufen
fashionable [ˈfæʃnəbl]	modisch
gap [gæp]	Lücke
to **come down to sth** [ˌkʌm ˈdaʊn tə]	auf etw hinauslaufen, auf etw ankommen
quality [ˈkwɒləti]	Qualität
emotional [ɪˈməʊʃənl]	gefühlsmäßig, emotional
thinking [ˈθɪŋkɪŋ]	Denken
to **go for sth** [ˈgəʊ fə]	etw nehmen, etw gut finden

page 19

consumer [kənˈsjuːmə]	Verbraucher/in, Konsument/in
choice [tʃɔɪs]	Wahl, Entscheidung
availability [əˌveɪləˈbɪləti]	Verfügbarkeit
affordable [əˈfɔːdəbl]	erschwinglich
though [ðəʊ]	aber, dagegen, allerdings
packaging [ˈpækɪdʒɪŋ]	Verpackung
to **affect** [əˈfekt]	beeinflussen, sich auswirken auf
background [ˈbækgraʊnd]	Herkunft
sportswear [ˈspɔːtsweə]	Sportkleidung
to **advertise sth** [ˈædvətaɪz]	etw bewerben, für etw werben
goods *pl* [gʊdz]	Waren, Güter
to **suggest** [səˈdʒest]	unterstellen, suggerieren
athlete [ˈæθliːt]	Sportler/in, Athlet/in
over-achiever [ˌəʊvərəˈtʃiːvə]	Überflieger
to **look for sb/sth** [ˈlʊk fə]	jdn/etw suchen
to **achieve sth** [əˈtʃiːv]	etw erreichen, etw leisten
to **display** [dɪˈspleɪ]	zeigen
value [ˈvæljuː]	Wert
belief [bɪˈliːf]	Überzeugung
depending on [dɪˈpendɪŋ ɒn]	je nach(dem)
to **persuade** [pəˈsweɪd]	überzeugen, überreden
including [ɪnˈkluːdɪŋ]	einschließlich
to **pack** [pæk]	verpacken
to **identify with sb/sth** [aɪˈdentɪfaɪ wɪð]	sich mit jdm/etw identifizieren
to **grow up** [ˌgrəʊ ˈʌp]	aufwachsen

page 20

sold out [ˌsəʊld ˈaʊt]	ausverkauft
to **rewrite** [ˌriːˈraɪt]	umformulieren, neu schreiben
position [pəˈzɪʃn]	Stelle, Stellung, Position
allowance [əˈlaʊəns]	Taschengeld
actually [ˈæktʃuəli]	in der Tat, eigentlich, wirklich
similarity [ˌsɪməˈlærəti]	Ähnlichkeit
discount [ˈdɪskaʊnt]	Rabatt, Nachlass
discount label [ˈdɪskaʊnt leɪbl]	Billigmarke
sweater [ˈswetə]	Pullover
preference [ˈprefrəns]	Vorliebe
to **celebrate** [ˈselɪbreɪt]	feiern
athletic [æθˈletɪk]	sportlich, athletisch
challenging [ˈtʃælɪndʒɪŋ]	anspruchsvoll, fordernd

page 21

comparison [kəmˈpærɪsn]	Steigerung *(von Adjektiven)*
crowded [ˈkraʊdɪd]	voll (mit Leuten), überfüllt
tasty [ˈteɪsti]	schmackhaft, lecker
to **download** [ˌdaʊnˈləʊd]	herunterladen
competitive [kəmˈpetətɪv]	konkurrenzfähig, *(Preise:)* günstig
to **collect sth** [kəˈlekt]	etw abholen
to **sponsor** [ˈspɒnsə]	(finanziell) unterstützen, sponsern
run [rʌn]	Lauf
it's not long before [ɪts nɒt ˌlɒŋ ˈbɪfɔː]	es dauert nicht lange, bis
to **pick sb/sth up** [ˌpɪk ˈʌp]	jdn/etw abholen
stripe [straɪp]	Streifen
(it's a) pity [ˈpɪti]	schade
you guys [ˌju ˈgaɪz]	ihr
gear [gɪə]	Ausrüstung, Kleidung
Thank goodness! [ˌθæŋk ˈgʊdnəs]	Gott sei Dank!
lovely [ˈlʌvli]	schön, nett, hübsch
What's up? [ˌwɒts ˈʌp]	Was gibt's? Was ist los?
fee [fiː]	Gebühr
entrance fee [ˈentrəns fiː]	Teilnahmegebühr
still [stɪl]	(immer) noch, dennoch
to **matter** [ˈmætə]	wichtig sein, darauf ankommen
to **feel comfortable** [ˌfiːl ˈkʌmftəbl]	sich wohlfühlen
affordability [əˌfɔːdəˈbɪləti]	Erschwinglichkeit, Bezahlbarkeit
to **interrupt** [ˌɪntəˈrʌpt]	unterbrechen, ins Wort fallen
to **pretend** [prɪˈtend]	vorgeben; so tun, als ob
sweatshop [ˈswetʃɒp]	Ausbeutungsbetrieb
What's going on? [ˌwɒts gəʊɪŋ ˈɒn]	Was ist los?
amateur [ˈæmətə]	Amateur(-), Hobby-
professional [prəˈfeʃənl]	Profi
to **meet up** [ˌmiːt ˈʌp]	sich treffen
to **cheer for sb** [ˈtʃɪə fə]	jdn anfeuern, jdm zujubeln
even though [ˈiːvn ðəʊ]	selbst wenn, obwohl
sports gear [ˈspɔːts gɪə]	Sportkleidung, Sportausrüstung

page 22

flap [flæp]	Umschlagklappe
cover ['kʌvə]	(Buch-)Umschlag, Einband
logical(ly) ['lɒdʒɪkl]	logisch
debate [dɪ'beɪt]	Diskussion, Debatte
to **make sure** [ˌmeɪk 'ʃʊə]	sicherstellen; dafür sorgen, dass
whenever [wen'evə]	jedes Mal, wenn; wann (auch) immer
to **pay attention to sth** [ˌpeɪ ə'tenʃn tə]	auf etw achten
to **give an opinion** [ˌgɪv ən ə'pɪniən]	eine Meinung äußern
to **give a reason** [ˌgɪv ə 'ri:zn]	eine Begründung anführen
to **disagree with sth** [ˌdɪsə'gri: wɪð]	einer Sache nicht zustimmen, gegen etw sein, etw ablehnen
to **keep sth safe** [ˌki:p 'seɪf]	etw aufbewahren
on the one hand [ɒn ðə 'wʌn hænd]	einerseits
in fact [ɪn 'fækt]	um genau zu sein, eigentlich
to **take sth into account** [ˌteɪk ɪntu ə'kaʊnt]	etw in Betracht ziehen, etw berücksichtigen
on the whole [ɒn ðə 'həʊl]	im Großen und Ganzen

page 23

victim ['vɪktɪm]	Opfer
either ... or [ˌaɪðə 'ɔ:]	entweder ... oder
(the) latest ['leɪtɪst]	der/die/das allerneueste/n
to **suit sb** [su:t]	*(Kleidung:)* jdm stehen
to **walk along sth** [wɔ:k]	etw *(Straße etc.)* entlanggehen
high street ['haɪ stri:t]	Hauptgeschäftsstraße, Einkaufsstraße
glossy ['glɒsi]	Hochglanz-
toned [təʊnd]	straff, durchtrainiert
to **photo-shop** ['fəʊtəʊ ʃɒp]	mit Photoshop bearbeiten
cover ['kʌvə]	Titelseite
fingernail ['fɪŋgəneɪl]	Fingernagel
to **squeeze oneself into sth** ['skwi:z ɪntə]	sich in etw hineinzwängen
skinny ['skɪni]	hauteng
copy ['kɒpi]	Nachahmung, Imitat
watch [wɒtʃ]	Armbanduhr
up to ['ʌp tə]	bis
to **admit** [əd'mɪt]	zugeben, (ein)gestehen
stuff [stʌf]	Zeug, Sache(n)
to **bet** [bet]	wetten
for what it's worth [fə wɒt ɪts 'wɜ:θ]	meiner (bescheidenen) Meinung nach
to **stick to sth** ['stɪk tə]	bei etw bleiben, sich an etw halten
item (of clothing) ['aɪtəm]	Kleidungsstück
to **suit sb/sth** [su:t]	zu jdm/etw passen
no matter ... [ˌnəʊ 'mætə]	ganz egal, ...
to **draw attention to sb/sth** [ˌdrɔ: ə'tenʃn tə]	Aufmerksamkeit auf jdn/etw ziehen
acne ['ækni]	Akne
Yuck! [jʌk]	Igitt! Bäh!
as far as I'm concerned [əz ˌfɑ:r əz ˌaɪm kən'sɜ:nd]	was mich betrifft
a bit [ə 'bɪt]	ein bisschen
tight [taɪt]	knapp, eng
to **stare at sb** ['steər ət]	jdn anstarren
matter ['mætə]	Angelegenheit, Sache
unique [ju'ni:k]	einzigartig
to **copy** ['kɒpi]	nachahmen, imitieren
to **experiment** [ɪk'sperɪmənt]	experimentieren
particular [pə'tɪkjələ]	bestimmt, speziell
secret ['si:krɪt]	Geheimnis
to **overdo it** [ˌəʊvə'du: ɪt]	es übertreiben
all at once [ˌɔ:l ət 'wʌns]	auf einmal
I'm afraid [aɪm ə'freɪd]	leider
criticism (of sb/sth) ['krɪtɪsɪzəm]	Kritik (an jdm/etw)
fake [feɪk]	Fälschung, Imitation
collection [kə'lekʃn]	Sammlung

page 24

bullet point ['bʊlɪt pɔɪnt]	Stichpunkt
preparation (for sth) [ˌprepə'reɪʃn]	Vorbereitung (auf etw)
waste of time [ˌweɪst əf 'taɪm]	Zeitverschwendung
to **keep up with sb/sth** [ˌki:p 'ʌp wɪð]	mit jdm/etw Schritt halten
to **influence** ['ɪnfluəns]	beeinflussen

UNIT 4

page 25

leisure ['leʒə]	Freizeit, Muße
to **surf the internet** [ˌsɜ:f ði 'ɪntənet]	im Internet surfen
to **mind sth** [maɪnd]	etw gegen etw haben
to **hang out** [ˌhæŋ 'aʊt]	rumhängen, sich rumtreiben
lack [læk]	Mangel
area ['eəriə]	Gegend, Region
riding ['raɪdɪŋ]	Reiten
lesson ['lesn]	(Unterrichts-)Stunde
photography [fə'tɒgrəfi]	Fotografie, Foto-
to **save up** [ˌseɪv 'ʌp]	sparen

page 26

instead [ɪn'sted]	stattdessen
to **interpret** [ɪn'tɜ:prɪt]	interpretieren
cartoon [kɑ:'tu:n]	Karikatur
to **analyse** ['ænəlaɪz]	analysieren
instructions *pl* [ɪn'strʌkʃnz]	Anleitung, Anweisung(en)
drawing ['drɔ:ɪŋ]	Zeichnung
speech bubble ['spi:tʃ bʌbl]	Sprechblase
to **relate to sth** [rɪ'leɪt tə]	sich auf etw beziehen
to **get sth** [get]	etw verstehen, etw kapieren
joke [dʒəʊk]	Witz
to **study sth** ['stʌdi]	sich etw genau ansehen
cartoonist [kɑ:'tu:nɪst]	Karikaturist/in
to **draw** [drɔ:]	zeichnen
to **make a point** [ˌmeɪk ə 'pɔɪnt]	ein Argument vortragen, etw sagen wollen
human being [ˌhju:mən 'bi:ɪŋ]	Mensch, menschliches Wesen

page 27

among [ə'mʌŋ]	unter, inmitten, zwischen
shopping mall ['ʃɒpɪŋ mɔ:l]	Einkaufspassage, Einkaufszentrum
curfew ['kɜ:fju:]	Sperrstunde
unless [ən'les]	es sei denn, außer wenn
to **put an end to sth** [ˌpʊt ən 'end tə]	mit etw Schluss machen, einen Schlussstrich unter etw ziehen
at least [ət 'li:st]	zumindest, mindestens
to **accompany** [ə'kʌmpəni]	begleiten
legal guardian [ˌli:gl 'gɑ:diən]	Vormund, Erziehungsberechtigte/r
to **approach sb** [ə'prəʊtʃ]	an jdn herantreten

to **provide** [prə'vaɪd]	zur Verfügung stellen
ID [ˌaɪ 'diː]	Personalausweis
although [ɔːl'ðəʊ]	obwohl
to **object to sth** [əb'dʒekt tə]	etw ablehnen, gegen etw Einwände haben
spokesman ['spəʊksmən]	Sprecher
to **argue** ['ɑːgjuː]	argumentieren, geltend machen
retailer ['riːteɪlə]	Einzelhändler/in
to **back** [bæk]	unterstützen
to **respect** [rɪ'spekt]	respektieren
incident ['ɪnsɪdənt]	Vorfall, Zwischenfall
complaint [kəm'pleɪnt]	Beschwerde, Klage, Reklamation
bid [bɪd]	Versuch
to **maintain sth** [meɪn'teɪn]	etw aufrecht erhalten
to **estimate** ['estɪmeɪt]	schätzen
to **state** [steɪt]	darlegen, festlegen
appropriate(ly) [ə'prəʊpriət]	angemessen, passend
...-oriented ['ɔːriəntɪd]	...orientiert
adequate(ly) ['ædɪkwət]	ausreichend, angemessen
to **cover** ['kʌvə]	bedecken
visible ['vɪzəbl]	sichtbar
undergarments *pl* ['ʌndəgɑːmənts]	Unterwäsche
permitted [pə'mɪtɪd]	erlaubt, gestattet
measure ['meʒə]	Maßnahme
to **divide** [dɪ'vaɪd]	teilen
intent [ɪn'tent]	Absicht
to **loiter** ['lɔɪtə]	herumlungern
initiative [ɪ'nɪʃətɪv]	Aktion, Initiative
to **escort sb** [ɪ'skɔːt]	jdn begleiten, jdn eskortieren
exemption [ɪg'zempʃn]	Ausnahme, Befreiung
to **boast sth** [bəʊst]	etw aufweisen (können)
to **abridge** [ə'brɪdʒ]	*(Text)* kürzen
to **adapt** [ə'dæpt]	*(Text)* bearbeiten

page 28

mediation [ˌmiːdi'eɪʃn]	Vermittlung
written ['rɪtn]	schriftlich
sense [sens]	Sinn
to **be aimed at sb** [bi 'eɪmd ət]	sich an jdn richten
to **paraphrase** ['pærəfreɪz]	umschreiben, paraphrasieren
sort [sɔːt]	Art, Sorte
to **re-read** [ˌriː 'riːd]	erneut lesen
colleague ['kɒliːg]	Kollege/-in
translation [træns'leɪʃn]	Übersetzung
to **mess around** [ˌmes ə'raʊnd]	herumalbern, herumgammeln
to **cause** [kɔːz]	verursachen
to **be on sale** [bi ɒn 'seɪl]	angeboten werden, zum Verkauf stehen
to **move house** [ˌmuːv 'haʊs]	umziehen
to **lift** [lɪft]	heben
to **complain** [kəm'pleɪn]	sich beschweren, sich beklagen

page 29

social skills *pl* [ˌsəʊʃl 'skɪlz]	Sozialkompetenz
to **exchange** [ɪks'tʃeɪndʒ]	austauschen
moans *pl* [məʊnz]	Gejammer, Genörgel
sex [seks]	Geschlecht
the opposite sex [ði ˌɒpəzɪt 'seks]	das andere Geschlecht
to **text** [tekst]	eine SMS schicken, simsen
to **post** [pəʊst]	*(im Internet)* posten
peer [pɪə]	Gleichaltrige/r, Altersgenosse
to **interact** [ˌɪntər'ækt]	interagieren, aufeinander eingehen
network ['netwɜːk]	Netz, Netzwerk
site [saɪt]	Website
to **get together** [ˌget tə'geðə]	sich treffen
apart from [ə'pɑːt frəm]	abgesehen von, außer
to **look after sb** [lʊk 'ɑːftə]	sich um jdn kümmern
siblings *pl* ['sɪblɪŋz]	Geschwister
nearby ['nɪəbaɪ]	in der Nähe
opportunity [ˌɒpə'tjuːnəti]	Gelegenheit, Möglichkeit, Chance
to **socialize** ['səʊʃəlaɪz]	sich treffen, unter Leute gehen
to **be pleased** [bi 'pliːzd]	sich freuen
to **keep in touch** [ˌkiːp ɪn 'tʌtʃ]	in Verbindung bleiben
face to face [ˌfeɪs tə 'feɪs]	persönlich
contact ['kɒntækt]	Kontakt, Verbindung
ability [ə'bɪləti]	Fähigkeit, Befähigung
especially [ɪ'speʃəli]	besonders, insbesondere

page 30

to **come round** [ˌkʌm 'raʊnd]	vorbeikommen
till [tɪl]	bis
all right by me [ɔːl ˌraɪt baɪ 'miː]	in Ordnung für mich
there's little point in doing sth [θeəz ˌlɪtl pɔɪnt ɪn 'duːɪŋ]	es hat wenig Sinn, etw zu tun

JOB SKILLS 1

page 31

vocational college [vəʊˌkeɪʃənl 'kɒlɪdʒ]	Fachoberschule, Berufskolleg
work experience ['wɜːk ɪkspɪəriəns]	Praktikum
writer ['raɪtə]	Verfasser/in
suggestion [sə'dʒestʃən]	Vorschlag
to **apply for a job** [əˌplaɪ fər ə 'dʒɒb]	sich auf eine Stelle bewerben
trainee [treɪ'niː]	Auszubildende/r
native language [ˌneɪtɪv 'læŋgwɪdʒ]	Muttersprache
secretary ['sekrətri]	Sekretär/in
backpacker ['bækpækə]	Rucksacktourist/in
hostel ['hɒstl]	Herberge, Wohnheim
sometime ['sʌmtaɪm]	irgendwann
Cheers! [tʃɪəz]	Tschüs! Mach's gut! Danke!
insight ['ɪnsaɪt]	Einblick
to **run** [rʌn]	*(Unternehmen)* führen, betreiben
at first hand [ət ˌfɜːst 'hænd]	aus erster Hand, hautnah
contact details *pl* ['kɒntækt diːteɪlz]	Kontaktdaten
to **mention** ['menʃn]	erwähnen
to **attach sth** [ə'tætʃ]	*(E-Mail:)* etw beifügen, etw anhängen
job advertisement ['dʒɒb ədvɜːtɪsmənt]	Stellenanzeige, -ausschreibung
to **let sb know sth** [ˌlet 'nəʊ]	jdm etw mitteilen
at the latest [ət ðə 'leɪtɪst]	spätestens
Yours sincerely [ˌjɔːz sɪn'sɪəli]	*(Brief:)* Mit freundlichen Grüßen

page 32

to **contrast** [kən'trɑːst]	gegenüberstellen, vergleichen
abbreviation [əˌbriːvi'eɪʃn]	Abkürzung
chatty ['tʃæti]	mitteilsam, geschwätzig
etiquette ['etɪket]	Etikette, Regeln
subject line ['sʌbdʒɪkt laɪn]	*(Brief:)* Betreffzeile
to **get into the habit of doing sth** [ˌget ɪntə ðə 'hæbɪt əv]	sich angewöhnen, etw zu tun
to **type sth in** [ˌtaɪp 'ɪn]	etw eintippen
capital letter [ˌkæpɪtl 'letə]	Großbuchstabe
spelling ['spelɪŋ]	Rechtschreibung
application [ˌæplɪ'keɪʃn]	Bewerbung
to **submit** [səb'mɪt]	einreichen, vorlegen, zusenden
to **take sth further** [ˌteɪk 'fɜːðə]	etw (weiter) verfolgen
to **confirm** [kən'fɜːm]	bestätigen
to **be available** [bi ə'veɪləbl]	*(Telefon:)* zu sprechen sein
set-up ['setʌp]	Aufbau

page 33

to **separate** ['sepəreɪt]	trennen, loslösen
to **soften** ['sɒfn]	mildern, abmildern
surname ['sɜːneɪm]	Nachname
proper name [ˌprɒpə 'neɪm]	Eigenname
line [laɪn]	Leitung
digit ['dɪdʒɪt]	Ziffer
separately ['seprətli]	einzeln
e.g. [ˌiː 'dʒiː]	z. B.
to **spell** [spel]	buchstabieren
to **put sb through** [ˌpʊt 'θruː]	*(Telefon:)* jdn durchstellen, jdn verbinden
to **leave a message** [ˌliːv ə 'mesɪdʒ]	eine Nachricht hinterlassen

page 34

as things turn out [əz ˌθɪŋz tɜːn 'aʊt]	wie sich herausstellt
appointment [ə'pɔɪntmənt]	Termin, Verabredung
to **bother sb** ['bɒðə]	jdn belästigen, jdn stören
luck [lʌk]	Glück
to **be unavailable** [bi ˌʌnə'veɪləbl]	*(Telefon:)* nicht zu sprechen sein
to **have a chat** [həv a 'tʃæt]	sich unterhalten, miteinander plaudern
leaflet ['liːflət]	Broschüre, Merkblatt
attachment [ə'tætʃmənt]	*(E-Mail:)* Anhang
definitely ['defɪnətli]	absolut, ganz sicher
to **hold the line** [ˌhəʊld ðə 'laɪn]	am Apparat bleiben
likely ['laɪkli]	wahrscheinlich
caller ['kɔːlə]	Anrufer/in
to **carry out** [ˌkæri 'aʊt]	durchführen, ausführen
to **respond to sth** [rɪ'spɒnd tə]	auf etw reagieren, auf etw antworten
to **take a message** [ˌteɪk ə 'mesɪdʒ]	etw ausrichten, eine Nachricht notieren
to **read sth back** [ˌriːd 'bæk]	etw (zur Kontrolle) vorlesen
to **enquire about sth** [ɪn'kwaɪər əbaʊt]	sich nach etw erkundigen
department [dɪ'pɑːtmənt]	Abteilung
accounts [ə'kaʊnts]	Buchhaltung
to **hold on** [ˌhəʊld 'ɒn]	warten
engaged [ɪn'geɪdʒd]	*(Telefon:)* besetzt

UNIT 5

page 35

virtual ['vɜːtʃuəl]	virtuell
role [rəʊl]	Rolle
poster ['pəʊstə]	Plakat
gallery ['gæləri]	Galerie
gallery walk ['gæləri wɔːk]	Galerierundgang
to **put sth up** [ˌpʊt 'ʌp]	etw *(Bild etc.)* aufhängen
per [pə]	pro

page 36

to **skim** [skɪm]	*(Text)* überfliegen
to **underline** [ˌʌndə'laɪn]	unterstreichen
bold [bəʊld]	fett(gedruckt)
type [taɪp]	Schrift, Type
italics *pl* [ɪ'tælɪks]	Kursivschrift
lonely ['ləʊnli]	einsam
habit ['hæbɪt]	Gewohnheit
Briton ['brɪtn]	Brite/Britin
average ['ævərɪdʒ]	Durchschnitt
poll [pəʊl]	Umfrage
to **suggest** [sə'dʒest]	darauf hindeuten, nahelegen
third [θɜːd]	Drittel
user ['juːzə]	Benutzer/in
quarter ['kwɔːtə]	Viertel
usage ['juːsɪdʒ]	Nutzung
to **exceed** [ɪk'siːd]	übersteigen
to **base on sth** ['beɪs ɒn]	auf etw basieren
to **carry out** [ˌkæri 'aʊt]	durchführen, ausführen
primary ['praɪməri]	Haupt-, hauptsächlich
reader ['riːdə]	Dozent/in
psychology [saɪ'kɒlədʒi]	Psychologie
to **tend to do sth** ['tend tə]	dazu neigen, etw zu tun
largely ['lɑːdʒli]	weitgehend, überwiegend
dependent on sth [dɪ'pendənt ɒn]	von etw abhängig
all the time [ˌɔːl ðə 'taɪm]	ständig, die ganze Zeit
to **cut sb off from sth** [ˌkʌt 'ɒf frəm]	jdn von etw abschneiden
several ['sevrəl]	mehrere
left out of sth [ˌleft 'aʊt əv]	von etw ausgeschlossen
to **isolate** ['aɪsəleɪt]	absondern, isolieren

page 37

at the expense of sth [ət ði ɪk'spens əv]	auf Kosten von etw
regardless of sth [rɪ'gɑːdləs əv]	ungeachtet einer Sache
update ['ʌpdeɪt]	Aktualisierung
to **engage with sb** [ɪn'geɪdʒ wɪð]	auf jdn zugehen
channel ['tʃænl]	Kanal
to **listen in** [ˌlɪsn 'ɪn]	mithören
presence ['prezns]	Anwesenheit, Präsenz
amount [ə'maʊnt]	Betrag
sum [sʌm]	Summe
representative [ˌreprɪ'zentətɪv]	repräsentativ
to **get involved with sb** [ˌget ɪn'vɒlvd wɪð]	mit jdm zu tun haben
account [ə'kaʊnt]	Konto
to **be called** [bi 'kɔːld]	heißen
unfit [ʌn'fɪt]	nicht fit
to **spell** [spel]	buchstabieren, (richtig) schreiben
handwriting ['hændraɪtɪŋ]	Handschrift
thumb [θʌm]	Daumen

childhood ['tʃaɪldhʊd]	Kindheit
to **hand sth in** [ˌhænd 'ɪn]	etw abgeben
suggestion [sə'dʒestʃən]	Vorschlag
to **take a vote** [ˌteɪk ə 'vəʊt]	abstimmen

page 38

entry ['entri]	*(Blog:)* Beitrag, Meldung
importance [ɪm'pɔːtns]	Bedeutung, Wichtigkeit
anecdote ['ænɪkdəʊt]	Anekdote
call for help [ˌkɔːl fə 'help]	Hilferuf
wall [wɔːl]	Wand, Pinnwand
conclusion [kən'kluːʒn]	Schlussfolgerung, Schluss
helpline ['helplaɪn]	Hotline, Sorgentelefon
to **suffer from sth** ['sʌfə frəm]	unter etw leiden
solution [sə'luːʃn]	Lösung
counsellor ['kaʊnsələ]	Berater/in
to **take a call** [ˌteɪk ə 'kɔːl]	einen Anruf entgegennehmen, ans Telefon gehen
to **go viral** [ˌgəʊ 'vaɪrəl]	sich (im Internet) rasend schnell verbreiten
to **laugh at sb** ['lɑːf ət]	über jdn lachen, jdn auslachen
to **point at sb/sth** ['pɔɪnt ət]	auf jdn/etw zeigen
desperate ['despərət]	verzweifelt
fully ['fʊli]	vollkommen, völlig
cruel [kruːəl]	grausam, gemein
to **trust** [trʌst]	vertrauen
appointment [ə'pɔɪntmənt]	Termin
talk [tɔːk]	Gerede
advice [əd'vaɪs]	(guter) Rat, Ratschläge
to **see sb** [siː]	zu jdm gehen
practical ['præktɪkl]	zweckmäßig, praktisch (umsetzbar)
to **delete** [dɪ'liːt]	löschen, tilgen
to **advise sb** [əd'vaɪz]	jdn beraten, jdm etw raten
to **contact sb** ['kɒntækt]	sich mit jdm in Verbindung setzen

page 39

to **block** [blɒk]	sperren
to **deactivate** [ˌdiː'æktɪveɪt]	stilllegen, deaktivieren
legal action [ˌliːgl 'ækʃn]	rechtliche Schritte
to **take legal action** [teɪk ˌliːgl 'ækʃn]	rechtliche Schritte unternehmen
setting ['setɪŋ]	Einstellung
to **bother sb** ['bɒðə]	jdn belästigen
right-hand ['raɪt hænd]	rechte/r/s, auf der rechten Seite
screen [skriːn]	Bildschirm
to **reactivate** [ˌrɪ'æktɪveɪt]	wieder in Betrieb nehmen, reaktivieren
at any time [ət ˌeni 'taɪm]	jederzeit
to **log in** [ˌlɒg 'ɪn]	sich einloggen
to **log out** [ˌlɒg 'aʊt]	sich ausloggen
deletion [dɪ'liːʃn]	Löschung, Tilgung
epitaph ['epɪtɑːf]	Grabinschrift
e.g. [ˌiː 'dʒiː]	z. B.
to **hire sb** ['haɪə]	jdn beauftragen, jdn engagieren
lawyer ['lɔːjə]	Anwalt/Anwältin
specialist lawyer [ˌspeʃəlɪst 'lɔːjə]	Fachanwalt/-anwältin
service ['sɜːvɪs]	Dienst, Dienstleistung
provider [prə'vaɪdə]	Anbieter
thousand ['θaʊznd]	tausend, Tausend

page 40

unwanted [ˌʌn'wɒntɪd]	unerwünscht
schoolboy ['skuːlbɔɪ]	Schuljunge
drunken ['drʌŋkən]	betrunken
crasher ['kræʃə]	ungeladener Gast
to **trash sth** [træʃ]	etw demolieren
pound [paʊnd]	Pfund
reveller ['revələ]	Feiernde/r
to **gatecrash** ['geɪtkræʃ]	uneingeladen erscheinen
damage ['dæmɪdʒ]	Schaden
vomit ['vɒmɪt]	Erbrochenes
terraced *BE* ['terəst]	Reihenhaus-
property ['prɒpəti]	Immobilie(n), Anwesen
riot ['raɪət]	Aufstand, Aufruhr
riot police ['raɪət pəliːs]	Bereitschaftspolizei
to **break up** [ˌbreɪk 'ʌp]	*(Menschenmenge)* zerstreuen
trouble ['trʌbl]	Ärger, Problem(e)
danger ['deɪndʒə]	Gefahr
details *pl* ['diːteɪlz]	Angaben
to **realise** ['rɪəlaɪz]	wissen, erkennen, klar sein
invitation [ˌɪnvɪ'teɪʃn]	Einladung
to **throw** [θrəʊ]	werfen
to **throw a party** [ˌθrəʊ ə 'pɑːti]	eine Party geben/schmeißen
privacy ['prɪvəsi]	Privatsphäre
absolutely ['æbsəluːtli]	absolut
essential [ɪ'senʃl]	wesentlich, unerlässlich
to **make sb aware of sth** [ˌmeɪk ə'weər əv]	jdn über etw informieren, jdn auf etw hinweisen
poisoning ['pɔɪzənɪŋ]	Vergiftung
laughing gas ['lɑːfɪŋ gæs]	Lachgas
canister ['kænɪstə]	Dose, Büchse
to **toss** [tɒs]	werfen
living room ['lɪvɪŋ ruːm]	Wohnzimmer
carpet ['kɑːpɪt]	Teppich(boden)
to **clean up** [ˌkliːn 'ʌp]	aufräumen, saubermachen
to **damage** ['dæmɪdʒ]	beschädigen
skylight ['skaɪlaɪt]	Oberlicht, Dachfenster
bouncer ['baʊnsə]	Türsteher/in
in advance [ɪn əd'vɑːns]	im Voraus
unable [ʌn'eɪbl]	nicht in der Lage, unfähig
to **cope (with sth)** ['kəʊp wɪð]	etw bewältigen, mit etw klarkommen, mit etw fertig werden
to **turn up** [ˌtɜːn 'ʌp]	auftauchen
shocked [ʃɒkt]	schockiert
to **drop sb off** [ˌdrɒp 'ɒf]	jdn (wohin)bringen
aged [eɪdʒd]	im Alter von
to **wreck** [rek]	demolieren
chaos ['keɪɒs]	Chaos
to **do sb harm** [du 'hɑːm]	jdm etwas (an)tun
apparently [ə'pærəntli]	anscheinend
reputation [ˌrepju'teɪʃn]	Ansehen, Ruf
to **shoot up** [ˌʃuːt 'ʌp]	rasant ansteigen

page 41

immediately [ɪ'miːdiətli]	unverzüglich, unmittelbar, sofort
to **get drunk** [ˌget 'drʌŋk]	sich betrinken
to **deal with sth** ['diːl wɪð]	mit etw zurechtkommen, mit etw umgehen
to **look sth up** [ˌlʊk 'ʌp]	etw *(Vokabel etc.)* nachschlagen
context ['kɒntekst]	Zusammenhang, Kontext
uninvited [ˌʌnɪn'vaɪtɪd]	un(ein)geladen
noise [nɔɪz]	Lärm
next door [ˌnekst 'dɔː]	nebenan
to **end up** [ˌend 'ʌp]	landen

page 42

text message ['tekst mesɪdʒ]	SMS
to **upload** [ˌʌp'ləʊd]	hochladen

page 43

mess [mes]	Chaos
to **expand** [ɪk'spænd]	erweitern
to **act out** [ˌækt 'aʊt]	spielen, vorspielen
horrified ['hɒrɪfaɪd]	entsetzt
invite ['ɪnvaɪt]	Einladung
to **wash** [wɒʃ]	abwaschen, abwischen
to **apologize** [ə'pɒlədʒaɪz]	sich entschuldigen
behaviour [bɪ'heɪvjə]	Benehmen, Verhalten
cancer ['kænsə]	Krebs *(Krankheit)*
fundraiser ['fʌndreɪzə]	Spendensammler/in
to **raise money** [ˌreɪz 'mʌni]	Geld beschaffen
charity ['tʃærəti]	Wohltätigkeit, wohltätige Zwecke
plight [plaɪt]	Notlage
to **spread** [spred]	sich verbreiten
to **diagnose sb with sth** ['daɪəgnəʊz wɪð]	etw *(Krankheit)* bei jdm feststellen/diagnostizieren
terminal ['tɜːmɪnl]	im Endstadium, tödlich
rather than ['rɑːðə ðən]	anstatt
to **dwell on sth** ['dwel ɒn]	sich mit etw aufhalten
misfortune [ˌmɪs'fɔːtʃuːn]	Unglück, Missgeschick
to **draw up** [ˌdrɔː 'ʌp]	*(Text)* verfassen, abfassen
bucket ['bʌkɪt]	Eimer
bucket list ['bʌkɪt lɪst]	*Dinge, die man getan haben sollte, bevor man stirbt*
skydive ['skaɪdaɪv]	Fallschirmsprung
drums *pl* [drʌmz]	Schlagzeug
final ['faɪnl]	Finale
initially [ɪ'nɪʃəli]	anfangs, anfänglich
to set out to do sth [ˌset 'aʊt tə]	sich vornehmen, etw tun
fundraising ['fʌndreɪzɪŋ]	Spendensammeln, Geldbeschaffung
campaign [kæm'peɪn]	Aktion, Kampagne
to **attract** [ə'trækt]	anlocken, anziehen
to **attract attention** [əˌtrækt ə'tenʃn]	Aufmerksamkeit erregen
inspirational [ˌɪnspɪ'reɪʃnəl]	anregend, inspirierend
to **benefit** ['benɪfɪt]	nutzen, Nutzen bringen, profitieren
to **research sth** [rɪ'sɜːtʃ]	etw recherchieren, Nachforschungen über etw anstellen
findings *pl* ['faɪndɪŋz]	Ergebnisse

page 44

encryption [ɪn'krɪpʃn]	Verschlüsselung
secure [sɪ'kjʊə]	sicher
messaging ['mesɪdʒɪŋ]	*Versenden von Nachrichten*
to **remain** [rɪ'meɪn]	bleiben
process ['prəʊses]	Verfahren
to **scramble** ['skræmbl]	verschlüsseln
to **apply sth to sth** [ə'plaɪ]	etw auf etw anwenden
algorithm ['ælgərɪðm]	Algorithmus
central to sth ['sentrəl tə]	von zentraler Bedeutung für etw
mathematical [ˌmæθə'mætɪkl]	mathematisch
complex ['kɒmpleks]	komplex
in theory [ɪn 'θɪəri]	theoretisch
to **decrypt** [ˌdiː'krɪpt]	entschlüsseln
symmetric [sɪ'metrɪk]	symmetrisch
secret ['siːkrɪt]	geheim
sender ['sendə]	Absender
recipient [rɪ'sɪpiənt]	Empfänger/in
to **intercept** [ˌɪntə'sept]	abfangen, abhören
asymmetric [eɪsɪ'metrɪk]	asymmetrisch
simultaneous(ly) [ˌsɪml'teɪniəs]	gleichzeitig
to **work sth out** [ˌwɜːk 'aʊt]	etw herausfinden
to **reverse sth** [rɪ'vɜːs]	umkehren, auflösen
to **restore** [rɪ'stɔː]	wiederherstellen, rekonstruieren
not … either [nɒt 'aɪðə]	auch nicht
by contrast [baɪ 'kɒntrɑːst]	im Gegensatz dazu, dagegen
to **discover** [dɪ'skʌvə]	entdecken, herausfinden
review [rɪ'vjuː]	Rezension, Kritik
feature ['fiːtʃə]	Merkmal, Eigenschaft

UNIT 6

page 45

advertising ['ædvətaɪzɪŋ]	Werbung
billboard ['bɪlbɔːd]	Reklametafel, Plakatwand
digital signage [ˌdɪdʒɪtl 'saɪnɪdʒ]	digitale Außenwerbung
ad, advert, advertisment [æd, 'ædvɜːt, əd'vɜːtɪsmənt]	Anzeige, Werbung
viral ad [ˌvaɪrəl 'æd]	Internet-Werbespot
element ['elɪmənt]	Baustein, Element
ambition [æm'bɪʃn]	Ziel, Ehrgeiz
emotion [ɪ'məʊʃn]	Gefühl, Emotion
entertainment [ˌentə'teɪnmənt]	Unterhaltung
excitement [ɪk'saɪtmənt]	Spannung, Aufregung
fascination [ˌfæsɪ'neɪʃn]	Faszination
horror ['hɒrə]	Schrecken
tragedy ['trædʒədi]	Tragödie
humour ['hjuːmə]	Humor
mystery ['mɪstri]	Rätsel, Rätselhaftigkeit
provocation [ˌprɒvə'keɪʃn]	Provokation
reward [rɪ'wɔːd]	Belohnung, Lohn
to **contain** [kən'teɪn]	enthalten

page 46

theory ['θɪəri]	Theorie
giant ['dʒaɪənt]	riesig, riesenhaft
note [nəʊt]	Ton, Note
likely ['laɪkli]	wahrscheinlich
to **be likely to do sth** [bi 'laɪkli tə]	etw wahrscheinlich tun (werden)
to **skip sth** [skɪp]	etw auslassen, etw überspringen
escalator ['eskəleɪtə]	Rolltreppe
in favor of doing sth *AE* [ɪn 'feɪvər əv]	um (stattdessen) etw zu tun
to **compose** [kəm'pəʊz]	komponieren
subway *AE* ['sʌbweɪ]	U-Bahn
to **view sth** [vjuː]	(sich) etw ansehen
concept ['kɒnsept]	Idee, Gedanke, Konzept
to **create** [kri'eɪt]	(er)schaffen, entwerfen, kreieren
ad(vertising) agency ['æd eɪdʒənsi]	Werbeagentur
goal [gəʊl]	Ziel, Absicht
do-good ['duː gʊd]	weltverbessernd
to **promote sth** [prə'məʊt]	für etw werben, etw bewerben
environmentally friendly [ɪnˌvaɪrənˌmentəli 'frendli]	umweltfreundlich

increasingly [ɪnˈkriːsɪŋli]	zunehmend
competitive [kəmˈpetətɪv]	umkämpft, wettbewerbsintensiv
eco- [ˈiːkəʊ]	Öko-
traditional [trəˈdɪʃənl]	herkömmlich
effective [ɪˈfektɪv]	wirksam, effektiv
competition [ˌkɒmpəˈtɪʃn]	Konkurrenz, Konkurrenzkampf
environmental(ly) [ɪnˌvaɪrənˈmentl]	umweltmäßig, Umwelt-
sound [saʊnd]	solide, untadelig
fierce [fɪəs]	heftig, erbittert
innovative [ˈɪnəveɪtɪv]	innovativ
approach [əˈprəʊtʃ]	Ansatz, Herangehensweise
deputy manager [ˌdepjəti ˈmænɪdʒə]	stellvertretende/r Geschäftsführer/in
commuter [kəˈmjuːtə]	Pendler/in
to **choose sth over sth** [ˈtʃuːz əʊvə]	etw. einer anderen Sache vorziehen
to **increase** [ɪnˈkriːs]	steigen, zunehmen
phase [feɪz]	Phase
release [rɪˈliːs]	Veröffentlichung
to **enter sth** [ˈentə]	an etw teilnehmen
contest [ˈkɒntest]	Wettbewerb
to **submit sth** [səbˈmɪt]	etw einreichen, etw einsenden
once [wʌns]	sobald
submission [səbˈmɪʃn]	Einsendung
thoughtful [ˈθɔːtfl]	wohlüberlegt, gut durchdacht
game machine [ˈgeɪm məʃiːn]	Videospielgerät, Spielautomat
to **turn sb/sth into sb/sth** [ˈtɜːn ɪntə]	jdn/etw zu jdm/etw machen
can [kæn]	Dose
to **encourage sb to do sth** [ɪnˈkʌrɪdʒ]	jdn ermuntern, etw zu tun
to **invent** [ɪnˈvent]	erfinden
bottle bank [ˈbɒtl bæŋk]	Glascontainer
arcade [ɑːˈkeɪd]	Spielautomat
amusement arcade [əˈmjuːzmənt ɑːkeɪd]	Spielhalle
noise [nɔɪz]	Geräusch
passer-by [ˈpɑːsə baɪ]	Passant/in
display [dɪˈspleɪ]	Bildschirm, Anzeige, Display
conventional [kənˈvenʃənl]	konventionell, herkömmlich

page 47

deep [diːp]	tief
rubbish [ˈrʌbɪʃ]	Müll, Abfall
rubbish bin [ˈrʌbɪʃ bɪn]	Mülltonne
crash [kræʃ]	Schlag, Krach
to **step** [step]	treten
to **be fun** [bi ˈfʌn]	Spaß machen
to **protect** [prəˈtekt]	schützen
metal [ˈmetl]	Metall
government [ˈgʌvənmənt]	Regierung, öffentliche Verwaltung
clever [ˈklevə]	intelligent, klug, schlau, clever
ground [graʊnd]	(Erd-)Boden
effect [ɪˈfekt]	Wirkung, Effekt

page 48

in addition [ɪn əˈdɪʃn]	außerdem, darüber hinaus
for this reason [fə ðɪs ˈriːzn]	aus diesem Grund
presentation [ˌpreznˈteɪʃn]	Vortrag, Referat, Präsentation
to **give a presentation** [gɪv ə ˌpreznˈteɪʃn]	ein Referat halten
slide [slaɪd]	Dia, (Overhead-)Folie
to **take turns** [ˌteɪk ˈtɜːnz]	sich abwechseln
spelling [ˈspelɪŋ]	Rechtschreibung
to **number** [ˈnʌmbə]	nummerieren
hand-held [ˈhænd held]	in der Hand gehalten
quick reference [ˌkwɪk ˈrefərəns]	schnelles Nachschlagen
presenter [prɪˈzentə]	Vortragende/r
to **form** [fɔːm]	bilden
to **present** [prɪˈzent]	vorstellen, präsentieren
invention [ɪnˈvenʃn]	Erfindung
tram [træm]	Straßenbahn, Tram
public transport [ˌpʌblɪk ˈtrænspɔːt]	öffentliche Verkehrsmittel
ticket inspector [ˈtɪkɪt ɪnspektə]	Fahrkartenkontrolleur/in
to **fine sb** [faɪn]	jdn mit einer Geldbuße belegen
to **stamp** [stæmp]	stempeln, abstempeln
lottery [ˈlɒtəri]	Lotterie, Verlosung
instant(ly) [ˈɪnstənt]	sofortig, augenblicklich
salary [ˈsæləri]	Gehalt
speed [spiːd]	Geschwindigkeit
speed camera [ˈspiːd kæmərə]	Geschwindigkeitsüberwachungskamera, Radarfalle
speed limit [ˈspiːd lɪmɪt]	Geschwindigkeitsbegrenzung
to **reward** [rɪˈwɔːd]	belohnen
fine [faɪn]	Geldbuße
traffic lights *pl* [ˈtræfɪk laɪts]	Ampel
motorist *BE* [ˈməʊtərɪst]	Autofahrer/in
to **jump red lights** [ˌdʒʌmp red ˈlaɪts]	bei Rot über eine Ampel fahren
driving licence [ˈdraɪvɪŋ laɪsns]	Führerschein
knowledge [ˈnɒlɪdʒ]	Wissen, Kenntnis(se)
visuals *pl* [ˈvɪʒuəlz]	visuelle Hilfsmittel
OHP transparency [ˌəʊ eɪtʃ ˈpiː trænspærənsi]	Overheadfolie
introductions *pl* [ˌɪntrəˈdʌkʃnz]	Vorstellen
to **hand over** [ˌhænd ˈəʊvə]	übergeben
in conclusion [ɪn kənˈkluːʒn]	abschließend, zum Schluss
to **be pleased to do sth** [bi ˈpliːzd tə]	etw gern tun

page 49

giant [ˈdʒaɪənt]	Riese
to **make the difference** [ˌmeɪk ðə ˈdɪfrəns]	entscheidend sein, den entscheidenden Unterschied ausmachen
to **start out** [ˌstɑːt ˈaʊt]	(zunächst) anfangen
office clerk [ˈɒfɪs klɑːk]	Büroangestellte/r
soap [səʊp]	Seife
dope [dəʊp]	Depp
managing director [ˌmænɪdʒɪŋ dəˈrektə]	Geschäftsführer/in
in-tray [ˈɪn treɪ]	Posteingang(skorb)
to **fire sb** [ˈfaɪə]	jdn feuern
to **hire sb** [ˈhaɪə]	jdn einstellen
I've never looked back. [aɪv ˌnevə lʊkt ˈbæk]	Ich habe es nie bereut.
to **set up** [ˌset ˈʌp]	*(Unternehmen)* gründen
manufacturer [ˌmænjuˈfæktʃərə]	Hersteller/in, Produzent/in
to **know sth inside out** [nəʊ ˌɪnsaɪd ˈaʊt]	etw in- und auswendig kennen

to **stand out** [ˌstænd 'aʊt]	auffallen, herausstechen
research [rɪ'sɜːtʃ]	Recherche, Nachforschungen, Untersuchungen
to **colour** ['kʌlə]	färben
hair care ['heəkeə]	Haarpflege
secret ['siːkrɪt]	heimlich, geheim
fascinating ['fæsɪneɪtɪŋ]	faszinierend
caller ['kɔːlə]	Anrufer/in
line [laɪn]	Leitung
to **legalize** ['liːgəlaɪz]	legalisieren
lying ['laɪɪŋ]	Lügen
seriously ['sɪəriəsli]	im Ernst
to **cook a meal** [ˌkʊk ə 'miːl]	eine Mahlzeit zubereiten, ein Essen kochen
to **paint** [peɪnt]	malen
trash [træʃ]	Müll
beetle ['biːtl]	Käfer
bare [beə]	kahl, nackt
college ['kɒlɪdʒ]	Fachhochschule
promotion [prə'məʊʃn]	Werbung
broke [brəʊk]	kaputt
niche [nɪtʃ]	Nische
targeted ['tɑːgɪtɪd]	gezielt
blanket ['blæŋkɪt]	pauschal, umfassend
to **be designed to do sth** [bi dɪ'zaɪnd tə]	dazu gedacht sein, etw zu tun; darauf ausgelegt sein, etw zu tun
maximum ['mæksɪməm]	maximal, Höchst-
to **be supposed to do sth** [bi sə'pəʊzd tə]	etw tun sollen
to **ship** [ʃɪp]	verschicken
to **bottle** ['bɒtl]	in Flaschen abfüllen
vending machine ['vendɪŋ məʃiːn]	(Verkaufs-)Automat
to **donate** [dəʊ'neɪt]	spenden
vacation *AE* [və'keɪʃn]	Urlaub
to **join** [dʒɔɪn]	mitmachen, *(Radio etc.:)* in einer Sendung sein, *(Telefon:)* (mit jdm) sprechen
washing powder ['wɒʃɪŋ paʊdə]	Waschpulver
sales *pl* [seɪlz]	Verkauf, Verkäufe, Absatz, Vertrieb
factor ['fæktə]	Faktor
life-cycle ['laɪf saɪkl]	Lebensdauer, Lebenszyklus
maximum ['mæksɪməm]	Höchstwert
car wash ['kɑː wɒʃ]	Autowaschanlage
hairdressing salon ['heədresɪŋ sælɒn]	Friseursalon
electrician [ɪˌlek'trɪʃn]	Elektriker/in
perfume ['pɜːfjuːm]	Parfüm
sports car ['spɔːts kɑː]	Sportwagen

page 50

to **intend** [ɪn'tend]	beabsichtigen
arrangement [ə'reɪndʒmənt]	Abmachung, Vereinbarung, Vorbereitung, Regelung
salesman ['seɪlzmən]	Verkäufer, Vertreter
deal [diːl]	Geschäft, Abschluss
profit ['prɒfɪt]	Gewinn, Profit
Head Office [ˌhed 'ɒfɪs]	Zentrale, Direktion, Hauptverwaltung
Human Resources (HR) [ˌhjuːmən rɪ'sɔːsɪz]	Personal(abteilung)
luck [lʌk]	Glück
Good luck! [ˌgʊd 'lʌk]	Viel Glück!
limited ['lɪmɪtɪd]	begrenzt, beschränkt
publisher ['pʌblɪʃə]	Verleger/in
straight [streɪt]	direkt, gleich
to **phone in** [ˌfəʊn 'ɪn]	(in einer Sendung) anrufen
to **get bored** [ˌget 'bɔːd]	sich langweilen
to **launch** [lɔːntʃ]	*(Produkt)* auf den Markt bringen, einführen

page 51

commercial [kə'mɜːʃl]	(Werbe-)Spot
to **pick sth out** [ˌpɪk 'aʊt]	etw heraussuchen
to **read sth closely** [ˌriːd 'kləʊsli]	etw genau (durch)lesen
capital letter [ˌkæpɪtl 'letə]	Großbuchstabe
to **come across sth** [ˌkʌm ə'krɒs]	auf etw stoßen
visionary ['vɪʒənri]	Visionär/in
genius ['dʒiːniəs]	Genie
to **brand a product** [ˌbrænd ə 'prɒdʌkt]	ein Markenprodukt schaffen
household name ['haʊshəʊld neɪm]	bekannter Name, Begriff
sunny ['sʌni]	sonnig
threatening ['θretnɪŋ]	bedrohlich
scary ['skeəri]	unheimlich, beängstigend
to **come up with sth** [ˌkʌm 'ʌp wɪð]	sich etw ausdenken, sich etw einfallen lassen
likeable ['laɪkəbl]	sympathisch
to **be about to do sth** [bi ə'baʊt tə]	im Begriff sein, etw zu tun; gerade dabei sein, etw zu tun
to **target sb** ['tɑːgɪt]	jdn ins Visier nehmen, auf jdn abzielen
strategy ['strætədʒi]	Strategie
high-end [ˌhaɪ 'end]	hochklassig, hochwertig
everyday ['evrideɪ]	alltäglich, Alltags-
constant ['kɒnstənt]	ständig, andauernd
to **discover** [dɪ'skʌvə]	entdecken
function ['fʌŋkʃn]	Funktion
powerful ['paʊəfl]	stark, mächtig, kräftig
manual ['mænjuəl]	Bedienungsanleitung
jargon ['dʒɑːgən]	Fachsprache, Jargon
entrepreneur [ˌɒntrəprə'nɜː]	Unternehmer/in
accessible [ək'sesəbl]	zugänglich, erreichbar, offen
to **feel sth** [fiːl]	etw anfassen, etw ertasten
mouse [maʊs]	Maus
to **survive** [sə'vaɪv]	überleben
to **rebuild** [ˌriː'bɪld]	umbauen, erneuern
series ['sɪəriːz]	Reihe, Serie

page 52

to **continue to do sth** [kən'tɪnjuː tə]	etw weiterhin tun
graph [grɑːf]	Diagramm, Kurve
chart [tʃɑːt]	Diagramm, Tabelle
bar chart ['bɑː tʃɑːt]	Säulendiagramm
figure ['fɪgə]	Zahl, Ziffer
statistics [stə'tɪstɪks]	Statistik(en)
visual ['vɪʒuəl]	visuell
change [tʃeɪndʒ]	Veränderung
spending ['spendɪŋ]	Ausgaben, Aufwendungen
billion ['bɪliən]	Milliarde
percent [pə'sent]	Prozent
note [nəʊt]	Hinweis
directory [də'rektəri]	Telefonbuch
source [sɔːs]	Quelle

page 53

axis ['æksɪs]	Achse
line chart ['laɪn tʃɑːt]	Liniendiagramm
upwards ['ʌpwədz]	steigend

downwards ['daʊnwədz]	fallend
percentage [pə'sentɪdʒ]	Prozentsatz, Anteil
point [pɔɪnt]	Komma
target group ['tɑːgɪt gruːp]	Zielgruppe
branded goods *pl* [ˌbrændɪd 'gʊdz]	Markenware, Markenartikel
writer ['raɪtə]	Autor/in, Schriftsteller/in

page 54

beacon ['biːkn]	Funkfeuer, Beacon
interactive [ˌɪntər'æktɪv]	interaktiv
radio transmitter ['reɪdiəʊ trænsmɪtə]	Sender, Funksender
to **employ** [ɪm'plɔɪ]	verwenden, einsetzen
specification [ˌspesɪfɪ'keɪʃn]	Spezifikation, Vorgabe, Richtlinie
range [reɪndʒ]	Reichweite
means [miːnz]	Mittel
proximity [prɒk'sɪməti]	(räumliche) Nähe
typically ['tɪpɪkli]	üblicherweise, normalerweise
special deal [ˌspeʃl 'diːl]	Sonderangebot
coupon ['kuːpɒn]	Gutschein
purchase ['pɜːtʃəs]	Kauf
to **ignore** [ɪg'nɔː]	nicht beachten, ignorieren
notification [ˌnəʊtɪfɪ'keɪʃn]	Benachrichtigung
additional [ə'dɪʃənl]	zusätzlich
customized ['kʌstəmaɪzd]	auf den Kundenbedarf zugeschnitten
owner ['əʊnə]	Besitzer/in
location [ləʊ'keɪʃn]	Lage, Standort, Ort
within [wɪ'ðɪn]	innerhalb, binnen
radio signal ['reɪdiəʊ sɪgnəl]	Funksignal
cloud [klaʊd]	Wolke, Cloud
relevant ['reləvənt]	relevant, passend
to **pioneer sth** [ˌpaɪə'nɪə]	bei etw Pionierarbeit leisten
to **combine** [kəm'baɪn]	kombinieren, verbinden, vereinen
contactless ['kɒntæktləs]	drahtlos
payment ['peɪmənt]	Zahlung, Bezahlung
automated ['ɔːtəmeɪtɪd]	automatisch
checkout ['tʃekaʊt]	Kasse
Near Field Communication [ˌnɪə fiːld kəˌmjuːnɪ'keɪʃn]	Nahfeldkommunikation
sales assistant ['seɪlz əsɪstənt]	Verkäufer/in
cashier [kæ'ʃɪə]	Kassierer/in
to **brainstorm** ['breɪnstɔːm]	Ideen sammeln
feature ['fiːtʃə]	Merkmal, Eigenschaft
to **design** [dɪ'zaɪn]	entwerfen, planen
explanation [ˌeksplə'neɪʃn]	Erläuterung, Erklärung
design [dɪ'zaɪn]	Entwurf, Plan

UNIT 7

page 55

beyond [bɪ'jɒnd]	darüber hinaus
Hinduism ['hɪnduːɪzəm]	Hinduismus
Catholicism [kə'θɒləsɪzəm]	Katholizismus, der katholische Glaube
Judaism ['dʒuːdeɪɪzəm]	Judaismus, Judentum
extended [ɪk'stendɪd]	erweitert
extended family [ɪkˌstendɪd 'fæməli]	Großfamilie
immediate [ɪ'miːdiət]	unmittelbar
peer group ['pɪə gruːp]	Altersgruppe, Bezugsgruppe, Umfeld
role model ['rəʊl mɒdl]	Vorbild
chore [tʃɔː]	(lästige Routine-)Aufgabe

page 56

safely ['seɪfli]	mit Gewissheit
twin [twɪn]	Zwilling
to **spoil** [spɔɪl]	*(Kind)* verwöhnen
to **turn to sb** ['tɜːn tə]	sich an jdn wenden
day-to-day [ˌdeɪ tə 'deɪ]	tagtäglich
chat [tʃæt]	Unterhaltung, Schwätzchen
to **go under** [ˌgəʊ 'ʌndə]	Pleite gehen
financial [faɪ'nænʃl]	finanziell, Finanz-
to **get sb through** [ˌget 'θruː]	jdn durchbringen; jdm helfen, etw zu überstehen
these days [ðiːz 'deɪz]	zur Zeit
freedom ['friːdəm]	Freiheit
root [ruːt]	Wurzel
what's more [wɒts 'mɔː]	zudem
to **set an example** [ˌset ən ɪg'zɑːmpl]	ein Beispiel setzen, mit gutem Beispiel vorangehen
to **have a hard time** [həv ə ˌhɑːd 'taɪm]	es schwer haben
to **be caught** [bi 'kɔːt]	festsitzen, in der Klemme sitzen

page 57

to **gossip** ['gɒsɪp]	tratschen, schwatzen
to **borrow sth** ['bɒrəʊ]	sich etw ausleihen
noisy ['nɔɪzi]	laut, lärmend
nuclear ['njuːkliə]	Kern-
various ['veəriəs]	verschieden, mehrere, allerlei
to **be involved in sth** [bi ɪn'vɒlvd ɪn]	sich an etw beteiligen, bei etw mitmachen
drama ['drɑːmə]	Schauspiel
whatever [wɒt'evə]	was auch immer
at the end of the day [ət ði end əv ðə 'deɪ]	letzten Endes, unterm Strich
cheerful ['tʃɪəfl]	fröhlich
tea *BE* [tiː]	*Zwischenmahlzeit am Nachmittag, Abendessen*
to **be a pain (in the neck)** [bi ə 'peɪn]	jdm auf die Nerven gehen
to **mind one's own business** [ˌmaɪnd wʌnz əʊn 'bɪznəs]	sich um seinen eigenen Kram kümmern
tension ['tenʃn]	Spannung
laugh [lɑːf]	Lachen, Gelächter
hill [hɪl]	Berg, Anhöhe, Hügel
grass [grɑːs]	Rasen, Gras
independent [ˌɪndɪ'pendənt]	unabhängig
unnecessary [ʌn'nesəsəri]	überflüssig, unnötig
abbreviation [əˌbriːvi'eɪʃn]	Abkürzung
needs *pl* [niːdz]	Bedürfnisse, Bedarf

page 58

lifestyle ['laɪfstaɪl]	Lebensweise, Lebensführung
to **tidy up** [ˌtaɪdi 'ʌp]	aufräumen
housework ['haʊswɜːk]	Hausarbeit
to **do (the/some) ironing** [duː 'aɪənɪŋ]	bügeln
paperwork ['peɪpəwɜːk]	Büroarbeit, Schreibarbeit
feature ['fiːtʃə]	Hintergrundbericht, Reportage
talent ['tælənt]	Begabung, Talent

page 59

drama club ['drɑːmə klʌb]	Schauspiel-AG
to **feel embarrassed** [ˌfiːl ɪm'bærəst]	sich genieren, sich schämen

to **raise sth** [reɪz]	etw *(Thema etc.)* ansprechen
to **respond (to sth)** [rɪ'spɒnd]	(auf etw) reagieren, (auf etw) antworten
sympathetic(ally) [ˌsɪmpə'θetɪk]	einfühlsam
to **point sth out** [ˌpɔɪnt 'aʊt]	auf etw hinweisen
informal [ɪn'fɔːml]	informell, locker
contracted [kən'træktɪd]	zusammengezogen
shy [ʃaɪ]	schüchtern
saying ['seɪɪŋ]	Sprichwort, Redensart

page 60

grade *AE* [greɪd]	Note
grade A student [ˌgreɪd 'eɪ stjuːdnt]	Einserschüler/in
ridiculous(ly) [rɪ'dɪkjələs]	lächerlich, unglaublich
to **make it** ['meɪk ɪt]	es schaffen
to **start on sb** [stɑːt]	jdn angreifen, jdn kritisieren
to **hoover** ['huːvə]	staubsaugen
load [ləʊd]	Ladung
washing ['wɒʃɪŋ]	Wäsche
plus [plʌs]	außerdem
nosey ['nəʊzi]	(auf unangenehme Weise) neugierig
receipt [rɪ'siːt]	Quittung
by the way [baɪ ðə 'weɪ]	übrigens, nebenbei erwähnt
part-time [ˌpɑːt'taɪm]	Teilzeit-
to **ban sb from doing sth** ['bæn frəm]	jdm verbieten, etw zu tun
to **feel left out** [fiːl ˌleft 'aʊt]	sich ausgeschlossen fühlen
to **turn into sth** ['tɜːn ɪntə]	zu etw werden
to **take sth** [teɪk]	etw ertragen
to **drive sb away** [ˌdraɪv ə'weɪ]	jdn vertreiben
to cut a long story short [tə kʌt ə lɒŋ ˌstɔːri 'ʃɔːt]	lange Rede, kurzer Sinn
benefits *pl* ['benɪfɪts]	Sozialleistungen
Department for Work and Pensions [dɪˌpɑːtmənt fə ˌwɜːk ən 'penʃnz]	*brit. Arbeits- und Sozialministerium*
to **manage** ['mænɪdʒ]	verwalten, regeln
welfare ['welfeə]	Sozialfürsorge, Sozialhilfe
benefits office ['benɪfɪts ɒfɪs]	Sozialamt
to **drop** [drɒp]	fallen, *(Noten:)* schlechter werden
properly ['prɒpəli]	richtig, ordentlich, korrekt
in order to [ɪn 'ɔːdə tə]	um … zu
to **find sb sth** [faɪnd]	jdm etw besorgen
brief(ly) [briːf]	kurz, knapp
grade *AE* [greɪd]	Note

page 61

idiomatic [ˌɪdiə'mætɪk]	idiomatisch, redensartlich
weekday ['wiːkdeɪ]	Werktag, Wochentag
suitable ['suːtəbl]	passend
as necessary [əz 'nesəsəri]	nötigenfalls
to **get on** [ˌget 'ɒn]	vorwärtskommen, zurechtkommen
to **get over sth** [ˌget 'əʊvə]	über etw hinwegkommen, etw verkraften
tiny ['taɪni]	winzig
stage [steɪdʒ]	Phase, Abschnitt
move [muːv]	Schritt, Umzug

page 62

mind [maɪnd]	Gedanken
to **go from bad to worse** [gəʊ frəm ˌbæd tə 'wɜːs]	immer schlimmer werden
ahead [ə'hed]	voraus, vorausliegend
to **step off** [ˌstep 'ɒf]	aussteigen
to **blow** [bləʊ]	wehen, blasen
steadily ['stedɪli]	ununterbrochen
to **pull sth tight** [ˌpʊl 'taɪt]	etw straff ziehen
lane [leɪn]	Weg, Gasse
towards sth [tə'wɔːdz]	zu etw hin, auf etw zu
to **return to sth** [rɪ'tɜːn tə]	sich wieder einer Sache zuwenden
youth [juːθ]	Jugend
to **fall behind** [ˌfɔːl bɪ'haɪnd]	zurückfallen, in Rückstand geraten
false start [ˌfɔːls 'stɑːt]	Fehlstart
respect [rɪ'spekt]	Achtung, Respekt
experienced [ɪk'spɪəriənst]	erfahren
efficient(ly) [ɪ'fɪʃnt]	effizient
first of all [ˌfɜːst əv 'ɔːl]	zuallererst
I suppose [aɪ sə'pəʊz]	wohl
shared house [ˌʃeəd 'haʊs]	Wohngemeinschaft
to **check sth out** [ˌtʃek 'aʊt]	sich etw ansehen
comfortable ['kʌmftəbl]	angenehm
to **get sth wrong** [ˌget 'rɒŋ]	bei etw einen Fehler machen, etw falsch machen
monthly ['mʌnθli]	monatlich
budget ['bʌdʒɪt]	Etat, Haushalt, Budget
heating ['hiːtɪŋ]	Heizung
bill [bɪl]	Rechnung
on time [ɒn 'taɪm]	pünktlich
credit rating ['kredɪt reɪtɪŋ]	(Bewertung/Einstufung der) Bonität, Kreditwürdigkeit
disaster [dɪ'zɑːstə]	Katastrophe
to **lend sb sth** [lend]	jdm etw leihen
it doesn't matter [ɪt dʌznt 'mætə]	es ist egal
by oneself [baɪ wʌn'self]	allein
strong advice [ˌstrɒŋ əd'vaɪs]	dringender Rat
washing up [ˌwɒʃɪŋ 'ʌp]	Geschirrspülen
and so on [ənd 'səʊ ɒn]	und so weiter
(French) fries *pl AE* [fraɪz]	Pommes frites
to **go wrong** [ˌgəʊ 'rɒŋ]	schieflaufen
to **get angry** [ˌget 'æŋgri]	sich ärgern
to **get upset** [ˌget ʌp'set]	sich aufregen
thought [θɔːt]	Gedanke
boomerang ['buːməræŋ]	Bumerang
to **rescue** ['reskjuː]	retten, bergen

page 63

usefulness ['juːsfəlnəs]	Nutzen, Zweckmäßigkeit
to **sniff sth** [snɪf]	an etw riechen
duvet cover ['duːveɪ kʌvə]	Bettdeckenbezug
raw [rɔː]	roh
chips *pl BE* [tʃɪps]	Pommes frites
nutrient ['njuːtriənt]	Nährstoff
to **be up to sth** [bi 'ʌp tə]	etw vorhaben
on a need-to-know basis [ɒn ə ˌniːd tə 'nəʊ beɪsɪs]	im (unumgänglichen) Bedarfsfall
alive [ə'laɪv]	lebendig, am Leben
sink [sɪŋk]	Spüle

page 64

robot ['rəʊbɒt]	Roboter
lawn mower ['lɔːn məʊə]	Rasenmäher
common ['kɒmən]	verbreitet, üblich
domestic [də'mestɪk]	Heim-
a varied bunch [ə ˌveərid 'bʌntʃ]	eine bunte Truppe

to **water** ['wɔːtə]	*(Pflanze)* gießen
to **feed** [fiːd]	füttern
pet [pet]	Haustier
to **hide** [haɪd]	sich verstecken, sich verbergen
mobile ['məʊbaɪl]	mobil
appliance [ə'plaɪəns]	Haushaltsgerät
to **perform sth** [pə'fɔːm]	etw ausführen, etw durchführen
multiple ['mʌltɪpl]	mehrere, vielfache
wheel [wiːl]	Rad
track [træk]	Schiene
manipulator arm [mə'nɪpjuleɪtər ɑːm]	Greifarm
to **handle sth** ['hændl]	mit etw umgehen, mit etw hantieren
general-purpose [ˌdʒenrəl 'pɜːpəs]	Allzweck-
programmable ['prəʊgræməbl]	programmierbar
platform ['plætfɔːm]	Plattform
continually [kən'tɪnjuəli]	kontinuierlich
to **acquire** [ə'kwaɪə]	erwerben
capability [ˌkeɪpə'bɪləti]	Fähigkeit
equipped with [ɪ'kwɪpt wɪð]	ausgestattet mit
attachment point [ə'tætʃmənt pɔɪnt]	Befestigungspunkt
accessories *pl* [ək'sesəriz]	Zubehör
standard ['stændəd]	genormt
interface ['ɪntəfeɪs]	Verbindung, Schnittstelle
third-party [ˌθɜːd 'pɑːti]	von Drittanbietern, fremd
to **install** [ɪn'stɔːl]	installieren
scenario [sə'nɑːriəʊ]	Szenario
roboticist [rəʊ'bɒtɪsɪst]	Robotiker/in, Roboter-ingenieur/in
in sight [ɪn 'saɪt]	in Sicht(weite), im Blick
pure [pjʊə]	rein
combination [ˌkɒmbɪ'neɪʃn]	Kombination, Vereinigung
chief executive (officer) [ˌtʃiːf ɪg'zekjətɪv ɒfɪsə]	Vorstandsvorsitzende/r
cofounder ['kəʊfaʊndə]	Mitbegründer/in
file [faɪl]	Datei
printer ['prɪntə]	Drucker
to **come to mind** [ˌkʌm tə 'maɪnd]	in den Sinn kommen, einfallen
to **fetch** [fetʃ]	holen
fridge [frɪdʒ]	Kühlschrank
to **operate sth** ['ɒpəreɪt]	etw bedienen
microwave ['maɪkrəweɪv]	Mikrowelle
to **clear the table** [ˌklɪə ðə 'teɪbl]	den Tisch abräumen
to **load the dishwasher** [ˌləʊd ðə 'dɪʃwɒʃə]	die Spülmaschine einräumen
to **unload the dishwasher** [ʌnˌləʊd ðə 'dɪʃwɒʃə]	die Spülmaschine ausräumen
to **pick sth up** [ˌpɪk 'ʌp]	etw aufheben
toy [tɔɪ]	Spielzeug
to **do laundry** [duː 'lɔːndri]	Wäsche waschen
original [ə'rɪdʒənl]	originell

UNIT 8

page 65

realistic [ˌriːə'lɪstɪk]	realistisch
doer ['duə]	Macher/in
investigative [ɪn'vestɪgətɪv]	erforschend, Untersuchungs-
thinker ['θɪŋkə]	Denker/in
organizer ['ɔːgənaɪzə]	Organisator/in
artistic [ɑː'tɪstɪk]	künstlerisch
creator [kri'eɪtə]	Schöpfer/in
enterprising ['entəpraɪzɪŋ]	geschäftstüchtig, risikofreudig
persuader [pə'sweɪdə]	*jd, der andere überzeugt und mitreißt*
helper ['helpə]	Helfer/in
mechanical [mɪ'kænɪkl]	mechanisch
mechanic [mɪ'kænɪk]	Mechaniker/in
carpenter ['kɑːpəntə]	Zimmerer/in, Schreiner/in
engineer [ˌendʒɪ'nɪə]	Ingenieur/in
police officer [pə'liːs ɒfɪsə]	Polizist/in
to **observe** [əb'zɜːv]	beobachten
to **investigate** [ɪn'vestɪgeɪt]	ermitteln, untersuchen
to **evaluate** [ɪ'væljueɪt]	bewerten, beurteilen
to **solve** [sɒlv]	lösen
psychologist [saɪ'kɒlədʒɪst]	Psychologe/-in
management consultant [ˌmænɪdʒmənt kən'sʌltənt]	Unternehmensberater/in
programmer ['prəʊgræmə]	Programmierer/in
clerical ['klerɪkl]	Büro-
numerical [njuː'merɪkl]	Zahl-, zahlenmäßig
instruction [ɪn'strʌkʃn]	Anweisung
accountant [ə'kaʊntənt]	Buchhalter/in
administrator [əd'mɪnɪstreɪtə]	Verwalter/in
intuitional [ˌɪntju'ɪʃnəl]	intuitiv
unstructured [ʌn'strʌktʃəd]	unstrukturiert
imagination [ɪˌmædʒɪ'neɪʃn]	Phantasie, Vorstellungskraft
creativity [ˌkriːeɪ'tɪvəti]	schöpferische Begabung, Kreativität
journalist ['dʒɜːnəlɪst]	Journalist/in
architect ['ɑːkɪtekt]	Architekt/in
designer [dɪ'zaɪnə]	Gestalter/in, Designer/in, Konstrukteur/in
dancer ['dɑːnsə]	Tänzer/in
organizational [ˌɔːgənaɪ'zeɪʃənl]	organisatorisch
economic [ˌiːkə'nɒmɪk]	wirtschaftlich
gain [geɪn]	Gewinn, Vorteil
politician [ˌpɒlə'tɪʃn]	Politiker/in
to **enlighten** [ɪn'laɪtn]	aufklären
caring ['keərɪŋ]	fürsorglich
to **be skilled with sth** [bi 'skɪld wɪð]	mit etw gut umgehen können
social worker ['səʊʃl wɜːkə]	Sozialarbeiter/in
nurse [nɜːs]	Krankenpfleger/-schwester
priest [priːst]	Priester/in, Geistliche/r
company car ['kʌmpəni kɑː]	Firmenwagen
flexible ['fleksəbl]	flexibel
working hours *pl* [ˌwɜːkɪŋ 'aʊəz]	Arbeitszeiten
pay [peɪ]	Bezahlung, Lohn
promotion [prə'məʊʃn]	Beförderung, (beruflicher) Aufstieg
promotion prospects *pl* [prə'məʊʃn prɒspekts]	Aufstiegschancen
working conditions *pl* [ˌwɜːkɪŋ kən'dɪʃnz]	Arbeitsbedingungen
job security [ˌdʒɒb sɪ'kjʊərəti]	sicherer Arbeitsplatz
insurance [ɪn'ʃʊərəns]	Versicherung
medical insurance [ˌmedɪkl ɪn'ʃʊərəns]	Krankenversicherung
category ['kætəgəri]	Kategorie
involved [ɪn'vɒlvd]	dazugehörig
to **involve** [ɪn'vɒlv]	mit sich bringen, umfassen

to **design** [dɪ'zaɪn]	konstruieren, planen
construction worker [kən'strʌkʃn wɜːkə]	Bauarbeiter/in
ideal [aɪ'diːəl]	ideal
baker ['beɪkə]	Bäcker/in
satisfying ['sætɪsfaɪɪŋ]	befriedigend
rewarding [rɪ'wɔːdɪŋ]	lohnend, erfüllend

page 66

job advertisement [ˌdʒɒb əd'vɜːtɪsmənt]	Stellenanzeige, -ausschreibung
work experience ['wɜːk ɪkspɪəriəns]	Praktikum
temporary ['temprəri]	vorübergehend, befristet
recruitment [rɪ'kruːtmənt]	Personalbeschaffung
job title ['dʒɒb taɪtl]	Stellenbezeichnung
full-time [ˌfʊl 'taɪm]	Vollzeit-
requirement [rɪ'kwaɪəmənt]	Voraussetzung, Bedingung, Anforderung
board and lodging [ˌbɔːd ənd 'lɒdʒɪŋ]	Kost und Logis
return airfare [rɪˌtɜːn 'eəfeə]	Kosten für Hin- und Rückflug
maximum (max.) ['mæksɪməm]	höchstens, maximal
to **apply (for a job)** [ə'plaɪ]	sich (um/auf eine Stelle) bewerben
to **email sb** ['iːmeɪl]	jdm eine E-Mail schicken
CV (curriculum vitae) [ˌsiː 'viː, kəˌrɪkjələm 'viːtaɪ]	Lebenslauf
cover letter ['kʌvə letə]	Anschreiben, Begleitschreiben
internship ['ɪntɜːnʃɪp]	Praktikum
charity ['tʃærəti]	Wohltätigkeitsorganisation
to **set sth up** [ˌset 'ʌp]	etw einrichten
community [kə'mjuːnəti]	Gemeinde, Gemeinschaft
to **staff** [stɑːf]	(mit Personal) besetzen
highly motivated [ˌhaɪli 'məʊtɪveɪtɪd]	hochmotiviert
intern ['ɪntɜːn]	Praktikant/in
to **volunteer to do sth** [ˌvɒlən'tɪə tə]	sich bereit erklären, etw zu tun
management ['mænɪdʒmənt]	Führung, Management
administration [ədˌmɪnɪ'streɪʃn]	Verwaltung
fully ['fʊli]	vollständig
fully equipped [ˌfʊli ɪ'kwɪpt]	vollausgestattet
location [ləʊ'keɪʃn]	Standort, Ort
to **insure** [ɪn'ʃʊə]	versichern
accommodation [əˌkɒmə'deɪʃn]	Unterkunft
homestay accommodation ['həʊmsteɪ əkɒmədeɪʃn]	Unterbringung bei Gasteltern
travel expenses *pl* ['trævl ɪkspensɪz]	Reisekosten, Fahrtkosten
registered ['redʒɪstəd]	eintragen, (staatlich) anerkannt
post [pəʊst]	Stelle, Posten
to **advertise a job** [ˌædvətaɪz ə 'dʒɒb]	eine Stelle ausschreiben
technician [tek'nɪʃn]	Techniker/in
allowance [ə'laʊəns]	Aufwandsentschädigung
asap (as soon as possible) [ˌeɪ es eɪ 'piː]	baldmöglichst
duration [dju'reɪʃn]	Dauer
to **be responsible for sth** [bi rɪ'spɒnsəbl fə]	für etw zuständig/verantwortlich sein
set [set]	Kulisse
lighting ['laɪtɪŋ]	Beleuchtung, Licht
prop [prɒp]	Requisite
maintenance ['meɪntənəns]	Wartung, Instandhaltung
equipment [ɪ'kwɪpmənt]	Ausrüstung, Geräte
candidate ['kændɪdət]	Bewerber/in
electrical [ɪ'lektrɪkl]	elektrisch, Elektro-
DIY (do-it-yourself) [ˌdiː aɪ 'waɪ]	Heimwerker-, Heimwerken
shift [ʃɪft]	Schicht
equal opportunities *pl* [ˌiːkwəl ɒpə'tjuːnətiz]	Chancengleichheit
employer [ɪm'plɔɪə]	Arbeitgeber/in

page 67

equivalent [ɪ'kwɪvələnt]	Entsprechung
to **administer** [əd'mɪnɪstə]	verwalten
to **accommodate** [ə'kɒmədeɪt]	unterbringen
to **maintain** [meɪn'teɪn]	warten, instand halten
equality [ɪ'kwɒləti]	Gleichheit
volunteer [ˌvɒlən'tɪə]	(freiwilliger) Helfer/in
voluntary ['vɒləntri]	freiwillig
administrative [əd'mɪnɪstrətɪv]	Verwaltungs-
technological [ˌteknə'lɒdʒɪkl]	technologisch
terms *pl* [tɜːmz]	Bedingungen, Konditionen
owner ['əʊnə]	Besitzer/in
medical ['medɪkl]	medizinisch
secretary ['sekrətri]	Sekretär/in
bank clerk ['bæŋk klɑːk]	Bankangestellte/r
elsewhere [ˌels'weə]	woanders, anderswo
to **supply** [sə'plaɪ]	liefern, bieten
sustainable [sə'steɪnəbl]	nachhaltig
treatment ['triːtmənt]	Behandlung

page 68

qualification [ˌkwɒlɪfɪ'keɪʃn]	Abschluss, Qualifikation
typing ['taɪpɪŋ]	Schreibmaschinenschreiben
standard ['stændəd]	Niveau
surgery ['sɜːdʒəri]	(Arzt-)Praxis
pleasant ['pleznt]	angenehm
as regards … [əz rɪ'gɑːdz]	was … betrifft
band [bænd]	Gehaltsstufe, Gehaltsklasse
pay scale ['peɪ skeɪl]	Lohntarif, Lohntabelle
secure [sɪ'kjuə]	sicher
shortage ['ʃɔːtɪdʒ]	Mangel
staff [stɑːf]	Personal, Belegschaft, Mitarbeiter/innen
satisfaction [ˌsætɪs'fækʃn]	Zufriedenheit
profession [prə'feʃn]	Beruf
caring profession ['keərɪŋ prəfeʃn]	Pflegeberuf
maths [mæθs]	Mathe(matik) *(Schulfach)*
trainee [treɪ'niː]	Auszubildende/r
cashier [kæ'ʃɪə]	Kassierer/in
to **cash a cheque** [ˌkæʃ ə 'tʃek]	einen Scheck einlösen
payment ['peɪmənt]	Zahlung
microwave ['maɪkrəweɪv]	Mikrowelle
entry level pay [ˌentri levl 'peɪ]	Einstiegsgehalt, Anfangsgehalt
customer services advisor [ˌkʌstəmə 'sɜːvɪsɪz ədvaɪzə]	Kundenberater/in

apprenticeship [ə'prentɪʃɪp]	Ausbildung, Lehre
qualified ['kwɒlɪfaɪd]	mit Abschluss, qualifiziert
crisis ['kraɪsɪs]	Krise
careers advisor [kə'rɪəz ədvaɪzə]	Berufsberater/in
entry level ['entri levl]	Einstieg, Anfang
a word of warning [ə ˌwɜːd əv 'wɔːnɪŋ]	Hinweis, Warnung
ambitious [æm'bɪʃəs]	ehrgeizig
plate [pleɪt]	Teller
to **offer sb sth on a plate** [ˌɒfər ɒn ə 'pleɪt]	jdm etw auf dem Silbertablett servieren
yearly ['jɪəli]	jährlich, Jahres-
income ['ɪnkʌm]	Einkommen
irregular [ɪ'regjələ]	unregelmäßig
salesperson ['seɪlzpɜːsn]	Vertreter/in, Verkäufer/in
to **work hard** [ˌwɜːk 'hɑːd]	hart arbeiten, fleißig sein
page 69	
workplace ['wɜːkpleɪs]	Arbeitsplatz
to **mind sth** [maɪnd]	auf etw achten
to **grab sth** [græb]	sich etw schnappen
wheely ['wiːli]	auf Rollen
filing cabinet ['faɪlɪŋ kæbɪnət]	Aktenschrank
to **make for sth** ['meɪk fə]	sich auf den Weg nach etw machen
to **be on the increase** [bi ɒn ði 'ɪŋkriːs]	auf dem Vormarsch sein, zunehmen
driving force [ˌdraɪvɪŋ 'fɔːs]	treibende Kraft
ever-improving [ˌevər ɪm'pruːvɪŋ]	stetig besser werdend
electronics *pl* [ˌɪlek'trɒnɪks]	Elektronik
employee [ɪm'plɔɪiː]	Angestellte/r, Beschäftigte/r
workforce ['wɜːkfɔːs]	Belegschaft
increase ['ɪŋkriːs]	Zunahme, Steigerung
to **cause sb to do sth** [kɔːz]	jdn dazu veranlassen, etw zu tun
to **rethink** ['riːθɪŋk]	überdenken
corporate ['kɔːpərət]	Unternehmens-, von Unternehmen
infrastructure ['ɪnfrəstrʌktʃə]	Infrastruktur
manufacturing [ˌmænju'fæktʃərɪŋ]	Fertigung
to **require** [rɪ'kwaɪə]	erfordern, benötigen
mobile ['məʊbaɪl]	mobil
pad [pæd]	(Notiz-)Block; Bude
minimum ['mɪnɪməm]	Mindestmaß, -menge, Minimum
by default [baɪ dɪ'fɔːlt]	automatisch
therefore ['ðeəfɔː]	daher, deshalb, demzufolge
meeting room ['miːtɪŋ ruːm]	Sitzungsraum, Besprechungsraum
to **plug in(to)** [ˌplʌg 'ɪn]	anschließen, einstecken
to **counteract sth** [ˌkaʊntər'ækt]	einer Sache entgegenwirken
loneliness ['ləʊnlinəs]	Einsamkeit
homing ['həʊmɪŋ]	Heimfindeverhalten *(z. B. von Brieftauben)*
instinct ['ɪnstɪŋkt]	Instinkt
to **acknowledge** [ək'nɒlɪdʒ]	anerkennen, zugeben
allotted [ə'lɒtɪd]	zugewiesen
car park ['kɑː pɑːk]	Parkplatz, -haus, -garage
to **tend to do sth** ['tend tə]	dazu neigen, etw zu tun
spot [spɒt]	Platz, Ort, Fleck, Punkt
gradual ['grædʒuəl]	schrittweise, allmählich

development [dɪ'veləpmənt]	
to **address** [ə'dres]	
concern [kən'sɜːn]	
wide-ranging ['waɪd reɪndʒɪŋ]	
cultural ['kʌltʃərəl]	
practice ['præktɪs]	Praxis, Ausübung, Verfahren, Ablauf, Praktik
informality [ˌɪnfɔː'mæləti]	Formlosigkeit, Ungezwungenheit
norm [nɔːm]	Norm
senior ['siːniə]	leitend
department [dɪ'pɑːtmənt]	Abteilung
legal department [ˌliːgl dɪ'pɑːtmənt]	juristische Abteilung
finance ['faɪnæns]	Finanz(-)
majority [mə'dʒɒrəti]	Mehrheit
to **be territorial** [bi ˌterə'tɔːriəl]	sein Revier verteidigen
open-plan office [ˌəʊpən plæn 'ɒfɪs]	Großraumbüro
to **personalise** ['pɜːsnəlaɪz]	individuell gestalten
barrier ['bæriə]	Hürde
to **cross** [krɒs]	überqueren, überwinden
to **judge** [dʒʌdʒ]	beurteilen
in time [ɪn 'taɪm]	rechtzeitig
page 70	
to **drop in** [ˌdrɒp 'ɪn]	vorbeikommen, hereinschauen
to **gravitate to sth** ['grævɪteɪt tə]	von etw angezogen werden
continuity [ˌkɒntɪn'juːəti]	Kontinuität, Fortdauer
belonging [bɪ'lɒŋɪŋ]	Zugehörigkeit
to **shake sth off** [ˌʃeɪk 'ɒf]	etw abschütteln
totally ['təʊtəli]	voll und ganz
suit [suːt]	Anzug
tie [taɪ]	Krawatte
to **dress down** [ˌdres 'daʊn]	sich leger kleiden
sector ['sektə]	Sektor, Bereich
global(ly) ['gləʊbl]	weltweit, global
to **downsize** ['daʊnsaɪz]	verkleinern, gesundschrumpfen
prestigious [pre'stɪdʒəs]	repräsentativ, prestigeträchtig
rapid(ly) ['ræpɪd]	rasch, schnell
centrally heated [ˌsentrəli 'hiːtɪd]	zentralbeheizt
moveable ['muːvəbl]	beweglich, mobil
fixed [fɪkst]	fest, festgelegt, fest installiert
routine [ruː'tiːn]	(fester) Ablauf, Routine
page 71	
to **store** [stɔː]	aufbewahren, lagern
file [faɪl]	Akte, Ordner
office block ['ɒfɪs blɒk]	Bürogebäude
sudden ['sʌdn]	plötzlich
to **employ sb** [ɪm'plɔɪ]	jdn beschäftigen, jdn einstellen
casual ['kæʒuəl]	leger, zwanglos
to **mediate** ['miːdieɪt]	vermitteln
technique [tek'niːk]	Methode, Technik
gist [dʒɪst]	das Wesentliche
to **take a seat** [ˌteɪk ə 'siːt]	Platz nehmen
premises *pl* ['premɪsɪz]	Geschäftsräume

ermanent ['pɜːmənənt]	dauerhaft
Must rush. [ˌmʌst 'rʌʃ]	Ich muss weg.
to **get back to sb** [ˌget 'bæk tə]	sich bei jdm (zurück)melden

page 72

finance director [ˌfaɪnæns də'rektə]	kaufmännische/r Leiter/in
chain [tʃeɪn]	Kette
market share [ˌmɑːkɪt 'ʃeə]	Marktanteil
competitor [kəm'petɪtə]	Konkurrent/in, Konkurrenz
to **break down** [ˌbreɪk 'daʊn]	zusammenbrechen
strike [straɪk]	Streik
to **go on strike** [ˌgəʊ ɒn 'straɪk]	streiken
receptionist [rɪ'sepʃənɪst]	Empfangsmitarbeiter/in
job rotation ['dʒɒb rəʊteɪʃn]	Arbeitsplatzrotation, (innerbetrieblicher) Arbeitsplatzwechsel
to **stand in for sb** [ˌstænd 'ɪn fə]	jdn vertreten
to **retrain** [ˌriː'treɪn]	umschulen

page 73

to **draw** [drɔː]	ziehen
to **split** [splɪt]	(sich) aufteilen
separate ['seprət]	getrennt, separat
to **conduct sth** [kən'dʌkt]	etw durchführen
to **ensure** [ɪn'ʃʊə]	sicherstellen; dafür sorgen, dass
to **conclude** [kən'kluːd]	schließen, beenden

page 74

to **be amongst …** [bi ə'mʌŋst]	zu … gehören
consultant [kən'sʌltənt]	Berater/in
vocational training [vəʊˌkeɪʃənl 'treɪnɪŋ]	Berufsausbildung
widely ['waɪdli]	weithin
particularly [pə'tɪkjələli]	besonders, insbesondere
currently ['kʌrəntli]	zur Zeit, aktuell
unemployment [ˌʌnɪm'plɔɪmənt]	Arbeitslosigkeit
unemployment rate [ˌʌnɪm'plɔɪmənt reɪt]	Arbeitslosenquote
employable [ɪm'plɔɪəbl]	(auf dem Arbeitsmarkt) vermittelbar
understandable [ˌʌndə'stændəbl]	verständlich
to **combine** [kəm'baɪn]	kombinieren, verbinden, vereinen
theoretical [ˌθɪə'retɪkl]	theoretisch
vocational school [vəʊˌkeɪʃənl 'skuːl]	berufsbildende Schule
to **provide sb with sth** [prə'vaɪd wɪð]	jdn mit etw versorgen
skilled [skɪld]	qualifiziert
equally ['iːkwəli]	gleichermaßen, genauso
beyond [bɪ'jɒnd]	jenseits, über
border ['bɔːdə]	Grenze
to **adopt** [ə'dɒpt]	einführen, anwenden
subsidiary [səb'sɪdiəri]	Niederlassung
aim [eɪm]	Ziel, Zweck
objective [əb'dʒektɪv]	Ziel, Zweck
to **adapt** [ə'dæpt]	anpassen
after all [ˌɑːftər 'ɔːl]	letztlich
to **import** [ɪm'pɔːt]	importieren, einführen
framework ['freɪmwɜːk]	Rahmen(bedingungen)
to **take sth into consideration** [ˌteɪk ɪntə kənˌsɪdə'reɪʃn]	etw berücksichtigen
to **depend on sth** [dɪ'pend ɒn]	von etw abhängen, auf etw angewiesen sein
cooperation [kəʊˌɒpə'reɪʃn]	Zusammenarbeit, Zusammenwirken
educational [ˌedʒu'keɪʃənl]	schulisch, Bildungs-
to **complement** ['kɒmplɪmənt]	ergänzen
relevant to sth ['reləvənt tə]	für etw relevant
medium-sized ['miːdiəm saɪzd]	mittelständisch
to **exist** [ɪg'zɪst]	bestehen, existieren
degree course [dɪ'griː kɔːs]	Studiengang
integrated ['ɪntɪgreɪtɪd]	integriert, ganzheitlich
to **be in touch** [bi ɪn 'tʌtʃ]	sich melden
secondary school ['sekəndri skuːl]	weiterführende Schule
advanced [əd'vɑːnst]	weiterführend, vertiefend
engineering design [endʒɪˌnɪərɪŋ dɪ'zaɪn]	Konstruktion
mostly ['məʊstli]	meistens
welding ['weldɪŋ]	Schweißen
lathe [leɪð]	Drehbank, Drehmaschine
design office [dɪ'zaɪn ɒfɪs]	Konstruktionsbüro
to **progress** [prə'gres]	vorankommen, fortschreiten
registered ['redʒɪstəd]	zugelassen, qualifiziert
engineering technician [ˌendʒɪ'nɪərɪŋ teknɪʃn]	Konstruktionsmechaniker/in
to **mention** ['menʃn]	erwähnen, nennen

JOB SKILLS 2

page 75

office assistant [ˌɒfɪs ə'sɪstənt]	Bürokaufmann/-frau
duty ['djuːti]	Aufgabe, Pflicht, Arbeit
located in [ləʊ'keɪtɪd ɪn]	in (… gelegen)
accurate ['ækjərət]	genau
to **be willing to do sth** [bi 'wɪlɪŋ tə]	bereit sein, etw zu tun
a must [ə 'mʌst]	ein Muss
plc [ˌpiː el 'siː]	AG
business studies ['bɪznəs stʌdiz]	Betriebswirtschaft
to **seek** [siːk]	suchen
to **update** [ˌʌp'deɪt]	aktualisieren
spreadsheet ['spredʃiːt]	Tabellenkalkulation
to **be equivalent to sth** [bi ɪ'kwɪvələnt tə]	einer Sache entsprechen
native speaker [ˌneɪtɪv 'spiːkə]	Muttersprachler/in
fluent ['fluːənt]	*(Sprache:)* fließend
oral ['ɔːrəl]	mündlich
intermediate [ˌɪntə'miːdiət]	mittlere/r/s *(Niveau)*
pressure ['preʃə]	Druck
reference ['refərəns]	Referenz, Zeugnis
referee [ˌrefə'riː]	Referenzgeber
on request [ɒn rɪ'kwest]	auf Wunsch, auf Verlangen

page 76

body ['bɒdi]	*(Brief:)* Hauptteil
complimentary close [ˌkɒmplɪˌmentri 'kləʊz]	*(Brief:)* Schlussformel
enclosure (encl.) [ɪn'kləʊʒə]	*(Brief:)* Anlage
inside address [ˌɪnsaɪd ə'dres]	Empfängeranschrift
salutation [ˌsælju'teɪʃn]	*(Brief:)* Anrede

signature [ˈsɪgnətʃə]	Unterschrift
writer's address [ˌraɪtəz əˈdres]	Absenderanschrift
attn. (= attention) [əˈtenʃn]	*(Brief:)* zu Händen
ref. (= reference) [ˈrefərəns]	*(Brief:)* Zeichen
copy [ˈkɒpi]	Ausgabe
currently [ˈkʌrəntli]	zur Zeit
to **be keen to do sth** [bɪ ˈkiːn tə]	etw unbedingt tun wollen
English-speaking [ˈɪŋglɪʃ spiːkɪŋ]	englischsprachig
in addition to sth [ɪn əˈdɪʃn tə]	zusätzlich zu etw
to **be an asset to sb** [bi ən ˈæset tə]	für jdn eine Bereicherung sein
to **appreciate** [əˈpriːʃieɪt]	zu schätzen wissen, schätzen
to **grant sb sth** [grɑːnt]	jdm etw gewähren
interview [ˈɪntəvjuː]	Vorstellungsgespräch

page 77

section [ˈsekʃn]	Abschnitt
applicant [ˈæplɪkənt]	Bewerber/in
to **compile** [kəmˈpaɪl]	erstellen, zusammenstellen
educational [ˌedʒuˈkeɪʃənl]	schulisch, Bildungs-
item [ˈaɪtəm]	Punkt, Gegenstand
correction [kəˈrekʃn]	Korrekturlesen, Korrektur
to **pin** [pɪn]	(mit einer Nadel) befestigen, anbringen

page 78

to **interview sb** [ˈɪntəvjuː]	mit jdm ein Vorstellungsgespräch führen
strength [streŋθ]	Stärke
weakness [ˈwiːknəs]	Schwäche
to **report to sb** [rɪˈpɔːt tə]	jdm unterstellt sein
surprised [səˈpraɪzd]	erstaunt, überrascht
superior [suːˈpɪəriə]	Vorgesetzte/r
to **invite sb to do sth** [ɪnˈvaɪt tə]	jdn auffordern, etw zu tun
Speaking. [ˈspiːkɪŋ]	*(Telefon:)* Am Apparat.
to **go backpacking** [ˌgəʊ ˈbækpækɪŋ]	auf Rucksacktour gehen
to **gain** [geɪn]	erwerben
to **take responsibility** [teɪk rɪˌspɒnsəˈbɪləti]	Verantwortung übernehmen
right away [ˌraɪt əˈweɪ]	sofort
careless [ˈkeələs]	nachlässig
as far as I'm concerned [əz ˌfɑːr əz ˌaɪm kənˈsɜːnd]	von mir aus, was mich betrifft
to **attend sth** [əˈtend]	an etw teilnehmen
reservation [ˌrezəˈveɪʃn]	Reservierung
assessment [əˈsesmənt]	Beurteilung, Einstufung
to **send sth out** [ˌsend ˈaʊt]	etw verschicken
interviewer [ˈɪntəvjuːə]	*Person, die ein Vorstellungsgespräch führt*
responsibility [rɪˌspɒnsəˈbɪləti]	Aufgabe, Zuständigkeit

UNIT 9

page 79

multiculturalism [ˌmʌltiˈkʌltʃərəlɪzm]	Multikulturalität, Multikulturismus, kulturelle Vielfalt
festival [ˈfestɪvl]	Fest, Festtag, Festival
to **light** [laɪt]	*(Kerze etc.)* anzünden
to **march** [mɑːtʃ]	marschieren
candle [ˈkændl]	Kerze
dragon [ˈdrægən]	Drachen
lantern [ˈlæntən]	Laterne
pipe band [ˈpaɪp bænd]	Dudelsackkapelle
New Year [ˌnjuː ˈjɪə]	Neujahr
lion [ˈlaɪən]	Löwe
display [dɪˈspleɪ]	Vorführung
parade [pəˈreɪd]	Parade
march [mɑːtʃ]	Marsch
ceilidh [ˈkeɪlɪ]	*geselliges Beisammensein mit Musik und Tanz (schottischer Brauch)*
midsummer [ˌmɪdˈsʌmə]	Mittsommer, Sommersonnenwende
cuisine [kwɪˈziːn]	Küche, Kochkunst
craft [krɑːft]	Handwerk

page 80

refugee [ˌrefjuˈdʒiː]	Flüchtling
coast [kəʊst]	Küste
to **separate** [ˈsepəreɪt]	trennen, abspalten
violent [ˈvaɪələnt]	heftig
given name [ˈgɪvn neɪm]	Vorname
soldier [ˈsəʊldʒə]	Soldat/in
to **kick sth down** [ˌkɪk ˈdaʊn]	etw eintreten
to **wave sth around** [ˌweɪv əˈraʊnd]	mit etw herumfuchteln
rifle [ˈraɪfl]	Gewehr
to **drag** [dræg]	zerren
to **force** [fɔːs]	zwingen
facing sth [ˈfeɪsɪŋ]	gegen etw, mit dem Gesicht zu etw
to **be in command** [bi ˌɪn kəˈmɑːnd]	das Kommando führen, die Befehle geben, das Sagen haben
inch [ɪntʃ]	Zoll *(= 2,54 cm)*
to **shudder** [ˈʃʌdə]	erschaudern, zittern
fear [fɪə]	Angst
to **tremble** [ˈtrembl]	beben, zittern
to **look on** [ˌlʊk ˈɒn]	zusehen
terrified [ˈterɪfaɪd]	entsetzt
to **shoot** [ʃuːt]	schießen
bullet [ˈbʊlɪt]	(Gewehr-)Kugel
to **scream** [skriːm]	schreien
peace [piːs]	Frieden
to **raise sth** [reɪz]	etw anheben, etw hochheben
to **point sth at sb** [ˈpɔɪnt ət]	etw auf jdn richten, mit etw auf jdn zielen
traitor [ˈtreɪtə]	Verräter/in
enemy [ˈenəmi]	Feind/in
forehead [ˈfɔːhed]	Stirn
mongrel [ˈmɒŋgrəl]	Mischling, Bastard
to **drop one's voice** [ˌdrɒp wʌnz ˈvɔɪs]	die Stimme senken
equally [ˈiːkwəli]	gleichermaßen, genauso
safety [ˈseɪfti]	Sicherheit
authority [ɔːˈθɒrəti]	Behörde
welcoming [ˈwelkəmɪŋ]	gastfreundlich

page 81

evil [ˈiːvl]	böse, schlecht
border [ˈbɔːdə]	Grenze
body [ˈbɒdi]	Leichnam
law [lɔː]	Justiz
kind [kaɪnd]	freundlich, gütig, nett
to **arrest** [əˈrest]	verhaften
detention centre [dɪˈtenʃn sentə]	Auffanglager, Haftanstalt

homeless ['həʊmləs]	obdachlos
unpleasant [ʌn'pleznt]	unangenehm, unschön
court [kɔːt]	Gericht(shof)
basket ['bɑːskɪt]	Korb
amount [ə'maʊnt]	Menge
tinned [tɪnd]	in Dosen, Dosen-
checkout ['tʃekaʊt]	Kasse
counter ['kaʊntə]	Schalter, Theke
to **drop one's eyes** [ˌdrɒp wʌnz 'aɪz]	den Blick senken
deal [diːl]	Abmachung, Geschäft
wallet ['wɒlɪt]	Brieftasche, (Herren-) Portemonnaie
voucher ['vaʊtʃə]	Gutschein
asylum seeker [ə'saɪləm siːkə]	Asylbewerber/in
change [tʃeɪndʒ]	Wechselgeld
queue [kjuː]	Warteschlange
courtroom ['kɔːtruːm]	Gerichtssaal
to **humiliate** [hjuː'mɪlieɪt]	demütigen, erniedrigen
meanwhile ['miːnwaɪl]	inzwischen, unterdessen
to **file** [faɪl]	feilen
nail [neɪl]	Nagel
to **comb** [kəʊm]	kämmen
exhibition [ˌeksɪ'bɪʃn]	Ausstellung
humiliation [hjuːˌmɪli'eɪʃn]	Demütigung, Erniedrigung
proud [praʊd]	stolz
penny ['peni]	Pfennig, Penny
to **reduce sb to sth** [rɪ'djuːs]	jdn zu etw bringen
to **amount to sth** [ə'maʊnt tə]	auf etw hinauslaufen
to **live off aid** [lɪv ˌɒf 'eɪd]	von Sozialhilfe leben
to **wonder** ['wʌndə]	sich fragen
mathematician [ˌmæθəmə'tɪʃn]	Mathematiker/in
promising ['prɒmɪsɪŋ]	vielversprechend
airline ['eəlaɪn]	Fluglinie
silent(ly) ['saɪlənt]	still, schweigend
to **shake one's head** [ˌʃeɪk wʌnz 'hed]	den Kopf schütteln
in disgust [ɪn dɪs'gʌst]	angewidert
to **shuffle** ['ʃʌfl]	schlurfen
line [laɪn]	Reihe
down the line [ˌdaʊn ðə 'laɪn]	weiter
death [deθ]	Tod

page 82

understanding [ˌʌndə'stændɪŋ]	Verständnis
to **make a point to sb** [ˌmeɪk ə 'pɔɪnt tə]	jdm etw zu verstehen geben
to **recognize** ['rekəgnaɪz]	(wieder)erkennen
to **jump the queue** [ˌdʒʌmp ðə 'kjuː]	sich vordrängeln
to **wait for one's turn** [ˌweɪt fə wʌnz 'tɜːn]	warten, bis man an der Reihe ist
to **face sb** [feɪs]	jdn konfrontieren
goal [gəʊl]	*(Ballspiel:)* Tor
to **behave** [bɪ'heɪv]	sich benehmen, sich verhalten

page 83

earnings *pl* ['ɜːnɪŋz]	Einkünfte, Verdienst
reduction [rɪ'dʌkʃn]	Verringerung, Senkung
pride [praɪd]	Stolz
on top of [ɒn 'tɒp əv]	auf
cupboard ['kʌbəd]	Schrank
health and safety [ˌhelθ ənd 'seɪfti]	Arbeitsschutz
cure [kjʊə]	Heilung, Therapie
cost of living [ˌkɒst əv 'lɪvɪŋ]	Lebenshaltungskosten
great-grandfather [ˌgreɪt 'grænfɑːðə]	Urgroßvater
to **take pride in sth** [ˌteɪk 'praɪd ɪn]	auf etw Wert legen, sich mit etw Mühe geben
excellent ['eksələnt]	ausgezeichnet, hervorragend
to **land** [lænd]	landen

page 84

purpose ['pɜːpəs]	Absicht, Zweck
What now for …? [ˌwɒt 'naʊ fə]	Wie steht es um …?
policy ['pɒləsi]	Politik, Kurs, Konzept
harmony ['hɑːməni]	Harmonie
to **have the guts to do sth** [həv ðe 'gʌts tə]	den Mumm haben, etw zu tun
law [lɔː]	Gesetz
to **pass a law** [ˌpɑːs ə 'lɔː]	ein Gesetz verabschieden
to **reject** [rɪ'dʒekt]	ablehnen, zurückweisen
to **deport** [dɪ'pɔːt]	abschieben
violent ['vaɪələnt]	gewalttätig
gang [gæŋ]	Bande
Muslim ['mʊzlɪm]	muslimisch, Moslem
to **take over** [ˌteɪk 'əʊvə]	die Macht übernehmen
to **save oneself sth** [seɪv]	sich etw ersparen
to **calm down** [ˌkɑːm 'daʊn]	sich beruhigen
not … either [nɒt 'aɪðə]	auch nicht
minority [maɪ'nɒrəti]	Minderheit
moderate ['mɒdərət]	gemäßigt, maßvoll
MP (Member of Parliament) [ˌem 'piː]	Parlamentsabgeordnete/r
wave [weɪv]	Welle
descendant [dɪ'sendənt]	Nachfahre, Nachkomme
contribution [ˌkɒntrɪ'bjuːʃn]	Beitrag
to **make a contribution** [ˌmeɪk ə ˌkɒntrɪ'bjuːʃn]	einen Beitrag leisten
to **be a two-way street** [bi ə ˌtuː weɪ 'striːt]	auf Gegenseitigkeit beruhen
vibrant ['vaɪbrənt]	dynamisch, voller Leben
peaceful ['piːsfl]	friedlich
varied ['veərid]	vielfältig, abwechslungsreich
to **hide (away)** [haɪd]	sich verstecken, sich verbergen
to **put sth down to sth** [ˌpʊt 'daʊn tə]	etw einer Sache zuschreiben
ethnic ['eθnɪk]	ethnisch, Volks-
to **integrate** ['ɪntɪgreɪt]	(sich) integrieren
He has a (good) point. [hiː ˌhæz ə 'pɔɪnt]	Da ist etwas dran. Da hat er recht.
migrant ['maɪgrənt]	Migrant/in
racial ['reɪʃl]	rassisch, Rassen-

page 85

lively ['laɪvli]	lebendig, lebhaft, rege
population [ˌpɒpju'leɪʃn]	Bevölkerung
struggle ['strʌgl]	Kampf
engine ['endʒɪn]	Motor

page 86

shipyard ['ʃɪpjɑːd]	Werft
to **fall in love with sb/sth** [ˌfɔːl ɪn 'lʌv wɪð]	sich in jdn/etw verlieben
to **emigrate** ['emɪgreɪt]	auswandern
to **build sth up** [ˌbɪld 'ʌp]	etw aufbauen

deportation [dɪpɔːˈteɪʃn]	Abschiebung	
to **escape from sth** [ɪˈskeɪp frəm]	einer Sache entkommen	
port [pɔːt]	Hafen, Hafenstadt	
parliament [ˈpɑːləmənt]	Parlament	
to **retire** [rɪˈtaɪə]	in den Ruhestand gehen, in Rente gehen	
unemployment [ˌʌnɪmˈplɔɪmənt]	Arbeitslosigkeit	
to **claim unemployment benefits** [ˌkleɪm ʌnɪmˈplɔɪmənt benɪfɪts]	Arbeitslosengeld beziehen	
housing [ˈhaʊzɪŋ]	Wohnungsbau, Wohnungen	
approximately (approx.) [əˈprɒksɪmətli]	zirka (ca.)	
presenter [prɪˈzentə]	Moderator/in	
agricultural [ˌægrɪˈkʌltʃərəl]	landwirtschaftlich, Landwirtschafts-	
free movement [ˌfriː ˈmuːvmənt]	Freizügigkeit	
rural [ˈrʊərəl]	ländlich	
uncontrolled [ˌʌnkənˈtrəʊld]	ungeregelt, unkontrolliert	
incomer [ˈɪnkʌmə]	Zuzügler, Ankömmling	
issue [ˈɪʃuː]	Streitpunkt, Frage, Problem, Thema	
the other way round [ði ˌʌðə weɪ ˈraʊnd]	umgekehrt	
economy [ɪˈkɒnəmi]	Wirtschaft	
war [wɔː]	Krieg	
replacement [rɪˈpleɪsmənt]	Ersatz, Ersetzung, Austausch	
unemployment rate [ˌʌnɪmˈplɔɪmənt reɪt]	Arbeitslosenquote	
pressure [ˈpreʃə]	Druck	

page 87

course of action [ˌkɔːs əv ˈækʃn]	Vorgehen, Maßnahmen
sir [sɜː]	mein Herr
jacket [ˈdʒækɪt]	Jacke, Jackett
to **deal with sth** [ˈdiːl wɪð]	mit etw zu tun haben
label [ˈleɪbl]	Beschriftung, Bezeichnung
explanation [ˌekspləˈneɪʃn]	Erläuterung, Erklärung
to **select** [sɪˈlekt]	auswählen
to **contrast** [kənˈtrɑːst]	gegenüberstellen, vergleichen
to **take sb in** [ˌteɪk ˈɪn]	jdn aufnehmen
host [həʊst]	Gastgeber
approximate [əˈprɒksɪmət]	ungefähr, angenähert
similarly [ˈsɪmələli]	in ähnlicher Weise, genauso, ebenso

page 88

to **pass sth** [pɑːs]	weitergeben
developing country [dɪˌveləpɪŋ ˈkʌntri]	Entwicklungsland
advanced [ədˈvɑːnst]	fortschrittlich, entwickelt
host [həʊst]	(Radio-/TV-)Moderator/in
passenger jet [ˈpæsɪndʒə dʒet]	Passagierflugzeug
vehicle [ˈviːəkl]	Fahrzeug
to **demand** [dɪˈmɑːnd]	fordern, verlangen
rapid rise [ˌræpɪd ˈraɪz]	steiler Aufstieg
economic power [iːkəˌnɒmɪk ˈpaʊə]	Wirtschaftsmacht
high speed rail [ˌhaɪ spiːd ˈreɪl]	Hochgeschwindigkeitsstrecken *(Eisenbahn)*
to **compete** [kəmˈpiːt]	konkurrieren, im Wettbewerb stehen
to **come up with sth** [ˌkʌm ˈʌp wɪð]	etw entwickeln
innovation [ˌɪnəˈveɪʃn]	Innovationen
original [əˈrɪdʒənl]	ursprünglich
to **re-innovate sth** [ˌriː ˈɪnəveɪt]	etw weiter verbessern, etw weiterentwickeln
folks *pl* [fəʊks]	Leute
bullet train [ˈbʊlɪt treɪn]	Hochgeschwindigkeitszug
quote [kwəʊt]	Zitat
to **attain** [əˈteɪn]	erreichen
pioneer [ˌpaɪəˈnɪə]	Pionier/in
to **deny** [dɪˈnaɪ]	leugnen
additional [əˈdɪʃənl]	zusätzlich
effort [ˈefət]	Anstrengung(en), Einsatz, Leistung
to **export** [ɪkˈspɔːt]	ausführen, exportieren
violation [ˌvaɪəˈleɪʃn]	Verletzung *(eines Vertrags)*
legal recourse [ˌliːgl rɪˈkɔːs]	Regressansprüche
to **sue sb** [suː]	jdn verklagen
in the meantime [ɪn ðə ˈmiːntaɪm]	in der Zwischenzeit
carmaker [ˈkɑːmeɪkə]	Autohersteller
to **be eager to do sth** [bi ˈiːgə tə duː]	darauf brennen, etw zu tun
given [ˈgɪvn]	angesichts der Tatsache, dass
to **succeed** [səkˈsiːd]	erfolgreich sein, Erfolg haben
dilemma [dɪˈlemə]	Zwiespalt, Dilemma
publicly [ˈpʌblɪkli]	in der Öffentlichkeit
to **strike a posture** [ˌstraɪk ə ˈpɒstʃə]	eine Haltung einnehmen
to **be willing to do sth** [bi ˈwɪlɪŋ tə]	bereit sein, etw zu tun
based in … [ˈbeɪst ɪn]	mit Sitz in, aus
industrialization [ɪnˌdʌstriəlaɪˈzeɪʃn]	Industrialisierung
motor vehicle [ˌməʊtə ˈviːəkl]	Kraftfahrzeug
theft [θeft]	Diebstahl, Klau
short-term [ˌʃɔːtˈtɜːm]	kurzfristig

UNIT 10

page 89

clothing bank [ˈkləʊðɪŋ bæŋk]	Altkleidersammelbehälter
beggar [ˈbegə]	Bettler/in
to **beg for sth** [ˈbeg fə]	um etw betteln
donation [dəʊˈneɪʃn]	Spende

page 90

blockbuster [ˈblɒkbʌstə]	Straßenfeger
poverty [ˈpɒvəti]	Armut
producer [prəˈdjuːsə]	Produzent/in
Not on our watch. [nɒt ɒn ˈaʊə wɒtʃ]	Nicht mit uns!
mission [ˈmɪʃn]	Auftrag, Mission
atrocities *pl* [əˈtrɒsətiz]	Gräueltaten
to **invite sb to do sth** [ɪnˈvaɪt]	jdn auffordern, etw zu tun
to **lobby sb** [ˈlɒbi]	auf jdn Einfluss nehmen
donor [ˈdəʊnə]	Spender/in
schooling [ˈskuːlɪŋ]	Schulbesuch, Schulbildung
benefactor [ˈbenɪfæktə]	Wohltäter/in
sponsorship [ˈspɒnsəʃɪp]	Förderung
accountancy [əˈkaʊntənsi]	Buchhaltung, Rechnungswesen
tear [tɪə]	Träne

loan [ləʊn]	Darlehen, Kredit
foundation [faʊn'deɪʃn]	Stiftung
to **feed** [fi:d]	ernähren, mit Nahrung versorgen
life saving ['laɪf seɪvɪŋ]	lebensrettend
medicine ['medsn]	Arznei(mittel), Medizin
handout ['hændaʊt]	Almosen
ongoing ['ɒŋgəʊɪŋ]	laufend
to **empower sb to do sth** [ɪm'paʊə]	jdn befähigen, etw zu tun
self-sustainable [ˌself sə'steɪnəbl]	selbsttragend, lebensfähig
to **enable** [ɪ'neɪbl]	befähigen
to **make a difference** [ˌmeɪk ə 'dɪfrəns]	etw bewirken
valuable ['væljuəbl]	wertvoll
along the way [əˌlɒŋ ðə 'weɪ]	dabei, währenddessen
to **value** ['vælju:]	wertschätzen, schätzen
from all walks of life [frəm ˌɔ:l wɔ:ks əv 'laɪf]	aus allen Gesellschaftsschichten, aus allen Lebensbereichen
currently ['kʌrəntli]	zur Zeit
to **trouble sb** ['trʌbl]	jdn bekümmern, jdm Schwierigkeiten bereiten
Salvation Army [sælˌveɪʃn 'ɑ:mi]	Heilsarmee
toddler ['tɒdlə]	Kleinkind
disadvantaged [ˌdɪsəd'vɑ:ntɪdʒd]	benachteiligt
day centre ['deɪ sentə]	Tagesstätte
companionship [kəm'pæniənʃɪp]	Gemeinschaft, Gesellschaft

page 91

homelessness ['həʊmləsnəs]	Obdachlosigkeit
psychological [ˌsaɪkə'lɒdʒɪkl]	psychologisch
armed [ɑ:md]	bewaffnet
home country [ˌhəʊm 'kʌntri]	Heimatland
in the long term [ɪn ðə 'lɒŋ tɜ:m]	langfristig
in the short term [ɪn ðə ˌʃɔ:t 'tɜ:m]	kurzfristig
horrific [hə'rɪfɪk]	schrecklich, entsetzlich
act [ækt]	Handlung, Tat
to **finance** ['faɪnæns]	finanzieren
(the) good [gʊd]	Wohl

page 92

giving ['gɪvɪŋ]	Spenden
level ['levl]	Grad, Höhe
gross domestic product (GDP) [ˌgrəʊs dəˌmestɪk 'prɒdʌkt]	Bruttosozialprodukt
tax [tæks]	Steuer
to **give to charity** [ˌgɪv tə 'tʃærəti]	(für wohltätige Zwecke) spenden
good cause [gʊd 'kɔ:z]	guter Zweck
disabled [dɪs'eɪbld]	behindert
surgery ['sɜ:dʒəri]	Operation
in need [ɪn 'ni:d]	bedürftig, in Not
regardless of sth [rɪ'gɑ:dləs əv]	ungeachtet einer Sache
religious [rɪ'lɪdʒəs]	religiös
funding ['fʌndɪŋ]	Finanzierung, Geldmittel
to **feel sorry for sb** [ˌfi:l 'sɒri fə]	jd tut einem leid
responsibility [rɪˌspɒnsə'bɪləti]	Verantwortung, Zuständigkeit
to **fund** [fʌnd]	finanzieren
charitable ['tʃærətəbl]	wohltätig, gemeinnützig
line graph ['laɪn grɑ:f]	Liniendiagramm
striking ['straɪkɪŋ]	auffallend, auffällig, hervorstechend
progression [prə'greʃn]	Entwicklung, Steigerung
to **rank sixth** [ræŋk 'sɪksθ]	den sechsten Platz einnehmen
times [taɪmz]	mal

page 93

attitude ['ætɪtju:d]	Einstellung, Haltung
walk [wɔ:k]	Spaziergang, Rundgang
gardening ['gɑ:dnɪŋ]	Gartenarbeit
target ['tɑ:gɪt]	Ziel
feedback ['fi:dbæk]	Reaktion(en), Rückmeldung(en)
English-speaking ['ɪŋglɪʃ spi:kɪŋ]	englischsprachig
pen friend ['pen frend]	Brieffreund/in

page 94

orphan ['ɔ:fn]	Waise
orphanage ['ɔ:fənɪdʒ]	Waisenhaus
Boxing Day ['bɒksɪŋ deɪ]	2. Weihnachtstag
to **strike** [straɪk]	treffen
fishing village ['fɪʃɪŋ vɪlɪdʒ]	Fischerdorf
to **be asleep** [bi ə'sli:p]	schlafen
scream [skri:m]	Schrei
to **smash** [smæʃ]	zertrümmern, zerstören
to **sweep away** [ˌswi:p ə'weɪ]	fortschwemmen, erfassen, wegreißen
whilst [waɪlst]	während
despite [dɪ'spaɪt]	trotz
blow [bləʊ]	Schlag
to **escape sth narrowly** [ɪˌskeɪp 'nærəʊli]	einer Sache knapp entkommen
to **hitch-hike** ['hɪtʃ haɪk]	per Anhalter fahren, trampen
embassy ['embəsi]	Botschaft
to **rejoin sb** [rɪ'dʒɔɪn]	jdn wieder treffen
to **adopt sb** [ə'dɒpt]	jdn adoptieren
ultimately ['ʌltɪmətli]	letztlich, letztendlich
strength [streŋθ]	Stärke, Kraft
humanitarian [hju:ˌmænɪ'tæriən]	humanitär
a great deal [ə ˌgreɪt 'di:l]	eine erhebliche Menge
to **hand sth out** [ˌhænd 'aʊt]	etw verteilen, etw ausgeben
confidence ['kɒnfɪdəns]	Selbstvertrauen, Zuversicht
to **knock sb off sth** [ˌnɒk 'ɒf]	jdn von etw herunterstoßen, von etw herunterfallen
to **be worse off** [bi ˌwɜ:s 'ɒf]	schlechter dran sein
independence [ˌɪndɪ'pendəns]	Unabhängigkeit
movement ['mu:vmənt]	Bewegung
enterprise ['entəpraɪz]	Unternehmen
to **found** [faʊnd]	gründen
commitment to sth [kə'mɪtmənt tə]	Engagement für etw, Einsatz für etw
portion ['pɔ:ʃn]	Teil
sole [səʊl]	alleinig
essentials *pl* [ɪ'senʃlz]	lebensnotwendige Güter
shelter ['ʃeltə]	Unterkunft
nutrition [nju'trɪʃn]	Nahrung, Ernährung
medication [ˌmedɪ'keɪʃn]	Arzneimittel
to **make an impact** [ˌmeɪk ən 'ɪmpækt]	etw bewirken, etw verändern

opening ['əʊpnɪŋ]	Eröffnung
memory of sb ['meməri]	Gedenken an jdn
to **mark** [mɑːk]	*(Jahrestag etc.)* begehen
anniversary [ˌænɪ'vɜːsəri]	Jahrestag

page 95

to **destroy** [dɪ'strɔɪ]	zerstören
force [fɔːs]	Gewalt, Kraft
ride [raɪd]	Fahrt
unpaid [ˌʌn'peɪd]	unbezahlt
intention [ɪn'tenʃn]	Absicht
hurricane ['hʌrɪkən]	Wirbelsturm
flood [flʌd]	Überschwemmung
fatality [fə'tæləti]	Todesfall, Todesopfer
NGO (non-government organization) [ˌen dʒiː 'əʊ]	Nichtregierungsorganisation
citizen ['sɪtɪzn]	Bürger/in
to **put in work** [pʊt ˌɪn 'wɜːk]	Arbeit leisten

page 96

occupation [ˌɒkju'peɪʃn]	Beruf, Tätigkeit, Beschäftigung
contribution [ˌkɒntrɪ'bjuːʃn]	(finanzielle) Zuwendung, Spende
madam ['mædəm]	gnädige Frau
banker ['bæŋkə]	Bankkaufmann/-frau
earthquake ['ɜːθkweɪk]	Erdbeben
to **have spare cash** [həv ˌspeə 'kæʃ]	Geld übrig haben
to **run** [rʌn]	*(Unternehmen etc.)* führen, betreiben
to **transfer** [træns'fɜː]	*(Geld)* überweisen
so far [ˌsəʊ 'fɑː]	bislang
medical student [ˌmedɪkl 'stjuːdnt]	Medizinstudent/in
walk-in medical centre [ˌwɔːk ɪn 'medɪkl sentə]	Ambulanz

page 97

saleswoman ['seɪlzwʊmən]	Verkäuferin
myth [mɪθ]	Mythos, Märchen
aid [eɪd]	Hilfe
disease [dɪ'ziːz]	Krankheit
common ['kɒmən]	verbreitet, üblich
misunderstanding [ˌmɪsʌndə'stændɪŋ]	Missverständnis
developing country [dɪˌveləpɪŋ 'kʌntri]	Entwicklungsland
to **treat** [triːt]	behandeln
corrupt [kə'rʌpt]	korrupt, bestechlich
official [ə'fɪʃl]	Beamte/r, Funktionär/in
concrete ['kɒŋkriːt]	konkret
mosquito net [məs'kiːtəʊ net]	Moskitonetz
farming ['fɑːmɪŋ]	Landwirtschaft
health care ['helθ keə]	Gesundheitswesen, medizinische Versorgung
preventable [prɪ'ventəbl]	vermeidbar
proverb ['prɒvɜːb]	Sprichwort
for a lifetime [fər ə 'laɪftaɪm]	ein Leben lang

page 98

border ['bɔːdə]	Grenze
engineering [endʒɪ'nɪərɪŋ]	(Ingenieur-)Technik
posting ['pəʊstɪŋ]	(Auslands-)Einsatz, Posten
annual ['ænjuəl]	jährlich
placement ['pleɪsmənt]	Vermittlung, Einsatz
freshwater supply ['freʃwɔːtə səplaɪ]	Trinkwasserversorgung
palm nut ['pɑːm nʌt]	Palmnuss
fuel ['fjuːəl]	Treibstoff
to **promote sth** [prə'məʊt]	etw fördern, sich für etw einsetzen
amongst [ə'mʌŋst]	unter, bei
awareness [ə'weənəs]	Bewusstsein, Kenntnis
decision-maker [dɪ'sɪʒn meɪkə]	Entscheidungsträger/in
impact ['ɪmpækt]	Einfluss, Auswirkung
to **entail** [ɪn'teɪl]	beinhalten
groundwater extraction ['graʊndwɔːtər ɪkstrækʃn]	Grundwasserförderung
depth [depθ]	Tiefe
machinery [mə'ʃiːnəri]	Maschinen
borehole ['bɔːhəʊl]	Bohrloch
to **upgrade** [ˌʌp'greɪd]	aufrüsten, verbessern
existing [ɪg'zɪstɪŋ]	bestehend, vorhanden
rig [rɪg]	Bohrturm
to **modify** ['mɒdɪfaɪ]	modifizieren
frame [freɪm]	Rahmen
welding shop ['weldɪŋ ʃɒp]	Schweißerei
pulley ['pʊli]	Rolle, Riemenscheibe
lightweight ['laɪtweɪt]	leicht
palm tree ['pɑːm triː]	Palme
to **squeeze** [skwiːz]	(aus)pressen
nut [nʌt]	Nuss, Kern
to **extract** [ɪk'strækt]	*(Rohstoff)* gewinnen
to **go to waste** [ˌgəʊ tə 'weɪst]	ungenutzt bleiben
reaction [ri'ækʃn]	Reaktion
fairly ['feəli]	ziemlich
thick [θɪk]	dickflüssig
presence ['prezns]	Gegenwart
catalyst ['kætəlɪst]	Katalysator
runny ['rʌni]	dünnflüssig
glycerine ['glɪsriːn]	Glyzerin
gravity ['grævəti]	Schwerkraft
creation [kri'eɪʃn]	Einrichtung
production plant [prə'dʌkʃn plɑːnt]	Produktionsanlage
to **mechanize** ['mekənaɪz]	mechanisieren
yield [jiːld]	Ertrag
sanitation [ˌsænɪ'teɪʃn]	Abwasserentsorgung
waste management ['weɪst mænɪdʒmənt]	Abfallentsorgung
transportation [ˌtrænspɔː'teɪʃn]	Transportwesen
to **adapt to sth** [ə'dæpt tə]	sich an etw anpassen
climate change ['klaɪmət tʃeɪndʒ]	Klimawandel

UNIT 11

page 99

reach [riːtʃ]	Reichweite
bread roll ['bred rəʊl]	Brötchen
cardboard ['kɑːdbɔːd]	Pappe
supply chain [sə'plaɪ tʃeɪn]	Lieferkette
item ['aɪtəm]	Artikel, Gegenstand
to **manufacture** [ˌmænju'fæktʃə]	fertigen, herstellen
raw product [ˌrɔː 'prɒdʌkt]	Ausgangsprodukt, Roherzeugnis
to **originate from** [ə'rɪdʒɪneɪt frəm]	kommen aus
within [wɪ'ðɪn]	innerhalb, binnen

to **grow** [grəʊ]	*(Pflanze)* anbauen
to **import** [ɪm'pɔːt]	importieren, einführen
wheat [wiːt]	Weizen
lettuce ['letɪs]	Kopfsalat

page 100

globalization [ˌgləʊbəlaɪ'zeɪʃn]	Globalisierung
case study ['keɪs stʌdi]	Fallstudie
growth [grəʊθ]	Wachstum, Zunahme
trade [treɪd]	Handel
influence ['ɪnfluəns]	Einfluss
to **spread** [spred]	sich ausbreiten, sich verbreiten
trader ['treɪdə]	Händler/in
trading ['treɪdɪŋ]	Handel
cooperative [kəʊ'ɒpərətɪv]	Genossenschaft
to **transform** [træns'fɔːm]	(völlig) verändern
to **raise sth** [reɪz]	etw steigern, etw erhöhen
to **switch to sth** ['swɪtʃ tə]	auf etw umstellen
organic [ɔː'gænɪk]	biologisch, Bio-
buyer ['baɪə]	Einkäufer/in
facilities *pl* [fə'sɪlətiz]	Anlage(n), Einrichtungen
to **process** [prəʊ'ses]	verarbeiten
finished product [ˌfɪnɪʃt 'prɒdʌkt]	Endprodukt
clinic ['klɪnɪk]	Klinik
secondary school ['sekəndri skuːl]	weiterführende Schule
textile ['tekstaɪl]	Textil-
back [bæk]	Rücken
to **care about sth** ['keər əbaʊt]	sich um etw kümmern
to **injure** ['ɪndʒə]	verletzen
to **collapse** [kə'læps]	einstürzen
deadline ['dedlaɪn]	Frist, Termin
order ['ɔːdə]	Auftrag, Bestellung
to **fill an order** [ˌfɪl ən 'ɔːdə]	einen Auftrag ausführen
union ['juːniən]	Gewerkschaft
to **take action** [ˌteɪk 'ækʃn]	handeln
offshore [ˌɒf'ʃɔː]	im/ins Ausland
folks *pl* [fəʊks]	Leute
carpentry ['kɑːpəntri]	Schreinerei
depressed [dɪ'prest]	*(Wirtschaft:)* flau, am Boden
to **re-skill** [ˌriː 'skɪl]	umschulen
computer-aided [kəm'pjuːtər eɪdɪd]	computergestützt
automated ['ɔːtəmeɪtɪd]	automatisiert
to **expand** [ɪk'spænd]	expandieren, ausweiten
electronic [ˌɪlek'trɒnɪk]	elektronisch, Elektronik-
component [kəm'pəʊnənt]	Bauteil
export ['ekspɔːt]	Ausfuhr, Export
to **turn out** [ˌtɜːn 'aʊt]	sich herausstellen
co-worker ['kəʊwɜːkə]	Kollege/-in
to **go inland** [gəʊ 'ɪnlænd]	ins Landesinnere gehen
employment [ɪm'plɔɪmənt]	Anstellung, Arbeit
people ['piːpl]	Volk

page 101

to **mention** ['menʃn]	erwähnen, nennen
to **change for the better** [ˌtʃeɪndʒ fə ðə 'betə]	sich zum Besseren verändern
point of view [ˌpɔɪnt əv 'vjuː]	Perspektive, Blickwinkel, Standpunkt
to **farm** [fɑːm]	*(Land)* bewirtschaften
to **govern** ['gʌvn]	regieren, verwalten, führen
agreement [ə'griːmənt]	Vereinbarung, Absprache
to **construct** [kən'strʌkt]	bauen, errichten, konstruieren
transformation [ˌtrænzfə'meɪʃn]	(grundlegende) Veränderung, Umwandlung
expansion [ɪk'spænʃn]	Ausweitung, Expansion
to **look a mess** [ˌlʊk ə 'mes]	fürchterlich aussehen
democracy [dɪ'mɒkrəsi]	Demokratie

page 102

petrol ['petrəl]	Benzin
petrol-driven ['petrəl drɪvn]	benzingetrieben
mass production [ˌmæs prə'dʌkʃn]	Massenproduktion
personal transport [ˌpɜːsənl 'trænspɔːt]	Individualverkehr
to **export** [ɪk'spɔːt]	ausführen, exportieren
complex ['kɒmpleks]	komplex
link [lɪŋk]	Verbindung, Verknüpfung, Beziehung
plant [plɑːnt]	Fabrik, Werk, Anlage
to **link** [lɪŋk]	verbinden, verknüpfen
aircraft ['eəkrɑːft]	Flugzeug
maker ['meɪkə]	Hersteller, -bauer
shared [ʃeəd]	gemeinsam
to **test** [test]	erproben, testen
even so ['iːvn səʊ]	dennoch, allerdings

page 103

order ['ɔːdə]	Bestellung
straight away [streɪt ə'weɪ]	sofort
particularly [pə'tɪkjələli]	besonders
related [rɪ'leɪtɪd]	zugehörig
to **consist of sth** [kən'sɪst əv]	aus etw bestehen
ironic [aɪ'rɒnɪk]	ironisch
to **remind sb (of sth)** [rɪ'maɪnd]	jdn (an etw) erinnern
secondly ['sekəndli]	zweitens
collapse [kə'læps]	Einsturz
sharp [ʃɑːp]	scharf
attack [ə'tæk]	Attacke, Angriff
care [keə]	Sorge, Fürsorge, Sorgfalt

page 104

to **re-shore** [ˌriː 'ʃɔː]	*(Industrie)* wieder im Inland ansiedeln, wieder ins Inland verlagern
head [hed]	Leiter/in, Chef/in
industrialized [ɪn'dʌstriəlaɪzd]	industrialisiert
low-cost [ˌləʊ'kɒst]	billig, kostengünstig
to **undercut** [ˌʌndə'kʌt]	unterbieten
section ['sekʃn]	Bereich, Teil
industrial [ɪn'dʌstriəl]	Industrie-
wasteland ['weɪstlənd]	Brachland
wage [weɪdʒ]	Lohn
floor care ['flɔː keə]	Bodenpflege
slight [slaɪt]	leicht, gering
overheads *pl* ['əʊvəhedz]	Fixkosten, Betriebskosten
rent [rent]	Miete
labour ['leɪbə]	Arbeit

page 105

demand [dɪ'mɑːnd]	Nachfrage
to **meet a demand** [ˌmiːt ə dɪ'mɑːnd]	eine Nachfrage befriedigen
delay [dɪ'leɪ]	Verzögerung
stock [stɒk]	(Lager-)Bestand, Vorrat
breakage ['breɪkɪdʒ]	Bruchschaden
faulty ['fɔːlti]	defekt, fehlerhaft
balance ['bæləns]	Bilanz, Saldo

water heater ['wɔːtə hiːtə]	Warmwasserbereiter, Boiler
cash machine ['kæʃ məʃiːn]	Geldautomat
rate [reɪt]	Tempo, Quote, Rate, Anteil
loss [lɒs]	Verlust
to **slow** [sləʊ]	sich verlangsamen, sich abschwächen
to **balance** ['bæləns]	ausgleichen
roughly ['rʌfli]	ungefähr

page 106

development [dɪ'veləpmənt]	*(Immobilie:)* Erschließung, Bau
to **hyphenate** ['haɪfəneɪt]	mit einem Bindestrich schreiben
to **decrease** [dɪ'kriːs]	abnehmen, zurückgehen
to **decline** [dɪ'klaɪn]	zurückgehen, fallen, sinken
sharp(ly) [ʃɑːp]	stark
steady ['stedi]	kontinuierlich, stabil
slightly [slaɪtli]	geringfügig, leicht
climb [klaɪm]	Anstieg
fall [fɔːl]	Absturz, Rückgang
decrease ['diːkriːs]	Abnahme, Rückgang
decline [dɪ'klaɪn]	Rückgang
to **remain** [rɪ'meɪn]	bleiben

page 107

sales *pl* [seɪlz]	Umsatz
sales director ['seɪlz dərektə]	Verkaufsleiter/in, Vertriebsleiter/in
to **identify** [aɪ'dentɪfaɪ]	erkennen, bestimmen, identifizieren
recession [rɪ'seʃn]	Rezession
flat [flæt]	*(Umsatz etc.:)* konstant, unverändert
to **face sth** [feɪs]	mit etw konfrontiert werden, sich einer Sache gegenüber sehen
to **fight back** [ˌfaɪt 'bæk]	sich wehren, sich zurückkämpfen
optimistic [ˌɒptɪ'mɪstɪk]	optimistisch
running ['rʌnɪŋ]	in Folge
to **cut costs** [kʌt 'kɒsts]	Kosten senken
to **go out of business** [gəʊ ˌaʊt əv 'bɪznəs]	das Geschäft aufgeben, Pleite gehen
partly ['pɑːtli]	teils, teilweise
operation [ˌɒpə'reɪʃn]	Betrieb, Geschäftstätigkeit
bottom line [ˌbɒtəm 'laɪn]	das, woraus es (unterm Strich) ankommt
to **last** [lɑːst]	dauern, andauern, so bleiben

page 108

cable ['keɪbl]	Kabel
submarine cable [sʌbməˌriːn 'keɪbl]	Tiefseekabel
telecommunications [ˌtelikəˌmjuːnɪ'keɪʃnz]	Telekommunikation
wireless ['waɪələs]	drahtlos, Funk-
connectivity [ˌkɒnek'tɪvəti]	Verbindung(en)
satellite ['sætəlaɪt]	Satellit
to **depend on sth** [dɪ'pend ɒn]	von etw abhängen, auf etw angewiesen sein
largely ['lɑːdʒli]	größtenteils, überwiegend
seabed ['siːbed]	Meeresgrund
vulnerable ['vʌlnərəbl]	verwundbar, anfällig
lifeline ['laɪflaɪn]	Lebensader
fibre optic cable [ˌfaɪbər ɒptɪk 'keɪbl]	Glasfaserkabel
ocean ['əʊʃn]	Ozean
undersea [ˌʌndə'siː]	Untersee-
rare(ly) [reə]	selten
underwater [ˌʌndə'wɔːtə]	Unterwasser-
landslide ['lændslaɪd]	Erdrutsch
anchor ['æŋkə]	Anker
net [net]	Netz
fishing boat ['fɪʃɪŋ bəʊt]	Fangschiff, Fischerboot
thick [θɪk]	dick, stark
armoured ['ɑːməd]	armiert, gepanzert
layer ['leɪə]	Lage, Schicht
steel [stiːl]	Stahl
wire ['waɪə]	Draht
shore [ʃɔː]	Küste
cable break ['keɪbl breɪk]	Kabelbruch
mostly ['məʊstli]	meistens
redundancy [rɪ'dʌndənsi]	Redundanz
to **reroute** [riː'ruːt]	umleiten
to **dig for sth** ['dɪg fə]	nach etw graben
copper ['kɒpə]	Kupfer
accidentally [ˌæksɪ'dentəli]	versehentlich
access ['ækses]	Zugang
neighbouring ['neɪbərɪŋ]	Nachbar-

UNIT 12

page 109

changing ['tʃeɪndʒɪŋ]	im Wandel
jobless ['dʒɒbləs]	arbeitslos
elderly ['eldəli]	älter; Senioren
pension ['penʃn]	Rente, Pension
burden ['bɜːdn]	Last, Belastung, Bürde
pensioner ['penʃənə]	Rentner/in
to **recover** [rɪ'kʌvə]	sich erholen
joblessness ['dʒɒbləsnəs]	Arbeitslosigkeit
millennial [mɪ'leniəl]	Jahrtausend-
to **campaign** [kæm'peɪn]	kämpfen
her native Pakistan [hə ˌneɪtɪv pækɪ'stɑːn]	ihr Geburtsland Pakistan
to **shoot sb** [ʃuːt]	jdn erschießen
to **be left for dead** [bi ˌleft fə 'ded]	als tot zurückgelassen werden
emergency [ɪ'mɜːdʒənsi]	Notfall, Not-
to **recover fully** [rɪˌkʌvə 'fʊli]	wieder völlig gesund werden

page 110

to **make room** [meɪk 'ruːm]	Platz machen
to **address sb** [ə'dres]	jdn ansprechen
to **pass sth on** [ˌpɑːs 'ɒn]	etw weitergeben, etw weiterreichen
degree [dɪ'griː]	Abschluss
to **juggle** ['dʒʌgl]	miteinander vereinbaren, jonglieren
casual job [ˌkæʒuəl 'dʒɒb]	Nebenjob
to **self-fund** [ˌself 'fʌnd]	selbst finanzieren
congressman ['kɒŋgresmən]	Kongressabgeordneter
retail ['riːteɪl]	Einzelhandel(s-)
to **make sb redundant** [ˌmeɪk rɪ'dʌndənt]	jdn (betriebsbedingt) entlassen
previous ['priːviəs]	vorherig, früher
to **land sth** [lænd]	etw an Land ziehen
middle management [ˌmɪdl 'mænɪdʒmənt]	mittlere Führungsebene
skilled [skɪld]	qualifiziert, erfahren
to **be sick of sth** [bi 'sɪk əv]	von etw die Nase voll haben
rather ['rɑːðə]	eher, lieber
endless ['endləs]	endlos, fortwährend
to **terminate** ['tɜːmɪneɪt]	beenden

full-time [ˌfʊl 'taɪm]	Vollzeit-
nannying ['næniɪŋ]	Kinderbetreuung
out-of-state [ˌaʊt əf 'steɪt]	in einem anderen Bundesstaat
application [ˌæplɪ'keɪʃn]	Bewerbung
applicant ['æplɪkənt]	Bewerber/in
pay packet ['peɪ pækɪt]	Lohntüte, Gehalt
minimum wage [ˌmɪnɪməm 'weɪdʒ]	Mindestlohn
editor ['edɪtə]	Herausgeber/in
to **take a chance on sb** [ˌteɪk ə 'tʃɑːns ɒn]	es mit jdm versuchen, jdm eine Chance geben
to **state** [steɪt]	erklären, feststellen
ought to ['ɔːt tə]	sollen
contributor [kən'trɪbjuːtə]	Autor/in *(von Zeitschriftenartikeln)*
entry-level ['entri levl]	Einstiegs-
to **be rigged against sb** [bi 'rɪgd əgenst]	jdn (systematisch) benachteiligen, gegen jdn arbeiten
graduate ['grædʒuət]	Absolvent/in
stream [striːm]	Strom
to **be unique to sth** [bi ju'niːk tə]	etw ausschließlich betreffen
lazy ['leɪzi]	faul
to **mooch off sth** [ˌmuːtʃ 'ɒf]	von etw schmarotzen
hopeless ['həʊpləs]	hoffnungslos

page 111

dole [dəʊl]	Arbeitslosengeld
dole bludger ['dəʊl blʌdʒə]	Sozialschmarotzer
useless ['juːsləs]	nutzlos
unexpected(ly) [ˌʌnɪk'spektɪd]	unerwartet
afterwards ['ɑːftəwədz]	danach, darauf
publication [ˌpʌblɪ'keɪʃn]	Veröffentlichung
edition [ɪ'dɪʃn]	Ausgabe
to **outline** ['aʊtlaɪn]	skizzieren, grob beschreiben

page 112

journalism ['dʒɜːnəlɪzəm]	Journalismus
assistance [ə'sɪstəns]	Hilfe, Unterstützung
graduation [ˌgrædʒu'eɪʃn]	(Schul-/Universitäts-) Abschluss
interview ['ɪntəvjuː]	Vorstellungsgespräch
interviewer ['ɪntəvjuːə]	*Person, die ein Vorstellungsgespräch führt*
interviewee [ˌɪntəvjuː'iː]	*Person, mit der ein Vorstellungsgespräch geführt wird*
shipbuilding ['ʃɪpbɪldɪŋ]	Schiffbau
to **interview sb** ['ɪntəvjuː]	mit jdm ein Vorstellungsgespräch führen
to **meet a deadline** [ˌmiːt ə 'dedlaɪn]	eine Frist / einen Termin einhalten

page 113

to **play the piano** [ˌpleɪ ðə pi'ænəʊ]	Klavier spielen
harbour ['hɑːbə]	Hafen
to **read sth back** [ˌriːd 'bæk]	etw (zur Kontrolle) vorlesen
to **edit** ['edɪt]	*(Text)* redigieren, bearbeiten
original material [əˌrɪdʒənl mə'tɪəriəl]	eigene Beiträge
to **confirm** [kən'fɜːm]	bestätigen

page 114

retirement [rɪ'taɪəmənt]	Ruhestand, Rente
to **age** [eɪdʒ]	altern
founder ['faʊndə]	Gründer/in
resource [rɪ'sɔːs]	Ressource
senior citizen [ˌsiːniə 'sɪtɪzn]	Senior/in, ältere/r Mitbürger/in
to **be still going strong** [bi ˌstɪl gəʊɪŋ 'strɒŋ]	gut dabei sein, immer noch in Form sein
startling ['stɑːtlɪŋ]	alarmierend, erschreckend, erstaunlich
scrapheap ['skræhiːp]	Schrotthaufen
to **retire sb** [rɪ'taɪə]	jdn in den Ruhestand versetzen
social engineering [ˌsəʊʃl ˌendʒɪ'nɪərɪŋ]	Änderung gesellschaftlicher Strukturen, angewandte Sozialwissenschaft
to **be past it** [bi 'pɑːst ɪt]	die besten Jahre hinter sich haben, jenseits von Gut und Böse sein
mental(ly) ['mentl]	geistig
to **ignore** [ɪg'nɔː]	nicht beachten, ignorieren
reliability [rɪˌlaɪə'bɪləti]	Zuverlässigkeit, Verlässlichkeit
wish [wɪʃ]	Wunsch
to **act as sth** ['ækt əz]	als etw fungieren
adviser [əd'vaɪzə]	Berater/in
lifetime ['laɪftaɪm]	(ganzes) Leben
to **guide** [gaɪd]	führen
heart-warming ['hɑːt wɔːmɪŋ]	herzerwärmend
to **team up with sb** [ˌtiːm 'ʌp wɪð]	mit jdm zusammenarbeiten, sich mit jdm zusammentun
home for the elderly [ˌhəʊm fə ði 'eldəli]	Altenheim
native speaker [ˌneɪtɪv 'spiːkə]	Muttersprachler/in
retirement home [rɪ'taɪəmənt həʊm]	Altersheim

page 115

ancient ['eɪnʃənt]	alt, historisch, antik
gay [geɪ]	schwul, lesbisch
equal society [ˌiːkwəl sə'saɪəti]	gerechte Gesellschaft

page 116

to **work sth out** [ˌwɜːk 'aʊt]	etw herausfinden
closely related [ˌkləʊsli rɪ'leɪtɪd]	eng verwandt
to **make sense** [ˌmeɪk 'sens]	Sinn ergeben, sinnvoll sein
characteristic [ˌkærəktə'rɪstɪk]	Merkmal, charakteristische Eigenschaft
wedding ['wedɪŋ]	Hochzeit
affluent ['æfluənt]	wohlhabend
construction company [kən'strʌkʃn kʌmpəni]	Baufirma
to **stop sb from doing sth** [stɒp]	jdn daran hindern, etw zu tun
to **carry on** [ˌkæri 'ɒn]	weitermachen
tiring ['taɪərɪŋ]	anstrengend
warehouse ['weəhaʊs]	Lager
forklift (truck) ['fɔːklɪft]	Gabelstapler

page 117

fuel ['fjuːəl]	Brennstoff, Treibstoff
sadly ['sædli]	leider
there's no escape from the fact that [ðeəz nəʊ ɪˌskeɪp frəm ðə 'fækt ðət]	man kann nicht außer Acht lassen, dass; man muss der Tatsache ins Auge sehen, dass
allowance [ə'laʊəns]	Zuschuss
per annum [pər 'ænəm]	pro Jahr

sensitive ['sensətɪv] – sensibel, *(Information:)* vertraulich
internal [ɪn'tɜːnl] – inländisch, Inlands-
to **post** [pəʊst] – *(Brief:)* einwerfen, schicken
anonymous(ly) [ə'nɒnɪməs] – anonym
police force [pə'liːs fɔːs] – Polizei
precaution [prɪ'kɔːʃn] – Vorkehrung, Sicherheitsmaßnahme
to **be willing to do sth** [bi 'wɪlɪŋ tə] – bereit sein, etw zu tun

page 128

to **defend** [dɪ'fend] – verteidigen
to **let oneself in for sth** [ˌlet wʌnself 'ɪn fə] – sich auf etw einlassen
to **harm sb** [hɑːm] – jdm schaden
self-defence [ˌself dɪ'fens] – Selbstverteidigung
specialist ['speʃəlɪst] – Spezial-, Fach-
request [rɪ'kwest] – Bitte, Wunsch, Anfrage
to **instruct sb to do sth** [ɪn'strʌkt] – jdn beauftragen, etw zu tun
to **install** [ɪn'stɔːl] – installieren
undetectable [ˌʌndɪ'tektəbl] – nicht erkennbar, nicht nachweisbar
spyware ['spaɪweə] – Spionagesoftware
to **transmit** [træns'mɪt] – übertragen, übermitteln, senden
to **track sb** [træk] – jds Spur verfolgen
to **log** [lɒg] – aufzeichnen, protokollieren
school-age ['skuːl eɪdʒ] – im Schulalter
to **intercept** [ˌɪntə'sept] – abfangen, abhören
to **be mistaken** [bi mɪ'steɪkən] – sich irren
keystroke ['kiːstrəʊk] – Tastenanschlag, Herunterdrücken einer Taste
handy ['hændi] – praktisch
to **input** ['ɪnpʊt] – eingeben
access code ['ækses kəʊd] – Zugangscode

page 129

silent ['saɪlənt] – stumm
microphone ['maɪkrəfəʊn] – Mikrofon
to **go unnoticed** [ˌgəʊ ʌn'nəʊtɪst] – unbemerkt bleiben
to **switch to sth** ['swɪtʃ tə] – auf etw umschalten
delivery [dɪ'lɪvəri] – Lieferung
van [væn] – Lieferwagen
lawnmower ['lɔːnməʊə] – Rasenmäher
to **refuse sth** [rɪ'fjuːz] – etw verweigern
to **knock sth off** [ˌnɒk 'ɒf] – etw abschlagen
mirror ['mɪrə] – Spiegel
to **stick sth on** [ˌstɪk 'ɒn] – etw befestigen
washing machine ['wɒʃɪŋ məʃiːn] – Waschmaschine
to **be priced at …** [bi 'praɪst ət] – … kosten
purchase ['pɜːtʃəs] – Kauf
to **advise** [əd'vaɪz] – (jdm etw) raten
to **save** [seɪv] – *(Daten)* sichern
embarrassing [ɪm'bærəsɪŋ] – peinlich, unangenehm
to **prompt sb to do sth** [prɒmpt] – jdn veranlassen, etw zu tun
to **withdraw** [wɪð'drɔː] – *(Geld)* abheben
untraceable [ˌʌn'treɪsəbl] – nicht ausfindig zu machen
to **be sick and tired of sth** [bi ˌsɪk ən 'taɪəd əv] – die Nase von etw gestrichen voll haben
straightaway [ˌstreɪtə'weɪ] – sofort, sogleich
nasty ['nɑːsti] – gemein, hässlich, böse
to **beg sb to do sth** [beg] – jdn anflehen, etw zu tun
to **concede** [kən'siːd] – eingestehen, einräumen
utter ['ʌtə] – völlig, vollkommen
defeat [dɪ'fiːt] – Niederlage
obtainable [əb'teɪnəbl] – erhältlich
suspicious [sə'spɪʃəs] – misstrauisch
spouse [spaʊz] – Ehegatte
to **spy on sb** ['spaɪ ɒn] – jdn ausspionieren
the small print [ðə 'smɔːl prɪnt] – das Kleingedruckte
tormentor [tɔː'mentə] – Peiniger
encrypted [ɪn'krɪptɪd] – verschlüsselt
in person [ɪn 'pɜːsn] – persönlich

page 130

means of transport [ˌmiːnz əf 'trænspɔːt] – Verkehrsmittel
to **obtain sth** [əb'teɪn] – etw erhalten, an etw gelangen
to **launch an attack** [ˌlɔːntʃ ən ə'tæk] – einen Angriff starten
consequence ['kɒnsɪkwəns] – Folge, Konsequenz
to **cancel** ['kænsl] – abbrechen, abblasen
cybercrime ['saɪbəkraɪm] – Cyberkriminalität
bank robbery ['bæŋk rɒbəri] – Banküberfall, Bankraub
to **rob a bank** [ˌrɒb ə 'bæŋk] – eine Bank überfallen, eine Bank ausrauben
to **hijack** ['haɪdʒæk] – kapern

page 131

extract ['ekstrækt] – Auszug, Ausschnitt
novel ['nɒvl] – Roman
to **associate** [ə'səʊʃieɪt] – in Verbindung bringen, assoziieren
term [tɜːm] – Begriff
to **publish** ['pʌblɪʃ] – veröffentlichen
fictional ['fɪkʃənl] – fiktiv
totalitarian [ˌtəʊtælɪ'tæriən] – totalitär
to **gaze** [geɪz] – starren, blicken
to **contrive** [kən'traɪv] – bewerkstelligen
beneath [bɪ'niːθ] – unterhalb, unter
telescreen ['telɪskriːn] – Televisor
whisper ['wɪspə] – Flüstern
field of vision [ˌfiːld əv 'vɪʒn] – Sichtfeld
plaque [plɑːk] – Platte, Tafel
to **command** [kə'mɑːnd] – beherrschen
to **plug in on sth** [ˌplʌg 'ɪn ɒn] – sich in etw einschalten
wire ['waɪə] – Draht
guesswork ['geswɜːk] – Mutmaßung, Spekulation
at any rate [ət eni 'reɪt] – auf jeden Fall
assumption [ə'sʌmpʃn] – Annahme
to **overhear** [ˌəʊvə'hɪə] – belauschen, aufschnappen
darkness ['dɑːknəs] – Dunkelheit
movement ['muːvmənt] – Bewegung
to **scrutinize** ['skruːtənaɪz] – genau ansehen, überprüfen
parallel ['pærəlel] – Parallele

page 132

CCTV (closed-circuit television) [ˌsiː siː tiː 'viː] – Videoüberwachung
CCTV camera [ˌsiː siː tiː 'viː kæmərə] – Überwachungskamera
to **be located** [bi ləʊ'keɪtɪd] – sich befinden
to **disclose** [dɪs'kləʊz] – offenlegen
campaigner [kæm'peɪnə] – Aktivist/in
care home ['keə həʊm] – Pflegeheim
scheme [skiːm] – Plan, Programm
invaluable [ɪn'væljuəbl] – unschätzbar, unbezahlbar

crime detection ['kraɪm dɪtekʃn] Aufdecken von Straftaten
evidence ['evɪdəns] Beweise, Beweismittel
murder ['mɜːdə] Mord
footage ['fʊtɪdʒ] Film-/Bildmaterial
to **be a stark reminder** [bi ə ˌstɑːk rɪ'maɪndə] etw jäh vor Augen führen, etw überdeutlich machen
potential(ly) [pə'tenʃl] potenziell
to **monitor** ['mɒnɪtə] überwachen
to **recognise** ['rekəgnaɪz] anerkennen, begreifen
democratic [ˌdemə'krætɪk] demokratisch
to **threaten** ['θretn] bedrohen

page 134

to **give off** [ˌgɪv 'ɒf] abgeben, ausstoßen
particle ['pɑːtɪkl] Teilchen, Partikel
electromagnetic [ɪˌlektrəʊmæg'netɪk] elektromagnetisch
space weather ['speɪs weðə] Weltraumwetter
coronal mass ejection [kəˌrəʊnl 'mæs ɪdʒekʃn] koronaler Massenauswurf
spectacular [spek'tækjələ] spektakulär
solar storm [ˌsəʊlə 'stɔːm] Sonnensturm
Northern Lights *pl* [ˌnɔːðən 'laɪts] Nordlicht, Polarlicht
disturbance [dɪ'stɜːbəns] Störung
magnetic field [mægˌnetɪk 'fiːld] Magnetfeld
extra-high voltage [ˌekstrə haɪ 'vəʊltɪdʒ] Höchstspannung
transformer [træns'fɔːmə] Transformator, Umspannwerk

vulnerable ['vʌlnərəbl] verwundbar, anfällig
matter ['mætə] Materie
to **travel** ['trævl] sich bewegen
solar flare [ˌsəʊlə 'fleə] Sonneneruption
to **confuse sth** [kən'fjuːz] etw verwechseln
to **emit** [ɪ'mɪt] ausstoßen
to **weigh** [weɪ] wiegen
tonne [tʌn] Tonne
terrifying ['terɪfaɪɪŋ] erschreckend, furchterregend
to **hit sth** [hɪt] etw erreichen, auf etw treffen

geomagnetic storm [dʒiːəʊmægˌnetɪk 'stɔːm] geomagnetischer Sturm
intense [ɪn'tens] stark
to **knock sth out** [ˌnɒk 'aʊt] etw lahmlegen
entire [ɪn'taɪə] ganz, gesamt
power grid ['paʊə grɪd] Stromnetz
to **generate** ['dʒenəreɪt] erzeugen
current ['kʌrənt] (elektrischer) Strom
power line ['paʊə laɪn] Stromleitung
to **put sth out of action** [pʊt ˌaʊt əv 'ækʃn] etw außer Gefecht setzen
surely ['ʃʊəli] bestimmt, (doch) wohl
severe [sɪ'vɪə] schwer, heftig
to **disrupt** [dɪs'rʌpt] unterbrechen, stören
to **occur** [ə'kɜː] auftreten
flash [flæʃ] Blitz
radiation [ˌreɪdi'eɪʃn] Strahlung
satellite ['sætəlaɪt] Satellit
to **rely on sth** [rɪ'laɪ ɒn] auf etw angewiesen sein
prediction [prɪ'dɪkʃn] Vorhersage
observatory [əb'zɜːvətri] Observatorium
to **detect** [dɪ'tekt] aufspüren, entdecken
sensitive ['sensətɪv] empfindlich
power cut ['paʊə kʌt] Stromausfall

sheet [ʃiːt] Blatt (Papier)
scenario [sə'nɑːriəʊ] Szenario
arrow ['ærəʊ] Pfeil
failure ['feɪljə] Ausfall, Defekt
ATM [ˌeɪ tiː 'em] Geldautomat
cash withdrawal ['kæʃ wɪðdrɔːəl] Geldauszahlung, Barabhebung
explanatory [ɪk'splænətri] erläuternd
petrol station ['petrəl steɪʃn] Tankstelle
rail network ['reɪl netwɜːk] Schienennetz, Eisenbahnnetz
reservoir ['rezəvwɑː] Wasserspeicher, Hochbehälter, Stausee
water supply ['wɔːtə səplaɪ] Wasserversorgung
emergency service [ɪ'mɜːdʒənsi sɜːvɪs] Notfalldienst

UNIT 14

page 135

solar ['səʊlə] Sonnen-, Solar-
biomass ['baɪəʊmæs] Biomasse
fossil fuel ['fɒsl fjuːəl] fossiler Brennstoff
geothermal power [dʒiːəʊˌθɜːml 'paʊə] Erdwärme
hydro-electric power [ˌhaɪdrəʊ ɪˌlektrɪk 'paʊə] Wasserkraft
methane ['miːθeɪn] Methan
nuclear power [ˌnjuːkliə 'paʊə] Kernkraft
solar power [ˌsəʊlə 'paʊə] Sonnenenergie
tidal power [ˌtaɪdl 'paʊə] Gezeitenkraft
wind power ['wɪnd paʊə] Windkraft
renewable [rɪ'njuːəbl] erneuerbar
breakdown ['breɪkdaʊn] Zusammenbruch
to **make sth up** [ˌmeɪk 'ʌp] etw ausmachen

page 136

climate ['klaɪmət] Klima
climate change ['klaɪmət tʃeɪndʒ] Klimawandel
angry ['æŋgri] aufgebracht, ungehalten
man-made ['mæn meɪd] künstlich, menschlichen Ursprungs

cause [kɔːz] Ursache
global warming [ˌgləʊbl 'wɔːmɪŋ] Erderwärmung
advocate ['ædvəkət] Befürworter/in
scientist ['saɪəntɪst] (Natur-)Wissenschaftler/in
denier [dɪ'naɪə] Leugner/in
carbon dioxide [ˌkɑːbən daɪ'ɒksaɪd] Kohlendioxid
carbon dioxide level [ˌkɑːbən daɪ'ɒksaɪd levl] Kohlendioxidkonzentration, -gehalt
previously ['priːviəsli] zuvor, vorher
variability [ˌveəriə'bɪləti] Schwankung, Unbeständigkeit

degree [dɪ'griː] Grad
CEO (Chief Executive Officer) [ˌsiː iː 'əʊ] Vorstandsvorsitzende/r
to **try sb** [traɪ] jdn vor Gericht stellen
high crime [ˌhaɪ 'kraɪm] Schwerverbrechen
humanity [hjuː'mænəti] Menschheit, Menschlichkeit

coal [kəʊl] Kohle
coal-fired ['kəʊl faɪəd] kohlegetrieben
power plant ['paʊə plɑːnt] Kraftwerk

to **be to blame** [bi tə 'bleɪm]	Schuld sein
to **quote** [kwəʊt]	zitieren
news anchor ['nju:z æŋkə]	Nachrichtensprecher/in
large-scale ['lɑ:dʒ skeɪl]	in großem Umfang/Ausmaß
greenhouse gas [ˌgri:nhaʊs 'gæs]	Treibhausgas
to **reflect** [rɪ'flekt]	reflektieren
to **escape** [ɪ'skeɪp]	entweichen
termperature ['temprətʃə]	Temperatur

page 137

atmospheric [ˌætməs'ferɪk]	atmosphärisch, in der Atmosphäre
to **pass** [pɑ:s]	überschreiten
beyond [bɪ'jɒnd]	jenseits, über
major ['meɪdʒə]	bedeutend, wichtig, groß
disastrous [dɪ'zɑ:strəs]	katastrophal, verheerend
unstoppable [ˌʌn'stɒpəbl]	unaufhaltsam
cyclone ['saɪkləʊn]	Wirbelsturm, Zyklon, Sturmtief
to **warm** [wɔ:m]	sich erwärmen
ocean ['əʊʃn]	Ozean, Weltmeer
ice sheet ['aɪs ʃi:t]	Eisdecke
to **melt** [melt]	schmelzen, abschmelzen
sea level ['si: levl]	Meeresspiegel
island ['aɪlənd]	Insel
coastal ['kəʊstl]	Küsten-
to **drown** [draʊn]	ertrinken, im Meer versinken
worrying ['wʌriɪŋ]	besorgniserregend
emission [ɪ'mɪʃn]	Ausstoß, Emission
panel ['pænl]	Gremium, Ausschuss
to **prepare** [prɪ'peə]	*(Bericht etc.)* erstellen, verfassen
as long as [əz 'lɒŋ əz]	solange
co-author [ˌkəʊ 'ɔ:θə]	Mitautor/in, Mitverfasser/in
economics [ˌi:kə'nɒmɪks]	Ökonomie, Wirtschaft(swissenschaft)
urgently ['ɜ:dʒəntli]	dringend, nachdrücklich
carbon ['kɑ:bən]	Kohlenstoff
investment [ɪn'vestmənt]	Investition
existing [ɪg'zɪstɪŋ]	bestehend, vorhanden
to **commute** [kə'mju:t]	(zur Arbeit) pendeln
to **pollute** [pə'lu:t]	(die Umwelt) verschmutzen
in turn [ɪn 'tɜ:n]	wiederum
quality of life [ˌkwɒləti əv 'laɪf]	Lebensqualität
to **limit** ['lɪmɪt]	begrenzen, einschränken
at the same time [ət ðə ˌseɪm 'taɪm]	gleichzeitig
to **encourage** [ɪn'kʌrɪdʒ]	fördern
largely ['lɑ:dʒli]	größtenteils, überwiegend
sceptic ['skeptɪk]	Skeptiker/in
flooding ['flʌdɪŋ]	Überschwemmung
to **call for sth** ['kɔ:l fə]	zu etw aufrufen

page 138

oil [ɔɪl]	Öl
natural gas [ˌnætʃrəl 'gæs]	Erdgas
to **power** ['paʊə]	antreiben, mit Energie versorgen
by contrast [baɪ 'kɒntrɑ:st]	im Gegensatz dazu, dagegen
to **flood** [flʌd]	überschwemmen

page 139

Head of Science [ˌhed əf 'saɪəns]	Fachbereichsleiter/in Naturwissenschaft
sixth-form college ['sɪksθ fɔ:m kɒlɪdʒ]	Oberstufenzentrum, Studienkolleg
grateful ['greɪtfl]	dankbar
to **specialize in sth** ['speʃəlaɪz ɪn]	sich auf etw spezialisieren
research [rɪ'sɜ:tʃ]	Forschung
plain [pleɪn]	schlicht
freely ['fri:li]	ungehindert, nach Belieben
unlike [ˌʌn'laɪk]	anders als
power station ['paʊə steɪʃn]	Kraftwerk, Elektrizitätswerk
ton [tʌn]	Tonne
to **provide sth** [prə'vaɪd]	für etw sorgen
pollution [pə'lu:ʃn]	Umweltverschmutzung

page 140

conference ['kɒnfərəns]	Konferenz
journey ['dʒɜ:ni]	Reise, Fahrt
sb's take on sth ['teɪk ɒn]	jds Einschätzung von etw
controversial [ˌkɒntrə'vɜ:ʃl]	umstritten
hydraulic [haɪ'drɔ:lɪk]	hydraulisch
to **fracture** ['fræktʃə]	brechen, aufbrechen
shale [ʃeɪl]	Schiefer
rock [rɒk]	Fels, Gestein
to **inquire** [ɪn'kwaɪə]	nachfragen, sich erkundigen
to **drill** [drɪl]	bohren
to **pump** [pʌmp]	pumpen
crack [kræk]	Spalte
surface ['sɜ:fɪs]	Oberfläche
well [wel]	Bohrloch
enthusiastic(ally) [ɪnˌθju:zi'æstɪk]	begeistert
requirement [rɪ'kwaɪəmənt]	Bedarf
to **rely on sth** [rɪ'laɪ ɒn]	sich auf etw verlassen, auf etw angewiesen sein
to **light up** [ˌlaɪt 'ʌp]	leuchten, aufleuchten
one by one [ˌwʌn baɪ 'wʌn]	der Reihe nach
tunnel ['tʌnl]	Tunnel
nuclear power station [ˌnju:kliə 'paʊə steɪʃn]	Kernkraftwerk
nuclear plant [ˌnju:kliə 'plɑ:nt]	Kernkraftwerk
to **close down** [ˌkləʊz 'daʊn]	stilllegen
working life [ˌwɜ:kɪŋ 'laɪf]	Betriebsdauer
barrage ['bærɑ:ʒ]	Staumauer

page 141

subsidy ['sʌbsədi]	Subvention
corrosion [kə'rəʊʒn]	Korrosion, Zersetzung
cost-effective [ˌkɒst ɪ'fektɪv]	rentabel
close to ['kləʊs tə]	nahe bei, in der Nähe von
onshore [ˌɒn'ʃɔ:]	an Land
to **become annoyed** [ˌbɪkʌm ə'nɔɪd]	sich ärgern, sich aufregen
wind farm ['wɪnd fɑ:m]	Windpark
offshore [ˌɒf'ʃɔ:]	auf See
to **invest** [ɪn'vest]	investieren
to **pick** [pɪk]	wählen, aussuchen
by chance [baɪ 'tʃɑ:ns]	zufällig

page 142

to **opt for sth** ['ɒpt fə]	sich für etw entscheiden
to **corrode** [kə'rəʊd]	korrodieren, zersetzen
vehicle ['vi:əkl]	Fahrzeug
to **turn sth on** [ˌtɜ:n 'ɒn]	etw an-/einschalten
structure ['strʌktʃə]	Bauwerk, Konstruktion
press conference ['pres kɒnfərəns]	Pressekonferenz

editor ['edɪtə]	Redakteur/in
commercial [kə'mɜːʃl]	gewerblich, kommerziell
planning permission ['plænɪŋ pəmɪʃn]	Baugenehmigung

page 143

electricity bill [ɪˌlek'trɪsəti bɪl]	Stromrechnung
to **beg** [beg]	flehen, eindringlich bitten
council ['kaʊnsl]	(Stadt-, Gemeinde-)Rat
application [ˌæplɪ'keɪʃn]	Antrag
farmland ['fɑːmlænd]	Ackerland, landwirtschaftliche Nutzfläche
drilling ['drɪlɪŋ]	Bohrung(en)
drilling rig ['drɪlɪŋ rɪg]	Bohrturm
waste water [ˌweɪst 'wɔːtə]	Abwasser
worries *pl* ['wʌriz]	Bedenken
councillor ['kaʊnsələ]	Ratsmitglied
to **leak** [liːk]	sickern, entweichen
groundwater ['graʊndwɔːtə]	Grundwasser
supplies *pl* [sə'plaɪz]	Vorräte, Vorkommen
tap [tæp]	Wasserhahn
on fire [ɒn 'faɪə]	in Flammen
concrete ['kɒŋkriːt]	Beton
steel [stiːl]	Stahl
well casing ['wel keɪsɪŋ]	Bohrlochverrohrung, Bohrlochwandung
regulation [ˌregju'leɪʃn]	Vorschrift
in return [ɪn rɪ'tɜːn]	im Gegenzug, als Ausgleich
to **be required to do sth** [bi rɪ'kwaɪəd tə]	etw tun müssen; verpflichtet sein, etw zu tun
community benefits *pl* [kə'mjuːnəti benɪfɪts]	Zahlungen an die Gemeinde
earnings *pl* ['ɜːnɪŋz]	Einnahmen, Gewinn
golf course ['gɒlf kɔːs]	Golfplatz
to **treat** [triːt]	*(Abwasser)* klären
to **weigh** [weɪ]	abwägen
to **calm** [kɑːm]	beruhigen
in principle [ɪn 'prɪnsəpl]	prinzipiell, grundsätzlich

page 144

appliance [ə'plaɪəns]	Haushaltsgerät
scrap [skræp]	Schrott
proportion [prə'pɔːʃn]	Anteil
broken ['brəʊkən]	kaputt, defekt
to **fit sth with sth** [fɪt]	etw mit etw ausstatten
tracking device ['trækɪŋ dɪvaɪs]	Ortungsgerät
trace [treɪs]	Spur
estimate ['estɪmət]	Schätzung
loudspeaker [ˌlaʊd'spiːkə]	Lautsprecher
fridge [frɪdʒ]	Kühlschrank
poisonous ['pɔɪzənəs]	giftig
arsenic ['ɑːsnɪk]	Arsen
lead [led]	Blei
mercury ['mɜːkjəri]	Quecksilber
to **forbid** [fə'bɪd]	verbieten, untersagen
to **dump** [dʌmp]	*(Müll)* (wild) abladen
toxic ['tɒksɪk]	giftig, Gift-
nationwide ['neɪʃnwaɪd]	landesweit
remaining [rɪ'meɪnɪŋ]	übrig, verbleibend
to **ship** [ʃɪp]	versenden, verschiffen
to **profit** ['prɒfɪt]	profitieren
battery pack ['bætəri pæk]	Akku
interval ['ɪntəvl]	(zeitlicher) Abstand
to **unload** [ˌʌn'ləʊd]	entladen
alarm [ə'lɑːm]	Alarmsignal
collection [kə'lekʃn]	Abholung
to **shine light on sth** [ˌʃaɪn 'laɪt ɒn]	Licht auf etw werfen
shadowy ['ʃædəʊi]	zwielichtig
customs *pl* ['kʌstəmz]	Zoll
powerless ['paʊələs]	machtlos, unfähig
stop [stɒp]	Station
dubious ['djuːbiəs]	zweifelhaft
dealer ['diːlə]	Händler/in
exporter [ɪk'spɔːtə]	Exporteur/in
wait [weɪt]	Warten, Wartezeit
capital ['kæpɪtl]	Hauptstadt
out in the open [ˌaʊt ɪn ði 'əʊpən]	im Freien
to **pile** [paɪl]	stapeln
mud [mʌd]	Schlamm
umbrella [ʌm'brelə]	Regenschirm
clearance sale ['klɪərəns seɪl]	Räumungsverkauf
farther ['fɑːðə]	weiter
mark [mɑːk]	Markierung, Zeichen
to **shake sth** [ʃeɪk]	an etw rütteln
to **activate** ['æktɪveɪt]	aktivieren
dump [dʌmp]	Müllhalde

page 145

hub [hʌb]	Drehkreuz, (Verkehrs-) Knoten
forwarding agency ['fɔːwədɪŋ eɪdʒənsi]	Spedition
shipping company ['ʃɪpɪŋ kʌmpəni]	Transportunternehmen, Spediteur, Reederei
middleman ['mɪdlmən]	Zwischenhändler
value chain ['væljuː tʃeɪn]	Wertschöpfungskette
to **break sth apart** [ˌbreɪk ə'pɑːt]	etw auseinandernehmen
to **set fire to sth** [ˌset 'faɪə tə]	etw anzünden
insulating foam ['ɪnsjuleɪtɪŋ fəʊm]	Isolierschaum
cable ['keɪbl]	Kabel
coating ['kəʊtɪŋ]	Ummantelung, (Kabel-) Mantel
copper ['kɒpə]	Kupfer
district ['dɪstrɪkt]	Bezirk
breeding ground ['briːdɪŋ graʊnd]	Brutplatz
migratory bird [ˌmaɪgrətri 'bɜːd]	Zugvogel
graveyard ['greɪvjɑːd]	Friedhof
to **poison** ['pɔɪzn]	vergiften
to **gut** [gʌt]	ausweiden, ausschlachten
worthless (to sb) ['wɜːθləs]	wertlos (für jdn)
scrapyard ['skræpjɑːd]	Schrottplatz
mystery ['mɪstri]	Rätsel, Geheimnis
to **get rid of sth** [ˌget 'rɪd əv]	etw loswerden

page 146

monitor ['mɒnɪtə]	Anzeigegerät, Überwachungsgerät
monitoring ['mɒnɪtərɪŋ]	Überwachung
wearable ['weərəbl]	(in der Kleidung) tragbar
sensing technology ['sensɪŋ teknɒlədʒi]	Messtechnologie, Sensortechnologie
to **detect** [dɪ'tekt]	aufspüren, entdecken
presence ['prezns]	Gegenwart, Vorhandensein
to **gather** ['gæðə]	sammeln, zusammentragen
respiratory [rɪ'spɪrətri]	Atemwegs-

condition [kən'dɪʃn]	Krankheit
to **keep tabs on sth** [ˌkiːp 'tæbz ɒn]	etw im Auge behalten
exposure to sth [ɪk'spəʊʒə tə]	Belastung durch etw
to **crowdsource sth** ['kraʊdsɔːs]	etw durch Freiwillige (übers Internet) beziehen
compound ['kɒmpaʊnd]	(chemische) Verbindung
wristband ['rɪstbænd]	Armband
geared toward sb ['ɡɪəd təwɔːd]	auf jdn zugeschnitten
prevention [prɪ'venʃn]	Vorbeugung, Prophylaxe
pollutant [pə'luːtənt]	Schadstoff
to **provoke sth** [prə'vəʊk]	etw hervorrufen
attack [ə'tæk]	Anfall
to **track** [træk]	verfolgen, aufzeichnen
concerned [kən'sɜːnd]	besorgt
forecast ['fɔːkɑːst]	Vorhersage
accurate ['ækjərət]	genau
readings *pl* ['riːdɪŋz]	Messwerte
initial [ɪ'nɪʃl]	erste/r/s
charged [tʃɑːdʒd]	(elektrisch) geladen
nanoparticle ['nænəʊpɑːtɪkl]	Nanoteilchen, Nanopartikel
carbon ['kɑːbən]	Kohlenstoff
to **swell** [swel]	anschwellen, aufquellen
vapor *AE* ['veɪpə]	Dampf
resistance [rɪ'zɪstəns]	Widerstand
circuit ['sɜːkɪt]	Stromkreis
sensitive ['sensətɪv]	empfindlich
municipal [mjuː'nɪsɪpl]	kommunal

UNIT 15

page 147

cactus ['kæktəs]	Kaktus
drought [draʊt]	Dürre
exploitation [ˌeksplɔɪ'teɪʃn]	Ausbeutung, Abbau *(von Rohstoffen)*
over-exploitation [ˌəʊvər eksplɔɪ'teɪʃn]	Raubbau, übermäßiger Abbau
stork [stɔːk]	Storch
famine ['fæmɪn]	Hungersnot

page 148

to **be equivalent to sth** [bi ɪ'kwɪvələnt tə]	einer Sache entsprechen
crop [krɒp]	Nutzpflanze, Feldfrucht
pastureland ['pɑːstʃəlænd]	Weideland
to **hit** [hɪt]	erreichen
crop production ['krɒp prədʌkʃn]	Pflanzenproduktion, pflanzliche Erzeugung
to **demand** [dɪ'mɑːnd]	nachfragen, verlangen
rich [rɪtʃ]	*(Nahrung)* gehaltvoll, reichhaltig
to **succeed** [sək'siːd]	erfolgreich sein, Erfolg haben
diet ['daɪət]	Ernährung, Kost
vital ['vaɪtl]	lebensnotwendig, unerlässlich
to **clear** [klɪə]	räumen, roden
prairie ['preəri]	Prärie
forest ['fɒrɪst]	Wald
ecosystem ['iːkəʊsɪstəm]	Ökosystem
ice-free ['aɪs friː]	eisfrei
agriculture ['æɡrɪkʌltʃə]	Landwirtschaft
species ['spiːʃiːz]	*(Biologie:)* Art
to **store** [stɔː]	speichern
catastrophe [kə'tæstrəfi]	Katastrophe
square mile ['skweə maɪl]	Quadratmeile
ice-covered ['aɪs kʌvəd]	eisbedeckt
undeveloped [ˌʌndɪ'veləpt]	*(Land:)* unbebaut
cropland ['krɒplænd]	Ackerland
to **plant** [plɑːnt]	pflanzen, anpflanzen

page 149

share [ʃeə]	Anteil
fresh water [ˌfreʃ 'wɔːtə]	Süßwasser
lake [leɪk]	(Binnen-)See
wetland ['wetlənd]	Feuchtgebiet, Sumpfgebiet
acre ['eɪkə]	Morgen *(ca. 4047 qm)*
variety [və'raɪəti]	(Pflanzen-)Sorte
greatly ['ɡreɪtli]	erheblich
farm chemicals *pl* ['fɑːm kemɪklz]	Landwirtschaftschemikalien
polluting [pə'luːtɪŋ]	umweltschädlich
fertilizer ['fɜːtəlaɪzə]	Dünger, Düngemittel
precious ['preʃəs]	kostbar
irrigation [ˌɪrɪ'ɡeɪʃn]	Bewässerung
biofuel [ˌbaɪəʊ'fjuːəl]	Biokraftstoff
grain [ɡreɪn]	Getreide
consumption [kən'sʌmpʃn]	Verbrauch, Konsum
to **consume** [kən'sjuːm]	verbrauchen, konsumieren
to **cut** [kʌt]	reduzieren, einschränken
use-by date ['juːs baɪ deɪt]	Haltbarkeitsdatum
cooperation [kəʊˌɒpə'reɪʃn]	Zusammenarbeit, Zusammenwirken

page 150

destruction [dɪ'strʌkʃn]	Zerstörung
equals ['iːkwəlz]	gleich
midday [ˌmɪd'deɪ]	Mittag
to **multiply** ['mʌltɪplaɪ]	multiplizieren
junior ['dʒuːniə]	Jung-, Nachwuchs-
dawn [dɔːn]	Morgendämmerung
garment ['ɡɑːmənt]	Kleidungsstück

page 151

graphic ['ɡræfɪk]	Grafik
to **join sth** [dʒɔɪn]	etw (miteinander) verbinden
divorce [dɪ'vɔːs]	Scheidung
to **work sth out** [ˌwɜːk 'aʊt]	etw ausrechnen
utility bills *pl* [juː'tɪləti bɪlz]	Rechnungen für Versorgungsleistungen
food pantry *AE* ['fuːd pæntri]	Tafel, karitative Essensausgabe
parcel ['pɑːsl]	Paket
to **take the point** [ˌteɪk ðə 'pɔɪnt]	den Standpunkt verstehen

page 152

GM (genetically modified) [ˌdʒiː 'em]	genmanipuliert
to **fear** [fɪə]	fürchten
selection [sɪ'lekʃn]	Auslese, Selektion
to **adapt (to sth)** [ə'dæpt]	sich (an etw) anpassen
adaptation [ˌædæp'teɪʃn]	Anpassung, Anpassungsleistung
gene [dʒiːn]	Gen
to **pass sth to sb** ['pɑːs tə]	jdm etw weiterreichen
to **reproduce** [ˌriːprə'djuːs]	sich fortpflanzen
to **become extinct** [bɪˌkʌm ɪk'stɪŋkt]	aussterben
to **breed** [briːd]	züchten
livestock ['laɪvstɒk]	Vieh
pre-historic [ˌpriː hɪ'stɒrɪk]	prähistorisch
selective [sɪ'lektɪv]	selektiv
breeding ['briːdɪŋ]	Zucht, Züchtung
feature ['fiːtʃə]	Merkmal, Eigenschaft

to **aim at sth** ['eɪm ət]	etw anstreben
wool [wʊl]	Wolle
sheep [ʃiːp]	Schaf
resistance [rɪ'zɪstəns]	Widerstandsfähigkeit, Resistenz
herd [hɜːd]	Herde
crop [krɒp]	Ernte
productive [prə'dʌktɪv]	produktiv
to **modify** ['mɒdɪfaɪ]	modifizieren
genetic [dʒə'netɪk]	genetisch
seed [siːd]	Samen, Saatgut
laboratory [lə'bɒrətri]	Labor
by laboratory design [baɪ lə,bɒrətri dɪ'zaɪn]	im Labor geplant
herbicide ['hɜːbɪsaɪd]	Unkrautvernichtungsmittel
spray [spreɪ]	Spritzmittel
weed [wiːd]	Unkraut
pollen ['pɒlən]	Blütenstaub, Pollen
to **fertilize** ['fɜːtəlaɪz]	befruchten
in no time [ɪn 'nəʊ taɪm]	im Nu
resistant to sth [rɪ'zɪstənt tə]	resistent gegen etw
chemical control (of pests) [,kemɪkl kən'trəʊl]	Schädlingsbekämpfung (smittel)
downside ['daʊnsaɪd]	Nachteil
hydroponics [,haɪdrəʊ'pɒnɪks]	Hydrokultur

page 153

hydroponic [,haɪdrəʊ'pɒnɪk]	Hydrokultur-
soil [sɔɪl]	Erde, Boden, Erdreich
thick [θɪk]	dick, stark
to **absorb** [əb'sɔːb]	aufnehmen, absorbieren
flow [fləʊ]	Strom, Fluss
to **take off** [,teɪk 'ɒf]	*(Flugzeug:)* abheben, starten
passenger ['pæsɪndʒə]	Passagier
to **take off** [,teɪk 'ɒf]	*(Produkt:)* gut anlaufen, gut ankommen
to **take up space** [,teɪk ʌp 'speɪs]	Platz einnehmen
vertical(ly) ['vɜːtɪkl]	senkrecht, vertikal
to **float** [fləʊt]	(auf dem Wasser) treiben
productivity [,prɒdʌk'tɪvəti]	Produktivität

page 154

to **trick sb into doing sth** [trɪk]	jdn (mit einer List) dazu bringen, etw zu tun
to **take sth on** [,teɪk 'ɒn]	*(Aufgabe)* übernehmen
to **take sb on** [,teɪk 'ɒn]	es mit jdm aufnehmen, gegen jdn antreten
to **hunt** [hʌnt]	jagen
protein ['prəʊtiːn]	Eiweiß, Protein
fishing ['fɪʃɪŋ]	Fischerei, Befischung
to maintain stocks [meɪn,teɪn 'stɒks]	den Bestand erhalten
population [,pɒpju'leɪʃn]	*(Biologie:)* Population
to **crash** [kræʃ]	abstürzen, zusammenbrechen
severe [sɪ'vɪə]	ernst, schwer
diamond-shaped ['daɪəmənd ʃeɪpt]	rautenförmig
cage [keɪdʒ]	Käfig
unpolluted [,ʌnpə'luːtɪd]	unverschmutzt

page 155

dome [dəʊm]	Kuppel
to **harvest** ['hɑːvɪst]	ernten
horizontal(ly) [,hɒrɪ'zɒntl]	waagrecht, horizontal
turn [tɜːn]	Runde, Umdrehung
running cost ['rʌnɪŋ kɒst]	Betriebskosten
frame [freɪm]	Rahmen
container [kən'teɪnə]	Behälter
shelf, shelves [ʃelf, ʃelfvz]	Regal, Regale
surprisingly [sə'praɪzɪŋli]	erstaunlicherweise
light bulb ['laɪt bʌlb]	Glühbirne
hectare ['hekteə]	Hektar
to **fail** [feɪl]	ausfallen
starvation [stɑː'veɪʃn]	Hunger
food security ['fuːd sɪkjʊərəti]	Ernährungssicherung
proposal [prə'pəʊzl]	Vorschlag
to **seek** [siːk]	suchen
redevelopment [,riːdɪ'veləpmənt]	Sanierung
splendid ['splendɪd]	prächtig
turbine ['tɜːbaɪn]	Turbine
hall [hɔːl]	Saal, Halle
Grade 1 building [,greɪd 'wʌn bɪldɪŋ]	denkmalgeschütztes Gebäude
to **pull down** [,pʊl 'daʊn]	*(Gebäude)* abreißen
to **redevelop** [,riːdɪ'veləp]	sanieren
committee [kə'mɪti]	Ausschuss, Kommission, Komitee
chairperson ['tʃeəpɜːsn]	Vorsitzende/r

page 156

scale [skeɪl]	Ausmaß, Umfang
to **depend on sth** [dɪ'pend ɒn]	von etw abhängen, auf etw angewiesen sein
cassava [kə'sɑːvə]	Maniok, Kassava
pest [pest]	Schädling
diversity [daɪ'vɜːsəti]	Vielfalt
to **deter** [dɪ'tɜː]	abschrecken, abhalten
to **certify** ['sɜːtɪfaɪ]	zertifizieren
credit ['kredɪt]	Verdienst
undergraduate [,ʌndə'grædʒuət]	Student/in *(vor dem ersten akad. Grad)*
non-profit [,nɒn'prɒfɪt]	gemeinnützig
to **lurch** [lɜːtʃ]	schlingern, taumeln
steep [stiːp]	steil
rutted ['rʌtɪd]	zerfurcht, ausgefahren
pickup ['pɪkʌp]	Pritschenwagen
to **green** [griːn]	begrünen
to **drift** [drɪft]	wehen
slope [sləʊp]	Hang
forested ['fɒrɪstɪd]	bewaldet
brick [brɪk]	Ziegel
partially ['pɑːʃəli]	teilweise
to **plaster** ['plɑːstə]	verputzen
corrugated metal [,kɒrəgeɪtɪd 'metl]	Wellblech
short-sleeved [,ʃɔːt 'sliːvd]	kurzärmlig
blouse [blaʊz]	Bluse
wraparound skirt [,ræpəraʊnd 'skɜːt]	Wickelrock
porch [pɔːtʃ]	Veranda
to **raise** [reɪz]	*(Pflanzen)* anbauen
passion fruit ['pæʃn fruːt]	Passionsfrucht
spinach ['spɪnɪtʃ]	Spinat
leafy vegetable [,liːfi 'vedʒtəbl]	Blattgemüse
backup ['bækʌp]	Ersatz, Reserve
strategic(ally) [strə'tiːdʒɪk]	strategisch
row [rəʊ]	Reihe
sunflower ['sʌnflaʊə]	Sonnenblume
whitefly ['waɪtflaɪ]	Mottenschildlaus

compost ['kɒmpɒst]	Kompost
runoff ['rʌnɒf]	Abfluss, abfließendes Wasser
to **contaminate** [kən'tæmɪneɪt]	verunreinigen, kontaminieren
stream [striːm]	Bach, Fließgewässer
life-altering ['laɪf ɔːltərɪŋ]	lebensverändernd
liberation [lɪbə'reɪʃn]	Befreiung
debt [det]	Schulden
crippling ['krɪplɪŋ]	lähmend, mörderisch
expense [ɪk'spens]	Kosten, Aufwand
annual ['ænjuəl]	jährlich
per capita income [pə ˌkæpɪtə 'ɪnkʌm]	Pro-Kopf-Einkommen

page 157

skeptical *AE* ['skeptɪkl]	skeptisch
to **be aware of sth** [bi ə'weər əv]	sich einer Sache bewusst sein, etw kennen
sweeping views *pl* [ˌswiːpɪŋ 'vjuːz]	atemberaubende Ausblicke, umwerfende Sicht
to **cultivate** ['kʌltɪveɪt]	bewirtschaften
terraced ['terəst]	terrassiert
scarred [skɑːd]	vernarbt, gezeichnet
to **erode** [ɪ'rəʊd]	erodieren
terrace ['terəs]	Terrasse
to **retain** [rɪ'teɪn]	zurückhalten, behalten, bewahren

page 158

drone [drəʊn]	Drohne
to **conjure sth up** [ˌkʌndʒər 'ʌp]	etw heraufbeschwören
sinister ['sɪnɪstə]	finster, unheimlich
remote-controlled [rɪˌməʊt kən'trəʊld]	ferngesteuert
harmless ['hɑːmləs]	harmlos, unbedenklich
radio-controlled [ˌreɪdiəʊ kən'trəʊld]	funkferngesteuert
toy [tɔɪ]	Spielzeug
sophisticated [sə'fɪstɪkeɪtɪd]	hochentwickelt, ausgeklügelt
civilian [sə'vɪliən]	zivil, Zivil-
emergency response [ɪ'mɜːdʒənsi rɪspɒns]	Notfallmaßnahmen
civil engineering [ˌsɪvl endʒɪ'nɪərɪŋ]	Hoch- und Tiefbau
grid [grɪd]	Raster, Gitter
crop health ['krɒp helθ]	Pflanzengesundheit
difficulty ['dɪfɪkəlti]	Schwierigkeit(en)
monitoring ['mɒnɪtərɪŋ]	Überwachung
dimensions *pl* [dɪ'menʃnz]	Abmessungen
farming ['fɑːmɪŋ]	Landwirtschaft
range [reɪndʒ]	Bandbreite, Reihe
hail [heɪl]	Hagel
insect pests *pl* ['ɪnsekt pests]	Schädlinge
bacterial [bæk'tɪəriəl]	bakteriell
viral ['vaɪrəl]	Virus-
fungal ['fʌŋgl]	Pilz-
variation [ˌveəri'eɪʃn]	Schwankung(en), Unterschied(e)
minerals *pl* ['mɪnərəlz]	Mineralien
to **keep track of sth** [ˌkiːp 'træk əv]	den Überblick über etw behalten
to **maximize** ['mæksɪmaɪz]	maximieren
yield [jiːld]	Ertrag
to **harvest** ['hɑːvɪst]	ernten
maize *BE* [meɪz]	Mais
overview ['əʊvəvjuː]	Überblick
precise [prɪ'saɪs]	exakt, genau, präzise
wingspan ['wɪŋspæn]	Spannweite
onboard ['ɒnbɔːd]	an Bord, Bord-
to **detect** [dɪ'tekt]	aufspüren, entdecken
flight path ['flaɪt pɑːθ]	Flugroute
in-flight [ˌɪn'flaɪt]	während des Flugs
diagnostics [ˌdaɪəg'nɒstɪks]	Fehlersuche, Diagnose
to **instruct sb to do sth** [ɪn'strʌkt]	jdm sagen, was er/sie tun soll
high-resolution [ˌhaɪ rezə'luːʃn]	hochauflösend
stressed [strest]	strapaziert, belastet
weed [wiːd]	Unkraut
guesswork ['geswɜːk]	Spekulation, Rätselraten
forestry ['fɒrɪstri]	Forstwirtschaft

UNIT 16

page 159

compass ['kʌmpəs]	Kompass
contraceptive [ˌkɒntrə'septɪv]	Verhütungsmittel
internal combustion engine [ɪnˌtɜːnl kəm'bʌstʃən endʒɪn]	Verbrennungsmotor
printing press ['prɪntɪŋ pres]	Druckerpresse
refrigeration [rɪˌfrɪdʒə'reɪʃn]	Kühlung, Kälteerzeugung
wheel [wiːl]	Rad

page 160

spread [spred]	Verbreitung, Ausbreitung
to **type in** [ˌtaɪp 'ɪn]	eintippen
café ['kæfeɪ]	Café
to **hit** [hɪt]	*(Taste)* drücken
transaction [træn'zækʃn]	(Geschäfts-)Vorgang, Transaktion
additional [ə'dɪʃənl]	zusätzlich
to **fail** [feɪl]	versagen
dramatic(ally) [drə'mætɪk]	dramatisch
colonial power [kəˌləʊniəl 'paʊə]	Kolonialmacht
to **lay cables** [ˌleɪ 'keɪblz]	Kabel verlegen
landline ['lændlaɪn]	Festnetz(-)
highway *AE* ['haɪweɪ]	Autobahn
textbook ['tekstbʊk]	Lehrbuch
(radio/TV) station ['steɪʃn]	(Radio-/Fernseh-)Sender
jungle ['dʒʌŋgl]	Dschungel
savannah [sə'vænə]	Savanne
button ['bʌtn]	Knopf, Button
merchant ['mɜːtʃənt]	Händler/in
to **access sth** ['ækses]	auf etw zugreifen
harvest ['hɑːvɪst]	Ernte
veterinarian [ˌvetərɪ'neəriən]	Tierarzt/-ärztin, Veterinär/in
to **function** ['fʌŋkʃn]	fungieren, funktionieren
substitute ['sʌbstɪtjuːt]	Ersatz
to **keep watch over sb** [ˌkiːp 'wɒtʃ əʊvə]	über jdn wachen, jdn beobachten
to **be in power** [bi ɪn 'paʊə]	an der Macht sein
cutting-edge [ˌkʌtɪŋ 'edʒ]	Spitzen-, auf dem neusten Stand
limitation [ˌlɪmɪ'teɪʃn]	Einschränkung
obstacle ['ɒbstəkl]	Hindernis
enabled [ɪ'neɪbld]	fähig
to **coax sth out of sth** [kəʊks]	etw aus etw herausholen

Unit word list

trajectory [trəˈdʒektəri]	Flugbahn, Weg
breed [briːd]	Rasse
calving [ˈkɑːvɪŋ]	Kalben
feed [fiːd]	Futter
fertility cycle [fəˈtɪləti saɪkl]	Fruchtbarkeitszyklus
illiterate [ɪˈlɪtərət]	Analphabet/in
to **practise** [ˈpræktɪs]	praktizieren
remote [rɪˈməʊt]	entlegen
diagnosis, diagnoses [ˌdaɪəgˈnəʊsɪs, ˌdaɪəgˈnəʊsiːs]	Diagnose, Diagnosen

page 161

epidemic [ˌepɪˈdemɪk]	Epidemie, Seuche
influential [ˌɪnfluˈenʃl]	einflussreich
consulting firm [kənˈsʌltɪŋ fɜːm]	Beratungsfirma
satisfied [ˈsætɪsfaɪd]	zufrieden(gestellt)
ranking [ˈræŋkɪŋ]	Rangliste
governance [ˈgʌvnəns]	Regierungshandeln
leadership [ˈliːdəʃɪp]	Führung
to **award sth to sb** [əˈwɔːd]	jdm etw verleihen, jdm etw zuerkennen
commendable [kəˈmendəbl]	vorbildlich
in a row [ɪn ə ˈrəʊ]	nacheinander
worthy of sth [ˈwɜːði əv]	einer Sache würdig
primarily [praɪˈmerəli]	vorrangig, hauptsächlich
civil society [ˌsɪvl səˈsaɪəti]	Bürgergesellschaft
border customs officer [ˌbɔːdə ˈkʌstəmz ɒfɪsə]	(Grenz-)Zollbeamte/r
to **extort** [ɪkˈstɔːt]	erpressen, abnötigen
to **pressure** [ˈpreʃə]	unter Druck setzen
election [ɪˈlekʃn]	Wahl
tribe [traɪb]	Stamm
to **overcome** [ˌəʊvəˈkʌm]	bewältigen, überwinden
isolated [ˈaɪsəleɪtɪd]	abgeschottet, abgeschieden, isoliert
to **sow** [səʊ]	säen
discord [ˈdɪskɔːd]	Zwietracht
commerce [ˈkɒmɜːs]	Handel
mid-century [ˌmɪd ˈsentʃəri]	Jahrhundertmitte
IT developer [ˌaɪ ˈtiː]	IT-Entwickler/in

page 162

addition [əˈdɪʃn]	Hinzufügung
convention [kənˈvenʃn]	Übereinkunft, Gepflogenheit, Konvention
to **speak up** [ˌspiːk ˈʌp]	lauter sprechen
to **answer the phone** [ˌɑːnsə ðə ˈfəʊn]	ans Telefon gehen

page 163

case [keɪs]	Koffer
trainers *pl* [ˈtreɪnəz]	Turnschuhe
for ages [fər ˈeɪdʒɪz]	ewig, eine Ewigkeit
library [ˈlaɪbrəri]	Bibliothek, Bücherei
at one time [ət ˌwʌn ˈtaɪm]	gleichzeitig
comprehensive school [kɒmprɪˈhensɪv skuːl]	Gesamtschule
to **confiscate** [ˈkɒnfɪskeɪt]	beschlagnahmen, konfiszieren

page 164

artificial intelligence [ɑːtɪˌfɪʃl ɪnˈtelɪdʒəns]	künstliche Intelligenz
aim [eɪm]	Absicht, Ziel, Zweck
scary [ˈskeəri]	gruselig, schaurig
tempting [ˈtemptɪŋ]	verlockend
to **dismiss sth as sth** [dɪsˈmɪs]	etw als etw abtun
notion [ˈnəʊʃn]	Vorstellung, Auffassung
to **point to sth** [ˈpɔɪnt tə]	auf etw hindeuten
progress [ˈprəʊgres]	Fortschritt(e)
driverless [ˈdraɪvələs]	führerlos
civilization [ˌsɪvəlaɪˈzeɪʃn]	Zivilisation
to **magnify** [ˈmægnɪfaɪ]	vergrößern, verstärken
eradication [ɪˌrædɪˈkeɪʃn]	Ausrottung
military [ˈmɪlətri]	Militär
autonomous [ɔːˈtɒnəməs]	autonom
superhuman [ˌsuːpəˈhjuːmən]	übermenschlich
to **outsmart** [ˌaʊtˈsmɑːt]	überlisten, austricksen
to **manipulate** [məˈnɪpjuleɪt]	manipulieren
institute [ˈɪnstɪtjuːt]	Institut
vastness [ˈvɑːstnəs]	unermessliche Weite
universe [ˈjuːnɪvɜːs]	Universum
The best is yet to come. [ðe ˌbest ɪs jet tə ˈkʌm]	Das Beste kommt noch. Die besten Zeiten stehen uns noch bevor.
meaningful [ˈmiːnɪŋfl]	wichtig, bedeutend, sinnstiftend
to **gather** [ˈgæðə]	sammeln, zusammentragen
completion [kəmˈpliːʃn]	Ausführung, Erledigung *(einer Aufgabe)*
course [kɔːs]	Weg, Vorgehensweise
either [ˈaɪðə]	eine/r/s *(von beiden)*
extinction [ɪkˈstɪŋkʃn]	Vernichtung, Ausrottung, Aussterben
crossroads [ˈkrɒsrəʊdz]	Scheideweg

page 165

outcome [ˈaʊtkʌm]	Ergebnis, Resultat
superior [suːˈpɪəriə]	überlegen
alien [ˈeɪliən]	außerirdisch
to **devote** [dɪˈvəʊt]	widmen
industrialist [ɪnˈdʌstriəlɪst]	Industrielle/r
general [ˈdʒenrəl]	General
to **reap the benefits** [ˌriːp ðə ˈbenɪfɪts]	die Früchte ernten, die Vorteile nutzen

page 166

to **enjoy oneself** [ɪnˈdʒɔɪ wʌnself]	sich (gut) amüsieren
vase [vɑːz]	Vase
missing [ˈmɪsɪŋ]	vermisst
test drive [ˈtest draɪv]	Testfahrt
road testing [ˈrəʊd testɪŋ]	Fahrversuche, Fahrerprobung, Straßentests
test track [ˈtest træk]	Teststrecke
to **perform** [pəˈfɔːm]	(leistungsmäßig) abschneiden
failure [ˈfeɪljə]	Ausfall, Defekt
(car) crash [kræʃ]	Autounfall
accident [ˈæksɪdənt]	Unfall
human error [ˌhjuːmən ˈerə]	menschliches Versagen
property damage [ˈprɒpəti dæmɪdʒ]	Sachschaden, Sachschäden
association [əˌsəʊsiˈeɪʃn]	Verband, Vereinigung
freeway *AE* [ˈfriːweɪ]	Autobahn
smooth(ly) [smuːð]	reibungslos
to **speed up** [ˌspiːd ˈʌp]	beschleunigen
to **slow down** [ˌsləʊ ˈdaʊn]	bremsen
tailback [ˈteɪlbæk]	Rückstau
gallon [ˈgælən]	Gallone *(= 3,78 l in den USA)*
service station [ˈsɜːvɪs steɪʃn]	Tankstelle

page 167

to **suffer from sth** ['sʌfə frəm]	unter etw zu leiden haben
in-car entertainment [ˌɪn kɑːr entə'teɪnmənt]	Unterhaltungselektronik im Auto
operator ['ɒpəreɪtə]	Betreiber/in
city planner ['sɪti plænə]	Stadtplaner/in
emergency service [ɪ'mɜːdʒənsi sɜːvɪs]	Notfalldienst
accident and emergency department (A&E) [ˌæksɪdənt ənd ɪ'mɜːdʒənsi dɪpɑːtmənt]	Notaufnahme
legislature ['ledʒɪsleɪtʃə]	Gesetzgebung
special committee [ˌspeʃl kə'mɪti]	Sonderausschuss
representative [ˌreprɪ'zentətɪv]	Repräsentant/in, Abgeordnete/r
pressures *pl* ['preʃəz]	Belastungen
robot ['rəʊbɒt]	Roboter
domestic [də'mestɪk]	heimisch, Inlands-
to **declare** [dɪ'kleə]	verkünden

page 168

robotics [rəʊ'bɒtɪks]	Robotertechnik
dishwasher ['dɪʃwɒʃə]	Spülmaschine
to **load the dishwasher** [ˌləʊd ðə 'dɪʃwɒʃə]	die Spülmaschine einräumen
to **unveil** [ˌʌn'veɪl]	enthüllen, vorstellen
to **manipulate** [mə'nɪpjuleɪt]	handhaben, bedienen
unfamiliar [ˌʌnfə'mɪliə]	unbekannt, ungewohnt
humanlike ['hjuːmənlaɪk]	menschenähnlich
grasp [grɑːsp]	Griff
outing ['aʊtɪŋ]	Ausflug, Ausfahrt
depth [depθ]	(räumliche) Tiefe
wrist [rɪst]	Handgelenk
to **calculate** ['kælkjuleɪt]	berechnen
to **grasp** [grɑːsp]	greifen, ergreifen
novel ['nɒvl]	neu, neuartig
robotic [rəʊ'bɒtɪk]	Roboter-
obstruction [əb'strʌkʃn]	Hindernis
to **go for sth** ['gəʊ fə]	etw wählen, etw wagen
collaborator [kə'læbəreɪtə]	Mitarbeiter/in
ambitious [æm'bɪʃəs]	ehrgeizig
a bunch of [ə 'bʌntʃ əv]	eine Menge
to **scatter** ['skætə]	verteilen, verstreuen
set [set]	Menge
to **figure out** [ˌfɪgər 'aʊt]	herausfinden
to **assign sb sth** [ə'saɪn]	jdm etw zuweisen, jdn mit etw beauftragen
duty ['djuːti]	Aufgabe, Pflicht
necessity [nə'sesəti]	Notwendigkeit
manipulative [mə'nɪpjələtɪv]	manipulativ
faculty ['fæklti]	Fähigkeit
cutlery ['kʌtləri]	Besteck
fiddly ['fɪdli]	knifflig, fummelig
symmetrical [sɪ'metrɪkl]	symmetrisch
to **represent** [ˌreprɪ'zent]	vertreten, repräsentieren
airborne drone [ˌeəbɔːn 'drəʊn]	Flugdrohne
novelty ['nɒvlti]	Neues, Neuartiges
to **perform sth** [pə'fɔːm]	etw ausführen, etw durchführen
alongside [əˌlɒŋ'saɪd]	neben
uncertainty [ʌn'sɜːtnti]	Ungewissheit

page 169

unstructured [ʌn'strʌktʃəd]	unstrukturiert
discipline ['dɪsəplɪn]	Disziplin
mechanical engineering [mɪˌkænɪkl ˌendʒɪ'nɪərɪŋ]	Maschinenbau
electrical engineering [ɪˌlektrɪkl ˌendʒɪ'nɪərɪŋ]	Elektrotechnik
unexpected [ˌʌnɪk'spektɪd]	unerwartet
setback ['setbæk]	Rückschlag
to **complicate** ['kɒmplɪkeɪt]	komplizieren
pinkie ['pɪŋki]	kleiner Finger
to **approach sth** [ə'prəʊtʃ]	sich einer Sache nähern
to **be keen to do sth** [bi 'kiːn tə]	etw unbedingt tun wollen
to **transfer** [træns'fɜː]	übergeben, weitergeben
bi-manual [ˌbaɪ 'mænjuəl]	beidhändig
to **lack sth** [læk]	etw nicht haben
sense of touch [ˌsens əf 'tʌtʃ]	Tastsinn
tactile sensing [ˌtæktaɪl 'sensɪŋ]	Tastempfinden
sufficient [sə'fɪʃnt]	ausreichend, hinreichend
to **operate** ['ɒpəreɪt]	tätig sein
enthusiastic about sth [ɪnˌθjuːzi'æstɪk əbaʊt]	von etw begeistert
acronym ['ækrənɪm]	Akronym, Abkürzung
homage ['hɒmɪdʒ]	Reverenz
flaxen-haired [ˌflæksn 'heəd]	strohblond, flachsblond
to **chuckle** ['tʃʌkl]	kichern, schmunzeln
unpredictable [ˌʌnprɪ'dɪktəbl]	launenhaft, unkalkulierbar

page 170

satellite ['sætəlaɪt]	Satellit
to **be fully operational** [bi ˌfʊli ɒpə'reɪʃənl]	vollständig in Betrieb sein
orbit ['ɔːbɪt]	Umlaufbahn
altitude ['æltɪtjuːd]	Höhe
to **occupy** ['ɒkjupaɪ]	besetzen, belegen
orbital plane [ˌɔːbɪtl'pleɪn]	Umlaufebene
inclined [ɪn'klaɪnd]	geneigt
angle ['æŋgl]	Winkel
equator [ɪ'kweɪtə]	Äquator
to **be spread evenly** [bi ˌspred 'iːvnli]	gleichmäßig verteilt sein
to **orbit** ['ɔːbɪt]	umrunden
spare [speə]	Reserve, Ersatz
stand-by ['stændbaɪ]	Bereitschaft
planner ['plænə]	Planer/in
constellation [ˌkɒnstə'leɪʃn]	Konstellation
in sight [ɪn 'saɪt]	in Sicht, im Blickfeld
hence [hens]	daher, folglich
to **determine** [dɪ'tɜːmɪn]	bestimmen
ranging signal ['reɪndʒɪŋ sɪgnəl]	Peilsignal
to **broadcast** ['brɔːdkɑːst]	senden, ausstrahlen
inclination [ˌɪnklɪ'neɪʃn]	Neigung, Neigungswinkel
coverage ['kʌvərɪdʒ]	Abdeckung, Erfassung
polar latitudes *pl* [ˌpəʊlə 'lætɪtjuːdz]	polare Breiten
to **serve** [sɜːv]	bedienen, versorgen
accurate(ly) ['ækjərət]	genau
high-rise city [ˌhaɪ raɪz 'sɪti]	Stadt mit Hochhäusern
overhead [ˌəʊvə'hed]	darüber, am Himmel
interoperable [ˌɪntər'ɒpərəbl]	interoperabel, vollständig kompatibel
extensive [ɪk'stensɪv]	umfangreich
positioning [pə'zɪʃnɪŋ]	Positionierung, Positions-
clock error ['klɒk erə]	Taktfehler, Uhrfehler
range [reɪndʒ]	Reichweite, Umfang
launch vehicle ['lɔːntʃ viːəkl]	Trägerrakete

Unit word list

to **draw sth up** [ˌdrɔː ˈʌp]	etw erstellen
timeline [ˈtaɪmlaɪn]	Zeitachse, Zeitleiste
completion [kəmˈpliːʃn]	Abschluss

JOB SKILLS 4

page 171

email exchange [ˈiːmeɪl ɪkstʃeɪndʒ]	E-Mail-Korrespondenz
initial [ɪˈnɪʃl]	erste/r/s
to **attend sth** [əˈtend]	an etw teilnehmen
member of staff [ˌmembər əf ˈstɑːf]	Mitarbeiter/in
to **get to know sb** [ˌget tə ˈnəʊ]	jdn kennen lernen
in good time [ɪn ˌgʊd ˈtaɪm]	rechtzeitig

page 172

seating [ˈsiːtɪŋ]	Bestuhlung
projector [prəˈdʒektə]	Beamer
reception [rɪˈsepʃn]	Empfang
handout [ˈhændaʊt]	Arbeitsblatt
refreshment [rɪˈfreʃmənt]	Erfrischung
name tag [ˈneɪm tæg]	Namensschild
place card [ˈpleɪs kɑːd]	Platzkarte, Tischkarte
to **leak** [liːk]	auslaufen
to **dry out** [ˌdraɪ ˈaʊt]	austrocknen
pad [pæd]	Notizblock
to **type sth up** [ˌtaɪp ˈʌp]	etw (am Computer) formulieren, etw ausarbeiten
agenda [əˈdʒendə]	Tagesordnung
on sb's behalf [ɒn bɪˈhɑːf]	in jds Namen
item [ˈaɪtəm]	Tagesordnungspunkt

page 173

break [breɪk]	Pause
cloud [klaʊd]	Wolke
gossip [ˈgɒsɪp]	Klatsch, Tratsch
taboo [təˈbuː]	Tabu
to **convince** [kənˈvɪns]	überzeugen
chilly [ˈtʃɪli]	kühl
Research and Development (R&D) [rɪˌsɜːtʃ ən dɪˈveləpmənt]	Forschung(s-) und Entwicklung(sabteilung)
section [ˈsekʃn]	Abteilung
to **get down to business** [get ˌdaʊn tə ˈbɪznəs]	zur Sache kommen

page 174

millennium [mɪˈleniəm]	Jahrtausend
talk [tɔːk]	Vortrag
to **customize** [ˈkʌstəmaɪz]	auf den Kundenbedarf zuschneiden
to **near** [nɪə]	sich nähern
to **get down to business** [ˌget ˈdaʊn tə ˈbɪznəs]	zur Sache kommen
focus [ˈfəʊkəs]	Schwerpunkt
to **distribute** [dɪˈstrɪbjuːt]	verteilen, austeilen
to conclude [tə kənˈkluːd]	abschließend
bit [bɪt]	Teil

TECHNICAL TOPIC 1

page 175

cloud [klaʊd]	Wolke, Cloud
computing [kəmˈpjuːtɪŋ]	Datenverarbeitung, Rechenwesen, Computer(-)
consultancy [kənˈsʌltənsi]	Beratung(sfirma)
subscription [səbˈskrɪpʃn]	Abonnement
to **interface with sth** [ˈɪntəfeɪs wɪð]	sich mit etw verbinden
to **back sth up** [ˌbæk ˈʌp]	eine Sicherungskopie von etw machen
assignment [əˈsaɪnmənt]	Aufgabe
hard drive [ˈhɑːd draɪv]	Festplatte
storage [ˈstɔːrɪdʒ]	*(Daten:)* Speicherung
line [laɪn]	Grenze, Trennlinie
fuzzy [ˈfʌzi]	unscharf, verschwommen
to **synchronize** [ˈsɪŋkrənaɪz]	abgleichen, synchronisieren
to **keep track of sth** [ˌkiːp ˈtræk əv]	den Überblick über etw behalten
unauthorized [ˌʌnˈɔːθəraɪzd]	unbefugt
to **disappear** [ˌdɪsəˈpɪə]	verschwinden
contact details *pl* [ˈkɒntækt diːteɪlz]	Kontaktdaten
financial records *pl* [faˌnænʃl ˈrekɔːdz]	Finanzunterlagen
backup [ˈbækʌp]	Sicherungskopie

page 176

recommendation [ˌrekəmenˈdeɪʃn]	Empfehlung
to **apply to sth** [əˈplaɪ tə]	für etw gelten, auf etw zutreffen
compatible [kəmˈpætəbl]	kompatibel
bandwidth [ˈbændwɪdθ]	Bandbreite
to **rent** [rent]	mieten
to **crowdfund** [ˈkraʊdfʌnd]	durch freiwillige Beiträge (übers Internet) finanzieren
to **convert** [kənˈvɜːt]	umbauen
occasional(ly) [əˈkeɪʒənl]	gelegentlich

page 177

explanatory [ɪkˈsplænətri]	erläuternd
dynamic [daɪˈnæmɪk]	dynamisch
to **update** [ˌʌpˈdeɪt]	aktualisieren, aufrüsten
application [ˌæplɪˈkeɪʃn]	Software, Programm
collaborative [kəˈlæbərətɪv]	kollaborativ, gemeinschaftlich
collaboration [kəˌlæbəˈreɪʃn]	Zusammenarbeit
to **centralize** [ˈsentrəlaɪz]	bündeln, zusammenfassen
planning [ˈplænɪŋ]	Planung
financial reporting [faɪˌnænʃl rɪˈpɔːtɪŋ]	Rechnungslegung
free of charge [ˌfriː əv ˈtʃɑːdʒ]	gebührenfrei, kostenlos
competency [ˈkɒmpɪtənsi]	Kompetenz
to **tie** [taɪ]	binden, knüpfen
to **house** [haʊz]	unterbringen
sales force [ˈseɪlz fɔːs]	Verkaufspersonal
sales rep(resentative) [ˈseɪlz rep]	Handelsvertreter/in, Verkäufer/in

TECHNICAL TOPIC 2

page 178

signage [ˈsaɪnɪdʒ]	Beschilderung, Anzeige
electric motor [ɪˌlektrɪk ˈməʊtə]	Elektromotor
to **demonstrate** [ˈdemənstreɪt]	zeigen, darlegen
engineering [ˌendʒɪˈnɪərɪŋ]	(Ingenieur-)Technik, Maschinenbau
bright [braɪt]	hell
to **light sth up** [ˌlaɪt ˈʌp]	etw erleuchten, etw erhellen
to **fade** [feɪd]	verblassen

to **fall apart** [ˌfɔːl əˈpɑːt]	auseinanderfallen
dazzling [ˈdæzlɪŋ]	überwältigend, verwirrend
array [əˈreɪ]	Reihe, Spektrum
to **revolutionize** [ˌrevəˈluːʃənaɪz]	revolutionieren
visibility [ˌvɪzəˈbɪləti]	Sichtbarkeit
high definition [ˌhaɪ defɪˈnɪʃn]	hohe (Bild-)Auflösung
exotic [ɪɡˈzɒtɪk]	exotisch
holographic [ˌhɒləˈɡræfɪk]	holografisch, Hologramm-
fog [fɒɡ]	Nebel
to **animate** [ˈænɪmeɪt]	animieren
pedestrian [pɪˈdestriən]	Fußgänger/in
pavement [ˈpeɪvmənt]	Bürgersteig, Gehweg
exhibition centre [ˌeksɪˈbɪʃn sentə]	Messezentrum
novel [ˈnɒvl]	neuartig
to **broadcast** [ˈbrɔːdkɑːst]	senden, übertragen
interactive [ˌɪntərˈæktɪv]	interaktiv
solid [ˈsɒlɪd]	massiv
page 179	
to **assess** [əˈses]	beurteilen, bewerten
sheet [ʃiːt]	Blatt (Papier)
by yourself [baɪ jɔːˈself]	allein
originality [əˌrɪdʒəˈnæləti]	Originalität, Neuheit
unusual [ʌnˈjuːʒʊəl]	ungewöhnlich
effectiveness [ɪˈfektɪvnəs]	Effektivität
gimmick [ˈɡɪmɪk]	Trick, (technische) Spielerei
tried and trusted [ˌtraɪd ən ˈtrʌstɪd]	seit Langem bewährt
board of directors [ˌbɔːd əv dəˈrektəz]	Vorstand, Geschäftsführung
unit [ˈjuːnɪt]	Gerät
roundup [ˈraʊndʌp]	Übersicht, Zusammenfassung
surrounded by sth [səˈraʊndɪd baɪ]	von etw umgeben
to **display** [dɪˈspleɪ]	anzeigen, darstellen
limitation [ˌlɪmɪˈteɪʃn]	Grenze
exhibition [ˌeksɪˈbɪʃn]	Messe
compact [ˈkɒmpækt]	kompakt
vaporizer [ˈveɪpəraɪzə]	Zerstäuber
to **emit** [ɪˈmɪt]	ausstoßen
droplet [ˈdrɒplət]	Tröpfchen
to **float** [fləʊt]	(in der Luft) schweben
fan [fæn]	Ventilator
vertical [ˈvɜːtɪkl]	senkrecht, vertikal
infrared [ˌɪnfrəˈred]	infrarot, Infrarot-
to **capture** [ˈkæptʃə]	erfassen
gesture [ˈdʒestʃə]	Geste
central processing unit [ˌsentrəl ˈprəʊsesɪŋ juːnɪt]	Hauptprozessor
feedback [ˈfiːdbæk]	Rückinformation, Feedback
page 180	
light-emitting [ˈlaɪt ɪmɪtɪŋ]	lichtabstrahlend
solid state [ˌsɒlɪd ˈsteɪt]	Festkörper(-)
to **convert** [kənˈvɜːt]	umwandeln
crystal [ˈkrɪstl]	Kristall
semiconductor [ˌsemikənˈdʌktə]	Halbleiter
silicon [ˈsɪlɪkən]	Silizium
to **attach** [əˈtætʃ]	anbringen, befestigen
to **seal** [siːl]	abdichten, einschließen
epoxy (resin) [ɪˈpɒksi]	Epoxidharz
current [ˈkʌrənt]	(elektrischer) Strom

to **flow** [fləʊ]	fließen, strömen
to **give off** [ˌɡɪv ˈɒf]	abgeben, ausstoßen
to **determine** [dɪˈtɜːmɪn]	bestimmen
wavelength [ˈweɪvleŋθ]	Wellenlänge
thus [ðʌs]	dadurch, damit
to **arrange** [əˈreɪndʒ]	anordnen
module [ˈmɒdjuːl]	Modul
equal [ˈiːkwəl]	gleich
rectangular [rekˈtæŋɡjələ]	rechteckig
grid [ɡrɪd]	Raster, Gitter
viewer [ˈvjuːə]	Betrachter/in
to **illuminate** [ɪˈluːmɪneɪt]	beleuchten
liquid [ˈlɪkwɪd]	flüssig
to **combine** [kəmˈbaɪn]	kombinieren, verbinden, vereinen

TECHNICAL TOPIC 3

page 181	
passive [ˈpæsɪv]	passiv
to **renovate** [ˈrenəveɪt]	renovieren
standard [ˈstændəd]	Norm, Richtlinie
radiator [ˈreɪdieɪtə]	Heizkörper
central heating [ˌsentrəl ˈhiːtɪŋ]	Zentralheizung
thermal bridge [ˌθɜːml ˈbrɪdʒ]	Kältebrücke, Wärmebrücke
to **remove** [rɪˈmuːv]	beseitigen
air conditioning [ˈeə kəndɪʃnɪŋ]	Klimaanlage(n-)
demand (for sth) [dɪˈmɑːnd]	Bedarf (an etw)
Alpine [ˈælpaɪn]	alpin, Gebirgs-
to **compensate for sth** [ˈkɒmpənseɪt fə]	etw ausgleichen
draft [drɑːft]	Luftzug, Zugluft
ventilation heating [ˌventɪˈleɪʃn hiːtɪŋ]	Warmluftheizung
insulation [ˌɪnsjuˈleɪʃn]	Isolierung
to **transfer** [trænsˈfɜː]	(ab-, weiter)leiten, übertragen
to **utilize** [ˈjuːtəlaɪz]	nutzen, nutzbar machen
recovery [rɪˈkʌvəri]	Rückgewinnung
subsoil heat exchange [ˌsʌbsɔɪl ˈhiːt ɪkstʃeɪndʒ]	Erdwärmeaustausch
durable [ˈdjʊərəbl]	langlebig, solide, strapazierfähig
page 182	
glazing [ˈɡleɪzɪŋ]	Verglasung
thermal bridging [ˌθɜːml ˈbrɪdʒɪŋ]	Wärmebrücken
airtightness [ˈeətaɪtnəs]	Luftdichtheit, Luftdichtigkeit
to **insulate** [ˈɪnsjuleɪt]	isolieren
envelope [ˈenvələʊp]	Hülle
airtight [ˈeətaɪt]	luftdicht
principle [ˈprɪnsəpl]	Prinzip, Grundsatz
heat transfer [ˈhiːt trænsfɜː]	Wärmeübertragung
triple-glazed [ˌtrɪpl ˈɡleɪzd]	dreifach verglast
sheet [ʃiːt]	(Glas-)Scheibe
interior [ɪnˈtɪəriə]	Innenraum, Innenbereich
the least resistance [ðə ˌliːst rɪˈzɪstəns]	der geringste Widerstand
conductive [kənˈdʌktɪv]	leitfähig, leitend
brick [brɪk]	Ziegel, Backstein
window frame [ˈwɪndəʊ freɪm]	Fensterrahmen
layer [ˈleɪə]	Schicht
to **recover** [rɪˈkʌvə]	(rück)gewinnen

thermal energy [ˌθɜːml 'enədʒi]	Wärmeenergie
exhaust air [ɪgˌzɔːst 'eə]	Abluft
counterflow heat exchanger [ˌkaʊntəfləʊ 'hiːt ɪkstʃeɪndʒə]	Gegenstromwärmetauscher
air flow ['eə fləʊ]	Luftstrom
supply air [sə'plaɪ eə]	Zuluft
pipe [paɪp]	Rohr, Röhre, Schlauch
thermal mass [ˌθɜːml 'mæs]	Wärmemasse, thermische Masse
cooling ['kuːlɪŋ]	Kühlung

page 183

channel ['tʃænl]	Kanal, Leitung
plate [pleɪt]	Platte
to **replenish** [rɪ'plenɪʃ]	(wieder)auffüllen, (wieder) ergänzen
extract air ['ekstrakt eə]	Abluft
savings *pl* ['seɪvɪŋz]	Einsparung(en), Ersparnis(se)
suitability [ˌsuːtə'bɪləti]	Eignung

TECHNICAL TOPIC 4

page 184

woodworking ['wʊdwɜːkɪŋ]	Holzbearbeitung, Holz-
carpenter ['kɑːpəntə]	Zimmerer/in, Schreiner/in
timber ['tɪmbə]	(Bau-)Holz
timber-framed house [ˌtɪmbə freɪmd 'haʊs]	Fachwerkhaus
to **struggle** ['strʌgl]	kämpfen, zu kämpfen haben
engineered timber [endʒɪˌnɪəd 'tɪmbə]	Ingenieurholz
machining [mə'ʃiːnɪŋ]	(maschinelle) Bearbeitung
curved [kɜːvd]	gebogen
glulam ['gluːlæm]	Brettschichtholz
beam [biːm]	Balken, Träger
to **glue** [gluː]	leimen, kleben
to **laminate** ['læmɪneɪt]	laminieren, schichten
application [ˌæplɪ'keɪʃn]	Anwendung
worktop ['wɜːktɒp]	Arbeitsplatte
structural beam [ˌstrʌktʃərəl 'biːm]	Trägerbalken
structural steel [ˌstrʌktʃərəl 'stiːl]	Baustahl, tragende Stahlelemente
motorway *BE* ['məʊtəweɪ]	Autobahn
to **cut down** [ˌkʌt 'daʊn]	*(Baum)* fällen
strength [streŋθ]	Festigkeit, Tragfähigkeit
ratio ['reɪʃiəʊ]	Verhältnis
glue [gluː]	Leim, Kleber
moisture ['mɔɪstʃə]	Feuchtigkeit
chlorine ['klɔːriːn]	Chlor
to **sequence sth** ['siːkwəns]	etw in eine Reihenfolge bringen
to **apply sth to sth** [ə'plaɪ tə]	etw auf etw anwenden, etw auf etw ausüben
lamella, lamellae [lə'melə, lə'melaɪ]	Lamelle, Lamellen
glue line ['gluː laɪn]	Verleimung
glue spreader ['gluː spredə]	Leimauftragsmaschine
log [lɒg]	(entasteter) Baumstamm
to **saw** [sɔː]	sägen
saw mill ['sɔː mɪl]	Sägewerk
plank [plæŋk]	Bohle, Brett
to **label** ['leɪbl]	etikettieren, auszeichnen
specification [ˌspesɪfɪ'keɪʃn]	Spezifikation, Vorgabe, technische Daten
construction site [kən'strʌkʃn saɪt]	Baustelle
workshop ['wɜːkʃɒp]	Werkstatt
to **fell** [fel]	fällen
sustainably managed [səˌsteɪnəbli 'mænɪdʒd]	nachhaltig bewirtschaftet
softwoods *pl* ['sɒftwʊdz]	Weichholz
plantation [plæn'teɪʃn]	Plantage, Pflanzung
kiln [kɪln]	Trockenofen, Trockenkammer
moisture content ['kɒntent]	Feuchtigkeitsgehalt
stable ['steɪbl]	stabil
to **split** [splɪt]	reißen
to **bend** [bend]	sich verziehen, sich werfen
finger-jointed ['fɪŋgə dʒɔɪntɪd]	keilgezinkt
to **feed sth through sth** [fiːd]	etw durch etw führen
planer ['pleɪnə]	Hobelmaschine
uniform ['juːnɪfɔːm]	gleichmäßig
thickness ['θɪknəs]	Stärke, Dicke
clamp [klæmp]	Schraubzwinge
firm(ly) [fɜːm]	fest
straight [streɪt]	gerade
to **cure** [kjʊə]	aushärten
zigzag ['zɪg zæg]	Zickzack(-)
to **apply sth to sth** [ə'plaɪ]	etw auf etw auftragen
smooth [smuːð]	glatt
finish ['fɪnɪʃ]	Oberfläche

page 185

strength grading ['streŋθ greɪdɪŋ]	Festigkeitssortierung
adhesive [əd'hiːsɪv]	Klebstoff
application [ˌæplɪ'keɪʃn]	Auftrag
clamping ['klæmpɪŋ]	Verpressen
planing ['pleɪnɪŋ]	Hobeln
finishing ['fɪnɪʃɪŋ]	Oberflächenbearbeitung, Endbearbeitung
CNC machining [ˌsiː en 'siː məʃiːnɪŋ]	CNC-Bearbeitung
milling machine ['mɪlɪŋ məʃiːn]	Fräsmaschine
computer numerical control [kəmˌpjuːtə njuːˌmerɪkl kən'trəʊl]	rechnergestützte numerische Steuerung
power tool ['paʊə tuːl]	Elektrowerkzeug
versatile ['vɜːsətaɪl]	vielseitig (einsetzbar)
end mill ['end mɪl]	Fräser
drill bit ['drɪl bɪt]	Bohrer, Bohrspitze
drill [drɪl]	Bohrer, Bohrmaschine
mill [mɪl]	Fräse
sideways ['saɪdweɪz]	seitlich, zur Seite
precision [prɪ'sɪʒn]	Präzision, Genauigkeit
axis, axes ['æksɪs, 'æksiːz]	Achse, Achsen
to **tilt** [tɪlt]	neigen, kippen
workpiece ['wɜːkpiːs]	Werkstück
to **rotate** [rəʊ'teɪt]	(sich) (um die eigene Achse) drehen

page 186

reliance on sth [rɪ'laɪəns ɒn]	Abhängigkeit von etw
operator ['ɒpəreɪtə]	(Maschinen-)Bediener/in
design [dɪ'zaɪn]	Konstruktion
manually operated [ˌmænjuəli 'ɒpəreɪtɪd]	handbetrieben, von Hand bedient
hand tool ['hænd tuːl]	Handwerkzeug
to **simulate** ['sɪmjuleɪt]	simulieren
manufacture [ˌmænju'fæktʃə]	Fertigung, Herstellung
prototype ['prəʊtətaɪp]	Prototyp

to **supervise** ['su:pəvaɪz]	überwachen, beaufsichtigen
craftspeople ['krɑ:ftspi:pl]	Handwerker
organic [ɔ:'gænɪk]	organisch
to **make sth obsolete** [ˌmeɪk 'ɒbsəli:t]	etw überflüssig machen
mortise ['mɔ:tɪs]	Nut, Zapfenloch
tenon ['tenən]	Zapfen
joint [dʒɔɪnt]	Verbindung
mortise and tenon joint [ˌmɔ:tɪs ən 'tenən dʒɔɪnt]	Zapfenverbindung
woodworker ['wʊdwɜ:kə]	Holzhandwerker, Schreiner/in
neat [ni:t]	sauber
to **wobble** ['wɒbl]	wackeln
house frame ['haʊs freɪm]	Holzskelett
nostalgia [nɒ'stældʒə]	Nostalgie
carpentry workshop ['kɑ:pəntri wɜ:kʃɒp]	Zimmerei, Schreinerei

TECHNICAL TOPIC 5

page 187

speech [spi:tʃ]	(gesprochene) Sprache
speech recognition ['spi:tʃ rekəgnɪʃn]	Spracherkennung
domestic appliance [dəˌmestɪk ə'plaɪəns]	Haushaltsgerät, Elektrogerät
to **implement** ['ɪmplɪmənt]	einbauen
to **brief sb** [bri:f]	jdn informieren, jdn einweisen
to **review** [rɪ'vju:]	*(Text)* redigieren, korrigieren
to **break sth down** [ˌbreɪk 'daʊn]	etw aufgliedern, etw in einzelne Teile zerlegen
analogue ['ænəlɒg]	analog
Practice makes perfect. [ˌpræktɪs meɪks 'pɜ:fɪkt]	Übung macht den Meister.
to **give sth a second thought** [gɪv ə ˌsekənd 'θɔ:t]	sich über etw Gedanken machen
computerized [kəm'pju:təraɪzd]	computergestützt
sophisticated [sə'fɪstɪkeɪtɪd]	hochentwickelt, ausgeklügelt
analogue-to-digital converter (ADC) [ˌænəlɒg tə ˌdɪdʒɪtl kən'vɜ:tə]	Analog-Digital-Wandler (AD-Wandler)
to **sample** ['sɑ:mpl]	abtasten
measurement ['meʒəmənt]	Messung, Messwert
at frequent intervals [ət ˌfri:kwənt 'ɪntəvlz]	in kurzen Abständen
to **digitize** ['dɪdʒɪtaɪz]	digitalisieren
acoustic model [əˌku:stɪk 'mɒdl]	akustisches Modell
segment ['segmənt]	Teilstück, Segment
match [mætʃ]	Übereinstimmung, Entsprechung
accuracy ['ækjərəsi]	Genauigkeit
end user ['end ju:zə]	Endbenutzer/in, Privatanwender/in
pattern ['pætn]	Muster
command [kə'mɑ:nd]	Befehl

page 188

to **annotate** ['ænəteɪt]	beschriften, mit Anmerkungen versehen
soundcard ['saʊndkɑ:d]	Soundkarte

page 189

translator [træns'leɪtə]	Übersetzer/in
captain ['kæptɪn]	Kapitän, Hauptmann
crew [kru:]	Mannschaft, Besatzung
to **seek sth out** [ˌsi:k 'aʊt]	nach etw suchen
civilization [ˌsɪvəlaɪ'zeɪʃn]	Zivilisation
universal [ˌju:nɪ'vɜ:sl]	universell, Universal-
fortunately ['fɔ:tʃənətli]	zum Glück
to **break down barriers** [breɪk ˌdaʊn 'bæriəz]	Grenzen beseitigen, Hürden überwinden
language barrier ['læŋgwɪdʒ bæriə]	Sprachbarriere
blocker (to sth) ['blɒkə]	Hemmnis (für etw)
vice president [ˌvaɪs 'prezɪdənt]	Vizepräsident/in
vice versa [ˌvaɪs 'vɜ:sə]	umgekehrt
to **demonstrate** ['demənstreɪt]	vorführen, demonstrieren
minor ['maɪnə]	klein, unbedeutend
galaxy ['gæləksi]	Galaxie
diplomacy [dɪ'pləʊməsi]	Diplomatie
multilingual [ˌmʌlti'lɪŋgwəl]	mehrsprachig
dictation [dɪk'teɪʃn]	Diktieren, Diktat
synthesis ['sɪnθɪsɪs]	Synthese
chief executive (officer) [ˌtʃi:f ɪg'zekjətɪv]	Vorstandsvorsitzende/r
neural net(work) [ˌnjʊərəl 'net]	neuronales Netz
to **generate** ['dʒenəreɪt]	erzeugen
nerve [nɜ:v]	Nerv
brain [breɪn]	Gehirn

TECHNICAL TOPIC 6

page 190

proprietary [prə'praɪətri]	urheberrechtlich geschützt
supporter [sə'pɔ:tə]	Anhänger/in, Befürworter/in
undecided [ˌʌndɪ'saɪdɪd]	unschlüssig
concise [kən'saɪs]	knapp, kurz (und bündig)
source code ['sɔ:s kəʊd]	Quellcode
modification [ˌmɒdɪfɪ'keɪʃn]	Änderung, Abwandlung, Modifizierung
enhancement [ɪn'hɑ:nsmənt]	Verbesserung
to **fix** [fɪks]	*(Fehler)* beheben, beseitigen
to **maintain control** [meɪnˌteɪn kən'trəʊl]	Kontrolle ausüben
exclusive [ɪk'sklu:sɪv]	ausschließlich, exklusiv
property ['prɒpəti]	Eigentum
license *AE* ['laɪsns]	Lizenz
expressly [ɪk'spresli]	ausdrücklich
to **permit** [pə'mɪt]	gestatten
to **alter** ['ɔ:ltə]	ändern
to **promote sth** [prə'məʊt]	etw fördern, sich für etw einsetzen
sharing ['ʃeərɪŋ]	Teilen, gemeinsame Nutzung
to **incorporate** [ɪn'kɔ:pəreɪt]	integrieren, aufnehmen
to **prevent sb from doing sth** [prɪ'vent]	jdn daran hindern, etw zu tun

page 191

alike [ə'laɪk]	gleichermaßen, wie
operating system ['ɒpəreɪtɪŋ sɪstəm]	Betriebssystem
bug [bʌg]	Programmierfehler
upgrade ['ʌpgreɪd]	Aktualisierung
to **spot sth** [spɒt]	etw entdecken
to **bother to do sth** ['bɒðə]	sich die Mühe machen, etw zu tun
permission [pə'mɪʃn]	Erlaubnis

to **distribute** [dɪ'strɪbjuːt]	verteilen, vertreiben
critical(ly) ['krɪtɪkl]	entscheidend, kritisch
obsolete ['ɒbsəliːt]	veraltet, überholt
to **troubleshoot** ['trʌblʃuːt]	Fehler suchen, Fehler beheben
compatibility [kəm,pætə'bɪləti]	Kompatibilität
documentation [,dɒkjumen'teɪʃn]	(technische) Dokumentation
ease of use [,iːz əv 'juːs]	Benutzerfreundlichkeit

page 192

bounty ['baʊnti]	Kopfgeld
crowdfunding ['kraʊdfʌndɪŋ]	*Finanzierung durch freiwillige Unterstützer*
delayed [dɪ'leɪd]	verzögert
extension [ɪk'stenʃn]	Erweiterung, Ergänzung
continued [kən'tɪnjuːd]	kontinuierlich, Weiter-
functionality [,fʌŋkʃə'næləti]	Funktion(en)
to **encourage sth** [ɪn'kʌrɪdʒ]	zu etw auffordern, zu etw animieren
to **come up with sth** [,kʌm 'ʌp wɪð]	etw entwickeln
desired [dɪ'zaɪəd]	gewünscht
core [kɔː]	Kern

TECHNICAL TOPIC 7

page 193

freight [freɪt]	Fracht, Frachtverkehr
logistics [lə'dʒɪstɪks]	Logistik
strict [strɪkt]	streng
transport mode ['trænspɔːt məʊd]	Beförderungsart, Transportart
overview ['əʊvəvjuː]	Überblick
transportation [,trænspɔː'teɪʃn]	Beförderung(swesen), Transport(swesen)
in terms of [ɪn 'tɜːmz əv]	hinsichtlich, bezüglich
with regard to [wɪð rɪ'gɑːd tə]	im Hinblick auf, hinsichtlich
bulk goods *pl* ['bʌlk gʊdz]	Massengut, Schüttgut
cement [sɪ'ment]	Zement
cargo ['kɑːgəʊ]	Fracht
high-value [,haɪ 'væljuː]	hochwertig
low-value [,ləʊ 'væljuː]	geringwertig
bulk freight ['bʌlk freɪt]	Massenfracht
woodchips *pl* ['wʊdtʃɪps]	Holzhackschnitzel
pipeline ['paɪplaɪn]	Rohrleitung
liquid ['lɪkwɪd]	Flüssigkeit
seafood ['siːfuːd]	Meeresfrüchte
dairy produce ['deəri prɒdjuːs]	Milchprodukte
to **expend** [ɪk'spend]	aufwenden
inefficient [,ɪnɪ'fɪʃnt]	ineffizient, unwirtschaftlich
unviable [ʌn'vaɪəbl]	undurchführbar, unmöglich
origin ['ɒrɪdʒɪn]	Ausgangsort, Ursprungsort
destination [,destɪ'neɪʃn]	Bestimmungsort
intermodal [,ɪntə'məʊdl]	*(Transport:)* multimodal, intermodal, kombiniert
to **load** [ləʊd]	laden, verladen
jet plane ['dʒet pleɪn]	Düsenflugzeug
supersonic plane [suːpə,sɒnɪk 'pleɪn]	Überschallflugzeug

page 194

road freight ['rəʊd freɪt]	Straßengüterverkehr
to **be around** [bi ə'raʊnd]	da sein, (es) geben
freight station ['freɪt steɪʃn]	Güterbahnhof
leg [leg]	Etappe
literally ['lɪtərəli]	(wort)wörtlich
heavy goods vehicle (HGV) [,hevi gʊdz 'viːəkl]	(Schwer-)Lastkraftwagen (Lkw)
inventory ['ɪnvəntri]	(Lager-)Bestand
to **minimize** ['mɪnɪmaɪz]	minimieren
labour costs *pl* ['leɪbə kɒsts]	Lohnkosten, Arbeitskosten
road train ['rəʊd treɪn]	Lastzug
torque [tɔːk]	Drehmoment
acceleration [ək,selə'reɪʃn]	Beschleunigung
long-distance [,lɒŋ'dɪstəns]	Langstrecken-
stage of development [,steɪdʒ ev dɪ'veləpmənt]	Entwicklungsstand, -stadium
shipping ['ʃɪpɪŋ]	Versand, Transport, Schifffahrt
to **be on the verge of doing sth** [bi ɒn ðə 'vɜːdʒ əv]	kurz davor stehen, etw zu tun
to **envision sth** [en'vɪʒn]	sich etw vorstellen
silver-skinned ['sɪlvə skɪnd]	mit silberner Haut
airship ['eəʃɪp]	Luftschiff
aloft [ə'lɒft]	oben, in der Höhe
to **drop sb** [drɒp]	jdn absetzen
triage ['triːɑːʒ]	(notfallmedizinische) Ersteinschätzung, Triage
disaster site [dɪ'zɑːstə saɪt]	Katastrophengebiet
to **deposit** [dɪ'pɒzɪt]	deponieren, absetzen
machinery [mə'ʃiːnəri]	Maschinen
airstrip ['eəstrɪp]	Landebahn
knot [nɒt]	Knoten
capacity [kə'pæsəti]	Fassungsvermögen, Kapazität
buoyancy ['bɔɪənsi]	Auftrieb
buoyancy control ['bɔɪənsi kəntrəʊl]	Tarierung
dirigible ['dɪrɪdʒɪbl]	Luftschiff
to **tether** ['teðə]	anbinden, anleinen
chamber ['tʃeɪmbə]	Kammer
descent [dɪ'sent]	Sinkflug
private sector [,praɪvət 'sektə]	Privatwirtschaft
convinced [kən'vɪnst]	überzeugt
air vessel ['eə vesl]	Luftfahrzeug, Luftschiff
holiday season ['hɒlədeɪ siːzn]	Weihnachtszeit
fleet [fliːt]	Flotte

page 195

sail [seɪl]	Segel
propulsion [prə'pʌlʃn]	Antrieb, Vortrieb
to **re-harness** [,riː 'hɑːnɪs]	wieder nutzbar machen
towing kite ['təʊɪŋ kaɪt]	Zugdrachen
launch and recovery system [,lɔːntʃ ənd rɪ'kʌvəri sɪstəm]	Start- und Landesystem
to **turn heads** [,tɜːn 'hedz]	für Aufsehen sorgen
to **come into force** [,kʌm ɪntə 'fɔːs]	in Kraft treten
auxiliary [ɔːg'zɪliəri]	Hilfs-, zusätzlich
to **offset** [,ɒf'set]	ausgleichen
to **amount to sth** [ə'maʊnt tə]	auf etw herauslaufen, sich auf etw belaufen
significant [sɪg'nɪfɪkənt]	bedeutend, erheblich
variable ['veəriəbl]	wechselnd, unbeständig
iteration [ɪtə'reɪʃn]	Version
vessel ['vesl]	Wasserfahrzeug, Schiff
to **prove** [pruːv]	belegen, nachweisen
fundamental [,fʌndə'mentl]	grundlegend

newbuild ['nju:bɪld]	(Schiffs-)Neubau
to **retrofit** ['retrəʊfɪt]	nachträglich ausstatten
maneuverable [mə'nu:vrəbl]	manövrierfähig
to **compromise** ['kɒmprəmaɪz]	beeinträchtigen
loading ['ləʊdɪŋ]	Beladung, Verladen
unloading [ˌʌn'ləʊdɪŋ]	Entladung, Entladen, Löschen *(von Ladung)*
appeal [ə'pi:l]	Attraktivität, Reiz
imagination [ɪˌmædʒɪ'neɪʃn]	Vorstellungskraft

TECHNICAL TOPIC 8

page 196

cybernetics [ˌsaɪbə'netɪks]	Kybernetik
RFID (radio frequency identification) [ɑ:r ˌef eɪ 'di:]	Funkerkennung (RFID)
implant ['ɪmplɑ:nt]	Implantat
humanity [hju:'mænəti]	Menschheit
acceptance [ək'septəns]	Akzeptanz
to **enhance** [ɪn'hɑ:ns]	verbessern, *(Sinne)* schärfen
deaf [def]	taub
thanks to ['θæŋks tə]	dank
cochlea ['kɒkliə]	Gehörschnecke, Cochlea
surgical(ly) ['sɜ:dʒɪkl]	chirurgisch
to **implant** [ɪm'plɑ:nt]	einpflanzen, implantieren
inner ear [ˌɪnər 'ɪə]	Innenohr
external [ɪk'stɜ:nl]	extern, Außen-
to **pick up** [ˌpɪk 'ʌp]	*(Klang, Ton)* aufnehmen
to **emphasize** ['emfəsaɪz]	hervorheben, betonen
transmitter [træns'mɪtə]	Sender
receiver [rɪ'si:və]	Empfänger
stimulator ['stɪmjuleɪtə]	Stimulator
to **embed** [ɪm'bed]	einbetten
skull [skʌl]	Schädel
electrode [ɪ'lektrəʊd]	Elektrode
impulse ['ɪmpʌls]	Impuls
deep brain stimulation [ˌdi:p breɪn stɪmju'leɪʃn]	Tiefenhirnstimulation
symptom ['sɪmptəm]	Symptom
pacemaker ['peɪsmeɪkə]	Herzschrittmacher

page 197

wireless(ly) ['waɪələs]	drahtlos, über Funk, Funk-
pill [pɪl]	Tablette, Pille
cybernetic [saɪbə'netɪk]	kybernetisch
to **unlock** [ˌʌn'lɒk]	aufschließen, entriegeln
eager ['i:gə]	begierig, ungeduldig
appearance [ə'pɪərəns]	Erscheinung(sbild)
plastic surgery [ˌplæstɪk 'sɜ:dʒəri]	plastische Chirurgie
superhuman [ˌsu:pə'hju:mən]	übermenschlich
sight [saɪt]	Sehvermögen
hearing ['hɪərɪŋ]	Gehör, Hörvermögen
ornamental [ɔ:nə'mentl]	schmückend, zierend
functional ['fʌŋkʃənl]	funktionell
to **make sb uncomfortable** [ˌmeɪk ʌn'kʌmftəbl]	jdm unangenehm sein
implication [ˌɪmplɪ'keɪʃn]	Folge, Auswirkung
unlikely [ʌn'laɪkli]	unwahrscheinlich
inequality [ɪnɪ'kwɒləti]	Ungleichheit
consensus [kən'sensəs]	Übereinstimmung, Konsens

page 198

to **forward** ['fɔ:wəd]	weiterleiten
sprawling ['sprɔ:lɪŋ]	ausgedehnt
marine engineering [məˌri:n endʒɪ'nɪərɪŋ]	Schiffsmaschinenbau
facility [fə'sɪləti]	Anlage, Werk
shipbuilder ['ʃɪpbɪldə]	Schiffsbauer
to **outfit sb with sth** ['aʊtfɪt]	jdn mit etw ausstatten
exoskeleton [ˌeksəʊ'skelɪtn]	Exoskelett
lead engineer [ˌli:d endʒɪ'nɪə]	Chefingenieur/in
arm [ɑ:m]	Zweig
pilot ['paɪlət]	Pilotversuch
assembly [ə'sembli]	Montage
alloy ['ælɔɪ]	Legierung
to **support** [sə'pɔ:t]	tragen, halten
to **engineer** [ˌendʒɪ'nɪə]	konstruieren
battery life ['bætəri laɪf]	Akkulaufzeit
pace [peɪs]	Tempo
mass [mæs]	Masse
to **strap** [stræp]	festschnallen
pad [pæd]	Unterlage, Polster
base [beɪs]	Fußteil, Sockel
padded ['pædɪd]	gepolstert
strap [stræp]	Gurt
thigh [θaɪ]	Oberschenkel
waist [weɪst]	Taille
chest [tʃest]	Brust
to **bear** [beə]	tragen
load [ləʊd]	Last
hydraulic [haɪ'drɔ:lɪk]	hydraulisch
joint [dʒɔɪnt]	Gelenk
backpack ['bækpæk]	Rucksack
crane [kreɪn]	Kran
to **boost** [bu:st]	verstärken
effectively [ɪ'fektɪvli]	tatsächlich, praktisch
trial ['traɪəl]	Versuch
repeatedly [rɪ'pi:tɪdli]	wiederholt, immer wieder
strain [streɪn]	Strapaze, Anstrengung

TECHNICAL TOPIC 9

page 199

biometric [ˌbaɪəʊ'metrɪk]	biometrisch
chemical engineering [ˌkemɪkl endʒɪ'nɪərɪŋ]	Chemietechnik, chemische Verfahrenstechnik
trade secret ['treɪd si:krɪt]	Betriebsgeheimnis
rival ['raɪvl]	Rivale, Konkurrent
authorized ['ɔ:θəraɪzd]	befugt
fingerprint ['fɪŋgəprɪnt]	Fingerabdruck
reader ['ri:də]	Lesegerät
to **assign sb** [ə'saɪn]	jdn *(einer Gruppe etc.)* zuteilen
taskforce ['tɑ:skfɔ:s]	Arbeitsgruppe
to **clone** [kləʊn]	klonen
thumbprint ['θʌmprɪnt]	Daumenabdruck
to **replicate** ['replɪkeɪt]	reproduzieren
print [prɪnt]	Abdruck
biometrics [ˌbaɪəʊ'metrɪks]	Biometrik
to **be considered sth** [bi kən'sɪdəd]	als etw gelten
insecure [ˌɪnsɪ'kjʊə]	unsicher
convention [kən'venʃn]	Tagung
close-up ['kləʊs ʌp]	Nahaufnahme
angle ['æŋgl]	Winkel
minister ['mɪnɪstə]	Minister/in
glove [glʌv]	Handschuh
presumably [prɪ'zju:məbli]	vermutlich
identification [aɪˌdentɪfɪ'keɪʃn]	Erkennung, Identifikation

voter ['vəʊtə]	Wähler/in
polling station ['pəʊlɪŋ steɪʃn]	Wahllokal
presidential [ˌprezɪ'denʃl]	Präsidenten-
static ['stætɪk]	statisch
trivial ['trɪviəl]	banal, einfach, simpel
to **forge** [fɔːdʒ]	fälschen
to **fake** [feɪk]	nachahmen, fälschen
cybersecurity [ˌsaɪbəsɪ'kjʊərəti]	Internetsicherheit

page 200

vein [veɪn]	Ader, Vene
gait [geɪt]	Gang, Gangart
motion ['məʊʃn]	Bewegung
possession [pə'zeʃn]	Besitz
to **exhibit sth** [ɪg'zɪbɪt]	etw an den Tag legen, etw haben
intensive care unit [ɪnˌtensɪv 'keə juːnɪt]	Intensivstation
to **indicate** ['ɪndɪkeɪt]	darauf hinweisen
blood pressure ['blʌd preʃə]	Blutdruck
unsafe [ˌʌn'seɪf]	unsicher
to **trick** [trɪk]	täuschen, überlisten, betrügen
documentary [ˌdɒkju'mentri]	*(Radio, TV:)* Dokumentation
ignition [ɪg'nɪʃn]	Zündung
lock [lɒk]	Schloss
to **capture** ['kæptʃə]	erbeuten, kapern
malware ['mælweə]	Schadsoftware
measurable ['meʒərəbl]	messbar
iris scanning ['aɪrɪs skænɪŋ]	Iris-Scan
gruesome ['gruːsəm]	grauenvoll
pitch [pɪtʃ]	Tonlage, Tonhöhe
rhythm ['rɪðəm]	Rhythmus
user ID ['juːzər aɪ diː]	Benutzername
signature ['sɪgnətʃə]	Unterschrift
on record [ɒn 'rekɔːd]	aufgezeichnet, hinterlegt
consistently [kən'sɪstəntli]	ständig, durchweg
pulse [pʌls]	Puls
complexity [kəm'pleksəti]	Komplexität, Aufwand
profile ['prəʊfaɪl]	Profil

page 201

authentication [ɔːˌθentɪ'keɪʃn]	Authentifizierung, Legitimation
criterion, criteria [kraɪ'tɪəriən, kraɪ'tɪəriə]	Kriterium, Kriterien
universality [ˌjuːnɪvə'sæləti]	Allgemeingültigkeit, Universalität
uniqueness [ju'niːknəs]	Einzigartigkeit
to **distinguish** [dɪ'stɪŋgwɪʃ]	unterscheiden, auseinanderhalten
permanence ['pɜːmənəns]	Beständigkeit, Dauerhaftigkeit
circumstances *pl* ['sɜːkəmstənsɪz]	Umstände
measurability [ˌmeʒərə'bɪləti]	Messbarkeit
acceptability [əkˌseptə'bɪləti]	Akzeptanz
biometric [ˌbaɪəʊ'metrɪk]	biometrische Eigenschaft
circumvention [ˌsɜːkəm'venʃn]	Umgehen, Überlistung
to **imitate** ['ɪmɪteɪt]	imitieren, nachahmen
trait [treɪt]	Merkmal, Eigenschaft
i.e. [ˌaɪ 'iː]	d. h.

with reference to [wɪð 'refrəns tə]	mit Bezug auf
convenient [kən'viːniənt]	praktisch, bequem
chief security officer [ˌtʃiːf sɪ'kjʊərəti ɒfɪsə]	Hauptsicherheitsbeauftragte/r

TECHNICAL TOPIC 10

page 202

electric vehicle [ɪˌlektrɪk 'viːəkl]	Elektrofahrzeug
hybrid electric vehicle [haɪbrɪd ɪˌlektrɪk 'viːəkl]	Hybridfahrzeug
to **shiver** ['ʃɪvə]	zittern
magnetic [mæg'netɪk]	magnetisch
attraction [ə'trækʃn]	Anziehung
pole [pəʊl]	Pol
to **repel** [rɪ'pel]	abstoßen
to **align** [ə'laɪn]	ausrichten
unlike [ˌʌn'laɪk]	ungleich, gegensätzlich
kinetic energy [kɪˌnetɪk 'enədʒi]	Bewegungsenergie
stator ['steɪtə]	Stator
rotor ['rəʊtə]	Rotor
polarity [pə'lærəti]	Polung, Polarität
synchronous ['sɪŋkrənəs]	synchron
three-phase AC motor [ˌθriː feɪz eɪ 'siː məʊtə]	Drehstrommotor
permanent magnet ['pɜːmənənt mægnɪt]	Permanentmagnet
electromagnet [ɪˌlektrəʊ'magnɪt]	Elektromagnet
coil [kɔɪl]	Spule
to **spin** [spɪn]	sich drehen

page 203

alternating current (AC) [ˌɔːltəneɪtɪŋ 'kʌrənt]	Wechselstrom
direction [də'rekʃn]	Richtung
cycle ['saɪkl]	Zyklus
set [set]	Gruppe
to **colour** ['kʌlə]	färben
to **attend sth** [ə'tend]	an etw teilnehmen
automotive [ˌɔːtə'məʊtɪv]	Automobil-, Kraftfahrzeug-
The future lies with … [ðə 'fjuːtʃə laɪz wɪð]	Die Zukunft gehört …
in a nutshell [ɪn ə 'nʌtʃel]	kurz gesagt
battery bank ['bætəri bæŋk]	Akku
configuration [kənˌfɪgə'reɪʃn]	Konfiguration
mild hybrid ['maɪld haɪbrɪd]	Mild-Hybrid
full hybrid ['fʊl haɪbrɪd]	Voll-Hybrid
series ['sɪəriːz]	seriell
micro hybrid ['maɪkrəʊ haɪbrɪd]	Mikro-Hybrid
pointless ['pɔɪntləs]	sinnlos, unsinnig
to **assist** [ə'sɪst]	unterstützen, helfen
fuel economy ['fjuːəl ɪkɒnəmi]	(wirtschaftlicher) Kraftstoffverbrauch
to **drive** [draɪv]	antreiben
drivetrain ['draɪvtreɪn]	Antrieb, Antriebsstrang

page 204

show [ʃəʊ]	Ausstellung, Messe
to **swap** [swɒp]	tauschen
regenerative [rɪ'dʒenrətɪv]	regenerativ
braking ['breɪkɪŋ]	Bremsen, Bremsvorgang
to **recharge** [ˌriː'tʃɑːdʒ]	Aufladen *(von Akkus)*

TECHNICAL TOPIC 11

page 205

ready meal ['redi mi:l]	Fertiggericht
transceiver [træn'si:və]	Transceiver, Sendeempfänger
antenna [æn'tenə]	Antenne
radio frequency field [ˌreɪdiəʊ 'fri:kwənsi fi:ld]	Hochfrequenzfeld
memory ['meməri]	(Daten-)Speicher
voltage ['vəʊltɪdʒ]	Spannung
stock item ['stɒk aɪtəm]	Bestandsartikel
limitless ['lɪmɪtləs]	grenzenlos
idle state ['aɪdl steɪt]	Ruhezustand
to **conserve** [kən'sɜ:v]	bewahren, sparen
to **initiate** [ɪ'nɪʃieɪt]	einleiten, initiieren
humidity [hju:'mɪdəti]	Luftfeuchtigkeit
asset ['æset]	Wirtschaftsgut, Anlagegut
toll [təʊl]	Maut

page 205

food processing industry ['fu:d prəʊsesɪŋ ɪndəstri]	nahrungsmittelverarbeitende Industrie
panel ['pænl]	Expertenrunde, Diskussionsrunde
beacon ['bi:kn]	Funksignal
taste [teɪst]	Geschmack
refrigerator [rɪ'frɪdʒəreɪtə]	Kühlschrank
cool room ['ku:l ru:m]	Kühlraum
to **dump** [dʌmp]	*(Abfall)* wegwerfen
oven ['ʌvn]	Ofen, Herd
volatile ['vɒlətaɪl]	flüchtig
to **pick** [pɪk]	pflücken
ethical ['eθɪkl]	ethisch, moralisch
pesticide residues *pl* ['pestɪsaɪd rezɪdju:z]	Pestizidrückstände
contamination [kənˌtæmɪ'neɪʃn]	Verunreinigung, Kontamination
equipped with [ɪ'kwɪpt wɪð]	ausgestattet mit
panellist ['pænəlɪst]	*(Podiumsdiskussion:)* Diskussionsteilnehmer, Experte
edible ['edəbl]	essbar
to **insert** [ɪn'sɜ:t]	hineinstecken, einführen
lifecycle ['laɪfsaɪkl]	Lebenszyklus

page 207

rainfall ['reɪnfɔ:l]	Regen, Niederschlagsmenge

TECHNICAL TOPIC 12

page 208

printing ['prɪntɪŋ]	Drucken, Drucktechnik
dummy ['dʌmi]	Dummkopf, Hirni
ceramic [sə'ræmɪk]	keramisch, Keramik-
stoneware ['stəʊnweə]	Steingut
vase [vɑ:z]	Vase
fancy ['fænsi]	raffiniert, ausgefallen
production line [prə'dʌkʃn laɪn]	Fertigungsstraße
ink [ɪŋk]	Tinte, Druckerschwärze
printing press ['prɪntɪŋ pres]	Druckerpresse, Druckmaschine
hot metal type [ˌhɒt 'metl taɪp]	Setzmaschine
drying rack ['draɪɪŋ ræk]	Trockengestell
microscope ['maɪkrəskəʊp]	Mikroskop
to **stain** [steɪn]	einfärben
slice [slaɪs]	Scheibchen
to **stick** [stɪk]	kleben, haften
hinge [hɪndʒ]	Scharnier
handlebars *pl* ['hændlbɑ:z]	(Fahrrad-)Lenker
saddle ['sædl]	Sattel
lorry *BE* ['lɒri]	Lkw

page 209

cost per item [ˌkɒst pɜ:r 'aɪtəm]	Stückkosten
economics *pl* [ˌi:kə'nɒmɪks]	Ökonomie, Wirtschaftlichkeit
to **stack up against sth** [ˌstæk 'ʌp əgenst]	einem Vergleich mit etw standhalten
stereolithography ['steriəʊlɪ'θɒgrəfi]	Stereolithographie
fused deposition modeling [ˌfju:zd depə'zɪʃn mɒdlɪŋ]	Schmelzschichtung
selective laser sintering [sɪˌlektɪv 'leɪzə sɪntərɪŋ]	selektives Lasersintern
to **deposit** [dɪ'pɒzɪt]	*(Material)* ablagern, auftragen
movable ['mu:vəbl]	beweglich
spool [spu:l]	Rolle, Spule
filament ['fɪləmnt]	Faser, Faden
to **squeeze** [skwi:z]	(aus)drücken
powder ['paʊdə]	Pulver
to **spread** [spred]	verteilen, auftragen
to **fuse** [fju:z]	schmelzen, verschmelzen
to **sinter** ['sɪntə]	sintern
focusing head ['fəʊkəsɪŋ hed]	Fokussierkopf
to **solidify** [sə'lɪdɪfaɪ]	verfestigen, erstarren
mass manufacturing [ˌmæs mænju'fæktʃərɪŋ]	Massenfertigung
pirate copy ['paɪrət kɒpi]	Raubkopie
to **get one's head around sth** [ˌget wʌnz 'hed əraʊnd]	etw begreifen, etw verstehen

page 210

to **self-assemble** [ˌself ə'sembl]	sich selbsttätig zusammenbauen
herald ['herəld]	Vorbote
self-assembly [ˌself ə'sembli]	selbsttätige Montage
lab [læb]	Labor
to **propose** [prə'pəʊz]	vorschlagen, anregen
to **transform** [træns'fɔ:m]	(sich) verwandeln, (sich) umformen
multi-layered ['mʌlti leɪəd]	mehrschichtig
strand [strænd]	Strang
to **expand** [ɪk'spænd]	sich ausdehnen
rigid ['rɪdʒɪd]	starr, steif
to **bend** [bend]	(sich) biegen, (sich) verbiegen
to **twist** [twɪst]	(sich) verdrehen
for the time being [fə ðə ˌtaɪm 'bi:ɪŋ]	einstweilen
to **explore** [ɪk'splɔ:]	erkunden, erforschen
to **dig up** [ˌdɪg 'ʌp]	*(Straße)* aufreißen
to **collaborate on sth** [kə'læbəreɪt ɒn]	bei etw *(Projekt etc.)* zusammenarbeiten
principal ['prɪnsəpl]	Chef(-)

A–Z word list

Dieses Wörterverzeichnis enthält alle Wörter in **Focus on Success – 5th edition: Ausgabe Technik** in alphabetischer Reihenfolge. Nicht aufgeführt sind die Wörter aus der *Basic word list* sowie internationale Wörter wie *hotel*, *email* usw.
Wörter, die in den Hörverständnistexten vorkommen, sind mit einem *T* hinter der Seitenzahl gekennzeichnet. Wörter, die in den *Files* vorkommen, sind mit einem *F* hinter der Seitenzahl gekennzeichnet.

A

abbreviation *32* Abkürzung
ability *29* Fähigkeit, Befähigung
about, to **be ~ to do sth** *51* im Begriff sein, etw zu tun; gerade dabei sein, etw zu tun
to **abridge** *27* *(Text)* kürzen
absolutely *40* absolut
to **absorb** *153* aufnehmen, absorbieren
acceleration *194T* Beschleunigung
to **accept** *11T* akzeptieren, gutheißen
acceptability *201* Akzeptanz
acceptance *196* Akzeptanz
to **access sth** *160* auf etw zugreifen
access: ~ to sth *108* Zugriff auf etw, Zugang zu etw; **wheelchair ~** *122* behindertengerechter Zugang; **~ code** *128* Zugangscode
accessibility *118* Barrierefreiheit
accessible *51* zugänglich, erreichbar, offen
accessories *pl* *64* Zubehör
accident *166T* Unfall; **~ and emergency department (A&E)** *167* Notaufnahme
accidentally *108* versehentlich
to **accommodate** *67* unterbringen
accommodation *66* Unterkunft; **homestay ~** *66* Unterbringung bei Gasteltern
to **accompany** *27* begleiten
according to *12* entsprechend, nach, gemäß; *14* laut, zufolge
account *37* Konto; to **take sth into ~** *22* etw in Betracht ziehen, etw berücksichtigen
accountancy *90* Buchhaltung, Rechnungswesen
accountant *65* Buchhalter/in
accounts *34* Buchhaltung
accuracy *187* Genauigkeit
accurate(ly) *75* genau
to **ache** *16* schmerzen, wehtun
to **achieve sth** *19* etw erreichen, etw leisten
achievement *10* Errungenschaft, Leistung
to **acknowledge** *69* anerkennen, zugeben
acne *23* Akne
acoustic model *187* akustisches Modell
to **acquire** *64* erwerben
acre *149* Morgen *(ca. 4047 qm)*
acronym *169* Akronym, Abkürzung
act *91* Handlung, Tat
to **act: ~ as sth** *114* als etw fungieren; **~ out** *43* spielen, vorspielen
action, legal ~ *39* rechtliche Schritte; to **put sth out of ~** *134T* etw außer Gefecht setzen; to **take ~** *100* handeln; to **take legal ~** *39* rechtliche Schritte unternehmen; **course of ~** *87* Vorgehen, Maßnahmen
to **activate** *144* aktivieren
actually *20* in der Tat, eigentlich, wirklich
ad *45* Anzeige, Werbung; **viral ~** *45* Internet-Werbespot; **~ agency** *46* Werbeagentur
to **adapt** *27* *(Text)* bearbeiten; *74T* anpassen; **~ to sth** *98* sich an etw anpassen
adaptation *152* Anpassung, Anpassungsleistung
addition *162* Hinzufügung; **in ~** *48* außerdem, darüber hinaus; **in ~ to sth** *76* zusätzlich zu etw
additional *54* zusätzlich
to **address** *69* *(Problem etc.)* ansprechen, angehen, thematisieren; **~ sb** *110* jdn ansprechen
address, inside ~ *76* Empfängeranschrift; **writer's ~** *76* Absenderanschrift
adequate(ly) *27* ausreichend, angemessen
adhesive *185* Klebstoff
to **administer** *67* verwalten
administration *66* Verwaltung
administrative *67* Verwaltungs-
administrator *65* Verwalter/in
to **admire** *11* bewundern
to **admit** *23* zugeben, (ein)gestehen
to **adopt** *74T* einführen, anwenden; **~ sb** *94* jdn adoptieren
advance, in ~ *40* im Voraus
advanced *74* weiterführend, vertiefend; *88* fortschrittlich, entwickelt
to **advertise: ~ sth** *19* etw bewerben, für etw werben; **~ a job** *66* eine Stelle ausschreiben
advert(isement) *45* Anzeige, Werbung; **job ~** *31* Stellenanzeige, -ausschreibung
advertising *45* Werbung; **~ agency** *46* Werbeagentur
advice *38T* (guter) Rat, Ratschläge; **strong ~** *62T* dringender Rat
to **advise** *129* (jdm etw) raten; **~ sb** *38* jdn beraten
adviser *114* Berater/in
advisor, careers ~ *68* Berufsberater/in; **customer services ~** *68T* Kundenberater/in
advocate *136* Befürworter/in
aerobics *12* Aerobic
to **affect** *19* beeinflussen, sich auswirken auf
affluent *116* wohlhabend
affordability *21T* Erschwinglichkeit, Bezahlbarkeit
affordable *19* erschwinglich
afraid, I'm ~ *23* leider
after all *74T* letztlich
afterwards *111* danach, darauf
to **age** *114* altern
age, for ~s *163* ewig, eine Ewigkeit
aged *40* im Alter von
agency *14* Agentur
agenda *172* Tagesordnung
agreement *101* Vereinbarung, Absprache
agricultural *86T* landwirtschaftlich, Landwirtschafts-
agriculture *148* Landwirtschaft
ahead *62* voraus, vorausliegend
aid *97* Hilfe; to **live off ~** *81* von Sozialhilfe leben
aim *74T* Ziel, Zweck, Absicht
to **aim at sth** *152* etw anstreben
aimed, to **be ~ at sb** *28* sich an jdn richten
air, exhaust ~ *182* Abluft; **extract ~** *183* Abluft; **supply ~** *182* Zuluft; **~ conditioning** *181* Klimaanlage(n-); **~ flow** *182* Luftstrom; **~ vessel** *194* Luftfahrzeug, Luftschiff
airborne drone *168* Flugdrohne
aircraft *102* Flugzeug
airfare, return ~ *66* Kosten für Hin- und Rückflug
airline *81* Fluglinie
airship *194* Luftschiff
airstrip *194* Landebahn
airtight *182* luftdicht
airtightness *182* Luftdichtheit, Luftdichtigkeit
alarm *144* Alarmsignal
alcoholic, non-~ *121* alkoholfrei
algorithm *44* Algorithmus

alien *165* außerirdisch
to **align** *202* ausrichten
alike *191* gleichermaßen, wie
alive *63* lebendig, am Leben
all, at ~ *16* überhaupt
allotted *69* zugewiesen
allowance *117T* Zuschuss
allowance *20* Taschengeld
allowance *66* Aufwandsentschädigung
alloy *198* Legierung
aloft *194* oben, in der Höhe
along the way *90* dabei, währenddessen
alongside *168* neben
Alpine *181* alpin, Gebirgs-
to **alter** *190* ändern
alternating current (AC) *203* Wechselstrom
although *27* obwohl
altitude *170* Höhe
amateur *21T* Amateur(-), Hobby-
ambition *45* Ziel, Ehrgeiz
ambitious *68* ehrgeizig
among *27* unter, inmitten, zwischen
amongst *98* unter, bei; to **be ~ ...** *74* zu ... gehören
amount *37* Betrag; *81* Menge
to **amount to sth** *81* auf etw hinauslaufen; *195* sich auf etw belaufen
amusement arcade *46* Spielhalle
analogue *187* analog; **~-to-digital converter (ADC)** *187* Analog-Digital-Wandler (AD-Wandler)
to **analyse** *26* analysieren
anchor *108* Anker; **news ~** *136* Nachrichtensprecher/in
ancient *115* alt, historisch, antik
and so on *62T* und so weiter
anecdote *38* Anekdote
angle *170* Winkel
angry *136* aufgebracht, ungehalten; to **get ~** *62T* sich ärgern
to **animate** *178* animieren
anniversary *94* Jahrestag
to **annotate** *188* beschriften, mit Anmerkungen versehen
to **announce** *14* verkünden, ankündigen
annoyed, to **become ~** *141* sich ärgern, sich aufregen
annual *98* jährlich
annum, per ~ *117T* pro Jahr
anonymous(ly) *127* anonym
to **answer the phone** *162* ans Telefon gehen
antenna *205* Antenne
apart from *29* abgesehen von, außer
to **apologize** *43* sich entschuldigen
apparently *40* anscheinend
appeal *195* Attraktivität, Reiz
to **appear** *7* auftreten, erscheinen; *15* scheinen
appearance *197* Erscheinung(sbild)
appliance *64* Haushaltsgerät; **domestic ~** *187* Haushaltsgerät, Elektrogerät
applicant *77* Bewerber/in
application *32* Bewerbung; *143T* Antrag; *177T* Software, Programm; *184T* Anwendung; *185* Auftrag (von Klebstoff etc.)
to **apply: ~ to sth** *176* für etw gelten, auf etw zutreffen; **~ sth to sth** *44* etw auf etw anwenden; *184* etw auf etw auftragen; *184* etw auf etw anwenden, etw auf etw ausüben; **~ for a job** *31* sich auf eine Stelle bewerben
appointment *34T* Termin, Verabredung
to **appreciate** *76* zu schätzen wissen, schätzen
apprenticeship *68T* Ausbildung, Lehre
approach *46* Ansatz, Herangehensweise
to **approach: ~ sb** *27* an jdn herantreten; **~ sth** *169* sich einer Sache nähern
appropriate(ly) *27* angemessen, passend
approximate *87* ungefähr, angenähert
approximately (approx.) *86* zirka (ca.)
arcade *46* Spielautomat; **amusement ~** *46* Spielhalle
architect *65* Architekt/in
area *11* Gebiet, Bereich, Feld; *25* Gegend, Region
to **argue** *27* argumentieren, geltend machen
arm *198* Zweig
to **arm sb** *126T* jdn bewaffnen
armed *91* bewaffnet; **~ forces** *pl* *126T* Streitkräfte
armoured *108* armiert, gepanzert
army *126* Armee; **Salvation A~** *90* Heilsarmee
around, to **be ~** *194T* da sein, (es) geben
to **arrange** *180* anordnen
arrangement *50* Abmachung, Vereinbarung, Vorbereitung, Regelung
array *178* Reihe, Spektrum
to **arrest** *81* verhaften
arrow *134* Pfeil
arsenal *124* Instrumentarium, Waffenlager
arsenic *144* Arsen
artificial intelligence *164* künstliche Intelligenz
artistic *65* künstlerisch
as things turn out *34* wie sich herausstellt
asap (as soon as possible) *66* baldmöglichst
asleep, to **be ~** *94* schlafen
aspect *15* Gesichtspunkt, Aspekt
assembly *198* Montage; **self-~** *210* selbsttätige Montage
to **assess** *179* beurteilen, bewerten
assessment *78T* Beurteilung, Einstufung
asset *205* Wirtschaftsgut, Anlagegut; to **be an ~ to sb** *76* für jdn eine Bereicherung sein
to **assign: ~ sb** *199* jdn *(einer Gruppe etc.)* zuteilen; **~ sb sth** *168* jdm etw zuweisen, jdn mit etw beauftragen
assignment *175* Aufgabe
to **assist** *203T* unterstützen, helfen
assistance *112* Hilfe, Unterstützung
assistant, office ~ *75* Bürokaufmann/-frau; **sales ~** *54* Verkäufer/in
to **associate** *131* in Verbindung bringen, assoziieren
association *166T* Verband, Vereinigung
assumption *131* Annahme
asylum seeker *81* Asylbewerber/in
asymmetric *44* asymmetrisch
at all *16* überhaupt
at least *27* zumindest, mindestens
athlete *19* Sportler/in, Athlet/in
athletic *20* sportlich, athletisch
ATM *134* Geldautomat
atmosphere *17T* Stimmung, Atmosphäre
atmospheric *137* atmosphärisch, in der Atmosphäre
atrocities *pl* *90* Gräueltaten
to **attach** *180* anbringen, befestigen; **~ sth** *31* *(E-Mail:)* etw beifügen, etw anhängen
attachment *34T* *(E-Mail:)* Anhang; **~ point** *64* Befestigungspunkt
attack *103* Attacke, Angriff; *123* Anschlag, Attentat; *146* Anfall; to **launch an ~** *130* einen Angriff starten
attacker *125* Attentäter/in
to **attain** *88T* erreichen
to **attend sth** *78T* an etw teilnehmen
attention *11T* Aufmerksamkeit, Beachtung; to **attract ~** *43* Aufmerksamkeit erregen; to **draw ~ to sb/sth** *23* Aufmerksamkeit auf jdn/etw ziehen; to **pay ~ to sth** *22* auf etw achten
attitude *93* Einstellung, Haltung
attn. (= attention) *76* *(Brief:)* zu Händen
to **attract** *43* anlocken, anziehen; **~ attention** *43* Aufmerksamkeit erregen
attraction *202* Anziehung
attractive *17* attraktiv, anziehend
audience *8* Publikum; **member of the ~** *8* Zuschauer/in
authentication *201* Authentifizierung, Legitimation
authority *80* Behörde
authorized *199* befugt
autograph *7* Autogramm
automated *54* automatisch; *100* automatisiert

automotive *203* Automobil-, Kraftfahrzeug-
autonomous *164* autonom
auxiliary *195* Hilfs-, zusätzlich
availability *19* Verfügbarkeit
available, to **be ~** *32* *(Telefon:)* zu sprechen sein
average *36* Durchschnitt
to **await** *124* erwarten, abwarten
to **award sth to sb** *161* jdm etw verleihen, jdm etw zuerkennen
aware, to **be ~ of sth** *157* sich einer Sache bewusst sein, etw kennen; to **make sb ~ of sth** *40* jdn über etw informieren, jdn auf etw hinweisen
awareness *98* Bewusstsein, Kenntnis
axis, axes *53* Achse, Achsen

B

back *100* Rücken; **~ yard** *124* Hinterhof
to **back** *27* unterstützen; **~ sth up** *175* eine Sicherungskopie von etw machen
background *10* Hintergrund; *19* Herkunft
backpack *198* Rucksack
backpacker *31* Rucksacktourist/in
backpacking, to **go ~** *78T* auf Rucksacktour gehen
backup *156* Ersatz, Reserve; *175* Sicherungskopie
bacterial *158T* bakteriell
baker *65* Bäcker/in
balance *105* Bilanz, Saldo
to **balance** *105* ausgleichen
to **ban sb from doing sth** *60* jdm verbieten, etw zu tun
band *68T* Gehaltsstufe, Gehaltsklasse
bandwidth *176* Bandbreite
bank: to **rob a ~** *130* eine Bank überfallen, eine Bank ausrauben; **~ clerk** *67* Bankangestellte/r; **~ robbery** *130* Banküberfall, Bankraub
banker *96T* Bankkaufmann/-frau
bar chart *52* Säulendiagramm
bare *49T* kahl, nackt
barrage *140* Staumauer
barrier *69* Hürde; **language ~** *189* Sprachbarriere; to **break down ~s** *189* Grenzen beseitigen, Hürden überwinden
base *198* Fußteil, Sockel
to **base on sth** *36* auf etw basieren
based in … *88T* mit Sitz in, aus
basket *81* Korb
to **bat an eyelid** *14* mit der Wimper zucken
battery: ~ bank *203T* Akku; **~ life** *198* Akkulaufzeit; **~ pack** *144* Akku
battlefield *124* Schlachtfeld
beacon *54* Funkfeuer, Beacon; *206T* Funksignal
beam *184* Balken, Träger; **structural ~** *184T* Trägerbalken
to **bear** *198* tragen
beetle *49T* Käfer
to **beg** *143* flehen, eindringlich bitten; **~ for sth** *89* um etw betteln; **~ sb to do sth** *129* jdn anflehen, etw zu tun
beggar *89* Bettler/in
behalf, on sb's ~ *172* in jds Namen
to **behave** *82* sich benehmen, sich verhalten
behaviour *43* Benehmen, Verhalten
being, human ~ *26* Mensch, menschliches Wesen
belief *19* Überzeugung
belonging *70* Zugehörigkeit
to **bend** *184* *(Holz:)* sich verziehen, sich werfen; *210* (sich) biegen, (sich) verbiegen
beneath *131* unterhalb, unter
benefactor *90* Wohltäter/in
to **benefit** *43* nutzen, Nutzen bringen, profitieren
benefit *17T* Nutzen, Vorteil, Pluspunkt
benefits *pl* *60* Sozialleistungen; **community ~** *143T* Zahlungen an die Gemeinde; to **claim unemployment ~** *86* Arbeitslosengeld beziehen; to **reap the ~** *165* die Früchte ernten, die Vorteile nutzen; **~ office** *60* Sozialamt
beside *16* neben
best, All the ~, *17* Mit besten Grüßen, Alles Gute; **The ~ is yet to come.** *164* Das Beste kommt noch. Die besten Zeiten stehen uns noch bevor.; **B~ wishes** *120* *(Brief:)* Mit den besten Wünschen
to **bet** *23* wetten
better, to **change for the ~** *101* sich zum Besseren verändern
beyond *55* darüber hinaus; *74T* jenseits, über
bid *27* Versuch
bill *62T* Rechnung
billboard *45* Reklametafel, Plakatwand
billion *52* Milliarde
bi-manual *169* beidhändig
biofuel *149* Biokraftstoff
biomass *135* Biomasse
biometric *199* biometrisch; *201* biometrische Eigenschaft
biometrics *199* Biometrik
bit *174* Teil; **a ~** *23* ein bisschen; **drill ~** *185* Bohrer, Bohrspitze
to **blame:** to **be to blame** *136* Schuld sein
blank *120* leer, frei
blanket *49T* pauschal, umfassend
to **block** *39* sperren
blockbuster *90* Straßenfeger
blocker (to sth) *189* Hemmnis (für etw)
blood: ~ pressure *200* Blutdruck; **~ vessel** *17* Blutgefäß
blouse *156* Bluse
to **blow** *62* wehen, blasen
blow *94* Schlag
bludger, dole ~ *111* Sozialschmarotzer
board: ~ and lodging *66* Kost und Logis; **~ of directors** *179* Vorstand, Geschäftsführung
to **boast sth** *27* etw aufweisen (können)
body *76* *(Brief:)* Hauptteil; *81* Leichnam
bold *36* fett(gedruckt)
bomb *124* Bombe
to **bomb sth** *124* einen Bombenanschlag auf etw verüben
bomber *125* Bombenattentäter
booking *119* Buchung
boomerang *62T* Bumerang
to **boost** *17T* ankurbeln; *198* verstärken
border *74T* Grenze; **~ customs officer** *161* (Grenz-)Zollbeamte/r
to **border with sth** *126T* an etw grenzen
bored, to **get ~** *50* sich langweilen
borehole *98* Bohrloch
to **borrow sth** *57* sich etw ausleihen
to **bother sb** *34T* jdn belästigen, jdn stören; **~ to do sth** *191T* sich die Mühe machen, etw zu tun
to **bottle** *49T* in Flaschen abfüllen
bottle bank *46* Glascontainer
bottom line *107T* das, worauf es (unterm Strich) ankommt
bouncer *40* Türsteher/in
bounty *192* Kopfgeld
Boxing Day *94* 2. Weihnachtstag
bracket *7* Klammer
brain *118* Gehirn; **deep ~ stimulation** *196* Tiefenhirnstimulation
to **brainstorm** *54* Ideen sammeln
braking *204* Bremsen, Bremsvorgang
brand *18* Marke
to **brand a product** *51* ein Markenprodukt schaffen
branded goods *pl* *53* Markenware, Markenartikel
bread roll *99* Brötchen
break *173* Pause
to **break: ~sth apart** *145* etw auseinandernehmen; **~ down** *72* zusammenbrechen; **~ sth down** *187* etw aufgliedern, etw in einzelne Teile zerlegen; **~ down barriers** *189* Grenzen beseitigen, Hürden überwinden; **~ sth up** *7* etw zertrümmern, etw demolieren; **~ up** *40* *(Menschenmenge)* zerstreuen
breakage *105* Bruchschaden
breakdown *135* Zusammenbruch
breathing *14* Atmung
breathless(ly) *124* atemlos
breed *160* Rasse
to **breed** *152* züchten
breeding *152* Zucht, Züchtung; **~ ground** *145* Brutplatz

brick *156* Ziegel, Backstein
to **bridge a gap** *118* eine Lücke schließen, eine Kluft überbrücken
bridge, thermal ~ *181* Kältebrücke, Wärmebrücke
bridging, thermal ~ *182* Wärmebrücken
to **brief sb** *187* jdn informieren, jdn einweisen
brief(ly) *60* kurz, knapp
bright *178* hell
Briton *36* Brite/Britin
to **broadcast** *170* senden, ausstrahlen
broke *49T* kaputt
broken *144* kaputt, defekt
bubble, speech ~ *26* Sprechblase
bucket *43* Eimer; ~ **list** *43 Dinge, die man getan haben sollte, bevor man stirbt*
budget *62T* Etat, Haushalt, Budget
buffet lunch *122* Lunchbuffet
bug *191* Programmierfehler
to **build sth up** *86* etw aufbauen
bulb, light ~ *155T* Glühbirne
bulk: ~ **freight** *193* Massenfracht; ~ **goods** *pl 193* Massengut, Schüttgut
bullet *80* (Gewehr-)Kugel; ~ **point** *24* Stichpunkt; ~ **train** *88T* Hochgeschwindigkeitszug
bunch, a ~ **of** *168* eine Menge; **a varied** ~ *64* eine bunte Truppe
buoyancy *194* Auftrieb; ~ **control** *194* Tarierung
to **burn** *17T* (sich) verbrennen
burden *109* Last, Belastung, Bürde
business: to **go out of** ~ *107T* das Geschäft aufgeben, Pleite gehen; to **get down to** ~ *173T* zur Sache kommen; to **mind one's own** ~ *57* sich um seinen eigenen Kram kümmern; ~ **contact** *121* Ansprechpartner/in, Geschäftspartner/in; ~ **studies** *75* Betriebswirtschaft
button *160* Knopf, Button
buyer *100* Einkäufer/in
by oneself/yourself *62T* allein
by the way *60* übrigens, nebenbei erwähnt

C

cable *108* Kabel; **fibre optic** ~ *108* Glasfaserkabel; **submarine** ~ *108* Tiefseekabel; to **lay** ~**s** *160* Kabel verlegen; ~ **break** *108* Kabelbruch; ~ **news** *124* TV-Nachrichtensender
cactus *147* Kaktus
caffeine *14* Koffein
cage *154* Käfig
to **calculate** *168* berechnen
call: to **take a** ~ *38T* einen Anruf entgegennehmen, ans Telefon gehen; ~ **for help** *38* Hilferuf
to **call for sth** *137* zu etw aufrufen
called *16* namens; to **be** ~ *37* heißen
caller *34* Anrufer/in
to **calm** *143* beruhigen; ~ **down** *84* sich beruhigen
calorie *17* Kalorie
calving *160* Kalben
to **campaign** *109* kämpfen
campaign *43* Aktion, Kampagne
campaigner *132* Aktivist/in
can *46* Dose
to **cancel** *16* absagen, stornieren; *130* abbrechen, abblasen
cancer *43* Krebs *(Krankheit)*
candidate *66* Bewerber/in
candle *79* Kerze
canister *40* Dose, Büchse
capability *64* Fähigkeit
capacity *194* Fassungsvermögen, Kapazität
capita, per ~ **income** *156* Pro-Kopf-Einkommen
capital *144* Hauptstadt
capital letter *32* Großbuchstabe
captain *189* Kapitän, Hauptmann
caption *8* Bildunterschrift
to **capture** *179T* erfassen; *200T* erbeuten, kapern
car: racing ~ *13* Rennwagen; **sports** ~ *49* Sportwagen; ~ **crash** *166T* Autounfall; ~ **park** *69* Parkplatz, -haus, -garage; ~ **wash** *49* Autowaschanlage
carbon *137* Kohlenstoff; ~ **dioxide** *136* Kohlendioxid; ~ **dioxide level** *136* Kohlendioxidkonzentration, -gehalt
cardboard *99* Pappe
cardiovascular *17* Herz-Kreislauf-
care *17T* Sorge, Fürsorge, Sorgfalt; **floor** ~ *104* Bodenpflege; **hair** ~ *49T* Haarpflege; **health** ~ *97* Gesundheitswesen, medizinische Versorgung; **intensive** ~ **unit** *200* Intensivstation; ~ **home** *132* Pflegeheim
to **care about sth** *100* sich um etw kümmern
career *8* Karriere, Laufbahn
careers advisor *68* Berufsberater/in
careless *78T* nachlässig
cargo *193* Fracht
caring *65* fürsorglich; ~ **profession** *68T* Pflegeberuf
carmaker *88T* Autohersteller
carpenter *65* Zimmerer/in, Schreiner/in
carpentry *100* Schreinerei; ~ **workshop** *186* Zimmerei, Schreinerei
carpet *40* Teppich(boden)
to **carry:** ~ **on** *116* weitermachen; ~ **out** *34* durchführen, ausführen
cartoon *26* Karikatur
cartoonist *26* Karikaturist/in
case *163* Koffer; ~ **study** *100* Fallstudie
cash: to **have spare** ~ *96T* Geld übrig haben; ~ **machine** *105* Geldautomat; ~ **withdrawal** *134* Geldauszahlung, Barabhebung
to **cash a cheque** *68T* einen Scheck einlösen
cashier *54* Kassierer/in
casing, well ~ *143T* Bohrlochverrohrung, Bohrlochwandung
cassava *156* Maniok, Kassava
casual *71* leger, zwanglos; ~ **job** *110* Nebenjob
catalyst *98* Katalysator
catastrophe *148* Katastrophe
category *65* Kategorie
to **cater** *122* Speisen und Getränke liefern; ~ **for sth** *122* auf etw eingehen
Catholicism *55* Katholizismus, der katholische Glaube
caught, to **be** ~ *56* festsitzen, in der Klemme sitzen
cause *136* Ursache; **good** ~ *92* guter Zweck
to **cause** *28* verursachen; ~ **sb to do sth** *69* jdn dazu veranlassen, etw zu tun
CCTV *132* Videoüberwachung; ~ **camera** *132* Überwachungskamera
ceilidh *79 geselliges Beisammensein mit Musik und Tanz*
to **celebrate** *20* feiern
celebrity *6* Prominente/r, Prominenz
cement *193* Zement
central: ~ **to sth** *44* von zentraler Bedeutung für etw; ~ **heating** *181* Zentralheizung; ~ **processing unit** *179T* Hauptprozessor
to **centralize** *177T* bündeln, zusammenfassen
centrally heated *70* zentralbeheizt
century *14* Jahrhundert; **mid-**~ *161* Jahrhundertmitte
CEO *136* Vorstandsvorsitzende/r
ceramic *208* keramisch, Keramik-
to **certify** *156* zertifizieren
chain *72* Kette; **supply** ~ *99* Lieferkette; **value** ~ *145* Wertschöpfungskette
chairperson *155* Vorsitzende/r
challenge *10* Herausforderung, (große) Aufgabe
challenging *20* anspruchsvoll, fordernd
chamber *194* Kammer
champion *13* Meister/in
chance: to **take a** ~ **on sb** *110* es mit jdm versuchen, jdm eine Chance geben
change *8* Wandel, Verwandlung; *52* Veränderung; *81* Wechselgeld; **by** ~ *141* zufällig
to **change:** ~ **sth into sth** *17* etw in etw umwandeln; ~ **for the better** *101* sich zum Besseren verändern
changing *109* im Wandel; ~ **room** *13* Umkleidekabine, Umkleide

channel *37* Kanal, Leitung
chaos *40* Chaos
characteristic *116* Merkmal, charakteristische Eigenschaft
to **charge sb with sth** *14* jdn einer Sache beschuldigen, jdn einer Sache anklagen
charge, free of ~ *177T* gebührenfrei, kostenlos
charged *146* (elektrisch) geladen
charitable *92* wohltätig, gemeinnützig
charity *7* Benefiz-, Wohltätigkeit(s-); *43* wohltätige Zwecke; *66* Wohltätigkeitsorganisation; to **give to ~** *92* (für wohltätige Zwecke) spenden
chart *52* Diagramm, Tabelle; **bar ~** *52* Säulendiagramm; **line ~** *53* Liniendiagramm
charts *pl* *11* Hitparade
to **chase sb** *14* jdn verfolgen, jdn jagen
chat *56* Unterhaltung, Schwätzchen; to **have a ~** *34T* sich unterhalten, miteinander plaudern
chatty *32* mitteilsam, geschwätzig
to **check sth out** *62T* sich etw ansehen
checkout *54* Kasse
to **cheer for sb** *21T* jdn anfeuern, jdm zujubeln
cheerful *57* fröhlich
cheers *pl* *8* Jubel, Applaus; **C~!** *31* Tschüs! Mach's gut! Danke!
chemical: ~ control (of pests) *152* Schädlingsbekämpfung(smittel); **~ engineering** *199* Chemietechnik, chemische Verfahrenstechnik
chemicals *pl*, **farm ~** *149* Landwirtschaftschemikalien
cheque, to **cash a ~** *68T* einen Scheck einlösen
chess *13* Schach; **~ set** *13* Schachspiel *(Figuren + Brett)*
chest *198* Brust
chief executive officer *64* Vorstandsvorsitzende/r
chief security officer *201* Hauptsicherheitsbeauftragte/r
childhood *37* Kindheit; **~ sweetheart** *10* Jugendliebe
chilly *173T* kühl
chips *pl BE* *63* Pommes frites
chlorine *184T* Chlor
choice *19* Wahl, Entscheidung
to **choose sth over sth** *46* etw. einer anderen Sache vorziehen
chore *55* (lästige Routine-)Aufgabe
Christian *126* christlich, Christ/in
to **chuckle** *169* kichern, schmunzeln
circuit *146* Stromkreis
circumstances *pl* *201* Umstände
circumvention *201* Umgehen, Überlistung
citizen *95* Bürger/in; **senior ~** *114* Senior/in, ältere/r Mitbürger/in
city planner *167* Stadtplaner/in
civil: ~ engineering *158* Hoch- und Tiefbau; **~ society** *161* Bürgergesellschaft
civilian *158* zivil, Zivil-
civilization *164* Zivilisation
to **claim** *124* behaupten; **~ unemployment benefits** *86* Arbeitslosengeld beziehen
clamp *184* Schraubzwinge
clamping *185* Verpressen
to **clean up** *40* aufräumen, saubermachen
to **clear** *148* räumen, roden; **~ the table** *64* den Tisch abräumen
clearance sale *144* Räumungsverkauf
clerical *65* Büro-
clerk, bank ~ *67* Bankangestellte/r; **office ~** *49T* Büroangestellte/r
clever *47* intelligent, klug, schlau, clever
climate *136* Klima; **~ change** *98* Klimawandel
climb *106* Anstieg
clinic *100* Klinik
clock error *170* Taktfehler, Uhrfehler
to **clone** *199* klonen
close *11* nah, dicht, eng; **~ to** *141* nahe bei, in der Nähe von; **complimentary ~** *76* *(Brief:)* Schlussformel
to **close sth down** *140* etw stilllegen
close-up *199* Nahaufnahme
closely, to **read sth ~** *51* etw genau (durch)lesen; **~ related** *116* eng verwandt
cloth, man of the ~ *126T* Geistlicher
clothing bank *89* Altkleidersammelbehälter
cloud *54* Wolke, Cloud
clue *8* Hinweis, Anhaltspunkt
CNC machining *185* CNC-Bearbeitung
coal *136* Kohle
coal-fired *136* kohlegetrieben
coast *80* Küste
coastal *137* Küsten-
coating *145* Ummantelung, (Kabel-)Mantel
co-author *137* Mitautor/in, Mitverfasser/in
to **coax sth out of sth** *160* etw aus etw herausholen
cocaine *14* Kokain
cochlea *196* Gehörschnecke, Cochlea
cofounder *64* Mitbegründer/in
coil *202* Spule
cold *13* Erkältung
to **collaborate on sth** *210* bei etw *(Projekt etc.)* zusammenarbeiten
collaboration *177T* Zusammenarbeit
collaborative *177T* kollaborativ, gemeinschaftlich
collaborator *168* Mitarbeiter/in
to **collapse** *100* einstürzen
collapse *103* Einsturz
colleague *28* Kollege/-in
to **collect** *7* sammeln; **~ sth** *21* etw abholen
collection *11T* Kollektion; *23* Sammlung; *144* Abholung
college *49T* Fachhochschule; **sixth-form ~** *139* Oberstufenzentrum, Studienkolleg; **vocational ~** *31* Fachoberschule, Berufskolleg
colonial power *160* Kolonialmacht
to **colour** *49T* färben
to **comb** *81* kämmen
combination *64* Kombination, Vereinigung
to **combine** *54* kombinieren, verbinden, vereinen
combustion, internal ~ engine *159* Verbrennungsmotor
to **come: ~ across sth** *51* auf etw stoßen; **~ down to sth** *18* auf etw hinauslaufen, auf etw ankommen; **~ round** *30* vorbeikommen; **~ up with sth** *51* sich etw ausdenken, sich etw einfallen lassen; *88T* etw entwickeln; **~ fourth** *14* Vierte/r werden
comfortable *62T* angenehm; to **feel ~** *21T* sich wohlfühlen
command *187* Befehl; to **be in ~** *80* das Kommando führen, die Befehle geben, das Sagen haben
to **command** *131* beherrschen
commander *124* Kommandant/in, Anführer/in
commendable *161* vorbildlich
commerce *161* Handel
commercial *51* (Werbe-)Spot; *142* gewerblich, kommerziell
commitment to sth *94* Engagement für etw, Einsatz für etw
committee *14* Ausschuss, Kommission, Komitee; **special ~** *167* Sonderausschuss
common *64* verbreitet, üblich
communication, near field ~ *54* Nahfeldkommunikation
community *66* Gemeinde, Gemeinschaft; **~ benefits** *pl* *143T* Zahlungen an die Gemeinde
to **commute** *137* (zur Arbeit) pendeln
commuter *46* Pendler/in
compact *179T* kompakt
companionship *90* Gemeinschaft, Gesellschaft
company car *65* Firmenwagen
to **compare** *9* vergleichen
comparison *21* Steigerung *(von Adjektiven)*
compass *159* Kompass
compatibility *191* Kompatibilität
compatible *176* kompatibel
to **compensate for sth** *181* etw ausgleichen
to **compete** *14* (bei einem Wettbewerb) antreten; *88T* konkurrieren, im Wettbewerb stehen
competency *177T* Kompetenz

competition *8* Wettbewerb, Wettkampf; *46* Konkurrenz, Konkurrenzkampf; to **enter a ~** *14* an einem Wettkampf/Wettbewerb teilnehmen
competitive *14* wettkampfmäßig; *21* konkurrenzfähig, *(Preise:)* günstig; *46* umkämpft, wettbewerbsintensiv
competitor *72* Konkurrent/in, Konkurrenz
to **compile** *77* erstellen, zusammenstellen
to **complain** *28* sich beschweren, sich beklagen
complaint *27* Beschwerde, Klage, Reklamation
to **complement** *74T* ergänzen
completion *164* Ausführung, Erledigung *(einer Aufgabe)*; *170* Abschluss
complex *44* komplex
complexity *200T* Komplexität, Aufwand
to **complicate** *169* komplizieren
complimentary close *76* *(Brief:)* Schlussformel
component *100* Bauteil
to **compose** *46* komponieren
compost *156* Kompost
compound *146* (chemische) Verbindung
comprehensive school *163* Gesamtschule
to **compromise** *195* beeinträchtigen
computer-aided *100* computergestützt
computerized *187* computergestützt
computing *175* Datenverarbeitung, Rechenwesen, Computer(-)
to **concede** *129* eingestehen, einräumen
to **concentrate on sth** *11T* sich auf etw konzentrieren
concept *46* Idee, Gedanke, Konzept
concern *69* Sorge, Befürchtung
concerned *146* besorgt; **as far as I'm ~** *23* von mir aus, was mich betrifft
concise *190* knapp, kurz (und bündig)
to **conclude** *73* schließen, beenden; **to ~** *174* abschließend
conclusion *38* Schlussfolgerung, Schluss; **in ~** *48* abschließend, zum Schluss
concrete *97* konkret; *143T* Beton
condition *146* Krankheit
to **conduct sth** *73* etw durchführen
conductive *182T* leitfähig, leitend
conference *140* Konferenz
confidence *94* Selbstvertrauen, Zuversicht
configuration *203T* Konfiguration
to **confirm** *32* bestätigen
confirmation *121* Bestätigung
to **confiscate** *163* beschlagnahmen, konfiszieren
conflict zone *126* Krisenregion, Konfliktzone
to **confuse sth** *134T* etw verwechseln
to **congratulate sb on sth** *11* jdm zu etw gratulieren
congressman *110* Kongressabgeordneter
to **conjure sth up** *158* etw heraufbeschwören
connection *15* Verbindung
connectivity *108* Verbindung(en)
consensus *197* Übereinstimmung, Konsens
consequence *130* Folge, Konsequenz
to **conserve** *205* bewahren, sparen
consideration, to **take sth into ~** *74T* etw berücksichtigen
considered, to **be ~ sth** *199* als etw gelten
to **consist of sth** *103* aus etw bestehen
consistently *200T* ständig, durchweg
constant *51* ständig, andauernd
constellation *170* Konstellation
to **construct** *101* bauen, errichten, konstruieren
construction: ~ company *116* Baufirma; **~ site** *184* Baustelle; **~ worker** *65* Bauarbeiter/in
consultancy *175* Beratung(sfirma)
consultant *74* Berater/in; **management ~** *65* Unternehmensberater/in
consulting firm *161* Beratungsfirma
to **consume** *149* verbrauchen, konsumieren
consumer *19* Verbraucher/in, Konsument/in
consumption *149* Verbrauch, Konsum
contact *29* Kontakt, Verbindung; *121* Ansprechpartner/in, Geschäftspartner/in; **~ details** *pl* *31* Kontaktdaten
to **contact sb** *38* sich mit jdm in Verbindung setzen
contactless *54* drahtlos
to **contain** *45* enthalten
container *155T* Behälter
to **contaminate** *156* verunreinigen, kontaminieren
contamination *206T* Verunreinigung, Kontamination
contest *46* Wettbewerb
context *41* Zusammenhang, Kontext
continually *64* kontinuierlich
to **continue to do sth** *52* etw weiterhin tun
continued *192* kontinuierlich, Weiter-
continuity *70* Kontinuität, Fortdauer
contraceptive *159* Verhütungsmittel
contract *8* Vertrag.
contracted *59* zusammengezogen
to **contrast** *32* gegenüberstellen, vergleichen
contrast, by ~ *44* im Gegensatz dazu, dagegen
contribution *84* Beitrag; *96* (finanzielle) Zuwendung, Spende; to **make a ~** *84* einen Beitrag leisten
contributor *110* Autor/in *(von Zeitschriftenartikeln)*
to **contrive** *131* bewerkstelligen
control, to **maintain ~** *190* Kontrolle ausüben
controversial *140* umstritten
convenient *201* praktisch, bequem
convention *162* Übereinkunft, Gepflogenheit, Konvention; *199* Tagung
conventional *46* konventionell, herkömmlich
to **convert** *176* umbauen; *180* umwandeln
converter, analogue-to-digital ~ (ADC) *187* Analog-Digital-Wandler (AD-Wandler)
to **convince** *173* überzeugen
convinced *194* überzeugt
to **cook a meal** *49T* eine Mahlzeit zubereiten, ein Essen kochen
cool: ~ down *17T* Abkühlen; **~ room** *206T* Kühlraum
cooling *182* Kühlung
cooperation *74T* Zusammenarbeit, Zusammenwirken
cooperative *100* Genossenschaft
to **cope (with sth)** *40* etw bewältigen, mit etw klarkommen, mit etw fertig werden
copper *108* Kupfer
copy *23* Nachahmung, Imitat; *76* Ausgabe
to **copy** *23* nachahmen, imitieren
core *192* Kern
coronal mass ejection *134* koronaler Massenauswurf
corporate *69* Unternehmens-, von Unternehmen
correction *77* Korrekturlesen, Korrektur
corridor *120T* Flur, Gang
to **corrode** *142* korrodieren, zersetzen
corrosion *141* Korrosion, Zersetzung
corrugated metal *156* Wellblech
corrupt *14* korrupt, bestechlich
cost: labour ~s *pl* *194T* Lohnkosten, Arbeitskosten; **running ~** *155* Betriebskosten; **~ of living** *83* Lebenshaltungskosten; **~ per item** *209* Stückkosten; **low-~** *104* billig, kostengünstig; to **cut ~s** *107T* Kosten senken
cost-effective *141* rentabel
council *143T* (Stadt-, Gemeinde-)Rat
councillor *143T* Ratsmitglied
counsellor *38T* Berater/in
counter *81* Schalter, Theke
to **counteract sth** *69* einer Sache entgegenwirken
counterflow heat exchanger *182* Gegenstromwärmetauscher
coupon *54* Gutschein

course *164* Weg, Vorgehensweise; **~ of action** *87* Vorgehen, Maßnahmen; **golf ~** *143T* Golfplatz
court *81* Gericht(shof)
courtroom *81* Gerichtssaal
cover *22* (Buch-)Umschlag, Einband; *23* Titelseite; **~ letter** *66* Anschreiben, Begleitschreiben
to **cover** *27* bedecken
coverage *170* Abdeckung, Erfassung
co-worker *100* Kollege/-in
crack *140* Spalte
craft *79* Handwerk
craftspeople *186* Handwerker
crane *198* Kran
to **crash** *154* abstürzen, zusammenbrechen
crash *47* Schlag, Krach; *166T* Autounfall
crasher *40* ungeladener Gast
craze *16* Modewelle, Trend
to **create** *46* (er)schaffen, entwerfen, kreieren
creation *98* Einrichtung
creativity *65* schöpferische Begabung, Kreativität
creator *65* Schöpfer/in
credit *156* Verdienst; **~ rating** *62T* (Bewertung/Einstufung der) Bonität, Kreditwürdigkeit
crew *189* Mannschaft, Besatzung
crime, high ~ *136* Schwerverbrechen; **~ detection** *132* Aufdecken von Straftaten
criminal justice *124* Strafjustiz
crippling *156* lähmend, mörderisch
crisis *68T* Krise
criterion, criteria *201* Kriterium, Kriterien
critical(ly) *191T* entscheidend, kritisch
criticism (of sb/sth) *23* Kritik (an jdm/etw)
to **criticize** *9* kritisieren
crop *148* Nutzpflanze, Feldfrucht; *152* Ernte; **~ health** *158* Pflanzengesundheit; **~ production** *148* Pflanzenproduktion, pflanzliche Erzeugung
cropland *148* Ackerland
cross *125* Kreuz
to **cross** *69* überqueren, überwinden
crossroads *164* Scheideweg
crowded *21* voll (mit Leuten), überfüllt
to **crowdfund** *176* durch freiwillige Beiträge (übers Internet) finanzieren
crowdfunding *192 Finanzierung durch freiwillige Unterstützer*
to **crowdsource sth** *146* etw durch Freiwillige (übers Internet) beziehen
cruel *38T* grausam, gemein
to **cry one's eyes out** *11* wie ein Schlosshund heulen
crystal *180* Kristall
cuisine *79* Küche, Kochkunst
cult *6* Kult
to **cultivate** *157* bewirtschaften
cultural *69* kulturell, kulturbezogen
cupboard *83* Schrank
cure *83* Heilung, Therapie
to **cure** *184* aushärten
curfew *27* Sperrstunde
current *10* aktuell; *134T* (elektrischer) Strom; **alternating ~ (AC)** *203* Wechselstrom
currently *74T* zur Zeit, aktuell
curved *184* gebogen
customer services advisor *68T* Kundenberater/in
to **customize** *174T* auf den Kundenbedarf zuschneiden
customized *54* auf den Kundenbedarf zugeschnitten
customs *pl 144* Zoll; **border ~ officer** *161* (Grenz-)Zollbeamte/r
cut, power ~ *134T* Stromausfall
to **cut** *149* reduzieren, einschränken; **~ down** *184T (Baum)* fällen; **~ sb off from sth** *36* jdn von etw abschneiden; **~ costs** *107T* Kosten senken; **to ~ a long story short** *60* lange Rede, kurzer Sinn
cutlery *168* Besteck
cutting-edge *160* Spitzen-, auf dem neusten Stand
CV (curriculum vitae) *66* Lebenslauf
cybercrime *130* Cyberkriminalität
cybernetic *197* kybernetisch
cybernetics *196* Kybernetik
cybersecurity *199* Internetsicherheit
cycle *203* Zyklus; **fertility ~** *160* Fruchtbarkeitszyklus
to **cycle on** *14* weiterradeln
cyclist *14* Radfahrer/in; **racing ~** *14* Radrennfahrer/in
cyclone *137* Wirbelsturm, Zyklon, Sturmtief

D

dairy produce *193* Milchprodukte
damage *40* Schaden
to **damage** *40* beschädigen
dance routine *17T* Tanzschritte
dancer *65* Tänzer/in
danger *40* Gefahr
darkness *131* Dunkelheit
data protection *123* Datenschutz
dawn *150* Morgendämmerung
day, at the end of the ~ *57* letzten Endes, unterm Strich; **these ~s** *56* zur Zeit; **~-to-day** *56* tagtäglich
day centre *90* Tagesstätte
dazzling *178* überwältigend, verwirrend
to **deactivate** *39* stilllegen, deaktivieren
dead, to **be left for ~** *109* als tot zurückgelassen werden
deadline *100* Frist, Termin; to **meet a ~** *112* eine Frist / einen Termin einhalten
deaf *196* taub
deal *50* Geschäft, Abschluss; *81* Abmachung; **a great ~** *94* erhebliche Menge; **special ~** *54* Sonderangebot
to **deal with sth** *41* mit etw zurechtkommen, mit etw umgehen; *87* mit etw zu tun haben
dealer *144* Händler/in
death *81* Tod
debate *22* Diskussion, Debatte
debt *156* Schulden
decade *14* Jahrzehnt; **throughout the ~s** *14* durch/über die Jahrzehnte
decision-maker *98* Entscheidungsträger/in
to **declare** *167* verkünden
decline *106* Rückgang
to **decline** *106* zurückgehen, fallen, sinken
decrease *106* Abnahme, Rückgang
to **decrease** *106* abnehmen, zurückgehen
to **decrypt** *44* entschlüsseln
deep *47* tief; **~ brain stimulation** *196* Tiefenhirnstimulation
default, by ~ *69* automatisch
defeat *129* Niederlage
defence, self-~ *128* Selbstverteidigung
to **defend** *128* verteidigen
to **define** *6* definieren
definitely *34T* absolut, ganz sicher
definition, high ~ *178* hohe (Bild-) Auflösung
degree *110* Abschluss; *136* Grad; **~ course** *74T* Studiengang
delay *105* Verzögerung
delayed *192* verzögert
to **delete** *38T* löschen, tilgen
deletion *39* Löschung, Tilgung
delivery *129* Lieferung
demand (for sth) *181* Bedarf (an etw)
demand *105* Nachfrage; to **meet a ~** *105* eine Nachfrage befriedigen
to **demand** *88T* fordern, verlangen; *148* nachfragen
democracy *101* Demokratie
democratic *132* demokratisch
to **demonstrate** *178* zeigen, darlegen; *189* vorführen, demonstrieren
denier *136* Leugner/in
to **deny** *88T* leugnen
department *34* Abteilung; **D~ for Work and Pensions** *60 brit. Arbeits- und Sozialministerium;* **legal ~** *69* juristische Abteilung
to **depend on sth** *74T* von etw abhängen, auf etw angewiesen sein
dependence *123* Abhängigkeit
dependent on sth *36* von etw abhängig
depending on *19* je nach(dem)

to **deport** 84 abschieben
deportation 86 Abschiebung
to **deposit** 194 deponieren, absetzen; 209T *(Material)* ablagern, auftragen
deposition, fused ~ modeling 209 Schmelzschichtung
depressed 100 *(Wirtschaft:)* flau, am Boden
depth 98 Tiefe
deputy manager 46 stellvertretende/r Geschäftsführer/in
descendant 84 Nachfahre, Nachkomme
descent 194 Sinkflug
desert 124 Wüste
to **deserve** 6 verdienen
design 54 Entwurf, Plan; 186 Konstruktion; **engineering ~** 74 Konstruktion; **~ office** 74 Konstruktionsbüro
to **design** 11T entwerfen, gestalten; 54 planen; 65 konstruieren
designed, to **be ~ to do sth** 49T dazu gedacht sein, etw zu tun; darauf ausgelegt sein, etw zu tun
designer 65 Gestalter/in, Designer/in, Konstrukteur/in
desired 192 gewünscht
desperate 38T verzweifelt
despite 94 trotz
destination 193 Bestimmungsort
to **destroy** 95 zerstören
destruction 150 Zerstörung
destructive 124 zerstörerisch
details *pl* 40 Angaben
to **detect** 134T aufspüren, entdecken
detention centre 81 Auffanglager, Haftanstalt
to **deter** 156 abschrecken, abhalten
to **determine** 170 bestimmen
devastating 125 verheerend
developing country 88 Entwicklungsland
development 69 Entwicklung; 106 *(Immobilie:)* Erschließung, Bau; **Research and D~ (R&D)** 120T Forschung(s-) und Entwicklung(sabteilung); **stage of ~** 194 Entwicklungsstand, -stadium
device, explosive ~ 125 Sprengsatz; **tracking ~** 144 Ortungsgerät
to **devote** 165 widmen
to **diagnose sb with sth** 43 etw *(Krankheit)* bei jdm feststellen/ diagnostizieren
diagnosis, diagnoses 160 Diagnose, Diagnosen
diagnostics 158T Fehlersuche, Diagnose
diamond-shaped 154 rautenförmig
dictation 189 Diktieren, Diktat
diet 148 Ernährung, Kost
dietary 122 Ernährungs
difference, to **make a ~** 90 etw bewirken; to **make the ~** 49T entscheidend sein, den entscheidenden Unterschied ausmachen
difficulty 118 Schwierigkeit(en)
to **dig: ~ for sth** 108 nach etw graben; **~ up** 210 *(Straße)* aufreißen
digit 33 Ziffer
digital signage 45 digitale Außenwerbung
to **digitize** 187 digitalisieren
dilemma 88T Zwiespalt, Dilemma
dimensions *pl* 158 Abmessungen
diplomacy 189 Diplomatie
direction 203 Richtung
directions *pl* 119 Wegbeschreibung; to **give ~** 119 den Weg beschreiben
directory 52 Telefonbuch
dirigible 194 Luftschiff
dirty 9 schmutzig
disability 13 Behinderung
disabled 92 behindert; **~ facilities** *pl* 122 behindertengerechte Toiletten
disadvantaged 90 benachteiligt
to **disagree with sth** 22 einer Sache nicht zustimmen, gegen etw sein, etw ablehnen
to **disappear** 175 verschwinden
disaster 62T Katastrophe; **~ site** 194 Katastrophengebiet
disastrous 137 katastrophal, verheerend
discipline 169 Disziplin
to **disclose** 132 offenlegen
discord 161 Zwietracht
discount 20 Rabatt, Nachlass; **~ label** 20 Billigmarke
to **discover** 44 entdecken, herausfinden
disease 97 Krankheit
disgust, in ~ 81 angewidert
dishwasher 168 Spülmaschine; to **load the ~** 64 die Spülmaschine einräumen; to **unload the ~** 64 die Spülmaschine ausräumen
to **dismiss sth as sth** 164 etw als etw abtun
display 46 Bildschirm, Anzeige, Display; 79 Vorführung
to **display** 19 zeigen; 179T anzeigen, darstellen
to **disrupt** 134T unterbrechen, stören
distance, long-~ 194 Langstrecken-; **within walking ~** 119 in Laufweite
to **distinguish** 201 unterscheiden, auseinanderhalten
to **distribute** 174 verteilen, austeilen; 191T (Waren) vertreiben
district 145 Bezirk
disturbance 134 Störung
diversity 156 Vielfalt
to **divide** 27 teilen
divorce 151 Scheidung
DIY (do-it-yourself) 66 Heimwerker-, Heimwerken
documentary 200 *(Radio, TV:)* Dokumentation
documentation 191 (technische) Dokumentation
doer 65 Macher/in
do-good 46 weltverbessernd
dole 111 Arbeitslosengeld; **~ bludger** 111 Sozialschmarotzer
dome 155 Kuppel
domestic 64 Heim-; 167 heimisch, Inlands-; **~ appliance** 187 Haushaltsgerät, Elektrogerät; **gross ~ product (GDP)** 92 Bruttosozialprodukt
to **dominate** 124 beherrschen, dominieren
to **donate** 49T spenden
donation 89 Spende
donor 90 Spender/in
doorbell, to **ring the ~** 13 (an der Tür) klingeln, läuten
dope 49T Depp
to **dope** 14 dopen
down the line 81 weiter
to **download** 21 herunterladen
downside 152 Nachteil
to **downsize** 70 verkleinern, gesundschrumpfen
downwards 53 fallend
draft 181 Luftzug, Zugluft
to **drag** 80 zerren
dragon 79 Drachen
drama 57 Schauspiel
drama club 59 Schauspiel-AG
dramatic(ally) 160 dramatisch
to **draw** 26 zeichnen; 73 ziehen; **~ up** 43 *(Text)* verfassen, abfassen; **~ sth up** 170 etw erstellen; **~ attention to sb/sth** 23 Aufmerksamkeit auf jdn/etw ziehen
drawing 26 Zeichnung
to **dress down** 70 sich leger kleiden
to **drift** 156 wehen
to **drill** 140 bohren
drill 185 Bohrer, Bohrmaschine; **~ bit** 185 Bohrer, Bohrspitze
drilling 143T Bohrung(en); **~ rig** 143T Bohrturm
drive, hard ~ 175 Festplatte; **test ~** 166T Testfahrt
to **drive** 203T antreiben; **~ sb away** 60 jdn vertreiben
driverless 164 führerlos
drivetrain 203T Antrieb, Antriebsstrang
driving: ~ force 69 treibende Kraft; **~ licence** 48F Führerschein
drone 158 Drohne; **airborne ~** 168 Flugdrohne
to **drop** 60 fallen, *(Noten:)* schlechter werden; **~ sb** 194 jdn absetzen; **~ in** 70 vorbeikommen, hereinschauen; **~ sb off** 40 jdn (wohin)bringen; **~ one's eyes** 81 den Blick senken; **~ one's voice** 80 die Stimme senken
droplet 179T Tröpfchen
drought 147 Dürre
to **drown** 137 ertrinken, im Meer versinken

drums *pl* *43* Schlagzeug
drunk, to **get** ~ *41* sich betrinken
drunken *40* betrunken
to **dry out** *172* austrocknen
drying rack *208* Trockengestell
dubious *144* zweifelhaft
due, to **be** ~ *121T* *(Flugzeug etc.:)* planmäßig ankommen; ~ **to** *118* aufgrund von, wegen
dummy *208* Dummkopf, Hirni
dump *145* Müllhalde
to **dump** *144* *(Müll)* (wild) abladen; *206T* *(Abfall)* wegwerfen
durable *181* langlebig, solide, strapazierfähig
duration *66* Dauer
duty *168* Aufgabe, Pflicht
duty *75* Aufgabe, Pflicht, Arbeit
duvet cover *63* Bettdeckenbezug
to **dwell on sth** *43* sich mit etw aufhalten
dynamic *177T* dynamisch

E

eager *197* begierig, ungeduldig; to **be** ~ **to do sth** *88T* darauf brennen, etw zu tun
ear, inner ~ *196* Innenohr
earnings *pl* *83* Einkünfte, Verdienst; *143T* Einnahmen, Gewinn
earthquake *96T* Erdbeben
ease of use *191* Benutzerfreundlichkeit
eco- *46* Öko-
economic *65* wirtschaftlich; ~ **power** *88T* Wirtschaftsmacht
economics *137* Ökonomie, Wirtschaft(swissenschaft); *209* Ökonomie, Wirtschaftlichkeit
economy *86T* Wirtschaft; **fuel** ~ *203T* (wirtschaftlicher) Kraftstoffverbrauch
ecosystem *148* Ökosystem
edible *206T* essbar
to **edit** *113* *(Text)* redigieren, bearbeiten
edition *111* Ausgabe
editor *110* Herausgeber/in; *142* Redakteur/in
educational *74T* schulisch, Bildungs-
effect *47* Wirkung, Effekt
effective *46* wirksam, effektiv
effectively *198* tatsächlich, praktisch
effectiveness *179* Effektivität
efficient(ly) *62T* effizient
effort *88T* Anstrengung(en), Einsatz, Leistung
e.g. *33* z. B.
either *164* eine/r/s *(von beiden);* ~ **… or** *23* entweder … oder; **not …** ~ *44* auch nicht
ejection, coronal mass ~ *134* koronaler Massenauswurf
elder center *AE* *118* Senioreneinrichtung
elderly *109* älter; Senioren; **home for the** ~ *114* Altenheim
election *161* Wahl
electric: ~ **motor** *178* Elektromotor; ~ **vehicle** *202* Elektrofahrzeug
electrical *66* elektrisch, Elektro-; ~ **engineering** *169* Elektrotechnik
electrician *49* Elektriker/in
electricity bill *143* Stromrechnung
electrode *196* Elektrode
electromagnet *202* Elektromagnet
electromagnetic *134* elektromagnetisch
electronic *100* elektronisch, Elektronik-
electronics *pl* *69* Elektronik
element *45* Baustein, Element
elsewhere *67* woanders, anderswo
to **email sb** *66* jdm eine E-Mail schicken
email exchange *171* E-Mail-Korrespondenz
embarrassed, to **feel** ~ *59* sich genieren, sich schämen
embarrassing *129* peinlich, unangenehm
embassy *94* Botschaft
to **embed** *196* einbetten
emergency *109* Notfall, Not-; ~ **exit** *120* Notausgang, Fluchtweg; ~ **exit plan** *120* Fluchtwegplan; ~ **response** *158* Notfallmaßnahmen; ~ **service** *134* Notfalldienst
to **emigrate** *86* auswandern
emission *137* Ausstoß, Emission
to **emit** *134T* ausstoßen
emotion *45* Gefühl, Emotion
emotional *18* gefühlsmäßig, emotional
to **emphasize** *196* hervorheben, betonen
to **employ** *54* verwenden, einsetzen; ~ **sb** *71* jdn beschäftigen, jdn einstellen
employable *74T* (auf dem Arbeitsmarkt) vermittelbar
employee *69* Angestellte/r, Beschäftigte/r
employer *66* Arbeitgeber/in
employment *100* Anstellung, Arbeit
to **empower sb to do sth** *90* jdn befähigen, etw zu tun
to **enable** *90* befähigen
enabled *160* fähig
enclosure (encl.) *76* *(Brief:)* Anlage
to **encounter sth** *118* auf etw treffen, auf etw stoßen
to **encourage** *137* fördern; ~ **sb to do sth** *46* jdn ermuntern, etw zu tun; ~ **sth** *192* zu etw auffordern, zu etw animieren
encrypted *129* verschlüsselt
encryption *44* Verschlüsselung
end: to **put an** ~ **to sth** *27* mit etw Schluss machen, einen Schlussstrich unter etw ziehen; ~ **mill** *185* Fräser;
~ **user** *187* Endbenutzer/in, Privatanwender/in
to **end up** *41* landen
ending *14* Schluss, Ende
endless *110* endlos, fortwährend
enemy *80* Feind/in
energy *16* Energie; **kinetic** ~ *202* Bewegungsenergie; **thermal** ~ *182* Wärmeenergie
to **engage:** ~ **in sth** *124* aktiv werden; ~ **with sb** *37* auf jdn zugehen
engaged *34* *(Telefon:)* besetzt
enforcement, law ~ *124* Gesetzesvollzug, Innere Sicherheit, Exekutive; **law** ~ **agency** *124* Strafverfolgungsbehörde, Exekutivorgan
engine *85* Motor; **internal combustion** ~ *159* Verbrennungsmotor
engineer *65* Ingenieur/in; **lead** ~ *198* Chefingenieur/in
to **engineer** *198* konstruieren
engineered timber *184* Ingenieurholz
engineering *98* (Ingenieur-)Technik, Maschinenbau; **chemical** ~ *199* Chemietechnik, chemische Verfahrenstechnik; **civil** ~ *158* Hoch- und Tiefbau; **electrical** ~ *169* Elektrotechnik; **marine** ~ *198* Schiffsmaschinenbau; **mechanical** ~ *169* Maschinenbau; **social** ~ *114* Änderung gesellschaftlicher Strukturen, angewandte Sozialwissenschaft; ~ **design** *74* Konstruktion; ~ **technician** *74* Konstruktionsmechaniker/in
English-speaking *76* englischsprachig
to **enhance** *196* verbessern, *(Sinne)* schärfen
enhancement *190* Verbesserung
to **enjoy oneself** *166* sich (gut) amüsieren
to **enlighten** *65* aufklären; ~ **about sth** *34* sich nach etw erkundigen
to **ensure** *73* sicherstellen; dafür sorgen, dass
to **entail** *98* beinhalten
to **enter:** ~ **sth** *46* an etw teilnehmen; ~ **a competition** *14* an einem Wettkampf/Wettbewerb teilnehmen
enterprise *94* Unternehmen
enterprising *65* geschäftstüchtig, risikofreudig
entertainment *45* Unterhaltung
enthusiastic(ally) *140* begeistert
entire *134T* ganz, gesamt
entirely *127* völlig, ganz
entrance fee *21T* Teilnahmegebühr
entrepreneur *51* Unternehmer/in
entry *38* *(Blog:)* Beitrag, Meldung
entry level *68* Einstieg, Anfang; ~ **pay** *68T* Einstiegsgehalt, Anfangsgehalt
entry-level *110* Einstiegs-
envelope *182* Hülle
environmental(ly) *46* umweltmäßig, Umwelt-; ~**ly friendly** *46* umweltfreundlich

F

feedback *93* Reaktion(en), Rückmeldung(en); *179T* Rückinformation, Feedback
to **feel: ~ sth** *51* etw anfassen, etw ertasten; **~ low** *17T* schlecht gelaunt sein, deprimiert sein; **~ sorry for sb** *92* jd tut einem leid
to **fell** *184* fällen
fertility cycle *160* Fruchtbarkeitszyklus
to **fertilize** *152* befruchten
fertilizer *149* Dünger, Düngemittel
festival *79* Fest, Festtag, Festival
to **fetch** *64* holen
fibre optic cable *108* Glasfaserkabel
fictional *131* fiktiv
fiddly *168* knifflig, fummelig
field, magnetic ~ *134* Magnetfeld; **near ~ communication** *54* Nahfeldkommunikation; **radio frequency ~** *205* Hochfrequenzfeld; **~ of vision** *131* Sichtfeld
fierce *46* heftig, erbittert
to **fight back** *107T* sich wehren, sich zurückkämpfen
figure *52* Zahl, Ziffer
to **figure out** *168* herausfinden
filament *209T* Faser, Faden
file *64* Datei; *71* Akte, Ordner
to **file** *81* feilen
filing cabinet *69* Aktenschrank
to **fill an order** *100* einen Auftrag ausführen
final *43* Finale
to **finance** *91* finanzieren
finance *69* Finanz(-); **~ director** *72* kaufmännische/r Leiter/in
financial *56* finanziell, Finanz-; **~ records** *pl* *175* Finanzunterlagen; **~ reporting** *177T* Rechnungslegung
to **find sb sth** *60* jdm etw besorgen
findings *pl* *43* Ergebnisse
fine *48F* Geldbuße
to **fine sb** *48F* jdn mit einer Geldbuße belegen
finger-jointed *184* keilgezinkt
fingernail *23* Fingernagel
fingerprint *199* Fingerabdruck
finish *184* Oberfläche
to **finish second** *8* Zweite/r werden
finished product *100* Endprodukt
finishing *185* Oberflächenbearbeitung, Endbearbeitung; **~ line** *124* Ziellinie
fire, on ~ *143T* in Flammen; to **set ~ to sth** *145* etw anzünden
to **fire sb** *49T* jdn feuern
firefight *124* Schusswechsel
firm(ly) *184* fest
first: ~ of all *62T* zuallererst; **~ name** *17* Vorname
fishing *154* Fischerei, Befischung; **~ boat** *108* Fangschiff, Fischerboot; **~ village** *94* Fischerdorf
to **fit** *16* passen; **~ sth with sth** *144* etw mit etw ausstatten
to **fix** *190* *(Fehler)* beheben, beseitigen
fixed *70* fest, festgelegt, fest installiert
flap *22* Umschlagklappe
flare, solar ~ *134T* Sonneneruption
flash *134T* Blitz
flat *107T* *(Umsatz etc.:)* konstant, unverändert
flaxen-haired *169* strohblond, flachsblond
fleet *194* Flotte
flexible *65* flexibel
flight path *158T* Flugroute
to **float** *153* (auf dem Wasser) treiben; *179T* (in der Luft) schweben
to **flood** *138* überschwemmen
flood *95* Überschwemmung
flooding *137* Überschwemmung
floor care *104* Bodenpflege
to **flow** *180* fließen, strömen
flow *153* Strom, Fluss
fluent *75* *(Sprache:)* fließend
foam, insulating ~ *145* Isolierschaum
focus *174* Schwerpunkt
to **focus on sth** *11* sich auf etw konzentrieren
focusing head *209* Fokussierkopf
fog *178* Nebel
folks *pl* *88T* Leute
follow-up *8* Folge-, Nachfolger
food: ~ pantry *AE* *151* Tafel, karitative Essensausgabe; **~ processing industry** *206* nahrungsmittelverarbeitende Industrie; **~ security** *155T* Ernährungssicherung
footage *132* Film-/Bildmaterial
footballer *11* Fußballer/in
to **forbid** *144* verbieten, untersagen
to **force** *80* zwingen
force *95* Gewalt, Kraft; **driving ~** *69* treibende Kraft; **police ~** *127* Polizei; **sales ~** *177* Verkaufspersonal; to **come into ~** *195* in Kraft treten
forces *pl*, **armed ~** *126T* Streitkräfte; **security ~** *126T* Sicherheitskräfte
forecast *146* Vorhersage
forehead *80* Stirn
forest *148* Wald
forested *156* bewaldet
forestry *158* Forstwirtschaft
to **forge** *199* fälschen
forklift (truck) *116* Gabelstapler
to **form** *48* bilden
formula *7* Formel
fortunately *189* zum Glück
fortune *7* Vermögen
to **forward** *198* weiterleiten
forwarding agency *145* Spedition
fossil fuel *135* fossiler Brennstoff
to **found** *94* gründen
foundation *90* Stiftung
founder *114* Gründer/in
to **fracture** *140* brechen, aufbrechen
frame *98* Rahmen; **house ~** *186* Holzskelett; **window ~** *182T* Fensterrahmen
framework *74T* Rahmen(bedingungen)
free: ~ movement *86T* Freizügigkeit; **~ of charge** *177T* gebührenfrei, kostenlos
freedom *56* Freiheit
freely *139* ungehindert, nach Belieben
freeway *AE* *166T* Autobahn
freight *193* Fracht, Frachtverkehr; **bulk ~** *193* Massenfracht; **road ~** *194* Straßengüterverkehr; **~ station** *194T* Güterbahnhof
French fries *pl AE* *62T* Pommes frites
frequency, radio ~ field *205* Hochfrequenzfeld
frequent, at ~ intervals *187* in kurzen Abständen
fresh water *149* Süßwasser
freshwater supply *98* Trinkwasserversorgung
fridge *64* Kühlschrank
fries *pl AE* *62T* Pommes frites
fuel *98* Brennstoff, Treibstoff; **fossil ~** *135* fossiler Brennstoff; **~ economy** *203T* (wirtschaftlicher) Kraftstoffverbrauch
to **fulfil** *11* erfüllen
full hybrid *203T* Voll-Hybrid
full-time *66* Vollzeit-
fully *38T* vollkommen, völlig; *66* vollständig; **~ equipped** *66* vollausgestattet
fun, to **be ~** *47* Spaß machen
to **function** *160* fungieren, funktionieren
function *51* Funktion
functional *197T* funktionell
functionality *192* Funktion(en)
fundamental *195* grundlegend
to **fund** *92* finanzieren
funding *92* Finanzierung, Geldmittel
fundraiser *43* Spendensammler/in
fundraising *43* Spendensammeln, Geldbeschaffung
fungal *158T* Pilz-
further *8* weitere/r/s
furthermore *117* darüber hinaus
to **fuse** *209T* schmelzen, verschmelzen
fused deposition modeling *209* Schmelzschichtung
future, The ~ lies with … *203T* Die Zukunft gehört …
fuzzy *175* unscharf, verschwommen

G

gain *65* Gewinn, Vorteil
to **gain** *78T* erwerben
gait *200* Gang, Gangart
galaxy *189* Galaxie
gallery *35* Galerie; **~ walk** *35* Galerierundgang
gallon *166T* Gallone *(= 3,78 l in den USA)*
game machine *46* Videospielgerät, Spielautomat

H

health: ~ **and safety** *83* Arbeitsschutz; ~ **care** *97* Gesundheitswesen, medizinische Versorgung
hearing *197* Gehör, Hörvermögen
heart-warming *114* herzerwärmend
heat, counterflow ~ **exchanger** *182* Gegenstromwärmetauscher; **subsoil** ~ **exchange** *181* Erdwärmeaustausch; ~ **transfer** *182T* Wärmeübertragung
heating *62T* Heizung; **central** ~ *181* Zentralheizung; **ventilation** ~ *181* Warmluftheizung
heavy goods vehicle (HGV) *194T* (Schwer-)Lastkraftwagen (Lkw)
hectare *155T* Hektar
helper *65* Helfer/in
helpline *38* Hotline, Sorgentelefon
hence *170* daher, folglich
herald *210* Vorbote
herbicide *152* Unkrautvernichtungsmittel
herd *152* Herde
hero *13* Held
to **hide (away)** *64* sich verstecken, sich verbergen
high: ~ **crime** *136* Schwerverbrechen; ~ **definition** *178* hohe (Bild-)Auflösung; ~ **-rise city** *170* Stadt mit Hochhäusern; ~ **speed rail** *88T* Hochgeschwindigkeitsstrecken *(Eisenbahn)*; ~ **spinal cord injury** *118* hoch gelegene Querschnittslähmung; ~ **street** *23* Hauptgeschäftsstraße, Einkaufsstraße; ~**-end** *51* hochklassig, hochwertig; ~**-resolution** *158T* hochauflösend; ~**-value** *193* hochwertig
to **highlight** *16* hervorheben
highly motivated *66* hochmotiviert
highway *AE 160* Autobahn
to **hijack** *130* kapern
hill *57* Berg, Anhöhe, Hügel
Hinduism *55* Hinduismus
hinge *208* Scharnier
hip *17T* Hüfte
to **hire sb** *39* jdn beauftragen, jdn engagieren; *49T* jdn einstellen
historical *14* historisch
to **hit** *118* *(Taste)* drücken; *148* erreichen; ~ **sth** *134T* etw erreichen, auf etw treffen; ~ **the headlines** *7* in die Schlagzeilen kommen, Schlagzeilen machen
to **hitch-hike** *94* per Anhalter fahren, trampen
to **hold:** ~ **on** *34* warten; ~ **sb back** *8* jdn bremsen; ~ **the line** *34T* am Apparat bleiben
holiday season *194* Weihnachtszeit
holographic *178* holografisch, Hologramm-
homage *169* Reverenz
home: ~ **country** *91* Heimatland; ~ **for the elderly** *114* Altenheim
homeless *81* obdachlos
homelessness *91* Obdachlosigkeit
homestay accommodation *66* Unterbringung bei Gasteltern
homing *69* Heimfindeverhalten *(z. B. von Brieftauben)*
hooked, to **get sb** ~ *17T* jdn anfixen
to **hoover** *60* staubsaugen
hopeless *110* hoffnungslos
horizontal(ly) *155* waagrecht, horizontal
horrific *91* schrecklich, entsetzlich
horrified *43* entsetzt
horror *45* Schrecken
host *87* Gastgeber; *88* (Radio-/TV-) Moderator/in
hostel *31* Herberge, Wohnheim
hot metal type *208* Setzmaschine
to **house** *177T* unterbringen
house, shared ~ *62T* Wohngemeinschaft; **timber-framed** ~ *184* Fachwerkhaus; to **move** ~ *28* umziehen; ~ **frame** *186* Holzskelett
household name *51* bekannter Name, Begriff
housework *58* Hausarbeit
housing *86* Wohnungsbau, Wohnungen
hub *145* Drehkreuz, (Verkehrs-) Knoten
huge *8* riesig, Riesen-
human: ~ **being** *26* Mensch, menschliches Wesen; ~ **error** *166T* menschliches Versagen; **H~ Resources (HR)** *50* Personal(abteilung)
humanitarian *94* humanitär
humanity *136* Menschheit, Menschlichkeit
humanlike *168* menschenähnlich
humidity *205* Luftfeuchtigkeit
to **humiliate** *81* demütigen, erniedrigen
humiliation *81* Demütigung, Erniedrigung
humour *45* Humor
to **hunt** *154* jagen
hurricane *95* Wirbelsturm
hybrid, full ~ *203T* Voll-Hybrid; **micro** ~ *203T* Mikro-Hybrid; **mild** ~ *203T* Mild-Hybrid; ~ **electric vehicle** *202* Hybridfahrzeug
hydraulic *140* hydraulisch
hydro-electric power *135* Wasserkraft
hydroponic *153* Hydrokultur-
hydroponics *152* Hydrokultur
to **hyphenate** *106* mit einem Bindestrich schreiben

I

ice sheet *137* Eisdecke
ice-covered *148* eisbedeckt
ice-free *148* eisfrei
ID *27* Personalausweis; **user** ~ *200T* Benutzername
ideal *65* ideal
identification *199* Erkennung, Identifikation
to **identify** *107* erkennen, bestimmen, identifizieren; ~ **with sb/sth** *19* sich mit jdm/etw identifizieren
identity *123* Identität
idiomatic *61* idiomatisch, redensartlich
idle state *205* Ruhezustand
idol *8* Idol
i.e. *201* d.h.
ignition *200T* Zündung
to **ignore** *54* nicht beachten, ignorieren
illegal *14* verboten, illegal
illiterate *160* Analphabet/in
to **illuminate** *180* beleuchten
imagination *65* Phantasie, Vorstellungskraft
to **imitate** *201* imitieren, nachahmen
immediate *55* unmittelbar
immediately *41* unverzüglich, unmittelbar, sofort
impact *98* Einfluss, Auswirkung; to **make an** ~ *94* etw bewirken, etw verändern
implant *196* Implantat
to **implant** *196* einpflanzen, implantieren
to **implement** *187* einbauen
implication *197T* Folge, Auswirkung
to **import** *74T* importieren, einführen
importance *38* Bedeutung, Wichtigkeit
impressed *120T* beeindruckt
to **improve** *14* (sich) verbessern, (sich) steigern; **ever-~ing** *69* stetig besser werdend
improvement in sth *14* Verbesserung bei etw
to **improvise** *16* improvisieren
impulse *196* Impuls
in-car entertainment *167* Unterhaltungselektronik im Auto
to **incorporate** *190* integrieren, aufnehmen
inch *80* Zoll *(= 2,54 cm)*
incident *27* Vorfall, Zwischenfall
inclination *170* Neigung, Neigungswinkel
inclined *170* geneigt
including *19* einschließlich
inclusive *118* inklusiv, offen
income *68* Einkommen; **per capita** ~ *156* Pro-Kopf-Einkommen
incomer *86T* Zuzügler, Ankömmling
to **increase** *46* steigen, zunehmen; ~ **sth** *17T* etw steigern
increase *69* Zunahme, Steigerung; to **be on the** ~ *69* auf dem Vormarsch sein, zunehmen
increasingly *46* zunehmend
independence *94* Unabhängigkeit
independent *57* unabhängig
to **indicate** *200* darauf hinweisen
industrial *104* Industrie-
industrialist *165* Industrielle/r
industrialization *88* Industrialisierung

industrialized 104 industrialisiert
inefficient 193 ineffizient, unwirtschaftlich
inequality 197 Ungleichheit
in-flight 158T während des Flugs
to **influence** 24 beeinflussen
influence 100 Einfluss
influential 161 einflussreich
informal 59 informell, locker
informality 69 Formlosigkeit, Ungezwungenheit
infrared 179T infrarot, Infrarot-
infrastructure 69 Infrastruktur
initial 146 erste/r/s
initially 43 anfangs, anfänglich
to **initiate** 205 einleiten, initiieren
initiative 27 Aktion, Initiative
to **injure** 100 verletzen
injury 14 Verletzung
ink 208 Tinte, Druckerschwärze
inland, to **go** ~ 100 ins Landesinnere gehen
inner ear 196 Innenohr
innocent 125 unschuldig
innovation 88T Innovationen
innovative 46 innovativ
to **input** 128 eingeben
to **inquire** 140 nachfragen, sich erkundigen
insect pests *pl* 158T Schädlinge
insecure 199 unsicher
to **insert** 118 einstecken; 206T hineinstecken, einführen
inside address 76 Empfängeranschrift
inside out, to **know sth** ~ 49T etw in- und auswendig kennen
insight 31 Einblick
to **inspire** 10 inspirieren, anregen
inspirational 43 anregend, inspirierend
to **install** 64 installieren
instance, for ~ 117 zum Beispiel
instant(ly) 48F sofortig, augenblicklich
instead 26 stattdessen; ~ **of** 16 anstatt
instinct 69 Instinkt
institute 164 Institut
to **instruct sb to do sth** 128 jdn beauftragen, etw zu tun; 158T jdm sagen, was er/sie tun soll
instruction 65 Anweisung; ~**s** *pl* 26 Anleitung, Anweisung(en)
instructor 16 Lehrer/in
to **insulate** 182 isolieren
insulating foam 145 Isolierschaum
insulation 181 Isolierung
insurance 65 Versicherung; **medical** ~ 65 Krankenversicherung
to **insure** 66 versichern
to **integrate** 84 (sich) integrieren
integrated 74T integriert, ganzheitlich
to **intend** 50 beabsichtigen
intense 134T stark
intensive care unit 200 Intensivstation
intent 27 Absicht
intention 95 Absicht
to **interact** 29 interagieren, aufeinander eingehen
interactive 54 interaktiv
to **intercept** 44 abfangen, abhören
interest (in sth) 13 Interesse (an etw)
interface 64 Verbindung, Schnittstelle
to **interface with sth** 175 sich mit etw verbinden
interior 182T Innenraum, Innenbereich
intermediate 75 mittlere/r/s *(Niveau)*
intermodal 193 *(Transport:)* multimodal, intermodal, kombiniert
intern 66 Praktikant/in
internal 127 inländisch, Inlands-
internal combustion engine 159 Verbrennungsmotor
internship 66 Praktikum
interoperable 170 interoperabel, vollständig kompatibel
to **interpret** 26 interpretieren
to **interrupt** 21T unterbrechen, ins Wort fallen
interval 144 (zeitlicher) Abstand; **at frequent** ~**s** 187 in kurzen Abständen
to **interview sb** 78 mit jdm ein Vorstellungsgespräch führen
interview 76 Vorstellungsgespräch
interviewee 112 *Person, mit der ein Vorstellungsgespräch geführt wird*
interviewer 78 *Person, die ein Vorstellungsgespräch führt*
in-tray 49T Posteingang(skorb)
introductions *pl* 48 Vorstellen
intuitional 65 intuitiv
invaluable 132 unschätzbar, unbezahlbar
to **invent** 46 erfinden
invention 48 Erfindung
inventory 194T (Lager-)Bestand
to **invest** 141 investieren
to **investigate** 65 ermitteln, untersuchen
investigative 65 erforschend, Untersuchungs-
investment 137 Investition
invitation 40 Einladung
to **invite sb to do sth** 78 jdn auffordern, etw zu tun
invite 43 Einladung
to **involve** 65 mit sich bringen, umfassen
involved 65 dazugehörig; ~ **in sth** 13 an etw beteiligt, bei etw engagiert; to **be** ~ **in sth** 57 sich an etw beteiligen, bei etw mitmachen; to **get** ~ **with sb** 37 mit jdm zu tun haben
iris scanning 200T Iris-Scan
ironic 103 ironisch
irregular 68 unregelmäßig
irrigation 149 Bewässerung
ironing, to **do (the/some)** ~ 58 bügeln
island 137 Insel
to **isolate** 36 absondern, isolieren
isolated 161 abgeschottet, abgeschieden, isoliert
issue 86T Streitpunkt, Frage, Problem, Thema
IT developer 161 IT-Entwickler/in
italics *pl* 36 Kursivschrift
item 77 Punkt, Gegenstand; 99 Artikel; 172 Tagesordnungspunkt; **stock** ~ 205 Bestandsartikel; ~ **of clothing** 23 Kleidungsstück; **item, cost per** ~ 209 Stückkosten
iteration 195 Version

J

jacket 87T Jacke, Jackett
jargon 51 Fachsprache, Jargon
jet: ~ **plane** 193 Düsenflugzeug; **passenger** ~ 88T Passagierflugzeug
jewellery 6 Schmuck
job: casual ~ 110 Nebenjob; to **advertise a** ~ 66 eine Stelle ausschreiben; ~ **advertisement** 31 Stellenanzeige, -ausschreibung; ~ **rotation** 72 Arbeitsplatzrotation, (innerbetrieblicher) Arbeitsplatzwechsel; ~ **security** 65 sicherer Arbeitsplatz; ~ **title** 66 Stellenbezeichnung
jobless 109 arbeitslos
joblessness 109 Arbeitslosigkeit
to **join** 16 beitreten, eintreten, mitmachen; 49T mitmachen, *(Radio etc.:)* in einer Sendung sein, *(Telefon:)* (mit jdm) sprechen; ~ **sth** 151 etw (miteinander) verbinden; ~ **together** 126T sich zusammenschließen
joint 98 Gelenk; 186 Verbindung; **mortise and tenon** ~ 186 Zapfenverbindung
joke 26 Witz
journalism 112 Journalismus
journalist 65 Journalist/in
journey 140 Reise, Fahrt
joy 17 Freude
Judaism 55 Judaismus, Judentum
judge 8 Richter/in, Juror/in
to **judge** 69 beurteilen
to **juggle** 110 miteinander vereinbaren, jonglieren
to **jump:** ~ **red lights** 48F bei Rot über eine Ampel fahren; ~ **the queue** 82 sich vordrängeln
jungle 160 Dschungel
junior 14 Junioren-; 150 Jung-, Nachwuchs-

K

keen, to **be** ~ **on sth** 12 auf etw versessen sein; to **be** ~ **to do sth** 76 etw unbedingt tun wollen
to **keep:** ~ **to the right/left** 119 sich rechts/links halten; ~ **up with sb/sth** 24 mit jdm/etw Schritt halten

keep-fit *12* Fitness(-)
keystroke *128* Tastenanschlag, Herunterdrücken einer Taste
to **kick sth down** *80* etw eintreten
kiln *184* Trockenofen, Trockenkammer
kind *81* freundlich, gütig, nett
kinetic energy *202* Bewegungsenergie
kiosk, public ~ *118* öffentliches Internet-Terminal
kite, towing ~ *195* Zugdrachen
to **knock: ~ sb off sth** *94* jdn von etw herunterstoßen, von etw herunterfallen; **~ sth off** *129* etw abschlagen; **~ sth out** *134T* etw lahmlegen
knot *194* Knoten
to **know: ~ sth inside out** *49T* etw in- und auswendig kennen; to **get to ~ sb** *171* jdn kennen lernen; to **let sb ~ sth** *31* jdm etw mitteilen, jdm etw sagen; **on a need-to-~ basis** *63* im (unumgänglichen) Bedarfsfall
knowledge *48F* Wissen, Kenntnis(se)

L

lab *118* Computerraum; *210* Labor
label *11* (Mode-)Firma, Marke; *87* Beschriftung, Bezeichnung; **discount ~** *20* Billigmarke
to **label** *184* etikettieren, auszeichnen
laboratory *152* Labor; **by ~ design** *152* im Labor geplant
labour *104* Arbeit; **~ costs** *pl* *194T* Lohnkosten, Arbeitskosten
lack *25* Mangel
to **lack sth** *169* etw nicht haben
lake *149* (Binnen-)See
lamella, lamellae *184* Lamelle, Lamellen
to **laminate** *184* laminieren, schichten
to **land** *83* landen; **~ sth** *110* etw an Land ziehen
landline *160* Festnetz(-)
landslide *108* Erdrutsch
lane *62* Weg, Gasse
language barrier *189* Sprachbarriere
lantern *79* Laterne
large print *118* große Schrift, Großdruck
large-scale *136* in großem Umfang/Ausmaß
largely *36* weitgehend, überwiegend, größtenteils
to **last** *107T* dauern, andauern, so bleiben
last but not least *17T* zu guter Letzt, nicht zuletzt
(the) latest *23* der/die/das allerneueste/n; **at the ~** *31* spätestens
lathe *74* Drehbank, Drehmaschine
latitude, polar ~s *pl* *170* polare Breiten
laugh *57* Lachen, Gelächter
to **laugh at sb** *38T* über jdn lachen, jdn auslachen
laughing gas *40* Lachgas
launch: ~ and recovery system *195* Start- und Landesystem; **~ vehicle** *170* Trägerrakete
to **launch** *50* *(Produkt)* auf den Markt bringen, einführen; **~ an attack** *130* einen Angriff starten
laundry, to **do ~** *64* Wäsche waschen
law *81* Justiz; *84* Gesetz; to **pass a ~** *84* ein Gesetz verabschieden; **~ and order** *126T* Recht und Ordnung; **~ enforcement** *124* Gesetzesvollzug, Innere Sicherheit, Exekutive; **~ enforcement agency** *124* Strafverfolgungsbehörde, Exekutivorgan
lawnmower *64* Rasenmäher
lawyer *39* Anwalt/Anwältin; **specialist ~** *39* Fachanwalt/-anwältin
to **lay cables** *160* Kabel verlegen
layer *108* Lage, Schicht
layered, multi-~ *210* mehrschichtig
lazy *110* faul
lead *144* Blei
lead engineer *198* Chefingenieur/in
leadership *161* Führung
leaflet *34T* Broschüre, Merkblatt
leafy vegetable *156* Blattgemüse
to **leak** *143T* sickern, entweichen
to **leak** *172* auslaufen
least, at ~ *27* zumindest, mindestens; **last but not ~** *17T* zu guter Letzt, nicht zuletzt
to **leave a message** *33* eine Nachricht hinterlassen
left: ~ out of sth *36* von etw ausgeschlossen; to **feel ~ out** *60* sich ausgeschlossen fühlen; to **be ~ for dead** *109* als tot zurückgelassen werden
leg *194T* Etappe
legal *15* erlaubt, legal; **~ action** *39* rechtliche Schritte; to **take ~ action** *39* rechtliche Schritte unternehmen; **~ department** *69* juristische Abteilung; **~ guardian** *27* Vormund, Erziehungsberechtigte/r; **~ recourse** *88T* Regressansprüche
to **legalize** *49T* legalisieren
legend *6* Legende
legislature *167* Gesetzgebung
leisure *25* Freizeit, Muße
to **lend sb sth** *62T* jdm etw leihen
lesson *25* (Unterrichts-)Stunde
to **let: ~ oneself in for sth** *128* sich auf etw einlassen; **~ sb know sth** *31* jdm etw mitteilen, jdm etw sagen
lettuce *99* Kopfsalat
level *8* Stufe, Niveau, Ebene; *92* Grad, Höhe; **carbon dioxide ~** *136* Kohlendioxidkonzentration, -gehalt; **sea ~** *137* Meeresspiegel
liberation *156* Befreiung
library *163* Bibliothek, Bücherei
licence, driving ~ *48F* Führerschein
license *AE* *190* Lizenz
life: from all walks of ~ *90* aus allen Gesellschaftsschichten, aus allen Lebensbereichen; **~-altering** *156* lebensverändernd; **~-changing** *8* lebensverändernd; **~ saving** *90* lebensrettend; **quality of ~** *137* Lebensqualität; **working ~** *140* Betriebsdauer
lifecycle *49* Lebensdauer, Lebenszyklus
lifeline *108* Lebensader
lifestyle *58* Lebensweise, Lebensführung
lifetime *114* (ganzes) Leben; **for a ~** *97* ein Leben lang
to **lift** *28* heben
light, to **shine ~ on sth** *144* Licht auf etw werfen; **~ bulb** *155T* Glühbirne
to **light** *79* *(Kerze etc.)* anzünden; **~ up** *140* leuchten, aufleuchten; **~ sth up** *178* etw erleuchten, etw erhellen
light-emitting *180* lichtabstrahlend
lighting *66* Beleuchtung, Licht
lights *pl*, **traffic ~** *48F* Ampel; to **jump red ~** *48F* bei Rot über eine Ampel fahren; **Northern ~** *134* Nordlicht, Polarlicht
lightweight *98* leicht
like *8* wie
likeable *51* sympathisch
likely *34* wahrscheinlich; to **be ~ to do sth** *46* etw wahrscheinlich tun (werden)
to **limit** *137* begrenzen, einschränken
limitation *160* Einschränkung; *179T* Grenze
limited *50* begrenzt, beschränkt
limitless *205* grenzenlos
line *33* Leitung; *81* Reihe; *175* Grenze, Trennlinie; **down the ~** *81* weiter; to **hold the ~** *34T* am Apparat bleiben; **finishing ~** *124* Ziellinie; **glue ~** *184* Verleimung; **power ~** *134T* Stromleitung; **production ~** *208* Fertigungsstraße; **~ chart** *53* Liniendiagramm; **~ graph** *92* Liniendiagramm
link *102* Verbindung, Verknüpfung, Beziehung
to **link** *102* verbinden, verknüpfen
lion *79* Löwe
liquid *180* flüssig; *193* Flüssigkeit
to **listen in** *37* mithören
literally *194T* (wort)wörtlich
lively *85* lebendig, lebhaft, rege
livestock *152* Vieh
living room *40* Wohnzimmer
load *60* Ladung; *198* Last
to **load** *193* laden, verladen
loading *195* Beladung, Verladen
loan *90* Darlehen, Kredit
to **lobby sb** *90* auf jdn Einfluss nehmen
located, ~ in *75* in (… gelegen); to **be ~** *132* sich befinden; to **be ~ in** *119* in … liegen
location *54* Lage, Standort, Ort

lock *200T* Schloss
lodging, board and ~ *66* Kost und Logis
log *184* (entasteter) Baumstamm
to **log** *128* aufzeichnen, protokollieren; **~ in** *39* sich einloggen; **~ out** *39* sich ausloggen
logical(ly) *22* logisch
logistics *193* Logistik
to **loiter** *27* herumlungern
loneliness *69* Einsamkeit
lonely *36* einsam
long, as ~ as *137* solange; **it wasn't ~ before ...** *16* es dauerte nicht lange, bis ...; **it's not ~ before** *21* es dauert nicht lange, bis
long-distance *194* Langstrecken-
to **look: ~ on** *80* zusehen; **~ after sb** *29* sich um jdn kümmern; **~ for sb/sth** *19* jdn/etw suchen; **~ forward to sth** *9* sich auf etw freuen; **~ sth up** *41* etw *(Vokabel etc.)* nachschlagen; **~ up to sb** *13* zu jdm aufsehen, jdn bewundern; **~ a mess** *101* fürchterlich aussehen; **I've never ~ed back.** *49T* Ich habe es nie bereut.
lorry *BE* *208* Lkw
to **lose** *13* verlieren; **~ weight** *17T* abnehmen
loss *105* Verlust; **memory ~** *118* Gedächtnisschwund
lottery *48F* Lotterie, Verlosung
loudspeaker *144* Lautsprecher
love, to **fall in ~ with sb/sth** *86* sich in jdn/etw verlieben
lovely *21T* schön, nett, hübsch
lover *10* Geliebte/r, Liebhaber/in
low, to **feel ~** *17T* schlecht gelaunt sein, deprimiert sein
low-cost *104* billig, kostengünstig
low-value *193* geringwertig
luck *34T* Glück; **Good ~!** *50* Viel Glück!
lung *17T* Lunge
to **lurch** *156* schlingern, taumeln
lying *49T* Lügen

M

machinery *98* Maschinen
machining *184* (maschinelle) Bearbeitung; **CNC ~** *185* CNC-Bearbeitung
madam *96T* gnädige Frau
magical *8* magisch, traumhaft
magnet, permanent ~ *202* Permanentmagnet
magnetic *202* magnetisch; **~ field** *134* Magnetfeld
magnification *118* Vergrößerung
to **magnify** *164* vergrößern, verstärken
mainly *17T* hauptsächlich
to **maintain** *67* warten, instand halten; **~ sth** *27* etw aufrecht erhalten; **~ control** *190* Kontrolle ausüben; **~ stocks** *154* den Bestand erhalten
maintenance *66* Wartung, Instandhaltung
maize *BE* *158T* Mais
major *137* bedeutend, wichtig, groß
majority *69* Mehrheit
to **make: ~ for sth** *69* sich auf den Weg nach etw machen; **~ sb up** *9* jdn schminken; **~ sth up** *6* etw erfinden, sich etw ausdenken; **~ sth up** *135* etw ausmachen; **~ it** *60* es schaffen; **~ sure** *22* sicherstellen; dafür sorgen, dass
maker *102* Hersteller, -bauer
malware *200T* Schadsoftware
man of the cloth *126T* Geistlicher
man-made *136* künstlich, menschlichen Ursprungs
to **manage** *60* verwalten, regeln; **sustainably ~ed** *184* nachhaltig bewirtschaftet
management *66* Führung, Management; **~ consultant** *65* Unternehmensberater/in
managing director *49T* Geschäftsführer/in
maneuverable *195* manövrierfähig
manhunt *124* Verbrecherjagd
to **manipulate** *164* manipulieren; *168* handhaben, bedienen
manipulative *168* manipulativ
manipulator arm *64* Greifarm
manual *51* Bedienungsanleitung
manually operated *186* handbetrieben, von Hand bedient
to **manufacture** *99* fertigen, herstellen
manufacture *186* Fertigung, Herstellung
manufacturer *49T* Hersteller/in, Produzent/in
manufacturing *69* Fertigung; **mass ~** *209* Massenfertigung
march *79* Marsch
to **march** *79* marschieren
marine engineering *198* Schiffsmaschinenbau
mark *144* Markierung, Zeichen
to **mark** *94* *(Jahrestag etc.)* begehen
marker *122* Filzstift
market share *72* Marktanteil
marvellous *120T* toll, phantastisch
mass *198* Masse; **thermal ~** *182* Wärmemasse, thermische Masse; **coronal ~ ejection** *134* koronaler Massenauswurf; **~ manufacturing** *209* Massenfertigung; **~ media** *pl* *124* Massenmedien; **~ production** *102* Massenproduktion
massive(ly) *126T* massiv
match *11* Spiel, Partie, Match; *187* Übereinstimmung, Entsprechung
material *14* Material, Werkstoff; **original ~** *113* eigene Beiträge
mathematical *44* mathematisch
mathematician *81* Mathematiker/in
maths *68T* Mathe(matik) *(Schulfach)*
to **matter** *21T* wichtig sein, darauf ankommen; **it doesn't ~** *62T* es ist egal
matter *23* Angelegenheit, Sache; *134T* Materie; **no ~ ...** *23* ganz egal, ...
to **maximize** *158T* maximieren
maximum *49* Höchstwert; *49T* maximal, Höchst-; *66* höchstens
meal, to **cook a ~** *49T* eine Mahlzeit zubereiten, ein Essen kochen; **ready ~** *205* Fertiggericht
meaningful *164* wichtig, bedeutend, sinnstiftend
means *54* Mittel; **~ of transport** *130* Verkehrsmittel
meantime, in the ~ *88T* in der Zwischenzeit
meanwhile *81* inzwischen, unterdessen
measurability *201* Messbarkeit
measurable *200T* messbar
measure *27* Maßnahme
to **measure** *17* messen
measurement *187* Messung, Messwert
mechanic *65* Mechaniker/in
mechanical *65* mechanisch; **~ engineering** *169* Maschinenbau
to **mechanize** *98* mechanisieren
medal *13* Medaille
to **mediate** *71* vermitteln
mediation *28* Vermittlung
medical *67* medizinisch; **~ insurance** *65* Krankenversicherung; **~ student** *96T* Medizinstudent/in; **walk-in ~ centre** *96T* Ambulanz
medication *94* Arzneimittel
medicine *90* Arznei(mittel), Medizin
medium-sized *74T* mittelständisch
to **meet: ~ up** *21T* sich treffen; **~ a deadline** *112* eine Frist / einen Termin einhalten; **~ a demand** *105* eine Nachfrage befriedigen
meeting room *69* Sitzungsraum, Besprechungsraum
to **melt** *137* schmelzen, abschmelzen
member: ~ of staff *171* Mitarbeiter/in; **~ of the audience** *8* Zuschauer/in
memory *120* Gedächtnis; *205* (Daten-)Speicher; **~ of sb** *94* Gedenken an jdn; **~ loss** *118* Gedächtnisschwund
mental(ly) *114* geistig
to **mention** *31* erwähnen, nennen
merchant *160* Händler/in
mercury *144* Quecksilber
mess *43* Chaos; to **look a ~** *101* fürchterlich aussehen
to **mess around** *28* herumalbern, herumgammeln
message, to **leave a ~** *33* eine Nachricht hinterlassen; to **take a ~** *34* etw ausrichten, eine Nachricht notieren

messaging *44* *Versenden von Nachrichten*
metabolism *17* Stoffwechsel
metal *47* Metall
methane *135* Methan
micro hybrid *203T* Mikro-Hybrid
microphone *129* Mikrofon
microscope *208* Mikroskop
microwave *64* Mikrowelle
mid-century *161* Jahrhundertmitte
midday *150* Mittag; ~ **management** *110* mittlere Führungsebene
middleman *145* Zwischenhändler
midnight *6* Mitternacht
midsummer *79* Mittsommer, Sommersonnenwende
migrant *84* Migrant/in
migratory bird *145* Zugvogel
mild hybrid *203T* Mild-Hybrid
military *164* Militär
mill *185* Fräse; **end** ~ *185* Fräser; **saw** ~ *184* Sägewerk
millennial *109* Jahrtausend-
millennium *174T* Jahrtausend
milling machine *185* Fräsmaschine
mind *62* Gedanken; to **come to** ~ *64* in den Sinn kommen, einfallen
to **mind:** ~ **sth** *25* etw gegen etw haben; *69* auf etw achten; ~ **one's own business** *57* sich um seinen eigenen Kram kümmern
minerals *pl* *158T* Mineralien
to **minimize** *194T* minimieren
minimum *69* Mindestmaß, -menge, Minimum; ~ **wage** *110* Mindestlohn
minister *199* Minister/in
minor *189* klein, unbedeutend
minority *84* Minderheit
mirror *129* Spiegel
misfortune *43* Unglück, Missgeschick
missing *166* vermisst
mission *90* Auftrag, Mission
mistaken, to **be** ~ *128* sich irren
misunderstanding *97* Missverständnis
to **mix and match** *122* individuell zusammenstellen
mixture *14* Mischung
moans *pl* *29* Gejammer, Genörgel
mobile *64* mobil
mobility *124* Mobilität
mode, transport ~ *193* Beförderungsart, Transportart
modeling, fused deposition ~ *209* Schmelzschichtung
moderate *84* gemäßigt, maßvoll
modernity *124* Moderne
modification *190* Änderung, Abwandlung, Modifizierung
to **modify** *98* modifizieren
module *118* Modul
moisture *184T* Feuchtigkeit; ~ **content** *184* Feuchtigkeitsgehalt
money, to **raise** ~ *43* Geld beschaffen
mongrel *80* Mischling, Bastard
monitor *146* Anzeigegerät, Überwachungsgerät
to **monitor** *132* überwachen
monitoring *146* Überwachung
monthly *62T* monatlich
to **mooch off sth** *110* von etw schmarotzen
more, what's ~ *56* zudem
moreover *117* überdies
mortise *186* Nut, Zapfenloch
mortise and tenon joint *186* Zapfenverbindung
mosquito net *97* Moskitonetz
mostly *74* meistens
motion *200* Bewegung
motivated, highly ~ *66* hochmotiviert
motor, electric ~ *178* Elektromotor; ~ **vehicle** *88* Kraftfahrzeug
motorist *BE* *48F* Autofahrer/in
motorway *BE* *184T* Autobahn
mouse *51* Maus
movable *209T* beweglich
to **move:** ~ **on** *8* weiterkommen, weitergehen; ~ **house** *28* umziehen
move *17T* Schritt, Bewegung; *61* Umzug
moveable *70* beweglich, mobil
movement *94* Bewegung; **free** ~ *86T* Freizügigkeit
MP (Member of Parliament) *84* Parlamentsabgeordnete/r
mud *144* Schlamm
multi-layered *210* mehrschichtig
multiculturalism *79* Multikulturalität, Multikulturismus, kulturelle Vielfalt
multilingual *189* mehrsprachig
multiple *64* mehrere, vielfache
municipal *146* kommunal
murder *132* Mord
muscle *16* Muskel
musical *17* musikalisch, Musik-
Muslim *84* muslimisch, Moslem
a must *75* ein Muss
mystery *45* Rätsel, Rätselhaftigkeit; *145* Geheimnis
myth *97* Mythos, Märchen

N

nail *81* Nagel
to **name** *16* nennen, benennen
name, first ~ *17* Vorname; **given** ~ *80* Vorname; **household** ~ *51* bekannter Name, Begriff; **proper** ~ *33* Eigenname; ~ **tag** *172* Namensschild
nannying *110* Kinderbetreuung
nanoparticle *146* Nanoteilchen, Nanopartikel
narrowly, to **escape sth** ~ *94* einer Sache knapp entkommen
nasty *129* gemein, hässlich, böse
national *14* Landes-, national
national team *13* Nationalmannschaft
nationwide *144* landesweit
native, her ~ **Pakistan** *109* ihr Geburtsland Pakistan; ~ **language** *31* Muttersprache; ~ **speaker** *75* Muttersprachler/in
natural gas *138* Erdgas
to **near** *174T* sich nähern
Near Field Communication *54* Nahfeldkommunikation
nearby *29* in der Nähe
neat *186* sauber
necessary, as ~ *61* nötigenfalls
necessity *168* Notwendigkeit
neck *118* Hals
need, in ~ *92* bedürftig, in Not
need-to-know basis, on a *63* im (unumgänglichen) Bedarfsfall
needs *pl* *57* Bedürfnisse, Bedarf
neighbour *6* Nachbar/in
neighbouring *108* Nachbar-
nerve *189* Nerv
nervous *9* aufgeregt, nervös
net *108* Netz
network *29* Netz, Netzwerk
neural net(work) *189* neuronales Netz
New Year *79* Neujahr
newbuild *195* (Schiffs-)Neubau
news anchor *136* Nachrichtensprecher/in
next door *41* nebenan
next to *120T* neben
NGO (non-government organization) *95* Nichtregierungsorganisation
niche *49T* Nische
nitroglycerine *14* Nitroglycerin
noise *41* Lärm; *46* Geräusch
noisy *57* laut, lärmend
non-alcoholic *121* alkoholfrei
non-profit *156* gemeinnützig
non-smoking *120* Nichtraucher-
norm *69* Norm
Northern Lights *pl* *134* Nordlicht, Polarlicht
nosey *60* (auf unangenehme Weise) neugierig
nostalgia *186* Nostalgie
note *46* Ton, Note; *52* Hinweis
notebook *15* Heft, Notizbuch
notification *54* Benachrichtigung
notion *164* Vorstellung, Auffassung
novel *131* Roman; *168* neu, neuartig
novelty *168* Neues, Neuartiges
now, What ~ **for …?** *84* Wie steht es um …?
nowhere, to **get you** ~ *126* zu nichts führen, nichts bringen
nuclear *57* Kern-; ~ **plant** *140* Kernkraftwerk; ~ **power station** *140* Kernkraftwerk
to **number** *48* nummerieren
numerical *65* Zahl-, zahlenmäßig; **computer** ~ **control** *185* rechnergestützte numerische Steuerung
nurse *65* Krankenpfleger/-schwester

nut *98* Nuss, Kern; **palm ~** *98* Palmnuss
nutrient *63* Nährstoff
nutrition *94* Nahrung, Ernährung
nutshell, in a ~ *203T* kurz gesagt

O

to **object to sth** *27* etw ablehnen, gegen etw Einwände haben
objective *74T* Ziel, Zweck
observatory *134T* Observatorium
to **observe** *65* beobachten
obsolete *191T* veraltet, überholt; to **make sth ~** *186* etw überflüssig machen
obstacle *160* Hindernis
obstruction *168* Hindernis
to **obtain sth** *130* etw erhalten, an etw gelangen
obtainable *129* erhältlich
occasional(ly) *176* gelegentlich
occupation *96* Beruf, Tätigkeit, Beschäftigung
to **occupy** *170* besetzen, belegen
to **occur** *14* vorfallen, geschehen; *134T* auftreten
ocean *108* Ozean, Weltmeer
off, to **be worse ~** *94* schlechter dran sein
to **offer sb sth on a plate** *68* jdm etw auf dem Silbertablett servieren
office: Head O~ *50* Zentrale, Direktion, Hauptverwaltung; **open-plan ~** *69* Großraumbüro; **~ assistant** *75* Bürokaufmann/-frau; **~ block** *71* Bürogebäude; **~ clerk** *49T* Büroangestellte/r; **~ supplies** *pl* *120T* Büromaterial
officer *126* Offizier/in; **border customs ~** *161* (Grenz-)Zollbeamte/r; **chief executive ~** *64* Vorstandsvorsitzende/r; **chief security ~** *201* Hauptsicherheitsbeauftragte/r; **police ~** *65* Polizist/in
official *97* Beamte/r, Funktionär/in
to **offset** *195* ausgleichen
offshore *100* im/ins Ausland; *141* auf See
OHP transparency *48* Overheadfolie
oil *138* Öl
Olympic *14* olympisch
onboard *158T* an Bord, Bord-
once *46* sobald; **all at ~** *23* auf einmal
one by one *140* der Reihe nach
ongoing *90* laufend
onshore *141* an Land
onto *8* auf
open, out in the ~ *144* im Freien
open-plan office *69* Großraumbüro
opening *94* Eröffnung
openness *11T* Offenheit
to **operate** *169* tätig sein; **~ sth** *64* etw bedienen
operating system *191* Betriebssystem
operation *107T* Betrieb, Geschäftstätigkeit
operational, to **be fully ~** *170* vollständig in Betrieb sein
operator *167* (Maschinen-)Bediener/in
opinion, to **give an ~** *22* eine Meinung äußern
opportunity *29* Gelegenheit, Möglichkeit, Chance
opposite, the ~ sex *29* das andere Geschlecht
to **opt for sth** *142* sich für etw entscheiden
optimistic *107T* optimistisch
oral *75* mündlich
to **orbit** *170* umrunden
orbit *170* Umlaufbahn
orbital plane *170* Umlaufebene
order *6* Reihenfolge; *100* Auftrag, Bestellung; to **fill an ~** *100* einen Auftrag ausführen; **in ~ to** *60* um ... zu; **law and ~** *126T* Recht und Ordnung
ordinary *11T* normal, gewöhnlich
organic *100* biologisch, Bio-; *186* organisch
organization *14* Organisation
organizational *65* organisatorisch
organizer *65* Organisator/in
...-oriented *27* ...orientiert
origin *193* Ausgangsort, Ursprungsort
original *64* originell; *88T* ursprünglich; **~ material** *113* eigene Beiträge
originality *179* Originalität, Neuheit
to **originate: ~ from** *99* kommen aus; **~ from sth** *124* von etw ausgehen, aus etw kommen
ornamental *197T* schmückend, zierend
orphan *94* Waise
orphanage *94* Waisenhaus
ought to *110* sollen
outcome *165* Ergebnis, Resultat
to **outfit sb with sth** *198* jdn mit etw ausstatten
outing *168* Ausflug, Ausfahrt
to **outline** *111* skizzieren, grob beschreiben
out-of-state *110* in einem anderen Bundesstaat
to **outsmart** *164* überlisten, austricksen
oven *206T* Ofen, Herd
over-achiever *19* Überflieger
to **overcome** *13* bewältigen, überwinden
to **overdo it** *23* es übertreiben
over-exploitation *147* Raubbau, übermäßiger Abbau
overhead *170* darüber, am Himmel
overheads *pl* *104* Fixkosten, Betriebskosten
to **overhear** *131* belauschen, aufschnappen
overnight, to **stay ~** *122* übernachten
overview *158T* Überblick
overweight *17* übergewichtig
own, on one's ~ *10* allein
owner *54* Besitzer/in

P

pace *198* Tempo
pacemaker *196* Herzschrittmacher
pacifist *126T* Pazifist/in
to **pack** *19* verpacken
packaging *19* Verpackung
pad *69* (Notiz-)Block; Bude; *198* Unterlage, Polster
padded *198* gepolstert
pain, to **be a ~ (in the neck)** *57* jdm auf die Nerven gehen
to **paint** *49T* malen
palm: ~ nut *98* Palmnuss; **~ tree** *98* Palme
panel *137* Gremium, Ausschuss; *206T* Expertenrunde, Diskussionsrunde
panellist *206T* *(Podiumsdiskussion:)* Diskussionsteilnehmer, Experte
to **panic** *17* in Panik geraten
pantry, food ~ *AE* *151* Tafel, karitative Essensausgabe
paperwork *58* Büroarbeit, Schreibarbeit
parade *79* Parade
paragraph *14* *(Text:)* Absatz
parallel *131* Parallele
to **paralyze** *118* lähmen
to **paraphrase** *28* umschreiben, paraphrasieren
parcel *151* Paket
parliament *86* Parlament
part, to **take ~ in sth** *9* an etw teilnehmen
partially *156* teilweise
participant *12* Teilnehmer/in
to **participate in sth** *118* an etw teilnehmen, an etw teilhaben
participation *118* Teilhabe, Teilnahme
particle *134* Teilchen, Partikel
particular *23* bestimmt, speziell
particularly *74T* besonders, insbesondere
partly *107T* teils, teilweise
part-time *60* Teilzeit-
party, third-~ *64* von Drittanbietern, fremd
to **pass** *137* überschreiten; **~ sth** *88* weitergeben; **~ sth on** *110* etw weitergeben, etw weiterreichen; **~ sth to sb** *152* jdm etw weiterreichen; **~ a law** *84* ein Gesetz verabschieden
passenger *153* Passagier; **~ jet** *88T* Passagierflugzeug
passer-by *46* Passant/in
passion fruit *156* Passionsfrucht
passive *181* passiv

past, to **be ~ it** *114* die besten Jahre hinter sich haben, jenseits von Gut und Böse sein
pastureland *148* Weideland
path, flight ~ *158T* Flugroute
pattern *187* Muster
pavement *178* Bürgersteig, Gehweg
pay *65* Bezahlung, Lohn; **entry level ~** *68T* Einstiegsgehalt, Anfangsgehalt; **~ packet** *110* Lohntüte, Gehalt; **~ scale** *68T* Lohntarif, Lohntabelle
to **pay attention to sth** *22* auf etw achten
payment *54* Zahlung, Bezahlung
peace *80* Frieden
peaceful *84* friedlich
pedestrian *178* Fußgänger/in
peer *29* Gleichaltrige/r, Altersgenosse; **~ group** *55* Altersgruppe, Bezugsgruppe, Umfeld
pen friend *93* Brieffreund/in
penny *81* Pfennig, Penny
pension *109* Rente, Pension; **Department for Work and P~s** *60 brit. Arbeits- und Sozialministerium*
pensioner *109* Rentner/in
people *100* Volk
per *35* pro; **~ annum** *117T* pro Jahr; **~ capita income** *156* Pro-Kopf-Einkommen
percent *52* Prozent
percentage *53* Prozentsatz, Anteil
to **perform** *8* singen, spielen, auftreten; *166T* (leistungsmäßig) abschneiden; **~ sth** *64* etw ausführen, etw durchführen
performance *14* Leistung, Abschneiden
perfume *49* Parfüm
permanence *201* Beständigkeit, Dauerhaftigkeit
permanent *71T* dauerhaft; **~ magnet** *202* Permanentmagnet
permission *191T* Erlaubnis; **planning ~** *142* Baugenehmigung
to **permit** *190* gestatten
permitted *27* erlaubt, gestattet
person, in ~ *129* persönlich
personal transport *102* Individualverkehr
personality *13* Persönlichkeit
to **personalise** *69* individuell gestalten
to **persuade** *19* überzeugen, überreden
persuader *65 jd, der andere überzeugt und mitreißt*
pest *156* Schädling; **insect ~s** *pl 158T* Schädlinge; **chemical control of ~s** *152* Schädlingsbekämpfung(smittel)
pesticide residues *pl 206T* Pestizidrückstände
pet *64* Haustier
petrol *102* Benzin; **~ station** *134* Tankstelle
petrol-driven *102* benzingetrieben
phase *46* Phase; **three-~ AC motor** *202* Drehstrommotor
phenomenon *14* Phänomen, Erscheinung
to **phone in** *50* (in einer Sendung) anrufen
photocopier *120T* Fotokopiergerät
photography *25* Fotografie, Foto-
to **photo-shop** *23* mit Photoshop bearbeiten
piano, to **play the ~** *113* Klavier spielen
to **pick** *141* wählen, aussuchen; *206T* pflücken; **~ sth out** *51* etw heraussuchen; **~ up** *196 (Klang, Ton)* aufnehmen; **~ sb/sth up** *21T* jdn/etw abholen; **~ sth up** *64* etw aufheben
pickup *156* Pritschenwagen
to **pile** *144* stapeln
pill *197* Tablette, Pille
pilot *198* Pilotversuch
to **pin** *77* (mit einer Nadel) befestigen, anbringen
pinkie *169* kleiner Finger
pioneer *88T* Pionier/in
to **pioneer sth** *54* bei etw Pionierarbeit leisten
pipe *182* Rohr, Röhre, Schlauch; **~ band** *79* Dudelsackkapelle
pipeline *193* Rohrleitung
pirate copy *209* Raubkopie
pitch *200T* Tonlage, Tonhöhe
pity, it's a ~ *21T* schade
place, to **take ~** *8* stattfinden; **~ card** *172* Platzkarte, Tischkarte
placement *98* Vermittlung, Einsatz
to **plague** *124* plagen, heimsuchen
plain *139* schlicht
plane, jet ~ *193* Düsenflugzeug; **supersonic ~** *193* Überschallflugzeug
planer *184* Hobelmaschine
planing *185* Hobeln
plank *184* Bohle, Brett
planner *170* Planer/in
planning *177T* Planung; **~ permission** *142* Baugenehmigung
plant *102* Fabrik, Werk, Anlage; **nuclear ~** *140* Kernkraftwerk; **power ~** *136* Kraftwerk; **production ~** *98* Produktionsanalge
to **plant** *148* pflanzen, anpflanzen
plantation *184* Plantage, Pflanzung
plaque *131* Platte, Tafel
to **plaster** *156* verputzen
plastic surgery *197* plastische Chirurgie
plate *68* Teller; *183* Platte; to **offer sb sth on a ~** *68* jdm etw auf dem Silbertablett servieren
platform *11T* Podium
to **play the piano** *113* Klavier spielen
plc *75* AG
pleasant *68T* angenehm
pleased, to **be ~** *29* sich freuen; to **be ~ to do sth** *48* etw gern tun
pleasure *11T* Vergnügen; **My ~.** *11T* Gern geschehen.
plight *43* Notlage
to **plug: ~ in(to)** *69* anschließen, einstecken; **~ in on sth** *131* sich in etw einschalten
plus *60* außerdem
point *53* Komma; to **make a ~** *26* ein Argument vortragen, etw sagen wollen; to **make a ~ to sb** *82* jdm etw zu verstehen geben; to **take the ~** *151* den Standpunkt verstehen; **He has a (good) ~.** *84* Da ist etwas dran. Da hat er recht.; **there's little ~ in doing sth** *30* es hat wenig Sinn, etw zu tun; **~ of view** *101* Perspektive, Blickwinkel, Standpunkt
to **point: ~ to sth** *164* auf etw hindeuten; **~ at sb/sth** *38T* auf jdn/etw zeigen; **~ sth at sb** *80* etw auf jdn richten, mit etw auf jdn zielen; **~ sth out** *59* auf etw hinweisen
pointless *203T* sinnlos, unsinnig
to **poison** *145* vergiften
poisoning *40* Vergiftung
poisonous *144* giftig
polar latitudes *pl 170* polare Breiten
polarity *202* Polung, Polarität
pole *202* Pol
police: riot ~ *40* Bereitschaftspolizei; **~ force** *127* Polizei; **~ officer** *65* Polizist/in; **~ station** *125* Polizeiwache
policy *84* Politik, Kurs, Konzept
politician *65* Politiker/in
poll *36* Umfrage
pollen *152* Blütenstaub, Pollen
polling station *199* Wahllokal
pollutant *146* Schadstoff
to **pollute** *137* (die Umwelt) verschmutzen
polluting *149* umweltschädlich
pollution *139* Umweltverschmutzung
popularity *6* Beliebtheit, Popularität
population *85* Bevölkerung; *154 (Biologie:)* Population
porch *156* Veranda
port *86* Hafen, Hafenstadt
portion *94* Teil
to **post** *29 (im Internet)* posten; *127 (Brief:)* einwerfen, schicken
position *20* Stelle, Stellung, Position
positioning *170* Positionierung, Positions-
possession *200* Besitz
post *66* Stelle, Posten
poster *35* Plakat
posting *98* (Auslands-)Einsatz, Posten
posture, to **strike a ~** *88T* eine Haltung einnehmen
potential(ly) *132* potenziell
pound *40* Pfund

poverty *90* Armut
powder *209T* Pulver; **washing** ~ *49* Waschpulver
power *18* Macht, Stärke, Kraft; to **be in** ~ *160* an der Macht sein; **economic** ~ *88T* Wirtschaftsmacht; **geothermal** ~ *135* Erdwärme; **hydro-electric** ~ *135* Wasserkraft; **solar** ~ *135* Sonnenenergie; **tidal** ~ *135* Gezeitenkraft; **wind** ~ *135* Windkraft; ~ **cut** *134T* Stromausfall; ~ **grid** *134T* Stromnetz; ~ **line** *134T* Stromleitung; ~ **plant** *136* Kraftwerk; ~ **station** *139* Kraftwerk, Elektrizitätswerk; **nuclear** ~ **station** *140* Kernkraftwerk; ~ **tool** *185* Elektrowerkzeug
to **power** *138* antreiben, mit Energie versorgen
powerful *51* stark, mächtig, kräftig
powerless *144* machtlos, unfähig
practical *38T* zweckmäßig, praktisch (umsetzbar)
practice *69* Praxis, Ausübung, Verfahren, Ablauf, Praktik; **P~ makes perfect.** *187* Übung macht den Meister.
to **practise** *9* üben, trainieren; *160* praktizieren
prairie *148* Prärie
to **pray** *126T* beten
prayer *126T* Gebet; ~ **vigil** *126T* Gebetswache
precaution *127* Vorkehrung, Sicherheitsmaßnahme
precious *149* kostbar
precise *158T* exakt, genau, präzise
precision *185* Präzision, Genauigkeit
to **predict** *8* voraussagen, vorhersagen
prediction *134T* Vorhersage
preference *20* Vorliebe
pre-historic *152* prähistorisch
premises *pl* *71T* Geschäftsräume
preparation (for sth) *24* Vorbereitung (auf etw)
to **prepare** *137* *(Bericht etc.)* erstellen, verfassen
presence *37* Anwesenheit, Präsenz; *98* Gegenwart, Vorhandensein
to **present** *48* vorstellen, präsentieren
presentation *48* Vortrag, Referat, Präsentation; to **give a** ~ *48* ein Referat halten
presenter *48* Vortragende/r; *86T* Moderator/in
presidential *199* Präsidenten-
press conference *142* Pressekonferenz
pressure *75* Druck; **blood** ~ *200* Blutdruck; **~s** *pl* *167* Belastungen; ~ **cooker** *124* Schnellkochtopf
to **pressure** *161* unter Druck setzen
prestigious *70* repräsentativ, prestigeträchtig
presumably *199* vermutlich
to **pretend** *21T* vorgeben; so tun, als ob
pretty *11T* ziemlich
to **prevent** *127* verhindern, verhüten; ~ **sb from doing sth** *190* jdn daran hindern, etw zu tun
preventable *97* vermeidbar
prevention *146* Vorbeugung, Prophylaxe
previous *110* vorherig, früher
previously *136* zuvor, vorher
price, rental ~ *122* Mietpreis
priced, to **be** ~ **at ...** *129* ... kosten
pride *83* Stolz; to **take** ~ **in sth** *83* auf etw Wert legen, sich mit etw Mühe geben
priest *65* Priester/in, Geistliche/r
primarily *161* vorrangig, hauptsächlich
primary *36* Haupt-, hauptsächlich
principal *210* Chef(-)
principle *182T* Prinzip, Grundsatz; **in** ~ *143* prinzipiell, grundsätzlich
print *199* Abdruck; **large** ~ *118* große Schrift, Großdruck; **the small** ~ *129* das Kleingedruckte
printer *64* Drucker
printing *208* Drucken, Drucktechnik; ~ **press** *159* Druckerpresse, Druckmaschine
priority *123* Priorität, Vorrang
privacy *40* Privatsphäre
private sector *194* Privatwirtschaft
to **process** *100* verarbeiten
process *17* Ablauf, Vorgang, Prozess; *44* Verfahren
processing unit, central ~ *179T* Hauptprozessor
produce, dairy ~ *193* Milchprodukte
producer *90* Produzent/in
product, finished ~ *100* Endprodukt; **raw** ~ *99* Ausgangsprodukt, Roherzeugnis; to **brand a** ~ *51* ein Markenprodukt schaffen
production: ~ **line** *208* Fertigungsstraße; ~ **plant** *98* Produktionsanlage
productive *152* produktiv
productivity *118* Produktivität
profession *68T* Beruf; **caring** ~ *68T* Pflegeberuf
professional *14* professionell, Profi-
profile *118* Profil
profit *50* Gewinn, Profit; **non-**~ *156* gemeinnützig
to **profit** *144* profitieren
programmable *64* programmierbar
programmer *65* Programmierer/in
to **progress** *74* vorankommen, fortschreiten
progress *164* Fortschritt(e)
progression *92* Entwicklung, Steigerung
projector *121* Beamer
promising *81* vielversprechend
to **promote sth** *46* für etw werben, etw bewerben; *98* etw fördern, sich für etw einsetzen
promotion *49T* Werbung; *65* Beförderung, (beruflicher) Aufstieg; ~ **prospects** *pl* *65* Aufstiegschancen
to **prompt sb to do sth** *129* jdn veranlassen, etw zu tun
prop *66* Requisite
proper name *33* Eigenname
properly *60* richtig, ordentlich, korrekt
property *40* Immobilie(n), Anwesen; *190* Eigentum; ~ **damage** *166T* Sachschaden, Sachschäden
proportion *144* Anteil
proposal *155* Vorschlag
to **propose** *210* vorschlagen, anregen
proprietary *190* urheberrechtlich geschützt
propulsion *195* Antrieb, Vortrieb
prospects *pl*, **promotion** ~ *65* Aufstiegschancen
to **protect** *47* schützen
protection, data ~ *123* Datenschutz
protein *154* Eiweiß, Protein
prototype *186* Prototyp
proud *81* stolz
to **prove** *11T* beweisen; *195* belegen, nachweisen
proverb *97* Sprichwort
to **provide** *27* zur Verfügung stellen; ~ **sth** *139* für etw sorgen; ~ **sb with sth** *74T* jdn mit etw versorgen
provider *39* Anbieter
provocation *45* Provokation
to **provoke sth** *146* etw hervorrufen
proximity *54* (räumliche) Nähe
psychological *91* psychologisch
psychologist *65* Psychologe/-in
psychology *36* Psychologie
public *11T* öffentlich; ~ **kiosk** *118* öffentliches Internet-Terminal; ~ **transport** *48F* öffentliche Verkehrsmittel
publication *111* Veröffentlichung
publicly *88T* in der Öffentlichkeit
to **publish** *131* veröffentlichen
publisher *50* Verleger/in
to **pull:** ~ **down** *155* *(Gebäude)* abreißen; ~ **sth tight** *62* etw straff ziehen
pulley *98* Rolle, Riemenscheibe
pulse *200T* Puls
to **pump** *140* pumpen
purchase *54* Kauf
pure *64* rein
purpose *84* Absicht, Zweck; **general-**~ *64* Allzweck-
to **put** *127* formulieren, sagen, in Worte fassen; ~ **sth down to sth** *84* etw einer Sache zuschreiben; ~ **sth up** *35* etw *(Bild etc.)* aufhängen; ~ **sb through** *33* *(Telefon:)* jdn durchstellen, jdn verbinden; unter etw ziehen;

~ **in work** *95* Arbeit leisten; ~ **sth out of action** *134T* etw außer Gefecht setzen; ~ **an end to sth** *27* mit etw Schluss machen, einen Schlussstrich

Q

qualification *68* Abschluss, Qualifikation
qualified *68T* mit Abschluss, qualifiziert
quality *18* Qualität; ~ **control** *120T* Qualitätskontrolle; ~ **of life** *137* Lebensqualität
quarter *36* Viertel
queue *81* Warteschlange; to **jump the** ~ *82* sich vordrängeln
to **queue** *7* sich (in einer Warteschlange) anstellen
quote *88T* Zitat
to **quote** *136* zitieren

R

race *7* Rennen
racial *84* rassisch, Rassen-
racing: ~ **car** *13* Rennwagen; ~ **cyclist** *14* Radrennfahrer/in
rack, drying ~ *208* Trockengestell
radiation *134T* Strahlung
radiator *181* Heizkörper
radicalization *123* Radikalisierung
to **radicalize** *124* radikalisieren
radio: ~ **frequency field** *205* Hochfrequenzfeld; ~ **signal** *54* Funksignal; ~ **transmitter** *54* Sender, Funksender
radio-controlled *158* funkferngesteuert
rail, high speed ~ *88T* Hochgeschwindigkeitsstrecken *(Eisenbahn)*; ~ **network** *134* Schienennetz, Eisenbahnnetz
rainfall *207* Regen, Niederschlagsmenge
to **raise** *156* *(Pflanzen)* anbauen; ~ **sth** *59* etw *(Thema etc.)* ansprechen; *80* etw anheben, etw hochheben; *100* etw steigern, etw erhöhen; ~ **money** *43* Geld beschaffen
range *54* Reichweite; *158T* Bandbreite, Reihe; *170* Umfang
ranging signal *170* Peilsignal
to **rank:** ~ **sb/sth** *6* jdn/etw einstufen, jdn/etw (ein-)ordnen; ~ **sixth** *92* den sechsten Platz einnehmen
ranking *121* Rangfolge
rapid(ly) *70* rasch, schnell
rare(ly) *108* selten
rate *105* Tempo, Quote, Rate, Anteil; **at any** ~ *131* auf jeden Fall; **unemployment** ~ *74T* Arbeitslosenquote
rather *110* eher, lieber; ~ **than** *43* anstatt
rating, credit ~ *62T* (Bewertung/Einstufung der) Bonität, Kreditwürdigkeit
ratio *184T* Verhältnis
raw *63* roh; ~ **product** *99* Ausgangsprodukt, Roherzeugnis
reach *99* Reichweite
reaction *98* Reaktion
to **reactivate** *39* wieder in Betrieb nehmen, reaktivieren
to **read:** ~ **sth back** *34* etw (zur Kontrolle) vorlesen; ~ **sth closely** *51* etw genau (durch)lesen
reader *36* Dozent/in; *199* Lesegerät
readings *pl* *146* Messwerte
ready meal *205* Fertiggericht
to **realise** *40* wissen, erkennen, klar sein
realistic *65* realistisch
to **reap the benefits** *165* die Früchte ernten, die Vorteile nutzen
reason, to **give a** ~ *22* eine Begründung anführen; **for this** ~ *48* aus diesem Grund;
reasonable *122* vernünftig
to **rebuild** *51* umbauen, erneuern
receipt *60* Quittung
receiver *196* Empfänger
reception *120T* Empfang
receptionist *72* Empfangsmitarbeiter/in
recession *107T* Rezession
to **recharge** *204* Aufladen *(von Akkus)*
recipient *44* Empfänger/in
to **recognise** *82* (wieder)erkennen; *132* anerkennen, begreifen
recognition, speech ~ *187* Spracherkennung; **voice** ~ *118* Spracherkennung
recommendation *176* Empfehlung
to **record** *14* aufzeichnen
record, on ~ *200T* aufgezeichnet, hinterlegt; ~ **company** *8* Plattenfirma
recourse, legal ~ *88T* Regressansprüche
to **recover** *109* sich erholen; *182* (rück)gewinnen; ~ **fully** *109* wieder völlig gesund werden
recovery *181* Rückgewinnung; **launch and** ~ **system** *195* Start- und Landesystem
recruitment *66* Personalbeschaffung
rectangular *180* rechteckig
to **redevelop** *155* sanieren
redevelopment *155* Sanierung
to **reduce** *17T* senken, reduzieren, verringern; ~ **sb to sth** *81* jdn zu etw bringen
reduction *83* Verringerung, Senkung
redundancy *108* Redundanz
redundant, to **make sb** ~ *110* jdn (betriebsbedingt) entlassen
ref. (= reference) *76* *(Brief:)* Zeichen
to **refer to sb/sth** *14* jdn/etw erwähnen, sich auf jdn/etw beziehen
referee *75* Referenzgeber
reference *75* Referenz, Zeugnis; ~ **to sth** *15* Verweis auf etw; **quick** ~ *48* schnelles Nachschlagen; **with** ~ **to** *201* mit Bezug auf
to **reflect** *136* reflektieren
refreshment *172* Erfrischung
refrigeration *159* Kühlung, Kälteerzeugung
refrigerator *206T* Kühlschrank
refugee *80* Flüchtling
to **refuse** *14* sich weigern; ~ **sth** *129* etw verweigern
regard, with ~ **to** *193* im Hinblick auf, hinsichtlich; **R~s** *121* *(Brief:)* Viele Grüße
to **regard: as regards …** *68T* was … betrifft
regardless of sth *37* ungeachtet einer Sache
regenerative *204* regenerativ
registered *66* eintragen, (staatlich) anerkannt; *74* zugelassen, qualifiziert
regulation *143T* Vorschrift
to **re-harness** *195* wieder nutzbar machen
to **re-innovate sth** *88T* etw weiter verbessern, etw weiterentwickeln
to **reject** *84* ablehnen, zurückweisen
to **rejoin sb** *94* jdn wieder treffen
to **relate to sth** *26* sich auf etw beziehen
related *103* zugehörig; **closely** ~ *116* eng verwandt; to **be** ~ **to sth** *10* mit etw in Zusammenhang stehen
relationship *10* Beziehung, Verhältnis
release *46* Veröffentlichung
to **release** *8* veröffentlichen
relevant *17* relevant, wichtig; *54* passend
reliability *114* Zuverlässigkeit, Verlässlichkeit
reliance on sth *186* Abhängigkeit von etw
religious *92* religiös
to **rely on sth** *134T* sich auf etw verlassen, auf etw angewiesen sein
to **remain** *44* bleiben
remaining *120* übrig, verbleibend
to **remind sb (of sth)** *103* jdn (an etw) erinnern
reminder, to **be a stark** ~ *132* etw jäh vor Augen führen, etw überdeutlich machen
remote *160* entlegen; **~-controlled** *158* ferngesteuert
to **remove** *181* beseitigen
renewable *135* erneuerbar
to **renovate** *181* renovieren
to **rent** *176* mieten
rent *104* Miete
rental price *122* Mietpreis
repeatedly *198* wiederholt, immer wieder
to **repel** *202* abstoßen
repetition *15* Wiederholung

to **replace** *16* ersetzen, austauschen
to **replenish** *183* (wieder)auffüllen, (wieder) ergänzen
replacement *86T* Ersatz, Ersetzung, Austausch
to **replicate** *199* reproduzieren
to **report to sb** *78* jdm unterstellt sein
to **represent** *168* vertreten, repräsentieren
representative *37* repräsentativ; *167* Repräsentant/in, Abgeordnete/r
to **reproduce** *152* sich fortpflanzen
reputation *40* Ansehen, Ruf
request *128* Bitte, Wunsch, Anfrage; **on ~** *75* auf Wunsch, auf Verlangen
to **request: as requested** *120* wie gewünscht
to **require** *69* erfordern, benötigen
required, to **be ~ to do sth** *143T* etw tun müssen; verpflichtet sein, etw zu tun
requirement *66* Voraussetzung, Bedingung, Anforderung; *140* Bedarf
to **re-read** *28* erneut lesen
to **reroute** *108* umleiten
to **rescue** *62T* retten, bergen
research *49T* Recherche, Nachforschungen, Untersuchungen; *139* Forschung; **R~ and Development (R&D)** *120T* Forschung(s-) und Entwicklung(sabteilung)
to **research sth** *43* etw recherchieren, Nachforschungen über etw anstellen
reservation *78T* Reservierung
to **reserve** *121* reservieren
reservoir *134* Wasserspeicher, Hochbehälter, Stausee
to **re-shore** *104* *(Industrie)* wieder im Inland ansiedeln, wieder ins Inland verlagern
resident *124* Anwohner/in, Bewohner/in
residue, pesticide ~s *pl 206T* Pestizidrückstände
resistance *146* Widerstand; *152* Widerstandsfähigkeit, Resistenz; **the least ~** *182T* der geringste Widerstand
resistant to sth *152* resistent gegen etw
to **re-skill** *100* umschulen
resolution, high-~ *158T* hochauflösend
resource *114* Ressource; **Human R~s (HR)** *50* Personal(abteilung)
to **respect** *27* respektieren
respect *62* Achtung, Respekt
respiratory *146* Atemwegs-
to **respond to sth** *34* auf etw reagieren, auf etw antworten
response, emergency ~ *158* Notfallmaßnahmen
responsibility *78* Aufgabe, Zuständigkeit; *92* Verantwortung; to **take ~** *78T* Verantwortung übernehmen
responsible *124* verantwortungsvoll; to **be ~ for sth** *66* für etw zuständig/verantwortlich sein
to **restore** *44* wiederherstellen, rekonstruieren
retail *110* Einzelhandel(s-)
retailer *27* Einzelhändler/in
to **retain** *157* zurückhalten, behalten, bewahren
to **rethink** *69* überdenken
to **retire** *86* in den Ruhestand gehen, in Rente gehen; **~ sb** *114* jdn in den Ruhestand versetzen
retirement *14* Rücktritt, Rückzug; *114* Ruhestand, Rente; **~ home** *114* Altersheim
to **retrain** *72* umschulen
to **retrofit** *195* nachträglich ausstatten
return, in ~ *143T* im Gegenzug, als Ausgleich; **~ airfare** *66* Kosten für Hin- und Rückflug
to **return to sth** *62* sich wieder einer Sache zuwenden
reveller *40* Feiernde/r
to **reverse sth** *44* umkehren, auflösen
review *44* Rezension, Kritik
to **review** *187* *(Text)* redigieren, korrigieren
to **revolutionize** *178* revolutionieren
reward *45* Belohnung, Lohn
to **reward** *48F* belohnen
rewarding *65* lohnend, erfüllend
to **rewrite** *20* umformulieren, neu schreiben
RFID (radio frequency identification) *196* Funkerkennung (RFID)
rhythm *200T* Rhythmus
rich *148* *(Nahrung)* gehaltvoll, reichhaltig
rid, to **get ~ of sth** *145* etw loswerden
ride *95* Fahrt
ridiculous(ly) *60* lächerlich, unglaublich
riding *25* Reiten
rifle *80* Gewehr
rig *98* Bohrturm; **drilling ~** *143T* Bohrturm
rigged, to **be ~ against sb** *110* jdn (systematisch) benachteiligen, gegen jdn arbeiten
right, ~ away *78T* sofort; **all ~ by me** *30* in Ordnung für mich
right-hand *39* rechte/r/s, auf der rechten Seite
rigid *210* starr, steif
riot *40* Aufstand, Aufruhr; **~ police** *40* Bereitschaftspolizei
rise, rapid ~ *88T* steiler Aufstieg; **high ~ city** *170* Stadt mit Hochhäusern
rival *199* Rivale, Konkurrent
road: ~ freight *194* Straßengüterverkehr; **~ testing** *166T* Fahrversuche, Fahrerprobung, Straßentests; **~ train** *194T* Lastzug
to **rob a bank** *130* eine Bank überfallen, eine Bank ausrauben
robbery, bank ~ *130* Banküberfall, Bankraub
robot *64* Roboter
robotic *168* Roboter-
roboticist *64* Robotiker/in, Roboteringenieur/in
robotics *168* Robotertechnik
rock *140* Fels, Gestein
role *35* Rolle; **~ model** *55* Vorbild
role-play *11* Rollenspiel
to **role-play** *11* mit verteilten Rollen spielen
room, to **make ~** *110* Platz machen
root *56* Wurzel
to **root sth out** *124* etw beseitigen, etw ausmerzen
to **rotate** *185* (sich) (um die eigene Achse) drehen
rotation, job ~ *72* Arbeitsplatzrotation, (innerbetrieblicher) Arbeitsplatzwechsel
rotor *202* Rotor
roughly *105* ungefähr
roundup *179T* Übersicht, Zusammenfassung
routine *70* (fester) Ablauf, Routine; **dance ~** *17T* Tanzschritte
row *156* Reihe; **in a ~** *161* nacheinander
rubbish *47* Müll, Abfall; **~ bin** *47* Mülltonne
rules *pl* **of the game** *13* Spielregeln
run *21* Lauf
to **run** *31* *(Unternehmen)* führen, betreiben
running *107T* in Folge; **~ cost** *155* Betriebskosten
runny *98* dünnflüssig
runoff *156* Abfluss, abfließendes Wasser
rural *86T* ländlich
to **rush, Must ~.** *71T* Ich muss weg.
rutted *156* zerfurcht, ausgefahren

S

saddle *208* Sattel
sadly *117T* leider
safe, to **keep sth ~** *22* etw aufbewahren
safely *56* mit Gewissheit
safety *80* Sicherheit; **health and ~** *83* Arbeitsschutz
sail *195* Segel
salary *48F* Gehalt
sale, to **be on ~** *28* angeboten werden, zum Verkauf stehen; **clearance ~** *144* Räumungsverkauf
sales *pl 49* Verkauf, Verkäufe, Absatz, Vertrieb; *107* Umsatz; **~ assistant** *54* Verkäufer/in; **~ director** *107* Verkaufsleiter/in, Vertriebsleiter/in; **~ force** *177* Verkaufspersonal;

~ **rep(resentative)** *177* Handelsvertreter/in, Verkäufer/in
salesman *50* Verkäufer, Vertreter
salesperson *68* Vertreter/in, Verkäufer/in
saleswoman *97* Verkäuferin
salutation *76* *(Brief:)* Anrede
Salvation Army *90* Heilsarmee
sample *14* Probe
to **sample** *187* abtasten
sanitation *98* Abwasserentsorgung
satellite *108* Satellit
satisfaction *68T* Zufriedenheit
satisfied *161* zufrieden(gestellt)
satisfying *65* befriedigend
savannah *160* Savanne
to **save** *129* *(Daten)* sichern; ~ **oneself sth** *84* sich etw ersparen; ~ **up** *25* sparen
savings *pl* *183* Einsparung(en), Ersparnis(se)
to **saw** *184* sägen
saw mill *184* Sägewerk
say, to **have one's** ~ *126* seine Meinung äußern, zu Wort kommen
saying *59* Sprichwort, Redensart
scale *156* Ausmaß, Umfang; **large-~** *136* in großem Umfang/Ausmaß; **pay** ~ *68T* Lohntarif, Lohntabelle
to **scan** *15* *(Text)* überfliegen
scared, to **be** ~ *8* Angst haben
scarred *157* vernarbt, gezeichnet
scary *51* unheimlich, beängstigend; *164* gruselig, schaurig
to **scatter** *168* verteilen, verstreuen
scenario *64* Szenario
scene *11T* Szene
sceptic *137* Skeptiker/in
scheme *132* Plan, Programm
school leaving party *17T* Schulabgangsfeier
school-age *128* im Schulalter
schoolboy *40* Schuljunge
schooling *90* Schulbesuch, Schulbildung
scientist *136* (Natur-)Wissenschaftler/in
to **scramble** *44* verschlüsseln
scrap *144* Schrott
scrapheap *114* Schrotthaufen
scrapyard *145* Schrottplatz
scream *94* Schrei
to **scream** *80* schreien
screen *39* Bildschirm; *121* Leinwand
script *9* Drehbuch
to **scrutinize** *131* genau ansehen, überprüfen
sea level *137* Meeresspiegel
seabed *108* Meeresgrund
seafood *193* Meeresfrüchte
to **seal** *180* abdichten, einschließen
season, holiday ~ *194* Weihnachtszeit
seat, to **take a** ~ *71T* Platz nehmen
seating *121* Bestuhlung
secondary school *74* weiterführende Schule
secondly *103* zweitens
secret *23* Geheimnis; *44* geheim; *49T* heimlich; **trade** ~ *199* Betriebsgeheimnis
secretary *31* Sekretär/in
section *77* Abschnitt; *104* Bereich, Teil; *173T* Abteilung
sector *70* Sektor, Bereich; **private** ~ *194* Privatwirtschaft
secure *44* sicher
security: job ~ *65* sicherer Arbeitsplatz; ~ **forces** *pl* *126T* Sicherheitskräfte; ~ **service** *127* Geheimdienst
to **see sb** *38T* zu jdm gehen
seed *152* Samen, Saatgut
segment *187* Teilstück, Segment
to **seek** *75* suchen; ~ **sth out** *189* nach etw suchen
to **select** *87* auswählen
selection *121* Auswahl; *152* Auslese, Selektion
selective *152* selektiv; ~ **laser sintering** *209* selektives Lasersintern
to **self-assemble** *210* sich selbsttätig zusammenbauen
self-assembly *210* selbsttätige Montage
self-defence *128* Selbstverteidigung
to **self-fund** *110* selbst finanzieren
self-sustainable *90* selbsttragend, lebensfähig
semiconductor *180* Halbleiter
to **send sth out** *78T* etw verschicken
sender *44* Absender
senior *69* leitend; ~ **citizen** *114* Senior/in, ältere/r Mitbürger/in
to **sensationalize sth** *125* reißerisch über etw berichten
sense *28* Sinn; to **make** ~ *116* Sinn ergeben, sinnvoll sein; ~ **of touch** *169* Tastsinn
sensing
sensing, tactile ~ *169* Tastempfinden; ~ **technology** *146* Messtechnologie, Sensortechnologie
sensitive *127* sensibel, *(Information:)* vertraulich; *134T* empfindlich
to **separate** *33* trennen, loslösen; *80* abspalten
separate *73* getrennt, separat
separately *33* einzeln
to **sequence sth** *184* etw in eine Reihenfolge bringen
series *51* Reihe, Serie; *203T* seriell
seriously *49T* im Ernst
to **serve** *170* bedienen, versorgen
service *39* Dienst, Dienstleistung; ~ **station** *166T* Tankstelle
session *16* Sitzung
set *66* Kulisse; *168* Menge; *203* Gruppe
to **set:** ~ **out to do sth** *43* sich vornehmen, etw tun; ~ **up** *49T* *(Unternehmen)* gründen; ~ **sth up** *66* etw einrichten; ~ **an example** *56* ein Beispiel setzen, mit gutem Beispiel vorangehen; ~ **fire to sth** *145* etw anzünden
setback *169* Rückschlag
setting *39* Einstellung; **~s** *pl* *118* Einstellungen
set-up *32* Aufbau
several *36* mehrere
severe *134T* schwer, heftig; *154* ernst, schwer
sex *29* Geschlecht; **the opposite** ~ *29* das andere Geschlecht
shadowy *144* zwielichtig
to **shake** *9* zittern; ~ **sth** *144* an etw rütteln; *17T* etw schütteln, mit etw wackeln; ~ **sth off** *70* etw abschütteln; ~ **one's head** *81* den Kopf schütteln
shale *140* Schiefer
share *149* Anteil; **market** ~ *72* Marktanteil
shared *102* gemeinsam; ~ **house** *62T* Wohngemeinschaft
sharing *190* Teilen, gemeinsame Nutzung
sharp(ly) *103* scharf; *106* stark
sheep *152* Schaf
sheet *134* Blatt (Papier); *182T* (Glas-)Scheibe; **ice** ~ *137* Eisdecke
shelf, shelves *155T* Regal, Regale
shelter *94* Unterkunft
shift *66* Schicht
to **shine light on sth** *144* Licht auf etw werfen
to **ship** *49T* verschicken; *144* versenden, verschiffen
shipbuilder *198* Schiffsbauer
shipbuilding *112* Schiffbau
shipping *194* Versand, Transport, Schifffahrt; ~ **company** *145* Transportunternehmen, Spediteur, Reederei
shipyard *86* Werft
to **shiver** *202* zittern
shocked *40* schockiert
to **shoot** *80* schießen; ~ **sb** *109* jdn erschießen; ~ **up** *40* rasant ansteigen
to **shop** *18* einkaufen
shopper *6* Käufer/in, Kunde/Kundin
shopping mall *27* Einkaufspassage, Einkaufszentrum
shore *108* Küste
short-sleeved *156* kurzärmlig
short-term *88* kurzfristig
shortage *68T* Mangel
show *9* (TV-, Radio-)Sendung; *204* Ausstellung, Messe
to **shudder** *80* erschaudern, zittern
to **shuffle** *81* schlurfen
to **shut down** *124* schließen
shy *59* schüchtern
siblings *pl* *29* Geschwister
sick,to be ~ **of sth** *110* von etw die Nase voll haben; to **be** ~ **and tired of**

sth *129* die Nase von etw gestrichen voll haben
sideways *185* seitlich, zur Seite
sight *197* Sehvermögen; **in ~** *64* in Sicht(weite), im Blick
to **sign** *8* unterschreiben; **~ in** *118* sich anmelden
signage *178* Beschilderung, Anzeige; **digital ~** *45* digitale Außenwerbung
signal, ranging *170* Peilsignal
signature *76* Unterschrift
significant *195* bedeutend, erheblich
silent *129* stumm
silent(ly) *81* still, schweigend
silicon *180* Silizium
silver-skinned *194* mit silberner Haut
similarity *20* Ähnlichkeit
similarly *87* in ähnlicher Weise, genauso, ebenso
simultaneous(ly) *44* gleichzeitig
to **simulate** *186* simulieren
since *13* seit
sincerely, Yours ~ *31* *(Brief:)* Mit freundlichen Grüßen
sinister *158* finster, unheimlich
sink *63* Spüle
to **sinter** *209T* sintern
sintering, selective laser ~ *209* selektives Lasersintern
sir *87T* mein Herr
site *29* Website
sixth-form college *139* Oberstufenzentrum, Studienkolleg
skeptical *AE 157* skeptisch
skill *8* Fähigkeit, Fertigkeit
skilled *74T* qualifiziert; *110* erfahren; to **be ~ with sth** *65* mit etw gut umgehen können
to **skim** *36* *(Text)* überfliegen
skinny *23* hauteng
to **skip sth** *46* etw auslassen, etw überspringen
skull *196* Schädel
skydive *43* Fallschirmsprung
skylight *40* Oberlicht, Dachfenster
slice *208* Scheibchen
slide *48* Dia, (Overhead-)Folie
slight *104* leicht, gering
slightly *106* geringfügig, leicht
slim *17* schlank
slope *156* Hang
to **slow** *105* sich verlangsamen, sich abschwächen; **~ down** *166T* bremsen
small print, the ~ *129* das Kleingedruckte
to **smash** *94* zertrümmern, zerstören
smooth(ly) *166T* reibungslos; *184* glatt
to **sniff sth** *63* an etw riechen
so far *96T* bislang
soap *49T* Seife
social: ~ engineering *114* Änderung gesellschaftlicher Strukturen, angewandte Sozialwissenschaft; **~ skills** *pl 29* Sozialkompetenz; **~ worker** *65* Sozialarbeiter/in
to **socialize** *29* sich treffen, unter Leute gehen
society, civil ~ *161* Bürgergesellschaft
to **soften** *33* mildern, abmildern
softwoods *pl 184* Weichholz
soil *153* Erde, Boden, Erdreich
solar *135* Sonnen-, Solar-; **~ flare** *134T* Sonneneruption; **~ power** *135* Sonnenenergie; **~ storm** *134* Sonnensturm
sold out *20* ausverkauft
soldier *80* Soldat/in
sole *94* alleinig
solid *178* massiv; **~ state** *180* Festkörper(-)
to **solidify** *209* verfestigen, erstarren
solution *38T* Lösung
to **solve** *65* lösen
sometime *31* irgendwann
sophisticated *158* hochentwickelt, ausgeklügelt
sorry, to **feel ~ for sb** *92* jd tut einem leid
sort *28* Art, Sorte
to **sort** *6* sortieren, einordnen
sound *46* solide, untadelig
soundcard *188* Soundkarte
source *52* Quelle; **~ code** *190* Quellcode
to **sow** *161* säen
space, to **take up ~** *153* Platz einnehmen; **~ weather** *134* Weltraumwetter
spare *170* Reserve, Ersatz; to **have ~ cash** *96T* Geld übrig haben
speaker *17* Sprecher/in
to **speak: ~ up** *162* lauter sprechen; **Speaking.** *78T* *(Telefon:)* Am Apparat.
special: ~ committee *167* Sonderausschuss; **~ deal** *54* Sonderangebot
specialist *128* Spezial-, Fach-; **~ lawyer** *39* Fachanwalt/-anwältin
to **specialize in sth** *139* sich auf etw spezialisieren
species *148* *(Biologie:)* Art
specification *54* Spezifikation, Vorgabe, Richtlinie; *184* technische Daten
spectacular *134* spektakulär
spectator *12* Zuschauer/in
speech *187* (gesprochene) Sprache; **~ bubble** *26* Sprechblase; **~ recognition** *187* Spracherkennung
speed *48F* Geschwindigkeit; **~ camera** *48F* Geschwindigkeitsüberwachungskamera, Radarfalle; **~ limit** *48F* Geschwindigkeitsbegrenzung; **high ~ rail** *88T* Hochgeschwindigkeitsstrecken *(Eisenbahn)*
to **speed up** *166T* beschleunigen
to **spell** *33* buchstabieren, (richtig) schreiben
spelling *32* Rechtschreibung
spending *52* Ausgaben, Aufwendungen
to **spin** *202* sich drehen
spinach *156* Spinat
spinal cord *118* Rückenmark; **high ~ injury** *118* hoch gelegene Querschnittslähmung
splendid *155* prächtig
to **split** *73* (sich) aufteilen; *184* reißen; **~ (up)** *10* *(Paar:)* sich trennen
to **spoil** *56* *(Kind)* verwöhnen
spokesman *27* Sprecher
to **sponsor** *21* (finanziell) unterstützen, sponsern
sponsorship *90* Förderung
spool *209T* Rolle, Spule
sports: ~ car *49* Sportwagen; **~ gear** *21* Sportkleidung, Sportausrüstung
sportswear *19* Sportkleidung
spot *8* Platz, Stelle; *69* Ort, Fleck, Punkt
to **spot sth** *191T* etw entdecken
spouse *129* Ehegatte
sprawling *198* ausgedehnt
spray *152* Spritzmittel
spread *160* Verbreitung, Ausbreitung
to **spread** *43* sich verbreiten; *100* sich ausbreiten, sich verbreiten; *209T* verteilen, auftragen; to **be ~ evenly** *170* gleichmäßig verteilt sein
spreader, glue ~ *184* Leimauftragsmaschine
spreadsheet *75* Tabellenkalkulation
to **spy on sb** *129* jdn ausspionieren
spyware *128* Spionagesoftware
square mile *148* Quadratmeile
to **squeeze** *98* (aus)pressen; *209T* (aus)drücken; **~ oneself into sth** *23* sich in etw hineinzwängen
stable *184* stabil
to **stack up against sth** *209* einem Vergleich mit etw standhalten
stadium *13* Stadion
staff *68T* Personal, Belegschaft, Mitarbeiter/innen; **member of ~** *171* Mitarbeiter/in
to **staff** *66* (mit Personal) besetzen
stage *8* Bühne; *61* Phase, Abschnitt; **~ of development** *194* Entwicklungsstand, -stadium
to **stain** *208* einfärben
to **stamp** *48F* stempeln, abstempeln
to **stand: ~ in for sb** *72* jdn vertreten; **~ out** *49T* auffallen, herausstechen; **~ up** *17T* aufstehen, sich hinstellen
stand-by *170* Bereitschaft
standard *64* genormt; *68T* Niveau; *181* Norm, Richtlinie
to **stare at sb** *23* jdn anstarren
to **start: ~ on sb** *60* jdn angreifen, jdn kritisieren; **~ out** *49T* (zunächst) anfangen
startling *114* alarmierend, erschreckend, erstaunlich
starvation *155T* Hunger

to **state** *27* darlegen, festlegen; *110* erklären, feststellen; *124* aussagen
state, idle ~ *205* Ruhezustand; **out-of-~** *110* in einem anderen Bundesstaat; **solid ~** *180* Festkörper(-)
statement *7* Aussage, Feststellung, Behauptung
static *199* statisch
station, (radio/TV) ~ *160* (Radio-/Fernseh-)Sender; **freight ~** *194T* Güterbahnhof
stationery *122* Schreibpapier, Schreibwaren
statistics *52* Statistik(en)
stator *202* Stator
status *6* Status, Stellung
steadily *62* ununterbrochen
steady *106* kontinuierlich, stabil
steel *108* Stahl; **structural ~** *184T* Baustahl, tragende Stahlelemente
steep *156* steil
step *11T* Schritt
to **step** *47* treten; **~ off** *62* aussteigen
stereolithography *209* Stereolithographie
to **stick** *208* kleben, haften; **~ sth on** *129* etw befestigen; **~ to sth** *23* bei etw bleiben, sich an etw halten
still *21T* (immer) noch, dennoch
to **stimulate** *14* anregen, stimulieren
stimulator *196* Stimulator
stock *105* (Lager-)Bestand, Vorrat; **~ item** *205* Bestandsartikel
stocks *pl*, to **maintain ~** *154* den Bestand erhalten
stoneware *208* Steingut
stop *144* Station
to **stop sb from doing sth** *116* jdn daran hindern, etw zu tun
storage *175* *(Daten:)* Speicherung
store *6* Geschäft, Laden
to **store** *71* aufbewahren, lagern; *148* speichern
storeroom *120* Lagerraum
stork *147* Storch
storm, geomagnetic ~ *134T* geomagnetischer Sturm; **solar ~** *134* Sonnensturm
story, to cut a long ~ short *60* lange Rede, kurzer Sinn
straight *50* direkt, gleich; *184* gerade; **~ ahead** *119* geradeaus; **~ away** *103* sofort, sogleich
strain *198* Strapaze, Anstrengung
strand *210* Strang
strap *198* Gurt
to **strap** *198* festschnallen
strategic(ally) *156* strategisch
strategy *51* Strategie
stream *110* Strom; *156* Bach, Fließgewässer
street, high ~ *23* Hauptgeschäftsstraße, Einkaufsstraße; to **be a two-way ~** *84* auf Gegenseitigkeit beruhen
strength *78* Stärke; *94* Kraft; *184T* Festigkeit, Tragfähigkeit; **~ grading** *185* Festigkeitssortierung
to **strengthen** *17T* kräftigen, stärken
stress *17T* Belastung, Stress
stressed *17T* angestrengt, gestresst; *158T* strapaziert, belastet
strict *193* streng
strike *72* Streik; to **go on ~** *72* streiken
to **strike** *94* treffen; **~ a posture** *88T* eine Haltung einnehmen
striking *92* auffallend, auffällig, hervorstechend
stripe *21T* Streifen
strong
strong, to **be still going ~** *114* gut dabei sein, immer noch in Form sein; **~ advice** *62T* dringender Rat
structural: ~ beam *184T* Trägerbalken; **~ steel** *184T* Baustahl, tragende Stahlelemente
structure *142* Bauwerk, Konstruktion
to **structure** *15* strukturieren
struggle *85* Kampf
to **struggle** *184* kämpfen, zu kämpfen haben
strychnine *14* Strychnin
study *14* Untersuchung, Studie
to **study sth** *6* etw genau betrachten; *26* sich etw genau ansehen
stuff *23* Zeug, Sache(n)
sub-heading *15* Teilrubrik, Zwischenüberschrift
subject line *32* *(Brief:)* Betreffzeile
submarine cable *108* Tiefseekabel
submission *46* Einsendung
to **submit** *32* einreichen, vorlegen, zusenden; **~ sth** *46* etw einreichen, etw einsenden
subscription *175* Abonnement
subsidiary *74T* Niederlassung
subsidy *141* Subvention
subsoil heat exchange *181* Erdwärmeaustausch
substance *14* Substanz, Stoff
substitute *160* Ersatz
subway *AE* *46* U-Bahn
to **succeed** *88T* erfolgreich sein, Erfolg haben
sudden *71* plötzlich
to **sue sb** *88T* jdn verklagen
to **suffer: ~ sth** *14* an etw leiden, etw erleiden; **~ from sth** *38* unter etw leiden; *167* unter etw zu leiden haben
sufficient *169* ausreichend, hinreichend
to **suggest** *16* vorschlagen; *19* unterstellen, suggerieren; *36* darauf hindeuten, nahelegen
suggestion *31* Vorschlag
suicide *125* Selbstmord; **~ bomber** *125* Selbstmordattentäter/in
suit *70* Anzug
to **suit: ~ sb** *23* *(Kleidung:)* jdm stehen; **~ sb/sth** *23* zu jdm/etw passen
suitability *183* Eignung
suitable *61* passend
sum *37* Summe
to **sum up** *15* zusammenfassen; **to ~ up** *15* zusammenfassend
to **summarize** *15* zusammenfassen
sunflower *156* Sonnenblume
sunny *51* sonnig
superhuman *164* übermenschlich
superior *78* Vorgesetzte/r; *165* überlegen
supersonic plane *193* Überschallflugzeug
to **supervise** *186* überwachen, beaufsichtigen
supplies *pl* *143T* Vorräte, Vorkommen; **office ~** *120T* Büromaterial
supply, freshwater ~ *98* Trinkwasserversorgung; **water ~** *134* Wasserversorgung; **~ air** *182* Zuluft; **~ chain** *99* Lieferkette
to **supply** *67* liefern, bieten; **~ sb with sth** *126T* jdn mit etw versorgen, jdm mit etw beliefern
support *11* Unterstützung, Hilfe
to **support** *117* *(Argument)* untermauern, stützen; *11T* unterstützen; *198* tragen, halten
supporter *190* Anhänger/in, Befürworter/in
to **suppose: I ~** *62T* wohl
supposed, to **be ~ to do sth** *49T* etw tun sollen
sure, to **make ~** *22* sicherstellen; dafür sorgen, dass
surely *134T* bestimmt, (doch) wohl
to **surf the internet** *25* im Internet surfen
surface *140* Oberfläche
surgery *68T* (Arzt-)Praxis; *92* Operation; **plastic ~** *197* plastische Chirurgie
surgical(ly) *196* chirurgisch
surname *33* Nachname
surprised *78* erstaunt, überrascht
surprisingly *155T* erstaunlicherweise
surrounded by sth *179T* von etw umgeben
surveillance *123* Überwachung
survey *12* Umfrage
to **survive** *51* überleben
suspect *124* Verdächtige/r
suspicious *129* misstrauisch
sustainable *67* nachhaltig; **self-~** *90* selbsttragend, lebensfähig
sustainably managed *184* nachhaltig bewirtschaftet
to **swap** *204* tauschen
sweater *20* Pullover
sweatshop *21T* Ausbeutungsbetrieb

T

torque *194T* Drehmoment
to **toss** *40* werfen
totalitarian *131* totalitär
totally *70* voll und ganz
touch *17T* Berührung; to **be in** ~ *74* sich melden; to **keep in** ~ *29* in Verbindung bleiben; **sense of** ~ *169* Tastsinn
to **tour** *7* auf Tour gehen
towards sth *62* zu etw hin, auf etw zu
towing kite *195* Zugdrachen
toxic *144* giftig, Gift-
toy *64* Spielzeug
trace *144* Spur
track *64* Schiene; to **keep** ~ **of sth** *158T* den Überblick über etw behalten
to **track** *146* verfolgen, aufzeichnen; ~ **sb** *128* jds Spur verfolgen
tracking device *144* Ortungsgerät
trade *100* Handel; ~ **fair** *120* Handelsmesse, Fachmesse; ~ **secret** *199* Betriebsgeheimnis
trader *100* Händler/in
trading *100* Handel
traditional *16* traditionell; *46* herkömmlich
traffic lights *pl* *48F* Ampel
tragedy *45* Tragödie
to **train** *11* trainieren
train, road ~ *194T* Lastzug
trainee *31* Auszubildende/r
trainers *pl* *163* Turnschuhe
trait *201* Merkmal, Eigenschaft
traitor *80* Verräter/in
trajectory *160* Flugbahn, Weg
tram *48F* Straßenbahn, Tram
transaction *160* (Geschäfts-)Vorgang, Transaktion
transceiver *205* Transceiver, Sendeempfänger
to **transfer** *96T* *(Geld)* überweisen; *169* übergeben, weitergeben; *181* (ab-, weiter)leiten, übertragen
transfer, heat ~ *182T* Wärmeübertragung
to **transform** *100* (völlig) verändern; *210* (sich) verwandeln, (sich) umformen
transformation *101* (grundlegende) Veränderung, Umwandlung
transformer *134* Transformator, Umspannwerk
translation *28* Übersetzung
translator *189* Übersetzer/in
to **transmit** *128* übertragen, übermitteln, senden
transmitter *196* Sender; **radio** ~ *54* Sender, Funksender
transport, means of ~ *130* Verkehrsmittel; **personal** ~ *102* Individualverkehr; **public** ~ *48F* öffentliche Verkehrsmittel; ~ **mode** *193* Beförderungsart, Transportart
transportation *98* Beförderung (swesen), Transport(swesen)
trash *49T* Müll
to **trash sth** *40* etw demolieren
to **travel** *134T* sich bewegen
travel expenses *pl* *66* Reisekosten, Fahrtkosten
to **treat** *97* behandeln; *143T* *(Abwasser)* klären
treatment *67* Behandlung
to **tremble** *80* beben, zittern
triage *194* (notfallmedizinische) Ersteinschätzung, Triage
trial *198* Versuch
triathlon *14* Triathlon
tribe *161* Stamm
to **trick** *200* täuschen, überlisten, betrügen; ~ **sb into doing sth** *154* jdn (mit einer List) dazu bringen, etw zu tun
tried and trusted *179* seit Langem bewährt
to **trip** *16* stolpern
triple-glazed *182T* dreifach verglast
trivial *199* banal, einfach, simpel
trouble *40* Ärger, Problem(e)
to **trouble sb** *90* jdn bekümmern, jdm Schwierigkeiten bereiten
to **troubleshoot** *191T* Fehler suchen, Fehler beheben
to **trust** *38T* vertrauen
try, to **give sth a** ~ *17T* etw ausprobieren
to **try sb** *136* jdn vor Gericht stellen
tunnel *140* Tunnel
turbine *155* Turbine
turn *155* Runde, Umdrehung; **in** ~ *137* wiederum; to **take** ~**s** *48* sich abwechseln; to **wait for one's** ~ *82* warten, bis man an der Reihe ist
to **turn:** ~ **into sth** *60* zu etw werden; ~ **sb/sth into sb/sth** *46* jdn/etw zu jdm/etw machen; ~ **sth on** *142* etw an-/einschalten; ~ **out** *100* sich herausstellen; ~ **to sb** *56* sich an jdn wenden; ~ **up** *40* auftauchen; ~ **heads** *195* für Aufsehen sorgen; ~ **right/left** *119* rechts/links abbiegen
twin *56* Zwilling
to **twist** *210* (sich) verdrehen
two-way street, to **be a** ~ *84* auf Gegenseitigkeit beruhen
type *36* Schrift, Type; **hot metal** ~ *208* Setzmaschine
to **type:** ~ **sth in** *32* etw eintippen; ~ **sth up** *172* etw (am Computer) formulieren, etw ausarbeiten
typically *54* üblicherweise, normalerweise
typing *68T* Schreibmaschinenschreiben

U

ultimately *94* letztlich, letztendlich
umbrella *144* Regenschirm
unable *40* nicht in der Lage, unfähig
unauthorized *175* unbefugt
unavailable, to **be** ~ *34T* *(Telefon:)* nicht zu sprechen sein
uncertainty *168* Ungewissheit
uncomfortable, to **feel** ~ *8* sich unbehaglich fühlen; to **make sb** ~ *197T* jdm unangenehm sein
uncontrolled *86T* ungeregelt, unkontrolliert
undecided *190* unschlüssig
to **undercut** *104* unterbieten
undergarments *pl* *27* Unterwäsche
undergraduate *156* Student/in *(vor dem ersten akad. Grad)*
to **underline** *36* unterstreichen
to **unload** *144* entladen
undersea *108* Untersee-
understandable *74T* verständlich
understanding *82* Verständnis
underwater *108* Unterwasser-
undetectable *128* nicht erkennbar, nicht nachweisbar
undeveloped *148* *(Land:)* unbebaut
unemployment *74T* Arbeitslosigkeit; to **claim** ~ **benefits** *86* Arbeitslosengeld beziehen; ~ **rate** *74T* Arbeitslosenquote
unexpected(ly) *111* unerwartet
unfamiliar *168* unbekannt, ungewohnt
unfit *37* nicht fit
unhealthy *17* nicht gesund
uniform *184* gleichmäßig
uninvited *41* un(ein)geladen
union *100* Gewerkschaft
unique *23* einzigartig; to **be** ~ **to sth** *110* etw ausschließlich betreffen
uniqueness *201* Einzigartigkeit
unit *179* Gerät
universal *189* universell, Universal-
universality *201* Allgemeingültigkeit, Universalität
universally *118* allgemein, überall
universe *164* Universum
unless *27* es sei denn, außer wenn
unlike *139* anders als; *202* ungleich, gegensätzlich
unlikely *197T* unwahscheinlich
unloading *195* Entladung, Entladen, Löschen *(von Ladung)*
to **unlock** *197* aufschließen, entriegeln
unnecessary *57* überflüssig, unnötig
unnoticed, to **go** ~ *129* unbemerkt bleiben
unpaid *95* unbezahlt
unpleasant *81* unangenehm, unschön
unpolluted *154* unverschmutzt
unpredictable *169* launenhaft, unkalkulierbar
unsafe *200* unsicher
unstoppable *137* unaufhaltsam

unstructured *65* unstrukturiert
untraceable *129* nicht ausfindig zu machen
unusual *179* ungewöhnlich
to **unveil** *168* enthüllen, vorstellen
unviable *193* undurchführbar, unmöglich
unwanted *40* unerwünscht
up, What's ~? *21T* Was gibt's? Was ist los?; **~ to** *23* bis; to **be ~ to sth** *63* etw vorhaben
update *37* Aktualisierung
to **update** *75* aktualisieren; *177T* aufrüsten
upgrade *191* Aktualisierung
to **upgrade** *98* aufrüsten, verbessern
to **upload** *42* hochladen
upset, to **get ~** *62T* sich aufregen
upwards *53* steigend
urban *124* städtisch, Stadt-
urgently *137* dringend, nachdrücklich
usage *36* Nutzung
use *8* Gebrauch, Nutzen; to **make ~ of sth** *8* von etw Gebrauch machen, etw nutzen
use-by date *149* Haltbarkeitsdatum
usefulness *63* Nutzen, Zweckmäßigkeit
useless *111* nutzlos
user *36* Benutzer/in; **~ ID** *200T* Benutzername
utility bills *pl* *151* Rechnungen für Versorgungsleistungen
to **utilize** *181* nutzen, nutzbar machen
utter *129* völlig, vollkommen

V

vacation *AE* *49T* Urlaub
valuable *90* wertvoll
value *19* Wert; **high-~** *193* hochwertig; **low-~** *193* geringwertig; **~ chain** *145* Wertschöpfungskette
to **value** *90* wertschätzen, schätzen
van *129* Lieferwagen
vapor *AE* *146* Dampf
vaporizer *179T* Zerstäuber
variability *136* Schwankung, Unbeständigkeit
variable *195* wechselnd, unbeständig
variation *158T* Schwankung(en), Unterschied(e)
varied *84* vielfältig, abwechslungsreich; **a ~ bunch** *64* eine bunte Truppe
variety *149* (Pflanzen-)Sorte
various *57* verschieden, mehrere, allerlei
vase *166* Vase
vastness *164* unermessliche Weite
vegetarian *121* vegetarisch
vehicle *88T* Fahrzeug; **electric ~** *202* Elektrofahrzeug; **heavy goods ~ (HGV)** *194T* (Schwer-)Lastkraftwagen (Lkw); **hybrid electric ~** *202* Hybridfahrzeug; **launch ~** *170* Trägerrakete; **motor ~** *88* Kraftfahrzeug
vein *200* Ader, Vene
vending machine *49T* (Verkaufs-)Automat
ventilation heating *181* Warmluftheizung
verge, to **be on the ~ of doing sth** *194* kurz davor stehen, etw zu tun
versatile *185* vielseitig (einsetzbar)
vertical *179T* senkrecht, vertikal
vertical(ly) *153* senkrecht, vertikal
vessel *195* Wasserfahrzeug, Schiff; **blood ~** *17* Blutgefäß
veterinarian *160* Tierarzt/-ärztin, Veterinär/in
vibrant *84* dynamisch, voller Leben
vice president *189* Vizepräsident/in
vice versa *189* umgekehrt
victim *23* Opfer
view, point of ~ *101* Perspektive, Blickwinkel, Standpunkt
to **view sth** *46* (sich) etw ansehen
viewer *180* Betrachter/in
vigil, prayer ~ *126T* Gebetswache
violation *88T* Verletzung *(eines Vertrags)*
violence *124* Gewalt
violent *80* heftig; *84* gewalttätig
viral *158T* Virus-; to **go ~** *38T* sich (im Internet) rasend schnell verbreiten; **~ ad** *45* Internet-Werbespot
virtual *35* virtuell
visibility *178* Sichtbarkeit
visible *27* sichtbar
vision *118* Sehkraft; **field of ~** *131* Sichtfeld
visionary *51* Visionär/in
visual *52* visuell; **~s** *pl* *48* visuelle Hilfsmittel
vital *148* lebensnotwendig, unerlässlich
vocational; ~ college *31* Fachoberschule, Berufskolleg; **~ school** *74T* berufsbildende Schule; **~ training** *74* Berufsausbildung
voice, to **drop one's ~** *80* die Stimme senken; **~ recognition** *118* Spracherkennung
volatile *206T* flüchtig
voltage *205* Spannung; **extra-high ~** *134* Höchstspannung
voluntary *67* freiwillig
volunteer *67* (freiwilliger) Helfer/in
to **volunteer to do sth** *66* sich bereit erklären, etw zu tun
vomit *40* Erbrochenes
vote, to **take a ~** *37* abstimmen
voter *199* Wähler/in
voucher *81* Gutschein
vulnerable *108* verwundbar, anfällig

W

wage *104* Lohn; **minimum ~** *110* Mindestlohn
waist *198* Taille
wait *144* Warten, Wartezeit
to **wait for one's turn** *82* warten, bis man an der Reihe ist
walk *93* Spaziergang, Rundgang; **from all ~s of life** *90* aus allen Gesellschaftsschichten, aus allen Lebensbereichen
to **walk along sth** *23* etw *(Straße etc.)* entlanggehen
walk-in medical centre *96T* Ambulanz
walking distance, within ~ *119* in Laufweite
wall *38* Wand, Pinnwand
wallet *81* Brieftasche, (Herren-)Portemonnaie
war *86T* Krieg
warehouse *116* Lager
to **warm** *137* sich erwärmen
warming, global ~ *136* Erderwärmung
warm-up *17T* Aufwärmen
warning, a word of ~ *68* Hinweis, Warnung
to **wash** *43* abwaschen, abwischen; **~ over sb/sth** *8* jdn überkommen, etw überschwemmen
washing *60* Wäsche; **~ machine** *129* Waschmaschine; **~ powder** *49* Waschpulver; **~ up** *62T* Geschirrspülen
waste *123* Müll; to **go to ~** *98* ungenutzt bleiben; **~ management** *98* Abfallentsorgung; **~ waste of time** *24* Zeitverschwendung; **~ water** *143T* Abwasser
wasteland *104* Brachland
watch *23* Armbanduhr; **Not on our ~.** *90* Nicht mit uns!; to **keep ~ over sb** *160* über jdn wachen, jdn beobachten
water: ~ heater *105* Warmwasserbereiter, Boiler; **~ supply** *134* Wasserversorgung
to **water** *64* *(Pflanze)* gießen
to **wave: ~ sth** *8* etw schwenken, mit etw wedeln; **~ sth around** *80* mit etw herumfuchteln
wave *84* Welle
wavelength *180* Wellenlänge
way, by the ~ *60* übrigens, nebenbei erwähnt; **the other ~ round** *86T* umgekehrt; **along the ~** *90* dabei, währenddessen; to **find one's ~ around** *120T* sich zurechtfinden
weakness *78* Schwäche
weapon *124* Waffe
wearable *146* (in der Kleidung) tragbar
wedding *116* Hochzeit
weed *152* Unkraut
weekday *61* Werktag, Wochentag
to **weigh** *134T* wiegen; *143T* abwägen
weight, to **lose ~** *17T* abnehmen

Y

Z

Geographical names

Abingdon ['æbɪŋdən]	Abingdon *(Stadt an der Themse in Oxfordshire)*
Accra ['ækrə]	Accra *(Hauptstadt von Ghana)*
Africa ['æfrɪkə]	Afrika
African ['æfrɪkən]	afrikanisch, Afrikaner/in
America [ə'merɪkə]	Amerika
American [ə'merɪkən]	amerikanisch, Amerikaner/in
Amsterdam ['æmstədæm]	Amsterdam
Anglo-Irish [ˌæŋgləʊ 'aɪrɪʃ]	anglo-irisch
Antarctic [ænt'ɑːktɪk]	Antarktis, antarktisch
Arab ['ærəb]	arabisch, Araber/in
Arctic ['ɑːktɪk]	Arktis, arktisch
Asia ['eɪʃə]	Asien
Asian ['eɪʃn]	asiatisch, Asiate/-in
Australia [ɒ'streɪliə]	Australien
Australian [ɒ'streɪliən]	australisch, Australier/in
Austria ['ɒstriə]	Österreich
Austrian ['ɒstriən]	österreichisch, Österreicher/in
Bangladesh [ˌbæŋglə'deʃ]	Bangladesch
Bangladeshi [ˌbæŋglə'deʃi]	bangladeschisch, Bangladescher/in
Bath [bɑːθ]	Bath *(Stadt in Somerset)*
Belgian ['beldʒən]	belgisch, Belgier/in
Belgium ['beldʒəm]	Belgien
Benin [be'niːn]	Benin
Birmingham ['bɜːmɪŋəm]	Birmingham
Black Forest [ˌblæk 'fɒrɪst]	Schwarzwald
Bosnia ['bɒzniə]	Bosnien
Brazil [brə'zɪl]	Brasilien
Brazilian [brə'zɪliən]	brasilianisch, Brasilianer/in
Bristol ['brɪstl]	Bristol *(Stadt in Südwest-england)*
Britain ['brɪtn]	Großbritannien
Briton ['brɪtn]	Brite/Britin
Brittany ['brɪtəni]	Bretagne
Brixton ['brɪkstən]	Brixton *(Stadtteil im Süden Londons)*
Brussels ['brʌslz]	Brüssel
Burkina Faso [bəˌkiːnə 'fæsəʊ]	Burkina Faso
California [ˌkælə'fɔːniə]	Kalifornien
Canada ['kænədə]	Kanada
Central America [ˌsentrəl ə'merɪkə]	Mittelamerika
Chicago [ʃɪ'kɑːgəʊ]	Chicago
China ['tʃaɪnə]	China
Chinese [tʃaɪ'niːz]	chinesisch, Chinese/-in
Colombo [kə'lɒmbəʊ]	Colombo *(Hauptstadt von Sri Lanka)*
Columbia [kə'lʌmbiə]	Kolumbien
Dallas ['dæləs]	Dallas
Danish ['deɪnɪʃ]	dänisch, Däne/-in
Denmark ['denmɑːk]	Dänemark
Dublin ['dʌblɪn]	Dublin
East Ham [ˌiːst 'hæm]	East Ham *(Stadtteil im Osten Londons)*
Edinburgh ['edɪnbərə]	Edinburgh
Egypt ['iːdʒɪpt]	Ägypten
England ['ɪŋglənd]	England
Eritrea [ˌerɪ'trɪə]	Eritrea
Eritrean [ˌerɪ'trɪən]	eritreisch, Eritreer/in
Ethiopia [ˌiːθi'əʊpiə]	Äthiopien
Ethiopian [ˌiːθi'əʊpiən]	äthiopisch, Äthiopier/in
Europe ['jʊərəp]	Europa
(the) Far East [ˌfɑːr 'iːst]	der Ferne Osten
Finland ['fɪnlənd]	Finnland
Florida ['flɒrɪdə]	Florida
France [frɑːns]	Frankreich
Germany ['dʒɜːməni]	Deutschland
Ghana ['gɑːnə]	Ghana
Ghanaian [gɑː'neɪən]	ghanaisch, Ghanaer/in
Glasgow ['glɑːsgəʊ]	Glasgow
Goa ['gəʊə]	Goa
Great Barrier Reef [ˌgreɪt 'bæriə riːf]	Großes Barriereriff
Greece [griːs]	Griechenland
Greenland ['griːnlənd]	Grönland
Guinea ['gɪni]	Guinea
Haiti ['heɪti]	Haiti
Hawaii [hə'waɪi]	Hawaii
Heathrow [ˌhiːθ'rəʊ]	Heathrow *(Flughafen west-lich von London)*
Highgate ['haɪgeɪt]	Highgate *(Staddteil im Norden Londons)*
Honolulu [ˌhɒnə'luːluː]	Honolulu *(Haupstadt von Hawaii)*
Hungary ['hʌŋgəri]	Ungarn
Iceland ['aɪslənd]	Island
India ['ɪndiə]	Indien
Indian ['ɪndiən]	indisch, Inder/in
Indian Ocean [ˌɪndiən 'əʊʃn]	Indischer Ozean
Indonesia [ˌɪndəʊ'niːziə]	Indonesien
Iran [ɪ'rɑːn]	Iran
Iranian [ɪ'reɪniən]	iranisch, Iraner/in
Iraq [ɪ'rɑːk]	Irak
Ireland ['aɪələnd]	Irland
Irish ['aɪrɪʃ]	irisch, Ire/Irin
Italy ['ɪtəli]	Italien
Jamaica [dʒə'meɪkə]	Jamaika
Jamaican [dʒə'meɪkən]	jamaikanisch, Jamaikaner/in
Kenya ['kenjə]	Kenia
Kenyan ['kenjən]	kenianisch, Kenianer/in
Kilimanjaro [ˌkɪlɪmən'dʒɑːrəʊ]	Kilimandscharo
Korea [kə'rɪə]	Korea
Korean [kə'rɪən]	koreanisch, Koreaner/in
Kosovo ['kɒsəvəʊ]	Kosovo
Kosovian [kə'səʊviən]	kosovarisch, Kosovare/-in
Latin America [ˌlætɪn ə'merɪkə]	Lateinamerika
Latin American [ˌlætɪn ə'merɪkən]	lateinamerikanisch, Lateinamerikaner/in
London ['lʌndən]	London
Malawi [mə'lɑːwi]	Malawi
Mali ['mɑːli]	Mali
Manchester ['mæntʃɪstə]	Manchester
Massachusetts [ˌmæsə'tʃuːsɪts]	Massachusetts
Miami [maɪ'æmi]	Miami
Milan [mɪ'læn]	Mailand
(the) Netherlands ['neðələndz]	die Niederlande
New York [ˌnjuː 'jɔːk]	New York
Niger ['naɪdʒə]	Niger
North America [ˌnɔːθ ə'merɪkə]	Nordamerika
North Sea [ˌnɔːθ 'siː]	Nordsee
Northern Ireland [ˌnɔːðən 'aɪələnd]	Nordirland
Oxford ['ɒksfəd]	Oxford
Oxford Circus [ˌɒksfəd 'sɜːkəs]	Oxford Circus *(Platz und U-Bahn-Station in der Londoner Innenstadt)*

Pacific Ocean [pəˌsɪfɪk 'əʊʃn]	Pazifischer Ozean
Pakistan [ˌpækɪ'stɑːn]	Pakistan
Pakistani [ˌpækɪ'stɑːni]	pakistanisch, Pakistaner/in
Panama ['pænəmɑː]	Panama
(the) Philippines ['fɪləpiːnz]	die Philippinen
Pittsburgh ['pɪtsbɜːg]	Pittsburgh *(Stadt in Pennsylvania)*
Poland ['pəʊlənd]	Polen
Polish ['pəʊlɪʃ]	polnisch, Pole/Polin
Portugal ['pɔːtʃʊgl]	Portugal
Portuguese [ˌpɔːtʃu'giːz]	portugiesisch, Portugiese/-in
Red Sea [ˌred 'siː]	Rotes Meer
River Clyde [ˌrɪvə 'klaɪd]	der Clyde *(Fluss in Schottland)*
River Thames [ˌrɪvə 'temz]	die Themse
Romania [ruː'meɪniə]	Rumänien
Romanian [ruː'meɪniən]	rumänisch, Rumäne/-in
Russia ['rʌʃə]	Russland
Russian ['rʌʃn]	russisch, Russe/Russin
Scotland ['skɒtlənd]	Schottland
Scot [skɒt]	Schotte/-in
Scottish ['skɒtɪʃ]	schottisch, Schotte/-in
Shanghai [ˌʃæŋ'haɪ]	Schanghai
Singapore [ˌsɪŋə'pɔː]	Singapur
South Africa [ˌsaʊθ 'æfrɪkə]	Südafrika
South America [ˌsaʊθ ə'merɪkə]	Südamerika
South Carolina [ˌsaʊθ ˌkærə'laɪnə]	South Carolina
South Pole [ˌsaʊθ 'pəʊl]	Südpol
Spain [speɪn]	Spanien
Spanish ['spænɪʃ]	spanisch, Spanier/in
Sri Lanka [ˌsriː 'læŋkə]	Sri Lanka
Staffordshire ['stæfədʃə]	Staffordshire *(Grafschaft in Mittelengland)*
Staines ['steɪnz]	Staines *(Stadt in Surrey)*
sub-Saharan Africa [sʌb səˌhɑːrən 'æfrɪkə]	Schwarzafrika
Sudan [su'dɑːn]	Sudan
Sudanese [ˌsuːdə'niːz]	sudanesisch, Sudanese/-in
Sweden ['swiːdn]	Schweden
Swede [swiːd]	Schwede/-in
Swedish ['swiːdɪʃ]	schwedisch, Schwede/-in
Switzerland ['swɪtsələnd]	Schweiz
Swiss [swɪs]	schweizerisch, Schweizer/in
Sydney ['sɪdni]	Sydney
Syria ['sɪriə]	Syrien
Tanzania [ˌtænzə'niːə]	Tansania
Texas ['teksəs]	Texas
Tokyo ['təʊkiəʊ]	Tokio
Turkey ['tɜːki]	Türkei
Turkish ['tɜːkɪʃ]	türkisch, Türke/-in
Uganda [ju'gændə]	Uganda
Ugandan [ju'gændən]	ugandisch, Ugander/in
United Kingdom (UK) [juˌnaɪtɪd 'kɪŋdəm]	Vereinigtes Königreich
United States (USA) [juˌnaɪtɪd 'steɪts]	Vereinigte Staaten
Vancouver [væn'kuːvə]	Vancouver
Wales [weɪlz]	Wales
Welsh [welʃ]	walisisch, Waliser/in
Warsaw ['wɔːsɔː]	Warschau
Wembley ['wembli]	Wembley *(Stadtteil im Nordwesten Londons)*
Wimbledon ['wɪmbldən]	Wimbledon *(Stadtteil im Süden Londons)*
Winchester ['wɪntʃɪstə]	Winchester *(Stadt im Süden Englands)*
Zambia ['sæmbiə]	Sambia

be	was/were	been	*sein*
beat	beat	beaten	*schlagen, besiegen*
become	became	become	*werden*
begin	began	begun	*anfangen, beginnen*
bend	bent	bent	*(sich) beugen*
blow	blew	blown	*wehen, blasen, ziehen*
break	broke	broken	*brechen*
breed	bred	bred	*sich vermehren, sich ausbreiten*
bring	brought	brought	*(mit)bringen*
build	built	built	*bauen*
burn	burnt/ burned	burnt/ burned	*(ver)brennen*
buy	bought	bought	*kaufen*
catch	caught	caught	*fangen, fassen, erreichen*
choose	chose	chosen	*(aus)wählen*
come	came	come	*kommen*
cost	cost	cost	*kosten*
cut	cut	cut	*schneiden*
deal (with)	dealt (with)	dealt (with)	*sich kümmern um, umgehen mit*
dig	dug	dug	*graben*
do	did	done	*tun, machen*
draw	drew	drawn	*zeichnen*
dream	dreamt/ dreamed	dreamt/ dreamed	*träumen*
drink	drank	drunk	*trinken*
drive	drove	driven	*fahren*
eat	ate	eaten	*essen*
fall	fell	fallen	*fallen*
feed	fed	fed	*füttern, ernähren*
feel	felt	felt	*(sich) fühlen, empfinden*
fight	fought	fought	*kämpfen*
find	found	found	*finden*
fit	fit/fitted	fit/fitted	*passen, anbringen, entsprechen*
fly	flew	flown	*fliegen*
forbid	forbade	forbidden	*verbieten*
forget	forgot	forgotten	*vergessen*
get	got	got (*AE* gotten)	*bekommen*
give	gave	given	*geben*
go	went	gone	*gehen, fahren*
grow	grew	grown	*wachsen*
hang	hung	hung	*hängen*
have	had	had	*haben*
hear	heard	heard	*hören*
hide	hid	hidden	*(sich) verstecken*
hit	hit	hit	*schlagen*
hold	held	held	*halten, festhalten*
hurt	hurt	hurt	*verletzen*
keep	kept	kept	*behalten*
know	knew	known	*kennen, wissen*
lay	laid	laid	*legen*
lead	led	led	*führen*
lean	leant/ leaned	leant/ leaned	*sich lehnen, sich beugen*
learn	learnt/ learned	learnt/ learned	*lernen*
leave	left	left	*abfahren, verlassen, weggehen*
let	let	let	*lassen*
lie	lay	lain	*liegen*
light	lit	lit	*anzünden, beleuchten*
lose	lost	lost	*verlieren*
make	made	made	*machen*
mean	meant	meant	*meinen, bedeuten*
meet	met	met	*treffen*
pay	paid	paid	*bezahlen*
put	put	put	*setzen, stellen, legen*
quit	quit/ quitted	quit/ quitted	*verlassen, aufhören*
read	read	read	*lesen*
ride	rode	ridden	*reiten, fahren*
ring	rang	rung	*anrufen, läuten*
rise	rose	risen	*(an)steigen*
run	ran	run	*laufen, rennen*
say	said	said	*sagen*
see	saw	seen	*sehen*
seek	sought	sought	*suchen*
sell	sold	sold	*verkaufen*
send	sent	sent	*senden, schicken*
set	set	set	*setzen, stellen*
shake	shook	shaken	*schütteln*
shine	shone	shone	*scheinen, glänzen*
show	showed	shown	*zeigen*
shrink	shrank	shrunk	*schrumpfen, zurückgehen*
shut	shut	shut	*schließen*
sing	sang	sung	*singen*
sink	sank	sunk	*sinken*
sit	sat	sat	*sitzen*
sleep	slept	slept	*schlafen*
slide	slid	slid	*(ab)rutschen, (ab) sacken*
smell	smelt/ smelled	smelt/ smelled	*riechen*
speak	spoke	spoken	*sprechen*
spell	spelt/ spelled	spelt/ spelled	*buchstabieren*
spend	spent	spent	*ausgeben, verbringen*
spread	spread	spread	*(sich) verbreiten*
stand	stood	stood	*stehen*
steal	stole	stolen	*stehlen*
swim	swam	swum	*schwimmen*
take	took	taken	*nehmen*
teach	taught	taught	*unterrichten, beibringen*
tell	told	told	*sagen, erzählen*
think	thought	thought	*denken*
throw	threw	thrown	*werfen*
understand	understood	understood	*verstehen*
wake	woke	woken	*aufwachen, -wecken*
wear	wore	worn	*tragen*
win	won	won	*gewinnen*
write	wrote	written	*schreiben*

Quellenverzeichnis

Bildrechte

Titelfoto: Shutterstock – Mikhail Zahranichny

S. 6: vario Images – o. l.: OJO Images / o. r.: OJO Images / m.l.: Cultura RF / m. r.: OJO Images / u. l.: Caiaimage / u. r.: Westend61 (RM); **S. 8:** Shutterstock – Featureflash; **S. 10:** Shutterstock – racorn (2); **S. 12:** Shutterstock – v. o. l.: Monkey Business Images / Carme Balcells / m.: Andresr / v. u. l.: Monkey Business Images / wavebreakmedia; **S. 14:** FOTOFINDER – PhotoAlto; **S. 18:** Shutterstock – v. l.: Luciano Mortula / mikecphoto; **S. 21:** Shutterstock – Monkey Business Images; **S. 22:** Shutterstock – Monkey Business Images; **S. 23:** Shutterstock – Monkey Business Images; **S. 24:** Shutterstock – Monkey Business Images; **S. 25:** v. o. l.: Shutterstock – Shane Gross / anthonymooney / merzzie / Syda Productions / Rommel Canlas / auremar; **S. 26:** Cartoonstock – Marty Bucella; **S. 27:** Glow Images – Blend Images LLC; **S. 29:** Shutterstock – David Pereiras; **S. 30:** Isobel Williams, Berlin; **S. 31:** Shutterstock – Minerva Studio; **S. 34:** Shutterstock – Minerva Studio; **S. 35:** Shutterstock – o. l.: Syda Productions / o. r.: Robert Kneschke / m. l.: Leigh J / m. m.: gpointstudio / m. r.: Antonio Guillem / u. l.: RossHelen / u. r.: Monkey Business Images; **S. 36:** Shutterstock – Photographee.eu; **S. 38:** Shutterstock – v. l.: Photographee.eu / Agenturfotografin; **S. 40:** Shutterstock – Catherine Murray; **S. 43:** action press – SWNSaction press; **S. 44:** Oxford Designers & Illustrators; **S. 45:** v. o. l.: Shutterstock – Evgeny Atamanenko / Syda Productions / Thinglass / rangizzz / in 1. v. o. l.: michaeljung / 1 Valentina Razumova / Fotolia – 2 Dirima / 3 Photocreo Bednarek / 4 Electrolux Hausgeräte GmbH; **S. 46:** VW 2009 – DDB Stockholm (2); **S. 47:** VW 2009 – DDB Stockholm; **S. 51:** Mauritius Images – Alamy; **S. 54:** Oxford Designers & Illustrators; **S. 55:** Shutterstock – 1 Goodluz / 2 Rawpixel / 3 qvist / 4 mato / 5 AntonioDiaz / 6 Goodluz / 7 wavebreakmedia / 8 Mark Skalny; **S. 56:** v. o.: Shutterstock – Alena Ozerova / vario images – Image Source; **S. 57:** Glow Images – Stockbroker; **S. 60:** Oxford Designers & Illustrators (6); **S. 63:** v. o. Oxford Designers & Illustrators / Shutterstock – wavebreakmedia; **S. 64:** Oxford Designers & Illustrators; **S. 65:** Oxford Designers & Illustrators; **S. 67:** Shutterstock – 1 Adam Gregor / 2 racorn / Glow Images – 3 GammaA / 4 Fancy; **S. 69:** vario Images – OJO Images; **S. 70:** Shutterstock – Gemenacom; **S. 74:** Shutterstock – Goodluz; **S. 75:** Shutterstock – Minerva Studio; **S. 79:** Mauritius Images – 1 Alamy / F1online – 2 Corbis Creative – ROBIN UTRECHT FOTOGRAFIE/HillCreek Pictures / Shutterstock – 3 Oliver Juneau / Photoshot – 4 Xinhua; **S. 80:** Oxford Designers & Illustrators (3); **S. 81:** Oxford Designers & Illustrators; **S. 84:** Shutterstock – v. o.: Daniel M Ernst / GSPhotography / dotshock / Nadino; **S. 88:** Shutterstock – ArtisticPhoto; **S. 89:** Shutterstock – v. o. l.: Monkey Business Images / Panaspics / Monkey Business Images /v. u. l.: wrangler / Glow Images – Ariel Skelley/Blend Images LLC / Shutterstock – u.: Leremy; **S. 90:** Shutterstock – v. o.: Leremy / Sylvie Bouchard / karelnoppe / Goodluz / bikeriderlondon; **S. 91:** Corbis – RICK WILKING/Reuters; **S. 92:** Shutterstock – A spotmatik / B scigelova / C Levent Konuk / D bikeriderlondon; **S. 94:** Bulls Press – Barcroft Media (2); **S. 96:** Shutterstock – Andresr; **S. 98:** o. l.: Shutterstock – dolphfyn / u. l.: Oxford Designers & Illustrators / r.: Christopher Cleaver; **S. 99:** Oxford Designers & Illustrators (2); **S. 100:** Shutterstock – v. o.: Sylvie Bouchard / mortalpious / Darryl Brooks / Stuart Jenner; **S. 102:** akg-images – v. l.: akg-images / Visum – ANDIA; **S. 103:** Cartoonstock – Hajo de Reijger; **S. 108:** Oxford Designers & Illustrators; **S. 109:** action press – Patrik Österberg/AOP Sweden / Oxford Designers & Illustrators (3); **S. 110:** Mauritius Images – Alamy; **S. 114:** Fotolia – v. l.: Hunor Kristo / Ermolaev Alexandr; **S. 117:** Shutterstock – Martina Ebel; **S. 118:** Shutterstock – Belushi; **S. 119:** Shutterstock – Minerva Studio; **S. 123:** Shutterstock – 1 arindambanerjee / 2 Jonathan Nafzger /3 eldeiv / 4 Pablo Hidalgo - Fotos593 / 5 alexmillos / 6 withGod / 7 Phatic-Photography / Fotolia – 8 Ingo Bartussek; **S. 124:** Shutterstock – fmua; **S. 126:** Shutterstock – v. l.: Daniel M Ernst / Charlotte Purdy / racorn / Kinga; **S. 128:** Fotolia – beugdesign; **S. 131:** Photoshot – UPPA; **S. 132:** Shutterstock – Vasin Lee; **S. 133:** Shutterstock – Dubova (2); **S. 134:** Shutterstock – l.: Nixx Photography / m.: James Thew / r.: jackit17; **S. 135:** Oxford Designers & Illustrators; **S. 138:** Topic Media; **S. 140:** Oxford Designers & Illustrators; **S. 143:** Oxford Designers & Illustrators; **S. 144:** Mauritius Images – Alamy; **S. 146:** Shutterstock – S.V.Art; **S. 147:** v. l.: Cagle – Dario Castillejos / The Christian Science Monitor – Bennett / Oxford Designers & Illustrators; **S. 148:** Oxford Designers & Illustrators; **S. 151:** Shutterstock – StockCube; **S. 153:** Oxford Designers & Illustrators; **S. 155:** action press – v. l.: KYODO NEWS / Corbis – EDGAR SU/Reuters; **S. 156:** Mauritius Images – Alamy; **S. 158:** PrecisionHawk (www.precisionhawk.com); **S. 159:** Shutterstock – a beboy / b Dimedrol68 / c Dja65 / Fotolia – d areeya_ann / Shutterstock – e Somchai Som / f kavione / g Denis Dryashkin / h catolla / i Nikonaft / j Mike Flippo / k pzAxe / l Anna Hoychuk; **S. 161:** Mauritius Images – Alamy; **S. 164:** Shutterstock – Mopic; **S. 166:** Shutterstock – Krivosheev Vitaly; **S. 168:** University of Birmingham; **S. 170:** European Space Agency (ESA)– J. Huart, 2014; **S. 171:** Shutterstock – Minerva Studio; **S. 175:** Shutterstock – racorn; **S. 176:** Shutterstock – o. l.: Regisson / o. r.: Alina Ku-Ku / u.: racorn; **S. 177:** Oxford Designers & Illustrators; **S. 178:** v. o.: Laif – Polaris Images / Corbis – Lisa Wiltse; **S. 179:** Displair (www.displair.com); **S. 180:** v. o.: Shutterstock – Kittipong Siriruttatanon / Oxford Designers & Illustrators; **S. 181:** Laif – Michael Loewa; **S. 182:** Oxford Designers & Illustrators; **S. 183:** Oxford Designers & Illustrators (3); **S. 184:** Shutterstock – JP Chretien; **S. 185:** v. o.: Oxford Designers & Illustrators / Shutterstock – ID 1974; **S. 186:** Oxford Designers & Illustrators; **S. 187:** Shutterstock – adpePhoto; **S. 188:** Oxford Designers & Illustrators; **S. 189:** action press – EVERETT COLLECTION; **S. 190:** Shutterstock – scyther5; **S. 192:** Shutterstock – b Tancha / c Boguslaw Mazur / d Vadim Ermak / e veronchick84 / f Butterfly Hunter / g Wiktoria Pawlak / h Studio_G / i ilttlethinkbigideas; **S. 193:** Oxford Designers & Illustrators **S. 194:** v. o.: Fotolia – Yuri Bizgaimer / Aeros Corporation (www.aeroscraft.com); **S. 195:** SkySails GmbH; **S. 196:** v. o.: action press – Unimediaimages, Inc. / Shutterstock – Elsa Hoffmann; **S. 197:** Shutterstock / o.: Picsfive / u. l.: Blend Images / u. m.: Valua Vitaly / u. r.: Valua Vitaly; **S. 199:** Shutterstock – chungking; **S. 200:** Shutterstock – wavebreakmedia; **S. 202:** Shutterstock – o.: Matej Kastelic / u.: bikeriderlondon; **S. 203:** v. o.: Oxford Designers & Illustrators / picture-alliance – Jan Haas; **S. 204:** Oxford Designers & Illustrators (3); **S. 205:** Fotolia – Albert Lozano-Nieto; **S. 206:** Shutterstock – v. o.: mihalec / Kurt Kleemann / Fedor Korolevskiy / Baloncici / Adisa / Monkey Business Images; **S. 207:** Oxford Designers & Illustrators; **S. 208:** Shutterstock – Hopsalka; **S. 209:** Oxford Designers & Illustrators (3); **S. 210:** Oxford Designers & Illustrators; **S. 212:** Oxford Designers & Illustrators (3); **S. 215:** Shutterstock – Radu Razvan; **S. 222:** Shutterstock – michaeljung; **S. 226:** Shutterstock – bikeriderlondon; **S. 230:** Fotolia – govicinity; **S. 236:** Shutterstock – Tish1; **S. 237:** Cartoonstock – S. Haris

Textrechte

S. 27: Daily Mail Reporter, "Life's so unfair! Shopping mall sets 6pm curfew for teenagers – unless they bring their parents". http://www.dailymail.co.uk/news/article-2142964/Lifes-unfair-Shopping-mall-sets-6pm-curfew-forcing-teenagers-hang-parent-tow.html; Daily Mail Online, 11. Mai 2012;
S. 36–37: Pat Hurst, "Britons spend 62m hours a day on social media – that's an average one hour for EVERY adult and child". http://www.independent.co.uk/life-style/gadgets-and-tech/news/; The Independent, 27. Januar 2015;

S. 40: Mark Duell, "'Don't have any parties': Last words of mother leaving for holiday to her public schoolboy son, 17: days before drunken Facebook crashers trashed trashed her £1m house". http://www.dailymail.co.uk/news/article-2442337/Drunken-revellers-trash-1m-house-gatecrashing-Facebook-party.html; Daily Mail Online, 4. Oktober 2013;
S. 43: Sian Lloyd, "Cancer fundraiser Stephen Sutton dies aged 19". http://www.bbc.com/news/uk-england-27408818; BBC News, 14. Mai 2014;
S. 46: Kelsey Ramos, "Volkswagen brings the fun: Giant piano stairs and other 'Fun Theory' marketing. http://latimesblogs.latimes.com/money_co/2009/10/volkswagen-brings-the-fun-giant-piano-stairs-and-other-fun-theory-marketing.html#sthash.krm3bWiS.dpuf; Los Angeles Times, 15. Oktober 2009;
S. 64: Erico Guizzo, "So, Where Are My Robot Servants?". http://spectrum.ieee.org/robotics/home-robots/so-where-are-my-robot-servants; IEEE Spectrum, 29. Mai 2014;
S. 69–70: Violet Johnstone, "'Mind how you move that chair – it's hot' Hot-desking is a growing trend, bringing a new culture writes Violet Johnstone". http://www.telegraph.co.uk/finance/4493463/Mind-how-you-move-that-chair-its-hot-Hot-desking-is-a-growing-trend-bringing-a-new-culture-writes-Violet-Johnstone.html; The Telegraph, 10. Oktober 2002;
S. 80–81: Benjamin Zephaniah, "Refugee Boy". Bloomsbury Publishing, 1. Auflage, 2001;
S. 90: Emily Buchanan, "What's it like to be a sponsored child?". http://www.bbc.com/news/world-13697855; BBC News World, 10. Juni 2011;
S. 90: Paul Abbott, "MicroLoan Foundation helps some of the poorest women". http://www.microloanfoundation.org.uk/what-we-do/; MicroLoan Foundation UK; Abruf September 2014;
S. 90: Elizabeth Scowcroft, "Benefits of volunteering for Samaritans". http://www.samaritans.org/volunteer-us/change-someone's-life-your-own; Samaritans Volunteering Department, Abruf September 2014;
S. 90: The Salvation Army, "Donate now: £26 could pay for ...". https://www.salvationarmyappeals.org.uk/site/SPageServer/?pagename=home; The Salvation Army United Kingdom Territory Territorial Headquarters, Abruf September 2014;
S. 94: Orphans for Orphans. http://www.gandysflipflops.com/orphans-for-orphans;
S. 98: Chris Cleaver in Sierra Leone. http://www.ewb-uk.org/node/4791; Engineers without Borders UK; Abruf Oktober 2014;
S. 110–111: Georgia Leaker, "Pass it on: give Gen Y more than a foot in the door". http://www.smh.com.au/comment/pass-it-on-give-gen-y-more-than-a-foot-in-the-door-20130708-2pm8v.html; The Sydney Morning Herald, 9. Juli 2013;
S. 118: Gregg Vanderheiden, "Benefits To Consumers". http://gpii.net/ConsumerBenefits; Raising the Floor International, Genf; Abruf Oktober 2014;
S. 124: Jonathan R. White, "The Nature of Modern Terrorism". http://www.huffingtonpost.com/jonathan-r-white/confusion-about-boston_b_3128995.html; Huffington Post, 21. April 2013;
S. 131: George Orwell, "Nineteen Eighty-Four". Penguin Books, 1949;
S. 132: David Barrett, "One surveillance camera for every 11 people in Britain, says CCTV survey". http://www.telegraph.co.uk/technology/10172298/One-surveillance-camera-for-every-11-people-in-Britain-says-CCTV-survey.html; The Telegraph, 10. Juli 2013;
S. 146: Rachel Metz, "An Air Quality Monitor You Take with You". http://www.technologyreview.com/news/530011/an-air-quality-monitor-you-take-with-you/; MIT Technology Review, 18. August 2014;
S. 156–157: Tim Folger, "The Next Green Revolution". http://www.nationalgeographic.com/foodfeatures/green-revolution/; National Geographic Magazine, Oktober 2014;
S. 160–161: Jan Puhl, "Silicon Savannah: Africa's Transformative Digital Revolution". http://www.spiegel.de/international/world/silicon-savannah-how-mobile-phones-and-the-internet-changed-africa-a-936307.html; Spiegel Online International, 5. Dezember 2013;
S. 168–169: Michael Eyre, "Boris the robot can load up dishwasher". http://www.bbc.com/news/science-environment-29168675; BBC News Science, 11. September 2014;
S. 170: ESA, "GALILEO: A Constellation of 30 Navigation Satellites". http://www.esa.int/Our_Activities/Navigation/The_future_-_Galileo/Galileo_a_constellation_of_30_navigation_satellites; © ESA–J.Huart, 15. Februar 2013;
S. 170: ESA, "Fact Sheet: What ist Galileo?". http://download.esa.int/docs/Galileo_IOV_Launch/Galileo_factsheet_2012.pdf; © ESA–J.Huart, 15. Februar 2013;
S. 189: Samuel Gibbs, "Microsoft's Star Trek voice translator available before the end 2014". http://www.theguardian.com/technology/2014/may/28/microsofts-star-trek-voice-translator-skype; The Guardian, 28. Mai 2014;
S. 190–191: Jason Hibbets, "What is open source?". http://opensource.com/resources/what-open-source; Red Hat Inc., 2014;
S. 194: Billy Witz, "Pursuing a Shipping Revolution as Big as His Airship". www.nytimes.comhttp://www.nytimes.com/2014/11/11/business/pursuing-a-shipping-revolution-as-big-as-his-airship.html?_r=0; The New York Times, 10. November 2014;
S. 195: Chris Lo, "SkySails: bringing wind back to ship propulsion". http://www.ship-technology.com/features/feature-skysails-bringing-wind-back-ship-propulsion/; Kabel Intellligence Ltd., 2. Dezember 2013;
S. 198: Hal Hodson, "Robotic suit gives shipyard workers super strength". http://www.newscientist.com/article/mg22329803.900-robotic-suit-gives-shipyard-workers-super-strength.html#.VMdcRFqRNz9; NewScientist, 4. August 2014;
S. 199–200: Zoe Kleinman, "Politician's fingerprint cloned from photos by hacker". http://www.bbc.com/news/technology-30623611; BBC News Technology, 29. Dezember 2014;
S. 208–209: Andrew Walker, "3D printing for dummies: How do 3D printers work?". http://www.independent.co.uk/life-style/gadgets-and-tech/features/3d-printing-for-dummies-how-do-3d-printers-work-8668937.html; The Independent, 21. Juni 2013;
S. 210: Jane Wakefield, "TED 2013: 4D printed objects make themselves". http://www.bbc.com/news/technology-21614176; BBC News Technology, 28. Februar 2013;
S. 215: James Delay, "Pedestrians are the great menace to cyclists". http://www.independent.co.uk/environment/green-living/james-daley-pedestrians-are-the-great-menace-to-cyclists-887017.html; The Independent, 7. August 2008;
S. 241–242: Steve Doughty, "Changing face of the British family: One in three now has a step-child". http://www.dailymail.co.uk/news/article-2552650/Changing-face-British-family-One-three-step-child.html#ixzz3Dw5waM1L; Daily Mail Online, 6. Februar 2014

Canada & United States of America

Abbreviations CANADA:

NB = New Brunswick
P.E.I. = Prince Edward Island

Abbreviations UNITED STATES:

CT = Connecticut
DE = Delaware
NH = New Hampshire
NJ = New Jersey
MA = Massachusetts
MD = Maryland
PA = Pennsylvania
RI = Rhode Island
VT = Vermont

to **support** [sə'pɔːt]	*(Argument)* untermauern, stützen
moreover [mɔːr'əʊvə]	überdies
furthermore [ˌfɜːðə'mɔː]	darüber hinaus
for instance [fə'rɪnstəns]	zum Beispiel

page 118

inclusive [ɪn'kluːsɪv]	inklusiv, offen
accessibility [əkˌsesə'bɪləti]	Barrierefreiheit
feature ['fiːtʃə]	Merkmal, Eigenschaft
magnification [ˌmægnɪfɪ'keɪʃn]	Vergrößerung
voice recognition [ˌvɔɪs ˌrekəg'nɪʃn]	Spracherkennung
universally [ˌjuːnɪ'vɜːsəli]	allgemein, überall
profile ['prəʊfaɪl]	Profil
to **sign in** [ˌsaɪn 'ɪn]	sich anmelden
settings *pl* ['setɪŋz]	Einstellungen
to **bridge a gap** [ˌbrɪdʒ ə 'gæp]	eine Lücke schließen, eine Kluft überbrücken
to **participate in sth** [pɑː'tɪsɪpeɪt ɪn]	an etw teilnehmen, an etw teilhaben
participation [pɑːˌtɪsɪ'peɪʃn]	Teilhabe, Teilnahme
productivity [ˌprɒdʌk'tɪvəti]	Produktivität
access ['ækses]	Zugang, Zugriff
to **encounter sth** [ɪn'kaʊntə]	auf etw treffen, auf etw stoßen
public kiosk [ˌpʌblɪk 'kiːɒsk]	öffentliches Internet-Terminal
vision ['vɪʒn]	Sehkraft
elder center *AE* ['eldə sentə]	Senioreneinrichtung
large print ['lɑːdʒ prɪnt]	große Schrift, Großdruck
to **insert** [ɪn'sɜːt]	einstecken
spinal cord [ˌspaɪnl 'kɔːd]	Rückenmark
high spinal cord injury [haɪ ˌspaɪnl 'kɔːd ɪndʒəri]	hoch gelegene Querschnittslähmung
to **paralyze** ['pærəlaɪz]	lähmen
neck [nek]	Hals
switch [swɪtʃ]	Schalter
to **hit** [hɪt]	*(Taste)* drücken
module ['mɒdjuːl]	Modul
lab [læb]	Computerraum
difficulty ['dɪfɪkəlti]	Schwierigkeit(en)
due to ['djuː tə]	aufgrund von, wegen
memory loss ['meməri lɒs]	Gedächtnisschwund
brain [breɪn]	Gehirn

JOB SKILLS 3

page 119

to **give directions** [ˌgɪv də'rekʃnz]	den Weg beschreiben
booking ['bʊkɪŋ]	Buchung
reservation [ˌrezə'veɪʃn]	Reservierung
to **be located in** [bi ləʊ'keɪtɪd ɪn]	sich in … befinden, in … liegen
directions *pl* [də'rekʃnz]	Wegbeschreibung
to **turn right/left** [ˌtɜːn 'raɪt, 'left]	rechts/links abbiegen
café ['kæfeɪ]	Café
within walking distance [wɪðɪn 'wɔːkɪŋ dɪstəns]	in Laufweite
straight ahead [ˌstreɪt ə'hed]	geradeaus
to **keep to the right/left** [ˌkiːp tə 'raɪt, 'left]	sich rechts/links halten

page 120

accounts [ə'kaʊnts]	Buchhaltung
storeroom ['stɔːruːm]	Lagerraum
marvellous ['mɑːvələs]	toll, phantastisch
corridor ['kɒrɪdɔː]	Flur, Gang
next to ['nekst tə]	neben
impressed [ɪm'prest]	beeindruckt
to **find one's way around** [faɪn wʌnz ˌweɪ ə'raʊnd]	sich zurechtfinden
photocopier ['fəʊtəʊkɒpiə]	Fotokopiergerät
office supplies *pl* ['ɒfɪs səplaɪz]	Büromaterial
Research and Development (R&D) [rɪˌsɜːtʃ ən dɪ'veləpmənt]	Forschung(s-) und Entwicklung(sabteilung)
quality control ['kwɒləti kəntrəʊl]	Qualitätskontrolle
reception [rɪ'sepʃn]	Empfang
remaining [rɪ'meɪnɪŋ]	übrig, verbleibend
blank [blæŋk]	leer, frei
memory ['meməri]	Gedächtnis
emergency exit [ɪ'mɜːdʒənsi eksɪt]	Notausgang, Fluchtweg
emergency exit plan [iˌmɜːdʒənsi 'eksɪt plæn]	Fluchtwegplan
to **exhibit** [ɪg'zɪbɪt]	ausstellen
trade fair ['treɪd feə]	Handelsmesse, Fachmesse
non-smoking [ˌnɒn'sməʊkɪŋ]	Nichtraucher-
as requested [əz rɪ'kwestɪd]	wie gewünscht
Best wishes [ˌbest 'wɪʃɪz]	*(Brief:)* Mit den besten Wünschen

page 121

to **be due** [bi 'djuː]	*(Flugzeug etc.:)* planmäßig ankommen
confirmation [ˌkɒnfə'meɪʃn]	Bestätigung
to **let sb know sth** [ˌlet 'nəʊ]	jdm etw mitteilen, jdm etw sagen
(business) contact ['kɒntækt]	Ansprechpartner/in, Geschäftspartner/in
Regards [rɪ'gɑːdz]	*(Brief:)* Viele Grüße
to **reserve** [rɪ'zɜːv]	reservieren
ranking ['ræŋkɪŋ]	Rangfolge
seating ['siːtɪŋ]	Bestuhlung
wheelchair ['wiːltʃeə]	Rollstuhl
projector [prə'dʒektə]	Beamer
screen [skriːn]	Leinwand
selection [sɪ'lekʃn]	Auswahl
non-alcoholic [ˌnɒn ælkə'hɒlɪk]	alkoholfrei
vegetarian [ˌvedʒə'teəriən]	vegetarisch
to **exceed** [ɪk'siːd]	überschreiten

page 122

wheelchair access ['wiːltʃeər ækses]	behindertengerechter Zugang
throughout [θruː'aʊt]	überall, in ganz …
disabled facilities *pl* [dɪsˌeɪbld fə'sɪlətiz]	behindertengerechte Toiletten
equipped with [ɪ'kwɪpt wɪð]	ausgestattet mit
stationery ['steɪʃənri]	Schreibpapier, Schreibwaren
dietary ['daɪətri]	Ernährungs
to **cater for sth** ['keɪtə fə]	auf etw eingehen
to **stay overnight** [ˌsteɪ əʊvə'naɪt]	übernachten
reasonable ['riːznəbl]	vernünftig
to **mix and match** [ˌmɪks ən 'mætʃ]	individuell zusammenstellen
marker ['mɑːkə]	Filzstift
to **cater** ['keɪtə]	Speisen und Getränke liefern
buffet lunch ['bʊfeɪ lʌntʃ]	Lunchbuffet
rental price ['rentl praɪs]	Mietpreis

UNIT 13

page 123

priority [praɪ'ɒrəti]	Priorität, Vorrang
data protection [ˌdeɪtə prə'tekʃn]	Datenschutz
waste [weɪst]	Müll
dependence [dɪ'pendəns]	Abhängigkeit
extremism [ɪk'striːmɪzm]	Extremismus
identity [aɪ'dentəti]	Identität
theft [θeft]	Diebstahl
radicalization [ˌrædɪklaɪ'zeɪʃn]	Radikalisierung
surveillance [sɜː'veɪləns]	Überwachung
terrorist ['terərɪst]	Terrorist/in, Terror-
attack [ə'tæk]	Anschlag, Attentat

page 124

finishing line ['fɪnɪʃɪŋ laɪn]	Ziellinie
pressure cooker ['preʃə kʊkə]	Schnellkochtopf
bomb [bɒm]	Bombe
to **explode** [ɪk'spləʊd]	explodieren
suspect ['sʌspekt]	Verdächtige/r
firefight ['faɪəfaɪt]	Schusswechsel
manhunt ['mænhʌnt]	Verbrecherjagd
to **shut down** [ˌʃʌt 'daʊn]	schließen
resident ['rezɪdənt]	Anwohner/in, Bewohner/in
urban ['ɜːbən]	städtisch, Stadt-
desert ['dezət]	Wüste
back yard [ˌbæk 'jɑːd]	Hinterhof
to **state** [steɪt]	aussagen
to **bomb sth** [bɒm]	einen Bombenanschlag auf etw verüben
to **claim** [kleɪm]	behaupten
to **radicalize** ['rædɪklaɪz]	radikalisieren
to **engage in sth** [ɪn'geɪdʒ ɪn]	aktiv werden
violence ['vaɪələns]	Gewalt
multiple ['mʌltɪpl]	mehrere, vielfach
to **dominate** ['dɒmɪneɪt]	beherrschen, dominieren
battlefield ['bætlfiːld]	Schlachtfeld
century ['sentʃəri]	Jahrhundert
commander [kə'mɑːndə]	Kommandant/in, Anführer/in
modernity [mə'dɜːnəti]	Moderne
impact ['ɪmpækt]	Einfluss, Auswirkung
mobility [məʊ'bɪləti]	Mobilität
to **originate from sth** [ə'rɪdʒɪneɪt frəm]	von etw ausgehen, aus etw kommen
weapon ['wepən]	Waffe
access to sth ['ækses tə]	Zugriff auf etw, Zugang zu etw
destructive [dɪ'strʌktɪv]	zerstörerisch
to **plague** [pleɪg]	plagen, heimsuchen
tactic ['tæktɪk]	Taktik
essentially [ɪ'senʃəli]	im Wesentlichen
law enforcement ['lɔː ɪnfɔːsmənt]	Gesetzesvollzug, Innere Sicherheit, Exekutive
criminal justice [ˌkrɪmɪnl 'dʒʌstɪs]	Strafjustiz
arsenal ['ɑːsnəl]	Instrumentarium, Waffenlager
law enforcement agency ['lɔː ɪnfɔːsmənt eɪdʒənsi]	Strafverfolgungsbehörde, Exekutivorgan
extension [ɪk'stenʃn]	Erweiterung, Ausbau
to **root sth out** [ˌruːt 'aʊt]	etw beseitigen, etw ausmerzen
mass media *pl* [ˌmæs 'miːdiə]	Massenmedien
cable news ['keɪbl njuːz]	TV-Nachrichtensender
responsible [rɪ'spɒnsəbl]	verantwortungsvoll
breathless(ly) ['breθləs]	atemlos
to **await** [ə'weɪt]	erwarten, abwarten

page 125

bomber ['bɒmə]	Bombenattentäter
explosive device [ɪkˌspləʊsɪv dɪ'vaɪs]	Sprengsatz
to **sensationalize sth** [sen'seɪʃənlaɪz]	reißerisch über etw berichten
suicide ['suːɪsaɪd]	Selbstmord
suicide bomber [ˌsuːɪsaɪd 'bɒmə]	Selbstmordattentäter/in
devastating ['devəsteɪtɪŋ]	verheerend
attacker [ə'tækə]	Attentäter/in
explosive [ɪk'spləʊsɪv]	Sprengstoff
innocent ['ɪnəsnt]	unschuldig
cross [krɒs]	Kreuz
guilty ['gɪlti]	schuldig
police station [pə'liːs steɪʃn]	Polizeiwache

page 126

to **have one's say** [həv wʌnz 'seɪ]	seine Meinung äußern, zu Wort kommen
threat [θret]	Bedrohung
to **be under threat** [bi ˌʌndə 'θret]	bedroht werden
Christian ['krɪstʃən]	christlich, Christ/in
army [ɑːmi]	Armee
officer ['ɒfɪsə]	Offizier/in
to **get you nowhere** [ˌget jə 'nəʊweə]	zu nichts führen, nichts bringen
conflict zone ['kɒnflɪkt zəʊn]	Krisenregion, Konfliktzone
host [həʊst]	(Radio-/TV-)Moderator/in
law and order [ˌlɔː ənd 'ɔːdə]	Recht und Ordnung
security forces *pl* [sɪ'kjʊərəti fɔːsɪz]	Sicherheitskräfte
armed forces *pl* [ˌɑːmd 'fɔːsɪz]	Streitkräfte
massive(ly) ['mæsɪv]	massiv
to **border with sth** ['bɔːdə wɪð]	an etw grenzen
to **supply sb with sth** [sə'plaɪ]	jdn mit etw versorgen, jdm mit etw beliefern
westerner ['westənə]	Mensch aus der westlichen Welt
to **arm sb** [ɑːm]	jdn bewaffnen
pacifist ['pæsɪfɪst]	Pazifist/in
to **be in favour of sth** [bi ɪn 'feɪvər əv]	für etw sein
man of the cloth [ˌmæn əv ðə 'klɒθ]	Geistlicher
prayer [preə]	Gebet
prayer vigil ['preə vɪdʒɪl]	Gebetswache
to **pray** [preɪ]	beten
to **join together** [ˌdʒɔɪn tə'geðə]	sich zusammenschließen

page 127

to **prevent** [prɪ'vent]	verhindern, verhüten
thorough(ly) ['θʌrə]	gründlich, sorgfältig
entirely [ɪn'taɪəli]	völlig, ganz
to **put** [pʊt]	formulieren, sagen, in Worte fassen
security service [sɪ'kjʊərəti sɜːvɪs]	Geheimdienst